JOHN MILTON
Life, Work, and Thought

JOHN MILTON

Life, Work, and Thought

GORDON CAMPBELL
THOMAS N. CORNS

OXFORD

UNIVERSITY PRESS

OXFORD
UNIVERSITY PRESS

Great Clarendon Street, Oxford OX2 6DP

Oxford University Press is a department of the University of Oxford.
It furthers the University's objective of excellence in research, scholarship,
and education by publishing worldwide in

Oxford New York

Auckland Cape Town Dar es Salaam Hong Kong Karachi
Kuala Lumpur Madrid Melbourne Mexico City Nairobi
New Delhi Shanghai Taipei Toronto

With offices in

Argentina Austria Brazil Chile Czech Republic France Greece
Guatemala Hungary Italy Japan Poland Portugal Singapore
South Korea Switzerland Thailand Turkey Ukraine Vietnam

Oxford is a registered trade mark of Oxford University Press
in the UK and in certain other countries

Published in the United States
by Oxford University Press Inc., New York

British Library Cataloguing in Publication Data

Data available

Library of Congress Cataloging in Publication Data

Data available

Typeset by SPI Publisher Services, Pondicherry, India
Printed in Great Britain
on acid-free paper by
Clays Ltd., St Ives plc

ISBN 978–0–19–928984–4

3

For Mary and Pat, our espoused saints

Contents

Contents

Illustrations

A Note on Dates

THE dates used in this biography take account of two peculiarities in the calendar of seventeenth-century England. First, the Julian calendar in use in England and in some Protestant countries on the continent was ten days behind the Gregorian calendar in use in Catholic countries; Shakespeare and Cervantes are sometimes said to have died on the same day (23 April 1623), but in fact Cervantes died ten days before Shakespeare, because Spain had adopted the Gregorian calendar. The Julian Calendar is known to historians as Old Style (OS) and the Gregorian, which was not adopted in Britain until 1752, as New Style (NS). In the chapter on Italy we use split dates, so Milton is said to have read a poem to the Svogliati on 6/16 September 1638, which means that it was 6 September in England and 16 September in Italy.

The second discrepancy concerns the start of the new year. In Scotland and on the continent the new year was generally reckoned to start on 1 January, and in England this convention was used for dates on printed title pages. In English documents written by hand (including dates written on books), however, the year is deemed to start on 25 March, the Feast of the Annunciation. Milton's *Tenure of Kings and Magistrates* was published on or about 13 February 1649, and has that year on its title page; a presentation copy now in Exeter Cathedral Library is dated (by hand) February 1648. Some scholars split the dates (13 February 1648/49), but we have chosen the simpler alternative of using the modern convention of dating from 1 January, so we would write 13 February 1648/49 as 13 February 1649.

Seventeenth-century documents are also dated by a range of alternative means. Latin documents, for example, are sometimes dated by the Roman system of counting backwards from the three divisions of the month (*calends*, *nones*, and *ides*) rather than by counting forwards in ordinal numbers from the beginning of the month. State papers are often dated by regnal year, except during the years 1649 to 1660. Legal proceedings are dated by reference to the law terms, but legal documents, like ecclesiastical documents, are sometimes dated by saints' days and festivals. In all such cases, we have silently given the date by modern conventions.

Finally, Milton dated ten of his poems by his age, using the formula *anno aetatis* ('in the year of [his] age'), but that formula is ambiguous: '*anno aetatis* 17', for example, might mean that Milton was in his seventeenth year, but it usually seems to mean that he was 17. One of his Latin elegies (number 7), however, is dated *anno aetatis undevigesimo* ('at the age of 19'), and in this instance the use of a Latin ordinal number is probably meant to be taken literally, and the phrase therefore means 'in his nineteenth year' rather than 'at the age of 19'. In cases of doubt, we discuss the problem rather than bury it.

Map 1. William Faithorne, *An Exact Delineation of the Cities of London and Westminster and the Suburbs thereof, together with the Burrough of Southwark* (London, 1658).

Map 2. David Loggan, *Cantabrigia illustrata, sive, Omnium celeberrimae istius universitatis collegiorum, aularum, bibliothecae academicae, scholarum publicarum, sacelli coll. regalis* (Cambridge, 1690).

Introduction

Writing a biography of John Milton seems seductively easy, for two powerful reasons. First, much of the necessary information appears to be readily available. In the closing decades of the seventeenth century five lives were written by people who knew Milton or could draw information from others who did. Edward Phillips prepared an account of his uncle's life for inclusion in an edition of Milton's state papers published in 1694.[1] The antiquary John Aubrey assembled a collection of notes on Milton's life (now in the Bodleian Library in Oxford), in part based on interviews with relatives, including Milton's brother Christopher and his widow Elizabeth.[2] An anonymous biographer who can now be identified with confidence as Milton's friend Cyriack Skinner wrote a life that survives in manuscript, again in the Bodleian Library.[3] The antiquary Anthony Wood attempted to claim Milton (and other Cambridge authors) for Oxford by adding a chronology of Oxford (including incorporations from Cambridge) to his *Athenae Oxonienses*; the entry on Milton in the *Fasti* includes an account of his life.[4] The freethinker and philosopher John Toland composed a life for his collected edition of Milton, so confirming the process whereby Milton was appropriated to the Whig cause.

The earlier lives have the authority of personal acquaintance for certain periods of Milton's life. The work of Wood and Toland is largely derivative, though Toland has some information not otherwise captured. A later life, by Jonathan Richardson (London, 1734) picks up a few anecdotes that others have missed.[5] Moreover, Milton frequently tells his readers about himself, in his vernacular prose, in his Latin defences and sometimes in his poetry. Additionally, his life records have been scrupulously assembled by J. Milton French, and much more information scooped together in the mighty second volume of William Riley Parker's own biography, and both projects have been supplemented and amended by fine scholars of the present day.[6]

Secondly, Milton's work does seem readily explicable in terms of his life: puritan son of puritan father, educated by puritans, writing on puritan themes against puritan enemies until the failure of a puritan revolution requires him to redirect those energies into the definitive puritan poem. Find and replace 'puritan' with 'revolutionary' or 'radical' or 'progressive' to taste.

Of course, the issues are not that simple. The early lives probably owe too much to Milton's prose writings, which in turn were shaped to meet the challenges of the fierce polemical exchanges in which he was engaged, and to the carefully crafted demonstrations of self-representation which occur frequently his poetry. The most useful and most influential for later biographers, those of Skinner and Phillips, are partisan apologias in defence of a good friend and a nurturing uncle, and they are designed to respond to the sorts of attack Milton's life and reputation had attracted. The documents which make up the life records require careful interpretation, which teases out their significance in their own age; placing them in their proper context sharply changes their meaning for the biographer. Perhaps the accounts that require the greatest measure of detachment are those in which Milton describes his own life (as in the *Defensio Secunda*) or speaks in the first person in his poems (as in the invocations to *Paradise Lost*). We have attempted to read these autobiographical passages in their generic contexts, with an eye to Milton's habit of shaping his life and his personas to suit the exigencies of particular pieces of writing.

We have scrupulously revisited the archival evidence, of which earlier examination had been inhibited by the conditions obtaining in the heroic age of Milton studies, when French and Parker were writing: both wrote during World War II, when they were unable to visit England (or Italy), and both had to rely on documentary research conducted by generalists who lacked the specialist expertise of French (in legal documents) and Parker (in ecclesiastical documents). This reliance on material being reported at second hand has left considerable scope for post-war scholars, notably Leo Miller, John Shawcross, Robert Fallon, Peter Beal, and Edward Jones, all of whom have discovered new documents and enhanced our understanding of documents that had only been glimpsed at a distance. One of the distinguishing features of this biography is that its account of the factual record is the first since Masson's to have been based on an inspection of all the available documents.

The second distinguishing feature of this biography is the historiography that underlies our understanding of the early and mid-seventeenth century. The relationship between Milton's life and art emerges as much more complex once both are set against our changing understanding of religious, social, and especially political life in the period. Stuart historiography has developed in the last thirty years with a vigour and subtlety in comparison with which even historically informed literary criticism sometimes seems jejune. Our debts here are enormous: among others, to Kenneth Fincham, Anthony Milton, Peter Lake, Richard Cust, Conrad Russell, Kevin Sharpe, Ann Hughes, Murray Tolmie, John Coffey, John Morrill, Mark Kishlansky, Ian

Gentles, Blair Worden, David Underdown, John Spurr, Ronald Hutton, David Cressy, and, critic turned historian, N. H. Keeble.

Milton, on our account, is flawed, self-contradictory, self-serving, arrogant, passionate, ruthless, ambitous, and cunning. He is also among the most accomplished writers of the Caroline period, the most eloquent polemicist of the mid-century, and the author of the finest and most influential narrative poem in English. Janus-faced, he looks back to the world of Shakespeare, Spenser, and Jonson, and forward to Dryden and to Pope. He is driven by engaging enthusiasms—for the culture of Italy, for music, for in some way matching the life and work of Virgil. He knows his own worth, his singularity, his specialness. He is the most scholarly of poets, a master of classical culture and learning, a humanist in the great tradition of Hugo Grotius or John Selden, and he had a thorough appreciation of modern writers of continental Europe, and particularly of Italy. He studied law, mathematics, history, philology, and theology. He was also a thoughtful and innovative teacher.

The stages of his radicalization are the spine that runs through our study, as he moves from a culturally advanced but ideologically repressive young manhood into the struggle for a new reformation of the church and on to defence of regicide and republicanism, finally working out how to retain political and spiritual integrity in the threatening context of the Restoration. The revolutionary nature of Milton's mature thought can disappear from modern view because he was the advocate of principles which seem now obvious and commonplace. On issue after issue he was so often on the side that, in the long term, prevailed. He argued that governments have no business meddling with the religious beliefs of their citizens; that how people worship and whether they worship should not be regulated by the legal machinery of the state. He also denied the right of his rulers to determine what could be printed and read. He claimed that marriage should be founded on mutual affection and intellectual compatibility and that, when those broke down, divorce should end the misery and permit both parties to attempt other relationships. He thought his rulers should be held to account for their actions and that the law was above them. He also contended the best kind of government was republican, an argument that has often prevailed, though not at present in his native land. Many of the civil rights on which modern democratic states are founded are adumbrated in his work. Revolutionaries in France appropriated Milton to their cause.[7] Similarly, American statesmen such as Benjamin Franklin, Thomas Jefferson, and John Adams drew on their wide reading of Milton both to shape their republicanism and to address specific issues such as British taxation in America (for which Franklin drew a parallel with the Chaos of *Paradise Lost*), the case for ecclesiastical disestablishment in Virginia (for which Franklin drew on the anti-prelatical tracts) and the wickedness of British rulers (whose arrogance Adams compared to Satan's).[8] In intellectual terms, Milton is one of the founding fathers of America.

But he is not our contemporary. Those grand ideals, which we piece together from many works and from polemical contexts that diffuse their clarity, come with other values and assumptions that belong emphatically to his own age. He was certainly no democrat and, though he spoke up for the rights of working people to preach and study freely, he nowhere advocates a widened franchise, nor indeed does he evince much enthusiasm for the electoral process. His social assumptions, about the rights of the propertied and the subordination of the servant class, occasionally emerge as little different from the majority of men of his social standing in his age. His perspective on the relative status of men and women may be defended only in the most relativistic of terms; indeed, others around him were more patriarchal and misogynistic. Similarly, his plain intolerance of Roman Catholicism can sometimes be defended—poorly—as less implacable than that of others and as originating in opportunism rather than conviction; after all, he did have Catholic friends, and wrote admiringly of Catholic figures. Even in our own time anti-Catholicism has not quite disappeared—John F. Kennedy famously felt constrained to confront the issue when he was running for President, and Catholics are still banned from the British throne.[9]

Milton was no philosopher, in the sense that Thomas Hobbes and John Locke were, and his thought necessarily must be assembled often tentatively from texts that are not works of abstraction but of imagination or polemic. Moreover, over a significant period of his intellectual maturity he was working as a political activist and a public servant. What he says is shaped to attack or defend, and his reticencies, which are often surprising, reflect the disciplines of those callings.

This is a hero's life, though his heroism is of a rare kind. He did not fight in the foreign or civil wars of the mid-seventeenth century, despite his partisanship and political commitments, and despite his own physical capacity to do so. At the time, he carried a sword and knew how to use it.[10] When, at the Restoration, martyrdom beckoned, he cautiously declined. His was a life too precious to be thus jeopardized. What he achieved in the face of crippling adversity, blindness, bereavement, political eclipse, remains wondrous.

I

1608–1632

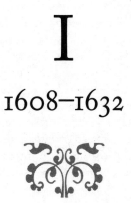

CHAPTER I

Childhood

J OHN Milton was born at 6.30 a.m. on Friday 9 December 1608[1] in the
house at the sign of the Spread Eagle, Bread Street, London, and on
20 December was baptized in nearby All Hallows Church.[2] He was the
second surviving child (after a sister called Anne) of a scrivener and composer
also called John Milton, and his wife Sara.

The future poet's paternal roots lay in Oxfordshire. His paternal great-
grandfather, Henry Milton (d. 1559),[3] had lived in the village of Stanton St
John with his wife Agnes.[4] Henry's son Richard, also of Stanton St John, was
a forest under-ranger in the Forest of Shotover who, according to one family
tradition, had been born in France.[5] What can be said with greater certainty is
that Richard was a recusant who was excommunicated on 11 May 1582 and
convicted of recusancy on 13 July 1601.[6]

On the account of the early lives, Richard's son John, father of the poet,
became a Protestant as a young man and was disinherited by his father.[7]
About 1583 John moved to London and entered the profession of scrivener.
Some uncertainty surrounds how that was achieved. Apprenticeships in such
professions were customarily based on a transaction in which the master
receives from the applicant's family a sum of money, in some ways like a
dowry, to accept the young man and take responsibility for his upkeep and
professional development. Evidence from the Jacobean period indicates payments of around £100 for entry into the higher professions.[8] However, the
early lives suggest that Richard Milton was unwilling to offer such support.
Three accounts point to an unnamed (and undiscovered) benefactor. John
Aubrey has it that he was 'brought up by a friend of his, was not his
Apprentice'. Cyriack Skinner has him 'beeing taken care of by a relation of
his a Scrivener'. Edward Phillips, grandson of John senior and nephew of the
poet, wrote that he became a scrivener, 'to which Profession he voluntarily
betook himself, by the advice and assistance of an intimate Friend of his,

Eminent in that Calling'. Professional companies did sometimes admit relatives of masters without formal apprenticeship, and it seems at least superficially unlikely that a young man in the depths of Oxfordshire would know a distinguished member of the trade except through family ties. John Milton senior's subsequent business dealings with the gentry of north Oxfordshire at least suggest that not all connection with the area was broken in the family discord that drove him to London.[9] Whatever the nature of the benefaction, he was admitted to the Company of Scriveners on 27 February 1600.[10]

Shortly thereafter he married Sara Jeffrey, the elder daughter of Paul Jeffrey(s), a merchant tailor, and his wife, Ellen,[11] who lived with John and Sara at the Spread Eagle in Bread Street from 1602 until her death in February 1611. Ellen's maiden name is not known, but if it was Bradshaw, the poet's relationship with Judge John Bradshaw might be more readily explicable.[12]

The house on Bread Street no longer exists: the City of London has twice been destroyed (in the fire of 1666 and the Blitz in 1940–1), but in the subsequent rebuilding the street layout was for the most part preserved on both occasions. The tenement known as the Spread Eagle, in a large building known as the White Bear, lay on the east side of the north end of Bread Street, a few yards from Cheapside. The property was owned by Eton College and leased to Sir Baptist Hicks,[13] the Miltons' landlord. On 16 October 1617 Eton College conducted a survey of the building (for purposes of renewing the lease to Hicks), and that survey still survives in Eton College.[14] The tenants of the White Bear included a girdler, a milliner, and a point-maker as well as the Miltons' of Spread Eagle. The accommodation rented by the Miltons, which was the most capacious of the tenements, was spread over five floors, plus a large cellar.[15] On the 'first storie', opening onto the street, was the scrivener's shop; on the second, a hall, a parlour and a kitchen; on the third, two bedrooms; on the fourth, a bedroom and a garret; on the fifth, another garret. When Milton was born, the household consisted of his parents, his sister Anne,[16] his grandmother Ellen Jeffrey, and a small number of servants who lived in the garrets;[17] short-lived daughters were born in 1612 (Sara) and 1614 (Tabitha), and a second son, Christopher, was to be born in 1615.[18] The neighbourhood, as Stow explained, was 'wholly inhabited by rich merchants';[19] John Milton senior had positioned himself at the heart of the London business community. There were, however, unruly visitors, for Mermaid Tavern was a few feet away at the top of the road (facing onto Cheapside but with an entrance on Bread Street) and drinkers, including Jonson and Shakespeare, would have walked down Bread Street to the river crossing.[20]

The business that the elder Milton conducted in his office was that of a scrivener: a professional scribe, but also a notary and money-lender. No evidence

1. C. J. Visscher, *Long Prospect of London* (detail) (London, 1616).

survives of the elder Milton's work as a scribe (which would have consisted of document preparation, though possibly he retained an interest in the more menial work of letter-writing for those who could not write), but his business as a notary and money-lender is amply documented,[21] and it is clear that he prospered. Indeed, over three and a half decades as freeman of his company he accumulated and invested enough capital to support himself and his family through a long retirement, at a time when most masters were working when they died and when bankruptcy was almost as common as retirement. Probably about 10 to 15 per cent of London businessmen actually managed to retire.[22] Business was his source of income; his passion, however, was music.

Milton the elder is known to have written twenty musical compositions. The music was all written for domestic use and is almost all sacred. Milton's earliest surviving composition, which is also his only known secular work, is a six-part madrigal called 'Fair Oriana in the morn', which was published in Thomas Morley's *Triumphs of Oriana* (1601). In 1614 he published four anthems in William Leighton's *The Tears or Lamentations of a Sorrowful Soul*. Three of his harmonizations of the York and Norwich psalm tunes are included in Thomas Ravenscroft's metrical psalter, *The Whole Book of Psalms* (1621). Milton's other surviving music was unpublished; these compositions survive in manuscripts

2. Sir William Leighton, *The Teares or Lamentacions of a Sorrovvfull Soule* (London, 1614), title page.

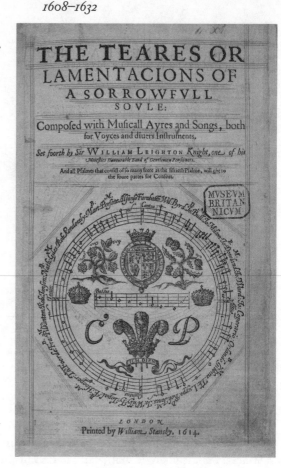

THE TEARES OR
LAMENTACIONS OF
A SORROWFVLL
SOVLE:

Compofed with Muficall Ayres and Songs, both
for Voyces and diuers Inftruments.

Set foorth by Sir WILLIAM LEIGHTON Knight, one of his
Maiefties Honourable Band of Gentlemen Penfioners.

And all Pfalmes that confift of fo many feete as the fiftieth Pfalme, will goe to
the foure partes for Confort.

MVSEVM
BRITAN
NICVM

LONDON
Printed by *William Stansby*, 1614.

associated with John Browne, clerk of the parliaments, and with Milton's friend Thomas Myriell.[23] The partbooks from the library of John Browne (now in Christ Church, Oxford), written in Myriell's hand, consist of three five-part fantasias and one six-part fantasia, all for consorts of viols, and a fantasia on 'In nomine' for voice and five viols; the collection also includes an anthem for four voices, 'If ye love me' (John 14: 15–16). Myriell's unpublished 'Tristitiae remedium' (now in the British Library) contains settings of five English biblical texts and of two verses (*incipit* 'Precamur sancte domine') of *Christe qui lux es*, a Latin hymn for compline. The passionate idiom of the *seconda practica* had advocates in England, and some English composers were writing light-hearted pieces, but the music of Milton and of the Myriell circle with which he was associated drew on a more conservative tradition and articulated the traditional values of the *prima practica* in its seriousness, abstraction, deployment of counterpoint, and even choice of instrument.

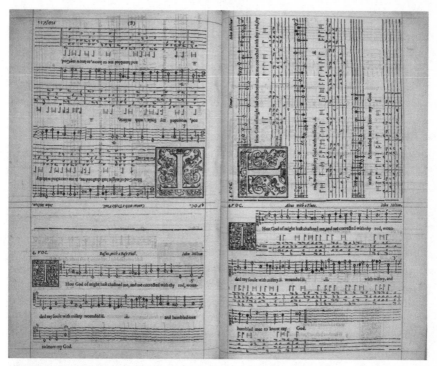

3. John Milton Senior, 'Thou God of might hast chastned me', part-song, from Leighton, *The Teares.*

How did the music of the elder Milton affect his son? In the case of singing, it is clear that the younger Milton created his own singing household when his nephews moved in with him; as John Aubrey notes, 'he made his Nephews Songsters, and sing from the time they were with him'.[24] Certainly tastes were passed on: the poet's preferences for part-singing, the organ, and the viol (as opposed to solo singing, the harpsichord, and the violin) place him in the same conservative musical tradition as his father. The fact that the music was designed for performance in private houses, without an audience, hints at the centrality of music in the Milton household; there Milton learned to sing in consorts and to play the organ and bass viol, and to rejoice in the pleasure of participating in music made purely for the benefit of the players. The music of the elder Milton is evidence of the religious sensibility of the household, and indicates a respect for liturgical and indeed ceremonial modes of worship. The clearest example is the setting of a Latin hymn for compline, which is the last of the canonical day-hours (said or sung before retiring for the night).

The Milton household was thus clearly musical: but it seems also to have been theatrical. Two recently discovered documents show that in 1620 the elder

Milton became a trustee of the Blackfriars playhouse. This may have been a purely financial arrangement, but it may hint at a previously unsuspected family link with the playhouses;[25] indeed, it is possible that the trusteeship was still active in May 1647, when the elder Milton died, in which case it would have belonged to the younger Milton until it was sold by William Burbage in 1651, although it is not unlikely that the trust was wound up once its principal beneficiary came of age in 1637. The trust was established in 1620 to meet difficulties posed by the death in 1619 of Richard Burbage, the great entrepreneurial genius behind the inexorable rise of the King's Men during the early Jacobean period. Richard had died, leaving a widow, a son, and a posthumously born daughter. Within the extended Burbage family and perhaps, too, among other shareholders of the King's Men, there was an evident concern that, should Winifred remarry, the property, which included the company's primary performing space (though they retained the reconstructed Globe too), could fall into the possession of her new husband, perhaps against the interest of the theatrical enterprise. A trust was established, under the supervision of two brewers, presumably solid citizens, Edward Raymond, a lawyer, and one 'John Milton'. The last has confidently been identified as the father of the poet, since he and Raymond had other, quite complex business dealings.

The location of an adult theatre company at Blackfriars in the heart of the city had long occasioned controversy among the civic elite. Indeed, not until 1609 had the King's Men taken over occupation from a company of boy actors, despite the Burbage family acquiring the property much earlier. Puritan opposition to theatres in general was well established, though in the case of the Blackfriars, its enemies sought to represent their concerns as essentially anxiety about civil order and public nuisance. The controversy entered a particularly heated phase in the period from December 1618 to March 1619, when a campaign, led by William Gouge, a prominent clergyman and influential puritan preacher,[26] petitioned the Lord Mayor and Corporation of London to close the theatre down.[27] The King's Men had royal patronage and protection, and plainly were able to resist the onslaught. The association of John Milton senior with the Burbage family and the playhouse in 1620 was a significant act of defiance of civic pressure, and a clear marker of where he lined up in the debate, within the City hierarchy, about the conflicting cultures of the theatre and the pulpit.

Similarly, it has recently been established that Thomas Morley, who published music by the elder Milton, may have been a link between the Miltons and Shakespeare. There are also strong hints of theatrical interests in the writings of the younger Milton. In Elegy I, a Latin verse letter written from London to his friend Charles Diodati, Milton refers to visits to a theatre that was covered by a roof (*sub tecto*, line 47); it is tempting to link the description to the Blackfriars. 'L'Allegro' celebrates the two greatest dramatists of Milton's youth:

Then to the well-trod stage anon,
If Jonson's learned sock be on,
Or sweetest Shakespeare, fancy's child,
Warble his native wood-notes wild.[28]

The possibility of a family link with Shakespeare is intriguing. The elder Milton may have contributed a poem to the First Folio (*incipit* 'We wondered, Shakespeare'), and the younger Milton's 'On Shakespeare' in the Second Folio was his first publication.[29]

The personal history of John Milton the poet, and indeed of other members of his family, must be traced against the larger backdrop of the interconnected crises, in religion and the state, that shaped English history through the seventeenth century. Already, in the older Milton's tastes in music, in domestic worship, perhaps in theatre, we see him taking sides in an increasingly polarized country. However, the crises, as they arise, come serially and in stages. Those among English Protestants and between Protestants and Catholicism are the most pertinent, but the issues in Milton's childhood differed sharply from those in his youth and maturity.

In the first decade of the century, the overwhelming majority of English Protestants were communicants of the Church of England. Separatists, that is puritans so hostile to the religion of the state that they withdrew to their own congregations, were rare in England, and their operation was so clandestine that they have left little trace. There were separatist churches in exile; in Amsterdam, for example.[30]

Within the Church of England three principal areas of controversy assume some significance at some points in the century: doctrine, the style of worship, and church government. In the early Jacobean period, the prevailing doctrinal position on the key article of faith, the doctrine of salvation (or soteriology), was Calvinist. The saved were predestinately saved, through no choice or merit in themselves, and the reprobate, in the most rigorous form of the doctrine, were predestinately reprobate. Alternative views, which attributed a role to the free will or the merit of individual believers, were relatively inchoate among churchmen, though they may well have had a wider currency in the larger community; they would shortly coalesce into anti-Calvinism or Arminianism. Style of worship was already keenly felt as a discriminating factor, as it had been from early in the reign of Elizabeth I, distinguishing those who favoured a heavily liturgical and ceremonial approach, with close attention to the vestments of the priest, from puritans who regarded ceremony and vestments as redolent of superseded Catholic practices. From time to time, presbyterian church government had had its advocates in England, though the issue was relatively dormant by the birth of Milton.

James I favoured episcopalian church government, and had been no friend of Presbyterianism in his years as king of Scotland, where it predominated. However, over a wide range of issues his approach was quite tolerant. As Kenneth Fincham puts it, 'For much of his reign, James I has claims to be regarded as the "common and ameliorating bond" who could favour both the Calvinist James Montagu and the anti-Calvinist Lancelot Andrewes, who was a patron of preaching yet questioned excessive preaching, who castigated Puritanism but tolerated moderate puritans, who could denounce the Pope as Antichrist and yet seek confessional unity.'[31] On these issues, the predisposition of individual clergymen and the more engaged laity was clear enough in the London of Milton's childhood. But the bitterness of the conflict, and an associated hostility towards Catholicism, was to come on in stages—in 1618 at the outbreak of the Thirty Years War, in 1623 when the Spanish Match, to marry Prince Charles off to the Infanta, was unsuccessfully pursued, and inexorably with the rise of William Laud after the accession of Charles in 1625. This drift towards an irreconcilable polarization crucially will shape our interpretation of Milton's life, work, and thought from his earliest student days onwards.

The north (Cheapside) end of Bread Street, where the Spread Eagle stood, was in the parish of All Hallows. The church of All Hallows, just to the south of the Spread Eagle (on the south-east corner of the intersection with Watling Street), was a crumbling building; the steeple had been struck by lightning in 1559 and demolished, but a full restoration was delayed until 1625.[32] It was in this church that Milton was baptized. The rector of All Hallows was Thomas Edmonds, who after many years of service was too ill to discharge his duties, so Milton was baptized by the curate, Richard Stock, who was to succeed Edmonds in 1611.

Richard Stock was a Yorkshireman who had studied at Cambridge, as did all five of the curates known to have assisted him at All Hallows.[33] He was a product of St John's College, which under the mastership of William Whitaker had been reformed along puritan lines; Whitaker had approved of Stock 'for his ingenuity, industry and proficiency in his studies'.[34] Stock was offered (and declined) a Fellowship at Sidney Sussex by the puritan James Montagu, a beneficiary of James's patronage. Thereafter Stock himself secured a series of valuable patrons. He became chaplain to the Sir Anthony Cope, who had been advocate for puritan causes in successive parliaments; then to one Lady Lane of Bourton on the Water, Gloucestershire; and finally to Sir William Knollys (later earl of Banbury), a prominent courtier and treasurer of the royal household.[35] Under the patronage of Knollys, Stock had become an anti-Catholic polemicist, and by the time Milton was born, he had published a translation of William Whitaker's *Ad rationes decem...responsio* (a rebuttal of Campion's *Rationes decem*), and a collection of anti-Catholic sermons; in 1609 he

4. Richard Stock, portrait
frontispiece to *A Learned and
Very Usefull Commentary
upon the Whole Prophesie of
Malachy* (London, 1641).

published an anti-Catholic Paul's Cross sermon (dedicated to James
Montagu). Thereafter he published nothing except for a funeral sermon (in
which he thanked Lucy countess of Bedford for her bounty), instead turning to
his true vocation, which was 'not to write, but to preach'. When he died in 1626
his funeral sermon was preached by Thomas Gataker, who praised his 'discreet
carriage in the catechizing of the younger sort'.[36] Stock was never accused of
nonconformist practices in his church, but in 1625 he was to align himself with
the puritan cause by becoming one of the founding Feoffees for Impropriations.[37] John Milton senior was living in Bread Street before Stock's arrival; he
did not move his home to be close to a puritan minister; rather a puritan
minister moved into his parish.

The young Milton surely heard Stock preach on many occasions, and may
also have been catechized by him. If so, the process failed to turn the young

Milton into a puritan. Nothing suggests that that induction, if it occurred, influenced the young Milton's personal assumptions about doctrine and discipline. In at least two other respects, however, Stock may have laid the foundations of habits of thought and behaviour that become manifest in Milton's conduct and writing in his student days. First, Stock was an early and vehement anti-Catholic. James had responded quite proportionately to the Gunpowder Plot of 1605, and was unwilling to place the persecution of recusancy high on his political agenda. Stock anticipated the idiom of the militant Protestantism much commoner after 1618 and especially after the fiasco of the Spanish Match. Of course, many who were anti-Catholic would not have considered themselves puritans. Second, Stock provided a role model for how a moderately talented scholar and divine could proceed to advancement in the church and the universities. He demonstrated the value of courting multiple patrons—and of accepting patronage fairly indiscriminately. Milton may have learned from Stock how the patronage system worked and how valuable it could be. As a young man Milton was to secure the patronage of the Bridgewater family, and throughout his life he seems to have enjoyed his association with aristocratic ladies from the Marchioness of Winchester to Viscountess Ranelagh.[38]

The close proximity to St Paul's Cathedral offered preaching of a different order. In November 1622 John Donne, who had (like Milton) been born in Bread Street, was installed as Dean of the Cathedral, a post that he was to occupy until his death in 1631. Little is known about his service as Dean (the act-books of the chapter during this period are lost), but he was obliged to preach on Christmas day, Easter day, and Whit Sunday and is known to have preached on other occasions. His sermons show that he was no friend of Puritanism, and his soteriology owed little to Calvinist theories of predestination. Donne's friends included the anti-Calvinist ceremonialists John Overall and Lancelot Andrewes, and the scholarly sympathizer Isaac Casaubon. When Hugo Grotius, a leading figure among the Dutch supporters of Arminius, came to London he used Casaubon to gain access to those who sympathized with Overall and Andrews, and Donne was part of that circle.[39]

Milton's education began at home. In *Ad patrem* ('To my Father') Milton was later to express his gratitude that his father had paid for lessons in Latin, Greek, Hebrew, French, and Italian. It is likely that instruction in these languages began with private tutors; although Milton went on to study the ancient languages at school, modern languages were not taught in schools, and it seems likely that all of Milton's instruction in French and Italian (and possibly Spanish) was given in the domestic setting.

The formal education of John Milton senior had finished early, although he was a cultivated man, experienced and competent in a demanding profession. He seems resolved that his children, or at least his eldest son, should have the gentleman's education he had probably been denied. The only tutor

5. Milton at the age of 10 (the 'Janssen portrait') (Morgan Library and Museum, New York).

of the young Milton whose name is known is Thomas Young, a Scottish schoolmaster and clergyman who was eventually to become master of Jesus College, Cambridge.[40] On moving to England, Young had worked as an assistant to Thomas Gataker in Rotherhithe, so it may have been Gataker's friend Richard Stock who arranged for Young to become the young Milton's tutor. This short-lived arrangement was effected in 1617 or 1618, and ended in April 1620 when Young was appointed as chaplain to the English Merchant Adventurers in Hamburg. It is not clear where the instruction took place: the comfortable assumption that tuition took place in Bread Street is destabilized by evidence that links Young to Rotherhithe and further afield (Essex, and Ware, in Hertfordshire). In any case, Milton seems to have established a good relationship with Young, and they were to correspond in later years; the surviving parts of the correspondence, all by Milton, consist of two verse epistles and a prose letter, all in Latin. They also exchanged gifts: Young gave a Hebrew Bible (now lost) to Milton, and Milton gave a copy of Thomas Cranmer's *Reformatio legum ecclesiasticarum* (now in Jesus College Cambridge) to Young.

Aubrey reported that Milton's schoolmaster 'was a Puritan in Essex, who cutt his haire short',[41] and that schoolmaster may or may not have been Young. (The clumsy syntax renders it impossible to be sure whether the haircut belonged to the boy or his master.) Alternatively, the term 'school-master' may imply a school rather than private tuition, so it is possible that Milton attended a school in Essex, where his mother had relatives. In *Reason of Church Government* (1641) Milton was to say that he was taught from his 'first years' by 'sundry masters and teachers both at home and at the schools'. No one other than Thomas Young can be named with certainty, but there is some evidence that another of his teachers was Patrick Young, who from 1621 to 1624 was Prebend and Treasurer of nearby St Paul's Cathedral.[42] If so, some measure of Patrick Young's vast learning would have been passed to the studious young boy.

It was during the period of Young's tutelage that Milton's portrait was first painted; he was 10 years old, and as Aubrey says (with reference to this painting) his hair is indeed cut fairly short. The small portrait (20 × 16 in.), which was in the possession of Milton's widow until her death in 1727 and is now in the Morgan Library and Museum in New York, is persistently assigned to Cornelius Janssen (or Johnson), but there is no documentary or stylistic evidence to support this attribution.[43] The portrait shows an elegantly dressed child with refined features, and so represents the aspirations of his father, an increasingly successful businessman who wished his elder son to become a gentleman. The next stage was formal schooling, and so Milton was enrolled at nearby St Paul's School.

CHAPTER 2

St Paul's School

S T Paul's School is now a major public school in West London (Barnes), to which it moved from Hammersmith in 1968. For many centuries, however, it was a one-room school that stood on the north side of the old St Paul's Cathedral,[1] a short walk from Milton's house. The school and all its records, together with the cathedral and much of the City, perished in the Great Fire of 1666, so the earliest record of Milton's attendance there is the admissions book of Christ's College, Cambridge. No extant record includes the dates of his attendance at St Paul's; he must have left near the end of 1624, but he may have entered the school any time between 1615 and 1621. The evidence is contradictory. Milton's nephew Edward Phillips said that his uncle 'was enter'd into the first Rudiments of Learning' at St Paul's, and Christopher Milton told John Aubrey that his brother 'went to school when he was very young'; these comments suggest an early date. On the other hand, Edward Phillips says that Milton was sent to St Paul's 'together with his brother';[2] if 'together' means 'at the same time', then it seems unlikely that Milton would have entered much before December 1622, when Christopher had his seventh birthday. In the *Defensio Secunda* Milton speaks of studying to midnight 'from the age of twelve',[3] and Christopher clearly associates this evening study with his brother's attendance at school;[4] John Milton became 12 on 9 December 1620.

The remote origins of St Paul's School may lie in late antiquity, but the earliest date at which it was constituted as a school is 1103. It is certainly possible that Thomas à Becket and Chaucer were educated there, but the school did not prosper, and by the sixteenth century, it was, in the view of John Colet, 'obviously a school of no importance'. Far from being content to deplore the state of the school, Colet, prompted and guided by Erasmus, took advantage of his position (dean of the cathedral) and his wealth (a large inheritance from his father in 1505) to rebuild it. He bought land on the north side of the cathedral and built a new schoolhouse, which was opened in 1509. He specified that there should be 153 pupils.[5] Colet delegated the governance and financial management of the school to the Mercers' Company (which still substantially retains these roles), and within Colet's lifetime St Paul's became one of the most important schools in England. It was this school, founded on the humanist principles of Erasmus and Colet, that Milton attended.

The school charged no fees, but boys were required to provide their own wax candles (a considerable expense[6]) and had to be able to read and write both English and Latin before they entered the school. The principal medium of instruction was Latin. Teaching in the school's large room was conducted by the high master and the surmaster (also known as the 'usher'); the latter was assisted by an under-usher in charge of the first form.[7] The first four forms were the responsibility of the surmaster, and the last four of the high master. In Milton's time the high master was Alexander Gil the elder; the surmaster was from 1603 to 1637 was William Sound and the under-usher from 1615 to 1621 was Oliver Smythe; neither is ever mentioned by Milton or any of his early biographers, which may imply that Milton did not attend the lower school, and began in the fifth form in 1621.

Alexander Gil the elder (1565–1635) was an Oxford graduate who in 1601 had published *A treatise concerning the trinitie of persons in unitie of the deitie*, an attack on the Anabaptist Thomas Mannering. On 10 March 1608 he was appointed high master of St Paul's School in succession to Richard Mulcaster. 'He had', says Wood, 'such an excellent way of training up youth that none in his time went beyond him; whence 'twas that many noted persons in church and state did esteem it the greatest of their happiness that they had been educated under him.'[8] Less deferential recollections were long enshrined in irreverent songs (quoted by Aubrey) about his enthusiasm for flogging boys, though it is possible that the actions of Gil the younger were, with the passage of time, wrongly attributed to the father who shared his name. Gil was not only famous as a schoolmaster, but was, as Wood attests, 'esteemed by most persons to be a noted Latinist, critic and divine'. His *Sacred Philosophie of the Holy Scripture* (1635) attempted to defend the truth of the Apostles' Creed against the rival creeds of Muslims, Jews, atheists, and heretics. He also wrote a dedicatory poem for John Speed's *Theatre of the Empire of Great Britaine* (1611), and a preface (in Latin) to Francis Anthony's *Apologia veritatis illucescentis, pro auro potabile* (1616) thanking him for curing his infant daughter and one of his sons by the administration of potable gold. His most important book was *Logonomia Anglica* (1619; rev. 1621), which champions a phonetic system of English spelling which may have influenced Milton's strongly held orthographical preferences.

The schoolroom of St Paul's was divided by a curtain, and in each half the four forms were ranged along the three walls and the curtain; the head boy of each form sat at a special desk. Gil taught the four upper forms in turn. In 1621, when Milton may have entered the fifth form,[9] he would have continued his study of Latin (reading Sallust's *Histories* and Virgil's *Eclogues*) and embarked on the study of Greek. In the sixth form (1622) he would have widened his study of Greek to include the *koiné* Greek of the New Testament, and his Latin reading would have included Cicero (probably the *De Officiis* and the *Letters*) and possibly Martial as well as more Virgil. In the seventh form (1623) his study of Attic and *koiné* Greek would have been supplemented by the principal Greek dialects (Aeolic, Doric, and Ionic) and literature written in those dialects, including Theocritus in Doric and Hesiod in Ionic; in Latin he would have read Horace and more Cicero (the *Orations*). Finally, in the eighth form (1624), Milton would have studied Hebrew (using the Hebrew Psalter) and extended his reading in Greek literature (Homer, Euripides, Isocrates, and possibly Demosthenes) and begun the Latin satirists (Persius and Juvenal); history reading was probably Dionysius of Halicarnassus, and science Aratus, both in Greek.[10]

Among those who were at St Paul's in Milton's time only two are known to have become his friends. One was the high master's son, Alexander Gil the younger, and the other was Charles Diodati. Alexander Gil the younger (1596/7–1642?) had attended St Paul's School, where he was taught by William Sound and, in the upper school, by his father. In 1612, at the age of 15, he had been admitted to Trinity College, Oxford, but the next year migrated to Wadham, where he took his BA, and then back to Trinity for his MA (1619). In January 1622 he succeeded Oliver Smythe as under-usher of St Paul's, but continued to prepare for his BD, which was awarded in 1627. Gil's interests included poetry, and in 1624 he had sent a cheerful poem (and some canary wine) to Thomas Farnaby, in whose school he had taught briefly after leaving Oxford.

Some of Gil's other early poetry had a less friendly purpose. Gil took revenge on Ben Jonson's slighting of his father in *Time Vindicated* (1623) by mocking Jonson's 'bed-ridden wit' (he had been paralysed by a stroke), abusing him for the failure of *The Magnetic Lady*, and suggesting that he go back to bricklaying. A similarly disturbing sensibility is expressed in Gil's poem on the death of some ninety Catholic worshippers, who perished when a secret chapel close to St Paul's collapsed on 15 November 1623. The event drew a compassionate response from some Protestants, but Gil celebrated by composing an exultantly vindictive poem, *In ruinam camerae papisticae*, in which he depicts the accident as God's revenge for the Gunpowder Plot.[11]

However, Gil's glee probably accorded more closely with the prevailing mood among English Protestants. In one of those critical shifts in popular sentiment which marked the increasing polarization in England, there was a wave of anti-Catholic sentiment in 1623. The mood of the country had changed in 1618, when the outbreak of the Thirty Years War saw much of continental Europe divided along what seemed like confessional lines. James I's son-in-law, Frederick, the Elector Palatine, the early leader of the Protestant cause, attracted much support among Englishmen, who thought their country, too, should be in arms against the legions of popery, as the forces of the Holy Roman Emperor and his allies were perceived to be. That sentiment intensified as the Protestants sustained numerous early defeats. As Anthony Milton notes, 'The English crown's personal link with the suffering Protestants of the Palatinate ... brought the conflicts of the Thirty Years War into every English parish church, where prayers for the Elector and his family were regularly read.'[12]

James's response, which was one of sustained neutrality, found limited favour, and his principal diplomatic initiative, which was to seek a marriage contract between his heir, Prince Charles, and the Spanish Infanta, caused anger and alarm. In February 1623 Charles, with the Marquis of Buckingham (soon to be created a duke) made a sudden and clandestine journey to Madrid. It ended in failure, to the general rejoicing of most of England. In the process it achieved the greatest public relations success of the early Stuart period, as fireworks, bonfire, peals of bells and extensive, bibulous merrymaking greeted their return.[13] Attitudes towards James's non-interventionist approach to the continental war divided sharply the political nation, and those who thought him still a cherished *rex pacificus*, the peace-maker king, were in a distinct minority. We shall shortly find Milton among their ranks (though his anti-Catholic enthusiasm would appear undimmed).[14]

Charles Diodati (1609/10–1638) may have been the closest friend that Milton ever had. His father was Theodore Diodati, a physician of Tuscan descent and the elder brother of the theologian Giovanni Diodati, whom Milton was to visit in Geneva in 1639; Charles's mother was an Englishwoman whose name is not known.[15] The Diodatis were members of the small Italian Protestant community whose church (which had closed in 1591) had reopened in 1609 in the Mercers' Chapel in Cheapside, a short distance east of Bread Street. Milton's friendship with a young Italian, and the proximity of an Italian expatriate community, may explain the fluency of Milton's spoken Italian and of the Italian sonnets that he was to write before his visit to Italy.[16]

Charles Diodati overlapped with Milton at St Paul's, but was admitted to Trinity College, Oxford in late 1621 or early 1622, and matriculated at the university on 7 February 1623, aged 13. He proceeded BA on 10 December 1625, just as Milton was preparing to go up to Cambridge as an undergraduate. Today this would be regarded as precocity, but the conventions were different in the early seventeenth century. The age entered in the university records was that attained in the academic year of matriculation, so Diodati, if his age was given correctly (some 15 per cent of ages were falsified) turned 13 before the end of Trinity term in June 1623. The Oxford degree took four years, so he must have been in residence at Trinity College when he was 11 or 12; this was the same age at which John Evelyn sent his eldest surviving son (also called John) to the same College.[17] The number of undergraduates under 13 was declining, and it is striking that they are clustered at the upper end of the social scale: many were the sons of peers, baronets, knights, and esquires; fewer the sons of gentlemen and clergy; and virtually none the sons of plebeians and paupers. The reason for this distribution is partly that members of aristocratic and gentry families had no intention of taking a degree, and partly that wealthy families could enrich the education of their sons by recourse to good schools and private tutors. Diodati went up to Oxford early not because he was clever, but because he had been well-educated.[18]

Both Milton and Diodati had poetic aspirations. In the case of Diodati, he wrote what was to be his sole published poem while at Oxford; it was an elegy in Latin alcaics on the death of William Camden.[19] A lifetime later, Milton's widow told John Aubrey that Milton was a poet at the age of 10. None of Milton's extant poems can be assigned to this date, but seven of his schoolboy juvenilia survive, and there are a few other poems that may date to his schooldays.

Milton's earliest datable poems are English paraphrases of psalms 114 and 136; when Milton printed them in 1645 he said that they 'were done by the Author at fifteen years old', which was in 1624. The term 'paraphrase' was not clearly distinguished from the term 'translation' (so the Targum, a translation from Hebrew into Aramaic, was known as the 'Chaldee Paraphrase'), and it seems likely that Milton was working from the Hebrew text, as he was studying Hebrew at St Paul's in 1624 (and may have learned it earlier from Thomas Young, who gave him a Hebrew Bible). What is striking about the poems is the extent to which Milton's lexical choices are influenced by his reading of Josuah Sylvester's English version of Du Bartas, the *Devine Weekes and Workes*. In Psalm 114, Sylvester's 'cleer Jordan's selfe . . . was fain to hide his head' becomes Milton's 'sought to hide his froth-becurled head . . . Jordan's clear streams recoil', and in Psalm 136 Sylvester's 'but contrarie the Red-sea did devower | The barbarous tyrant with his mighty power' become's Milton's 'But full soon they did devour | The tawny king with all his power'.[20] To some modern literary tastes the stylistic influence of Sylvester's Du Bartas, in Milton's psalms as elsewhere, may sometimes seem deleterious, but in late sixteenth- and early seventeenth-century Protestant England, his style was widely praised and hugely influential. As Wordsworth remarked, 'Who is there that can now endure to read *The Creation* of Dubartas? Yet all of Europe once resounded with his praise.'[21] That praise ceased to resound in the age of Dryden,[22] but Milton remained an admirer, and in *Paradise Lost* both the content (especially the invocations and Michael's vision in the closing books) and the style are indebted to Sylvester's Du Bartas.[23]

Milton's paraphrase on Psalm 114 has slipped into scholarly obscurity, but his version of Psalm 136 has become a well-known hymn:

> Let us with a gladsome mind
> Praise the Lord, for he is kind,
>   For his mercies ay endure
>   Ever faithful, ever sure.[24]

It is not clear whether Milton intended to set his words to music, or whether he did so; the version that is now sung (the 'Monkland' tune) does not derive from a Miltonic original. It is the work of John Bernard Wilkes, who in 1861 set Milton's words to a tune written in 1790 by the American composer John Antes (1740–1811), a stalwart of the Moravian Brethren who had arranged a Moravian melody published in *Geistreiches Gesangbuch* (1704).[25]

Milton's other surviving schoolboy poems were written in Latin or Greek. They include an imitation of Mantuan[26] entitled *Apologus de rustico et hero* ('The Fable of a Peasant and his Master')[27] and a Greek epigram with a Latin title, *Philosophus ad regem* ('A philosopher to a king'); both are probably school exercises. The Latin poem is one of several from the period that imitate the same fable from Mantuan, and Milton thought highly enough of it to publish it in his 1673 *Poems*; the reason for its absence from the 1645 collection is not known. The Greek epigram was published in both the 1645 and 1673 *Poems*. The quality of the Greek is unsteady, possibly because of the difficulty of printing Greek accurately, but in 1673 Milton, by then long blind, cared sufficiently about the poem to rework the penultimate line.

In 1874 a page (now in Austin, Texas) apparently in Milton's youthful hand came to light; it contains a prose theme on early rising and two Latin poems, all on the subject of getting out of bed early. The theme is a rhetorical amplification of *Mane citus lectum fuge* ('rise early in the morning'), a maxim that appears in Lily's *Grammar*, which was used at St Paul's. The structure of the exercise follows the method of the late fourth-century Greek sophist and rhetorician Aphthonius of Antioch, whose *Progymnasmata* was available in Latin translation and was widely used in schools in England and Germany. The language of the theme is a tissue of idioms and phrases that reflect Milton's reading, mostly of Cicero's *De Senectute*, but also of Virgil (*Eclogues* and *Georgics*), Plautus, Livy, and Lucan. The two poems are written on the other side of the sheet: one is entitled *Carmina Elegiaca* ('verses written in elegiacs') and the other is an untitled poem (*incipit: Ignavus satrapam*; 'kings should not oversleep') written in asclepiads.[28] Like the prose themes, these two poems demonstrate wide reading in their lexical choices; they also mark the beginning of Milton's lifelong interest in prosody, both in the ancient languages and in English.

Throughout Milton's years at St Paul's he was living at home. In 1621 Thomas Ravenscroft's *Whole Book of Psalmes* was published, and it contained six musical settings by the elder Milton; in the same year John Lane, for whom the elder Milton had composed a sonnet, responded by alluding in a poem to 'those sweet sweet parts Meltonus did compose'.[29]

In 1623 the most important family event of the period occurred: Milton's sister Anne was married to a Chancery official called Edward Phillips. The wedding took place on Saturday 22 November 1623 at the Church of St Stephen, Walbrook;[30] the rector, who conducted the wedding, was Thomas Myriell, almost certainly the man of the same name who was the musical friend of Milton's father. It is not clear why the wedding was held at St Stephen's rather than All Hallows Bread Street, but perhaps friendship or music was a deciding factor. The marriage settlement records a substantial dowry payment of £800 to Edward Phillips.[31] After the wedding, Anne and Edward settled in Westminster, where they lived initially on the Waterside of the Strand and then the Landside, near Charing Cross;[32] it was a very respectable address, as befitted a senior Chancery official (soon to be Deputy Clerk of the Crown Office in Chancery) and the daughter of a prosperous businessman.

The details of the wedding contract allow us to make a better estimate of where John Milton senior stood in the economic hierarchy of contemporary London. Basing his case for the most part on evidence drawn somewhat later, Peter Earle concludes that 'all merchants and wholesalers in the city or in Westminster would be worth more than £1000, sometimes very much more', while 'poorer shopkeepers, in the backstreets and in the poor suburbs, would rarely be worth £1000 and might be worth very much less'.[33] The poet's father evidently could afford £800 for a daughter's dowry, indicative, surely, of considerable affluence in the late Jacobean period; he was among the wealthier businessmen in a thriving business community. No doubt a man who would spend that much on a daughter would not stint himself in providing for his sons, and the scrivener's aspirations for John and Christopher soon became evident, as their childhood, prosperous, culturally and academically stimulating, and untroubled by mortality in the immediate family, drew to a close.

CHAPTER 3

Cambridge: The Undergraduate Years

I N December 1624 Milton turned 16, and this may have been the month in which he finished his education at St Paul's School.[1] Milton's friend Charles Diodati had gone to Oxford two years earlier (aged 11 or 12), but the time when students would choose universities on the basis of friendships or other personal preferences lay centuries ahead. In the seventeenth century choice lay with the father rather than the son, and the most important choice was not that of university or college, but rather of tutor. The principal factor that governed the choice of tutor was the type of spiritual and intellectual guidance that would be given. Milton's father arranged for his son to study under the tutelage of William Chappell, a 42-year-old Fellow of Christ's College in Cambridge.[2]

We have considered already the increasing polarization of practice and belief within the Church of England during Milton's childhood. Those tensions were felt keenly in the universities, where rival positions and principles were more clearly articulated. Cambridge had its anti-ceremonialist and Calvinist hothouses, for example in Emmanuel and Sidney Sussex Colleges. Christ's was more difficult to place on the spectrum, but Chappell and its most illustrious scholar, Joseph Mede, belonged with the Arminians and ceremonialists. The latter group achieved a new momentum over the middle years of the 1620s. Its leading figures had taken to meeting in Durham House, the London palace of Richard Neile, bishop of Durham. William Laud provided much of the energy and political drive for the movement, while Richard Mountague supplied the theological underpinning and controversial dynamism. Its great intellectual precursor and current mentor was Lancelot Andrewes, bishop of Winchester, a figure hugely respected by Prince Charles in the closing years of his father's reign. Career-minded academics—all college fellows, heads of house, and university professors were required to take holy orders—knew to position themselves with respect to this group, for them or against them. (Both options carried opportunities for patronage and dangers of alienating the wrong people, nor, in 1625, could the outcome of the developing struggle be with certainty predicted.) Chappell made his decision, and Milton's father chose him to educate his son.

By the time Milton arrived in Cambridge, William Chappell had forsaken his youthful puritanism and Calvinism, and had become a prominent sacramental Arminian. As early as 1619 John Preston, who was then at Queens' College and belonged to the anti-ceremonialist tendency, told James Ussher[3] that Chappell was suspected of Arminianism, and by the late 1620s Chappell was openly espousing Arminian views, and was regarded as the successor to Richard 'Dutch' Thomson as the university's most outspoken Arminian; as a later commentator noted,

lately there sprung up a new brood of such as did assist Arminianism, as Dutch Thomson of Clare Hall, and Mr William Chappell, Fellow of Christ's College, as the many pupils that were Arminianized under his tuition show.[4]

Eventually the obloquy to which such a position exposed Chappell led to a mental breakdown, and he was rescued from Cambridge by William Laud, by then bishop of London, who in 1633 arranged for his appointment as dean of Cashel, in Ireland.

The unit of accommodation in Cambridge is now the room (for undergraduates) or the set of rooms (for resident dons). In the early seventeenth century, the unit of accommodation was the chamber,[5] which tutors shared with their pupils. When Milton arrived at Christ's College he therefore moved in to William Chappell's chamber. The identity of his chamber-fellows is not known, though they may have included Robert Pory. Just as in inns strangers were expected to share beds,[6] so boys shared beds with each other and with their tutors. Milton's was the last generation to live in such close proximity to their tutors. Modern notions of privacy, which are clearly in evidence in the living arrangements of the mid-seventeenth century, were yet to emerge, though some Cambridge colleges were soon to erect partitions in chambers. In 1652, by which time student numbers had fallen throughout the university, Gonville and Caius College was to express its aspiration to assign a whole chamber to every student. When Milton was in residence, however, the chamber was a communal living space, and in the case of tutors who took a significant number of undergraduates (at Christ's, Chappell and Mede), the accommodation was crowded and intimate.

In 1625 Cambridge University consisted of sixteen colleges;[7] during term time some 2,900 academics and students shared the town with some 7,750 local people.[8] The town was contained within a bend of the River Cam, and

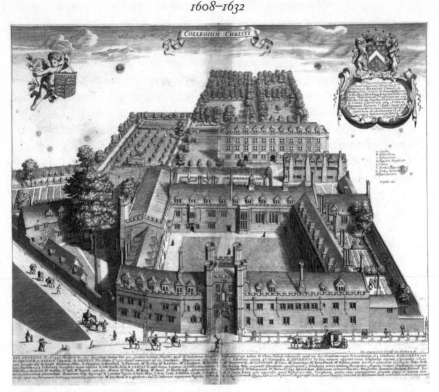

6. Christ's College, Cambridge (from Loggan, *Cantabrigia illustrata* (Cambridge: 1690)).

the presence of the King's Ditch joining two points in the river meant that much of the town was contained on a small island.[9] The medieval town had been built along the river, and so separated the colleges from the river. During the reign of Henry VI, however, the process of clearing the land between the colleges and the river began; the cleared ground was not land-scaped until the eighteenth century (when the gardens now known as the Backs were created), but rather remained as waste ground or was used as pasture or for growing fruit.

When Milton arrived in 1625, the academic staff of Christ's College, which was the third largest after the two huge colleges of Trinity and St John's, consisted of a Master and thirteen Fellows.[10] The most distinguished, the polymath Joseph Mede, was a friend of Milton's tutor. He was at the height of his powers, working to complete his *magnum opus*, the *Clavis Apocalyptica*, which first appeared in 1627. He had secured his Fellowship through the patronage of Lancelot Andrewes, and his own inclinations were certainly ceremonial and Arminian, but he nursed an anxiety that his insistence on equating the pope with the Antichrist perhaps made him appear to be a puritanical zealot in the eyes of those whose support he courted, though for him it was a conclusion founded on his study of the Revelation of St John the Divine.[11] Preferment, the career academic or divine's recurrent concern, often constituted a perplexing quest. But no such problems immediately confronted Milton as he settled into college life, which was centred on the chamber, the chapel, the library, and the hall.[12]

At Cambridge (both then and now) admission to a college was distinct from matriculation at the university. Milton was admitted to Christ's College on Saturday 12 February 1625; the entry in the Admissions Book in the College Archives may be translated

John Milton of London, son of John, inducted into the elements of letters under Mr Gill, high master of St Paul's School, was admitted as a pensioner on 12 February 1624/25, under Mr Chappell. He paid an entrance fee of 10 shillings.[13]

This entry, which constitutes the only documentary evidence that Milton attended St Paul's School, describes Milton as a minor pensioner. There were four classes of undergraduates: fellow-commoners (also known as major pensioners or greater pensioners), pensioners (also known as lesser pensioners or minor pensioners), sizars, and scholars. In the term in which Milton was admitted, the only fellow-commoner to be admitted was Richard (later Sir Richard) Earle of Stragglesthorpe, Lincolnshire, who paid a fee of 20 shillings; he too was assigned to Chappell, but because of his rank dined at high table with the Fellows and was entitled to separate accommodation. At the other end of the class hierarchy, some students were admitted as sizars, and so paid a modest fee of 5 shillings and worked for wealthy students to supplement their income, and others were admitted as scholars, and so paid no fees for tuition or board, but rather were supported by the endowments of the college. Students from Milton's social background were normally pensioners, and constituted the largest group at Christ's. This was the status of Robert Pory, whose name follows Milton's in the Admissions Book; he had been an exact contemporary at St Paul's, and was later to be sequestered because of his Arminianism.[14]

As the Lent term of 1625 drew to a close, news arrived that King James had died (27 March); on 30 March King Charles was proclaimed at the market cross in Cambridge. The university dutifully marked the transition with a collection of poems, *Cantabrigiensium Dolor et Solamen: seu Decessio Beatissimi Regis Jacobi Pacifici: et Successio Augustissimi Regis Caroli* (Cambridge, 1625). Senior academics, titled alumni, and graduates predominate; the absence of a scrivener's son, in his first year as an undergraduate, need not detain us long. Moreover, Milton's great burst of commemorative poems mourning the death of public figures lay more than a year in the future. The title at once rehearses James's favoured epithet, *pacificus*, and discloses some uncertainty about what the accession of Charles ushered in; he is, vaguely, *augustissimus*. Any uncertainty would soon be resolved. James had held the rival wings of the Church of England in a politic equilibrium; Charles allowed and promoted the victory of the Arminians in general—and William Laud in particular.

The Lent term ended on Friday 8 April, and the next day Milton matriculated at the university, presenting himself along with six other undergraduates from Christ's (including Robert Pory) to James Tabor, the long-serving Registrary (from 1600 to 1645). His matriculation is recorded in the University Matriculation Book. This was the formal beginning of his university (as opposed to college) career, and when the Easter term began on 27 April, it was the first of the twelve terms that Milton had to complete for his BA; four years later he was to be pronounced BA by the Proctor, at the end of the Lent term in 1629. Milton's four years of residence (*quadriennium*) required for his degree spanned five academic years, which was entirely normal during this period; six students who joined Christ's College in the same term as Milton finished at the same time as he did;[15] of the six with whom he matriculated, two (including Pory[16]) were to be admitted BA alongside him.

The syllabus at Cambridge has long been the Cinderella topic in studies of the university in the seventeenth century, partly because evidence is in short supply, but also because historians have been more concerned with the university as a national institution than with the student experience. W. T. Costello's pioneering study[17] of the problem (1958) identified some of the issues, but erred in seeing the syllabus as an anachronism in the age of new learning. The topic did not receive a thorough investigation until Mordechai Feingold's researches were published in 1997 in the seventeenth-century volume of *The History of the University of Oxford*.[18] It may seem odd that an investigation of Oxford should yield an understanding of Cambridge, but in matters of curriculum and teaching methods there was no significant difference between the universities, a fact that enables Feingold to use Cambridge material to flesh out his account of Oxford. In our account we will use Feingold's Oxford material to illuminate Cambridge, and also draw on Victor Morgan's recently published volume of *A History of the University of Cambridge*.[19] The statutes of 1570, which were in force in modified form when Milton was at Cambridge, stipulated in broad terms that 'the first year shall teach rhetoric, the second and third logic, the fourth shall add philosophy'. Under these capacious headings what was actually studied was classical languages and literature. The subject matter of the texts studied extended beyond literature and philosophy (both moral and natural) to include history, logic, Roman law, and the mathematical sciences. The intensity of study varied very considerably: aristocratic students who did not plan to take a degree were content to dabble; similarly, those who planned to move to one of the Inns of Court before embarking on formal disputations in their third year were unlikely to be serious students. However, those who planned to take a degree and stay on for the MA (three more years) and possibly the BD (seven years after the MA) or even DD (five years after the BD), were expected to be committed to a life of study, and their tutors were accordingly more demanding.

Examination was by disputation (a form of debate) and declamation (a rhetorical plea), and so lectures were supplemented by practice for participation in these genres. Some tutors gave lectures in their chambers, occasionally from the comfort of their beds, and all tutors arranged structured Latin conversations with groups of pupils, who were encouraged to be disputatious. Within the colleges there were exercises, some more solemn than others, designed to prepare students for university disputations in the building known as the Public Schools (now known as the Old Schools); college and university lecturers also read lectures to groups of students.

Twenty-first century students tend to return to their homes during vacations, but this was not necessarily the pattern in the seventeenth century; indeed, some students remained at university for the duration of their studies. In 1625 the Easter term ended on 8 July, but it is unlikely that Milton returned home to Bread Street, because an epidemic of plague was ravaging London,[20] and many undergraduates chose to remain in college because Cambridge was not yet affected. By the end of July, however, the epidemic had spread to Cambridge, and on 1 August all public gatherings at the university were discontinued. It seems likely that Milton left Cambridge at this point and joined his family at a retreat in the countryside. Oxford was unaffected (on 1 August Parliament was adjourned from Westminster to Oxford), so it possible that the Miltons returned to the part of Oxfordshire where John Milton senior had grown up.

By autumn the plague had abated, and Michaelmas term began on 10 October. In December Milton turned 17, and the following day his friend Charles Diodati received his BA at Oxford. Two letters from Diodati to Milton survive in the British Library. Both are in simple Greek prose written in a hand that uses conventional contractions and abbreviations (rather than copying printed forms), which implies a relaxed ease with the language. The Greek, however, is unambitious and not perfect, and in one of the letters there is a marginal correction in what seems to be Milton's hand. The letters are undated, and may have been written any time between Diodati's departure for Oxford in 1623 and Milton's departure for Italy in 1638. What is striking about the letters is their playful erotic charge. In one of the letters, which seems to imply a joint excursion the following day, Diodati assures Milton that 'all will be fine tomorrow, and air and sun and river and trees and birds and men will laugh and (if I may say without giving offence) dance with us'. J. Milton French, who adapted Masson's earlier translation, omitted the suggestion of dancing, which makes it deeply unclear how offence might have been given.[21] The teasing reference to dancing is immediately followed by a deft and disarming citation of a line from *Iliad* (2.408) in which Menelaus comes uninvited (and so eagerly) to join his brother Agamemnon. The sexual frisson in the other letter is similarly poised. Diodati asks Milton to be the noble companion that will give him happiness, and concludes 'enjoy yourself, but not like Sardanapalus in Soli'. The Greek word *paize* hovers between innocent play and sexual enjoyment, but the comparison to the effeminate Assyrian king Sardanapalus (an adumbration of the 'Lady of Christ's' tag) is overtly sexual. The explicitness is again immediately subverted, this time by the reference to Soli, the eponym of the English word 'solecism' (the Attic dialect of the colonists in the Cilician town of Soli was deemed to be corrupt), so Diodati is playfully warning Milton against sexual and lexical deviation.

In April 1626, Milton composed the verse-letter now known as *Elegia Prima*, which was addressed to Diodati, who was then living in Chester.[22] Lent term had ended on 31 March, and Milton had returned to London; Easter term was to begin on 19 April, and Milton was preparing to go back to Cambridge. The letter is a spirited hymn of praise to metropolitan life, contrasting the dreariness of remote Cambridge with the joys of London. Milton speaks of exile, and this has sometimes been interpreted as a reference to his rustication; more likely, as John Carey has observed, Milton's 'exile' is merely the university vacation.[23]

In the autumn of 1626 four public and university figures died, and Milton decided to write commemorative poems for all four.[24] Lancelot Andrewes, the bishop of Winchester, died on 25 September. Richard Ridding, the University Beadle, expired the following day. On 5 October it was the turn of Nicholas Felton, the bishop of Ely. Finally, the anatomist John Gostlin, who was Regius Professor of Physic, master of Gonville and Caius, and the university's vice-chancellor, died on 21 October.[25]

No evidence better establishes the ideological perspective of young Milton than the poem he wrote for Lancelot Andrewes, *Elegia Tertia, In Obitum Praesulis Wintoniensis* ('Elegy 3, On the Death of the Bishop of Winchester'). Andrewes was the founding father of English ceremonial Arminianism, advocating that cause long before it was expedient or even safe to do so. Indeed, early in the reign of James he had been warned off public criticism of the doctrine of predestination. Laud in his diary called him 'the great light of the Christian world', and Charles I appointed Laud as co-editor of a posthumous edition of his sermons. In the poem, Andrewes is translated to a baroque heaven where Milton depicts him in bright alb, the celestial equivalent of elaborate ecclesiastical vestments: 'A star-like radiance shone from his

7. Lancelot Andrewes, (portrait frontispiece from his *XCVI. Sermons by the Right Honourable, and Reverend Father in God, Lancelot Andrewes, late Lord Bishop of Winchester. Published, by His Majesties speciall command*, 2nd edition (London, 1631)).

bright face, a white robe flowed down to his golden feet and his god-like head was circled by a white band.'[26]

Richard Ridding had been the Esquire Bedel of the university since 1596; he had resigned his post on 16 September 1626, signed his will on the 19th and died on the 26th. The two Bedels[27] at Cambridge, where they are known as Esquire Bedels, are now holders of purely ceremonial posts (that of processional mace-bearers who walk in front of the vice-chancellor), but in the seventeenth century they were also executive officers of the university; the mace that Ridding carried in academic processions (mentioned in the first line of Milton's poem) is still owned by the university.[28] Milton's poem, *Elegia secunda, In Obitum Praeconis Academici Cantabrigiensis* ('Elegy Two, On the Death of the Bedel of the University of Cambridge') commemorates one whom Milton would have seen in a procession, but would not have met.

Nicholas Felton, the bishop of Ely, another ceremonialist, was a friend of Lancelot Andrewes, who had supported him for the Mastership of Pembroke Hall. Milton's commemorative poem, *In Obitum Praesulis Eliensis* ('On the Death of the Bishop of Ely'), is markedly similar to the poem for Lancelot Andrewes, whose own death receives mention here.[29] The metre of the Felton poem is an experiment in epodics (iambic lines with alternating trimeters and dimeters), which may reflect Milton's reading of Horace's first ten *Epodes*; similarly, his allusion to the 'Greek poet' in line 20 glances adeptly at Archilochus, who was thought to have invented the metre. Milton commemorates Felton as '*rex sacrorum*', king of the sacred rites,[30] in his diocese, and the poet's grief is assuaged by the appearance of the dead bishop who describes, in a baroque extravaganza, his apotheosis.

John Gostlin was a physician, academic, and politician whose career had been impeded by suspicions of popery; he was eventually elected master of Gonville and Caius after his religious credentials were attested by the Arminian bishop George Mountain (or Montaigne), whom Milton was memorably to castigate for his 'canary-sucking, and swan-eating palat'.[31] That was in 1641, by which time Milton had been radicalized. While at Cambridge fifteen years earlier, however, he took a different view. His *In Obitum Procancellarii Medici* ('On the Death of the Vice-Chancellor, a Doctor') imitates Horace's alcaic ode metre (each stanza has two pentameters and two trimeters), and when Milton printed it in his 1645 *Poemata*, he placed it first. Milton's friend Diodati had written an elegy for Camden in the same difficult metre, and in his prosodic choice Milton's eye may have been on Diodati as much as on Horace.[32]

At about the same time, Milton wrote *In Quintum Novembris* ('On the Fifth of November'), which must have been completed by the anniversary of the Gunpowder Plot.[33] Celebrating the overthrow of a Catholic coup not only afforded an opportunity for mildly riotous behaviour, it also allowed ceremonialists and Arminians to distance themselves from the taint of popery without much controversial ingenuity. The defeat of the conspirators was marked every year by sermons, and those who had given such sermons included Lancelot Andrewes (who had given the first, in Whitehall, in 1606) and John Donne (in St Paul's, in 1622); in Cambridge there was an annual sermon in St Mary's Church and an oration in the King's College Chapel. These arrangements are known because they were stipulated in a decree of 1606. There were no such decrees for Colleges, but it seems safe to assume that there were similar events at College level, and that *In Quintum Novembris* was a contribution to the marking in Christ's College of the twenty-first anniversary of the defeat of the Plot.[34] In the event, Milton also wrote four terse epigrams on the subject of the deliverance of the king and a fifth on the inventor of gunpowder (*In Inventorem Bombardae*). These poems may have been written in successive years or in a single creative burst. The poem in praise of gunpowder is probably part of the sequence (in which case it must be ironic), but it is possible that it is an unconnected encomium. Intermittently through poems which are essentially demonstrations of learned but still adolescent wit Milton demonstrates his endorsement of James's abiding image as the *rex pacificus*. Indeed, he uses that very epithet—despite the fact that England, by the time of writing *In Quintum Novembris* had entered into ill-advised and unsuccessful wars with Spain and France. Thus, England and Scotland are represented in the former neutralist days of high Jacobean prosperity: 'this island, blessed with wealth and joyful peace, with its fields cram-full of Ceres's gifts.' Celebration of James's escape from the plot is both ceremonially devotional and joyfully riotous: 'Pious incense is burned and grateful honours paid to God. There is merry-making at every crossroads and smoke rises from the festive bonfires.'[35]

In 1627 Milton embarked on his third year at Cambridge, and so was required to participate in disputations and to deliver declamations. The long shadow that these forms were to cast includes 'L'Allegro' and 'Il Penseroso', which recall the disputation, and *Areopagitica*, which is a latter-day declamation. Indeed, Milton's extant disputations show a mastery of Latin prose and an understanding of the combative stratagems of polemic, both of which were essential to his much later roles as controversialist in general and as defender of the republic in particular.

Disputations were raucous public debates in colleges and in the Public Schools. In 1600 students at Cambridge had been admonished to stop 'standinge upon stalles, knockinge, hissinge and other immoderate behaviour'; in 1630 the Provost of Queen's College, Oxford, was told that such occasions were characterized by 'great riots, tumults, abuses and disorders'.[36] At the end of his life Milton published some of his contributions to these academic exercises as *Prolusiones*, and they are known to students of Milton as prolusions. The numbering of the prolusions in the 1674 edition is not a safe guide to the order in which they were delivered. More importantly, it is not clear how the prolusions relate to the requirements for the BA and MA. At the end of the first year, undergraduates began to attend disputations as observers but did not participate. In the course of the last two years of their undergraduate study, students were required to contribute (as proponent or opponent) to two disputations in the Public Schools and two in College; the MA required three contributions as proponent in the Public Schools (each opposed by someone who had already proceeded to the MA), two college exercises in which the candidate responded to someone of his own standing, and one declamation in the Public Schools. Milton's Prolusion 6 may be part of the statutory exercises, if that requirement could be fulfilled by a ribald address to his fellow students at a College entertainment (known as a 'salting') on the eve of a long vacation. Of the other six, four (1, 2, 3, and 7) are orations (*declamationes*) and two (4 and 5) are Milton's half of formal debates (*disputationes*).[37] Prolusions 2, 3, and 5 were read in the Public Schools, and Prolusions 1, 4, and 7 were read in Christ's College; Prolusion 7 was read in the chapel, and the others either there or in the hall. It is not possible to map Milton's prolusions onto the exercises required by the university, and there are anomalies: why, for example, did Milton give two orations in the Public Schools (2 and 3) when only one was required? The answer may be that one of these orations was prepared for an occasion that has not been identified.

Disputations typically took place three times a week in college, and tutors sometimes conducted additional disputations in their rooms. At university level, disputations took place during the Lent term. The most important disputations were those held on formal occasions such as a royal visit or Commencement. The topics for disputations were assigned, and it is difficult to generalize about the extent to which the personal views of the participants are represented in their speeches. On the one hand, as Richard Steele remarked in a *Spectator* article in 1712, 'those who have been present at publick Disputes in the University, know that it is usual to maintain Heresies for Argument's sake. I have heard a Man a most impudent socinian for half an hour, who has been an Orthodox Divine all his Life after.' On the other hand, as was claimed at St John's College in the 1570s, 'factyious & seditious Questions are sometime propounded & contradictions maynteyned in bravery which move altercation & strife'.[38] In other words, the form of the disputation allowed speakers either to defend opinions that might be utterly contrary to their own or to articulate dissenting opinions without fear of reprisal.[39]

Various attempts have been made to date and order the prolusions, but for the most part hard evidence is wanting.[40] Of the four delivered in College, Prolusion 4 ('In the Destruction of any Substance there can be no resolution into First Matter') and Prolusion 1 ('Whether Day or Night is Better') may be undergraduate pieces, but in Prolusion 7 ('An Oration in Defence of Learning'), Milton mentions that he has spent the summer in the country; as the motive for such relocations was escape from the plague, and as 1630 was a plague year, it seems likely that this prolusion was delivered in the autumn of 1630. Indeed, the sheer quality of Prolusion 7, both in terms of its Latinity and its rhetorical power, implies that this is a relatively mature work, and its title hints that it may have been the declamation that Milton was required by statute to deliver for his MA. Prolusion 6 has traditionally been dated 1628, but there are good reasons for assigning it to 1631. Of the three prolusions delivered in the Public Schools, Prolusions 3 ('An attack on the Scholastic Philosophy') and 5 ('There are no partial forms in an animal in addition to the whole') are jejune pieces, but Prolusion 2 ('On the harmony of the spheres') is another powerfully eloquent piece that would seem to be a product of

Milton's postgraduate years. We shall therefore consider Prolusions 4, 1, 3, and 5 in the context of Milton's undergraduate career, and defer discussion of 7, 6, and 2 until we come to Milton's years as a postgraduate.

In Prolusion 4 Milton was the proponent, and had to argue that when any substance is destroyed, there can be no resolution into primary matter; his opponents were obliged to refute his argument. Milton argues his assigned perspective vigorously, but suddenly interrupts himself to say to his opponents 'I don't know whether I have bored you, but I have certainly bored myself'. He then expresses the hope that he will be able to reduce his opponents to primary matter, or preferably to annihilate them altogether. This adept use of *captatio benevolentiae*, the rhetorical strategy of securing the good will of the audience and of the moderator who would judge the debate, was to become a feature of Milton's polemical works, and even appears in the preface to *De Doctrina Christiana*.

In Prolusion 1 Milton was again the proponent in a College disputation, this time arguing that day is better than night. On this occasion he chooses to mock the convention of *captatio benevolentiae*, insisting that he is so disliked that he has no hope of persuading his audience that day is superior to night. The obloquy that he suffers, he assures his audience, is heartily reciprocated, for they are so shallow and ignorant that they are incapable of understanding his argument. Four centuries later, it is impossible to judge the tone of these remarks, especially as they are the written record of an oral occasion. Was Milton actually isolated from his fellow students, or was he sufficiently confident of their affections to feign a mutual dislike? One sentiment anticipates a familiar assertion of Milton's late poems, namely, that he values the opinion of the few over that of the multitude; this sentiment anticipates 'fit audience though few' in *Paradise Lost* and the contempt of the Jesus of *Paradise Regained* for the 'miscellaneous rabble'.[41] Many of Milton's opinions changed in the course of his lifetime, but he never claimed to be a populist or to worry much about his own singularity.

The Lent term in 1627 ended on 17 March, and Milton returned to London. On 26 March he wrote from London to Thomas Young in Hamburg, thanking him in Latin prose for the gift of a Hebrew Bible and enclosing a copy of a verse letter which was later published as *Elegia quarta*.[42] In the prose letter Milton addresses Young as his former tutor, apologizing that his earlier letters (all now lost) have been few in number, short in length and remote in time—he has not written at all for three years. Young, like Milton, was to turn against the Laudian church in the late 1630s, but at this stage he seems to have been fully accommodated to episcopal church government, and was steadily building his career. The Merchant Adventurers of Hamburg occupied a fine early fifteenth-century house on the Alte Gröningerstrasse. Young's formal position was that of chaplain to the merchant court, in which capacity he also conducted services in the ornate chapel on the second floor of the Englisches Haus.

Unlike Puritans such as Thomas Cartwright in Antwerp, who was never nominated by the Merchants, Young was their official chaplain, and so was not a puritan exile. When Milton asks why their homeland has driven its children abroad and forced them to forage on foreign shores,[43] he is not alluding to the exiled Puritans, but rather expressing extravagant regret that Young is so far away. Indeed, the following year (27 March 1628) Young returned to England, where he was presented with the living of St Peter and St Mary, Stowmarket (Suffolk), a post that he was to retain, sometimes pluralistically, for the rest of his life, even during the period of Laudian reform, during which time the floor of the chancel was raised. Similarly, Milton depicts Young as surrounded by battles, but Hamburg was not attacked during the Thirty Years War, nor had there been any battle within 150 miles.

What Milton has to say about the war merits careful attention. As much as any issue, it served as an ideological touchstone. Among particularly the zealous and puritanical, the Protestant cause was one actively to be espoused, even to the extent of direct military involvement, while James's non-interventionism was repugnant, a betrayal of coreligionaries. Milton's comments in *Elegia Quarta* place him firmly in support of the *rex pacificus*. The conflict is not represented as a crusade for religion or a struggle to regain England's honour, lost when the Elector Palatine was expelled from his homeland. Instead, it is a confessionally undifferentiated threat to Young and his family: 'Rumour...reports that wars are breaking out in the lands which border yours, that you and your city are surrounded by cruel-looking soldiers, and that Saxon leaders have already prepared their weapons for battle.'[44] Saxony fought on the Protestant side.

The Easter term of 1627 began on 4 April, and Milton may have returned to Cambridge in time for the start of term. However, the fact that he signed documents in London on 25 May and 11 June,[45] during term time, may imply that this was the term in which he incurred the wrath of his tutor. The evidence for the incident is twofold.[46] First, on 9/19 May 1654 the exiled royalist Bishop John Bramhall wrote from Antwerp to his son (code-named John Pierson) to excoriate Milton as

one who was sometime Bishopp Chappell's pupil in Christ Church in Cambridge, but turned away by him, as he well deserved to have been both out of the University and out of the society of men. If Salmasius his friends knew as much of him as I, they would make him go near to hang himself.[47]

Bramhall was hardly an unbiased witness, as will become apparent in Chapter 11,[48] but it seems likely that his source was Chappell, his fellow Irish bishop.

'Out of the society of men' may imply a sexual offence; such offences were not unprecedented either in Bramhall's world (his friend John Atherton, who was also an Irish bishop, had been hanged for incest and sodomy) or in Milton's (William Power, the senior Fellow of Christ's, was suspected by Chappell's friend Joseph Mede of being a sodomite).[49] Any hint of a homoerotic sexual scandal could well originate in the events that disrupted Milton's progress partway through his undergraduate course.

The second source is Milton's brother Christopher Milton, who told John Aubrey that:

His 1st Tutor there was Mr Chapell, from whom receiving some unkindnesse, he was afterwards (though it seemed [contrary to] ye rules of ye Coll:) transferred to the Tuition of one Mr Tovell, who dyed Parson of Lutterworth.[50]

Above the word 'unkindnesse', Aubrey (then or later) wrote 'whip't him'. The hostile account of Bishop Bramhall implies that Milton had committed a serious offence; the friendly account of Christopher Milton implies a private altercation in which fault lay with the unkindness of Chappell, though 'unkindnesse' could itself be some sort of euphemism or a laconic dismissal of an episode of corporal punishment. If Bramhall's view is correct, Milton may have been rusticated, though there seems to be no record of such a rustication in the college or university archives. If the latter is correct, Milton may simply have withdrawn from Cambridge and asked his father to find another tutor. It is certainly possible that Milton was whipped; just as he later perhaps whipped John and Edward Phillips, so he may have received the same punishment himself.[51] Whipping was not normally used to punish students of Milton's age, but it was a punishment used from time to time, and at Christ's the right to whip seems to have been reserved to the praelector and the deans; Chappell was neither, so if Milton was whipped it was not an official punishment for an offence that would have been recorded, but rather a private affair in Chappell's chamber.

The nature and date of the dispute are not clear, nor is the evidence for whipping conclusive, but whatever happened Milton returned to London. Even the return to London for a term may have another explanation: the requirement in the Elizabethan statutes of twelve terms of residence had been relaxed in 1578 by a formal decree that allowed students to be excused from one of the twelve terms, and Milton's difficulties with Chappell may have occasioned his taking advantage of that abatement.

While in London, Milton seems to have walked on the fashionable city promenades and in the fields outside the walls.[52] The city promenade and the 'prospects' to be enjoyed in the nearby countryside were markers by which the urban élite distinguished themselves and inspected possible mates. Milton's account of these walks is the subject of *Elegia Sexta*,[53] which culminates in a story of love at first sight that draws on Latin poets for its phrasing (Horace,

Ovid, Buchanan) and Italian poets for its content (Dante, Petrarch, and their successors); perhaps the closest analogy is Dante's first sight (also on 1 May) of Beatrice, as recorded in the *Vita Nuova*.

The dispute with Chappell propelled Milton's father into action, as he needed to secure another tutor for his son. He might have learned of Nathaniel Tovey from Richard Stock (the late rector of All Hallows, who had died in April 1626) or Dr Diodati (the father of Charles), because both had links with the Harington family, whose patronage had extended to John Tovey and his son Nathaniel.[54] Milton's new tutor, like Chappell, was later to be deprived as a Laudian in the 1640s (the charges included refusing to use the *Directory* instead of the *Book of Common Prayer*, railing in the altar, and raising the steps in the chancel), so the change of tutor nevertheless ensured a continuity of Arminian and ceremonialist influence, which presumably satisfied a significant criterion as John Milton senior made his choice. The new arrangement seemed to work satisfactorily, and one measure of its success was that five years later, when Milton's younger brother Christopher went up to Christ's College, he too became the pupil of Nathaniel Tovey.

The episode of Milton's return to London coincided with, and may have occasioned, the decision of Milton's father to make some financial provision for his elder son. On 11 June 1627 Milton the elder lent £300 to Richard Powell, the indigent squire of Forest Hill, in Oxfordshire;[55] Forest Hill is less than a mile from Stanton St John, the childhood home of Milton's father, so borrower and lender had probably known each other for many years. Security for the loan took the form of a statute staple[56] for £500 payable to the younger Milton, who was also a signatory to the agreement. The loan, at 8 per cent,[57] would earn £24 in interest annually, payable in two instalments on or about 12 June and 12 December every year. In the event, Powell was to service the debt for 17 years before defaulting on 12 June 1644. More significantly, the financial arrangement almost certainly played a part in Milton's marriage to Richard Powell's daughter.[58]

Milton returned to Cambridge for the beginning of the Lent term on 13 January 1628. Shortly after he arrived, his niece Anne Phillips, daughter of Anne and Edward, died; she was buried on 22 January.[59] The evidence is mixed,[60] but it seems likely that the death of Anne was the occasion for Milton's composition of 'On the death of a fair infant', which is (apart from translations) Milton's earliest surviving poem in English. For ten stanzas the poet addresses the fair infant in a classical idiom that may not have been familiar to the child's mother, but in the final stanza Milton addresses his sister with a consolation phrased in wholly accessible language:

> Then thou the mother of so sweet a child
> Her false imagined loss cease to lament,
> And wisely learn to curb thy sorrows wild;
> Think what a present thou to God hast sent,
> And render him with patience what he lent;
>   This if thou do he will an offspring give
> That till the world's last end shall make thy name to live.[61]

The final lines imply that there will be more children, which must have seemed a safe assumption, because Milton's sister was pregnant.[62]

On 2 July 1628 Milton wrote to Alexander Gil from Cambridge, and described his furtive contribution to Commencement the previous day. One of the Fellows of Christ's had had to act as respondent in a disputation, and in keeping with the custom of the occasion had arranged for printed 'act verses' on the theme of the disputation to be distributed during his opening speech.[63] The Fellow had deputed the task of composing the verses to Milton, who enclosed a copy to Gil. Neither the Fellow nor the theme of the verses is disclosed in the letter, but the Fellow was probably Robert Gell, who proceeded BD at the ceremony and was the only Fellow of Christ's to be graduating that summer. Gell, who seems to have been an Arminian, was in 1663 to preside over the marriage of Milton to his third wife, so it is possible that he and Milton remained in touch in the intervening years.[64] The poem in question is lost, but may be an earlier version of either *Naturam non pati senium* ('that nature is not subject to old age') or *De Idea Platonica* ('on the Platonic idea'), both of which, as John Hale has shown, are related to the genre of the act verse.[65]

Milton's letter to Gil goes on to complain about the lack of learning in his fellow students, many of whom would soon become clergymen. He observes (in Latin) that

There is really hardly anyone among us, as far as I know, who, almost completely unskilled and unlearned in Philology and Philosophy alike, does not flutter off to Theology unfledged, quite content to touch that also most lightly, learning barely enough for sticking together a short harangue by any method whatever and patching it with worn-out pieces from various sources—a practice carried far enough to make one fear that the priestly Ignorance of a former age may gradually attack our Clergy.[66]

In later years Milton would come to doubt the necessity of learning for clergymen, but as a student he remained committed to the notion of a learned clergy, and like William Laud himself, worried about their inadequacies.

University disputations were delivered in the Lent term by senior sophisters (fourth year undergraduates) about to graduate, so it seems likely that Prolusions 3 and 5 were delivered in the Public Schools during the Lent terms of 1628 (13 January–4 April) and 1629 (13 January–27 March), though there is no indication of which might be earlier. Prolusion 3 is an attack on scholasticism focused (as the allusion to the 'subtle doctors' shows) on the philosophical tradition of Duns Scotus, who in the eyes of humanists and Reformers encapsulated all that was repugnant about scholastic philosophy; a variant spelling of his name (and birthplace) produced the English word 'dunce', which in the seventeenth century was still strongly linked to the Doctor Subtilis. The Catholic Church (especially in Spain) continued to champion Scotist thought (and in 1993 he was beatified), but for learned Protestants he represented scholastic philosophy at its most incomprehensible. Opposition to the Scotist tradition therefore represented both Protestant sentiments and a principled opposition to the complexity of scholastic thought. What is distinctive about Milton's approach is the adverse judgement of scholasticism by the Horatian criteria of pleasure and instruction; this ploy enables Milton to contrast scholasticism with 'divine poetry, with its heaven-sent power', which 'elevates the mind and sets it amongst the heavenly mansions'.

Prolusion 5 defends the unappetizing Thomistic contention that 'there are no partial forms in an animal in addition to the total form'. Whereas in Prolusion 3 Milton had attacked the Franciscan Duns Scotus, here he invokes the Dominican Chrysostomus Javellus, borrowing a supportive argument 'from the dung-heap of his crude style', presumably the style of his commentaries on the *Physics* of Aristotle and the *Summa* of Thomas Aquinas. The substance of the prolusion is unlikely to engage the attention of anyone other than a student of scholasticism, but its learning, like that of Prolusion 3, is of interest because it is indicative of the range of Milton's reading in this unfashionable field, and also for his sympathy with earlier humanist attacks on scholastic thought (Erasmus et al.), by now over a century old.

The Lent term of 1629 was Milton's last as an undergraduate, and these disputations completed the requirements for the BA degree. He was deemed to have completed his four years in residence (*quadriennium*) since his matriculation at the university. Milton was required to supplicate for his degree and to subscribe to the three Articles of Religion. Christ's College presented thirty students, of whom twenty-seven had been admitted at the same time as Milton and six had been contemporaries at St Paul's. John Fenwick of Christ's assembled the thirty undergraduates and, to save time, dictated the formula for supplication and then signed each of the forms; the supplication is therefore in Milton's hand (except for Fenwick's signature).[67]

Milton was also obliged to subscribe to the three Articles of Religion specified by revised Canons of 1604 (number 36), whose purposes included the countering of puritanism. Milton signed the Latin version that had been drawn up by Bancroft (then bishop of London), as this was the sole authoritative text. In signing he affirmed, willingly and seriously (*ex animo*),

1. that the King's Majesty, under God, is the only supreme governor of this realm....
2. that the Book of Common Prayer, and of Ordering of Bishops, Priests and Deacons contained in it nothing contrary to the Word of God, and that it may lawfully so be used
3. that we allow the Book of Articles of Religion agreed upon...in 1552, and acknowledge all and every the Articles therein contained, being in number Nine-and-Thirty.

Milton would in due course become an opponent of the monarchy, of the Book of Common Prayer, of episcopacy and of several of the 39 Articles, but at the age of 20 all available evidence indicates that he was still an ecclesiastical and theological conservative, and so contentedly signed the subscription. On Tuesday 26 March 1629 he was declared by the Proctor to be a Bachelor of Arts. There was no grand ceremony comparable to Commencement, which took place in July for the conferring of degrees of master and doctor, but Milton had time to draw breath after a taxing term, and used some of that time to write poetry.

One poem that was almost certainly written at this time is *Elegia Quinta*, a poem on the coming of spring (*In adventum veris*). It is also a poem about the burgeoning of sexuality. The Ovidian *poscit opus* (line 8), as Parker coyly remarked, 'implies a returning potency not altogether poetical'.[68] The phrase evokes Ovid's *Amores* (3. 7. 67–8):

> quae nunc, ecce, vigent intempestiva valentque,
> nunc opus exposcunt militiamque suam

In Christopher Marlowe's translation,

> Now, when he should not jet, he bolts upright,
> And craves his task, and seeks to be at fight.

The explicitness is startling, but it is also a reminder that Milton felt more unbuttoned in Latin than in English. The description of spring admits little of the green world, but uses the idiom of classical antiquity to welcome the voluptuous baring of breasts and the breath of passion.

Two other poems, both in English, may have been written in the same spring. One is a cheerful 'Song: On May Morning' that resembles *Elegia Quinta* both in its subject and in its suggestion that May inspires 'warm desire'. Milton was still experimenting with style, and this aubade reminds his readers that he could write in the style of Ben Jonson. The second poem on the same theme is a sonnet (later numbered 'Sonnet 1'), of which the opening lines are a paraphrase of two lines (25–6) in *Elegia Quinta*:

> O nightingale, that on yon bloomy spray
> Warblest at eve, when all the woods are still

Iam Philomela tuos foliis adoperta novellis
Instituis modulos, dum silet omne nemus[69]

(Now Philomel, hidden by new leaves, begin your melodies while all the woods are silent)

The nightingale's song is contrasted with the sound of the cuckoo (the 'bird of hate'), which is first heard at the same time of year; both birds sing through the thick cover of leaves, so the poet's interest is in sound rather than sight. The comparison derives from the pseudo-Chaucerian 'The Cuckoo and the Nightingale', in which the nightingale stands for love and the cuckoo its profanation. This was the first of Milton's twenty-three sonnets, and one of only two in English (the other is Sonnet 7) to be written before the 1640s, when he was to expand the range of subjects thought appropriate for treatment in sonnet form. However, Milton establishes here the metrical form that also governs his later sonnets. Instead of following the English (Shakespearean) convention of three quatrains and a couplet, Milton follows the Italian (Petrarchan) convention of two quatrains and two tercets; the quatrains always used the 'enclosed order' of the rhyme scheme abba abba, but the tercets, in Milton as in Petrarch, are variously rhymed.

Graduates were free to leave the university, but Milton decided to stay on. The Easter term at Cambridge ended on 4 July 1629, and Milton was probably still in Cambridge for Commencement on 7 July; this was the university's principal festival, and on this occasion it had particular significance for Milton, because his friend Charles Diodati was present for the incorporation of his Oxford MA.[70] Milton was still in Cambridge on 21 July, when he wrote (in Latin prose) to Thomas Young. His former tutor had returned from Hamburg to Stowmarket, and had suggested that Milton might like to visit him. This letter is Milton's reply to Young's lost letter, articulating his hope of taking up the invitation. The central conceit is of Stowmarket as a rural retreat: it is the stoa of the Iceni, the portico of Zeno, the villa of Cicero, and Young is a latter-day Serranus or Curius.[71] The extravagance is genial in tone, but Milton is still contriving to impress his tutor.

Cambridge in the late Jacobean and early Caroline period seethed with ecclesiastical intrigue and debate, and Milton can certainly be seen positioning himself amid those tensions and controversies. National politics of a different kind eventually intruded, at least vicariously, on the young poet. Under the prompting of Charles and the Duke of Buckingham, James had reluctantly gone to war, with Spain, in which case his irenic overtures had been rejected, and with France, where there was denominational pressure to defend the Protestant Huguenots from a new surge of persecution. Both wars had gone badly, not least because of the ineptness of the English high command, where Buckingham was supreme. In September 1628, a few weeks before Milton returned to Cambridge, his friend Alexander Gil the younger, sitting in an Oxford tavern with some friends, drank the health of John Felton, who had assassinated Buckingham a week earlier. It was not clear at that point whether Felton had acted alone or as part of a conspiracy, and the wider context of England's war with France provided fertile soil for heightened government anxiety. Two days later, while drinking in the cellar of Trinity College, Oxford, Gil imprudently disparaged King Charles and his late father, King James. William Chillingworth, who was present, reported Gil's actions to his godfather William Laud, then bishop of London. Gil was arrested at St Paul's School on Laud's orders, and imprisoned in the Gate-house at Westminster. The rooms of Gil's friend William Pickering in Trinity College were searched, and incriminating 'libels and letters' by Gil were found.[72] Gil was examined by Laud, who, given the public nature of the outrage, could scarcely have done otherwise, and who reported his findings to the king; on 6 November the court of Star Chamber sentenced Gil to be degraded from the ministry, dismissed from his ushership at St Paul's, deprived of his university degrees, fined £2,000, to lose one ear in the pillory at Westminster and the other in Oxford, and to be imprisoned in the Fleet Prison at the king's pleasure. Gil's father successfully petitioned for a miti-gation of the fine and a remission of the corporal punishment, but Gil seems to have been imprisoned for about two years before receiving a royal pardon on 30 November 1630.

Milton never wrote about the experience of his friend, so it is difficult to assess how he felt. He was himself broadly aligned with Laud on major issues, and yet it was Laud who had led the prosecution of his friend. In the end, there was reconciliation. When Gil collected his poems (*Parerga*, 1632), he included a profoundly respectful poem addressed to Laud. In 1639, when Gil was dismissed from the high mastership of St Paul's for unleashing his violent temper on a young boy, he appealed to the king, who referred the petition to Laud; the archbishop decided to defend Gil.[73]

Much remains unknown about Milton's time as an undergraduate in Cambridge. Little is known about the musical life that may have interested him, but there is evidence that plays were performed in colleges by students[74] and that on some occasions Milton was in the audience. In a passage of polemical autobiography in *An Apology* (1642) he recalls:

That Playes must have bin seene, what difficulty was there in that? when in the Colleges so many of the young Divines, and those in next aptitude to Divinity have been seene so oft upon the Stage writhing and unboning their Clergie limms to all the antick and dishonest gestures of Trinculo's, Buffons, and Bawds; prostituting the shame of that ministery which either they had, or were nigh having, to the eyes of Courtiers and Court-Ladies, with their Groomes and *Madamoisellaes*. There while

8. Portrait of a young man identified as John Milton, by an unknown artist (*c.* 1629) (National Portrait Gallery, London).

they acted, and overacted, among other young scholars, I was a spectator; they thought themselves gallant men, and I thought them fools, they made sport, and I laught, they mispronounc't and I mislik't, and to make up the *atticisme*, they were out, and I hist.[75]

The allusion to Trinculo is not to an otherwise unknown performance of *The Tempest*, or of Thomas Tomkys' *Albumazar* (acted at Trinity College in 1614), whose protagonist has the same name; it points to a pamphlet published several months earlier, and to a passage through which Milton filtered his own recollections:

Such also I reckon amongst scandalous Ministers as doe fill their neighbours eares and eys, with obscaen & wanton words and carriages, making lascivious ribaldry the fittest musique at a table-meeting. *Tom Trinkilo* was never more acted to the life, then by many of these, who go under the name of the Angells of the Church of *England*, and by their mimicall, apish and ridiculous cariages seek to please the humours of the brave sparks and gallants of our times.[76]

Clearly objections to clerical acting were in the air in the months before the closing of the theatres. Milton's attitude to such acting had changed in the intervening years, but the passage is nonetheless clear evidence that he chose to attend plays as a student at Cambridge.[77] The one part of his recollection that rings true is that he had been censorious of the pronunciation of the actors, a detail characteristic of Milton and perhaps suggestive (like the ending of *Madamoisellaes*) of the possibility that the plays were Latin comedies. Milton's views were continuously evolving, but on subjects such as pronunciation were remarkably constant (and Erasmian).[78]

About the time that Milton finished his undergraduate studies, his portrait was again painted, not in academic dress but in a black tunic and white ruff. The relationship between the original of this painting, which Milton's widow showed to Aubrey in about 1681, and the painting (known as the 'Onslow' portrait) now in the National Portrait Gallery in London, is uncertain. Milton was said by his widow to have been about 20 when the picture was painted, but the picture seems to portray a youth in his early teens; if it is Milton, his appearance must have been extraordinarily youthful. There is also a difficulty about eye colour. In the portrait painted when he was 10, the eyes are grey, and in taking notes on the 'age 20' portrait Aubrey noted 'his eie a darke gray'. In the Onslow portrait, and in its two copies painted by Benjamin van der Gucht in 1792 (one in Milton's Cottage in Chalfont, the other owned by descendants of the Earl of Harcourt), the eyes are clearly brown. In short, it is clear that Milton was painted in the dress of a young Caroline gentleman when he was about 20, and it is possible that this is the painting in the National Portrait Gallery, but the link between the two is not secure.[79]

CHAPTER 4

Cambridge: The Postgraduate Years

MILTON's undergraduate studies concluded in a pivotal year in early Stuart history. After the death of the duke of Buckingham, Charles I took stock of the militant foreign policy he and his favourite had pursued. It had signally failed in its primary objectives. The Protestant cause in continental Europe had not been advanced. The Palatinate remained a problem and a taint on the honour of his dynasty. The French Protestant Huguenots had gained little from his abortive interventions. Furthermore, the need to finance the war had led the early Caroline administration into a series of dubious fiscal manoeuvres, the alleged illegality of which would not be forgiven. Such measures as the 'Forced Loan', demanded in 1626, and the subsequent clash of authorities could only have been justified in the eyes of the political nation if the wars with France and Spain had gone well. But they did not, and the 'shift in attitudes' among propertied Englishmen broke the consensus between the government and the governed.[1]

Moreover, Charles, to secure the supply necessary to prosecute his foreign policy, necessarily sought the support of a succession of short-lived parliaments, which became, increasingly, the forum for articulating the criticism of a progressively vociferous and confident opposition, which was often minded to link failures of foreign policy and fiscal sharp practice with the growing ceremonial and authoritarian tendency within the national church. What was to be the last session of parliament for eleven years was held from 20 January to 2 March 1629. It was dissolved by an exasperated monarch, who thus initiated 'the Personal Rule'. He also arrested the more prominent of his opponents, the leader of whom, Sir John Eliot, would die in the Tower of London, without trial, in 1632.

Gradually, Charles regained control of the country. He made peace with France and Spain, thus obviating a dependence on supply, and over the early 1630s a new confidence grew in government. The direction that had been set for ecclesiastical affairs since his accession advanced rapidly. Since 1627 William Laud had been the bishop of London and a privy councillor, and only the longevity of Abbot kept him from the archiepiscopate of Canterbury. During the attempts to secure supply from parliament, he had necessarily proceeded cautiously, but its dissolution left him 'free to pursue his objectives in the church more wholeheartedly, even though Abbot remained archbishop of Canterbury until his death on 4 August 1633'.[2] To the victors the spoils. We have hitherto characterized the ascendant tendency within the church as anti-Calvinist, Arminian, and ceremonialist; we may now, appropriately, term it Laudian, though the ideology was pervasive among many English Protestants, rather than simply the programme of one man. Peter Lake establishes the term nicely when he writes:

In using the term Laudian I do not mean to imply anything about the role of Laud in either originating or disseminating the views [to be discussed]. I am employing it merely as a handy shorthand term for the policies and religious temper of the Personal Rule....Laudianism...did exist as a coherent, distinctive and polemically aggressive vision of the Church, the divine presence in the world and the appropriate ritual response to that presence.[3]

Shifts in ecclesiastical policy and the rise of the Laudians were keenly tracked by the alert and ambitious churchmen of the universities, and Milton in 1629 surely understood, from his perspective at Cambridge, the direction in which power was flowing.

He persevered, probably watchfully, with his studies. The MA degree at Cambridge (and Oxford) is now taken without residence or examination, and the origins of this practice lie in the period in which Milton was a student. The statutes of 1570 made clear that students who had completed the BA course would study for the MA 'by their own industry'. In 1608 this statute was formally interpreted as exempting MA candidates from any residence requirement.[4] Milton's decision to remain in residence was therefore a matter of choice, not compulsion, and at times he seems not to have kept term. In considerable measure Milton was able to pursue his own interests, of which one of the most prominent in late 1629 was Italian; modern languages were not part of the syllabus, but the arrival of upper-class students in the universities did stimulate interest in the study of French and Italian.[5]

It is not known where or when Milton learned Italian. His friend Charles Diodati was part of London's small Protestant Italian community, which was centred in Cheapside, close to where Milton lived, and Milton's tutor was almost certainly a member of that community. A recent study by Stefano

Villani of the Italian church in Cheapside shows that there were at least two teachers of Italian, as well as amateur teachers that might have been drawn from the clergy or educated families such as the Burlamacchi and the Diodati.[6] There is also evidence that Milton was reading in Italian. In December 1629 he bought a copy of *Rime e Prose di Giovanni della Casa* for tenpence; the book is bound with Dante's *L'Amoroso Convivio* (Venice, 1529) and Benedetto Varchi's *Sonnetti* (Venice, 1555), and marginalia in the Della Casa and Varchi seem to be in Milton's hand.[7]

In the closing days of December 1629 Milton wrote *Elegia VI*, a verse-letter to Charles Diodati, who was staying with friends in the countryside. Diodati had written on 13 December (the letter is now lost) describing the convivial holiday that he was enjoying, but explaining that the festivities had compromised the quality of his poetry. Milton exuberantly takes up the theme, arguing in the first half of the poem that feasting enhances the quality of poetry, and then reversing the argument in the second half to argue that a great poet can only drink water. In the closing lines the tone shifts sharply, and Milton describes what he is writing. He explains that he is composing a poem as a birthday gift to Jesus (a reference to the 'Nativity Ode', of which more below), and he adds that he has been composing poems 'on your native country's pipes',[8] poems which he looks forward to reciting to Diodati. These poems are Milton's five Italian sonnets (subsequently numbered 2–6) and an interpolated *canzone*.

The poems are love sonnets in honour of a lady, who like Dante's Beatrice and Petrarch's Laura, may hover between fact and fiction. At one extreme, she may be a member of the Cheapside Italian community in whom Milton had declared an interest; at the other extreme she may be a purely literary creation; in between, she may have been a real person but Milton's interest may have been undisclosed and purely poetical, just as the sculptor may be detached from the model. Milton does seem to hint at her name. In the first sonnet (Sonnet 2) the poet addresses the lovely lady (*donna leggiadra*) and declares her name to be an honour to the grassy valley of Reno and the glorious ford (*il cui bel nome onora | L'erbosa val di Reno, e il nobil varco*);[9] as the Reno is a river in the region of Emilia, and the Rubicon (the glorious ford) is also in Emilia, it seems possible that the lady's name is Emilia.[10] In the second sonnet (Sonnet 3) he explains that in singing for his lady, he has exchanged the Thames for the Arno: the river of Florence stands for the Tuscan language, which in the early seventeenth century was being established as the literary language of the peninsula. These two sonnets are followed by a 15-line *canzone*,[11] which is again concerned with the paradox of an Englishman writing about love in Italian; the reason, as the lady declares in the *commiato*, is that Italian is the favourite language of *Amore*. The fourth poem (Sonnet 4) is addressed to the conventional figure of the male friend, who in this case is Charles Diodati.

More details of the beloved emerge: she speaks more than one language, and her singing would distract the 'labouring moon' (*E 'l cantar che di mezzo l' emisfero | Traviar ben può la faticosa Luna*); the striking final phrase would eventually reappear in *Paradise Lost*.[12] The fifth poem (Sonnet 5) is a conventional Petrarchan piece about the lady's eyes and the lover's sighs. Finally, Sonnet 6 pledges the lover's heart to his lady.

The sonnets are chiefly remarkable for their native-speaker fluency, which raises the question of how a young Londoner who had never been to Italy could achieve such a standard. It is true that Milton's Latin poetry was already achieving a very high standard, but the evidence for his proficiency in Greek, which he had studied for many years, implies a limited command of the language. How, in this context, could Milton's Italian be so good? The likely answer is that such fluency was unattainable, and that the Italian sonnets are not Milton's unaided work: he probably had a collaborator from the Italian community who could ensure that his proficient Italian could be raised to the level of a native speaker; it is even possible that the poems are exercises corrected by his Italian teacher. As Milton's wholly independent work, they are too good to be true. That said, the quality of Milton's spoken Italian was praised throughout his life, and it is possible that the texts of the sonnets were revised before publication in 1645, by which time Milton had visited Italy.

The other poem mentioned in *Elegia VI* was 'On the morning of Christ's Nativity', which is now known as the 'Nativity Ode'. This is the first of a series of poems on church festivals (the others are 'The Passion' and, perhaps a few years later, 'On the Circumcision'), the celebration of which was a marker of ritualistic sympathies. The Laudian concern with the liturgical year is well explained by Lake, who draws on the veteran ceremonialist Robert Shelford:[13]

The great festivals of the Christian year both figured and extended to all believers the benefits conferred on fallen humanity by Christ's life, passion and resurrection. 'They which come to God's house upon the day of Christ's nativity (coming in faith and love as they ought) are,' argued Robert Shelford, 'partakers of Christ's birth; they which come upon the day of circumcision are with him circumcised from the dominion of the flesh....'... It was this which allowed Shelford to conclude that the keeping 'of the holy feast of the Church' was one of the main offices of holiness.[14]

There is no hint of the anti-trinitarian theology of Milton's maturity: here the pre-incarnate Son sits in 'the midst of trinal unity'. The religious sensibility of the poem is characteristic of Milton's sympathy for the ethos of ceremonial Arminianism. Nor is it appropriate to regard the poem as morbid or heterodox in its association of the nativity with the Atonement (which occurs in lines 151–3: 'The babe lies yet in smiling infancy, | That on the bitter cross | Must redeem our loss'[15]). The connection was made in the readings for the communion service for Christmas day, as Diane McColley has noted.[16] The connection certainly occurs in other seventeenth-century poems on the Nativity.[17]

The poet does not appear to be especially millenarian in his orientation, or at least he is not exceptionally inclined to expect imminently the Second Coming. Certainly, at the core of poem he places an invocation to the music of the spheres that will accompany Christ when he comes in judgement as surely as it accompanied him at the Creation and at his birth on the first Christmas. A sense that the end of the world could be nigh, though often associated with religious radicalism, was perfectly orthodox theologically. James I apparently felt 'the latter days drawing on'.[18] Moreover, Joseph Mede, the most distinguished scholar whom Milton had by this time personally encountered, had published his great work on the prophecies of the Revelation of St John the Divine only two years earlier.[19] Yet Milton is not proclaiming that the terminal event would happen soon, though he does celebrate it as something dearly wished for and vividly imagined. In terms of his personal faith, it points to a complete equanimity about the fate of his own soul. John Donne, in a poem similarly contemplating the Second Coming, agonizingly craved a postponement to give time to address his own spiritual health. Young Milton betrays no such anxieties.

The poem provides a good insight into the development of the vernacular poet. The Nativity Ode shares much common ground with other poetry on the same subject and with devotional verse more generally. Some *topoi* can be identified both in Milton's and in the work of older contemporaries—Donne, Ben Jonson, George Herbert, and Robert Herrick and in numerous minor poets of the early Stuart period, where we also find the poem functioning as a gift, analogies between the poet and the shepherds or the magi, wordplay on Son (of God) and sun; and so on. This is not a source study, nor can we be sure which poems, mostly still in manuscript in 1629, could have been available to him, though he does seem in some sense to be answering or matching 'An Hymne of the Ascension' by William Drummond of Hawthornden, the most distinguished Scottish poet of the era, which he could have read only in manuscript.[20] University colleges often maintained a communal anthology of verse, drawing for the most part on works circulating in manuscript, and many of Milton's contemporaries, students, academics, inns-of-court men, and gentry families, did the same. No collection of Miltonic provenance is extant, but, more sharply than anything he had written before, the Nativity Ode shows us a poet in the making who is at home with the broader tradition of early Stuart verse.

Milton's ode evidently had much in common with the milieu in which he lived and with the dominant ideology of the period. But the poem shows, too, what was singular about him. In part, that rests in the confidence—not only that, when Christ returns in judgement, he will be fit and ready to stand before him, but also in its declarative cultural assurance. When other poets represent themselves as bringing the gifts along modestly, perhaps following behind the shepherds, Milton would have his poem 'prevent', that is arrive before, the magi. His ode may be 'humble' but he claims for it 'the honour first, thy Lord to greet'.[21] Secondly, Milton's religious sensibility appears out of alignment with that of contemporaries. What he finds to celebrate about the incarnate Christ is not the tenderness of the neonate, the compassion of his mother, or the circumstances of his birth; it is his power. The poem rehearses as some length the potency of Christ's mission for all false gods, as he strips, mutilates, blinds, and ejects them. Milton's Christ-child is an infant Hercules, strangling Typhon in his cradle: 'Our babe to show his Godhead true, | Can in his swaddling bands control the damned crew.'[22] Thus, he anticipates his representation, in Book 6 of *Paradise Lost*, of the irresistible might of the Son of God.

The second poem in the series, 'The Passion', may have been written on the following Good Friday (26 March 1630); it was Milton's only attempt to compose a vernacular poem in the baroque idiom he had used in some of his funeral elegies. The poem breaks off with an aesthetically unconvincing couplet ('Might think the infection of my sorrows loud, | Had got a race of mourners on some pregnant cloud'), whereupon Milton abandoned the poem. When he came to print it, he added a note: 'this subject the author finding to be above his years when he wrote it, and nothing satisfied with what was begun, left it unfinished.'[23] This policy smacks of arrogance—the poet doesn't much like what he has written but readers perhaps will find it interesting—and the poem has had a poor critical reception. Yet we hesitate to condemn it. Protestant poets found it difficult to focus on the tortured body of Christ, which appears so central to the devotional practices of the Counter-Reformation. Even Donne, indebted though he was to the Catholic tradition, recognizes the problem, which he makes the informing principle of 'Goodfriday, 1613. Riding Westward', perhaps the greatest English poem on the topic. There he depicts himself as literally and symbolically travelling away from the site of Golgotha, seeking a penitential progression that would allow him to turn to look on the crucifixion.

Milton never did find a way of representing that scene. In *Paradise Lost* the death of the Son receives briefer treatment than Nimrod,[24] while in *Paradise Regained* he averts the reader's gaze from the grisly phase of the Atonement to its more serene precursor. Richard Crashaw, with a Catholic sensibility, shows what could be achieved in the baroque idiom Milton had attempted:

> They have left thee naked, LORD, O that they had
> This garment too I would they had deny'd.
> Thee with thyself they have too richly clad,
> Opening the purple wardrobe in thy side.[25]

Milton will grow to a grandeur that Crashaw could never approach—perhaps in the Nativity Ode he had done so already—but Crashaw takes readers into uncomfortable territory, at the edge of what seems endurable to contemplation. Milton's apparent abandonment of 'The Passion' may seem a lame defeat by comparison. Yet arguably this is a poem about the inadequacy of the poet's idiom to capture the enormity of Christ's sacrifice; 'just as Milton as a believer cannot really bring himself to contemplate the tortured Christ, so Milton as poet cannot commemorate the event.'[26]

One other poem can be assigned to 1630, but its precise date of composition is not known. The poem is 'On Shakespeare', published in the Second Folio (1632) of Shakespeare's plays; it was Milton's first publication. How did an unknown poet manage to publish an appreciative poem in the Second Folio? The question has no ready answer, but there are several tantalizing possibilities. One is that the I.M. who published a poem (*incipit* 'We wondered, Shakespeare') in the First Folio (1623) was Milton's father. Another is that there was a connection through Thomas Morley between Shakespeare (who was Morley's near neighbour) and Milton's father (whose music had been published by Morley). A third is that Milton's father being a trustee of the Blackfriars Playhouse may be indicative of wider theatrical connections.[27] Whatever the reason, the Second Folio was a prestigious publication, and Milton's poem is entirely worthy of its august surroundings. Like Ben Jonson, Milton contrasts 'slow-endeavouring art' (which presumably includes his own) with that of Shakespeare, whose 'easy numbers flow', and insists that the monument of Shakespeare is the 'wonder and astonishment' of those who live after him. The poem is indicative of the early growth of the cult of Shakespeare; at this stage Milton had no reputation, but in succeeding centuries it became apparent that the only English poet to whom Milton paid substantial tribute in his own verse was the only English poet whose verse was to be judged superior to Milton's.

On 7 April 1630 the Easter term at Cambridge began, and about the same time Charles Diodati left for Geneva. On 16 April he matriculated at the Geneva Academy, where his uncle was a professor.[28] The Academy had been founded by Calvin in 1559; it was run on brutal disciplinarian principles.[29] Whether the decision to enrol was Diodati's or his father's is not known. He was still at the Academy on 15 September 1631 but it is not known how long he remained in residence. He subsequently decided not to enter the church, and instead followed his father into medicine. There is no record of Diodati having studied medicine at a university, so he may have been apprenticed to his father.

On 20 May Milton was for some reason back in London, from where he wrote to Alexander Gil,[30] who had enclosed his poem celebrating 'the capture of the city by Henry of Nassau'. The Stadhouder Frederik Hendrik, Prince of Orange, had captured 's-Hertogenbosch on 14 September 1629 (after a five-month siege in which English soldiers had participated), and his victory was regarded throughout Protestant Europe as a turning point in the war against the Habsburgs. Gil's celebratory poem, which was to be published in his *Parerga* (1632) as *In Sylvam-Ducis*, is described by Milton in terms of majesty and Virgilian genius. Cool judgement can be compromised by friendship and by the decorum of praise.

On 10 June 1630 Edward King, who was later to be commemorated as Milton's 'Lycidas', was appointed to a Fellowship at Christ's College by royal mandate. King had entered the College in June 1626, more than a year after Milton, and was admitted BA in 1630; a few months later he became a Fellow.[31] Royal mandates were common in the early seventeenth century, as they were a mechanism (like regius professorships) whereby the crown could exercise influence within the universities. Milton's friendship with King may already have been established, and there is no reason to think that he would not have been pleased by the appointment. The myth that Milton was aggrieved because he had been robbed of the Fellowship for which he was destined was invented in the eighteenth century, and is based on the groundless assumption that an academic post, with its attendant obligations of celibacy and ordination in the Church of England, would have been the highest calling to which Milton might have aspired. In fact Milton never showed the slightest interest in joining the Fellowship, and in any case would have been ineligible for election, because the statutes of the college prohibited the election of more than one Fellow from any county; Michael Honywood was, like Milton, a native of London, and so Milton could not have been elected to a Fellowship as long as Honywood was in post.

On New Year's Day 1631 Thomas Hobson, the Cambridge carrier, died at the age of 85. He was a businessman of considerable standing and wealth; one of his daughters had married a baronet, and a portrait of Hobson painted in 1629 shows him in the attire of a gentleman.[32] In 1568 Hobson had inherited the business (and land in Grantchester) from his father, who had been one of the treasurers of the Corporation of Cambridge. This was not a humble packhorse business: at first Hobson had used two-wheeled carts, but these were replaced by four-wheeled wagons drawn by teams of six or seven horses. He ran a regular service to London, carrying passengers as well as freight; the latter included fresh fish for the royal household. His customers for the London service included many students. He often travelled on the London service (which terminated at the Bull Inn in Bishopsgate Street Within), but as a proprietor rather than a driver; the driving was done by servants. In

9. Thomas Hobson, by an unknown artist (1629) (National Portrait Gallery, London; hung at NPG exhibition, Montacute House, Somerset).

addition to his business as a carrier, Hobson was a landowner: as the account in the *Oxford Dictionary of National Biography* explains,

In 1627 he acquired the site of the priory of Anglesey, with the manor of Anglesey-cum-Bottisham, Cambridgeshire. He was also owner of the manors of Crowlands, Lisles, and Sames in Cottenham, and, as lessee of the crown, held the Denny Abbey estate, with the manors of Waterbeach and Denny. His will mentions other property in Cambridge, Chesterton, Tidd St Giles, and Moulton. On 30 July 1628 he conveyed to the university and town of Cambridge the ground on which was erected the structure commonly known as the Spinning House, but more correctly called 'Hobson's Workhouse'.

By the time Milton arrived in Cambridge Hobson had become a local legend. In 1617 a pamphlet called *Hobson's Horse Load of Letters, or, Precedents for Epistles of Business* had been published. Hobson's insistence of hiring out his hackney horses in rotation, insisting that customers take 'this or none', gave rise to the expression 'Hobson's choice'; the principle is still observed at London taxi ranks. In his will he left money to raise a conduit on Market Street, and so the conduit became known as Hobson's Conduit;[33] his name is still preserved in the name of the conduit and of a street in Cambridge.

Hobson had continued to travel regularly to London until 1630, when the plague had forced the suspension of the service. It was shortly after this period of enforced idleness that Hobson died; as a man of standing, he was buried inside St Bene't's Church, not in the churchyard. The poets of the university, who used Latin to commemorate university members, thought it appropriate to commemorate Hobson in English verse. As he had died at a great age, the tone of the surviving poems is affectionate rather than grief-stricken. Milton composed two poems 'On the University Carrier', and may have been the author of a third.[34] One measure of the popularity of these three poems is that they variously appear in more than twenty-five manuscripts. The two that are securely Milton's are very different. The last twenty lines of 'Here lieth one' erupt into a sustained series of puns (e.g. 'too long vacation hastened on his term') that is rare in Milton's writing, but was to resurface again in his epics. 'Here lies old Hobson', on the other hand, begins in a tone of bantering recollection, but ends with a moving image of Death personified as a chamberlain (i.e. a room attendant) in an inn. Hobson had arrived at his journey's end and gone to his inn, where Death

> In the kind office of a chamberlain
> Showed him his room where he must lodge that night,
> Pulled off his boots, and took away the light.
> If any ask for him, it shall be said,
> 'Hobson has supped, and's newly gone to bed.'[35]

It would be hard to think of a gentler or more gracious description of death anywhere in English poetry.

In 1631 the Lent term began on 13 January, and on this occasion he returned to Cambridge with his 15-year-old brother Christopher, who on 15 February was formally admitted to Christ's College under Nathaniel Tovey. The brothers shared a tutor, and lived together in his chamber; when Milton graduated the following year, his brother was to leave Cambridge (in his case for the Inner Temple) at the same time. At some point in the year Milton bought (for 2*s.* 6*d.*) a copy of the edition of Aratus's *Phenomena* and *Diosemeia* published in Paris in 1559; he later annotated the volume, which is now in the British Library.[36]

On 15 April 1631, Jane Savage, the Marchioness of Winchester, died of a throat infection at the age of 23; Milton commemorated her with 'An Epitaph on the Marchioness of Winchester'. Lady Winchester was the daughter of a prominent Catholic nobleman, Thomas, Viscount Savage, who after the accession of Charles I became Chancellor to his Catholic queen Henrietta Maria; his wife Elizabeth, also a Catholic, became a lady of the bedchamber. At the age of 15 Jane had married John Paulet, a Catholic who in 1629 became the fifth Marquess of Winchester; in the same year she had given birth to Charles Paulet, the future sixth Marquess, and at the time of her death was again pregnant. It is remarkable that Milton should write a poem in memory of a Catholic aristocrat whom he had never met, and that he should choose to publish it a few months after Cromwell's storming of Basing House, the Winchester family seat, in October 1645, when the Marquess had been committed to the Tower and his lands confiscated.[37]

Milton was not alone in composing a poem in memory of Lady Winchester. Ben Jonson and William Davenant had also written poems, and it is possible that a university miscellany was planned or anticipated: Lady Winchester was related to the University Chancellor (Henry Rich, earl of Holland), and in his poem Milton makes the point that Cambridge is 'devoted to thy virtuous name'. Milton's poem certainly circulated before it was published: a manuscript version in the hand of John Walrond, secretary to Francis, Baron Willoughby,[38] seems to derive from a pre-publication draft. The poem may be a conventional tribute, but it is a marker of Milton's social attitudes in the spring of 1631: it is deferential to the aristocracy, and shows a respectful knowledge of its hierarchy: Lady Winchester was 'a viscount's daughter', then 'an earl's heir' (through her mother), then a marchioness (through marriage) and finally 'no marchioness, but now a queen'.

Prolusion 6 is Milton's best-known academic exercise. It consists of three parts: an oration on the contention that light-hearted entertainments are not prejudicial to philosophical studies; a second section (headed 'Prolusio') which introduces a student entertainment and ends with an announcement that Milton is about to leap over the wall of college regulations forbidding the use of English; and a third section consisting of the English poem 'At a Vacation Exercise in the College'. The exercise has long been considered to have been performed on or shortly before 4 July 1628, when Milton was an undergraduate, and that may be right;[39] most of the evidence, however, points to the comparable date (the last day of the Easter term) three years later, on 8 July 1631. First, Milton's letters to Alexander Gil (2 July 1628) and Thomas Young (21 July 1628) make no reference to Milton's starring role in the occasion. Second, Milton says that the exercises had not been held the previous year, and that points to 1631 (in 1630 exercises were cancelled because of plague) rather than 1628.

The third strand of evidence is a series of allusions to members of the college, some of which can be dated. Milton's command for 'Rivers' to arise seems to be addressed to either George Rivers or his brother Nizell, both of whom were admitted on 10 May 1628. Similarly, Milton says of the student actor playing the part of Substance that 'o'er all his brethren he shall reign as king', which would seem to be an allusion to one of the King brothers, but they were so numerous that one or more of the brothers was in residence at every possible date.[40] The 'spark-flashing Cerberus' who stands at the threshold must be the porter who is named in the college accounts (from 1626–32) as Sparks; the 'burning furnace' would seem to be Edward Furnise, who had been admitted on 29 May 1628. The passage in which Milton enumerates various birds seems to allude to many members of the college. The two Irish birds are presumably two of the King brothers, as they were the only Irish undergraduates. Even if we set aside undergraduates called Philip (who could be construed as sparrows) and those whose names include ornithic elements (e.g. Roger Hawkridge, Richard Ducket, William Fincham, and Brian Fowler), the roll-call of Christ's as set out in its Admissions Book flutters with bird-names. A few months after Milton matriculated William Finch (BA 1629, MA 1632) was admitted (2 July 1625). Jeremiah Goose (BA 1631, MA 1634) was admitted on 25 April 1627 and his younger brother John Goose (who left without a degree) on 26 January 1630; if Milton's joke about geese refers to these brothers, 1628 would seem to be too early.[41] The birds also include Thomas Bird (BA 1631), who was admitted on 27 January 1627, and his younger brother Samuel (BA 1632, MA 1635), who was admitted on 17 May 1628. Finally, George Cocke was admitted on 28 January 1628 and his younger brother Robert on 24 February 1631. This evidence is not conclusive, but it would seem that the birds only begin to flock in large numbers if the date of the prolusion is 1631.[42]

As William Riley Parker said of the date, 'the shadow of doubt could be completely removed if we could date the student prank [an attack on the town's water supply] described by Milton as causing the sudden departure of the real leader of the Sophisters'.[43] At the opening of the oration Milton explains that he is a last-minute substitute for someone who had led a force of fifty sophisters to Barwell Field, wrecking the aqueduct and forcing the town to surrender from thirst. No record of an attack on the town's water supply has ever been found, and the archives of Christ's College and of the university record no disturbances involving the students of Christ's in 1628 (though Trinity students rioted in June 1628). The records of the Vice-Chancellor's Court do contain, however, a fragmentary account of an incident involving five students (two postgraduates and three undergraduates) of Christ's College in April 1631.[44] The students were drinking in Chesterton (close by Barwell Field, and now part of Cambridge), and their rowdy behaviour caused them to be arrested by the local constables and incarcerated in a room of a tavern called the Green Dragon (which still exists). They were released by customers at the tavern, and after another drinking session with their liberators, walked back to college, where they were recaptured by the Chesterton constables. Two of the students are said to have effected a rescue at the 'backside' of Christ's, which would seem to imply that one of their number had fallen into the King's Ditch (which had been rebuilt in 1610 and was filled with water). The attack on the water supply to which Milton alludes was presumably a reference to either the polluting effect of the student in the ditch or to the fact that the drunken students (then as now) had urinated into the river.

In 1982 it was established that the genre of Prolusion 6 is that of the salting, and an awareness of the conventions of the genre explains an enormous amount about Milton's prolusion.[45] A salting was an initiation ritual in which new undergraduates made a speech; if it was judged to have been well done, the speaker was rewarded with a cup of caudle (spiced gruel), and if badly done a salted drink. In Cambridge saltings of the 1620s, a master of ceremonies pretended to be a college tutor, and so became the 'father' of his 'sons', the new students. He named his sons (who then replied) and then gave a satirical speech that typically lampooned the college, the university and the town; the humour was at once learned and low, and puns on the word 'salt' proliferate. Milton's prolusion broadly conforms to these conventions. In his case his sons are Aristotelian categories; the learnedly coarse humour is typified by a passage (brilliantly translated by John Hale) in which he challenges any member of the audience who is sitting like a sphinx and not laughing to 'express some gastric riddles to us, not from his sphinx but from his sphincter, his Posterior Anal-ytics'.

It is in this prolusion that Milton first mentions his nickname, 'the Lady'. In the Latin of the prolusion he says that he has lately heard himself called *domina*, so in this context he is deemed to be a lady in the sense of being married to a lord. The English version of the name was first reported by Milton's widow, who told Aubrey that 'he was so faire that they called him the Lady of Christ's College'. All autobiographical passages in Milton are constructed with a view to conveying a particular impression or association to the reader, and this one is no exception: Milton is recalling the *Vita Donati*, one of the ancient lives of Virgil, in which the fourth-century grammarian Aelius Donatus asserts the exemplary moral conduct of Virgil when he was a student in Naples by adducing his nickname: *Parthenias vulgo appellatus sit* ('he was usually called the Lady'). The Greek loan-word *parthenias* does not of course carry the same sense as Latin *domina*, but its suggestion of maidenliness is consonant with the phrase 'Lady of Christ's'. Milton may have acquired the nickname because of the fairness of his complexion, or because his manner or appearance was youthful or effeminate, but he prized it because it was Virgil's nickname.

Milton's twin poems, 'L'Allegro' and 'Il Penseroso', may have been written at any time in the 1630s, and may not have been written at the same time, but there is circumstantial evidence that makes the summer of 1631 less unlikely than the alternatives: Prolusion 7, written a few months later, recalls a long vacation spent in the countryside during which Milton was favoured by the muses; the poems are absent from the collection of drafts now known as the Trinity Manuscript, the earliest pages of which seem to date from 1632;

the opposing views of the poems, and their rhetorical openings, seem to point to a time when Milton was still at Cambridge.

'L'Allegro' is a poem in praise of the happy man, and 'Il Penseroso' praises the contemplative man. Each begins by banishing a parodic version of that which is celebrated in the other poem, and then turns to the celebration of its chosen virtue. Most of 'L'Allegro' draws its pleasure from an idealized version of the countryside, with whistling ploughmen and singing milkmaids; like the pastorals of Theocritus, they reflect the experience of a comfortable city-dweller in the countryside, not that of one who has ploughed a field or milked a cow. The poem then turns to 'towered cities', and celebrates 'pomp and feast and revelry, | With masque and antique pageantry', before turning to the comedies of Jonson and Shakespeare and finally arriving at the highest pleasure, that of music 'married to immortal verse'. These are not the pleasures of a radical-in-waiting, but of one who loves cakes and ale.

'Il Penseroso' celebrates another kind of joy, that of the life of the mind and spirit. It honours a pastoral version of a 'pensive nun, devout and pure'. The poet bids the nun

> Come, but keep thy wonted state,
> With even step, and musing gait,
> And looks commercing with the skies,
> Thy rapt soul sitting in thine eyes:
> There held in holy passion still,
> Forget thyself to marble.[46]

At a time when there were no nuns in England (the religious community at Little Gidding was to be established in 1636 and attacked as an 'Arminian nunnery' in 1641), this seems a remarkable figure to find in an English poem. However, as Anthony Milton notes, 'In Laudian Cambridge, even medieval contemplative monasticism (usually the object of sharp criticism) was beginning to find its supporters.'[47] When the poem moves to the city it is tragedy that is celebrated, and finally the poem moves to a religious vision that has no counterpart in 'L'Allegro'. The poet first describes ecclesiastical architecture, explaining how he will

> walk the studious cloister's pale,
> And love the high embowed roof,
> With antique pillars' massy proof
> And storied windows richly dight,
> Casting a dim religious light.[48]

Puritans had a studied dislike of religious buildings, famously stabling horses in cathedrals and smashing stained glass, but the poet of 'Il Penseroso' is moved by his experience of sanctified buildings, and the scene is commemorated in terms that illuminate the Laudian concern with 'the beauty of holiness'. He then moves to music:

> There let the pealing organ blow,
> To the full-voiced choir below,
> In service high, and anthems clear,
> As may with sweetness, through mine ear,
> Dissolve me into ecstasies,
> And bring all heaven before mine eyes.[49]

The passage seems close to Crashaw in its assumption that the senses can carry the mind to ecstatic vision. In *Eikonoklastes* (1649) Milton would pour scorn on 'painted windows', the 'chanted Service-Book', the 'Singing men' and even the 'Organs'.[50]

The summer of 1631 was not entirely taken up with the composition of poetry: on 12 August Milton's brother-in-law, Edward Phillips, made a will with the assistance of Milton's father, and on 25 August he was buried 'in the church at night', a procedure that circumvented the obligations and high costs of an heraldic funeral.[51] His widow Anne had a 1-year-old child (Edward Phillips) and was pregnant with another child (John Phillips, who would be born in October). Less than five months later (5 January 1632) Anne married Thomas Agar, a widower who had succeeded her late husband as Deputy Clerk of the Crown Office in Chancery.[52]

Prolusion 7 ('An Oration in Defence of Learning') was delivered in the chapel of Christ's College, possibly in the Michaelmas (autumn) term of 1631. The inconclusive evidence for this dating is that Milton mentions that he has spent the summer in the countryside; his family moved in April 1631 (or perhaps a little earlier) from London to Hammersmith, and in 1631 Hammersmith was still a village. The sheer quality of Prolusion 7, both in terms of its Latinity and its rhetorical power, implies that this is a relatively mature work: its title hints that it may have been the declamation that Milton was required by statute to deliver for his MA, but its college setting means that it need not have been delivered in his final term—though it may have been. While it is true that orations never touched openly on controversial subjects, the notion that learning was a wholly virtuous activity which required no defence would not have been apparent to a seventeenth-century university audience. There was a suspicion of experimental science, and the notion of forbidden knowledge (or 'knowledge within bounds') to which Milton's Raphael would later subscribe had adherents among Puritan sympathizers. As Samuel How asserted in *The Sufficiencie of the Spirit's Teaching without Human Learning* (1639),

> The Spirit's teaching in a cobbler's shop
> Doth Oxford and Cambridge o'ertop.

This was a view that Milton was later to adopt himself, but in 1631 the topic accorded well with his own evident scholarly enthusiasm.

In 1632 Milton embarked on his final months as a student. The public events of the Lent term included a royal visit at which two plays were performed, and the subsequent suicide of the vice-chancellor,[53] but Milton has left no record of his attendance at the former or his reaction to the latter, perhaps because he was absent at the time. None of the surviving prolusions can be associated with confidence with the academic exercises that Milton was obliged to complete, nor can any poems be assigned to the first half of the year. It is possible that Prolusion 2 was performed in the Public Schools on some occasion that has not been identified, but it may simply have been delivered as one of the required academic exercises: its quality implies that Milton has risen to an occasion, but the nature of that occasion is not known, beyond the fact that Milton's brief oration follows those of a series of distinguished speakers. Its subject, the music of the spheres, is unremarkable, though Milton boldly declares Pythagoras to have entered his body and to be speaking through him. What is remarkable is the soaring quality of Milton's Latin prose: the carefully modulated Latin follows the exposition of the central Pythagorean conceit with a consummate skill that is never glimpsed in Milton's earlier Latin prose, and would not be realized again until Milton wrote the visionary passages of the *Defensio Prima*.

Milton supplicated for his degree, and later signed the Subscription Book (3 July 1632), whereupon he proceeded MA, having once again subscribed to the supremacy of the crown, the Book of Common Prayer, episcopacy and the Thirty-Nine Articles. Of the twenty-seven members of Christ's College who signed the Book that day, Milton's name stands first; perhaps this was only coincidence, but a small honour may be implied.[54] The oaths that Milton took included one to continue his regency at the university for another five years.[55] This oath, which was required by statute, was simply a matter of form, but it is possible that Milton took seriously the commitment to continue academic study; that was certainly his principal activity for the next seven years.

II

1632–1639

CHAPTER 5

Hammersmith

F OR centuries it was assumed that in the course of Milton's final year at
Cambridge his father retired and the family moved in 1632 to the village
of Horton, a few miles from Windsor, where Milton was said to have lived
until he left for Italy in 1638. Two discoveries have obliged biographers to
reconfigure this period. In 1949 the discovery of four Chancery dispositions
in the Public Record Office made it clear that from 14 September 1632 (and
perhaps earlier) to 8 January 1635 (and perhaps later), the Miltons lived not at
Horton, but at Hammersmith. In 1996 documents were discovered in the
Hammersmith and Fulham Record Office that show that the Miltons were
living in Hammersmith by 30 April 1631, and that Milton's father may have
been serving as a churchwarden in the Laudian chapel-of-ease.[1]

Hammersmith is now an Inner London borough, but in the 1630s it was
a hamlet on the muddy north bank of the Thames, some seven miles west
of London. It lay on the main road from Westminster that ran through
Kensington westwards to Hammersmith and on to Windsor and the west of
England. Hammersmith was part of the Manor of Fulham, which had
belonged to the bishops of London for a millennium; the residence of the
bishops was Fulham Palace, which still stands on Bishop's Avenue, though it
ceased to be the official residence in 1973. The parish church, All Saints, was a
mile south of Hammersmith, and residents without horses found the journey
difficult in winter. In December 1629 Edmund Sheffield, earl of Mulgrave,[2]
who lived in nearby Butterwick House, petitioned William Laud, who was
then bishop of London, for a chapel-of-ease in Hammersmith. The chapel
would still be part of the parish (and was to remain so till 1834), and divine
service would be conducted by a curate. The petition referred movingly to the
length and foulness of the way to Fulham, and emphasized that in winter it
was most toilsome to travel over ploughed land.[3] Another strand of argument
asserted that many chose not to attend church, instead spending the
appointed time in profane alehouses and ungodly exercises. Finance was

raised by local subscription, notably the £700 contribution of Nicholas (later Sir Nicholas) Crispe, whose riverside mansion (later Brandenburgh House) was in the parish. Sheffield was later to become a parliamentarian and Crispe a royalist, but in 1629 they were both prepared to support the erection of a chapel within Laud's domain. The chapel was a brick building, 48 feet by 80 feet, and had a 58-foot tower with a peal of eight bells that now hang in St Paul's Church, which was built on the site of the chapel in 1889. The chapel was consecrated by Bishop Laud on 7 June 1631; his prayer survives among the Hammersmith papers in the Hammersmith archive, and is included in the collected edition of his works.[4]

Milton's father is not named in the petition, nor is he listed in the poor relief assessment of 1630 for 'Hammersmith side', but he was assessed on 30 April 1631, and that year paid poor relief on 24 June, 29 September, and 25 December.[5] The timing of the move implies that the attraction of Hammersmith for Milton's father was the opening of a Laudian chapel that accorded with his ecclesiastical preferences. There is no record of those attending the ceremony of consecration, so we cannot know whether Milton travelled from Cambridge to join his parents.

It was to this house, the precise location of which is unknown, that Milton moved on coming down from Cambridge after the award of his MA on 3 July 1632. His decision to live at home in order to study probably reflects an intention to take an STB (Sanctae Theologiae Baccalaureus, the degree now known as a BD), for which Cambridge MAs could supplicate after seven years; residence was unnecessary, so Milton decided to study at home, in the shadow of Laud's palace. There was no episcopal library, but Laud's own substantial library (dispersed after his incarceration) was housed in the palace; it is not known whether scholars in the neighbourhood had access. Milton's brother Christopher, who seems to have left Cambridge at the same time as his brother (having spent five terms in residence) did not return to Hammersmith. Instead he entered the Inner Temple, where the register describes him (in Latin) as a gentleman, and as the second son of John Milton.[6]

Soon after he arrived in Hammersmith Milton began to enter drafts of his poems into the first of a series of manuscripts that he accumulated until about 1658; the later entries were of necessity written by scribes. Long after Milton's death these loose papers were bound together, and they are now known collectively as the Trinity Manuscript, which is housed in the Wren Library of Trinity College Cambridge; an early cataloguer described it accurately as 'Miltons juvenile poems &c'. The first jottings in the earliest notebook are drafts of *Arcades*, a pastoral entertainment which was performed at Harefield (about 10 miles north-west of Hammersmith, now just inside the M25 orbital motorway) in honour of Alice, dowager countess of Derby. The date of the performance is unknown, but it seems likely to be after Milton came down from Cambridge in July 1632 and before the Bridgewater family embarked on their progress through Wales in July 1634. A good case has been made for the late summer of 1632;[7] the countess's seventy-fifth birthday on 4 May 1634 is another possibility.[8] *Arcades* is described as 'part of an entertainment'. It was written for a private performance before an aristocratic audience, and published in 1645 as one of three occasional pieces (together with 'Lycidas' and *A Masque presented at Ludlow Castle*) at the end of the volume. The reason for the choice of Milton for the commission of *Arcades* (and subsequently of *A Masque at Ludlow* for the same family) remains conjectural.

Alice Spencer had been born into a noble family and had twice married well. Her first husband was Ferdinando Stanley, Lord Strange (later earl of Derby). Lord Strange was a potential successor to Queen Elizabeth, but he died in 1594. His acting company, Lord Strange's Men, became the Countess of Derby's Men, which soon merged with the Lord Chamberlain's Men; the Company's principal playwright was Shakespeare. In 1600 the countess married again (this time secretly), becoming the third wife of Sir Thomas Egerton; as part of the same alliance Alice's daughter Frances was betrothed to John Egerton, Sir Thomas's son and heir (and the future earl of Bridgewater). The marriage of Lady Alice and Sir Thomas was characterized by acrimony and misery. In the words of Sir John Baker,

she was haughty, profligate, greedy, and ill-tempered, and added greatly to her husband's burdens for the last seventeen years of his life. 'I thank God I never desired long life', wrote Egerton in 1610, 'nor ever had less cause to desire it than since this, my last marriage, for before I was never acquainted with such tempests and storms.'[9]

The marriage ended with the death of Sir Thomas in 1617, whereupon Lady Alice withdrew to Harefield and lived the life, in Milton's felicitous phrase, of a 'rural queen'.[10] The dowager countess had been a notable patron for decades, and her patronage was acknowledged by poets and dramatists such as Robert Greene, Thomas Nashe, Edmund Spenser, John Davies of Hereford, John Harrington, and John Marston.[11] She had performed in court masques, such as Samuel Daniel's *Vision of the Twelve Goddesses* (1604) and Ben Jonson's *Masque of Blackness* (1605) and *Masque of Beauty* (1608), and she played a part in Milton's *Arcades*. Her patronage continued at Harefield, where she mounted masques in which her grandchildren could act.

In 1631 the family was engulfed in a national scandal: the trial and execution of Mervin Touchet, second earl of Castlehaven.[12] In the course of his first marriage, Touchet and his wife Elizabeth seem to have become Roman Catholics (though they denied it), and their children were certainly Catholics: James Touchet (the third earl) was to fight throughout the 1640s with Catholic forces in Ireland, and George Touchet was to become a Benedictine monk and chaplain to Queen Catherine of Braganza. After he was widowed,

10. Alice Spencer, dowager countess of Derby, by an unknown artist (National Portrait Gallery, London).

Mervin Touchet reverted to the Church of England and married Lady Anne Brydges, the widow of Grey Brydges, the fifth Baron Chandos and the eldest daughter of Alice, the dowager countess of Derby. On marrying Mervin Touchet, Anne moved to Fonthill Gifford (the family seat in Wiltshire) with her eldest daughter Elizabeth, but her sons George and William, and perhaps her youngest daughter Frances, remained at Harefield in the care of their grandmother Alice.

In 1628 Anne's daughter Elizabeth, aged 13, was married to Castlehaven's heir, James, Lord Audley, who was her step-brother. The marriage was not a success. Within a year Lord Audley had left Fonthill Gifford and his wife then entered into a sexual relationship with one Henry Skipwith, who was a favourite of Castlehaven; it is not clear whether the relationship was consensual or whether Castlehaven had gifted his daughter-in-law to Skipwith. The cuckolded Lord Audley fell out with his father; the dispute escalated, and eventually Audley

11. Mervin Touchet, earl of Castlehaven (frontispiece and title page from Anon., *The arraignment and conviction of Mervin Lord Avdley, Earle of Castlehaven* (London, 1642)).

appealed to the king.[13] The ensuing Privy Council investigation concluded that there was a *prima facie* case for Castlehaven being tried for a cluster of crimes, including rape and sodomy.

English law recognized the right to be tried by one's equals, and members of the House of Lords (other than bishops and life peers, who were not deemed to be ennobled in blood) were until 1948 entitled to be tried by other members of the House for felony or treason. When the case came to trial on 25 April 1631, Parliament was in recess, and under such circumstances the Lord High Steward (in this case Thomas Coventry, the Lord Keeper) was obliged to preside over the trial and to adjudicate on points of law; he was assisted by a jury of twenty-seven peers, including most of the Privy Council. The trial took place in Westminster Hall, where platforms were erected to accommodate the large number of spectators. Castlehaven was charged with committing sodomy with a male servant (Florence Fitzpatrick) and restraining his wife Anne while she was raped by another servant (Giles Broadway). The depositions of the countess and the household servants painted a lurid picture of a debauched household in which Castlehaven had sexual relations with prostitutes and serving boys, ordered servants to expose themselves to the countess and encouraged her to have sexual relations with his favourites. Castlehaven defended himself vigorously, insisting that the allegations were a family plot aimed at the securing of his estate, accusing his wife of adultery and infanticide, his son of greed, and his daughter-in-law of promiscuity. The ad hoc court made some odd rulings on points of law. Rape was defined as forced intercourse *per vaginam*, and necessitated penetration, but not necessarily emission. Giles Broadway insisted that he had ejaculated prematurely, and so had not penetrated Lady Castlehaven; he was nonetheless deemed to be guilty of rape. Similarly, Florence Fitzpatrick confessed under a promise of immunity that he had engaged with Castlehaven in mutual masturbation but not in sodomy, but the noble lords ruled that sodomy did not necessitate penetration *per anum*.

Lord Coventry had a vote, so there were twenty-eight possible votes, and a simple majority was required; twenty-six peers voted to convict on the charge of acting as an accessory to rape (which made Castlehaven liable to the same punishment as the principal felon), but only fifteen on the charge of sodomy. Three weeks later, on 14 May 1631, Castlehaven was beheaded at Tower Hill. The immunity granted to Fitzpatrick was set aside, and he was hanged along with Broadway. The verdicts were inevitable, but there are certain features of the trial that raise mild doubts about its impartiality. There were accusations of the suborning of witnesses, and it is striking that neither Henry Skipwith nor John Anktill (a reprobate who had married Castlehaven's eldest daughter) was tried, even though they were named in the original allegations. Why should favourites be immune? Possibly memories of Buckingham and alertness to the sensitivities of the royal court had influenced the judgement of the attorney-general.

The trial cast a long shadow over the family. Castlehaven's widow never remarried and his daughter-in-law was never reconciled with her husband. In 1633 Castlehaven's sister, the prophet Lady Eleanor Davies, published the first of three tracts designed to exonerate her late brother.[14] A steady stream of poems and polemics followed, and those who were to protest Castlehaven's innocence included Edward Hyde (later earl of Clarendon). Such was the state of the family when Milton composed *Arcades* and *A Masque at Ludlow*, and some have argued that the text of the latter responds to the scandal.[15]

Who were the 'noble persons' of Lady Alice's family who participated in *Arcades*? The dowager countess had had three daughters by her marriage to Ferdinando Stanley. Lady Anne, the eldest daughter, married Grey Brydges, fifth Baron Chandos; the marriage produced two sons (George, later the sixth baron, and William, later the seventh baron) and two or three daughters (Elizabeth, Frances, and possibly Anne); her subsequent marriage to the earl of Castlehaven produced no children. Both sons and possibly Frances were already living at Hatfield, but Anne and her daughter Elizabeth were tainted by the scandal, and Lady Alice was not quick to offer them refuge at Hatfield. She wrote to the Secretary of State (Dudley Carleton, Viscount Dorchester) that

My daughter and she [Elizabeth] may be so happie to receive their pardon from the King, and till such time I shall never willinglie yield to see either of them. for the sight of them would but Increase my griefs, whose hart is almost wounded to death already wth thinking of so fowle a business.[16]

The question of the presence of Anne and Elizabeth at the performance of *Arcades* cannot be resolved, as the pardons can be dated (November 1631[17]) but the date of *Arcades* is not known.

Lady Frances, Alice's second daughter, married her step-brother, John Egerton (later earl of Bridgewater); the marriage produced eight daughters and two sons. By 1634 seven daughters had married, and it was the remaining three children (Lady Alice, John and Thomas) who acted in the *Masque at Ludlow*. The third daughter, Lady Elizabeth, married Henry Hastings, who became earl of Huntingdon; the family was eminent but crushed by inherited debt. The marriage produced two sons (Ferdinando and Henry, Baron Loughborough) and two daughters (Alice and Elizabeth). Her grandchildren included Lady Mary and Lady Alice Egerton (daughters of the earl and countess of Bridgewater), whose music master since 1627 (and perhaps earlier) had been Henry Lawes, a Gentleman of the Chapel Royal who had in 1631 been appointed to the King's Musick as a lutenist and singer. Milton's commission for *Arcades* could have come from the countess, but it seems more likely that it was Lawes who commissioned Milton to write both *Arcades* and *A Masque at Ludlow*.

Arcades is a pastoral entertainment designed to honour the dowager countess. In an early draft Milton headed it 'part of a Maske', but then changed his mind and called it 'part of an entertainment'; in some ways it resembles a masque, but its action does not seem to be designed to lead to courtly revels. It also resembles country-house entertainments of a sort used to welcome eminent visitors (e.g. the visit of Queen Elizabeth to Harefield in 1602, when she was met at a dairy farm in the park of the estate), but its action is focused on the exaltation of the countess, not on her visitors.[18] Confusion about the last point has led critics to follow Masson's whimsical suggestion that *Arcades* was performed outdoors, but it was performed indoors, presumably in the great hall of Harefield. The central action of the entertainment is straightforward: members of her family and hired musicians, dressed in pastoral clothes, profess to have come from Arcadia. They are bidden to come to Harefield, where the noble lady whose home it is has made a new Arcadia. The countess was seated on a 'state', which was a raised chair, probably with a canopy indicative of her rank, and the Arcadians are guided to her by a servant-musician in the guise of the Genius of the Wood. The noble Arcadians approach the state and kiss the hem of the dowager countess's dress, whereupon two songs that Milton has written inaugurate the celebration of the virtue of the countess. *Arcades* may only be 'part of an entertainment', but it is sufficiently substantial (especially in the speech of Genius) to demonstrate the poise and grace of which Milton was capable, even in a piece of occasional writing.

On 9 December 1632 Milton marked his twenty-fourth birthday, and about this time he wrote 'How soon hath time' (Sonnet 7),[19] which refers to the end of his 'three and twentieth year'. He frets that he is getting older but has accomplished little: 'but my late spring no bud or blossom sheweth'. In the second quatrain he comments on his youthful appearance, explaining that it 'might deceive the truth, | That I to manhood am arrived so near'.[20] The sestet begins with a 'turn' on the word 'yet' and adopts a tone of resignation to the divine will: the course of his life will be the lot 'toward which time leads me, and the will of heaven'. The sonnet is remarkable both for form and content. The form, as befits the author of a series of Italian sonnets, is resolutely Italianate, as may be seen in features such as the rhyme scheme, the turn (Italian *volta*) and the internal balancing of the lines ('Yet be it less or more, or soon or slow'). The content marks the beginning of Milton's use of the sonnet for subjects other than love, in this case for the type of inward meditation that, shorn of its religious content, would re-emerge as an important genre in the Romantic period. As such, it is an early example of the confidence with which Milton, recurrently through his career as poet, pushed and extended the limitations of the genres which he adopted.

Perhaps later in the same month, Milton wrote 'On Time',[21] though the poem cannot be dated with confidence. It shares a subject with Sonnet 7, but the formal constraints of the sonnet form are cast off in favour of a carefully modulated combination of long and short lines that govern a gathering storm of words culminating in the final alexandrine, 'Triumphing over Death and Chance and thee O Time'. Milton was becoming a master of the short poem, but he was not to achieve such total control of pace and tone again until he wrote his sonnet on the Piedmont Massacre in the early 1650s.

The Feast of the Circumcision falls on 1 January, and it is possible that on New Year's Day 1633 Milton wrote 'Upon the Circumcision', the third in his sequence of poems (following the 'Nativity Ode' and 'The Passion') celebrating the ritual year. Circumcision was not (and is not) a rite of the Church of England, and it occurred only infrequently in early modern England, and then purely as a surgical procedure. Yet the Feast held an important place in the liturgical year, as an occasion for sombre reflection amid the traditional period of Christmas merry-making, which ended on Twelfth Night, and it figures not infrequently in early Stuart poetry. Robert Herrick explicitly interpreted the Feast of the Circumcision as a corrective to the encompassing rejoicing: 'let no Christmas mirth begin | Before ye purge, and circumcise | Your hearts, and hands, lips, eares, and eyes.'[22] Milton's own effort, the most conventional of his poems on the events of the liturgical year, conforms closely to the practices of other celebrations of the Feast. His association of Christ's circumcision with his Atonement on Good Friday may strike modern readers as morbidly inappropriate: 'O ere long | Huge pangs and strong | Will pierce more near his heart.'[23] However, contemporary analogues abound. Francis Quarles, for example, observes: 'The drops this day effused, were but laid | For his Good-Frydayes earnest.'[24]

Early in the new year, perhaps January 1633, Milton wrote the letter now known as the 'Letter to a Friend' or 'Letter to an unknown friend', which survives in two drafts in the Trinity MS; it should not be confused with the 'Letter to a Friend Concerning the Ruptures of the Commonwealth', which was written in 1660.[25] The names given to the letter derive from its closing phrase, 'Yo^r true & unfained freind'; the phrase is formulaic, and offers no hint of the friend's identity.[26] The letter continues the theme of the unrealized life articulated in Sonnet 7 (of which he encloses a copy) and 'On Time': his life, he explains, is 'as yet obscure, & unserviceable to mankind'. The friend observed in a meeting the previous day that 'too much love of Learning is in fault, & that I [that is, Milton] have given up my selfe to dreame away my Yeares in the arms of studious retirement like Endymion wth the Moone';[27] Milton deflects the suggestion of time-wasting with mocking self-deprecation.

The final poem that seems to have been written during this period is 'At a solemn music'. Again the Italian influence is apparent: the stanza form is modelled on Petrarch's 'Vergine bella', a *canzone* to the Virgin, and the opening sentence (Italian *fronte*) is sustained for twenty lines, followed by a four-line *coda*. The title alludes to attendance at a religious service, perhaps Choral Evensong (called 'Evening Prayer' in the 1552 Book of Common Prayer which Milton would have used), and the poem describes the vision of heaven to which Milton's mind is transported by the marriage of voice and verse. Many years later, in *Eikonoklastes* (1649), Milton would condemn the 'chanted Service-Book' and the 'singing men' who performed at such services,[28] but in the 1630s Milton could celebrate the glories of sacred music, nor does he ever really fall out of love with choral music. The theme returns in '*Ad Patrem*'.[29] Moreover, even in *Paradise Lost* a role remains for sacred song in praising the Father and the Son. Angels, whose harps are 'ever tuned', sing to 'waken raptures high . . . such concord is in heaven'.[30]

In 1634 Milton continued to read (his purchases included editions of Lycophron and Euripides[31]), but for him the principal event of the year was the commissioning of the Ludlow masque, often known as *Comus*. This title may seem inappropriate (it is as if *Paradise Lost* were known as *Satan*), but it has been in use since 1698, and is not going to go away. However, we retain Milton's own title, *A Masque presented at Ludlow Castle, 1634*, in modern spelling (in 1637 it is spelt 'Maske').

On 26 June 1631 King Charles appointed the lawyer and politician John Egerton, first earl of Bridgewater, as president of the Council in the Marches of Wales (informally known as the Council of Wales), with official residence at Ludlow Castle, Shropshire. On 8 July 1631 he was appointed lord lieutenant of Shropshire, Worcestershire, Herefordshire, Monmouthshire, and north and south Wales. The reason for these appointments in the English border counties is that the jurisdiction of the Council included both Wales and the Tudor lands in the marches. The Council was subject to the general supervision of the Privy Council (of which Bridgewater was a member), but exercised independent conciliar jurisdiction by authority of the king's commission, acting as both a local Star Chamber and a local Chancery; more contentiously, it also exercised jurisdiction in common law, which brought it into conflict with the courts of Westminster. Bridgewater's background made him well suited to the post: he was the son of an attorney-general, and had not only attended university but had also graduated and gone on to undertake legal training at Lincoln's Inn.[32] This legal background was to be a prominent feature of Bridgewater's presidency of the Council in the Marches of Wales. He defended the jurisdiction of the Council against encroachments by neighbouring English counties and other courts, and maintained the Council's casebooks in his own hand. He presided over more than 1,000 civil cases a year within the Council's chancery jurisdiction. Bridgewater also heard common law cases, of which the first high-profile example was that of Marjorie Evans, who successfully appealed to the Council after a lower court had declined to prosecute an alleged rapist.[33]

After many delays, Bridgewater embarked on a progress through the lands for which he had assumed responsibility.[34] The ceremonial journey began at Ashridge, the Hertfordshire seat of the Egerton family. At the end of June 1634, before the formal departure, Bridgewater visited Harefield (16 miles away from Ashridge); the party included the young earl of Castlehaven, who at the swing of the executioner's axe had inherited his father's earldom. On 1 July the earl and his family set out on the four-day journey to Ludlow; arriving in Worcester, they were greeted by bells of welcome for the new lord lieutenant.

On this occasion the earl stayed in Ludlow for several weeks before leaving at the end of the law term for a tour of the territories for which he was responsible. At the furthest point of the journey was Lyme (now Lyme Park), north of Macclesfield. The journey to Lyme might have been accomplished

12. Ludlow Castle.

in a few days, but Bridgewater took three weeks to get there, stopping *en route* at the homes of noble families; his party included the court musician Henry Lawes, to whom Bridgewater extended his patronage throughout the 1630s and 1640s. Lawes and Milton knew each other, and although the origins of their acquaintance are uncertain, it is possible that the musical culture of London had brought them together at an early stage. At some point they became friends, and Milton was to write a sonnet in honour of Lawes.[35]

The families that Bridgewater visited on this tour were either holders of posts related to his official duties (members of the Council of Wales or deputy lords lieutenant) or powerful families to which he was related. The family first stopped at Eyton Hall, the Shropshire home of Richard Newport (Baron Newport after his purchase of a peerage in 1642), a member of the Council of Wales.[36] They then travelled to Chirk Castle, a magnificent border fortress in Denbighshire which since 1595 had been owned by Sir Thomas Myddelton (or Middleton), the son and namesake of a founder of the East India Company who had invested profitably in the voyages of Drake, Raleigh, and Hawkins, and had converted Chirk into a stately home.[37] He had settled the castle on his son, Sir Thomas Myddelton the younger, in 1612, and the younger Myddelton, Bridgewater's host, had for long served as deputy lieutenant for Denbighshire and was the county's *custos rotulorum*.[38] At Chirk there was a banquet entertainment at which the earl, the countess, and the three children who were soon to act in *A Masque* were all given speaking parts written by Sir Thomas Salusbury.[39]

13. John Milton, *A Maske
Presented at Ludlow Castle, 1634*
(London, 1637), title page.

From Chirk the party journeyed into the Clywd Valley, presumably staying at Bachymbyd Fawr (seat of the Salusbury family), and then north to the coast, where they stayed at Mostyn Hall, then as now the seat of the Mostyn family; their host was Sir Roger Mostyn, who was a deputy lord lieutenant (for Flintshire) and justice of the peace. They then moved to Bretton Hall (Flintshire), which was the childhood home of the earl's parents (who were step-brother and sister) and thence via Cholmondeley Castle; this was the Cheshire seat of Robert Cholmondeley, who had become Viscount Kells when Irish peerages were offered at a reduced price of £1,500; he was also a deputy lord lieutenant of Cheshire and a justice of the peace. The penultimate stop was the newly constructed Dunham Massey Hall, the home of Bridgewater's niece Lady Vere Booth). Finally the family arrived at Lyme, the home of Sir Peter Legh, an important Cheshire figure to whom Bridgewater was related by marriage.[40]

The visit to Lyme lasted for three weeks, and on 15 September the family departed for Ludlow, where they arrived on the evening of Wednesday 17 September. Twelve days later, on Monday 29 September, Milton's *Masque*, the last and grandest of the peripatetic entertainments associated with the earl's installation, was acted in the hall of Ludlow Castle. Quite probably, preparations began while the family was travelling, since, once Ludlow was reached, there was not much time to mount the production and rehearse the young actors. Lawes, who travelled with them, could have facilitated the rehearsal of the spoken parts and the song the Lady sings. Preparing the dance may have been more problematic, since, as we know from the practice of masque rehearsal at the royal court, this could be very time-consuming. We are unaware of any choreographer in the earl's travelling party.

The script they had to work with was written by someone who had never visited Ludlow, a point evident in his uncertainties about staging: the opening stage direction, 'The Attendant Spirit descends or enters' reflects a lack of knowledge about whether there was sufficient ceiling space for a descent or a door convenient for an entrance. The date, however, was fixed well in advance, because a guest list for the banquet which preceded the masque had to be drawn up several weeks before the event. The civic records and household accounts are fragmentary, but guests included members of the judiciary and civic dignitaries. This was an occasion of state, not a children's entertainment.[41] Similarly, it was not in any sense a belated reaction to the Castlehaven scandal,[42] but was rather what it was intended to be: a masque in honour of the appointment of the earl of Bridgewater as president of the Council of Wales.

The music for the masque was written by Henry Lawes, who, as we noted above, had probably commissioned Milton to compose the text. The masquers were the earl's three youngest children: 15-year-old Lady Alice Egerton, 11-year-old John, Viscount Brackley and 9-year-old Thomas Egerton.[43] Henry Lawes acted the part of the Attendant Spirit, and unnamed professional actors played the parts of Comus and Sabrina, and most probably the members of Comus's rout, which functions substantially as a sort of antimasque. Musicians were professionals, perhaps drawn from the King's Musick, perhaps from theatre musicians or even the London waits, who sometimes supplemented the royal ensemble at court masques. Possibly, members of the earl's household could have constituted the rout of Comus and the attendants of Sabrina, though this was a grand event, and the case for, unstintingly, hiring in skilled performers, as was the custom at court, may have been overwhelming. There is no evidence that Milton made the journey from London, nor is it certain that, as hired help not needed for the performance, he would have gained admittance.

September 29 is Michaelmas Day, or, in the language of the Book of Common Prayer, the Feast of St Michael and All Angels. Michaelmas was one of the quarter-days in England and Wales (and so in common law had legal standing as a day on which rent was paid), and its legal significance is reflected in the name given to the autumn sitting of the Council; it was also the day on which magistrates began their terms of office, and so was appropriate to the inauguration of the earl's appointment as chief magistrate. The earthly guardians of the kingdom are magistrates, and the heavenly guardians are angels, so the association with the feast that celebrated guardian angels was entirely natural. The guardian of the young masquers was the Attendant Spirit, who had been despatched by Jove as their 'defence and guard'. It is clear that Milton wrote the part for Henry Lawes; his part includes a deft compliment, for he assumes the

> likeness of a swain
> That to the service of this house belongs
> Who with his soft pipe, and smooth-dittied song,
> Well knows to still the wild woods when they roar,
> And hush the waving woods.[44]

The parts that Milton wrote for Lady Alice and her brothers also reflect some foreknowledge of the actors: Alice was of marriageable age, and so virginity was an issue of proper concern, but her younger brother was more interested in 'nectared sweets'.[45]

Lawes, in the guise of the Attendant Spirit, introduces the action of the masque, beginning with an acknowledgement of the earl and then turning to his children:

> And all this tract that fronts the setting sun
> A noble peer of mickle trust and power
> Has in his charge, with tempered awe to guide
> An old and haughty nation proud in arms;
> Whereto his fair offspring nursed in princely lore,
> Are coming to attend their father's state,
> And new-entrusted sceptre.[46]

The earl's children are on a journey to attend him. This is, like some court masques of the early Stuart period, a story of a retarded journey, for the children are delayed by the arrival of Comus, a figure of temptation whose name (in Greek) means 'revelry'. This is not the vulgar 'god of cheer or the belly' of Jonson's *Pleasure reconciled to Virtue*, whose big-bellied Comus derives from Rabelais's Gaster, but rather the handsome youth of classical antiquity, and so a plausible tempter. His true nature, however, is demonstrated by the anti-masquers, a 'rout of monsters headed like sundry sorts of wild beasts' and so redolent of the sailors transformed by Circe.

The lines that Milton gives to Comus reflect his reading of the volume of Euripides that he had purchased that year, in that his speech imitates the dithyrambic monody of Euripides; the dithyramb is an ecstatic song, a genre seldom attempted in English (though Dryden's 'Alexander's Feast' is another fine post-banquet example). This form implies that the lines were sung or

14. Henry Lawes portrait by an unknown artist (Faculty of Music, University of Oxford).

spoken in recitative. Lawes's music for five of the songs in *A Masque* survives,[47] but there is none for this speech. At this point the nameless Lady (played by Lady Alice) enters, in search of her brothers. After a speech that reflects Milton's reading in late Shakespeare ('And airy tongues that syllable men's names | On sands and shores') the Lady sings, invoking 'sweet Echo'; unusually, within the genre, Echo does not reply: the Lady is alone and vulnerable. Comus sees his chance and engages her in conversation, disguised as a shepherd; he then leads her offstage to a cottage.

The action shifts to the brothers, to whom Milton gives extraordinarily demanding lines. They speak like adults, though the younger brother defers to the elder:

ELDER BROTHER: My sister is not so defenceless left
As you imagine, she has a hidden strength
Which you remember not.
SECOND BROTHER: What hidden strength
Unless the strength of heaven, if you mean that?

ELDER BROTHER: I mean that too, but yet a hidden strength
  Which if heaven gave it, may be termed her own:
  'Tis chastity, my brother, chastity:
  She that has that, is clad in complete steel.[48]

A modern audience might smile fondly, but the seventeenth-century notion of the child, especially the aristocratic child, was quite different, and so would the reaction have been. The speeches demonstrate to the audience in the great hall that the boys had been 'nursed in princely lore', and are preparing to assume the obligations of the ruling class. The Attendant Spirit enters, and with the brothers plans to rescue the Lady; their speeches bring the scene in the 'wild wood' to an end.

The second scene is set at a banquet in a 'stately palace', and as it opens the Lady is seated in an enchanted chair. Comus appears 'with his rabble' and offers the Lady a drink. She declines, and they enter into a debate. Comus speaks about the need to use the gifts of nature; his is on one level the speech of a Don Juan trying to seduce a young lady, but its emphasis on the need to use the body and its contempt for virginity echo puritan arguments about the ungodliness of celibacy, arguments which Milton himself was to deploy in *Paradise Lost*.[49] The Lady replies in eloquent defence of 'the sage | And serious doctrine of virginity', defending her own abstinence but also, by implication, that of clerical celibates in the tradition of Lancelot Andrewes and, indeed, Laud himself. The debate ends abruptly as 'the Brothers rush in with swords drawn' and rescue their sister, but allowing Comus and his rout to escape. Comus has taken his wand, so the rescuers cannot free the Lady from the chair. The Attendant Spirit proposes to invoke the assistance of Sabrina, a Severn nymph. He sings to her, and she rises and sings, so freeing the Lady.

The third and final scene is set in 'Ludlow Town and the President's Castle'. First country dancers—London professionals, or, just conceivably, locals or members of the earl's household—perform, and then the Attendant Spirit presents the three children to the earl and countess. This presentation of 'three fair branches of your own' is the dramatic conclusion of the journey. The masque finishes with an epilogue by the Attendant Spirit, and again the metre implies that it was sung. The earl has been honoured, and complemented through his children. The importance of godly governance, which was to prove a constant theme in Milton's ever-evolving politics, has been affirmed and has been associated with the prospects for the earl's gubernatorial role. Bridgewater was to honour those expectations.

Early Stuart masque, as a genre, valued innovation and its formal structures changed considerably, even within the work of a single writer. Ben Jonson, over his career as masque-writer, altered radically the role of the anti-masque and introduced elements of political satire. Among those who followed him, William Davenant, Thomas Carew, Aurelian Townshend, scripts were shaped to support the spectacular creativity of the designer, Inigo Jones.[50] Yet one convention remained unchanged: the aristocratic performers danced but they neither spoke nor sang. Milton pushes the genre expectations by an infusion of practices adapted from the rarer form of court entertainment, pastoral drama of the kind liked and performed by Henrietta Maria herself. His aristocratic performers do speak and the Lady sings. Again, other masque writers—and pre-eminently the learned Jonson— had written scripts that were allusive to classical mythology and which took on large and controversial themes, as well as fulfilling the simpler role of courtly compliment. While satisfying the requirements for praise and for spectacle, Milton takes the genre to a new level of high seriousness, for his is an Arminian masque.[51]

The theology needs some teasing out, since it is expressed, through allegory, in the intellectually fashionable idiom of a syncretic Neoplatonism. The knowing reader or spectator recognizes that the Lady's journey, though literally through a wood to meet her father, represents something altogether more spiritual, a journey into the world of the senses and back to a higher realm. It is a journey that many attempt and fail to complete, opting instead 'To roll with pleasure in a sensual sty'.[52] Those who hold fast to virtue are aided by divine intervention, though their own endeavours are not sufficient: 'if Virtue feeble were, | Heaven itself would stoop to her.'[53] The Attendant Spirit has some of the characteristics of grace, as conceptualized in Arminian soteriology. He seeks out those who are striving for salvation and through a synergetic relationship allows the achievement of that objective, while leaving the unregenerate to their fate, in this case, to serve in the rout of Comus. Those who are saved are not predestined to be so but reach out, actively, towards salvation: 'some there be that by due steps aspire | To lay their just hands on that golden key | That opes the palace of eternity.'[54] The sentiment recurs in *Paradise Lost*, enunciated by God the Father: 'Man shall not quite be lost, but saved who will, | Yet not of will in him, but grace in me | Freely vouchsafed.' The reprobate, who corresponds to the deformed followers of Comus, 'may stumble on, and deeper fall'.[55]

Yet a clear theological distinction separates the routes to salvation in the masque and the epic. In the latter, redemption comes through a wholly personal and internalized process of meditation on culpability, on justification by faith, and subsequently of spiritual regeneration. But in the masque, as in Laudian Arminianism, external agencies function as vital catalysts. This is the role that the clergy and the ceremonies they promote have within the church. In part, that role is discharged by some aspects of the Attendant Spirit, in part also by the Brothers, but most significantly by Sabrina. Her intervention is highly ceremonial as she liberates the Lady through a ritual sprinkling redolent of church sacraments, in an elegant display of the beauty of holiness:

> Thus I sprinkle on thy breast
> Drops that from my fountain pure,
> I have kept of precious cure,
> Thrice upon thy finger's tip,
> Thrice upon thy rubied lip,
> Next this marble venomed seat
> Smeared with gums of glutinous heat
> I touch with chaste palms moist and cold,
> Now the spell hath lost his hold.[56]

We note, too, a near-obsession with sacred or magical objects. Once more, Peter Lake's comments have a pertinence:

God's presence in the church suffused the whole structure and all the physical impedimenta used in his worship with an aura of holiness. While a physical object used in that worship could lay no claim to 'inherent sanctity' such objects were to be esteemed 'holy in relation to the holy use whereto it is assigned'. And in this sense times, places, oil, bread and several utensils . . . when they be applied to divine worship are holy.[57]

Ceremonial impedimenta break Comus's spell, in the imaginary plant (haemony) that is opposed to the magic of his cup and in the drops Sabrina sprinkles. *A Masque* constitutes the most complex and thorough expression of Laudian Arminianism and Laudian style within the Milton oeuvre, and indeed, the high-water mark of his indulgence of such beliefs and values.

The masque was an ephemeral genre, only fully realized as a fusion of stage design, dance, song, music, and speech in its usually unique performance. But Milton was not prepared to let his words die. The Trinity manuscript, which contains early drafts of *A Masque*, also (surprisingly) records textual revisions that seem to have been entered after the performance. There is also a presentation copy (in which Milton's role is unclear) that was given to the earl. Milton then prepared the text for the press in 1637, though Henry Lawes in the epistle dedicatory explicitly takes responsibility for the publication. Milton's name appears nowhere, and Lawes affirms it appeared 'Although not openly acknowledg'd by the Author'. He attests to the positive reception the script had received: he has brought it to press since 'it hath tir'd my pen to give my severall friends satisfaction'.[58] It was by far Milton's most substantial publication to date and his hesitation in publicly acknowledging it seems puzzling. Jonson's masque scripts had sometimes been published after the performance. Perhaps Milton felt or affected a squeamishness about the so-called stigma of print, an idea with some contemporary currency that gentlemen do not send their work to the press and that poems should be published only posthumously. John Donne was the most influential advocate of the prejudice.[59] Milton, however, took an obvious pride in what he had written, revising it yet again for publication in his *Poems* of 1645. Some of these changes are substantial, such as the Lady's augmentation of her explanation of temperance with a celebration of the value of chastity.[60] It is difficult to be confident about which words were spoken at the performance, because the actors' scripts are lost, but it is clear that Milton cared deeply about the text: *A Masque* was one of the most important artistic achievements of his youth, and Milton rightly valued it, as did discerning readers such as Sir Henry Wotton.

In November 1634 Milton's friend Alexander Gil, who had published a collection of poems (*Parerga*) in 1632, wrote a bawdy 75-line epithalamium (in Latin hendecasyllabics) for the wedding on 20 November of Elizabeth Noel, daughter of Edward Noel, second Viscount Campden, to John, Baron Chaworth of Armagh; the poem was recovered and published by Leo Miller in 1990.[61] On Tuesday 2 December Gil wrote to Milton, enclosing a copy of the poem; two days later Milton replied, enclosing by way of reciprocation a recently composed translation of Psalm 114 into Greek verse. Milton's letter, in Latin prose (*Epistolae Familiares* 5), promises he will meet Gil in London the following Monday (8 December, the day before Milton's birthday); the appointed place for the meeting is 'among the booksellers', which probably means St Paul's Churchyard, which was until the Great Fire the principal centre of the London book trade. He concludes by asking Gil to intervene with respect to business with the doctor who is this year's President of the College. The president and the college are not identified, nor is the nature of the business explained. There were, however, only two *collegia* in London headed by a *praeses* who was chosen annually: the College of Physicians and Sion College. In 1634 the president of the College of Physicians was Simeon Foxe (son of the martyrologist and friend of John Donne) and the college was situated in Amen Corner, in Paternoster Row beside St Paul's; if this was the *collegium*, it is possible that Milton and Gil were attempting to assist Diodati to secure a licentiate from it,[62] as such licences were (in theory) required for all physicians practising in London. The other possibility is Sion College, of which the president in 1634 was Thomas Worrall, rector of St Botolph's Bishopsgate and sometime chaplain of the bishop of London. Both colleges had libraries in which Milton might have had an interest, and although the holdings of the College of Physicians were not wholly medical,[63] the small library of Sion College had a theological emphasis that might better have suited Milton's purposes.[64] London was easily reached from Hammersmith by road or river, so both libraries were accessible to him.

Milton describes his translation of Psalm 114 as his first Greek composition since he left St Paul's, adding in a complaint that reverberates through the centuries that whoever in this age lavishes time on Greek composition will end up singing to the deaf. At St Paul's he had composed an English paraphrase of the same psalm, working from the Hebrew text. On this occasion he returned to the Hebrew text, and translated into Homeric Greek hexameters; in the first two lines, he manages the extraordinary feat of recreating the balanced structure of the Hebrew (Israel and Egypt, house of Jacob, and people of barbarous language) in Greek that Homer would have recognized. The Greek of the printed text is, however, peppered with minor errors, and the 1673 text is more inaccurate than 1645; the phenomenon whereby the correction of errors in Greek creates still more errors is familiar to modern scholars, and in Milton's case his blindness exacerbated the problem. Some of the mistakes are Milton's, but all are the product of slightly rusty Greek. Setting aside the misplaced breathings and accents, the lexical gaffes and the false quantities, all of which have been adversely judged by the uncompromising standards of the Victorian public school (Landor remarked that no sixth-former would dare submit such shoddy work) and badly treated by the printers, we are left with a poem that captures the effects of one language in another, and eschews pedantic correctness in favour of a tightly controlled rhythm and euphonious lexical choices.

In 1635, according to Wood, Milton's Cambridge MA was incorporated at Oxford. No record of any incorporation from this year survives: during the tenure of John French as registrary, as Wood explains, French failed to enter any Cambridge incorporations into the university records. That Milton did incorporate, Wood insists, was attested by Milton himself, 'from his own mouth to my friend, who was well acquainted with, and had from him, and from his Relations after his death, most of this account of his life and writings following'.[65] Incorporation of degrees at Oxford is now restricted to members of Cambridge and Trinity College Dublin, but in the early modern period supplicants included members of universities in Scottish and continental universities. The motives for incorporation were varied: some had had degrees refused at their own universities for theological or political reasons, and in such cases the time spent at the other university counted towards the required residence at Oxford; some had been beneficed or employed as schoolmasters near Oxford; some had been elected to fellowships at Oxford colleges. Milton is not alone in fitting none of these categories (Diodati is another, in his incorporation at Cambridge), but there is a possible motive for Milton's incorporation: in 1635 Milton may still have been planning to take a BD (for which he would have become eligible in 1639), and he may have thought it prudent or decorous or appropriate to take the degree in the university which in the course of the 1620s had become a predominantly Arminian institution (from 1630 with Archbishop Laud as its chancellor) rather than in one in which a puritan consensus was emerging.

The procedures for incorporation were tightened up in the Laudian statutes[66] enacted the year after Milton took his degree at the July ceremony, but it may be assumed that the procedure for Milton was broadly similar: a testimony from Cambridge was read aloud in Congregation, and an MA of Oxford University proposed a grace to the effect that Milton should be allowed to supplicate for an Oxford MA. Milton then supplicated for incorporation, requesting that he be admitted to the same degree, state, and dignity in Oxford (*admittatur ad eundem gradum, statum et dignitatem apud Oxonienses*) that he had enjoyed in Cambridge. He then swore an oath to observe the statutes, privileges, customs and franchises of Oxford University, to which he was formally admitted by the vice-chancellor, Robert Pinck,[67] who had been appointed by Archbishop Laud. The following year Milton was to move with his family to Horton, from which Oxford could be reached in a day, though it carried him significantly further from the metropolis.

CHAPTER 6

Horton

ON 12 May 1636 Milton's father was discharged at his own request as Assistant to the Company of Scriveners because of his 'removal to inhabit in the country'.[1] A few months earlier, the family had moved to the village of Horton, which is now in Berkshire (near Heathrow Airport) but was until 1974 in Buckinghamshire. The motive for the move is not known, but it may be related to a lawsuit that had been lodged against Milton's father, and may have been prompted by plague in Hammersmith.[2] The reason for the choice of this particular village is not known, but people called Milton and Jeffery (the maiden name of Milton's mother) flit through the parish records of the neighbourhood (there were Miltons in Eton and Jeffreys in Colnbrook), and it is possible that there was a family connection with the village.

The village of Horton lay some seventeen miles west of London and Westminster, from which the main road west passed through Colnbrook, a market town about a mile from Horton. The village of Horton had a manor house, a church, a substantial rectory and a scattering of houses. The manor house was the seat of the Bulstrode family, who were minor gentry; in 1602 one of the daughters of the family, Elizabeth Bulstrode, had married James (later Sir James) Whitlocke; their son was Bulstrode Whitlocke, who was to become Keeper of the Great Seal and a member of Cromwell's Council of State.[3] Though the location had few obvious advantages for the younger Milton (and its attractions for his parents are now difficult to imagine), the move allowed him to continue a programme of scholarship on which he had evidently embarked. Milton devoted much of his time to reading. Beyond his personal collection, which he expanded with occasional purchases,[4] there were two libraries within walking distance, and further afield were the libraries of London and Oxford; access to the latter, some thirty-five miles away, may have been Milton's reason for incorporating his MA at Oxford. Eton College was about five miles away from Horton, and Milton may have had access to the college library; certainly he had scholarly contacts in the college. The Kedermister Library[5] in Langley

Marish was only two miles from Horton, and Milton may have read or consulted some of its 300 volumes; some 40 of the authors represented in the collection were to be cited by Milton in his Commonplace Book (27 titles from 16 authors) or in his published writings. If he was preparing for the BD at Cambridge or Oxford (the incorporated MA would have given him the choice), the Kedermister Library would have been the most convenient resource.

At some point in the 1630s, perhaps the autumn of 1637, Milton began to keep a Commonplace Book in which he copied passages from books that he was reading, organizing them under three broad headings: ethics, economics and politics; each of these headings was divided into a large number of sub-topics. Milton was to write in the book until he went blind, and thereafter dictated entries to amanuenses; it is now in the British Library.[6] The Commonplace Book is not a complete record of Milton's reading: there is, for example, no classical literature, and theological material seems to have been gathered in a separate notebook.[7] The entries are difficult to date, but a single letter offers some assistance: before he went to Italy, Milton wrote the letter 'e' using the Greek form (ϵ) common in secretary hand, whereas after his return he gradually adopted the italic form (*e*) used by humanists.[8] Similarly, his spelling preferences seem to shift slightly, so 'their' is spelt 'thire' until about 1641 and 'thir' thereafter.

The rector of the church throughout the period that the Miltons lived in the village was a Cambridge graduate to whom the living had been presented in 1631 by Henry Bulstrode.[9] Edward Goodall clearly belonged to the wing of the Church of England that had resisted the rise of Laudianism and now paid the price of defeat—and was currently engaged in organizing some resistance. His first post after coming down from Cambridge had been at Rotherhithe (on the south bank of the Thames), where he had been the assistant of the puritan divine Thomas Gataker; this was the same post as had been held by Thomas Young, Milton's childhood tutor. Gataker, rather like Edmund Calamy, with whom Milton would later be associated,[10] was a divine of impeccable scholarly credentials and a resilient and influential opponent of the ceremonialists. Like Calamy and the East Anglian group around him, he would develop his critique of episcopacy along increasingly Presbyterian lines, and, again like Calamy, would play an important part in the early work of the Westminster Assembly of Divines. He would not have chosen Goodall as his assistant had he not been confident of his ecclesiastical ideology. Moreover, Goodall's appointment to the Horton rectorship probably tells us something about the beliefs and practices of Horton's leading family.

In Hammersmith the Miltons had been able to worship in a chapel-of-ease that suited their Laudian tastes, but the church of St Michael in Horton reflected the puritan convictions of its incumbent, who refused to wear the priestly vestments insisted on by ceremonialists. In 1633 Goodhall had

15. St Michael, the parish church, Horton.

married Sara Valentine of Chalfont St Giles (the village to which Milton was to move more than thirty years later); her father was Thomas Valentine, who ran afoul of Laud and Richard Neile, was suspended in 1636 and successfully petitioned to regain his living; he was later to be a member of the Westminster Assembly. Goodall's radical credentials were impeccable.

Milton did not have the means to live independently, and so perforce had followed his parents to Horton. His attitude towards the move cannot now be recovered: to modern eyes it perhaps seems idyllic, but it may have felt to Milton like rural banishment. Certainly many Cambridge graduates who had become country priests found village life intolerable. Nathaniel Tovey, his former tutor, complained from remote Leicestershire that whenever his Cambridge friends stopped writing, he lived 'in darkness and ignorance',[11] and the poet Robert Herrick famously spoke of his banishment to 'loathed Devonshire'.[12] Milton's own description of the Horton period in the *Defensio Secunda* (1651) as one of self-education and leisure (Latin *otium*) articulates the Ciceronian ideal of *otium cum dignitate*,[13] but his representation of Horton answers the polemical needs of the *Defensio*, and should not be construed as an authoritative account of the Horton years.[14]

Milton, like Goodall, had left behind both Cambridge and the metropolis. They had both moved from their networks of friends, in the rector's case from the circle of scholarly puritans forming in the London area, in Milton's from university poets and academics and from Alexander Gil and perhaps others still living in the City. Goodall and Milton probably had a mutual friend in Thomas Young. They were, most likely, the only two Cambridge graduates permanently in residence for several miles in any direction. If indeed they fell into each other's company, as seems highly plausible, Goodall would have been the first documented puritan with whom the adult Milton engaged on a personal level. Goodall's associations suggest his adherence to a Calvinist theology; on theories of salvation, Milton did not budge, although his mature soteriology would be much closer to the radical Arminian John Goodwin, than to that of the Laudians.[15] But on other issues, over the Horton years, albeit unevenly and indistinctly, Milton's radicalization began.

In the early 1630s the Laudian church offered to families like the Miltons attractive features such as the pursuit of the beauty of holiness and the rejection of Calvinist predestination. Through the mid-years of the decade, however, some less attractive features emerged: authoritarianism, sacerdotalism, and an enthusiasm for improving its own financial well-being. The Jacobean church had been characterized by a pluralism held in delicate balance by the guileful intelligence of James I. Charles had appointed Laud to develop the programme that they shared, and he was equal to the task. Kenneth Fincham characterizes well those policies and their implementation:

Anti-Calvinist ideas prospered after the accession of Charles I. The call for strict discipline was embraced by the new king, whose aesthetic preferences for order and reverence were sharpened by his fears of a puritan conspiracy in Church and state. The instructions given by Nathaniel Brent, Archbishop Laud's vicar-general, in metropolitan visitations in twenty dioceses between 1634 and 1637 express the priorities of the Caroline regime. First, full liturgical and ceremonial conformity was enforced. Ministers were to read divine service in its entirety with no omissions and hold services on Wednesdays and Fridays as the Prayer Book stipulated. Proper clerical attire was essential: this meant 'constantly' wearing the surplice during services, and outside Church 'never' failing to use a canonical cloak, that symbol of the priestly caste. A premium was placed on reverent conduct during services: parishioners should bow at the name of Jesus and stand at the creed and gospels, as canon 18 stated. Most significant of all, the communion table was ordered to be 'set at the upper end of the chancel north and south and a rail before it or round about it'.[16]

The Milton family would shortly feel directly the effect of a visitation informed by this brief. For the clergy, sanctions ranged from exclusion from preferment to actual suspension. As we shall see, open criticism of such measures carried the risk of far graver punishment. The emphasis on the separation of clergy from laity reflects a belief in the special role of the former in the spiritual life of the nation; it approached the sorts of sacerdotalism evident in the Catholic church, and it posed a challenge to the self-esteem of learned and devout lay Protestants like Milton. At the same time, Laud recognized that the cultural revolution he was implementing could not be achieved without funds, and a new emphasis on securing the income of the church caused some alarm among propertied laity.

To outsiders, much of this innovation smacked of popery, and that charge was laid, with increasing confidence, as the decade drew to its close. It was fed, too, by an anxiety about the influence of the openly and ostentatiously devout Catholic queen, Henrietta Maria, and a concern lest converts be drawn from the highest ranks around the king: 'throughout the years of the personal rule . . . this latent fear was never far below the surface of the nation's consciousness. . . . Stories of conversions, swelled by report beyond all proportion, spread from the capital to the country.'[17]

The most important year of Milton's Horton period is 1637, which in many ways marks a turning point in his life. On 27 January Milton's father was served with a summons in connection with a lawsuit initiated by Sir Thomas Cotton in the Court of Requests.[18] For almost forty years John Cotton had invested money with John Milton the elder, who had used the money for loans that attracted interest; the total investment was approximately £3,000.[19] The arrangement had run smoothly until mid-1630, when there was a proposal that Cotton surrender the bonds to the elder Milton and his partner, Thomas Bower.[20] In Cotton's version of what had happened, Milton and Bower had persuaded Cotton that the investments were unsound, and offered to buy the bonds for £2,000;[21] in the elder Milton's version of what happened, Cotton offered to sell the bonds to Milton, who declined, because he interpreted the offer as a slight to his professionalism.[22] Cotton then approached Thomas Bower separately, and on 25 November 1630 sold the bonds to Bower for £2,000, and issued a receipt that consisted of a signed inventory of the bonds.[23] In 1635 Cotton had died (his will was proved on 29 January 1636[24]), and his executor, who was his grand-nephew Sir Thomas Cotton,[25] brought suit against Bower and Milton's father, accusing them of collusion and conspiracy to defraud. He also alleged that they had colluded with Thomas Houlker (John Cotton's lawyer) and Thomas Colwell (John Cotton's landlord) to steal part of John Cotton's estate. A writ was issued on 23 January 1637, and as Milton the elder and Bower failed to reply, the court declared both to be in contempt, fining Milton 20 shillings (which was forfeited to Thomas Cotton) and committing Bower to the Fleet prison.[26]

When Milton the elder eventually received the summons, he quickly engaged a lawyer, George Miller, who replied to the Court of Requests that his client was too old and infirm to travel, and that he had prepared a writ of *dedimus potestatem*[27] that would enable the old man to prepare his reply at home. A writ issued on 10 March[28] authorized the commissioners for Buckinghamshire to receive Milton's answers under oath, to certify their authenticity, and to communicate them to the Court of Requests within three weeks of Easter, which in 1637 fell on 9 April. By this time the Milton family in London had rallied round, so the writ of 10 March was sent to Thomas Agar (the scrivener's son-in-law) and John Agar;[29] on 1 April Christopher Milton, who was still studying at the Inner Temple, submitted an affidavit to the Court of Requests explaining that his father, 'beinge aged about 74 yeares is not by reason of his said aige and infirmitye able to travel to the Cittye of westm^r to make his perfect answere to the said bill without much p^{r}iudice to his health hee livinge at Horton . . . about 17 miles distant'.[30] Whether this was the statement of a fledgling lawyer stretching the truth to protect his client, or the truthful statement of a worried son, cannot now be ascertained, though a sceptic might note that in the years to follow Milton the elder moved first to Reading and then to London.

On 3 April 1637 Henry Perry (Sir Thomas Cotton's solicitor) wrote to his client summarizing progress to date in the lawsuit.[31] On the same day, in Horton, the lawsuit was eclipsed by the death of Sara Milton.[32] The Miltons enjoyed the standing requisite for burial within the church, and Sara was buried under a stone in the floor of the chancel. The inscription, which is still clearly visible, says 'Heare lyeth the Body of Sara Milton the wife of John Milton who Died the 3rd of April 1637'.

Litigation does not tarry over death, and on 13 April Milton the elder submitted his answer to Sir Thomas Cotton's suit, denying either participating in or even knowing about the agreement between Cotton and Bower. He requested that the case against him be dismissed and, with admirable chutzpah, demanded that his legal expenses be reimbursed. Thereafter the case went quiet while all parties awaited the decision of the court. The matter was finally resolved in Milton the elder's favour on 1 February 1638, when the suit was dismissed, and Milton was awarded 20 shillings for his 'costs herein wrongfully susteyned'.[33] The scrivener had been vindicated. But the case had surely brought home to the Milton family facts which they would have preferred not to contemplate. Four-hundred years on, the probity of the esteemed father of a major cultural icon may appear self-evident. But perhaps that probity was not so clear at the time; more certainly, the case demonstrated that it could be seriously questioned, in ways that would have reduced

16. The gravestone of Sara Milton, Horton.

the family to disgrace and perhaps penury, had the charges been upheld. Any easy assumptions the Miltons may have held, about their secure position within the propertied classes of an ordered and immutable society, were broken by the recognition that, for the middling sort dependent on accumulated capital, rather than on the broad acres of the upper gentry, ruin could come swiftly and unexpectedly.

On 14 June 1637 another equity court, the Court of Star Chamber,[34] pronounced sentence on three radicals who had been convicted of sedition: the lawyer William Prynne, the divine Henry Burton, and the physician John Bastwick. All three had previously been active puritan critics of the regime, and had continued to publish 'vituperative treatises against the church'.[35] The corporal punishment that was part of their sentences was carried out on 30 June in the palace yard at Westminster, and it is entirely possible that Milton was present in the profoundly sympathetic crowd who witnessed it: 'Some dipped their handkerchiefs in their blood.'[36] Prynne, whose ears had been clipped in 1633 after his previous indictment by the Star Chamber, had the stumps completely removed with a hot iron; his nose was slit, and the initials 'S L' ('Seditious Libeller') were burnt into his cheeks. Prynne was later to remark that the letters stood for *Stigmata Laudis*, the marks of Laud.[37] Like Burton and Bastwick, who also lost their ears, he was also sentenced to be fined £5,000 and to suffer perpetual imprisonment.

The mutilation of the three radicals by a court that was seen as a vehicle of Laud's authoritarianism (Laud had spoken memorably and at great length at the trial, though he had declined to cast his vote at the judgement) polarized the nation. In some respects, the impact of the spectacular punishment on men of Milton's social status was analogous to that of the legal case against his father: it demonstrated that the lives of the middling sort were in some respects as fragile as those of the unpropertied. Corporal punishment, delivered in the public gaze, was commonplace in early modern England, but it was usually a lesson in social hierarchy written on the bodies of the poor, of prostitutes, vagrants, petty criminals. Laud and Charles, in their folly, had reached into the professional classes, and inscribed on the representatives' bleeding bodies the unequivocal message that they, too, were subject to their will. As Peter Heylin, Laud's chaplain, observed, their punishment 'was a very great trouble to the spirits of many very *moderate and well-meaning men*, to see the three most eminent professions ... to be so wretchedly dishonoured'.[38] Milton had been a contented Laudian both in his personal loyalties and in his theology, and he had probably entertained little sympathy hitherto with William Prynne, the apparent ringleader. His earlier punishment had been for the publication of *Histrio-mastix: The Players Scourge, or, actors tragaedie*, with an attack on masques, which appeared the year before Milton wrote the script for the Ludlow entertainment. No love was lost between them through the 1640s and 1650s.[39] But in 1637 Milton began to bid William Laud good night.

The process of disengagement seems to have been gradual, and a year later (as will be seen in the next chapter) Milton was still content to mix in Laudian circles in Paris, but the journey towards an anti-Laudian stance had begun, and the securing of a BD and a subsequent career in the Laudian church seemed less attractive than it once had done. Certainly the turning point could have been Laud's brutal treatment of the godly radicals, but it is equally possible that an event closer to home had encouraged disillusionment with the Laudian church.

That event was an episcopal visitation. Horton, which is now in the diocese of Oxford, was then in the enormous diocese of Lincoln. The bishop of Lincoln, John Williams, had personally visited his entire diocese in 1634, but was not involved in the visitation of Buckinghamshire in 1637, because he had been imprisoned in the Tower of London at the king's pleasure.[40] The visitation nonetheless went ahead, and on 8 August 1637 the archdeacon visited Horton.[41] He noted approvingly Laudian details such as the kneeling bench by the rails, but was concerned that some of the seats were too high, including that of 'Mr Millton', and noted that the rector's surplice did not conform to requirements. He also noted that 'the two Tombestones in the Chancel in the pavement are laid the wronge way'; the two tombstones in the floor of the chancel include that of Sara Milton. The transgressions seem venial, but may well have touched a nerve exposed by the spectacle in the palace yard. The Laudian church was not only persecuting godly men of professional standing, but was also interfering with the family pew and declaring the gravestone of Sara Milton to have been improperly orientated. It is difficult to judge the impact of this visitation on the Miltons. Possibly they shrugged it off, but it is also possible that it contributed to the erosion of the younger Milton's allegiance to the Caroline church, evident in his only major vernacular poem of the Horton period, 'Lycidas'. As plate 16 clearly shows the tombstone was indeed unorthodox in its orientation, implying that Sara's feet lie to the east. The inscription is read facing the west end, not the altar. Furthermore, the Milton family plainly resisted successfully its repositioning in compliance with the requirement of the visitation.

On 10 August 1637 Edward King,[42] a young Fellow of Christ's College, drowned off the coast of Anglesey while en route to Ireland. King was one of the nine children of Sir John King (d. 1637), a Yorkshireman who had served in Ireland in various administrative capacities since 1585, and his wife, Catherine, née Drury (d. 1617), whose father, Robert, was the nephew of Sir William Drury, lord deputy of Ireland. Edward's godfather was his uncle (and namesake) Edward King, bishop of Elphin. Of his brothers and sisters the most prominent were Robert King (who became a member of Cromwell's council of state), John (who became clerk of the hanaper), Mary (later Lady Charlemont), Margaret (later wife of Sir Gerald Lowther, chief justice of common pleas in Ireland), and Dorothy Durie (whose second husband was the Protestant divine John Durie, a friend of Milton). Edward was educated at Thomas Farnaby's school in Goldsmiths' Alley, Cripplegate, London. On 9 June 1626 Edward and his brother Roger were admitted as lesser pensioners to Christ's College, Cambridge, and were assigned to William Chappell, who had recently rusticated Milton. Edward proceeded BA in 1630 and MA in 1633. Soon after his MA he would have taken holy orders.

King's final term as an undergraduate began on 7 April 1630, but teaching was soon discontinued because of plague. As the Fellows and undergraduates were preparing to leave it became known that Andrew Sandelands intended to resign his Fellowship. On 10 June, while most of the Fellows were still absent, the vacant Fellowship was filled by royal mandate; King Charles appointed King to replace Sandelands. King (like Milton) was technically ineligible, because he was deemed, despite his Irish birth, to be a Yorkshireman, on the grounds that the family seat was Feathercock Hall, near Northallerton, and the college already had a Yorkshireman in the Fellowship (William Power). The royal mandate, however, stipulated that King should be appointed 'notwithstanding any statute'. Appointment by mandate, like the regius professorships, was an act of royal patronage whereby the crown exerted control over the universities and their constituent colleges. King was loyal, and his family was of the requisite social standing for such an act by the crown; Milton's was not. King held his Fellowship for the remaining seven years of his short life. During that period he took only thirteen undergraduates because he was not dependent on undergraduate fees for his income.

King was conspicuously loyal to the royal family. Of his ten published poems (all in Latin), seven were written to mark the birth of royal children; of the other three, one celebrates the recovery of King Charles from smallpox in the winter of 1632 and another gives thanks for Charles's safe return from his coronation in Scotland in 1633. Support for the royal family in these poems sometimes touched on sensitive areas. There is, for example, an approving reference to the royal fleet in a poem published in 1637, the year in which John Hampden was tried for refusing to pay ship-money, that could not have been politically neutral. Similarly the assertion in a poem written in 1636 that 'sancta maiestas Cathedræ | Dat placidam Italiæ quietem' ('the holy sovereignty of the church grants Italy its calm serenity') may have been appropriate in a poem addressed to a Catholic queen but it is indicative of an unusual degree of tolerance for Roman Catholicism.

Sir John King died in Lichfield on 4 January 1637 and was buried at Boyle Abbey on 30 March. Edward King decided to travel to Ireland that summer, probably with a view to seeing his relatives (his brother Robert, his sisters Mary and Margaret, and his uncle Bishop King) and his former tutor William Chappell, who was provost of Trinity College, Dublin; he may also have intended to visit his father's grave in Roscommon. Piracy and the threat of storms made travelling across the Irish Sea a perilous undertaking so King drew up a will (dated 30 July, with a codicil dated two days later) before he left for Chester, where his ship sailed on the spring tide of 10 August. The ship struck a rock off the coast of Anglesey and quickly sank. King was drowned, and his body was carried out to sea and never recovered.

The death of Ben Jonson on 16 August, six days after the death of Edward King, was marked in Oxford by a collection of memorial poems entitled *Jonsonus Virbius*. It is possible that this volume provided a stimulus for the poets of Cambridge to assemble a rival volume in memory of King, who had lacked Jonson's great gifts as a poet, but had nonetheless published ten competent Latin poems. Milton was asked to contribute a poem, and in

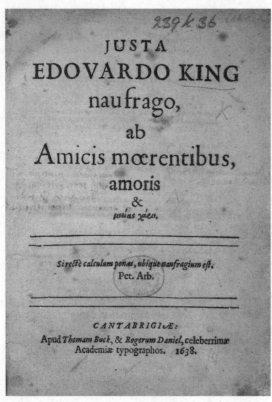

17. *Justa Edouardo King naufrago, ab amicis moerentibus, amoris & mneias charin* (Cambridge, 1638), title page.

November 1637 copied a draft of 'Lycidas' into a part of what is now the Trinity Manuscript. The poem was published in *Justa Edouardo King naufrago ab amicis moerentibus, amoris &* μνείας χάριν. ('Obsequies to Edward King, drowned by shipwreck, in token of love and remembrance, by his grieving friends') late in 1638. Milton had chosen to write in English, and his poem was placed at the end of the English section of the volume, which had a separate title page (*Obsequies to the Memory of Mr Edward King*). Most of the poems in the volume were written in the fashionable idioms adopted by followers and imitators of Donne or Jonson. Milton chose to ignore this contemporary enthusiasm for wittily expressed or lapidary grief, turning instead to the genre of the pastoral elegy and thus invoking a tradition that stretched through Spenser and Petrarch to Virgil and Theocritus. His poem commemorated King, but in the act of composition Milton transcended his ostensible subject and produced a meditation on human mortality that retains the power to move readers centuries after the death of King and those who mourned him. It is beyond dispute his greatest memorial poem, one that is arguably the finest short poem in the English language.

The poem poses considerable challenges to interpretation. Sometime after his return from Italy—we can date the addition by his handwriting; he uses an italic 'e'—he added to the manuscript version in the Trinity Manuscript, 'In this Monodie the author bewails a lerned friend unfortunatly drownd in his passage from Chester on the Irish seas 1637', a necessary piece of information once the poem is detached from the collection in which it appeared. However, when Milton reprinted it in his first collection, in 1645, he further added the words, 'And by occasion foretells the ruin of our corrupted clergy then in their height'.[43] From the vantage point of 1645, the year of Laud's execution, Milton can represent his poem as precisely prophetic and as such offer it as evidence of an early godly radicalism. The parts fall into place: the bad shepherds who push away their moral superiors are Laudian clergy; the prizes they scrabble for lucrative benefices; the punishment that awaits them ejections, exiles, imprisonment, and, in Laud's own case, execution.

But in 1637 the issues would not have seemed so clear. Milton's poem, without the second sentence of its header, is a more guarded rehearsal of an anti-Laudian critique and a more uncertain expression of an incipient unease with the Church of England. Among the men whose company Milton keeps in the *Justa* are plenty who were currently enjoying considerable preferment in the university and church and who would continue to do so, at least until ejection, from fellowships or livings, in the mid-1640s, in some cases followed by significant reward at the Restoration. John Pearson, for example, became master of Trinity College, Cambridge, and bishop of Chester; Michael Honywood, after years in exile, was appointed dean of Lincoln.[44] Most whom we can certainly identify were still actively pursuing their careers in 1637. Probably none would have wished to associate a loyal and generally Laudian volume with Milton's elaborate suicide note for his own academic and ecclesiastical career, unless, of course, that note were so deeply encrypted as to render it safe.

Milton's broad onslaught on the corrupt clergy accords with his chosen idiom, adapted most immediately from Spenser. There is nothing recognizably puritan in the poem's attack on ecclesiastical failures. Edward King was certainly not an oppositional figure, and had received his Fellowship at Christ's by royal mandate. Laud, like Milton, worried about the failings of churchmen and about the ignorance he found in some of them. Milton's sally at those who 'for their bellies sake | Creep and intrude and climb into the fold'[45] is a sentiment that could have been applauded by Laud himself, since he too was fiercely ascetic in lifestyle and he was active in the prosecution of ecclesiastical malpractice.[46] The poem can scarcely be perceived as anti-prelatical since it attributes the starkest indictment of the clergy to St Peter, regarded as the founder of the episcopacy.

Yet, with hindsight, the unease appears palpable enough. Besides the general failings of the church, the poem picks up, specifically though in code, on its inadequate response to the success achieved, or thought to be achieved, by

20

Reason not limits them that weep,
But bids them lanch into the deep;
Tells us they not exceed, that drain
In tears the mighty Ocean;
Nor all that in these tears are found
As in a generall deluge drown'd.

T. Norton.

Lycidas.

YEt once more, O ye laurels, and once more,
Ye myrtles brown, with ivy never-sere,
I come to pluck your berries harsh and crude,
And with forc'd fingers rude
Shatter your leaves before the mellowing yeare.
Bitter constraint, and sad occasion deare
Compells me to disturb your season due:
For Lycidas is dead, dead ere his prime,
(Young Lycidas!) and hath not left his peere.
Who would not sing for Lycidas? he knew *well*
Himself to sing, and build the lofty rhyme.
He must not flote upon his watry biere
Unwept, and welter to the parching wind
Without the meed of some melodious tear.
  Begin then, Sisters of the sacred well
That from beneath the seat of Jove doth spring;
Begin, and somewhat loudly sweep the string;
Hence with deniall vain, and coy excuse.
So may some gentle Muse
With lucky words favour my destin'd urn,
And as he passes, turn
And bid fair peace be to my sable shroud.

For

21

For we were nurst upon the self-same hill,
Fed the same flock, by fountain, shade, and rill;
Together both, ere the high Lawns appear'd
Under the glimmering eye-lids of the morn,
We drove a-field, and both together heard
What time the gray-fly winds her sultry horn,
Batt'ning our flocks with the fresh dews of night,
Oft till the ev'n-starre bright
Toward heav'ns descent had slop'd his burnisht wheel.
Mean while the rurall ditties were not mute
Temper'd to th' oaten flute;
Rough Satyres danc'd, and Fauns with cloven heel
From the glad sound would not be absent long,
And old Damoetas lov'd to heare our song.
  But oh the heavy change, now thou art gone,
Now thou art gone, and never must return!
Thee shepherds, thee the woods, and desert caves
With wild thyme and the gadding vine oregrown,
And all their echoes mourn.
The willows and the hasil-copses green
Shall now no more be seen
Fanning their joyous leaves to thy soft layes.
As killing as the canker to the rose,
Or taint-worm to the weanling herds that graze,
Or frost to flowers that their gay wardrobe weare,
When first the white-thorn blowes;
Such, Lycidas, thy losse to shepherds eare.
  Where were ye Nymphs, when the remorseless deep
Clos'd ore the head of your *Lord* Lycidas? *'Lord'*
For neyther were ye playing on the steep,
Where *your* old Bards the famous Druids lie,
Nor on the shaggie top of Mona high,
Nor yet where Deva spreads her wisard streame:
Ah me, I fondly dream!
Had ye been there——for what could that have done?
What could the Muse her self that Orpheus bore,

rhe

18. *Justa*, 20-1, showing Milton's corrections to 'Lycidas' (Cambridge University Library (Adv.d.38.5)).

Catholicism, in the lines, 'what the grim with privy paw | Daily devours apace, and nothing said'.[47] As the commentary tradition notes, the probable allusion is to the Catholic church. The arms of the founder of the Jesuits, Ignatius Loyola, included two grey wolves. Again, for anyone who was aware of the sufferings of Bastwick, Burton, and Prynne, Milton's allusion to the abhorred shears of the blind Fury and the trembling ears of the author have an obvious resonance.[48] In 1645 Milton told his readers that this poem marked his godly puritanism. Though its prophetic perspicacity, from the perspective of 1637, was not apparent, the stirrings of a new direction are there to be seen. The process of ideological relocation was protracted. Indeed, it was also unending, as there is evidence that decade by decade Milton grew more radical.

In November, when Milton was drafting 'Lycidas', he clearly spent time in London. That month he twice wrote to Diodati, and on both occasions gave his address as London rather than Horton; Diodati is said in the first letter to be lingering amongst the Hyperboreans, which probably means that he was in Chester. These letters, which in the printed version of 1674 are wrongly said to have been written in September,[49] are composed in Latin prose, and are filled with the exuberance that characterizes their correspondence. In the first letter (2 November) Milton speaks about having undertaken a journey at the beginning of autumn (which may imply September), but does not say where he went. The journey took Milton to London, where he visited Diodati's brother John, so his ultimate destination seems unlikely to have been Oxfordshire; Cambridge is a possibility, as a traveller would have to go to London to catch the coach for Cambridge at the Bull Inn in Bishopsgate.

The letter concludes that he is writing in haste because he was returning the following day to Horton. Diodati quickly replied, but his letter is lost. A few weeks later, however, Milton was back in London, where he again wrote to Diodati (23 November 1637).[50] Milton describes his reading, and discloses that he is planning to move into one of the Inns of Court. It is hard to interpret this plan with confidence.

In this period most students at the Inns of Court were the sons of country gentry, and their interest in the law was minimal, sometimes nil.[51] Many wanted to secure enough command of the law to be able to deal with lawsuits that characterized an increasingly litigious society, but others concentrated on lessons in dancing, fencing, and music, and enjoyed the masques and plays that were performed. Some, like Donne and Sir John Davies, wrote poetry, some, like John Ford, wrote plays, and others spent time in the court and the city. Some studied subjects such as anatomy or natural science or mathematics or theology or modern languages. A minority (including Christopher Milton) who intended to be called to the bar remained for sixteen terms (four years), studying common law (canon and civil law were studied at the universities and at Doctors' Commons), but there was neither personal tuition nor a syllabus. There were opportunities to attend moots, case-puttings and readings, and for attending sessions of the courts during term-time, but learning mostly took the form of private reading. Milton's family was not gentry, in the sense that its income did not derive directly from land, but rather came from capital investment, but it looked like gentry, it was socially ambitious, and Milton was soon to embark on a continental tour of a type ordinarily associated with gentry and aristocracy. It therefore seems possible that Milton was intending to spend some time as a gentleman student at one of the Inns. His legal knowledge was eventually to become formidable, but there is no evidence that he aspired to join the profession.[52] In any event, the plan to move to one of the Inns was abandoned, and Milton returned to Horton. Three days later (26 November), however, his brother Christopher was 'restored into commons' by a vote of the Parliament of the Inner Temple.[53] The meaning of this entry is unclear, but it may imply an hiatus in Christopher's residence, one that required a vote for him to be readmitted; alternatively, it may mean that he paid an overdue bill.

Milton remained for the first part of 1638 in England, but much of his time was spent preparing for the continental tour that would realize his Italophile aspirations. No poem can be attributed with confidence to these months, but Milton's widowed father was aging and Milton was shortly to leave the country, so it is possible that *Ad Patrem* ('To my father') was written during this period (though dates ranging from 1631 to 1645 have been advanced). The poem has a valedictory tone, and even a sense of reckoning, in that Milton attempts to sum up the gifts that he has received from his father; these gifts include languages, for his father had paid for tuition in Latin, Greek, French, Italian, and Hebrew. Milton also notes that they have complementary skills, in that he is a poet and his father a musician. The most puzzling aspect of the poem is Milton's portrayal of his father as a despiser of poetry. This seems unlikely, partly because his father had composed a few poems,[54] but also because he had set verse to music; it seems more likely to be a rhetorical trope. Milton thanks his father for not forcing him into the law or the world of commerce, but it is possible that the elder Milton wanted his son to have a profession, even as he had combined the profession of scrivener with the avocation of musician.

Milton published the poem while his father was still alive, so on one level it is a public document, but it is also a communication between son and father, and so inevitably contains private understandings. Milton was not confident that his father would still be alive at the end of the Italian journey, or indeed that he would survive the journey himself (in his imagination murderous Jesuits lay in wait), so the poem articulates feelings of gratitude that in normal circumstances would remain unspoken.

CHAPTER 7

Italy

I N the spring of 1638 Milton finalized his plans for a journey to Italy. There
was a steady trickle of young aristocrats travelling to Italy, a precursor of
the Grand Tour of the eighteenth century, but it was relatively unusual for a
Protestant of Milton's class to undertake such a journey:[1] he was neither a
merchant nor a pilgrim, and he had no particular interest in the visual arts.
The journey may represent social aspirations or an escape from his family (he
was unemployed and living in Horton with his recently widowed father) or
from some scandal[2] or from his father's wish to remove him from the
attentions of a government that had mutilated and imprisoned Prynne,
Bastwick, and Burton, if indeed he had responded intemperately to these
events; Italy offered a musical culture in which Milton was interested and
learned societies to which he had access by virtue of his class, linguistic ability,
and (possibly) letters of introduction. Whatever the reason, he decided to
explore fresh woods and pastures new. He needed a passport, some letters of
introduction, and quite a lot of money.

First, a passport. This was a document required not, as now, to enter a
country, but rather to leave one's own. It was a combination of what would
now be called an exit visa and a safe conduct. In the spring of 1638 Milton
applied to the Lord Warden of the Cinque Ports[3] for a passport. As he had
no direct access to the Warden (Theophilus Howard, second earl of Sussex[4]), Milton asked Henry Lawes to assist him. The passport is lost, but the
covering letter with which Lawes enclosed the passport survives in the
British Library:

Sir, I have sent you wth this A letter from my Lord Warden of the Cinque Portes
under his hand & seale, wch wilbe A sufficient warrant, to Justify yor goinge out of the
Kings Dominions. if you intend to [ryde?] yo^rselfe you cañot have a safer convoy for
both, than from Suffolke House, but that I leave to yor Owne Consideration &
remaine yor faithfull friend & servant Henry Lawes.[5]

The word 'both' is the first indication that Milton would not be travelling alone, but would be accompanied by a servant or companion; his identity is not known. The allusion to Suffolk House may be a metonym for the earl of Suffolk (the Warden) or to the use of his residence[6] as a point of departure travellers departing in 'convoy', as opposed to riding alone.

Milton also needed letters of introduction, and the opportunity to secure them came during a visit to Eton (a few miles from Horton), where he met Sir Henry Wotton, the retired diplomat (and poet) who had become Provost of Eton College. After meeting Wotton Milton wrote a letter of thanks (6 April 1638; now lost) and enclosed a copy of *A Masque at Ludlow*. Wotton was clearly enchanted by the masque, and on 13 April 1638 he replied to Milton, saying that 'I should much commend the tragical part if the lyrical did not ravish me with a certain Dorique delicacy in your songs and odes, whereunto I must plainly confess to have seen nothing parallel in our language';[7] Milton carefully preserved the letter, and published it in his 1645 *Poems*. The letter contains several puzzles beyond the question of which part of *A Masque* Wotton thought tragic. The meeting was effected by one to whom Wotton calls 'Mr H' and describes as Milton's 'learned friend'. Mr H could be John Harrison, one of the Fellows of Eton, but the adjective 'learned' points to the 'ever-memorable' John Hales, the prodigiously learned Fellow whose earlier posts had included the regius professorship of Greek at Cambridge and a period at the Synod of Dort (as chaplain to Sir Dudley Carleton), of which he later said 'there, I bid John Calvin good-night'.[8] His love of learning, his Arminianism and possibly his personal friendship with Laud may point to common ground with Milton. The other friend mentioned in the letter is the 'Mr R', whose poems had recently been posthumously printed in Oxford. This must be the poet and playwright Thomas Randolph, who had died in March 1635, and whose *Poems* had been printed in Oxford in 1638.[9] He was Milton's contemporary at Cambridge, and both wrote saltings, so it is possible that a friendship was forged there. Randolph's dissolute life thereafter may not have precluded the possibility that a friendship continued—on his return Milton was to seek out the boon companionship of Inns of Court men.[10]

After dealing with these literary matters, Wotton turns to Milton's journey. He assumes that Milton will be travelling through Paris, and so includes a letter of introduction to 'Mr M.B. whom you shall easily find attending the young Lord S. as his Governour'. M.B. is Michael Branthwait, who had been the English agent in Venice, and so was well placed to advise Milton on his itinerary. As for 'Lord S.', the difficulty is that there were two ambassadors in Paris, the earl of Leicester and Viscount Scudamore of Sligo. The 'young Lord S' could conceivably be Algernon Sidney, the 17-year-old son of the earl of Leicester, or his brother Philip Sidney (Viscount Lisle), or James Scudamore (1624–68), but it is more likely that Branthwait was tutor to young Scudamore; the evidence is simply that it was Lord Scudamore that Milton met.[11] Finally, Wotton passed on some advice that he had been given in 1592 while visiting Siena:

At Siena I was tabled in the house of one Alberto Scipioni, an old Roman courtier in dangerous times, having been steward to the Duca di Pagliano, who with all his family were strangled, save only this man … At my departure towards Rome … I had won his confidence enough to beg his advice how I might carry myself there without offence of others or of my own conscience. '*Signor Arrigo mio*', says he, '*i pensieri stretti ed il viso sciolto*'.

Wotton had told the same story before, and had translated the final line as 'My Signor Harry, your thoughts close and your countenance loose'.[12] This formula offered a solution to the problem of how a Protestant visiting Rome could be true to his own convictions while not giving offence: be silent and keep smiling.

Thirdly, Milton needed money. The source of his finance was sufficiently inconspicuous for Salmasius to suggest that he had financed his journey by working as a catamite,[13] but the truth is rather more mundane. On 1 February 1638 Milton lent £150 to Sir John Cope and others, and accepted a bond of £300 for security. The money was probably put up by Milton's father as a means of generating some income for his son, in this case £12 a year, paid quarterly.[14] The figures are not large (and the investment was a poor one), but it may be indicative of a process whereby Milton's father started to generate an income for his unemployed son. Similarly, in April 1638 the Miltons completed the sale of a property in St Martin in the Fields, which had been jointly held in the name of father and son[15]; the buyer was the tenant, Sir Matthew Lister,[16] who paid £100 for the property.[17] It seems likely that this income contributed substantially to the cost of Milton's journey.

Milton's first stop was Paris, though his route is not clear. If he took the packet to Calais and proceeded to travel south-east (along the route now taken by the motorway to Paris), he would within a few miles have entered the Spanish Netherlands, which included what is now the *département* of Nord and the northern half of the *département* of Pas-de-Calais. It is possible that Milton went that way, but it is perhaps more likely that he turned south in Calais and proceeded to Paris on roads wholly within French territory.

The two ambassadors in Paris, who were on implacably hostile terms, re-presented the deepening rift in English ecclesiastical politics. The ambassador-extraordinary, who had been sent at the behest of Henrietta Maria, was Robert Sidney, earl of Leicester; he was a Calvinist with good French who defied Laud by worshipping with his family at the French Reformed Church at Charenton. The ambassador-in-ordinary, who had been sent at the behest of his friend Archbishop Laud, was John Scudamore, viscount Sligo, who spoke Latin for diplomatic purposes, but had no inclination to speak French and so solved the difficulty of a finding a suitable Anglophone place of worship by constructing a full-scale Laudian chapel in his house. This chapel, at which hallowed times such as Lent were honoured, communion was administered monthly, auricular confession was heard, and altar plate and eucharistic implements were displayed, was an affront to French Huguenots and visiting English Protestants alike.

Lord Scudamore's circle of friends in Paris included the Dutch jurist Hugo Grotius (Huig van Groot), who was then the ambassador of Queen Kristina of Sweden. Grotius's Arminianism had incurred the enmity of the Calvinist leader Maurice of Nassau, and in 1618 he had been sentenced to life imprisonment. Twenty months later, he had been smuggled out of prison by his wife, who had arranged for him to be carried in a laundry basket. He sought refuge in Paris, where the books that he wrote included *De iure belli ac pacis* (1625), the founding text of modern international law, *De veritate religionis christianae* (1627), a tolerationist statement of moderate Protestantism from an Arminian perspective, and *Annotationes in Vetus et Novum Testamentum* (1642), which set aside the usual concentration on divine inspiration in favour of the historical and philological approach favoured by Scaliger (and later to be favoured by Milton in *De Doctrina Christiana*). The legal and theological sides of Grotius's writing are related in two ways: the emphasis on history and philology links his analytical approach to both the Bible and the corpus of Roman law, and his insistence on the centrality of the ecclesiastical tradition reflects his jurisprudential view of the importance of customary law.

Milton expressed a wish to meet Grotius, and Lord Scudamore obliged with letters of introduction and the loan of several retainers to accompany Milton on his visit. According to Edward Phillips, '*Grotius* took the Visit kindly, and gave him [Milton] Entertainment suitable to his Worth, and the high Commendations he had heard of him.'[18] As there is no mention of the visit in the Scudamore–Grotius correspondence,[19] it seems possible that the visit made more of an impression on Milton than on Grotius. Milton is never mentioned in the printed works of Grotius, but Grotius is mentioned respectfully in *Tetrachordon* ('yet living, and one of prime note among learned men') and *Doctrine and Discipline of Divorce* ('a man of these times, one of the best learned'); in the address to Parliament that prefaces *The Judgement of Martin Bucer*, Milton praises Grotius as an 'able assistant', because his commentary on Matthew's gospel supported Milton's view.[20] None of this gives any hint of what might have been said at the meeting. They had in common Lord Scudamore (who had discussed a possible union of the English and Swedish churches with Grotius) and Dr Theodore Diodati (who had matriculated at Leiden on the same day as Grotius) and experience of the politics of Arminianism, and Milton's nascent intellectual interests overlapped with those of Grotius, but it is just as likely that the meeting consisted of an

19. Genoa (from Johann Heinrich Pflaumer, *Mercurius Italicus* (Aug. Vind. [that is, Augsburg]: 1625)).

exchange of pleasantries; it does, however, mark Milton's cultural and scholarly aspirations.

There were others whom Milton might have met, as Lord Scudamore moved in the circle of Marin Mersenne (which included Thomas Hobbes and Sir Kenelm Digby), but Milton wanted to move on. As Cyriack Skinner explained, 'in this Kingdom, the manners & Genius of which hee had in no admiration, hee made small stay, nor contracted any Acquaintance, save that...hee waited on Hugo Grotius.'[21] Lord Scudamore furnished Milton with letters to English merchants in places where he would be stopping, and Milton travelled on to Nice.

In the south of what is now France Milton passed into the independent duchy of Savoy; there was a ducal connection with the English crown, in that Christina duchess of Savoy was the sister of Henrietta Maria. Savoy included what are now the French *départements* of Savoie and Haut Savoie and the Italian regions of Valle d'Aosta and Piedmont (which includes Turin, then the duchy's capital); the territory of Savoy extended south in a narrow corridor to the Mediterranean, where its port was Nice. The language of Savoy was

Savoyard, a Romance language quite distinct from French and Occitan and Italian; the French language had made inroads into southern France, but not into Savoy. In entering the duchy Milton was encountering a distinctive culture which, like England, was fragmenting under the pressure of religious divisions: Geneva had finally seceded in 1603, and there were attempts to convert the Waldenses by force; much later he would take up their cause.[22] Milton did not tarry for long. On reaching Nice he secured a passage to Genoa, leaving not from the present harbour to the east of the fortified headland, but from the west side, where the river then ran into the sea.

Genoa was an independent republic whose bankers, the financiers of the Habsburg Empire, had succeeded the Fuggers as the most powerful in Europe. The wealth of Genoa would be quickly apparent to a visiting Englishman walking past the mannerist and baroque façades of the palaces on what are now the Strada Nova and the Via Balbi. It was Milton's first visit to a republic, one whose constitution (modelled on Venice's) had been modified by Andrea Doria to limit the rule of the Doge to two years. At the time of Milton's visit, the doge was Agostino Pallavicini, a member of a patrician family who had previously served as governor of Corsica (then a Genoese possession) and ambassador to the Papal State (where his portrait, now in the Getty, was painted by Anthony van Dyck). Milton seems not to have visited the court, but would not have needed to do so in order to glimpse the model of government by a constitutional oligarchy. This was not the civic government of a city-state, but the government of a regional power so influential that Braudel was later to describe the previous century of European history as 'the age of the Genoese'. Milton may not have stayed long in Genoa,[23] and certainly did not write the 'breif description of Genoa' that has sometimes been attributed to him.[24] Instead he sailed on to Livorno[25] and sailed into the Porto Mediceo, which had been completed in 1620, docking at the jetty built by Cosimo I de' Medici in 1571. He had arrived at last in Tuscany.

Livorno was sufficiently familiar to Englishmen to have been given an exonym (Leghorn) that survived well into the twentieth century. A century earlier, however, it had been a village. The silting of the port of Pisa had led Cosimo to commission a new port at Livorno; the design of the port and fortifications was largely the work of Bernardo Buontalenti, who had also built the canal between Livorno and Pisa. The grand dukes had populated the new city by extending invitations to settle to Italians, Armenians, Germans, Greeks, Jews, Moors, Persians, Portuguese, Spaniards, Turks, and 'other men of the East and West'; Milton had never experienced religious toleration on such a scale. English merchants were included among the newcomers to this cosmopolitan city, which they used as a staging post. The English had not yet achieved the cultural domination of the city that they were to achieve in succeeding centuries, but had nonetheless settled in sufficient numbers to have established an English church. Milton may have worshipped in the church, but nothing else can be safely inferred. He may have noticed the cathedral façade (attributed to Inigo Jones) or the synagogue that had been opened in 1581 (there were no synagogues in England) or the images of enslaved Turks in the *Monumento dei Quattro Mori* (the memorial to Grand Duke Ferdinando I, installed in 1624), but there is no evidence that he did any of these things. He had, however, been furnished by Lord Scudamore with letters of introduction to English merchants, and as Livorno had the largest concentration of English merchants in the Mediterranean, it seems likely that Milton had some contact with the merchant community. In terms of hard knowledge, however, we know only that he landed at Livorno and proceeded to Pisa, probably but not certainly along the canal that had been dug in 1573.

Pisa had a magnificent past as a maritime nation, but its subjugation by Florence in 1406, the crushing of a rebellion in 1509 (when Machiavelli was Secretary of the Florentine Ten of War) and the recent relocation of the port to Livorno had meant that it was a city in decline; even the tower beside the cathedral was leaning dangerously, a tribute to poor engineering. Milton seems simply to have passed through Pisa (in Cyriack Skinner's phrase) before following the Arno for forty-five miles to Florence. Milton describes his visit to Florence in *Defensio Secunda*:

In that city, which I have always admired above all others because of its elegance, not just of its tongue, but also of its wit, I lingered for about two months. There I at once became the friend of many gentlemen eminent in rank and learning, whose private academies I frequented—a Florentine institution which deserves great praise not only for promoting humane studies but also for encouraging friendly intercourse. Time will never destroy my recollection—ever welcom and delightful—of you, Jacopo Gaddi, Carlo Dati, Frescobaldi, Coltellini, Buonmattei, Chimentelli, Francini, and many others.[26]

We do not know precisely when Milton arrived in Florence (perhaps June 1638), but passages such as this show that he visited several private academies, and that may afford a hint of one of the purposes of his Italian journey. There were many such academies in Florence, ranging from grand institutions such as the Accademia Fiorentina and the Accademia della Crusca to informal discussion groups. Milton became a member of two academies, the Svogliati and the Apatisti.

The best documented of Milton's Florentine visits are those to the Accademia degli Svogliati;[27] the laconic name ('men without will') is typical of academies of the time. It was long thought that Milton visited the Svogliati in the palace of Jacopo Gaddi in Piazza Madonna, but the census of 1632 places *Iacopo Gaddi e fratelli* a few yards away in the family's new palazzo in Via del Giglio, in the building that is now the Hotel Astoria.[28] Members of the Svogliati that Milton mentions include Jacopo Gaddi (the founder),

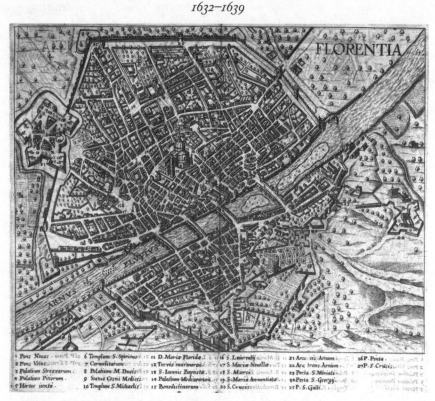

20. Florence (from Pflaumer, *Mercurius Italicus*).

Vincenzo Galilei (illegitimate son of the astronomer), the poet Antonio Malatesti, and the scholar Benedetto Bonmattei.

Jacopo Gaddi was only a few years older than Milton, but already had an established reputation as a published poet (in Latin and Italian) and had become an important figure in the literary and intellectual life of the city.[29] The weekly meetings of his Academy (on Thursdays) were minuted by Gaddi, and the Minute Book survives in the Biblioteca Nazionale in Florence. On 28 June/6 July 1638 an unnamed English man of letters (letterato Inglese) attended a meeting of the Academy and expresses a desire to become a member.[30] The following Thursday (5/15 July), an unnamed person, probably Milton, was elected to membership. He may have attended any or all of the meetings in the weeks that followed (there is not always a list of those present), but he certainly attended on 6/16 September, when he read one of his poems at the weekly meeting; the poem was written in Latin hexameters, and is likely to have been either '*Ad Patrem*' or '*Naturam non pati senium*.[31] Whichever poem it was, the view of the academicians was recorded in the Minute Book: they thought it *molto erudita*.

It is possible that Milton wrote home to describe his triumph, and it is equally possible that a letter with family news was sent to him at about the same time. Two pieces of news from home may have reached him: the first was that his friend Charles Diodati had died,[32] and the second was that Milton's brother Christopher had impregnated Thomasine Webber, a tailor's daughter, and a wedding had been hastily arranged for 13 September 1638.[33]

The significance of Milton's meetings with members of the Svogliati (who were often also members of other academies) had consequences that extended beyond polite applause. In September 1637 the poet Antonio Malatesti had composed an erotic sonnet sequence called *La Tina equivoci rusticali*, and subsequently decided to dedicate the collection *al grande poeta inghilese Giovanni Milton Londra*.[34] Milton had become 'the great English poet', and clearly remembered the compliment; he was to send cordial greetings to Malatesti in a letter to Carlo Dati written nine years later.[35] Milton had also met the scholar-priest Benedetto Buonmattei,[36] who was completing a grammar of Tuscan that he was shortly to publish as *Della Lingua Toscana, Libri Due*. With some temerity, Milton suggested that Father Benedetto might usefully add a chapter on pronunciation and furnish the reader with a list of Tuscan authors (perhaps including comedy, tragedy, dialogues, and letters) whose language might be exemplary. Buonmattei seems to have expressed polite interest, and so Milton decided to press the suggestions by writing to Buonmattei, not in Tuscan but in the Latin of which Milton had extraordinary mastery.[37] The letter is an encomium to Tuscan, to Buonmattei, and to the calling of the grammarian. As no draft of *Della Lingua Toscana* survives, it is difficult to tell whether Milton's suggestions were completely ignored or merely partly ignored: there is no chapter on pronunciation, nor is there a list of exemplary authors, but there are comments on pronunciation scattered throughout the volume.

Milton's letter is of particular interest because it takes sides in the pan-European debate about the rival claims of Latin and the vernaculars,[38] and within the latter the form of the languages that should be used. Milton's letter endorses a Tuscan cause, one that in the end proved to be victorious. It was not obvious at the time, however, that it was the language of fourteenth-century Tuscany that was to become the basis of the literary language of Italy. The claim for this form of the language had only recently been revived: the *Vocabulario* (1612) of the Accademia della Crusca (of which Buonmattei was a member) was the founding document. Until this point, the *questione della lingua* had involved competing claims for a language tempered by the speech of the northern courts (the *lingua cortigiana* championed by Castiglione and Trissino), the language of contemporary Tuscany (championed by

Machiavelli) or the archaic language of fourteenth-century Tuscany (championed by Bembo), of which the exemplars were Petrarch and Boccaccio.[39] Milton chose to support the antiquarian option. It is difficult to ascertain whether this was an allegiance formed in the heat of the moment or a settled opinion, but it must have helped to shape his eventual view that in Latin classical forms were to be preferred, but that for most literary purposes English in a form that had literary precedent was the ideal medium. As he took a similar view of Italian, he chose to cultivate the written and spoken forms of the language used in Tuscany.

Most important of all, Milton had met Vincenzo Galilei, the natural son of the astronomer; it was probably Vincenzo who arranged for Milton to meet Galileo. The only evidence for the visit is Milton's allusion to the meeting in *Areopagitica*: recalling his Italian journey many years earlier, Milton ringingly says that 'there it was I found and visited the famous *Galileo*, grown old, a prisner to the Inquisition, for thinking in Astronomy otherwise then the Franciscan and Dominican licencers thought'.[40] The recollection is slightly inaccurate, in that the *Dialogo sopra i due massimi sistemi de mondo* (Leiden, 1632) had been licensed,[41] but its publication had nonetheless incurred the displeasure of Urban VIII and the Roman Inquisition,[42] which had placed Galileo under a form of house arrest.

The restrictions on Galileo in the wake of his trial did not preclude receiving foreign visitors at Il Gioiello, his villa in Arcetri, and it is possible that Milton visited him there. It is equally possible, however, that the meeting took place in Florence. On 13 February 1638 the Florentine Inquisitor had written to Rome to explain that Galileo was ill and close to death.[43] This report formed the basis of the decision to lift the sentence of house arrest in order for Galileo to receive palliative medical treatment at Vincenzo's house on the Costa San Giorgio; he was, however, forbidden to receive visitors in Florence, and at least one eminent visitor, Constantijn Huygens, was prevented from seeing Galileo that summer. That, however, was intended as a formal occasion, as Huygens had intended to present his friend with a gold chain in acknowledgement of Galileo's work on the calculation of longitude. Milton was not an international celebrity, so may have slipped unnoticed into Vincenzo's house. Galileo's movements can in some measure be tracked through the summer of 1638, and it is clear that he spent more time in Florence than in Arcetri, but Milton could have made the short journey to Arcetri.

Nothing is known of what was said at Milton's meeting with Galileo, and it is difficult to assess what impact it had on Milton. With hindsight it is possible to see an image of Milton's own old age in the blind astronomer whose life was nearly forfeited because of his writings, but at that stage the world lay all before Milton. Galileo's science made little or no difference to Milton's cosmology, and this lack of intellectual influence may explain why

21. Palazzo Gaddi (now the
Astoria Hotel), Florence.

Milton failed to mention Galileo in his account of the Italian journey in *Defensio Secunda*, in which he chooses instead to emphasize the praise with which his poetry was greeted.

The second academy of which Milton became a member was the Apatisti ('Dispassionates'); his admission has only recently been confirmed. The founder was Agostino Coltellini, and other academicians known by Milton include Benedetto Buonmattei (discussed above), Carlo Dati, Piero Frescobaldi, Valerio Chimentelli, Antonio Francini, and Francesco Rovai.

Agostino Coltellini was four years younger than Milton.[44] He was a small man (*piccolissima statura*), which may have helped to endear him to Milton, who was sensitive about his modest height. Coltellini was by profession a lawyer, but most of his energies were devoted to the promotion of learning, for which his principal vehicle was the academy that he had founded and which met in his house on Via dell' Oriolo. The term 'Apatisti' is cognate with English 'apathy', but, far from implying indolent indifference, is intended to evoke the aspiration to Stoic detachment and a principled indifference to the passions. There was long thought to be no documentary evidence that Milton attended the meetings of the Apatisti in Coltellini's house in Via dell' Oriolo. There are indeed no seventeenth-century records of the Apatisti, but in the eighteenth century a learned member called Anton Francesco Gori compiled a handwritten account of its early history. This manuscript was transcribed and published in 1983, but not noted by a Milton scholar until 1998, when Estelle Haan discussed its significance.[45] It includes a list of new members for 1638, and the list includes 'Giovanni Milton inglese'.

Carlo Roberto Dati,[46] the only member of the group with whom Milton is known to have remained in contact in subsequent years, was the literary prodigy of Florence. He had been born on 2 October 1619, so when Milton met him he was only 18, and yet his eloquence and scientific and historical knowledge were already widely acknowledged. He was soon to establish a

European reputation, and is now valued as the first art historian to attempt a documentary history of painting in classical antiquity. The praise that he lavished on Milton in a Latin letter written while Milton was still in Florence came from one whose judgement Milton rightly respected. Milton saved the letter, and printed it in the *testimonia* that preface his 1645 *Poemata*.

The learned priest Piero Frescobaldi[47] at the time of Milton's visit held the benefice of the church of SS Maria e Leonardo in Artimino (Carmignano), near the Medici villa of La Ferdinanda; his duties were probably discharged by a curate. In Florence he was a member of the Apatisti, and enjoyed a reputation for being quick-witted and scholarly (*solertissimo et studiosissimo*, in Coltellini's phrase). He left no evidence of these qualities, but progressed in the church, and in the year of his death was consecrated as bishop of San Miniato.

Valerio Chimentelli was a young priest with a reputation in humanist circles for formidable learning; he subsequently became professor of Greek (and later Eloquence and Politics) at Pisa.[48] According to Thomas Warton, in 1762 'the late Mr Thomas Hollis examined the Laurentian library at Florence for six Italian sonnets of Milton, addressed to his friend Chimentelli . . . said to be remaining in manuscript in Florence'.[49] The fact that Hollis was searching for six sonnets (the number of Italian sonnets that Milton wrote) raises the possibility that underlying this unverifiable story there is a kernel of truth that might help to explain the extraordinary fluency of Milton's sonnets; perhaps Chimentelli was the friend who helped to bring the Italian of Milton's sonnets to native-speaker proficiency.

Antonio Francini was a young poet whose principal medium was Italian. His verse circulated in manuscript, and only a few pieces have survived in print. For students of Milton, his most important composition was an 84-line ode, *Al Signor Gio[vanni] Miltoni Nobile Inglese*, which he presented to Milton in Florence; as with Dati's letter, Milton printed it in the *testimonia* at the beginning of his *Poemata*; an Italian poem broke the decorum of Latin (in which the other testimonials are written), but it was too good to be omitted. The ode to Milton is extravagant, as befits the genre, but its particularities ring true, especially when Dati praises Milton's linguistic ability: *Ch'ode oltr'all' Anglia il suo più degno Idioma | Spagna, Francia, Toscana, e Grecia e Roma* ('for not only England hears you speak her worthy language, but also Spain, France, Tuscany, Greece and Rome'). The same ability is praised in Dati's letter, which is addressed *Polyglotto, in cujus ore linguæ iam deperditæ sic reviviscunt* ('to a polygot on whose lips languages already dead come to life again'). Dati's praise of Milton's Spanish may imply that he presented his poem to Milton as he returned to Florence on his northward journey from Naples, where he would have spoken Spanish at the vice-regal court.[50]

To these five names a sixth can be added from Carlo Dati's letter to Milton of 22 October/1 November 1647, in which Dati asks for some verses to commemorate Francesco Rovai, who had been well known to Milton.[51] Rovai was a poet with a gift for languages, and he was to die young without having published his works (though a posthumous collection was assembled).

Many of those whom he met in the academies of Florence long remained in Milton's mind. In his letter to Carlo Dati of 20 April 1647 Milton mentions several members of the 'Gaddian Academy' (Coltellini, Francini, Frescobaldi, Malatesta, and Chimentelli), and in Dati's letter to Milton of 24 November/4 December 1648 he passes on news of Chimintelli (who had been appointed to a chair of Greek at Pisa) and the affectionate good wishes of Frescobaldi, Coltellini, Francini, and Vincenzo Galilei. In the *Defensio Secunda* (1654) Milton mentions Gaddi, Dati, Frescobaldi, Coltellini, Buonmattei, Chimintelli, and Francini. What effect did Milton's encounters with the academies have on him? Milton was to supply the answer himself, in *Reason of Church Government* (1641):

In the privat Academies of *Italy*, whither I was favor'd to resort, perceiving that some trifles which I had in memory, compos'd at under twenty or thereabout (for the manner is, that every one must give some proof of his wit and reading there), met with acceptance above what was lookt for, and other things which I had shifted in scarsity of books and conveniences to patch up amongst them, were receiv'd with written Encomiums, which the Italian is not forward to bestow on men of this side the *Alps*.[52]

The praise lavished on Milton as a poet and a polyglot constituted international recognition of his talents, and he carefully preserved the written encomia for future use in the 1645 *Poemata*. Such honours were clearly precious to Milton.

The mention of Vallombrosa in *Paradise Lost* was the sandy foundation of a belief that while in Florence Milton made an excursion to the remote monastery of Vallombrosa, and that recollection of this visit eventually re-emerged as the image of the fallen angels who lay 'thick as autumnal leaves that strew the brooks | In Vallombrosa, where the Etrurian shades | High overarched imbower'.[53] There is not a shred of evidence for this visit, which was not on the itinerary of seventeenth-century travellers,[54] but the absence of evidence did not dampen the enthusiasm of nineteenth-century travellers such as Wordsworth (1837), Mary Shelley (1842), and Elizabeth Barrett Browning (1847). Mrs Browning, accompanied by dog Flush and husband Robert, was hauled up to the monastery in a wine basket mounted on a sledge pulled by four white oxen, only to be told on arrival that the monastery could not accommodate women (especially, one suspects, women who announced their intention of staying for three months to escape the heat of Florence).

On leaving Florence Milton travelled south through Siena (which had been incorporated into Tuscany in 1555) and then passed into the Papal State, a large sovereign state (the fifth on Milton's tour) which extended from sea to sea and reached as far north as Bologna (since 1506) and Ferrara (since 1598). Milton's goal was Rome, which was dominated by St Peter's Basilica, which had been completed in 1614 and consecrated in 1626 but had not yet been framed by Bernini's Doric colonnade, added between 1656 and 1671.[55] On this visit Milton stayed in Rome for about two months (possibly October–November 1638), during which only one day can be documented: on 20/30 October Milton dined at the English College.

The English College[56] (since 1818 known as the Venerable English College) was originally a resthouse for English pilgrims, but in 1578 had been reconstituted as a Jesuit seminary whose graduates were intended for service in England. Between that date and Milton's visit some thirty-two of its graduates (including Robert Southwell) had been martyred in England, the most recent in 1616. In its new capacity the College continued to receive English visitors to Rome (who in 1636 had included the physician William Harvey and in 1644 would include the diarist John Evelyn). The Pilgrim Book, which is still in the College, records the names of the visitors. The entry for 20/30 October 1638 records

A die 30. pransi st. in Coll° nřo Ill[ms.] D.N. Cary, frater Baronis de Faukeland. Doctor Holdingus Lancastrensis, D.N. Fortescuto, et Dñs Miltonus, cū famulo nobiles Angli. et excepti st. Laute.

'D.N.' is the usual abbreviation for Dominus Noster, 'Our Lord', and 'Dñs' an abbreviation for Dominus (i.e. 'Mr'), so the entry might be translated 'On 30 October were entertained in our College the illustrious Lord Cary, brother of Baron Falkland, Dr Holding of Lancaster, Lord Fortescue and Mr Milton with his servant, distinguished Englishmen, and they were magnificently received.' Who were Milton's fellow guests?[57] Lord Carey is Patrick Carey, the 14-year-old younger son of Viscount Falkland, then known as Brother Placid and later to be a published poet.[58] Dr 'Holding' is Henry Holden, then agent of the English Catholic clergy in Rome, and the holder of a Sorbonne doctorate.[59] Lord Fortescue is probably Sir Nicholas Fortescue, but could be his brother Sir John Fortescue.[60] In addition to these Roman Catholic guests, there is Milton's servant, whose identity remains a mystery. The Latin term is *famulus*, the same word that Milton was to use in *Defensio Secunda*. No servants are listed for the other guests, but that may be because they were resident in Rome for longer periods. The phrase *nobiles Angli* is inserted above the line with a caret, and so need not include the *famulus*, but his inclusion in the Pilgrim Book may imply a servant of some rank, probably not of the standing of Ben Jonson's servant Richard Brome, but possibly someone analogous to a sizar at a Cambridge college.

Those whom Milton met in Rome on his first or second visit (or both) include Lukas Holste and Cardinal Francesco Barberini (both of whom will be discussed in the context of the second visit), the youthful prodigy

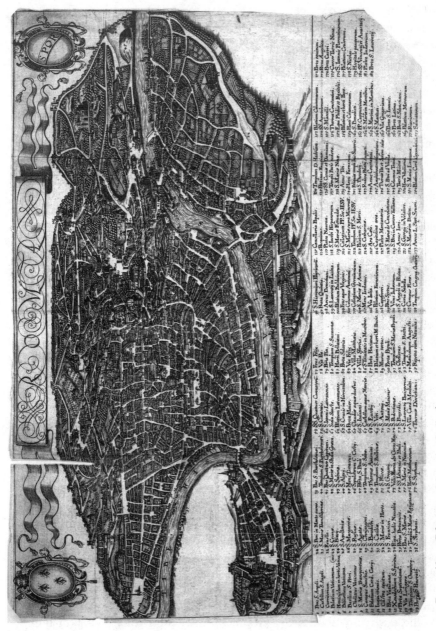

22. Rome (from Pfaumer, *Mercurius Italicus*).

Alessandro Cherubini, the poet Giovanni Salzilli, the poet Selvaggi and the Englishman Thomas Gawen. Cherubini, whom Milton mentions in a letter to Holste, was a youthful polymath who may already have been mortally ill when he met Milton; he was soon to die at the age of 28, leaving no publications to testify to his erudition.

Little is now known of the poet Giovanni Salzilli.[61] He contributed fifteen Italian poems (mostly sonnets) to a collection published in 1637, and he wrote a four-line Latin encomium for Milton which was later to be printed in the *testimonia* of the 1645 *Poemata*. It is entitled 'An Epigram by Giovanni Salsilli of Rome to John Milton, Englishman, who deserves to be crowned with the triple laurel of poetry, certainly Greek, Latin and Etruscan', and compares Milton, the poet of the Thames, to three poets whom he names by metonymy through their rivers: Meles (Homer), Mincius (Virgil), and Sebetus (Tasso): 'Yield Meles; let Mincius yield with lowered urn; let Sebetus cease to speak all the time of Tasso. But let the victorious Thames flow more deeply than all other rivers, for through you, Milton, he alone will be equal to all three.' Even by the generous conventions of encomium the praise seems extravagant, and it is little wonder that Milton treasured the poem, or that when Salzilli fell ill, Milton composed a poem in his honour. The nature of the illness is not known, but the metre of *Ad Salsillum* may imply that one of the symptoms was lameness: Milton chose to write in choliambs, the 'limping' iambic trimeter metre in which a comic or bathetic effect is created by the reversal of the penultimate syllable. His Latin prosody is, as ever, adventurous and wholly assured.

'Selvaggi' is the name appended to a Latin couplet (modelled on Propertius) in the *testimonia* of the 1645 *Poemata*: 'Let Greece boast of Homer and Rome of Virgil; England boasts of Milton, the equal of them both. Selvaggi.' It seems likely that Selvaggi is Matthew Savage (Matteo Selvaggio), the alias of the English Benedictine David Codner;[62] the name may derive from Codner's close association with the family of Jane Savage, marchioness of Winchester, whose death Milton had commemorated in the spring of 1631. The evidence of his surviving letters implies that Codner's Italian was so proficient that he could pass himself off as a native Roman, at least to a visiting Englishman, so Milton may not have known that he was English; alternatively, Milton may have known that Selvaggi was Codner but chose for reasons that cannot now be recovered to print the couplet with Codner's pseudonym.

Though younger than Milton, Thomas Gawen had already been elected to a perpetual Fellowship of New College, Oxford.[63] He had come to Italy to learn more about the society and to enhance his language skills. He was eventually to convert to Roman Catholicism, but it is not clear whether he already harboured such leanings. According to Anthony Wood, Gawen

NEAPOLIS

Mare Mediterraneum

1 *Arx S. Hermi.*   7 *Castellum Oui.*   13 *S. Petri ad Aram.*   19 *S. Ioannis in Carbonaria.* 25 *Palatium Ducis Grauinæ.* 31 *Porta Regalis.*
2 *Castellum Nouum.*   8 *Mons Pizzafalconis.*   14 *Forum.*   20 *S. Mariæ Nouæ.*   26 *Porta Fori.*   32 *Porta Romana.*
3 *Turris S. Vincentij.*   9 *Portus.*   15 *S. Mariæ Carmeli.*   21 *S. Pauli.*   27 *Porta Nolana.*
4 *Naualia.*   10 *Fons in Portu.*   16 *S. Dominici.*   22 *S. Martini.*   28 *P. Capuana.*
5 *Palatium Proregis.*   11 *Basilica Cathedralis.* 17 *Montis Oliueti.*   23 *S. Petri Martyris.*   29 *P. S. Ianuari.*
6 *Horti Palatini.*   12 *S. Mariæ Annunciatæ.* 18 *S. Claræ.*   24 *Curia seu Vicaria.*   30 *P. S. Mariæ Cõstãdinop.*

23. Naples (from Pflaumer, *Mercurius Italicus*).

'accidentally sometimes fell into the company of John Milton', a phrase that does not imply a burgeoning friendship; both Milton and Gawen were to become writers, but neither mentioned the other in print.

It was probably in December 1638 that Milton left Rome to travel to Naples. The Kingdom of Naples, which included most of southern Italy, was a vice-regal province of Spain; the suzerainty of Spain had been finally established in 1502 and, despite the insurrection led by the philosopher Tommaso Campanella in 1598, was to continue until 1707. Milton travelled from Rome to Naples in the improbable company of a hermit. Under the pressure of the Counter-Reformation hermits had all but disappeared, though there were eremetical elements in the life of the Carthusians and Carmelites. As contemplative hermits were not normally travellers, it seems more likely that Milton's companion belonged to the religious order variously known as Augustinian Hermits or Augustinian Friars or Friars Hermit; it was a reformed congregation of this order to which Martin Luther had belonged. The friars had originally lived in remote places, but gradually came to

24. Palazzo Reale (Royal Palace), Naples.

concentrate educational, pastoral, and missionary work in towns. It seems likely that Milton's hermit was not in one of the reformed congregations active in the area (the Augustinian Recollects and the Discalced Augustinians), but rather in the original order; the evidence is that he was a well-connected hermit who moved in the best circles in Naples. It was he who introduced Milton to Giambattista Manso, marquis of Villa,[64] who was in turn an habitué of the vice-regal court.

Manso lived in a seaside villa close to the hill of Posillipo and the town of Pozzuoli.[65] He entertained foreign visitors there, but it is not clear that he received Milton in the villa: Milton says that he stayed at an inn, where Manso visited him on several occasions. Manso shepherded Milton around the city and the Palazzo Reale,[66] the palace of the Spanish Viceroy (*qui et ipse me per urbis loca et Proregis aulam circumduxit*). Was Milton granted an audience with the viceroy, Ramiro Felipe de Guzmán, duke of Medina de las Torres? The Latin is ambiguous, but *circumduxit* seems to imply being 'led around' rather than being presented to the viceroy; the records of the court now in the Archivo General de Simancas have not yielded any record of an audience, and in the absence of such evidence it seems safer to assume that Milton visited the palace (where he could try out his spoken Spanish) but was not presented.

Manso was a patron of the arts, and had, for example, commissioned Caravaggio's *Seven Works of Mercy*, which still hangs in the church of Pio Monte della Misericordia in Naples. Milton's interest, however, lay in his

literary patronage: many years earlier Manso had been the patron of Torquato
Tasso and Giovanbattista Marino, both of whom he had befriended after
periods of imprisonment. In 1611 Manso had founded the Accademia degli
Oziozi (whose name celebrates the learned leisure of classical *otium*), which
soon became the most famous of the literary academies of Naples; on
returning to Naples in 1624 Marino had been elected as its *principe*. For
decades Neapolitan poetry had been constricted by the dead hand of
Petrarch, but the Oziozi revived the earlier tradition of experimental poetry
and became the principal centre of *concettismo*; the term is cognate with
English 'conceit', and the style was the equivalent of *culteranismo* in Spain
and to the idiom of Donne and his closer imitators. Milton had moved on
from that kind of writing, present to some extent in his poems on events of
the liturgical year, to a rediscovery of a longer English tradition that flowed
from Spenser, and so he was hardly in sympathy with the literary aspirations
of the Oziozi. Yet he had a poet's appreciation of the value of patronage, and
seems to have seen himself as third in a line of succession that had begun with
Tasso and Marino.

Manso had not only befriended Milton, but had composed a Latin distich
in his honour: in English translation it says 'if your religious convictions were
as your mind, your form, your elegance, appearance and manner, then you
would not be an Englishman, but, by Hercules, a true angel'. The reservation
about the misplaced piety of the Protestant Milton is gracefully subverted by
the reworking of the phrase attributed to Gregory the Great.[67] As in the case
of the poems written by his Florentine admirers, Milton garnered this one for
use in his *testimonia*. In this case, however, he also composed a poem of
thanks, perhaps the most gracious thank-you note he ever wrote.[68] *Mansus*
celebrates Manso as a befriender of poets, and Milton clearly thought that a
noble role. He presents himself as a young stranger from a northern land, but
one whose poetry has been touched by Virgil.[69]

Milton claimed in *Defensio Secunda* (1654) that it had been his intention to
travel on to Sicily and then to Greece, but 'the sad tidings of civil war from
England summoned me back'.[70] This retrospective account is puzzling for
several reasons. First, there was no civil war in England: King Charles was to
declare war on the Scots on 26 January 1639, but Milton had left on his
return journey by the time the news could have reached Naples; as for a civil
war within England, that began on 22 August 1642, when Charles raised his
standard at Nottingham. Second, for a man returning in haste Milton took
an inordinately long time, proceeding overland at a stately pace via Venice
and Geneva and reaching home six months later. Third, it is possible that
Milton aspired to follow in the footsteps of William Lithgow and George
Sandys to Sicily[71] (then ruled from Spanish Naples) to see the Fountain of
Arethusa in Syracuse, which had in antiquity been the second city (after

Athens) of the Greek world, but Greece seems an unlikely aspiration, except perhaps in retrospect: Greece was part of the Ottoman Empire, and did not become an extension of the Grand Tour until the mid-eighteenth century. Greece was not a place for cultured travellers accustomed to travelling in comfort, and the few Englishmen who had travelled there had been disappointed. William Lithgow,[72] for example, wrote that

In all this countrey of Greece, I could find nothing, to answer the famous relations, given by Auncient Authors, of the excellency of that land, but the name onely; the barbarousnesse of Turkes and Time, having defeated all the Monuments of Antiquity.

In short, it is neither unreasonable nor uncharitable to conclude that Milton had no serious intention of proceeding to Greece and that the reasons that he gave for turning back were constructed in the light of later events and his polemical purpose in 1654 rather than recalled from his time in Naples.

Milton decided to return home via Rome, despite, on his own account, having received a warning from English merchants to the effect that the Jesuits planned to kill him should he return there. Such paranoia about the Jesuits of Rome was quite normal in Protestant circles, rather like fear of communists in the 1950s or of Muslims in the post 9/11 world, and in all three cases the threat is imagined rather than real. The motif of the escape from Rome was well established in English travel writing,[73] and in Milton's case the threat of violence from Roman Jesuits may have been intensified by the belief that John Tovey, the father of Milton's second tutor at Cambridge, had been poisoned by the same Jesuits.[74] It would not be safe to assume that something had gone terribly wrong when Milton had dined with the Jesuits in Rome.

In January 1639 Milton returned to Rome, and on this visit his movements are better documented than in his earlier sojourn. It is entirely possible that on his first visit he had met some of those with whom his meetings are documented for the return visit.

The grandest public occasion of Milton's second visit occurred on 17/27 February 1639, when Milton attended the comic opera *Chi soffre, speri*, which was mounted by Cardinal Francesco Barberini[75] to inaugurate the newly constructed theatre[76] of the Palazzo Barberini. The libretto of the opera had been written by Cardinal Giulio Rospigliosi (the future Pope Clement IX), the music composed by Virgilio Mazzocchi and Marco Marazzoli,[77] and the stage set and costumes designed by Gianlorenzo Bernini, the papal sculptor, painter and architect who was later to design the colonnade of St Peter's. The theatre was vast, and on this occasion accommodated 3,500 guests, including Cardinal Mazarin. Milton was later to recall that he was greeted at the door by the Cardinal; this may be an accurate recollection, but another member of the audience (Raimondo Montecuccoli, emissary of the duke of Modena) recalled that it was Cardinal Antonio Barberini the younger[78] who greeted guests at the door, and that his brother Cardinal Francesco instead moved among the benches to welcome the guests. The entertainment, which lasted for five hours, consisted of a succession of loosely connected scenes more remarkable for their spectacle and music than for their dramatic power.[79]

The following day Milton had a private audience with Cardinal Francesco Barberini, whose responsibilities included the foreign policy of the Papal State and the work of the Sacred College of the Roman Inquisition; in the latter capacity he had been one of the ten judges in Galileo's trial, where he had argued for leniency. He was also Protector of the English, and in that capacity regularly offered hospitality and assistance to English travellers, most of whom were Catholic. There is no record of what was said at the meeting, which may have been entirely formal.

The other musical occasion at which Milton was probably present was a recital by the soprano Leonora Baroni,[80] the most celebrated singer in Rome. The evidence is Milton's three Latin epigrams *Ad Leonoram Romae canentem* ('To Leonora singing in Rome'). Leonora was often accompanied by her mother Adriana (who played the lyre), and the allusion to the golden strings of her mother's lyre implies that Adriana Basile was present on this occasion.[81] Extravagant poems of praise for Leonora were all the rage in Rome in 1639, and later that year a collection of such poems was to be published.[82] Milton's epigrams are his contributions to the genre, and were written for the benefit of Milton's Roman friends, not for the lady herself.

The contributors to the Leonora volume included Lukas Holste,[83] the librarian of Cardinal Francesco Barberini (who also owned a copy of the Leonora volume[84]). Holste (Latin Holstenius) was a German geographer and patristic scholar who had visited England in pursuit of his geographical research and had subsequently converted to Catholicism; he was later to become Vatican Librarian and to be chosen by Pope Alexander VII to receive the abjuration of Protestantism by Queen Kristina of Sweden. It is not known how Milton came to meet Holste, but it is possible that he had a letter of introduction from Patrick Young, who was a correspondent of Holste.[85] Whatever the reason, Holste invited Milton to meet him at the Vatican, where he showed him the Library, which was situated (then as now) in Fontana's building of 1587-9, bisecting (and diminishing the effect of) Bramante's Belvedere Court. Holste showed Milton the Greek material on which he had been working. The common interest in Hellenic scholarship seems to have been more powerful than the religious differences, and there are three clear signs of the warmth of their relationship. First, Holste asked a favour: as Milton was going to be passing through Florence, Holste wondered if he would be willing to copy some passages from a Medicean codex in the Laurentian Library. Second, Holste presented Milton with a copy of his newly published bilingual edition of the axioms of the later Pythagoreans.[86]

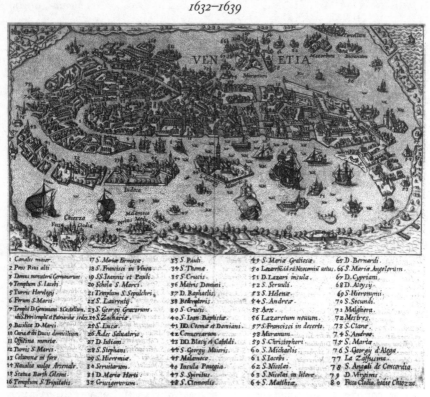

1 Canalis maior.
2 Pons Riui alti.
3 Domus mercatorū Germanorum.
4 Templum S.Iacobi.
5 Turris Horologij.
6 Forum S.Marci.
7 Templ D.Geminani 8.Castellum.
  ubi S.Petri templū et Patriarche sedes.
9 Basilica D.Marci.
10 Curia et ibi Ducis domicilium.
11 Officina monetæ.
12 Turris S.Marci.
13 Columna in foro.
14 Naualia uulgo Arsenale.
15 Statua Barth Coleoni.
16 Templum S.Trinitatis.

17 S.Moriæ Firmosæ.
18 S.Francisci in Vinea.
19 SS.Ioannis et Pauli.
20 Schola S.Marci.
21 Templum S.Sepulchri.
22 S.Laurentij.
23 S.Georgij Græcorum.
24 S.Zachariæ.
25 S.Lucæ.
26 Ædes Saluatoris.
27 D.Iuliani.
28 S.Stephani.
29 S.Hieremiæ.
30 Seruitarum.
31 D.Maria Horti.
32 Crucigerorum.

33 S.Pauli.
34 S.Thomæ.
35 S.Crucis.
36 Matris Domini.
37 D.Raphaelis.
38 Redemptoris.
39 S.Crucis.
40 S.Ioan.Baptistæ.
41 DD.Cosmæ et Damiani.
42 Conuersarum.
43 DD.Blasij et Casoldi.
44 S.Georgij Maioris.
45 Malamoco.
46 Insula Pouegia.
47 S.Spiritus.
48 S.Clementis.

49 S.Maria Gratiosæ.
50 Lazarū id ē Nosocomiū uetus.
51 D.Lazari insula.
52 S.Seruuli.
53 S.Helenæ.
54 S.Andreæ.
55 Arx.
56 Lazaretum nouum.
57 S.Francisci in deserto.
58 Muranum.
59 S.Christophori.
60 S.Michaelis.
61 S.Iacobi.
62 S.Nicolai.
63 S.Nicolai in litore.
64 S.Matthiæ.

65 D.Bernardi.
66 S.Maria Angelorum.
67 D.Cypriani.
68 D.Aloysy.
69 S.Hieronymi.
70 S.Secundi.
71 Malghera.
72 Mestres.
73 S.Claræ.
74 S.Andreæ.
75 S.Martæ.
76 S.Georgij d'Alega.
77 La Zaffusina.
78 S.Angali de Concordia.
79 D.Virginis.
80 Fossa Clodia, hodie Chiozza.

25. Venice (from Pflaumer, *Mercurius Italicus*).

Third, on 19/29 March 1639 Milton wrote a fulsome letter to Holste from Florence; the holograph is still in the Vatican Library, one of only two letters in Milton's hand.[87]

In March 1639 Milton left Rome for the last time and travelled north to Florence, where he tried unsuccessfully to secure permission to copy the manuscript in the Biblioteca Laurenziana for Holste; that failure was the immediate cause of his memorable letter. He lingered in Florence for several weeks, attending meetings of the Svogliati on 7/17 March, 14/24 March and 21/31 March; on the first two occasions he read Latin verses to his fellow academicians. He also undertook an excursion to Lucca (then a large independent city-state with a republican constitution); the reason for this journey is not known, but it may well be related to the Diodati family in this area.

In April Milton travelled to Bologna and Ferrara (both part of the Papal State) en route to Venice, which was an independent maritime city-state with a considerable empire. That empire been reduced in the Aegean by Ottoman incursions, and Cyprus had been lost in 1573, but at the time of Milton's visit the mainland territories of Venice extended to the plains of Lombardy (and so included cities such as Vicenza, Verona, Brescia and Bergamo), and its island possessions included Crete (Venetian Candia). The republican institutions of Venice were widely admired by European intellectuals as the realization of an ideal of stability and justice. The 'myth of Venice',[88] as this adulation of Venetian republicanism is known, was to be invoked by Dutch republicans seeking independence from Spain, by English republicans during the Interregnum and by secessionists in revolutionary America. Perhaps the seeds of Milton's later engagement with republicanism were planted in Venice; certainly the combination of a virtuous leader, a beneficent ruling class and the responsible representation of other citizens seem consistent with Milton's thinking in the later years of the English republic.[89]

Milton stayed in Venice for a month, and spent some of his time organizing a shipment to England of the books that he had collected in his travels. The consignment included at least one case of music books with works by Claudio Monteverdi, Luca Marenzio, Orazio Vecchi, Antonio Cifra, and Carlo Gesualdo.[90] He then proceeded through Verona (a Venetian possession) to Milan, which was then a Spanish dependency in which travellers did not tend to tarry; the city's population had been halved by the plague of 1631, and the city was heavily garrisoned.

There were two routes across the Alps that a traveller to Geneva could take: the Simplon (through Valais, an independent republic since 1628) or the Great St Bernard (through Savoy). It is not clear which Milton chose, as he did not comment on mountains. Like all travellers of the pre-Romantic period, Milton favoured landscapes that were flat and fertile; mountains were merely dangerous obstacles. In either case Milton travelled along Lake Geneva (then known as Lake Lausanne) to Geneva, either along the north shore through Vaud or the south shore through Savoy.

Geneva, like Valais, did not join the Swiss Confederation till 1815; Milton never visited the country now known as Switzerland. Geneva had finally gained its independence from Savoy in 1603, the year after the Savoyard attack known as the Escalade was repelled and the 83-year-old Beza had led the service of thanksgiving. The city had been rigidly run by Calvin, who in 1553 had burnt Servetus for esposing anti-Trinitarian views remarkably similar to those of the mature Milton. In 1559 Calvin had founded the Geneva Academy (the antecedent institution of the University of Geneva), at which Charles Diodati had studied in 1630 and 1631. At the Academy discipline was rigorously enforced; as recently as 1628, two students had been accused of mocking their tutors in ribald songs and making jokes about the Bible; disciplinary committees had more authority then than now, and both students were condemned to death, though both were eventually reprieved after appeals for mercy from their families.[91]

For those who failed to conform Geneva was brutal, but for Protestants of a certain stripe who sought refuge there, it was a safe place to live. One such émigré was Giovanni (French: Jean) Diodati, the resolutely Calvinist uncle of Milton's late friend Charles. It was long assumed that Milton stayed in the Villa Diodati where Byron lived, but that property was not owned or occupied by the Diodati family in the seventeenth century. The location of Giovanni Diodati's residence is not known, nor can it be assumed that Milton stayed with him, but Milton says that they spoke daily. If he had not heard the news of Charles's death earlier, Milton may have been told in Geneva; alternatively Milton may have broken the news to Giovanni Diodati.

On Monday 10 June 1639 Milton signed the autograph book (*album amicorum*) of Camillo Cardoini, a member of a Protestant Neapolitan family that had settled in Geneva.[92] Milton's inscription consists of a quotation of the final lines of *A Masque at Ludlow* ('if Vertue feeble were | Heaven it selfe would stoope to her), which implies that Cardoini could read English, and a line from the *Epistles* of Horace (1. 11. 27) that might be translated 'When I cross the sea I change my sky but not my mind'. The line sounds intransigent, and if it implied that Milton had not been changed by his Italian journey would be absurd; in the theocratic state of Geneva, however, the line was merely an affirmation of Milton's unwavering Protestantism.

From Geneva Milton travelled home, retracing his route through France. He arrived back in England with a new perspective on his own country and his place in it. He had tasted the intellectual richness of Italy, but increasingly defined himself as an Englishman, an act that had not been necessary when virtually everyone he knew was English. The poems of his Italian admirers addressed him as Anglus, and he had signed the Cardoini album 'Joannes Miltonius Anglus'. He had, however, come back to a different England from the one that he had left some fifteen months earlier; this was an increasingly divided England, one in which the king's subjects felt compelled more and more to take sides as the seemingly unchallengeable ascendancy of Charles and Laud started to fragment. It was also an England without Charles Diodati, whom Milton decided to commemorate in Latin, partly because he could write more expressively in that language, but also because it could be understood both by his English and Italian friends.[93]

Milton had left England clear about the careers and interests he would not follow; he would not be a priest, an academic, a lawyer, a scrivener. (He seems never to have contemplated medicine, the option of Charles Diodati after a similar period of uncertainty.) Yet he had written nothing that could substantiate any claim to scholarship, despite the personal studies he had assiduously pursued since leaving Cambridge. He had produced what are now recognized as one of the best liturgical poems of the early Stuart period, probably the finest script for an aristocratic entertainment, and certainly its finest pastoral elegy. He was known and admired by some, though in a fairly narrow circle: Henry Lawes, some Cambridge poets and academics, Sir Henry Wotton, one or two metropolitan friends, themselves on the periphery of Caroline literary culture. '*Ad Patrem*' showed a need to justify himself, even to his staunchest supporter, his own father, while 'Lycidas' betrayed a recognition that, were he himself to die young like Edward King, there would be little worldly acclaim of what he had achieved.

The journey to Italy gave new confidence and direction; he knew he could be—and perhaps only be—a poet, a commitment and a vocation without obvious parallel among the courtly, academic, and clerical writers of his own age, though, in the event, the emerging crises in church and state soon drew him in other directions. But for the moment he glowed with the assurance of a youngish man who had, in his own terms, achieved a cultural triumph. He had met towering figures—Grotius, pre-eminently for Milton, and Galileo. He had moved among cardinals who had received him courteously. He had written poems to an Italian *diva*. He had entered the academies of the learned and encountered there a level of sophistication, scholarship, and civility without precedent in an England where so much patronage and cultural activity remained within the orbit of the royal court. Most important, his poetry had been acclaimed—and it wasn't even the best poetry he had written!

Other uncertainties that had been manifest in 1637 found resolution. For the first time, he could compare the Laudian church, both as he knew it at home and in its extreme manifestation in Scudamore's chapel, with the practices of reformed Protestantism on the Genevan model, inevitably recognizing some truth in the old puritan assertion that the English reformation retained too many elements of popery. Catholic practices were all around him, in France and Italy, for comparison. His anti-Catholic anxieties, shared with so many of his countrymen, were confirmed in his encounters with English Jesuits, though much qualified by the gratifying friendships formed with humanist intellectuals, who happened to be Catholic. Less important for the immediate future, he had encountered civil government on the republican model. Not to mention some decent cooking.

III

1639–1649

CHAPTER 8

The Crisis of Government

THE precise date of Milton's return from continental Europe remains uncertain. He himself, writing in 1654, recalls, 'I returned home after a year and three months, more or less, at almost the same time as Charles [I] broke the peace and renewed the war with the Scots, which is known as the second Bishops' War.'¹ The skirmish at Newburn-on-Tyne to which he alludes took place on 28 August 1640. If the usual assumption, that he left England about May 1638, is correct, and if he has remembered the length of his absence, the date of his return would have been about August 1639. Though no life record certainly locates Milton in England before the later date, his probable progress through Europe, together with accounts in the early lives of his activities on his return, suggests a date close to August 1639 is the more likely. Indeed, in the next paragraph in the *Defensio Secunda* he proceeds to conflate the two parliaments called in 1640 into a single account; perhaps his recollection of the two Bishops' Wars are similarly confused. Charles's setback in the First Bishops' War, the retreat at Kelso, happened on 3 June 1639.

As Milton's narrative suggests, the failure of the king's expedition to quell opposition in his northern realm was indeed a pivotal episode in the fall of the monarchy. The Scottish crisis had its origins earlier in the decade, though it developed rapidly during Milton's continental travels. Charles was, of course, monarch of three kingdoms, but he had never visited Ireland and his relationship with the Scots was remote and intermittent. He had had his father's dream project, of uniting the countries politically and economically, celebrated by Peter-Paul Rubens in a fine panel on the ceiling of the Banqueting House at Whitehall,² but the project remained a fading aspiration. Charles ruled in Scotland through a series of proxies. He had delayed his Scottish coronation till 1633. Yet he dabbled in northern politics in ways which alarmed his subjects with uncertainties about his intentions and which indicated a clear sense of his prerogative powers, should he choose to exercise them. While there to be crowned, among other measures, he secured a statute authorizing him to prescribe clerical dress, a sensitive area, given the traditional austerities of Scottish Protestantism and Charles's well-known enthusiasm for elaborate clerical vestments. Kevin Sharpe, his most sympathetic modern biographer, concludes, 'When Charles left Edinburgh, he left a city which harboured resentments and worries about the future,' although 'There is no indication that the king or English Council regarded the progress as anything other than a spectacular success.'[3]

Thus encouraged, Charles pressed the Scottish bishops into writing and imposing a Book of Common Prayer and associated canons to bring the kirk into uniformity with the English church. They responded dutifully and imposed the liturgy with no significant consultation, provoking the kinds of resistance that Archbishop Laud had anticipated.[4] Matters of liturgical detail escalated into a crisis of governance. In February 1638, two or three months before Milton left England, a Covenant had been drawn up, not only asserting a commitment to Calvinism and Presbyterianism and a rejection of Arminianism and episcopacy, but also questioning the king's authority and exercise of power. Its terms would shortly resonate through political discourse in England. 'Covenanters' took effective control of Scotland, remaining so intransigent that eventually Charles raised an English army to confront them. He did so against the advice of many in his Council and without recourse to a parliament, 'the first occasion since 1323 when England had gone to war without a Parliament'.[5]

The debacle that followed left Charles obliged to agree a treaty, the Pacification of Berwick, though the causes of the conflict remained unresolved. The Covenanters increasingly addressed pamphlets to an English readership, among whom issues of church discipline and royal authority were reinvigorated: 'Even beyond puritan circles, the Scots war and the debates it generated transformed the perceptions of events and the language and taxonomy of politics.'[6] We have only Milton's account of his own radicalization. But across the English political nation, thousands followed the same trajectory, towards a more confident and explicit opposition to the politics of the Personal Rule and the ceremonialism of the Caroline church.

In the months following Milton's return, Charles, seemingly unaware of the political damage he had sustained,[7] worked to retrieve his position, while the emboldened Covenanters suppressed episcopacy and prepared to resist another invasion. For this second campaign, Charles needed a subsidy and that could come only through a parliamentary vote of supply. In April 1640, after eleven years of government without parliaments, what would come to be known at the Short Parliament assembled. Yet the vote of supply was deferred till the grievances of the 1630s has been addressed, even though another expeditionary force was in preparation. In early May, Charles dissolved it, a move precipitated perhaps by the government's anticipation of an imminent plan to bring a Scots declaration of their grievances before the Commons in a manoeuvre to align the oppositional forces in both kingdoms. Despite the lack of parliamentary subsidy, the king's forces were launched northwards, though the only engagement, the minor skirmish at Newburn just outside Newcastle, precipated an immediate loss of confidence. The English army withdrew from Newcastle, allowing the Covenanters to occupy it. The truce that followed left a large Scots army on English soil threatening to pillage the northern counties unless they received English funds to maintain them, together with a substantial and costly English force still in arms. Amid increasing concerns about civil order—including a large and violent demonstration outside Lambeth Palace—another parliament, 'the Long Parliament', met in early November, no better disposed to easing the king's troubles than its predecessor had been.

Milton had returned to a London in which the political future was bewilderingly uncertain. In the early months, life records are infrequent, though the outline of his material, cultural, and political progress may be discerned.

He seems to have decided against a return to his father's home in Horton. The account of his elder nephew, Edward Phillips, is singularly helpful, not least because his association with Milton became much closer at this time. Milton first 'took him a Lodging in St. *Brides* Church-yard, at the House of one *Russel*, a Taylor',[8] and undertook the education of his sister Anne's two sons, the younger of whom seems also from that time to have lodged with him. He shortly afterwards moved to a property off Aldersgate Street[9] large enough to accommodate his collection of books and 'other Goods fit for the furnishing of a good handsome House'. He found what he needed, 'a pretty Garden-House... at the end of an Entry, and therefore the fitter for his turn, by reason of the Privacy, besides that there are few Streets in *London* more free from Noise then that.' It was the first of several properties Milton was, at various times, to occupy on the north-west edge of the City, and no doubt constituted a pleasant change from the cramped alleyways around St Bride's. Here Edward joined his younger brother as a lodger.[10]

That he should have taken children of 9 and 10 into his household has sometimes surprised modern biographers. Fostering out, however, was a very common practice. As Lawrence Stone observes, 'the infants of the landed, upper-bourgeois and professional classes... seem normally to have left home very young, some time between the ages of seven and thirteen, with about ten as the commonest age, in order to go to boarding-school.'[11] Milton's sister Anne had remarried on the death of her first husband, the father of these children, and she herself died about the time they left home. Her husband, Thomas Agar, certainly behaved towards his step-sons in a manner typical of his social standing at that time, though it seems considerate that they joined their uncle rather than venturing the challenging lifestyle probable at most residential schools. Simple kindness may have motivated Milton, but his young charges could have repaid him, as they matured, with clerical assistance, and they provided the opportunity for testing his theories about the education of the young.[12] Others subsequently joined his little academy. We have no evidence as to whether Milton was paid for the services he rendered.

His household also contained a maid called Jane Yates, or at least it did so when a Poll Tax levy was raised in July 1641.[13] Indeed, since the tax applied only to people over the age of 16, there could have been younger children working for him. Edward Phillips recalled that he and his brother shared their uncle's life of 'hard Study, and spare Diet', though he adds an intriguing anecdote:

once in three Weeks or a Month, he would drop into the Society of some Young Sparks of his Acquaintance, the chief whereof were Mr. *Alphry*, and Mr. *Miller*, two Gentlemen of *Gray's*-Inn, the *Beau's* of those Times, but nothing near so bad as those now-a-dayes; with these Gentlemen he would so far make bold with his Body, as now and then to keep a Gawdy-day.[14]

As Parker resignedly concludes, 'the two young sparks have not been satisfactorily identified'.[15] Inns of Court men, for the most part, were relatively wealthy, certainly in comparison with the average university student, and included many young men who entertained no intention of pursuing a legal career.[16] Phillips is not an artless writer, and readers should be attentive to his tone. 'Spark' carried a depreciatory edge, while 'beau' was a word not current in Milton's own day, and certainly not in the 1640s. Both suggest foppishness and perhaps affectation. A 'gaudy' meant general merry-making as well as specific festivals at a college or an inn of court. When Cleopatra promises her sad captains a gaudy night, she offers a drinking spree.[17] Phillips's assurance that their conduct fell short of young gentlemen 'now-a-days' comes from someone who had lived through the numerous and highly visible outrages, both sexual and violent, perpetrated by the drunken rakehells of Restoration London. Milton with his dandyish friends, we are probably meant to recognize, was intermittently a binge drinker, though they stopped short of whoring and brawling (presumably the distinction Phillips hints at in distinguishing Milton and his pals from libertines later in the century). Phillips has little to gain from fabricating this account, and the naming of the fellow roisterers adds authenticity. However, the passage serves to correct, for his original readers as it should for modern biographers, the simpler image of Milton as a uniformly austere puritan.

Probably in the first few months after his return Milton produced and published *Epitaphium Damonis* (London, n.d.). The little booklet, a single quarto sheet, appeared without title page and bears no imprint. It survives in only a single copy in the British Library. We may reasonably assume that it was printed privately, presumably at the author's expense, and intended for circulation among friends and relatives of both the subject and the poet.

As its argument explains, it laments the death of Charles Diodati, Milton's friend of long standing, whose relationship to the poet has stimulated speculations and denials in equal measure. Some scholarly endeavour has been invested in establishing where and when on his peregrinations Milton would have heard news of Diodati's death.[18] Diodati had died in the August after Milton left England, and he had stayed with his uncle in Geneva on his way home. Did he hear of the death then or earlier in Italy? He could have been the person who broke the news to the uncle.[19] What Milton actually says may surprise modern readers: 'Thyrsis [i.e. the poet] . . . de obitu Damonis nuncium accepit. Domum postea reversus et rem ita esse comperto, se, suamque solitudinem hoc carmine deplorat' ('Thyrsis . . . received news of Damon's death. Later, when he had returned home and found that this news was true, he bewailed his lot and his loneliness in this poem').[20] On this account, he had reserved judgement on the veracity of Diodati's reported death till he could confirm it once back in London. Milton would have gained nothing from making this up. The poem itself starts with open lamentation, spoken as if by the poet now confirmed in his grief. Disclosure of the sequence by which he knew of the death—unreliable 'news' unconfirmed till his return—is wholly gratuitous, except to pre-empt the obvious comment that grief had not sooner driven him home.

The poem is a perfect exercise in neo-Latin elegy, showing a complete accomplishment in the idiom of Virgilian pastoral. It remains reticent about his affection for Diodati. Their activities together are simple acts of intellectual companionship. At one point he tropes the loss as a bird's loss of a dead mate, but immediately suppresses any notion of the mourning turtle. Even the sparrow, losing one friend, quickly finds another; but humankind are a less sociable and affectionate species: 'Vix sibi quisque parem de millibus invenit unum' ('It is hard for a man to find one kindred spirit among thousands of his fellows').[21] Loneliness is a recurrent concern of the poem.

The consolation offered by the poem is of a familiar kind: Diodati is memorialized by Milton and translated heavenward by his purity. Milton stresses both his chastity—he is a virgin—and his youth. Of course, by 1640 neither he nor Milton, his coeval, were really young. Milton had turned 30 in the December of 1639; Diodati was about 28 at his death. The claim for their youthfulness works thematically: it fits the prevailing idiom of pastoral elegy and makes the death seem especially untimely and poignant. But it perhaps meets a Miltonic anxiety that he, like Diodati, had not achieved much that was tangible; indeed, had not married, and possibly had no sexual experience whatsoever.

While the poem praises the dead it also pays complement to recent acquaintances from his Italian visit, recalling, in two cases by their real names, the intellectuals who had welcomed him to the Florentine academies. Some of the printed copies were sent back to the scene of what he represents as his recent cultural triumph.[22] The other, perhaps surprising, digression describes his creative progress since returning home, as he announces his intention to retell the foundation myths of the English or British people.[23] Though he concludes this section, in a close imitation of Virgil, by renouncing pastoral, hanging his shepherd's pipe from a pine,[24] he does not explicitly say he is writing a national epic. Indeed, the Trinity Manuscript contains eight pages, often ascribed to roughly this period, in which he jots down possible themes for neoclassical tragedies, which include the earliest notes towards *Paradise Lost*, or at least a closet drama on the theme of the fall, numerous other biblical stories that could be reworked, and a substantial list drawn from early British history.

Epitaphium Damonis, like the pages of notes, shows Milton looking for new engagements. These were political as well as cultural. The decision to live in London placed him close to the developing crisis, which till civil war broke out, would be in the conflict between the parliaments sitting in Westminster and the king and his Council, installed together till January 1642 in Whitehall. Though of course religious issues figured among the concerns expressed in the Short Parliament and in the early years of the Long Parliament, secular grievances predominated, and secular politicians, albeit of a puritan disposition, led the opposition to the crown. Pre-eminent were the earl of Warwick, Lord Saye and Sele, Lord Brooke, John Pym, John Hampden, and Sir Walter Erle, all of whom Charles suspected of collaborating with agents of the Covenanters.[25] Lord Brooke would later draw on Milton's early prose and in turn be singled out for praise by Milton. However, no life records suggest Milton had any connection with or access to these leading political figures. Indeed, the political connections he had were unhelpful to an aspiring opposition activist. His brother-in-law, Thomas Agar, had succeeded to Anne's first husband's post of Deputy Clerk of the Crown in the Crown Office in Chancery. As such, he had access to the Lord Keeper of the Seal and to the Lord Chancellor.[26] As we have seen, Milton was in contact with Agar after his return to England. Agar could probably have secured for Milton the role of some minor functionary in the Caroline government in its terminal phase.

Alexander Gil the younger had certainly seemed an oppositional figure in the late 1620s, when imprudent disparagement of Charles I, his late father, and the recently murdered Duke of Buckingham brought him to the attention of Star Chamber and subsequently to severe punishment.[27] By the time of Milton's return Gil was already deeply in trouble of a different kind and evidently in no shape to assume an oppositional role, had he been so inclined. Gil, who succeeded his father as headmaster of St Paul's, was an enthusiastic sadist, whose savage temper led him into what Aubrey described as 'whipping fits'. In one particularly nasty incident, he allegedly lifted a boy up by the jaws, beat him, and kicked him up and down the school. A subsequent petition initiated a series of events that ended with his dismissal. By early 1640 he was reduced to supplicating to the king and thereafter Laud for protection and reinstatement.[28] Gil, thus disgraced and dependent, could scarcely offer an avenue for access to the secular opposition.

But Milton had already proved himself expert at getting through the doors of the famous and privileged. He has secured a recommendation from one former ambassador, currently Provost of Eton, which got him into the company of another ambassador in Paris; he had met with the most famous jurist of his day, the father of international law and himself an ambassador for Sweden; he had found his way into Italian academies and into the company of cardinals, the pope's nephews, and Galileo himself. As the political crisis deepened, Milton sought out his connections with activists among the more puritanical clergy, in so doing probably ensuring that his initial foray into prose polemic concerned matters of church rather than state.

Thomas Young had been among his boyhood tutors, and their intermittent subsequent relationship is clear.[29] Young had come back from his post in Hamburg in 1628 and had been appointed to the living of Stowmarket on his return. In the late 1630s a loose alliance of anti-Laudian clergy, mostly in Suffolk and Essex, emerged, probably under the protection and patronage of Francis Russell, fourth earl of Bedford. Through the crises of 1639–40 Bedford positioned himself at the centre of an aristocratic grouping that was both critical of the government under the Personal Rule and generally Calvinist and anti-ceremonial. Inner-circle politics in those crucial months are intricate and often conflicted.[30] But evidently Laud's opponents at court and among the senior clergy were actively negotiating alternative models of church government and of church discipline that would have allowed a new consensus to emerge. Young's group cohered around another minister of Puritan inclination, Edmund Calamy, and attracted, too, William Spurstowe, Matthew Newcomen, and Stephen Marshall.[31] By 1640 they were meeting regularly at Calamy's London home at St Mary Aldermanbury, and Milton's subsequent involvement suggests, though no records confirm this, that he may at least intermittently have moved among them, though this was over-whelmingly a conclave of divines.

Relations between anti-Laudian episcopalians and this group took two, seemingly contradictory, trajectories. Senior clergy averse to Laud, pre-eminently John Williams, bishop of Lincoln, and James Ussher, archbishop of Armagh, opened up lines of negotiation, with a focus on developing an episcopalian model which reduced the roles of bishops from the grand ambitions of Laud to a status which could be represented as closer to their

26. William Prynne, *Rome for Canterbury, or, A true Relation of the Birth and Life of William Laud, Arch-bishop of Canterbury* (London, 1641), title page.

role in the primitive church. This would have been a settlement that the Calamy group would have accepted with alacrity in the late 1630s.

However, during 1640, less pliant supporters of episcopacy found an able public voice in Joseph Hall, bishop of Exeter, whose *Episcopacy by Divine Right Asserted* was published probably in February, 1640. Hall seemed to draw the line beyond which most episcopalians would not retreat. He had been hitherto regarded as anti-Laudian, an old Calvinist, not disinclined to engage in the sorts of dialogue Williams and Ussher allowed. However, as extant correspondence confirms, he worked on his tract with the encouragement and direction of Laud himself. Unlike most participants in the debate about church government, Hall had an accomplished and distinctive prose style, and developed a plausible persona, indulgent, patient, irenic, and no doubt to his opponents gratingly patronizing: 'And for you, my dearly beloved Brethren, at home; For Christs sake, for the Churches sake, for your soules sake, be exhorted to hold fast to this holy Institution of your blessed Saviour.'[32]

Ultimately, however, this is a firm statement of episcopalian principle, declaring the continuity between bishops of apostolic times and the present day, asserting the necessity for high salaries for prelates ('Little do these men think what charges do necessarily attend our places, what hospitality is expected from us'),[33] and asserting the divinely ordained status of the prelacy.

Positions hardened as the political crisis between king and parliament grew deeper, and in January 1641, in the same month that parliament passed a bill for the defacing of images in churches and a couple of months before it ordered the arrest and imprisonment of Laud, Hall's *An Humble Remonstrance to the High Court of Parliament* initiated a major controversy in print. It tersely restates much of his earlier arguments, and once more those rest on an interpretation of the history of the primitive church. The tone, if anything, has become smugger, remarkably for a man now contemplating the eclipse of his faction, probable unemployment and possible incarceration: 'Heare, I beseech you, the words of truth and confidence.'[34]

The Calamy group switched its attention from dialogue with episcopalians tractable to reform, to countering Hall's perhaps engaging initiative. There is strong evidence that Milton from the outset sought to assist them. Their first response, *An Answer to a Booke Entituled, An Humble Remonstrance*, which appeared in late March 1641, concluded with 'A Postscript', a methodologically and ideologically distinct coda, first attributed to Milton by David Masson,[35] a conjecture substantially confirmed by recent stylometric analysis.[36] The Calamy group's team, Stephen Marshall, Calamy himself, Thomas Young, and William Spurstowe, writing under the acronym 'Smectymnuus', carefully answered Hall, point by point, patiently following him over his arguments from antiquity, in the attempt to establish that the equivalent of the bishops in the primitive church held an office, status, and role very different from those of modern bishops. The main treatise ended on the last recto of a gathering, and concludes unequivocally with 'FINIS'. The Postscript starts on a new sheet.[37] The evidence points towards the later printing of the coda, perhaps as an afterthought. Certainly it is introduced tentatively. These are a 'variety of Histories' that have been 'given us', and they are 'subjoyne[d] by way of *appendix*' because the principal authors did not want 'to break the thread of our discourse'.[38]

Milton's section shows every sign of imperfect composition, suggesting that he had supplied notes, which he expected to be reworked in the body of the Smectymnuans' text, rather printed up in this way. The argument, however, points clearly to how implacably he now loathed bishops. His review of prelatical malpractice from the days of Augustine to the present is a historical overview drawn for the most part from English historians and demonstrating that the office and structure of prelacy are so malign that England suffers, no matter whether the malefactors are Protestant or

Catholic. The dialogue sometimes sought by Calamy's group is irreconcilable with Milton's analysis.

Possibly the Smectymnuans already felt uneasy about their lay ally, though he may have contributed at least one idea to the body of their tract. They observe, 'Doe we not know, the drunkennesse, profanenesse, superstition, Popishnesse of the English Clergie rings at *Rome* already?'[39] Milton, recently returned, was better placed to assert this information than a cluster of divines who had not travelled recently and in some cases had not travelled at all.

The debate about prelacy was merely one element in a complex collision of ideologies. Charles had immediate problems to resolve, most pressingly the conclusion of a treaty with the Scots that would have led to the withdrawal of their army. His opponents in parliament were concerned with pursuing their campaign against Strafford, executed in mid-May 1641. Moreover, mindful that Charles, once free from his Scottish troubles, would see no advantage in the continuation of parliament, they passed a bill ensuring that parliament would not dissolve without its members' consent, a measure with which the temporizing king agreed. No evidence indicates that Milton engaged actively in any of the secular agitation, though the internal politics of the city of London were contemporaneously heated as both sides battled to command its seats of power such as control of the Tower of London, whose artillery could cow the citizens, and the government of the city itself.

Hall and Smectymnuus exchanged blows through the late spring and into the early summer, though neither advanced their arguments significantly, and both became increasingly prolix.[40] Assessing which side had the best of the exchange can scarcely have been easy, even for contemporaries. Hall's objective was probably rather different from his opponents'. Episcopalians, under persistent attack in parliament and pulpit by critics newly liberated from the constraints of the Laudian ascendancy, needed to hear their case defended in order to be reassured of the sanctity and antiquity of the church government they believed in. Indeed, Hall's contributions to the debate were among his collected works lavishly published in 1662, when they served to define for a new age the central tenets of the Church of England.[41] He was probably less concerned with winning the middle ground than with rallying the confidence of partisans. He persistently brought to the exchange a capacity, lacking in the Smectymnuans, for sustained contempt: 'I am sorry, Brethren [i.e. the Smectymnuans], that your own importunities will needs make you guiltie of your own further shame: Had you sate down silent in the conscience of a just reproof, your blame had been by this time dead, and forgotten.'[42]

Hall had savaged the Postscript to the first Smectymnuan tract as 'a goodly *Pasquin* borrowed (for a great part) out of *Sion's Plea*, and the Breviate'.[43] Milton seems to have left the Smectymnuans to defend him as best they could.[44] But in the early summer of 1641 he entered the controversy with three publications of his own, *Of Reformation touching Church-Discipline in England: And the Causes that hitherto have hindred it* (London: May or perhaps June, 1641), *Of Prelatical Episcopacy, and Whether it may be deduc'd from the Apostolical times by vertue of those Testimonies which are alledg'd to that purpose in some late Treatises: One whereof goes under the Name of James Arch-bishop of Armagh* (London: June or July, 1641), and *Animadversions upon The Remonstrants Defence against Smectymnuus* (London: July, 1641). The titles promise treatises much in the manner of Smectymnuus, though each offers a radically different kind of reading experience. They appeared in such quick succession that all must have been in gestation together. They constitute three mutually distinctive kinds of polemic, though together they made a remarkable contribution to an already mature debate.

In *Of Reformation* Milton returned to the argument of the Postscript, demonstrating, in what Hall had not unfairly censured in the former work as 'a rhapsodye of Histories',[45] the malign influence of episcopacy on the English state and people. The argument is at least open to the challenge that the confusion of pre- and post-Reformation bishops in the same narrative falsifies the evidence. But that stratagem is central to Milton's thesis: namely, that there has been no proper reformation in England. However, it is not the thesis, but how that thesis is articulated, that lifts this pamphlet above the humbler achievements of the Smectymnuans. Consider this typical paragraph:

So that in this manner the *Prelates* both then and ever since comming from a meane, and Plebeyan *Life* on a sudden to be Lords of stately Palaces, rich furniture, delicious fare, and *Princely* attendance, thought the plaine and homespun verity of *Christs* Gospell unfit any longer to hold their Lordships acquaintance, unlesse the poore thred-bare Matron were put into better clothes; her chast and modest vaile sur-rounded with celestiall beames they overlai'd with wanton *tresses*, and in a flaring tire bespeccl'd her with all the gaudy allurements of a Whore.[46]

The modern reader could be struck first by the length and elaboration of the sentence, though both would have seen less remarkable to Milton's original audience. Syntactically, Milton's style broadly resembles that of the first Smectymnuan pamphlet.[47] The imagery is highly distinctive—brilliantly conceived, wonderfully vivid, and hitting multiple targets as it ties together the excesses of prelatical life styles and the excrescences of episcopalian embellishment of gospel simplicities. The lofty vocabulary ('*Plebeyan* life', 'celestiall beames', 'wanton *tresses*', and so on) is cut down with the stark crudeness with which the sentence concludes. Milton in his early pamphlets uses more similes and metaphors than Hall and far more than the Smectym-nuans, and his imagery often has this level of complexity.[48]

The sustained vehemence manifest here is pervasive and similarly distinct-ive. Milton offers a reiterated picture of bishops, throughout history, as vile, appetitive monsters, cramming rich livings into their 'many-benefice-gaping mouth[s]', to satisfy their 'canary-sucking, and swan-eating' palates.[49] The tract ends with a heady millenarian fantasy, somewhat surprising in a debate that had been hitherto concerned with the taxonomy of church offices in the early centuries of the Christian era. It is couched in what Hall would no doubt have censured as a 'big-mouthed prayer', and a singularly undisciplined example of the form at that. The penultimate paragraph offers a beatific vision in which the godly 'shall clasp inseparable Hands with *joy*, and *blisse* in over measure for ever'.[50] The vocabulary anticipates the vision extended by Michael to Adam at the close of *Paradise Lost*, with its promise of 'joy and eternal bliss'.[51] Here, however, the millennium seems imminent. The last paragraph replaces beatification with unrelenting vindictiveness. Milton describes the fate of prelates and their like. He anticipates 'a shamefull end in this *Life* (which *God* grant them)'. The phrase may well imply execution. Indeed, Strafford was beheaded about the time Milton was bringing his text to press. Laud had been incarcerated, like him, in the Tower of London since the start of March, though he was not brought to the block till 1645; the original, savage sentence of hanging, drawing and quartering was commuted to simple beheading.[52] Thereafter, the bishops will be confined to the lowest circle of hell, where all the other damned will have as their only comfort to right and duty of exercising 'a *Raving* and *Bestiall Tyranny* over them as their *Slaves* and *Negro's*'.[53]

The respectable middle-age Puritan divines gathered around Calamy could not have failed to recognize the zeal of their younger associate. Perhaps they were alarmed by it. Milton's next publication, *Of Prelatical Episcopacy*, superficially moved closer to the core issues of the Smectymnuan controversy. Its title page links it with a recent pamphlet by James Ussher, archbishop of Armagh, for long regarded as a moderate episcopalian with whom Calamy and his associates could do business. Ussher had issued in May 1641 *The Judgement of Doctor Rainoldes touching the Originall of Episcopacy. More largely confirmed out of Antiquity* (London). It substantially endorsed the arguments based on the history of the early Christian church that had been advanced by Hall, in the process invoking, perhaps spuriously, the endorsement of John Rainolds, a leading Elizabethan and Jacobean theologian of a moderate puritan inclination.[54]

Milton initially seems to play by the rules of the game, though a radically different perspective soon emerges. Instead, he impugns the evidence base previously used by participants in the controversy. He ridicules sources as documents tainted by the hagiographical tradition, as later reconstructions, and as the polluted remnants of texts corrupted by centuries of Catholic editorial intervention. To these he opposes the plain, unmediated Gospel:

we doe injuriously in thinking to tast better the pure Euangelick Manna by seasoning our mouths with the tainted scraps, and fragments of an unknown table; and searching among the verminous, and polluted rags dropt overworn from the toyling shoulders of Time, with these deformedly to quilt, and interlace the intire, the spotlesse, and undecaying robe of Truth, the daughter not of Time, but of Heaven, only bred up heer below in Christian hearts, between two grave & holy nurses the Doctrine, and Discipline of the Gospel.[55]

Of course, no other contributor to the debate writes prose of such imaginative power. As in *Of Reformation*, theological choice becomes almost a function of sensibility: the godly are drawn to Gospel simplicities, the ungodly to whatever is confused, adulterated, embellished, and corrupt. But if Milton's perspective prevails, then it marginalizes the contribution of scholarly divines on both sides. The attack on prelacy may be moved to more straightforward issues. Indeed, in the event the fate of episcopalian church government was determined, ultimately, by puritan politicians backed by the power of a puritan army.

Animadversions also seems initially familiar, in that Milton, like Smectymnuus and Hall, pursues a point-by-point refutation of his opponent's publication. Yet once more Milton carries the Smectymnuan case in an unusual and unpredictable direction, leavening academic disputation with the mordant irreverence of a Cambridge 'salting'. The spirit of *Prolusion 6* recurs in a surprising context, subverting the gravity of earlier exchanges.[56] But his target is not fellow students but a bishop esteemed for his elegance of expression. One would scarcely guess this from the tone of the exchange. Milton quotes Hall: 'D. *Hall* whom you name, I dare say for honours sake.' He responds: 'Y'are a merry man Sir, and dare say much.' He quotes Hall again: '...we have a Liturgy, and so had they [members of the primitive church].' He responds: 'A quick come off. The ancients us'd Pikes, and Targets, and therefore Guns, and great Ordnance, because wee use both.' He quotes again: 'No one Clergie in the whole Christian world yeelds so many eminent schollers, learned preachers, grave, holy and accomplish'd Divines as this Church of *England* doth at this day.' He responds: 'Ha, ha, ha'.[57] Perhaps the Smectymnuans may have reflected that they, too, were in holy orders in that church; there is a note of an incipient anti-clericalism, as well as anti-episcopalianism, to be heard here.

Milton brought, then, a new, undeferential, incisive, vivid, violent, and vindictive perspective to the Smectymnuan cause, but to what effect? None of Milton's first three pamphlets saw republication in his own lifetime. Yet he may well have found at least one deeply influential reader. Robert Greville, second Baron Brooke, seems to draw directly on *Of Prelatical Episcopacy* as he appraises the reliability of patristic records in *A Discourse Opening the Nature of that Episcopacie, which is Exercised in England* (London: November, 1641), a tract which may be more generally informed by the arguments of *Of*

Reformation in its critique of the old episcopal assertion that kingship is supported by prelacy.[58] Lord Brooke, like Milton, shows an overarching concern with excluding from the political agenda the sorts of compromises that Calamy and his circle had clandestinely pursued with Williams and Ussher. No life records directly connect him with Milton, though his father-in-law was the late earl of Bedford, to whom the Calamy circle looked for patronage and protection, his tract anticipates some of the argument of Milton's fourth pamphlet, and, after his death, Milton would praise him in *Areopagitica*.[59]

Milton becomes difficult to track over the last half of 1641. The summer saw the onset of a quite serious visitation of the plague and a smallpox epidemic. Indeed, the latter had killed the earl of Bedford in May. In August the two diseases accounted for over 250 deaths in the city.[60] If Milton were to have taken the sensible course of action for a fairly wealthy man with few business ties to the capital, he would have indulged a sojourn elsewhere. His father had probably already moved with Christopher and his family to Reading, one possible destination. In early August, Milton defaulted on the payment of a trivial tax, which may suggest he had temporarily quit Aldersgate Street.[61] There is no indication whether, if he indeed left, the Phillips boys went with him.

The political crises and controversies were, in any case, running out of steam. Hall issued his final rebuff to Smectymnuus, *A Short Answer*, probably about the time *Animadversions* appeared. The Smectymnuans did not rise to the challenge. In mid-August, to the surprise of most, Charles I withdrew from Whitehall and embarked on a visit to his northern kingdom. Parliament went into recess from 9 September to 20 October. The king did not return till late November.

The period from November to January proved crucial for the processes that led to civil war, and for Milton's own political development. Parliament set to work drafting the Grand Remonstrance, which grew into a mighty indictment of the government of the realm since the inception of the Personal Rule, a 'declaration of the state of the nation', with over two hundred separate complaints, presented to the king on 1 December.[62] Their first concern, however, had been finally to pass the legislation to exclude bishops from the House of Lords.

Charles, too, was busily confrontational. In mid-November Hall migrated to the see of Norwich, not a more senior appointment than Exeter though handier for the metropolis and its printing presses. On 23 November the king made his triumphal entry into the city of London to mark his return from Scotland. Shortly after, he filled the vacant archbishopric of York with John Williams. Agitation against the bishops mounted in late December, producing anti-episcopalian street demonstrations in London. One prompted

Williams, in a political miscalculation, to organize a remonstrance signed by himself and other prelates who happened to be in the capital at the time, which was read in parliament on 30 December. The next day the signatories, among them Joseph Hall, were arrested and imprisoned in the Tower. Four days later Charles attempted a *coup d'état*, marching with a large and armed entourage to Westminster in an abortive attempt to arrest in the House of Commons five leaders of the opposition to him. They had already escaped downriver to the safety of the City. Within a week the king had left London, by mid-March establishing in effect an alternative seat of government at York.

Both sides organized themselves for civil war. In late February Henrietta Maria went off to the continent with the crown jewels, looking to buy armaments. In April Charles made an abortive attempt to enter Hull and commandeer its arsenal. By then parliament had passed an ordinance to reorganize the militia in London and the areas where it could depend on support under the command of its supporters. Neither side responded adequately to the emergency in Ireland, first reported in early November, caused by a major insurrection by the predominately Catholic indigenous people against English and Scottish settlers.[63] From the king's departure an utter intransigence entered both sides, and, as Russell observes, 'The delay in the outbreak of civil war is... a measure of how extraordinarily demilitarized a country England had become.'[64]

In 'Lycidas' Milton had celebrated 'Fame' as 'That last infirmity of noble mind'.[65] Over the winter of 1641–2 he had his first encounter with its uglier sibling, notoriety.

Milton's attack on Hall provoked a substantial response, the anonymous *Modest Confutation of A Slandrous and Scurrilous Libell, Entituled, Animadversions upon the Remonstrants Defense against Smectymnuus* (London, 1642). This pamphlet shows evidence of being produced in difficult circumstances. Its authorship was and remains the subject of speculation. Milton claims to have heard that it was the work of 'Father and Son', that is, Hall and one of his sons.[66] Hall himself was incarcerated in the Tower till early May, and if he contributed he did so while in a constrained but not impossible condition. Most telling, unlike all Hall's earlier contributions to the debate and the pamphlets of Smectymnuus and Milton himself, it carries on its title page the name of neither printer nor bookseller. No stationer registered it. Contrary to its modern editor's view, the dates used on title pages corresponded for the most part to the modern calendar year, and so '1642' does not suggest 'publication after March 24, 1642', and, as he adds, internal evidence 'suggests composition before... February 5'.[67] It could well have been published or in press by the time Milton's fourth pamphlet, *The Reason of Church-government Urg'd against Prelaty* appeared. Again, dating is problematic. This carries '1641' on its title page, but certainly alludes to the imprisonment of the bishops on the last day of the modern calendar year.[68] If the anonymous author had indeed experienced difficulty finding a printer to take his manuscript on, knowledge that a brutal rebuttal of *Animadversions* had been written could have been widely rumoured around the London book trade, where Milton, as a currently active author, certainly had contacts, even if the work had not yet seen the light of day.

The speculation is significant since it could explain the most remarkable element in *The Reason of Church-government*, its extraordinary autobiographical digression. *A Modest Confutation* seeks to put Milton in his place, and it does so quite effectively. Milton may well have thought what posterity would generally concede, that among participants in the Smectymnuan debate, whatever the others' pretences to patristic lore, his was the towering intellect, the withering analysis, the persuasive rhetoric, and the potent style. But in the eyes of contemporaries, he was indeed a novice, with no pertinent publication record, holding neither church nor university office, and, unlike Lord Brooke for example, of relatively modest social standing. His father was a retired businessman, and he had no evident source of income apart from what his father supplied. Indeed, the Modest Confuter, while often wrong in detail, lands some shrewd blows. He claims 'to have no further notice of him [Milton], than he hath been pleased, in his immodest and injurious Libell to give of himselfe'.[69] But he has learnt or successfully surmised that he is relatively recently come to London, that he is in effect an unemployed and fairly recent graduate of one of the universities, and that he has neither an ecclesiastical post nor a wife: 'A rich Widow, or a Lecture, or both, contents you.'[70]

The autobiographical digression in *Reason of Church-government* meets or pre-empts such an attempted character assassination. Milton begins by disputing a central proposition of *The Modest Confutation*, that the vehemence against the prelates arises in 'stomach, virulence and ill nature'. He then describes his liberal education and his 'retired thoughts [paid for] out of the sweat of other men', an enigmatic phrase that perhaps acknowledges paternal subvention. He claims that he participates in controversial writing only reluctantly, using 'as I may account it, but of my left hand',[71] a dubious way of recommending himself to a reader who has bought the pamphlet on the assumption that its author will be using all his powers and resources. Thence follows an account, so frequently drawn on by subsequent biographers, of his education, his visit to Italy, his literary ambitions and how they relate to classical and Italian models, and his aspirations to be a national poet. Interestingly, as if to meet the Modest Confuter's charge that he has been frequenting 'the Play-Houses, or the Bordelli',[72] he distinguishes the poetry he would write from 'the writings and interludes of libidinous and ignorant Poetasters'.[73] He concludes with an account of his decision not to enter holy orders. Far from thirsting after a lucrative church lectureship, he decided, he tells us, that the Caroline church was tyrannical, and he declined to take an oath which would have required him to accept prelatical church government and to subscribe to the thirty-nine Articles of the Church of England. Though he had sworn a similar oath as he proceeded to his bachelor's and master's degrees, he now represented himself as 'Church-outed by the Prelats'.[74]

There is, of course, nothing apologetic, in the modern sense of the word, about Milton's *Apology*, which largely reiterates, expands, and defends the strictures of *Animadversions*, while taking issue, with similar irreverent vehemence, with the Modest Confuter. Inevitably, much of the defence against accusations of personal misconduct once more becomes autobiographical. He gives us another account of his honourable university career, assuring us that he stayed aloof from college drama, and describes again his taste in literature and his aspirations as a poet.[75] Perhaps he discloses here some disquiet about how off-course he has been blown by the controversies he has felt obliged to engage in.

One charge, that he sought a rich widow or a church lectureship, elicits a response that has fascinated recent commentators:

For this I cannot omit without ingratitude to that providence above, who hath ever bred me up in plenty, although my life hath not bin unexpensive in learning, and voyaging about.... I care not if I tell him thus much profestly, though it be to the losing of my *rich hopes*, as he calls them, that I think with them who both in prudence and elegance of spirit would choose a virgin of mean fortunes honestly bred, before the wealthiest widow.[76]

His principal concern is to demonstrate his status as the comfortably maintained son of a prosperous father: anyone who can live off a paternal allowance and indulge in 'voyaging about' plainly is not constrained to scrounge a living through church preferment. We have no record of how enthusiastically his father viewed this condition of permanent dependency. Yet, as most modern biographers note, that allusion to the 'virgin of mean fortunes' indicates either that he was generally contemplating marriage to such a person or, indeed, that he was specifically contemplating marriage to Mary Powell, who later in 1642 would be his bride.

The psychological profile suggested here is intriguing. Since mortality rates were high among young adults in the early modern period, 'the median duration of marriage...was probably somewhere about seventeen to twenty years' and 'remarriage was very common, about a quarter of all marriages being a remarriage for the bride or groom'.[77] It was commonplace, as it is not now, for a man of 33 to marry a widow. Milton goes out of his way to stress a preference for a sexually inexperienced partner, and one who would be wholly dependent upon him. His defence also discloses a prickly sensitivity and an aversion to a taste of his own medicine, traits unhelpful for one whose later career would carry him into many spitefully argued controversies. He was evidently aggrieved that the Modest Confuter is 'as good at dismembring and slitting sentences, as his grave Fathers the Prelates have bin at stigmatizing & slitting noses'.[78] In fact, though his adversary sometimes abbreviates or extracts phrases from their context, his practice is markedly more scrupulous than Milton's own in quoting Hall or the Modest Confuter himself.[79]

The Reason of Church-government, however, is a far richer text than *An Apology* in terms of its contribution to a developing debate among English puritans. Episcopalian apologists habitually claimed that only a prelatical church government could control schism and heresy and that the displacement of bishops from their traditional role had allowed the emergence in England of what the Modest Confuter called 'furious, hot-brain'd Hereticks, Schismaticks, &c.'[80] Moderate puritans like Calamy and those around him were acutely mindful of the charge and were currently exercised about how best to reform the national church without allowing the emergence of such heterodoxy. Their deliberations were substantially shaped by a handful of highly influential Scottish ministers, George Gillespie, Alexander Henderson, and Robert Baillie, who were in London from November 1640 to July 1641, acting as 'commissioners' or representatives of the Scottish kirk.

These Scots were themselves Presbyterians and powerful advocates for the adoption of a Presbyterian model of church government in England. They enjoyed access not only to influential pulpits but also to leading puritan divines. The details of the emergence of English Presbyterians as a dominant element remain disputed among church historians. Thus, R. S. Paul, albeit with some important caveats, locates the origins of English Presbyterianism among the Smectymnuans, while Tom Webster asserts this 'proves difficult to sustain'.[81] Webster's larger argument about Smectymnuus is that the tracts are more concerned in blocking Hall's ceremonial episcopalianism than with promulgating an alternative. Indeed, at the outset they could scarcely have anticipated the rapid decline and fall of the bishops, and arguably their work could be read as endorsing a primitive, reduced episcopacy rather than its complete elimination. By early 1642, however, filling the void left by the overthrow of the bishops was surely recognized as a pressing concern by those reluctant to allow a fragmentation of the national church and the development of heterodox groups outside it. *The Reason of Church-government* sits uncomfortably among the changing priorities of English puritanism. It completes Milton's critique of episcopalian arguments founded on the history of the early church. Its immediate occasion was a perceived need to answer *Certaine Briefe Treatises, Written by Diverse Learned Men, Concerning the Ancient and Moderne Government of the Church* (Oxford, 1641). This was a compendium of short tracts by learned divines, all except two of whom were already dead. Milton's engagement with them, even with the work of Lancelot Andrewes, perceived by puritans as Laud's ideological forebear, and Ussher, with whom he clashed in *Of Prelatical Episcopacy*, is neither close nor vehement. His real concerns evidently lie elsewhere.

Though Milton says in the autobiographical digression that he would rather be writing poems, he behaves as though he would rather be writing a tolerationist tract (rather than an anti-prelatical one). The argument is persistently diverted to consideration of the status of puritans more radical than Presbyterians, the sectaries. In part, Milton has been pushed out of position by polemical exigencies. He feels constrained to argue that sectaries pose no greater threat under a newly reformed church government than under a prelatical one, that godly ministers can contain and control them just as well as Laud did but more humanely, more in a spirit of Christian amity. Sectaries emerge, not as a gangrene of the state church, to anticipate the informing metaphor of Thomas Edwards's heresiography, but as symptoms of its health.[82] Because of its fitness, the new church government can respond less repressively to such groups.

Masson's account of the relationship of this tract to the mainstream of mid-seventeenth-century puritanism is singularly helpful and perceptive:

[Milton] confines himself to mentioning the smallest unit and the largest [of the presbyterian system of church government as practiced contemporaneously in Scotland]...: the *Parochial Consistory*, or court of the individual parish or congregation, answering to what the Scots call the *Kirk-session*; and the complete territorial or national Council, which he expressly calls by its Scottish name of *General Assembly*.... There is no distinct mention of the two bodies intermediate, in the Scottish Presbyterian system, between the Kirk-session and the General of National Assembly: to wit, the *Presbytery*, specially so called, or periodical meeting of office-bearers of a cluster of contiguous parishes, and the *Provincial Synod*, or periodical meeting of all the Presbyters of a shire or other large district.[83]

Masson probably errs when he concludes that Milton's scheme would have found favour with Scottish presbyterian cadres currently promoting reform on that model.[84] But he is closer the mark with his observation that, in Milton's model, 'as well as in his obvious indifference...to the alarms...about...the increase of sects, one traces the effects of his recent readings of tracts from the Independent side'.[85]

Milton's selective approach leaves important instruments of church control on the shelf while selecting the national assembly and the congregation. The former, which would shortly take flesh in the guise of the Westminster Assembly of Divines, is vital to his campaign against bishops, in that to its remit should fall those matters of discipline, especially ceremonialism, which Milton's earlier antiprelatical pamphlets found so reprehensible. But more interesting is his developing notion of congregational discipline, which separates power over the individual communicant from the national church and—

crucially—from the state and the secular arm of civil law. The model church which he would oppose to prelacy seems much closer to congregational independency at this point: 'God...hath committed this...office of preserving in healthful constitution the inner man, which may be term'd the spirit of the soul, to his spiritual deputy the minister of each Congregation; who being best acquainted with his own flock, hath best reason to know all the secretest diseases likely to be there.'[86] Milton no doubt still thinks in terms of a national reformation of a national church, but the product is a far looser structure than contemporary Presbyterians sought, and its discipline is wholly spiritual and congregational.

The appearance of *An Apology* concluded Milton's writing against prelacy. He would not turn again to explicit arguments about church government till 1659. Cyriack Skinner relates the conclusion of that business to the inception of new concerns, courtship and marriage. Skinner notes that Milton, 'according to his practice of not wasting that pretious Talent', moved swiftly, as if using a window that had opened in his busy schedule.[87] Edward Phillips among early biographers has the fullest account:

About *Whitsuntide* [29 May in 1642] it was, or a little after, that he took a Journey into the Country; no body about him certainly knowing the Reason, or that it was any more than a Journey of Recreation: after a Month's stay, home he returns a Married-man, that went out a Batchelor; his Wife being *Mary*, the Eldest Daughter of Mr. *Richard Powell*, then a Justice of Peace, of *Forrest-hil*, near *Shotover* in *Oxfordshire*.[88]

The Milton family had had a financial agreement with Richard Powell since 1627, when John Milton senior lent him £300, receiving as security a staple bond for £500 made payable to John Milton junior. The loan, at 8 per cent, the maximum allowed under statute but by no means atypically high, would earn £24 interest per annum, payable on or about 12 June and 12 December every year.[89] It is unclear whether Milton usually collected the income in person. Certainly it was paid while Milton was away on his continental travels. A rudimentary banking system had long since evolved to transfer money around the country using bills of exchange in settlement of debts and invoices, and it was particularly easy to send money from Oxford to London, since parents of students needed to send money in the opposite direction to support their offspring. Milton's father, as a scrivener, would have known the system well and would have used it frequently.[90] However, the marriage arrangements do point to Milton already knowing the Powell family and it is reasonable to surmise that he had at least occasionally called on his debtor (and probably an important source of secure income) in earlier years. Other ties, with his family's roots in that part of Oxfordshire, less than a mile away, may also have carried him there.

Much about the marriage remains enigmatic. No record survives of its date or even its location. Since Milton was already in Oxfordshire and since, on Edward Phillips's recollection, he had assembled no entourage of groomsmen to attend him, the performance of the ceremony in his bride's parish would have been the straightforward option. Phillips is clear, however, that the associated revels were protracted on the couple's return to Aldersgate Street, accompanied by 'some few of her nearest Relations', where 'the Feasting' continued 'for some days in Celebration of the Nuptials'.[91]

Milton had written of the advantages of marrying a poor virgin. The Powells were not obviously poor. Richard Powell, his father-in-law, was the most eminent gentry figure in his immediate locality, though his manor house and his lifestyle were maintained through borrowing, and he had recently taken on some considerable debts.[92] Both he and Milton belonged to social groups where dowries were central to marriage settlements. Typically, a dowry would have been paid by the bride's father to the groom's father, who would then disburse it appropriately to support the bride and in due course her offspring.[93] After Milton's death, his brother Christopher recalled that he had told him that £1,000 had been agreed though none of it had been paid.[94] Since Powell, though a considerable landowner, was cash-poor, some other arrangement would have been likelier, perhaps the annual payment of interest on the outstanding principle alongside the £24 he continued to pay his son-in-law. In the event, on Christopher's recollection of his assertion, he received nothing.

Milton may well have seemed a good match for a squire's eldest daughter. He was the elder son (and thus principal heir) of a wealthy businessman who, as an octogenarian, could reasonably be expected to die quite soon. He was evidently cultured, lived without working, and his authorship of *A Masque* pointed to an association with at least the periphery of the highest social circles. His immediate ideological orientation could well have appeared at the least uncertain. However, even the briefest sojourn in Aldersgate Street, where one saw him among his puritanical books and pamphlets, some of his own composition, and among fellow activists, would have been enough to dispel any uncertainties about where he would line up once the civil war began.

The onset of open hostilities was very close indeed by the time Milton married Mary Powell. Throughout the previous weeks peers and then MPs loyal to the king were drifting from parliament to join him in York, his provisional capital. Few of the political nation were surprised when Charles moved southward to Nottingham and, on 22 August, raised his standard, formally acknowledging that his was a country at war with itself.

CHAPTER 9

The First Civil War

M ILTON's marriage very quickly took an unsatisfactory turn. The early
biographers broadly agree, though Cyriack Skinner and Edward
Phillips wrote long after the event, albeit that the former was probably
reporting events he witnessed and the latter was certainly living in his uncle's
household over this period. Phillips was probably John Aubrey's only source
for that part of his narration. All agree that Mary Milton returned to her
family home in Forest Hill. Phillips says that, once those family members
who had travelled to London with her and Milton had gone home, she
herself remained 'for a Month or thereabouts', though Skinner puts it at 'a
few days' and adds the otherwise uncorroborated detail that she returned 'into
the Country with her Mother'. All three postulate reasons for her conduct.
Skinner has her 'beeing not well pleas'd' with Milton's 'reserv'd manner of
life'. In Phillips's version she is prompted by the 'earnest suit by Letter' of her
friends, 'possibly incited by her own desire', in turn stimulated by an aversion
to the 'Philosophical Life' she was now obliged to lead. He seems to hint that
Milton not only expected to be able to continue his own studies without
compromise but also expected Mary, like his nephews, to join in.

Aubrey's account is certainly flawed, in that he assumes Milton had
brought Mary home, not to the house in Aldersgate Street, but to his earlier
and meaner lodgings in St Bride's Churchyard. However, he has a detail
missing from the others, presumably gleaned from Phillips: 'she found it very
solitary: no company came to her, often-times heard his Nephews cry, and
beaten.'¹ That detail has a plausibility, and its omission from the accounts of
Phillips and Skinner, both pupils of Milton, is wholly explicable in terms of
grown men's reluctance to give weight to the everyday sufferings of their
younger selves. Child abuse of this kind was utterly commonplace in the early
modern period. Stone concludes confidently that 'There can be no doubt . . .
that more children were being beaten in the sixteenth and early seventeenth
centuries, over a longer age span, than ever before', and that 'Whipping was

27. *King Charles I and his Adherents,* after Sir Anthony Van Dyck and unknown artists (National Portrait Gallery, London).

[a] ... normal part of a child's experience'.[2] Only the egregious sadism of the kind manifest by Alexander Gil would attract investigation or even merit comment.[3]

Phillips notes that Mary had left 'on condition of her return at the time appointed, *Michalemas*, or thereabout'.[4] Milton, then, expected her back on or about 29 September 1642. In the event she did not return till 1645. Milton and his wife very soon found themselves separated by the battlelines that emerged shortly after the inception of the war. Indeed, a village six miles east of Oxford was probably the least accessible and, as the catastrophe of the royalist cause developed, the least congenial place for Mary to be, though had she attempted to return punctually she would have found safe enough passage. We have no evidence to explain her delay. Perhaps the relationship was close to breakdown; more simply, anxieties about placing a young woman on the open road in time of war or of returning her to a city that could soon be sacked could have motivated her or her parents to delay. Phillips, however, attributed her reluctance to the partisanship and perhaps opportunism of her family, fearing marriage to a supporter of parliament 'would be a blot in their Escutcheon'.[5]

By early October, Charles I, after wheeling from Nottingham to unite with forces raised elsewhere, descended south towards London with an obvious menace. He was soon into the southern Midlands, which were to become, in some respects, the principal cockpit of war for the next three years. Near the borders of Oxfordshire and Warwickshire in late October the first major engagement of the war, the battle of Edgehill, occurred, ending in a bloody stalemate that nevertheless left the king's army intact and operationally fit to continue its advance. Oxford itself had briefly been held for the king when a squadron of horse, fleeing a skirmish, had occupied it. That the university would initially at least receive the king sympathetically was certain, though the support of the townsfolk was less reliable. After the battle, the royal army advanced to occupy it. Till its eventual capitulation in June 1646 it would remain the royal capital and for much of that time the residence of the king.

For these purposes it had many advantages. College buildings adapted fairly well to accommodate the royal court. Charles established himself in the grand surrounding of Christ Church. Henrietta Maria was later installed in Merton, handily adjacent. The university buildings could scarcely accommodate court and scholars, and very few new undergraduates were matriculated during the occupation.[6] Moreover, the field armies of the king for the most part could not be quartered within the walls. Furthermore, royalist strategists favoured the development of outlying redoubts around their principal strongholds. Richard Powell's Forest Hill manor-house was garrisoned and probably fortified.[7] Powell and his sons soon emerged as royalist partisans. If they had not been, anything useful from the estate would simply have been confiscated. Even so, Powell no doubt found himself obliged to offer quarters and forage, and probably suffered the compulsory purchase of horses and carts for the cavalry and baggage train of the royal field armies.[8] Local historians of the southern Midlands record the plummeting fortunes of yeomen and minor gentry living in the war zone. Living so close to a major centre of royalist military concentration, Powell would have found neutrality scarcely an option and his partisanship probably did not save him from severe financial hardship. In the event, perhaps surprisingly, he did not default on at least the payment to Milton of his half-yearly interest until June 1644, which in itself points to some expectation that relations could be mended in the future. By that time, presumably, Charles's prohibition of October 1643 on trade between royalist and parliamentarian areas had started to bite and with it the possibility of cash transfers between Oxford and London.[9]

The aftermath of Edgehill had another impact on Milton's family. While the king turned to Oxford, Prince Rupert of the Rhine pushed on to quarter his cavalry in Reading. Milton's brother Christopher had moved there from Horton, taking with him his wife and John Milton senior.[10] The subsidy returns and churchwarden accounts for the parish of St Laurence, Reading indicate that the Christopher and his father were residents of that parish by April 1641. Both took the Protestation Oath in 1642 and remained in residence until after the siege of April 1643. Reading was in alarming proximity to the capital, though it was an obvious target for early recovery once the tide of war turned. Its occupation further obstructed access to Oxford. Meanwhile, Milton's surviving parent and sibling were living in a royalist stronghold, with all the associated risks. Christopher's only surviving child at this time was a little over a year old.

So far as we know, Milton stayed in London throughout the civil wars. Life in the metropolis was largely sheltered from the circumambient horrors that confronted Richard Powell. The capital preserved its links with the rich agricultural lands of the eastern counties and its port was open to foreign trade. It lost, however, access to the north-eastern coalfields, and the 'sea-coal' on which Londoners had come to depend for winter fuel.

Despite the zeal with which Milton had urged on the campaign against episcopacy, nothing suggests that he fought for parliament or even that he joined trained bands raised to protect London and its environs. As Charles and Rupert united their forces and in mid-November marched on London, approaching from the west, Milton may have responded with a poem, Sonnet 8, entitled in the Trinity Manuscript, 'When the assault was intended to the Citty', though it bears, too, a deleted earlier title, 'On his dore when the Citty expected an assault':[11]

Captain or colonel, or knight in arms,
  Whose chance on these defenceless doors may seize,
  If deed of honour did thee ever please,
Guard them, and him within protect from harms,
He can require thee, for he knows the charms
  That call fame on such gentle acts as these,
  And he can spread thy name o'er lands and seas,
Whatever clime the sun's bright circle warms.
Lift not thy spear against the muses' bower,
  The great Emathian conqueror bid spare
  The house of Pindarus, when temple and tower
Went to the ground: and the repeated air
  Of sad Electra's poet had the power
  To save the Athenian walls from ruin bare.[12]

The poem has deeply puzzled commentators. Is it a joke? If so, is it in appallingly bad taste? It seems unlikely that it was indeed pinned to the door in Aldersgate Street as Charles and Rupert came on, though it may have functioned as a spoof between uncle and nephews, and one whose levity could have given some comfort to the young and probably frightened orphans. In the Trinity Manuscript it has been transcribed in what appears to be a child's hand. At the least, it seems an extraordinarily courteous way to address cavaliers. Another explanation may merit consideration. When a walled town or city was threatened with imminent siege, the standard military tactic was to clear buildings away from the outside of the walls, to deny the enemy shelter and create a free-fire zone. In Oxford, for example, once the parliamentary forces began to threaten it, the houses to the south of the city walls were demolished. Clearing Aldersgate Street, or at least the part where Milton lived, would have seemed a sensible procedure under the circumstances, and Milton may address those charged with this task to pass his house by.

In the event, the royalist forces, confronted at Turnham Green by the troops, the assembled trained bands and militias that parliament's London supporters could muster, checked and fell back. Aldersgate Street remained intact, and Milton continued seemingly withdrawn. The poem points to a renewed commitment to the arts of peace; this is the 'muses' bower', a phrase echoed by Phillips.[13] Its occupant writes poetry and no longer exercises his rhetorical skills in partisan controversy. The role of Cinna the Poet, however, poses problems for Milton's modern admirers, since it may seem like simple pusillanimity, for it would have been easy enough to volunteer for one of the London trained bands; Milton was still fit and fairly young, and, according to himself and his early biographers, a reasonably competent swordsman. But he knew nothing of practical soldiering. Moreover, the soldier's trade, at least before the apparent heroism and discipline of the troops of Fairfax and

Cromwell, was widely despised. The construction of the stereotype of the whoring, drunken, swearing cavalier 'dammee' was premised on a much older antipathy to the dissoluteness long attributed in popular belief to military men.[14] Milton's decision to work at his vocation and educate his orphaned nephews, rather than trail the puissant pike, is unremarkable.

It was probably over the winter of 1642–3 that Milton sought actively the return of his wife. Ideologically suspect visitors from London were subject to rough treatment in royalist strongholds alert to the danger from spies. Indeed, both sides attempted undercover intelligence-gathering, though the agents certainly risked summary execution. At least one parliamentary spy was hanged at Reading during the royalist occupation.[15] Edward Phillips, straining to recall events so long ago ('to the best of my remembrance'), describes how Milton sent 'a Foot-Messenger with a Letter, desiring her return', only for him to be 'dismissed with some sort of Contempt'.[16] Given the jitteriness of royalist garrisons, he did well to return otherwise unscathed. Milton's Commonplace Book contains a series of notes on divorce, the inception of which may be tentatively attributed to about this time.[17]

Winter campaigning through the civil wars was usually low key. With spring came a parliamentary offensive to drive the royalists from Reading. In October 1642 Christopher Milton's name appeared in the muster-role of those defending the town. The simplest explanation is that he had under-taken to fight alongside the royalist garrison when and if the forces of parliament appeared before their defences.[18] The siege began on 15 April under the direction of the earl of Essex, who offered generous terms, on which the royalists soon settled. On 27 April the town surrendered. The defenders were allowed to march out in good order, evidently without giving undertakings as to their future neutrality. The town was not sacked, and the non-combatant occupants were not maltreated. The terms allowed 'they who could leave the town might have free leave and passage safely to go to what place they would, with their goods, within the space of six weeks after the surrender'.[19] John Milton senior moved back to London, the city where he had accumulated the wealth on which he and at least his elder son had subsequently lived, joining the poet in Aldersgate Street. He lived with his elder son until his death in 1647. Christopher's wife, already heavily pregnant, also returned to London, where she gave birth to a son, John, baptized at St Clement Dane's on 29 June 1643. Parker's surmise, that she went to live with her widowed mother, seems eminently likely, given the relative smallness of John Milton junior's house.[20] Christopher spent the rest of the first civil war in the service of the royalist cause, as royalist commissioner for sequestrations with responsibility for three counties, squeezing resources out of supporters of parliament living within regions under the king's control.[21]

The civil war continued over the summer months, with success and failure evenly distributed between the sides. Milton's life records and the accounts of the early biographers are thin, though evidently his intellectual and creative energies had been diverted from the grand plans he had entertained to a more narrowly focused and personal concern. On 1 August 1643, carrying neither his name nor initials, there appeared *The Doctrine and Discipline of Divorce: Restor'd to the Good of Both Sexes, From the bondage of Canon Law, and other mistakes, to Christian freedom, guided by the Rule of Charity, Wherein also many places of Scripture, have recover'd their long-lost meaning: Seasonable to be now thought on in the Reformation intended.* The title discloses a larger context besides personal hurt. It is seasonable because the ordinance calling into being the Westminster Assembly of Divines had passed parliament in mid-June and on 1 July it met for the first time, to complete the work of Reformation along puritan lines. The terms 'doctrine' and 'discipline' may seem curious ones to foreground in a discussion about divorce, but both figure in the ordinance. The assembled divines, with a smaller cohort of lay members, are to 'confer and treat among themselves of such matters and things concerning the liturgy, discipline and government of the Church of England, or the vindicating and clearing of the doctrine of the same from all false aspersions and misconstructions as shall be proposed unto them by either or both of the . . . Houses of Parliament'.[22] The idiom, like Milton's, is one of restoration and the purging of accreted and erroneous interpretation. Milton's assumption that the Assembly would freely engage with non-members unsupported by parliament was without basis and may have contributed to his decision to address the second edition of the tract 'To the Parlament of *England* with the Assembly', which acknowledged where parliament had intended real power should abide.

Milton stresses on the title page the policy he adopts in the tract, a close adherence to premissing his argument on biblical texts. The Assembly's remit, in the ordinance, specifically charged it with finding solutions 'most agreeable to the Word of God', and, as Paul observes, 'because the scriptures were the one indisputable authority, this was recognized as the primary basis for all the Assembly's future debates'.[23] His decision to attempt to change canon laws on divorce through public debate may soon have seemed at best overly optimistic and at worst crassly naive. It reflected, however, the mood among puritan activists confident that they, not the bishops, were in control of the conduct of religious observance in England.

At an unknown point in the mid-1640s, between 1643 and 1645, Milton again turned to verse, and wrote two more sonnets.[24] Sonnet 9 is an untitled poem (*incipit* 'Lady that in the prime') addressed to an unidentified woman in 'the prime of earliest youth' who has dedicated herself to a life of service and contemplation. The young woman whose life Milton commends has been variously (and fancifully) identified with Mary Powell, Lady Alice Egerton,

Lady Margaret Ley, the mysterious Miss Davis, and one of the two Thomason daughters (Katharine or Grace), but none of these identifications convinces, and speculation is otiose. The use of the term 'lady' may imply a member of the gentry or aristocracy, and the comparison to the biblical figure of Ruth may imply a widow who had chosen to stay with her mother-in-law rather than seek a new husband; none of the candidates advanced by scholars was in that position. The sonnet is conventional in its sentiments, but such sentiments are not normally found in a sonnet. Milton is again stretching the genre to accommodate emotions that are unPetrarchan.

Sonnet 10, which in the Trinity Manuscript is entitled 'To the Lady Margaret Ley', is addressed to Margaret Hobson, who was, together with her husband John Hobson, a neighbour of Milton in Aldersgate Street. Edward Phillips records that 'this Lady being a Woman of great Wit and Ingenuity, had a particular Honour for him [Milton], as likewise her husband Captain Hobson'.[25] Milton's use of Margaret's maiden name in the manuscript may imply that he began the poem before she married on 30 December 1641, but seems more likely to have been used to emphasize her parentage; there is a sense in which the poem is complimenting the father rather than the daughter. Margaret, as the opening lines of the poem explain, was 'Daughter to that good Earl, once President | Of England's Council and her Treasury'. James Ley (1550–1629) was a lawyer who had served as Lord Chief Justice of the King's Bench, Lord Treasurer of England, and President of the Privy Council; in 1626 he had been created earl of Marlborough. Milton's sonnet eulogizes Marlborough as 'unstained with gold or fee' and as having been broken by 'the sad breaking of that Parliament'. Neither contention seems to have been true. Sir James Whitelock recorded that Marlborough was known as 'Vulpone' and had accepted loans from judges; Henry Sherfield declared him to be corrupt and recalled carrying to him a gift of gilt plate from a litigant.[26] Marlborough had already retired from public life to prepare himself to die, and there is no evidence that the news of the collapse of parliament in March 1629 had hastened the anticipated end. Milton is whitewashing Marlborough both to please his daughter and to serve a political purpose, that of suggesting that the wickedness of the king in proroguing the parliament had occasioned the death of a good, just man.

Milton's prose writings from 1643 to 1647 should be contextualized in the increasingly ferocious encounters within the Assembly and parliament, and in their relations with radical elements outside. Five principal groups are to be identified. At the outset, the dominant group within the former, with some support in parliament, was the moderate puritan faction led by divines like Edmund Calamy and Stephen Marshall, whose Smectymnuan efforts Milton had seconded. These would probably have settled for a reformed and primitive episcopacy conforming to some notion of apostolic practice, had that option been more purposefully pursued in previous years. Over the course of the Assembly, they would recognize the attractions of Presbyterian church government and advocate its adoption. Marshall, at least, remained open to dialogue with more radical puritans. The Presbyterian position was stiffened by the arrival of the four Scottish commissioners to the Assembly. Alexander Henderson and George Gillespie arrived in September 1643, followed by Robert Baillie and Samuel Rutherford in November.[27] The Scottish representatives brought a firm commitment to Presbyterian church government to be imposed by the state on all its citizens, with an associated suppression of heterodoxy and radical dissent. From 1644, though increasing the following year, London saw what Ann Hughes has called 'the presbyterian mobilization', a newly animated movement of militantly anti-tolerationist conviction Presbyterianism, inspired in part by the intransigence of the Scottish delegation.[28]

Many in parliament and some in the Assembly, particularly among its lay members, were suspicious of the more doctrinaire form of Presbyterianism, recognizing in the Scottish model and, indeed, in recent Scottish history the dangers of clerical interference in the affairs of state. These 'Erastians', as they were termed, manifested a range of opinion, but the group cohered around a refusal to allow ministers to dictate the terms of church settlement and an aversion to clerical attempts to claim a divine sanction for any proposed model; 'Beyond that, the Erastians were not deeply concerned about the form of churchmanship the Assembly might recommend, although they shared the Puritan prejudice against diocesan prelacy.'[29]

A small but influential cluster of divines within the Assembly favoured a much looser model of church government than the Presbyterians advocated. They looked instead to the non-separating congregationalism of the New England church, in which congregations were allowed considerable latitude of doctrine and discipline within a national church. The group included a small number of ministers returned from New England, though its leaders, among whom Philip Nye was the most prominent, had merely supported the North American initiative or had lived recently in the United Provinces. Though in the event the New England congregations had developed closely similar practices and indeed a degree of intolerance of dissent, the Assembly 'Independents' were drawn to a position that was essentially tolerant of a range of beliefs more radical than their own.

The separatist churches and sects were unrepresented in the Assembly and probably in parliament, at least in the early 1640s. They originated in groups that had operated either clandestinely or in exile through the later Tudor and early Stuart period. The largest group, the Particular Baptists, were as severely Calvinist in their soteriology as the staunchest Presbyterian, though their model for church government asserted the independence of each congregation, membership of which was to be confirmed through believers' baptism. Another influential group, the General Baptists, probably had at least five congregations in London in the early 1640s. They adopted a different soteriology, general redemption, premised on the assumption that salvation stood open to all, which approximated to Arminianism, though of course stripped of the sacerdotal and ceremonial elements that distinguished it in the Laudian church.

Unusually, in the case of the crisis within English puritanism in the 1640s history has been written by the defeated. The authors of the Presbyterian mobilization, pre-eminently Thomas Edwards and Robert Baillie, configure the ideological landscape as deeply fissured, with stark divisions between Presbyterians on one side and Independents and those more extreme groups for whom they advocated toleration on the other. In reality, interactions were more complex. Moderate Presbyterian divines like Stephen Marshall certainly retained a dialogue with moderate Independents like Philip Nye. Not only did they collaborate in various negotiations with the Scots but also were connected by a marriage alliance; Marshall's daughter Elizabeth married Nye's nephew, John Nye.[30] At the same time, Nye developed a multifaceted dialogue with leading separatists, which developed into a wide-ranging tolerationism. Again, Independents shared common ground with Erastians in their profound disquiet at the prospect of the establishment of a Presbyterian national church on the Scottish model.

Milton fits uneasily into this landscape. Intellectually, he was probably closest to the Erastians. Their most learned representative in the Assembly and the Commons was John Selden, polyglot, polymath, jurist, and friend of poets, who in his life and work in some respects could be seen a sort of role model for Milton, who was over twenty years his junior. *Areopagitica*, in its rhetoric at least, certainly reflects an Erastian commitment to the supremacy of the state over the church. Milton probably retained friendly relations with the Smectymnuans, though in terms of their views on the sectaries they had been drifting apart since *The Reason of Church-government*. No Smectymnuan ever attacked Milton by name in print or, so far as we know, in the pulpit, nor did he attack them. In terms of church government, by 1643 Milton was probably close to the Assembly Independents with their posture of irenic toleration for more radical groups. Yet *The Doctrine and Discipline of Divorce* does mark him as a heterodox thinker of growing confidence. As we shall see, by the mid-decade he probably shared a lot of common ground with radical sectaries, not only in the imagination and strictures of Presbyterian heresiographers but also in terms of heretical beliefs to which he and they subscribed.

The first divorce tract in the circumstances of its production gives every indication of being rooted in harsh personal experience, though, since it is a carefully crafted argument, directed at an austerely puritanical readership in parliament and the Assembly, it should not be regarded as a window into Milton's own sexuality or his relationship with Mary. Milton fashions a version of himself which is wholly to his polemical purpose. He appears severely orthodox in other aspects of belief, gratuitously dismissing '*Anabaptism, Famelism, Antinomianism*, and other *fanatick* dreams' and anticipating a reform of sexual morality when 'fornication shall be austerely censur'd, adultery punisht'.[31] Milton's larger argument requires him to subordinate sexuality to companionship as the basis for marriage, and he has a clear interest in fending off the suggestion that liberated divorce legislation would open up the marriage bond in ways that favoured the licentious. Unsurprisingly, then, the sexual act is demeaningly represented:

> How vain therefore is it, and how preposterous in the Canon Law to have made such carefull provision against the impediment of carnall performance, and to have had no care about the unconversing inability of minde, so defective to the purest and most sacred end of matrimony: and that the vessell of voluptuous enjoyment must be made good to him that has tak'n it upon trust without any caution, when as the minde from whence must flow the acts of peace and love, a far more precious mixture then the quintessence of an excrement, though it be found never so deficient and unable to performe the best duty of mariage in a cheerfull and agreeable conversation, shall be thought good anough, how ever flat & melancholious it be, and must serve though to the eternall disturbance and languishing of him that complains him. Yet wisdom and charity waighing Gods own institution, would think that the pining of a sad spirit wedded to lonelines should deserve to be free'd, aswell as the impatience of a sensuall desire so providently reliev'd.[32]

Rather than common law, canon law, restated in the canons of 1604,[33] governed divorce in England, and allowed for divorce with the option of marrying again only on the grounds of want of capacity and want of true consent. The former could be precontract (a previous marriage, as in Henry VIII and Anne of Cleves, who had a precontract *per verba de praesenti*—a verbally declared marriage that would be binding in common law—with François de Lorraine), consanguinity, affinity (the fact that Henry had had intercourse with Mary Boleyn rendered void his marriage to her sister), and impotence or invincible frigidity at the time of marriage. The latter included duress, insanity, error, or being too young. Divorce *a mensa et thoro*, on the other hand, did not allow remarriage, but could be granted for adultery, cruelty, sodomy, heresy, or fear of future injury. This all came under strain in 1548, when the marquess of Northampton divorced his wife for adultery but then petitioned to remarry. Cranmer equivocated, so the marquess went ahead with the ceremony, which was ratified both by the Court of Delegates and by act of parliament. The precedent was followed but then overruled in 1572 (Sir John Stawell's case), which in effect restored the old rules (no divorce *a vinculo matrimonii* for adultery).

There is one more consideration. The purpose of the means by which Henry divorced Katherine and Anne was to bastardize their children, but when Mary and Elizabeth became queens, they both restored their legitimacy by act of parliament. That meant (as did the case of the marquess of Northampton) that parliament could overrule the ecclesiastical courts in their applications of the rules. In 1670, parliament ruled that Lord Roos (divorced for adultery) could remarry, and that opened the door for private divorce bills in parliament. Cranmer had wanted to introduce divorce for adultery and cruelty, but he did not manage it, and legislation had to wait for centuries. In effect, it was almost impossible for all but a few of the very rich to achieve a full divorce with permission to remarry. There was a handful in the early Elizabethan period, but then none until after 1670.

Milton's advocacy of reconsideration of divorce legislation was particularly timely in that the ecclesiastical courts 'ceased to function in the early 1640s', and in due course, in 1646, 'church control over marriage was abolished, authority being shifted in theory to secular authorities'.[34] Since canon law had provided for at least partial redress in the case of sexual incapacity or immorality, Milton argues that, because affectionate interaction is more important than mere copulation, provision should be made, too, for emotional incompatibilities. Of course, this argument leaves him with a clear agenda of writing down sexuality and writing up companionableness within marriage. Hence he writes dismissively of 'the quintessence of an excrement', a curious but resonant phrase, or his more straightforward indictment of 'those whose grosse and vulgar apprehensions conceit but low of matrimoniall purposes, and in the work of male and female think they have all'.[35]

Yet Milton does not deny the role of sexuality in marriage. The best marriages may indeed offer a companionable experience, but the worst still provide the opportunity for physical gratification. Even his grossest images carry an acknowledgement of carnal imperatives. When he ponders the status of 'the offspring of a former ill-twisted wedlock, begott'n only out of a bestial necessitie', he nevertheless recognizes at least male desire as an unavoidable impulse.[36] He recognizes the strength of that longing in his reflection that the fugitive from a bad marriage may 'piece up his lost contentment by visiting the Stews, or stepping to his neighbours bed . . . or els by suffering his usefull life to wast away and be lost under a secret affliction of an unconscionable size to humane strength'.[37] Milton writes as a youngish man tortured by a year of unlooked-for celibacy after a brief honeymoon of sexual experience.

The Doctrine and Discipline is Milton's first essay in controversial theology. Following the practice of the Assembly, he grounds his argument in a thorough exegesis of particular biblical texts. In a debate on divorce in the seventeenth century, that would anyway have been the inevitable starting point for discussion. The key texts are from the gospel of Matthew, where Jesus warns 'whosoever shall put away his wife, save for the cause of fornication, causeth her to commit adultery: and whosoever shall marry her that is divorced committeth adultery' (5: 32), and 'Whosoever shall put away his wife, except it be for fornication, and shall marry another, committeth adultery: and whoso marrieth her which is put away doth commit adultery' (19: 9). He who would argue for divorce on the grounds of emotional or intellectual incompatibility, with the permission for remarriage, plainly has an uphill struggle in the light of these texts.

Milton's response gives good earnest of his exegetical skills, which are both subtle and bold. He has to argue that Jesus's words here, as in some other places, should not be interpreted literally. Jesus speaks in a polemical context, to rebuff the Pharisees, 'who came unto him, tempting him'.[38] Moreover, 'this [Jesus's prohibition of divorce and remarriage] can be no new command, for the gospel enjoyns no new morality, save only the infinit enlargement of charity, which in this respect is call'd the *new Commandement* by St. *John*; as being the accomplishment of every command.'[39] So Jesus's mission is not to add to the prohibitions of the Mosaic code and other Old Testament laws, but to complete and interpret those rules in accordance with the charity of his mission. With this established, Milton can review the origins in Genesis of the institution of marriage, where it functions not only as the framework for reproduction ('be fruitful and multiply'[40]), but also as a cure for Adam's lonely isolation.[41] In face of the apparent plain-speaking of Jesus, Milton assembles a coherent argument. If God made Eve for Adam to mitigate the suffering of his single status, and if Jesus's mission is in charity to ease the severity of the Old Testament laws, then the strictures found in Matthew's gospel cannot be interpreted literally. As he concludes his treatise, echoing the words of Paul, 'God the Son hath put all other things under his own feet; but his Commandments he hath left all under the feet of charity.'[42]

Neither parliament nor the Assembly responded to the pamphlet, though it seemed rapidly to find a readership. It was the first of his publications to go into a second edition, and by June 1645 the tract, on his own account, had been '*twice printed, twice bought up*';[43] it was reprinted twice more in 1645, making it easily the most successful in terms of readership of his early prose works.

That success may have owed something to its notoriety. From late 1643 to 1646 and a little beyond Milton's writings on divorce were implacably hounded by the enemies of toleration, who characterized them as examples of the depravity permitted by the slackness encouraged by Independency. In the epistle to parliament with which he prefaced *The Judgement of Martin Bucer*, published in July 1644, he lamented '*that some of the Clergie began to inveigh and exclaim on what I was credibly inform'd they had not read*'.[44] The following month that same parliament was addressed by Herbert Palmer, a regular preacher on their fast-days, a clerical member of the Assembly, recently appointed master of Queens' College, Cambridge, and an influential advocate of a Presbyterian church settlement.[45] The sermon, the printed version of which runs to some sixty-six densely printed pages, urges action 'against the ungodly Toleration pleaded for under pretence of LIBERTY of CONSCIENCE'.[46] His attack on Milton is sandwiched between denunciations of refusals to take oaths and refusals to bear arms for parliament:

If any plead Conscience for the Lawfulnesse of *Polygamy*; (or for divorce for other causes then Christ and His Apostles mention; Of which a *wicked booke* is abroad and *uncensured*, though *deserving to be burnt*, whose *Author* hath been so *impudent* as to *set his Name* to it, and *dedicate it to your selves*,) or for Liberty to *marry incestuously*, will you grant a *Toleration* for all *this*?[47]

Palmer certainly seems to have seen the book, and in its revised second edition, and may even have read at least the epistle, at the end of which Milton placed his name; the first edition had been anonymous.[48]

Within a fortnight, the Stationers' Company presented a petition to parliament, which elicited as a response the decision 'to inquire out the Authors, Printers, and Publishers, of the Pamphlet against the Immortality of the Soul, and concerning Divorce'.[49] The first edition of *The Doctrine and Disciple* did have the initials and address of its printers; the second had no names or initials of printers or booksellers. Milton finds himself in interesting company. *Mans Mortallitie* by R. O. (almost certainly Richard Overton, the future Leveller) carried an Amsterdam imprint and promulgated the heresy, to be adopted by Milton at some point, that the soul dies and is resurrected with the body. In September, the lawyer and veteran puritan activist, William Prynne, though now an Erastian, launched a sustained attack on the tolerationism of Independency. Again he linked the divorce and the mortalist tracts, listing them alongside anabaptist and antinomian opinions, and linking them with the third member of what becomes a hateful trinity of books for burning, that 'late dangerous *Licentious Booke*' by Roger Williams, *The Bloudy Tenent of Persecution for cause of Conscience* (London, 1644).[50]

In November 1644, Palmer's sermon was printed, and the only book-length engagement with *The Doctrine and Discipline* appeared, the anonymous *Answer to a Book, Intituled, The Doctrine and Discipline of Divorce, or, A Plea for Ladies and Gentlewomen, and all other Maried Women against Divorce*. Milton could scarcely have encountered a less congenial opponent. The answerer is as openly hostile as other respondents to his initiative. While conceding it is 'sugred over with a little neat language', he calls *The Doctrine and Discipline* 'so immeritous and undeserving, so contrary to all humane learning, yea, truth and common experience it self, that all that reade it must needs count it worthie to be burnt by the Hangman'.[51] Plainly, he is not an accomplished theologian. Milton later claims to have discovered he is a serving man turned solicitor,[52] and he obviously has more appetite for the legal niceties and social consequences of divorce than for the exegetical argument. Milton's delicate attempts at teasing out a non-literal interpretation for Christ's pronouncement on divorce are bluntly dismissed: 'this your glosse is not only intolerable abuse of Scripture, but smels very strongly of little lesse then blasphemie against Christ himself.' With a similarly robust simplicity, he refutes the claim that the primary reason for creating Eve was not for reproduction but for companionship, 'for then it would have been more pleasant and beneficiall to *Adam* to have had another man created, then a woman'.[53] (The charge of sexism, so often laid at Milton, should perhaps be contextualized by reference to writers like the answerer.)

While such arguments and assertions reflect an intellectual clumsiness and an inability to engage at the right theoretical level, he becomes more persuasive when he turns to the social consequences of Milton's proposals, under which a man 'may unchristianly thrust his Wife out of dores with a bare Bill of Divorce in her hand to seek her living'. Social disintegration would follow: 'who sees not, how many thousands of lustfull and libidinous men would be parting from their Wives every week and marrying others: and upon this, who should keep the children of these divorces which somtimes they would leave in their Wives bellies?'[54] Here are issues which resonated with an early modern readership. Indeed, when the ecclesiastical courts still functioned, episcopal and archidiaconal visitation enquiries 'always included an item asking the churchwardens for the names of married couples...who were living separately', and 'Clearly, what bothered the churchwardens was that the burden of maintenance in...cases of separation fell on the parish.'[55] Milton had no arguments to silence anxiety about such unlooked for impositions on the respectable and propertied.

By the end of 1644, mere vituperation had turned into a much more serious threat. Parliament had instructed the Stationers' Company to seek out information relating to a recent 'libel', currently unidentified, that plainly had exercised them. The stationers' officers evidently failed, claiming that the letterpress used was too common to allow the identification of the printer. But they covered their shortcoming by once more raising the issue of 'frequent Printing of scandalous Books by divers', naming as examples Hezekiah Woodward and Milton.[56] Once more, he is made to keep interesting company. Woodward, like himself a vehement anti-prelatical activist, was also an educationalist and friend of Samuel Hartlib.[57] But he, too, had fallen foul of the Presbyterian mobilization in his advocacy of toleration, and, like Milton, he was no friend of William Prynne, whom he had made his target in his *Inquiries into the Causes of our Miseries* (London, 1644), part of which had been seized while in the press.[58]

Events proved how imperfect was the Presbyterians' seeming control of parliament. Woodward and Milton were to be brought 'before the Judges' under arrest by the Gentleman Usher, and to be interrogated in the presence of the Stationers' representatives. However, Woodward was merely released on bail. There is no record of any further action against Milton, though Cyriack Skinner, who probably erroneously attributes the action to the prompting of the Assembly, suggests he was arraigned before the House of Lords and released: 'that house, whether approving the Doctrin, or not favoring his Accusers, soon dismiss'd him.'[59] The latter speculation seems the likelier, since there is no evidence of any of the Lords still sitting espousing the cause of divorce reform, and ample evidence of a growing parliamentary concern about the political encroachments of Presbyterianism.

The polemical strategy of the Presbyterian mobilization and its broad spectrum of support was by then well established. It listed examples of extravagantly heterodox opinions and practices and attributed their currency to the indulgence of Independent tolerationism. The defining genre of the movement was heresiography, and Milton figured in the most developed and influential (as did Williams and R. O., by now his apparent associates). Among the most influential was Ephraim Pagitt's *Heresiography: or, A description of the Heretickes and Sectaries of these latter times* (London, May, 1645), although the aged Pagitt himself was scarcely a Presbyterian, but rather a strict Calvinist whose work was used somewhat opportunistically. The book serves as a sort of field guide to extravagant opinion. It proved immensely popular, and was reprinted numerous times over the late 1640s, the 1650s, and into the 1660s, and spawned a shorter version, apparently edited down by another hand, which also reproduces Pagitt's strictures on Milton.[60] He figures in the epistle dedicatory to the first edition, in close proximity to R. O., as the author of 'a tractate of divorce in which the bonds are let loose to inordinate lust'.[61]

Towards the end of 1645, Robert Baillie, looking to steel Presbyterians in the Assembly and the City, published his scholarly *A Dissuasive from the Errours of the Time*, in which he carefully drew on a wide range of Independent and sectary texts to chart a complex history, linking the current problems with Brownist separatism, tracing the movement to Amsterdam and New England, and showing, to his own satisfaction at least, Independency to be as obnoxious as the most outrageous tub-preaching. His comments on Milton disclosed an uncertainty about how exactly he fitted into the contemporary landscape: 'I doe not know certainely whither this man professeth *Independency*.' However, he demonstrates some continuities, unacknowledged by Milton himself, between his doctrine of divorce and that of 'men of renown among the *New-English Independents*'.[62]

The most sustained heresiography was Thomas Edwards's *Gangraena: or A Catalogue and Discovery of many of the Errours, Heresies, Blasphemies and pernicious Practices of the Sectaries of this time*, published in London in three very substantial sections in February, May, and December 1646. Edwards was 'an extreme figure' in 'the struggle for a Presbyterian religious and political settlement... centred on the city of London in alliance with the Scots and elements in parliament'. Edwards himself was outside the charmed circle around men like Marshall, never preaching a fast sermon, joining the Assembly, or securing a decent living, but, in Hughes's words, 'The summer of 1644 marked Edwards out as a man whose time had come'.[63] Though he was early into the field, with *Antapologia*, his substantial attack on *The Apologetically Narration*, *Gangraena* was the text that secured his place among Presbyterian writers most hated by Independents and sectaries. Hughes has best analysed his treatment of Milton, concluding, in its selectivity and its refusal to engage with the subtleties of his argument, 'This is not a misleading account... but a stark summary of its most obvious and controversial position.'[64] But Milton's argument holds no interest for Edwards, beyond its exemplary status as evidence that toleration breeds immorality. He confirms the point by associating Milton with a lacemaker, Mrs Attaway, a mildly notorious woman preacher, who, according to Edwards's source, would 'look more into' the arguments of *The Doctrine and Discipline* to support her intention 'in running away with another womans husband'.[65]

Milton described his bewilderment at the treatment he received in 'Sonnet 12. On the Detraction which followed upon my Writing Certain Treatises', where his divorce writings occasion an immediate and unexpected response: 'I did but prompt the age to quit their clogs | By the known rules of ancient liberty, | When *straight* a barbarous noise environs me.'[66] Milton's views probably find fullest expression in 'On the new forcers of conscience', which was written at an unknown date in 1646 or early 1647. The poem is an attack on Presbyterianism and Presbyterians. The freedom of conscience given by Christ is being overridden by 'a classic hierarchy'. The phrase alludes to the 'classis' or presbytery which sat as an ecclesiastical court, and the hierarchy of courts under the Presbyterian system.[67] At the outset of the poem Milton deploys a pun on lord/Laud, and at the conclusion he slams home his point with more wordplay: 'New *Presbyter* is but old *Priest* writ large' glances at Laud the 'old priest', but also draws on the etymology of the words ('priest' is a contracted form of Latin *presbyter*) to show that Laudianism and Presbyterianism amount to much the same thing, in that both deny liberty of conscience. The poem is twenty lines long, but is nonetheless a sonnet, of the type known in Italian as a 'tailed sonnet' (*sonnetto caudato*); each tail (*coda*) consists of a half line followed by a couplet, and Milton's poem has two tails. The structure reflects contemporary Italian practice rather than English practice; Milton's subject was English and Scottish, but the form in which he expresses it is Italian, an oblique assertion of the high culture his detractors did not share.

Whatever pain these poems, unpublished for many years, disclose, Milton regained the offensive. For the first time in his polemical career, he demonstrated (as others attacked in the Presbyterian mobilization also did) that he was indeed pugnacious, brave, and resourceful, though his analysis of those ranged against him sometimes lacks the clarity, for example, of Roger Williams.

Whereas the first edition of *The Doctrine and Discipline* appeared directed at the Assembly, the second, published in February 1644, primarily addressed secular authority, with a new and substantial epistle '*To the* PARLIAMENT OF ENGLAND, with the ASSEMBLY', thus recognizing that, while a constructive engagement with the latter now seemed unlikely, parliament was emerging as much more equivocal in its support for the emerging, Scottish-led Presbyterian agenda.[68] The text is much altered, far more so than any other work by Milton to go into a plurality of lifetime editions. Overwhelmingly, he supplemented what he had written, adding little to the argument but much to its rhetorical embellishment. In the first edition Milton had experimented with a new and more austere style, using few of those flamboyant and extensive similes and metaphors which had distinguished his anti-prelatical pamphlets from other contributions to the Smectymnuan controversy. That was a prose voice that appeals, in a sober, scholarly discourse, to sober and scholarly divines. In contrast, the material he added to the second edition is so heavy with imagery that its plain sense is sometimes quite hard to follow.[69] Though the life records are unhelpful for the period between the editions, there were evidently more pulpit attacks than had survived, since Milton's additional epigraph on the title page discloses his incipient frustration with the shallow engagement the first edition had promoted: 'Prov.18.13. *He that answereth a matter before he heareth it, it is a folly and a shame unto him.*' In the second edition he called upon his creativity to carry arguments hitherto ignored when coolly advanced.

The title page epigraph to his next divorce tract, *The Judgement of Martin Bucer, Concerning Divorce* (London, August, 1644), shows similar tetchiness with clerical opposition: 'John 3. 10. *Art thou a teacher of Israel, and know'st not these things?*' Though the impulse to continue the campaign came mainly in response to the attacks of divines, Milton's estrangement from the Assembly as an appropriate audience is marked by its omission from the dedication, which is wholly 'To the PARLAMENT'.[70] Milton, evidently, has been researching more widely since his attempt to argue from biblical texts alone, and he has found in Martin Bucer (1491–1551) a decidedly useful precursor. He could scarcely have done better. Bucer was an early Protestant reformer and supporter of Luther, who had been driven from Strasbourg to a prosperous exile, under the protection of Edward VI, as a Cambridge professor. He had suffered a posthumous martyrdom of sorts when in the reign of Mary I his corpse was exhumed and burned. For Milton, his chief attraction was his respectability, as associate of Luther, as protégé of an iconic English Protestant king, and as opponent of anabaptists. The last point rendered him paritcularly close in terms of religious ideology to Milton's own immediate adversaries. Milton translated a section of his *De Regno Christi*, published posthumously in Basel in 1557. Milton prefaces the translation with 'Testimonies of the high approbation Which learned men have given of *Martin Bucer*', of course made up of worthies with impeccable mainstream Protestant credentials, among them Calvin, Sir John Cheke, Beza, and John Foxe. To Bucer, he added the equally venerable figure of Paul Fagius, who died in 1549 while holding the readership in Hebrew at the University of Cambridge, and whose views on divorce were also broadly conformant with Milton's own. The strategy was crude but difficult to counter; indeed, so difficult that no one tried. It laid the axe at the root of Presbyterian arguments that equated all heteroxy with those outside the pale of religious and indeed social respectability, and it demonstrated the diversity of Protestant belief. As he concludes his epistle to parliament, his detractors '*must else put in the fame of* Bucer *and of* Fagius, *as my accomplices and confederates into the same in same endightment* [as himself]... *they must attaint with new attaintures which no Protestant ever before aspers't them with*'.[71]

Colasterion: A Reply to a Nameles Answer against The Doctrine and Discipline of Divorce (London, March, 1645) played a similar game though using a radically different tactic to deconstruct the Presbyterian dichotomy of tolerable and intolerable doctrines. Here Milton demonstrated his social and cultural affinities with men like Marshall and Calamy while postulating a view of the footsoldiers of the Presbyterian mobilization which set them at a social and cultural disadvantage. Indeed, Milton may have been disappointed that the author of *An Answer to the Doctrine and Discipline of Divorce* was unequal to engagement with the theological arguments. But in other respects, his modest attainments made him a vulnerable target. An obtrusive disingenuousness surrounds Milton's claim that he 'Gladly' received the intended refutation, and that he 'very attentively compos'd' himself to read, 'hoping that som good man had voutsaft the pains to instruct mee better, then I could yet learn out of all the volumes which for this purpos I had visited'.[72]

Once more, Milton's polemic is simple and coherent. He produced within the text a version of himself as a scholarly, gentlemanly searcher after truth, speaking to his social equals and fellow intellectuals about a parvenu who has overreached himself in assailing one of his superiors. Milton has discovered, or purports to have discovered, that he was 'an actual Serving-man' who had improved his personal circumstances by becoming some kind of junior law-agent, 'if any can hold laughter'.[73] Numerous jokes about the serving-man-turned-solicitor permeate the tract, building a community of values between the author and his target readers as he speaks as a gentleman to gentlemen about their social inferior. In the process, Milton subverts the Presbyterian stratagem of associating Independents, in their tolerationist stance, with low-class sectaries. Thus, for example, he has it that his adversary 'goes on to untruss my Arguments, imagining them his maisters points'; 'hee windes up his Text with much doubt and trepidation; for it may bee his trenchers were not scrap't.'[74] Milton makes a double thrust. He suggests that the Presbyterian mobilization has drawn on supporters who are socially inferior to those whom they attack, and he claims his own status both socially and intellectually, speaking to the elite theologians in the Assembly and the propertied men sitting in parliament. It also gives him a facile escape from the damaging objections to the social consequences of divorce, particularly for the children of the union, including those conceived but not born before separation; evidently, it is 'good news for Chamber-maids, to hear a Serving-man grown so provident for great bellies'.[75]

Milton's remaining contribution to his divorce campaign appeared, like *Colasterion*, in early March, 1645: *Tetrachordon: Expositions upon The foure chief places in Scripture, which treat of Mariage, or nullities in Mariage*. With hindsight, it is the book he should have written in the first place, instead of rushing somewhat naively into print with the first edition of *The Doctrine and Discipline*. Stylistically, it resembles that first edition in terms of its spare functionalism and its relatively low incidence of vivid imagery. It is what it seems: a highly technical exercise in biblical exegesis. Here, however, he worked much more patiently through the pertinent proof texts. Moreover, adopting the policy developed in *The Judgement of Martin Bucer*, Milton carefully cites earlier divines who broadly concur with his position. One section works through those 'among the fathers' who 'have interpreted the words of Christ concerning divorce, as is heer interpreted', together with 'what the civil law of Christian Emperors in the primitive Church determin'd', before turning to the compliant witness of 'reformed Divines', 'the famousest' of whom 'have taught according to the assertion of this booke'.[76] Thereafter, Milton fell silent on the subject of divorce. Perhaps, in the absence of a worthy adversary, there was no more to be said; perhaps, because his wife had returned from Oxford and was living with him, further comment would have been hurtful to her and damaging to the renewed relationship.

Tetrachordon was addressed to parliament, despite being written in an idiom better suited to learned divines like those currently sitting in the Assembly. Milton, by then, can have expected little to come from those deliberations, though he retained a conviction in the value of addressing parliament somewhat longer than other radicals among whose ranks he should now be numbered. Midway through the sequence of divorce tracts, in November 1644, he had addressed to them what became in the liberal academic tradition and more widely his most esteemed prose work, *Areopagitica; A Speech of Mr. John Milton For the Liberty of Unlicenc'd Printing, To the Parlament of England*. Of course, Milton was not free literally to address a speech to parliament (though, as we have seen, shortly later he would be called to give an account of his recent publications). Only members of parliament could freely address it, and even the reporting and circulation of the speeches they made, technically, were constrained by parliamentary privilege. Parliament was not a public sphere. But Milton, while giving a priority to a parliamentary readership, worked to establish that, in the relative freedom currently enjoyed by the press, something akin to the openness of Periclean Athens had been allowed to develop in the English metropolis.

Despite the confident posture, Milton remained outside the significant institutions of decision-making and power. But the tract is not as maverick as it may seem, since it is driven by two strong currents of public sentiment. It is fiercely anti-Catholic at a time when opposition to popery was going through one of those periodical highs that blight English political life through the seventeenth century and beyond. Under the Personal Rule of Charles I, active persecution of Catholics, including the priesthood, had almost ceased. However, the puritan critique of that regime, growing in intensity through the 1640s, at once attacked that laxness and sought to associate the ceremonialism of William Laud and of Charles himself with Catholic devotionalism. Reports of the massacres occasioned by the Irish uprising of 1641 massively increased the hostility. Milton himself seems to have been sufficiently moved by the plight of Irish Protestants to have made in June 1642 a substantial donation of £4 for their relief.[77] In the early 1640s persecution of Catholics returned with a renewed zeal. Between 1641 and 1646 twenty-four Catholic priests were executed, sometimes with a ferocious brutality. In Dorchester, a puritan stronghold, in 1642 the crowd kicked around as though it were a football the head of a dismembered priest. In London in the months before the civil war started, assaults on Catholics and their property rapidly intensified: 'Mobs attacked worshippers at mass in the queen's chapel and the Lord Mayor of London was forced to provide guards for the Catholic embassies to protect them against mob attack.'[78] In his strident assertion that the freedom for which he argues should not be extended to Catholics ('I mean not tolerated Popery' that 'should be extirpat'[79]) Milton expresses the uncompromising hostility of most of those who lived around him to a faith community to whom they attributed atrocities which placed them beyond the reach of mercy or forgiveness, let alone toleration. To the 1670s, Milton's expressed perspective on Catholicism remained inimical and often vengeful. In *Areopagitica* that spirit is embodied in the long and improbable history of licensing that lays its origins at the doors of the Catholic Counter-Reformation.

The second current with which Milton aligned himself was a minority one, though in time it was to become dominant, or at least profoundly influential: tolerationism. After the Independents in the Assembly had shown their hand in *The Apologeticall Narration*, a dialogue developed between them and more radical thinkers which probably proved the stimulus for the publication in 1644 of several landmark tracts on widening the range of opinion that should be tolerated within Protestant England. The broadest toleration was advocated by Roger Williams, the founder of Rhode Island, a colony that entertained the settlement of those excluded by the non-separating congregationalists who ran Massachusetts. Milton's tract has often been compared, to its disadvantage, with Williams's *The Bloudy Tenent of Persecution* (London, 1644).[80] Williams's arguments, however, place human history against a vision of the imminent onset of the final days, nor had he an engagement with the complexities of English ecclesiastical politics. He had returned home two months before *Areopagitica* appeared. John Goodwin's *Theomachia, or, The grand imprudence of men running the hazard of fighting against God in suppressing any way, doctrine, or practice concerning which they know not certainly whether it be from God or no* (London, 1644) was based on sermons preached to his Coleman Street congregation. Like Milton's, his concerns were essentially tactical and engaged with the developing crisis. He argues that uncertainties about doctrine and its divine sanction require a spirit of of open-minded enquiry among a wide spectrum of Protestant belief 'till we have security upon security, conditions as cleer as the noon-day, that they [erroneous doctrinal and disciplinary positions] are counterfeits and pretenders only'.[81]

Milton's aims are more modest still. To him, no pulpit was open, nor had he actual access to parliament or the Assembly; the press was crucial to his immediate campaign for divorce reform and to his conception of a new political order, in which the eloquent and right-minded, though unelected, could sway decision-making. To that end, he targeted the recent reintroduction through the licensing order of June 1643 of the requirement that books be examined by appointed officers before publication. To secure the success of his argument he made huge concessions to the mainstream puritans in parliament: of course, after publication, books may be burnt and authors prosecuted.[82] For recent critics, the disparities between the grandness of the rhetoric, in its enthusiastic celebration of the triumphs of truth over falsehood, and the limitations of the toleration the tract seeks have posed major interpretative problems. They reflect, in our view, the curious moment to which the pamphlet belongs. Already the Presbyterian backlash had shown itself, but Milton still believed he was in dialogue with moderate, rational, scholarly men like Calamy and Marshall, his erstwhile comrades. By 1646, once Edwards and the other heresiographers had done their worst, he can have entertained no such misconceptions.

Shifting fortunes of war had already reached deeply into Milton's personal circumstances, as the fall of Reading to the forces of parliament returned his father to London to live with him, separated his sister-in-law from Christopher, and placed the latter in effect on active service in the interest of the king. At some point in 1645 Mary Powell returned to London. From 29 January to 22 March a truce was observed between the warring sides to allow peace negotiations to be held at Uxbridge. Possibly, she took advantage of that lull to venture across the lines and back to the capital. Alternatively, her return may have occurred in the summer of 1645, when the temporary raising of the siege once more allowed communications. Skinner places the dates of the reconciliation rather later than Edward Phillips, after the fall of Oxford in late June 1646, though here he must err, since Anne, the first child of John and Mary, was born five weeks later, on 29 July of that year. Edward Phillips placed the reunion 'within a year' of the birth.[83]

In Skinner's narrative, Mary returned to Milton because she had no alternative. Phillips offers a much fuller account:

there fell out a passage, which though it altered not the whole Course he was going to Steer, yet it put a stop or rather an end to a grand Affair, which was more than probably thought to be then in agitation: It was indeed a design of Marrying one of Dr. *Davis's* Daughters, a very Handsome and Witty Gentlewoman, but averse, as it is said, to his Motion; however, the Intelligence hereof, and the then declining State of the King's Cause, and consequently of the Circumstances of Justice *Powell's* family, caused them to set all Engines on Work, to restore the late Married Woman to the Station wherein they a little before had planted her; at last this device was pitch'd upon. There dwelt in the Lane of St. *Martins Le Grand*, which was hard by, a Relation of our Author's, one *Blackborough*, whom it was known he often visited, and upon this occasion the visits were the more narrowly observ'd, and possibly there might be a Combination between both Parties; the Friends on both sides concentring in the same action though on different behalfs. One time above the rest, he making his usual visit, the Wife was ready in another Room, and on a sudden he was surprised to see one whom he thought to have never seen more, making Submission and begging Pardon on her Knees before him; he might probably at first make some shew of aversion and rejection; but partly his own generous nature, more inclinable to Reconciliation than to perseverance in Anger and Revenge; and partly the strong intercession of Friends on both sides, soon brought him to an Act of Oblivion, and a firm League of Peace for the future; and it was at length concluded, That she should remain at a Friends house, till such time as he was settled in his New house at *Barbican*, and all things for her reception were in order; the place agreed on for her present abode, was the Widow *Webber's* house in St. *Clement's* Churchyard, whose Second Daughter had been Married to the other Brother many years before.[84]

Phillips was only about 14 at the time, nor does he claim to have been a witness to the reconciliation. Moreover, this is not artless writing, despite the occasional syntactical clumsiness. The account seems in part at least mediated by literary recollections; Mary/Eve seeks the forgiveness of Milton/Adam in the manner of *Paradise Lost*, Book X. The playful allusion to the Restoration settlement and its Act of Oblivion serves his larger argument, that Milton was a reluctant servant of the Commonwealth. Furthermore, the final stages of the Presbyterian assault

28. Thomas Fairfax,
third Lord Fairfax of
Cameron, by William
Marshall, after Edward
Bower (1647).

on Milton saw him traduced as a brutal divorcer, cudgelling or casting aside his wife.[85] Phillips's account carefully negates that image.

Yet the wealth of circumstantial detail gives the narrative some plausibility. The Blackborough family were indeed Milton's kin, well located to act as go-betweens, though who the London friends of the Powells were defies even speculation. Placing Mary with the widow Webber made sense; Christopher's wife, who had returned to London as her husband took to the road in support of the king's cause, was probably living there already, another abandoned royalist perhaps sympathetic to Mary's own perspective on events. 'Dr. Davis' has not been identified, though the potential scandal Phillips describes offers a fascinating and surprising insight into his uncle. Milton presumably was seeking a sexual liaison that could not possibly have been within wedlock as long as Mary lived. Customary concubinage was rare among the propertied classes, not least because to the problems it posed in terms of the protection and inheritance of wealth,[86] and in any case the heresiographers would soon have ferreted out the scandal. Miss Davis probably had a lucky escape, whatever part the incident played in Mary's return.

The Cheife places in the
Citie obserued by severall letters

29. Anon., *Oxforde as it now lyeth* (n.p., 1644).

Her final months around and perhaps in Oxford cannot have been pleasant. In 1643 an epidemic of typhus swept the city, followed in 1644 and 1645 by
more typhus, together with plague and smallpox. The plight of the area
became desperate. There were serious food shortages, and loans were levied
from the better off to pay the garrison and keep it from mutiny. Richard
Powell can scarcely have escaped such impositions. Moreover, as parliament's
grip on the south midlands tightened, outlying strongholds, probably including Forest Hill, were abandoned. By the time the king quit Oxford and the
siege finally ended Powell had moved within the city itself.[87] On 27 June 1646,
Powell secured from Fairfax, who had taken the city, a pass allowing him to
leave. In a move that belies the usual assumptions about hostility between
Milton and his father-in-law, he departed with his wife and at least five of
their children to live with Milton in London. His estate was utterly devastated. Much of the equity of the gentry class was in stands of timber, which in

turn was in great demand through the mid-1640s, not least for work of reconstruction.[88] Even before Oxford fell, Powell shared the fate of many other royalist squires. In mid-June his household goods were sold by the parliamentary sequestrators of Oxfordshire. His timber, worth £400, was confiscated and granted to the town of Banbury, just north of Oxford, for long a puritan stronghold though one which had suffered greatly under a royalist occupation and a subsequent damaging parliamentary siege. It was used 'for the repair of the Church and Steeple, and rebuilding of the Vicarage House and Common Gaol there', and what was left over was disposed of 'to well affected persons' of the town for rebuilding their houses.[89] Sorting out his father-in-law's affairs would occupy Milton for years to come.

Oxford had been among the last defeats and capitulations of the first civil war. In June 1645 Cromwell and Fairfax had destroyed the major field army of the king at the battle of Naseby. Carlisle fell to parliament in the same month. Cromwell's victory at Langport in July confirmed the tide now ran ineluctably against the king. In September, Bristol surrendered. In October, the stronghold of Basing House was overrun, with considerable loss of life among its defenders.[90] In early May 1646, Charles gave himself up to the Scottish army encamped at Newark, and in June he issued a general order directing the governors of his remaining garrisons to surrender, though some continued to resist and the last, in Harlech Castle, did not give up till March 1647, thus formally ending the first civil war.[91] Amid the catastrophe, Exeter surrendered in April 1646. For the previous seven months, Christopher Milton had lived and worked there as a loyal servant of the king. However, he was allowed to leave and to return to London, thus rejoining his wife and children, still presumably living with his widowed mother-in-law in St Clement's Churchyard.

Christopher's fortunes were in disarray. His support for the royalist cause had been rewarded by his appointment as Royal Commissioner of Sequestrations with responsibility for three counties, but the defeat of royalist forces meant royalists themselves were subject to a Committee of Parliamentary Sequestrations, which deemed Christopher's support for the crown to be culpable. He was in Exeter when it fell, and so was subject to the Articles of the Treaty of Surrender, according to which his property was to be subject to sequestration, but he was allowed to compound. Christopher quickly took the Covenant and the Oath;[92] he then admitted that his service as a royal commissioner constituted delinquency and, claiming the benefit of the Articles of Surrender (by confirming that he had been resident in Exeter for seven months before the surrender of the city), lodged a petition to compound with Committee for the Composition of Property owned by Delinquents at Goldsmiths Hall.[93] The Committee consented to the petition, and on 25 August 1646 was fined £200 'at a third' and £80 'at a tenth'; this opaque formula reflected what was in practice the standard penalty for delinquents, a fine that reflected the rental value of his estate (both real and personal) for two years. Christopher had no personal estate, but he did have real estate, and that formed the basis of the fine.[94] In the event, Christopher paid the £80 fine in two instalments,[95] but not the £200 fine. It is possible that he defaulted, but it seems more likely that the fine was somehow mitigated at the behest of his brother: Edward Phillips records that Christopher's 'composition [was] made by the help of his Brother's Interest, with the then prevailing Power'.[96]

Milton's father-in-law, Richard Powell, had undergone the same process as Christopher Milton. He too had been a beneficiary of articles of surrender (but of Oxford rather than Exeter), and had been deemed a delinquent by the Committee of Parliamentary Sequestrations. He returned to London, but unlike Christopher (who had a lawyer's sense of his own interest) did not immediately subscribe to the Covenant. Powell's petition to compound arrived at the Goldsmiths' Hall Committee on 6 August, the day before Christopher's petition. Powell's estate was inventoried for compounding, and he submitted an account of his debts. He then took the Covenant and Oath and stated his debts under oath, and on 8 December his fine was set at £180;[97] he died in Milton's house on 1 January 1647, without having paid the fine.

These events had a serious impact on Milton, because he was one of Powell's creditors. The summary of debts included repayment of £300 that Powell had borrowed from Milton's father in 1627; Powell had paid interest for seventeen years before defaulting in June 1644. Milton had also been promised a dowry of £1,000 on his marriage to Mary Powell, but that debt was never paid, and was to be recalled in Milton's will. Powell's financial arrangements were bewilderingly complex, and his incompetence seems to have been compounded by fraud, but it was clear that his debts were greater than the value of his estate,[98] so Milton decided to recover what he could. In mid-December 1646, a fortnight before Powell's death, Milton presented the statute staple bond of 11 June 1627 to Sir Thomas Hampson, the same Clerk of the Staple who had certified the bond in 1627. This endorsement enabled Milton to secure a writ of extent (a mechanism for debt recovery) which was presented to William Cope, the sheriff of Oxfordshire. Cope was then obliged to empanel a jury with a view to deciding which part of the estate should be seized to satisfy the debt. Milton's targets were the manor of Forest Hill, which Powell had let to Sir Robert Pye,[99] and a second property, at Wheatley, which Powell had bequeathed to his widow. In the event, Milton did not secure Forest Hill, the freehold of Wheatley was seized by the crown, and on 20 November 1647 Milton was granted possession. He was to hold the property for nine years before returning it to the Powells, and during that period he treated his mother-in-law generously, paying the widow's third to which she was entitled and waiving more than £500 that was due to him. With respect to the dowry, however, he did not waive his claim, but he was never able to recover it.[100]

Probably in the autumn of 1645 Milton moved from the relatively small house in Aldersgate Street to a larger property less than half a mile away in Barbican. On Edward Phillips's account the move was designed to facilitate the establishment of a small school in response to the requests 'by several Gentlemen of his acquaintance, for the Education of his Sons'.[101] The house, number 17 Barbican, survived till the 1860s, and an illustration made shortly before its demolition shows it to be substantial though narrow fronted, with four stories and a double oriel window on its street-facing elevation.[102] Evidently the notoriety of his divorce tracts had not damaged Milton's reputation in the eyes of all who knew him. In the event the larger property facilitated Mary's renewed cohabitation, and it was to this house that the Powell family withdrew after the fall of Oxford. Milton's father moved there too.

Deaths soon reduced the inhabitants. On 30 December 1646 Milton witnessed his father-in-law's last will and testament, as Richard Powell desperately tried to set his affairs in some kind of order.[103] The consequent legal wranglings, as we have seen, would much exercise Milton thereafter. On 1 January Powell died in the Barbican house.[104] His wife and children, excluding Mary, left shortly afterwards. Sometime in March 1647, just as the last royalist strongholds were surrendering, John Milton senior died. He was buried on 15 March in St Giles' Cripplegate, in a vault below the chancel end of the nave, where, twenty-seven years on, his son John would also be interred. His will has not survived. However, among the equity inherited by his elder son was a short-dated lease on a property, known as the Red Rose, a large house on the west side of Bread Street. Milton renewed the lease for a further twenty-one years, at the cost of £200 in April 1649; otherwise it would have expired in 1653. The house perished in the Great Fire of 1666, though by then Milton had relinquished his interest in the property.[105] Milton's early biographers write of him living frugally on a 'moderate Patrimony', though from 1649 his income as a government servant was considerable. At no time could his circumstances be described as seriously straitened, either before that appointment or after the Restoration. Moreover, he could evidently raise £200 in 1649, presumably from part of his inheritance. A man tutored in financial management by an astute scrivener like John Milton senior would have diversified his investments more widely. Almost certainly Milton had other investments, perhaps in other properties, perhaps in private loans, perhaps both. To his dying day, he enjoyed the security and prosperity of a rich man's heir.

His decision to establish a small school can scarcely have been driven primarily by the need to earn fees from his young charges, though appropriate recompense for teaching and in some cases accommodating the children of his acquaintances may well have been received. He was, in any case, obligated to house and educate his nephews. Milton, moreover, had been thinking about education. Much as reflection on his personal circumstance had stimulated his divorce tracts and the associated research, evidently as he taught the Phillips boys and perhaps one or two others of his earliest pupils he worked out a theory and philosophy of education.

This project was in step with a renewed interest among an influential circle of intellectuals in issues of pedagogy. Francis Bacon's educational writings, pre-eminently his *Two Bookes of the Proficience and Advancement of Learning* (London, 1605), had argued for a refreshment of educational provision in the service of the rational, secular, functional, evidence-based accumulation, and dissemination of knowledge. It remained influential through the century, clearly felt, for example, in Thomas Sprat's great apologia for the new science, *The History of the Royal Society of London, for the Improving of National Knowledge* (London, 1667). Some aspects of Bacon's thinking are a pervasive presence in the Milton oeuvre. Yet the immediate stimulus to the upsurge of pedagogic theorizing and publication in the 1640s was not of English origin. Jan Amos Komenský, known as Johannes Amos Comenius, the Czech reformer, wrote extensively on the merits of universal education and on the development of a more efficient pedagogy to meet that context. In England, his ideas were disseminated by a German émigré, Samuel Hartlib, who in 1641 persuaded Komenský to visit London. Around Hartlib there developed a circle of like-minded reformers, encouraged by Hartlib to advance the debate about educational reform. Though personal contact certainly was central to Hartlib's promotional operation, the Comenian agenda was embodied in a considerable series of publications across the late 1630s and the 1640s, of which the most immediately significant were Hartlib's translation of Comenius, *A Reformation of Schooles* (London, 1642) and the frequently reprinted Thomas Horne's translation, *Janua linguarum reserata: or a seed-plot of all languages and sciences* (London, 1636). This group of educational reformers included men who, like Milton, were to become leading figures of the new establishment that emerged after 1649. William Petty was prominent in the Cromwellian administration of Ireland. John Dury became deputy keeper of what had been the king's library and undertook numerous diplomatic missions.[106]

Milton on his own account knew Hartlib personally by the time he wrote *Of Education*, published in June 1644. The tract, which takes the form of an open letter to Hartlib, speaks of his 'earnest entreaties, and serious conjurements' to contribute to the debate on educational reform. Hartlib certainly received and engaged with the tract, and, somewhat mysteriously, appears to have at least begun to make a transcription of the printed book. He may well have sent a copy to Dury, and certainly sent one to John Hall, like Milton and

Dury, a future salaried employee of the Commonwealth and protectorate. Hall, indeed, sought to use Hartlib as a means to meet Milton.[107]

Milton's little tract, a mere eight pages long, seems to have been intended for private circulation. It resembles the *Epitaphium Damonis* in that it is a single quarto sheet, without imprint or title page. The author distributed copies himself, evidently sending a few to Hartlib. As Ernest Sirluck has well demonstrated, the tract is much less Comenian in content than it .has sometimes appeared, though it shares Comenius's enthusiasm for accelerating and facilitating the learning of Latin for practical purposes, as 'the instrument convaying to us things usefull to be known'.[108] The then predominant system of school followed by university simply wasted too much time through poor organization and a weak pedagogy that required children to compose as well as read in Latin and Greek. Milton's more original contribution to the debate about educational reform is the proposal to replace that binary structure with academies to educate young people between the age of 12 and 20.[109] Milton's project is not universal but is, rather, designed to produce a ruling elite for a puritan state, men who can 'perform justly, skilfully and magnanimously all the offices both private and publicke of peace and war'.[110] In a detailed and developed fantasy, Milton sketches out the daily and weekly round for the inmates of his projected establishment, listing books they should read along the way, and determining the routine for the Officer Training Corps, imagining his young charges scrambled into the action of mock battles and exercises when 'about two hours before supper' they are to roused 'by a sudden alarum or watch word'.[111]

Repressive, prescriptive, elitist, masculinist, militaristic, dustily pedantic, class-ridden, and affectionless, Milton's nightmarish model for English education would, of course, have been unendurable to anyone as instinctively oppositional as its designer.[112] But at least one early reader, Sir Cheney Culpepper, 'an intriguing virtuoso with a fascination for technical change',[113] found it sufficiently enticing as a possible establishment for his son that he approached Hartlib for advice about 'the charge on w[hi]ch a schollar may be w[i]th Mr Milton'.[114]

It remains uncertain how closely Milton's own establishment resembled the one he projects. Cyriack Skinner and Edward Phillips, writing many years later, seem to turn to *Of Education* to flesh out their recollections of the educational programme they followed.[115] Clearly, however, there were considerable differences between the reality and the imagined ideal. *Of Education* projects an enrolment of 150 pupils in each model academy, whereas, Edward Phillips recalls, 'the accession of Scholars was not great'.[116]

The period immediately following Mary's return saw Milton not only smoothing the bed of death but also, for the first time, preparing a major literary manuscript for the press for publication late in 1645.[117] Henry Lawes had claimed responsibility for bringing out in print *A Maske Presented At Ludlow Castle, 1634.*[118] 'Lycidas', of course, was published in an anthology of elegies. Only Milton himself can have pulled together the contents of *Poems of Mr. John Milton, Both English and Latin, Compos'd at several times*, explicitly endorsed on the title page, '*Printed by his true Copies*', though evidently he had worked up the project with the bookseller, Humphrey Moseley. Indeed, Moseley must have collaborated in the literary joke Milton perpetrated on the portrait frontispiece, engraved by William Marshall, who had produced illustrations for several attacks on radical puritans, including Daniel Featley's *The Dippers Dipt* (London, 1645) which had attacked *The Doctrine and Discipline.*[119] At some stage in the production process, Milton, inevitably with Moseley's connivance, had a Greek poem inscribed beneath the portrait. Milton rarely composed in Greek, so the joke probably included the added pleasure of having Marshall himself copy it unknowingly onto the intaglio plate, whereas he could have tumbled to the significance had it been written in Latin. It reads: 'You would say, perhaps, that this picture was drawn by an ignorant hand, when you looked at the form that nature made. Since you do not recognize the man portrayed, my friends, laugh at this rotten picture of a rotten artist.'[120]

That Milton should have established a working relationship with Moseley may seem superficially remarkable. Moseley was at the earliest stage of what would prove to be an immensely successful career as publisher of creative writing. He had just released a new edition of the poems of Edmund Waller. Over the years to come, he responded to a strong market for printed plays and verse, no doubt stimulated by the disruptions to live theatre, closed since 1642, and to the coterie circulation in manuscript, which had been rendered almost impossible by the courtly diaspora of the 1640s and the disruptions to the universities and the inns of court. He published, among others, Beaumont and Fletcher, Jonson, Massinger, Middleton, Shirley, and Webster. His poetry list was to be as impressive, perhaps the more so since he evidently sought out new copy. It included Carew, Davenant, Fanshawe, Stanley, Crashaw, Cartwright, Cleveland, and Cowley. The preponderance of royalist writers in his catalogue is unmistakable, and inevitably provokes the question of what Milton was doing in such company.

One could try to argue that Moseley's own royalism may not have been apparent to Milton in 1645. Yet it was surely evident even in the epistle, 'The Stationer to the Reader'. Moseley's lament, that '*the slightest Pamphlet is nowadayes more vendible then the Works of learnedest men*', is a familiar royalist comment on the abuses of the press in the early 1640s.[121] Moseley certainly had developed an intelligent sense of the cultural orientation of Milton's early verse. He noted, for example, Milton's debt to '*our famous* Spencer . . . *whose Poems in these English ones are as rarely imitated, as sweetly excell'd*'.[122] Milton's

POEMS 113
OF
Mr. *John Milton*,
BOTH
ENGLISH and LATIN,
Compos'd at several times.

Printed by his true Copies.

The SONGS were set in Musick by
Mr. HENRY LAWES Gentleman of
the KINGS Chappel, and one
of His MAIESTIES
Private Musick.

———*Baccare frontem*
Cingite, ne vati noceat mala lingua futuro,
Virgil, Eclog. 7.

Printed and publish'd according to
ORDER.

Jan. 2ᵈ *LONDON,*
Printed by *Ruth Raworth* for *Humphrey Moseley,*
and are to be sold at the signe of the Princes
Arms in S. *Pauls* Church-yard. 1645.

30. John Milton, *Poems of Mr. John Milton*, title page and portrait frontispiece (London, 1645).

poems contained nothing indicative of his current fierce anti-prelatism, save for 'Lycidas'; he made no allusion to the current civil war, except for the enigmatic sonnet, 'When the assault was intended to the City'; and much of the early verse celebrated figures that the most die-hard royalist would have been happy to acknowledge as at least sound and in some cases saintly.

We cannot be certain why Milton chose to publish his collected early verse at this time. Much of it, after all, had remained in his private papers, seemingly uncirculated, for over a decade. Three hypotheses, by no means mutually exclusive, suggest themselves. Moseley in his epistle claims that he had actively solicited the poems, which could have stimulated Milton to pull the volume together.[123] In the context of the vicious campaign against him, Milton could have been minded to challenge the crude stereotyping by Presbyterians and the like of the tub-preaching fanatic with a definitive demonstration of his own, very different, cultural history.[124] Finally, the collection could mark a current inclination, evident elsewhere, of irenic rediscovery of former friendships.[125]

The title page noted 'The Songs were set in Musick by Mr. Henry Lawes Gentleman of the Kings Chappel, and one of His Maiesties Private Musick', a formula Moseley was to use repeatedly as he vouchsafed the poetry of the personal rule to print. Indeed, Lawes was evidently much in Milton's mind at the time, for in a poem dated in the Trinity Manuscript 'Feb. 9. 1645' (i.e. 1646), he addressed him as the composer who best served with music the words of the lyricist, who 'First taught our English music how to span | Words with just note and accent'.[126] Henry's brother William, also a composer, now best remembered for the setting of Herrick's 'Gather ye rosebuds', had died in late September at Rowton Heath in arms for the king. A wistfulness seems to shroud Milton's life and works at this time. Indeed, his sonnet to Henry first saw print as part of the front matter to *Choice Psalmes Put into Musick*, also published by Humphrey Moseley, a collection prefaced with a portrait of the king, to whom it is dedicated.

On 12 December 1646 Catharine Thomason, the wife of Milton's friend George Thomason, was buried in the south aisle of St Dunstan in the West, in Fleet Street.[127] George Thomason was one of a group of influential Presbyterians who had called for a personal treaty with the captured king; this was an unpopular position, and in common with his fellow petitioners he was to be deprived of office (he was a common councillor for the ward of Farringdon Within) following Pride's Purge in December 1648. Catharine was the ward and niece of Henry Fetherstone, a bookseller in St Paul's Churchyard, and Thomason's will refers to his wife's library. It would seem that she was another of those bookish women whose company Milton seems to have sought. His opening phrase, 'when faith and love', alludes to the conventional distinction in systematic theology between (as Milton phrases it in *Civil Power*) 'faith and charitie; or beleef and practise'.[128] Catharine embodied the two principal aspects of Milton's faith. Certainly his affection for Catharine is palpable in the sonnet, as is his admiration of her faith and 'good endeavour'.

At an unknown date after the publication of *Tetrachordon* and *Colasterion* in March 1645 Milton bound ten of his tracts (only *Of Education* is excluded) into one volume, which he inscribed and sent to Patrick Young, the King's Librarian.[129] The inscription makes clear that the volume is a personal gift to Young (not to the king's library), whose network of continental intellectuals overlapped with Milton's. It is possible that Young was one of Milton's childhood tutors, and possible that he effected Milton's introduction to the scholar-librarian Lukas Holste in Rome, but the contours of the relationship between Milton and Young remain blurred.[130]

In January 1647 Milton also sent a replacement copy of his poems to John Rouse, the Librarian of the Bodleian Library, in the recently liberated royalist capital of Oxford. Once more, the theme of friendship is sounded—the request has come from 'Docto...amico', his learned friend.[131] Just as Milton was renewing and perhaps mending relationships with his brother and his father-in-law, he was, in a mode more familiar from the behaviour and idiom of royalist poets, celebrating personal loyalties, committing his verse to print, and seeking out a quieter life. Whatever the successes of the New Model Army, Milton, bloodied and battered by the Presbyterian mobilization, seems to have adopted the emotional survivalism of the defeated.

CHAPTER 10

The Road to Regicide

Life records are singularly sketchy for the period from the death of Milton's father in March 1647 to the publication of *The Tenure of Kings and Magistrates* in February 1649, which marks his open engagement with the act of regicide. The complex legal process associated with Richard Powell's estate, discussed above, continued.[1] In September or October 1647, presumably because his household was now reduced by the death of his and Mary's fathers and by the removal of his mother-in-law and the dependant children that had accompanied her, Milton moved once more, quitting 'his great House in *Barbican*' for 'a smaller in *High Holbourn*, among those that open backward into *Lincolns-Inn* Fields', as Edward Phillips recalled.[2] Edward and his brother continued to live and study with their uncle, but the move reflects a decision to abandon any grander plans for the establishment of a formal academy, perhaps because the scheme was rendered less attractive after the inheritance of his patrimony and the return of steady investment income after the tide of war had shifted. On 25 October 1648, about six weeks before Milton's fortieth birthday, Mary gave birth to their second child, a daughter also called Mary, who was baptized on 7 November.[3]

On 20 April 1647 Milton wrote to Carlo Dati in Florence. There was no postal system, so the letter was carried to Italy by 'Bookseller James' or by 'his master'; James is James Allestree, who was apprenticed to Milton's friend George Thomason and would later become one of Milton's publishers. The letter, which survives in the New York Public Library,[4] responds to one (now lost) from Dati. Milton happily recalls his time in Florence, asking that his best wishes be passed to his friends, and alludes to the civil war, to the death of Diodati and to his English publications; he does not mention his marriage or his child, though there is a veiled reference to his father-in-law. Dati received the letter, and on 1 November (22 October in the English calendar) replied to Milton, flattering him by replying in Italian (Tuscan) to Milton's Latin.[5] Dati's long and effusive letter reminds Milton that he had promised to send a copy of his *Poemata*, and asks him to compose a memorial poem for inclusion in a memorial volume for Francesco Rovai; if Milton obliged, his letter never arrived, because there is no poem by Milton in the published collection.[6]

The attacks by Presbyterians and their allies, which had so characterized the middle years of the decade, continued, though more sporadically. Pagitt's *Heresiography* appeared in 1647 and 1648 in its third and fourth editions,[7] now with an engraved title page, depicting, among other depravities, the behaviour of the 'Divorser'. An anonymous broadside of 1647, *A Catalogue of the severall Sects and Opinions in England and other Nations*, offers another graphic image of a cudgel-wielding 'Divorcer', among cartoons of Adamites, Arminians, 'Libertins' and others. Milton, however, is not named (unlike Rhys Evans, 'a Welch man' lately committed to prison 'for saying he was Christ').[8] In another broadside of 1647, *These Trades-men are Preachers in and about the City of LONDON*, Milton's divorce views, 'That a man may lawfully put away his wife if she be not a meet helper', appears as heresy 27, between extreme tolerationism and the view 'That God is the Author of the sinfulnesse of his people'. A curious publication, it lists the fair gamut of heresies beneath cartoons of confectioners, smiths, soap-boilers, 'chicken-men' (that is, poulterers) and the like, going about their daily work. From later 1647 the attacks peter out with the political eclipse of the Presbyterians.[9]

The life records disclose a widening readership for Milton's prose and poetry. Edward Hyde, holed up in Jersey, received at least one of the divorce tracts in April 1647.[10] Robert Baron, a very young royalist writer near the beginning of his career, drew heavily on Milton's first poetry collection in his prose romance, *Erotopaignion, or The Cyprian Academy* (London, 1647). Baron's own ideological orientation is plainly signed: the epistle dedicatory is to James Howell, frequent panegyrist of the king, currently in prison, and the prose romance 'contains a thinly veiled portrait' of Cromwell as a 'rabble-rousing orator'.[11] Borrowings from Milton (along with Waller, Webster, Shakespeare, Suckling, and Lovelace) pepper the inset verse sections, sometimes somewhat incongruously. Thus, a 'Chorus of Fairies' begin a song with 'Ring out yee Christall Spheares', as a prelude to praising Queen Mab.[12] But at least the text shows an appreciation of Milton's status from across the political divide. So, too, does the manuscript anthology of William Sancroft, future archbishop of Canterbury, who was shortly to be deprived of his Fellowship at Emmanuel for his royalist sympathies. He transcribed both Psalm 136 ('Let us with a gladsome mind') and the Nativity Ode.[13]

Edward Phillips characterized these years as a return to the contemplative life, amid large events which scarcely touched Milton, before the trial of the king recalled him to a public role. Milton in the little house in High Holborn 'liv'd a private and quiet Life, still prosecuting his Studies and curious Search into Knowledge, the grand Affair perpetually of his Life'.[14] By the time he moved house, the political climate of England in general and London in particular had changed drastically. The summer of 1647 marked the zenith of Presbyterian power and influence, and the events which followed disclosed that their tactical strength, within the metropolis, had disguised their strategic weakness. While the polemicists of the Presbyterian mobilization had harried Independents and sectaries alike, catching up Milton himself in their onslaught, an alliance of London ministers, urged on by their Scottish mentors, came close to securing a national church settlement on the Presbyterian model. In stark contrast to the political dynamics of London, the prevailing religious character of the New Model Army was radical and pluralist. Of the forty-three chaplains known to have served with the army between 1645 and 1651, no more than four were Presbyterian at the outset and by 1649 this number had dwindled to extinction. The chaplains were appointed personally by the higher officers and so reflected the religious complexion of those army grandees. Lay preaching was permitted, itself an admission of tolerationist principles, and the senior officers and their chaplains furthermore 'devised an elaborate programme of religious exercises to occupy the army when it was not fighting'.[15] Mark Kishlansky has influentially argued that concerns about pay delays and the like more strongly motivated and radicalized the rank and file than religious or political beliefs.[16] But the orientation of the men who emerged in control of the New Model Army, particularly Cromwell and those closest to him, was plain to see in the sorts of religious practice they encouraged and sanctioned.

More militant Presbyterians had hoped that the Scottish army's contribution to the military campaign against the king would strengthen their own position. But that army was marginalized in the overwhelming victories of 1645–6, and by the spring of 1647 it had returned home. Men like Edwards monitored anxiously the religious temper and practices of the New Model Army, and successive parts of *Gangraena* reported the extravagant beliefs and behaviour of officers and men.[17]

From 1646 the political conflict between parliamentary Presbyterians and the commanders of the New Model Army shaped English politics, as the former sought to disband much of the forces once the war was effectively won. From early 1647, some regiments were moved closer to London, to counterbalance the relative decline of the Independents within parliament, city government, and the pulpit. Issues were further sharpened by the group in parliament around Denzil Holles and Sir Philip Stapleton, who not only sought to reduce the New Model Army but also advocated conscription of its troops to a new expeditionary force to intervene in Ireland.[18]

Meanwhile fruitless negotiations continued with the captive Charles I, provoking army anxieties about a possible Presbyterian plan to transfer him back into the hands of the Scots.[19] In June, the army snatched the king from the control of parliament. In London, plans were advanced for mobilizing an alternative force under the Presbyterian Colonel Edward Massey, MP, whose field brigade had been disbanded by Fairfax in October 1646. In August 1647, shortly before Milton left the Barbican house, Fairfax and Cromwell marched on London, ostensibly in response to riotous attacks on parliament by city-based Presbyterian supporters. They met no resistance, and leading Presbyterians slipped away into self-imposed exile, among them Massey and Thomas Edwards, while an irenic alliance of Philip Nye and Stephen Marshall preached sermons of reconciliation. Milton's enemies since the publication of his first divorce tract were effectively routed without any help or indeed response from himself. Edwards, who found refuge in Amsterdam with the Presbyterian English church, died in exile in February 1648, though others, included parliamentary Presbyterians, drifted back to London.

So far as we know, Milton remained aloof or detached from the process which led to the killing of the king and which provided the necessary conditions for his own emergence as apologist for the regicide state, though he observed events closely and reflectively. Two related crises carried events onward. In November 1647 Charles fled the captivity of the army, thus signalling that his seemingly passive acceptance of his fate was specious and that his ambition to recover his position was unabated; he had 'secretly abandoned the settlement being crafted by the army grandees and their parliamentary allies', and had opened negotiations with the Scots.[20] He and his advisers miscalculated in seeking refuge in the Isle of Wight, whose governor made him prisoner in Carisbrooke Castle. He and his supporters had done enough to stimulate the new outbreak of armed conflict in May 1648, the Second Civil War, which threatened the control wielded over England by the New Model Army. Uprisings in Kent and Wales were suppressed quite easily, though a Scottish incursion and a revolt in Essex posed challenges of a different order. The latter ended in late August 1648, when, after an eleven-week siege, 'perhaps the bitterest episode of either civil war',[21] Colchester surrendered to Fairfax. Of its royalist commanders, two were promptly executed and three others carried off to await the judgement of parliament. The Scottish incursion had been delayed by the opposition of the Kirk and the most able military commanders declined to serve; the Solemn League and Covenant still carried some weight north of the border.[22]

The political initiative thereafter remained with the army grandees, who decided that parliament was, despite recent events, poised to conclude a treaty which would see the king 'summoned to London amidst popular acclamation'.[23] In early December, regiments were moved into Westminster and Whitehall. After some vacillation, four days later, Colonel Thomas Pride, aided by foot-soldiers of his regiment, arrested as they entered parliament MPs identified as inimical to the interests of the army. Pride's Purge left

31. *Charles I and his Opponents*, by an unknown artist (National Portrait Gallery, London).

a purged parliament, known much later as 'the Rump', which acquiesced in the trial of the king before a High Court of Justice, whose commissioners, both military and civilian, or at least those who were minded to attend, duly found the king guilty. He was brought to execution on 30 January 1649.

Milton, it seems, was only tenuously connected with these events. John Bradshaw, the President of the court, had been engaged as his lawyer in the Chancery case of Milton vs. Sir Robert Pye in 1647.[24] Milton would later work with him and praise him in the *Defensio Secunda*, and they may have been related.[25] There is some evidence of contact around the time of the trial, in that a copy of *The Tenure of Kings and Magistrates* endorsed 'ex dono authoris feb 1648 [i.e. 1649]' could well have been Bradshaw's.[26]

Milton does, however, comment directly in a sonnet first published by Edward Phillips in 1694. In the Trinity Manuscript it bears the title, scored through, 'On the Lord Gen. Fairfax at the siege of Colchester':[27]

> Fairfax, whose name in arms through Europe rings
>   Filling each mouth with envy, or with praise,
>   And all her jealous monarchs with amaze,
>   And rumours loud, that daunt remotest kings,
> Thy firm unshaken virtue ever brings
>   Victory home, though new rebellions raise
>   Their hydra heads, and the false North displays
>   Her broken league, to imp their serpent wings,
> O yet a nobler task awaits thy hand;
>   For what can war, but endless war still breed.
>   Till truth and right from violence be freed,
> And public faith cleared from the shameful brand
>   Of public fraud. In vain doth valour bleed
>   While avarice, and rapine share the land.[28]

Precise dating is uncertain. As others have noted, the present tense, used for the Scottish incursion, may imply that Milton had not yet heard of Cromwell's defeat of the Scots at Preston on 17 August.[29] Perhaps, though the battle of Preston did not end Scottish resistance, as Cromwell recaptured Berwick and Carlisle, which had fallen into enemy hands, and pressed on into Scotland itself.[30] The deleted title, however, may suggest that the siege is continuing as the poet writes. More interesting are the ideological reverberations. Milton displays an evident hostility to monarchs and monarchy in his contrast between Fairfax's assurance and the imagined 'daunting' of distant monarchs, which anticipates Andrew Marvell's later fantasy of the Cromwell who would be 'A Caesar... ere long to Gaul, | To Italy an Hannibal'.[31] Whatever the public stance to be taken in *The Tenure of Kings and Magistrates*, Milton here hints at a systemic republicanism. He seems clear, too, that the military power must be called in to correct the corruptions of civilian government, and indeed to save religion from the depredations of simony. 'Avarice, and rapine' are charges that would be laid against Presbyterian divines in *The Tenure of Kings and Magistrates*.[32]

Milton's second observation on the developing crisis is much more incidental: his translation of Psalms lxxx–lxxxviii. When first he published them, in his poetry collection of 1673, he prefaced them with 'April. 1648. J.M.'[33] Why he selected this cluster of psalms to work on has been the subject of some critical speculation. William B. Hunter noted that the Westminster Assembly had appointed a committee to revise Francis Rous's psalter and that for the purposes of committee work the psalms were divided into four sections, of which the third began at Psalm lxxx. As has often been remarked, the psalms chosen have a particular resonance in the context of the impending second civil war.[34] An embattled quality pervades the text, though with some expectation of divine deliverance:

> 6 A strife thou mak'st us *and a prey*
> To every neighbour foe,
>   Among themselves they laugh, they play,
> And flouts at us they throw
> 7 Return us, *and thy grace divine*,
> O God of Hosts *vouchsafe*
>   Cause thou thy face on us to shine,
> And then we shall be safe.[35]

The implied equation of England and Israel as chosen nations protected by God's providence obliquely asserts optimism amid circumambient gloom.

Though Milton completed little and published less during these years, there is evidence of at least early work on a number of projects that would not be published till the final decade of his life. A note in the papers of Samuel Hartlib makes mention of his engagement on 'not only... a universal history of England but also an epitome of all Purchas's volumes', which would eventually appear as *The History of Moscovia* in 1682.[36] Edward Phillips notes that he had 'made some progress' with it before he took up public office.[37] He could well have been working on *Samson Agonistes* and on the earliest stages of *Paradise Lost*. The dating of the composition of the former remains problematic, and some commentators, most influentially Parker, attribute the work to the 1640s.[38]

The prosodic experiments of Milton's exquisite translation of Horace's Pyrrha Ode (1. 5) resemble those of *Samson Agonistes*, but the Ode is the most undatable work in the Milton canon, and so affords no assistance. As a translation, it comes as close as is possible in English to approximating Horace's poise, delicacy, and smiling gravity; it is, as Milton claims in his headnote, 'as near as the language will permit'. Its occasion is not known, though something like the courtship of the mysterious Miss Davis is possible. The poem is little known to students of Milton, but widely praised by those who can sense Horace's choriambic rhythm beneath the surface of Milton's assonant unrhymed lines: as the classic work on the English ode proclaims, 'it is hardly too much to say that if by chance the rest of Milton's work had been lost, this translation would suffice to prove that he had been a great artist'.[39]

Milton had long since announced his epic ambitions,[40] and could just possibly have been at an early stage in writing *Paradise Lost*. Edward Phillips, who played a pivotal role in the 1660s in preparing it for publication, recalled that some of it—he quotes book four, lines 32–41—was intended for a verse drama, and was 'shewn to me, and some others', 'several Years before the Poem was begun'.[41] However, the recollection occurs in a passage primarily concerned with Milton in the 1650s, and Edward Phillips for the most part proceeds chronologically.

Milton may well have been working on the earliest stages of his systematic theology. The epistle to *De Doctrina Christiana* describes its inception in some detail as a progression towards greater confidence and autonomy.[42] Thus, once his study of the testaments in their original languages had reached a level of competence, he turned to some of the shorter systematic accounts of theology, what he terms 'Theologorum Systema aliquot breviora'. Thereafter, taking them as his model, he started a sort of theological commonplace book, before moving to more voluminous and controversial treatises, none of which satisfied him. So, drawing on the Bible alone ('solo Dei verbo'), he compiled his own treatise, explicitly as an aid to his own faith, always to have it to hand ('ad manum mihi esset').[43] If, as we surmise, Milton wrote the epistle around 1659–60, the earliest stages of that study and compilation could well have been in the 1640s.[44]

By considering Milton's writings from 1645–6 and from 1649 in conjunction with the evidence of the psalms he translated and the sonnet to Fairfax, we may with some confidence trace the process of political transformation that made him an apologist for regicide. Plotting the development of his theological thought is necessarily more speculative. From the mid-decade we have the evidence of his implacable hostility to ceremonialism and to an enforced Presbyterian settlement, his advocacy of divorce reform, and his defence of toleration. But only with his tracts of 1659–60, with *De Doctrina Christiana*, which was last worked on about that time, and with *Paradise Lost* (1667) does he return to explicit engagement with doctrinal issues. There we see the extent of his anti-clericalism and his heterodoxy on soteriology and the Trinity.[45] We cannot be sure of the *terminus a quo* for the formulation of these positions, though some may well have developed in step with his political radicalization. Were that the case, how should he be contextualized in the devotional landscape of London in the late 1640s?

In some respects, his closest affinities are with General Baptists. Thomas Lambe, by trade a soap-boiler, had his congregation in Bell Alley, Coleman Street, within a ten-minute stroll of Aldersgate Street or Barbican. He not only exemplified the role of a preaching laity, but also was the probable author of the 'most elaborate published statement of General Baptist doctrine in this period', *The Fountain of Free Grace Opened* (London, 1645).[46] General Baptists held to the doctrine of general redemption, a position akin to the soteriology of Arminianism, and while they anticipated in their privileging of 'inner light' aspects of Quakerism, like Milton they diverged significantly

from the Quakers in their biblicism. They shared the enthusiastic appreciation of lay-preaching and the profound anti-clericalism of Milton's tracts of
1659 (views also central to the Quakers), and some were mortalists, and they
may also have advocated divorce for reasons other than those sanctioned
under the old canon law.[47]

Lambe's church, uniquely among non-parochial congregations, regularly
held meetings which were open to the public.[48] No evidence connects Milton
directly with it, though there are numerous examples of non-members frequenting Coleman Street to test themselves and their faith among the extremer sectaries, in a milieu which seems to have functioned in part as a sort of
Speakers' Corner.[49] As we have elsewhere demonstrated, much of the heterodoxy to be identified in Milton's theology, as it emerges in *De Doctrina
Christiana* and *Paradise Lost*, could be found in the patristic tradition and in
Protestant systematic theologians.[50] We doubt he had much to learn from *The
Fountain of Free Grace Opened*. Socially, the General Baptists were for the most
part poorly educated petty masters, their families and employees, several points
on the London social scale beneath a Cambridge-educated, independently
wealthy son of a prosperous scrivener. Moreover, as religious belief spilled
over into political action, again they diverged from Milton; from their ranks
emerged much of the civilian support for the Leveller movement.[51] Yet it is
important to recognize that contemporaries laboured to make associations
between Milton and such extreme groups. Mrs Attaway, 'the most notorious
woman preacher in London', began her career in Lambe's congregation.[52] If, in
the broadside *These Trades-men are Preachers in and about the City of* LONDON
we are to recognize Milton as the unnamed author of heresy 27, Lambe is just
as surely to be seen in the cartoon of the soap-boiler.

Socially, theologically, and in terms of their later political trajectories,
Milton's closest affinity was with another Coleman Street activist, the Cambridge-educated John Goodwin. Goodwin's early career could be seen as the
road not taken when Milton chose to eschew holy orders. In 1633 he had been
appointed vicar of St Stephen, Coleman Street. He spent the late 1630s
developing a puritan inclination while retaining a low profile. Though he
was not a member of the Westminster Assembly, he was broadly aligned with
the Independents, and achieved some notoriety as a polemicist for toleration.
At the same time, he proved a theologian of a heterodox originality. Historians of the mid-century church often associate him with Milton as leading
puritan thinkers, in Gerald Aylmer's elegant phrase, 'intellectual mandarins
to their fingertips'.[53] Theologically, Goodwin moved, over the 1640s, towards
convergence with Milton's own Arminian doctrine of salvation. Like Milton,
he attracted sustained attacks from the Presbyterian mobilization. As his
ecclesiology moved in the direction of independency, he attempted to run a
gathered church alongside his parochial congregation in St Stephen. It gave

the Presbyterians a route to dismiss him, and in May 1645 he was ejected from his living. He was not reinstated till 1649.[54] Like Milton, he was to defend in print the trial and killing of the king; few other ministers explicitly endorsed Pride's Purge and supported the Purged Parliament, at least in its earliest days. His major defence of the regicide, *The Obstructors of Justice*, was published in May, 'with his name and portrait emblazoned on the title page'; it drew on Milton's own first tract of 1649.[55]

⁂

Milton returned to writing prose polemic with *The Tenure of Kings and Magistrates: Proving, That it is Lawfull, and hath been held so through all Ages, for any, who have the Power, to call to account a Tyrant, or wicked KING, and after due conviction, to expose, and put him to death, if the ordinary MAGISTRATE have neglected, or deny'd to doe it.* It was published on or about 13 February 1649, a fortnight after the execution of the king. For the first time Milton addressed issues of essentially secular political concern, if we accept that *Areopagitica* was primarily a contribution to the debate about toleration. It constitutes Milton's most sustained exposition of political philosophy. Yet the discourse veers frequently towards the theological implications of political decisions. Moreover, for much of the time, Milton is engaging Presbyterian divines and their allies, as though reviving, in drastically changed circumstances, the mutual animosities of earlier years. His principal concession to the abstractions of theory is to leave his adversaries for the most part unnamed. However, once more, he enters an already mature controversy in which the terms of reference have largely been set by others. We hear much from the outset of new apologists for the king who had formerly 'curs'd him all over in thir Pulpits and thi Pamphlets'.[56] William Prynne is demeaningly alluded to in a comment on 'barking monitaries and memento's'.[57] Indeed, Merritt Y. Hughes has convincingly demonstrated that many of the points Milton makes are shaped to refute arguments articulated in Presbyterian publications critical of the trial and execution of the king.[58]

Milton seems intermittently uncertain of his audience. As Blair Worden long ago noted, the immediate priority for apologists for the Purged Parliament was to lull former allies, now alienated or excluded, into at least a passive acceptance of the new regime. Milton explicitly concedes this to be an objective; he offers 'Instruction' to those who would now backslide from their former 'just and pious resolution'.[59] Yet his resolve is subverted by his unmistakable, profound, and vengeful antipathy to the activists of the Presbyterian mobilization. Of course, as we have seen, he retained friendships with Presbyterians, nor did he and the Smectymnuans fall to open disputation. But for the likes of the late Thomas Edwards, who had fled into exile in mid-1647 in anticipation of radical reprisals, a rabid hostility, bordering on a more general anti-clericalism, breaks through from time to time, and the tract ends in a high-flown denuciation of the 'pack of hungrie Church-wolves, who in the step of *Simon Magus* thir Father, following the hot sent of double Livings and Pluralities . . . have got possession, or rather seis'd upoon the Pulpit, as the strong hold and fortress of thir sedition and rebellion against the civil Magistrate'.[60]

Milton builds the case against the Presbyterian royalists primarily in terms of their hypocrisy. On his account, they had encouraged the war, during which, with their approval, the armies of parliament had fought the king, placing his life in jeopardy on the field of battle. Their changed perspective originated in a resentment of the powers assumed by the leaders of the New Model Army; when Fairfax had marched his troops into the city in August 1647, he had frustrated the conspiracy among metropolitan divines and politicians to suppress heterodoxy and impose Presbyterian church government, thus eliminating in-dependent congregationalism, separatists, and sectaries. The New Model Army, encamped in and around London, underwrote the tolerationist ambitions of Milton and men like John Goodwin. Milton asserts that Presbyterian divines opposed the execution of the king out of pique that their own project had signally foundered: 'Nor did they Treat or think of Treating with him, till thir hatred to the Army that deliverd them, not thir love or duty to the King, joyn'd them secretly with men sentenc'd so oft for Reprobates in thir own mouthes.'[61]

He is somewhat constrained by a clause in the Solemn League and Covenant, agreed by nearly all who at the outset had opposed the king. It proclaimed an undertaking 'to preserve the rights and defend the King's Majesty's person and authority', and called on the world to witness 'that we have no thoughts or intentions to diminish His Majesty's just power and greatness'.[62] For Milton, the clause appears supererogatory in a document really drawn up to bind English and Scottish puritans to the promotion of church reform.[63] Moreover, as he often does in this tract, he falls back on to the core principles of English law, specifically the law of contract: 'If I make a voluntary Covnant as with a man, to doe him good, and he prove afterward a monster to me, I should conceave a disobligement. If I covnant, not to hurt an enemie, in favour of him & forbearance, & hope of his amendment, & he, after that, shall doe me tenfould injury and mischief . . . to what may tend to my destruction, I question not but that this his after actions release me.'[64]

Though Milton largely works to meet the exigencies of a mature contro-versy, he does develop some larger arguments in political philosophy, though they emerge loosely aligned rather than closely interdependent. He explicitly establishes that this is not a republican tract, but rather an argument for the deposition and trial of tyrants, repeating the themes established on the title page: 'look how great a good and happiness a just King is, so great a mischiefe is a Tyrant; as hee the public father of his Countrie, so this the common enemie.'[65] How may we know Charles was a tyrant? In part, that remains for others to determine: 'who in particular is a Tyrant cannot be determin'd in a general discours, otherwise then by supposition; his particular charge, and the sufficient proof of it must determin that: which I leave to Magistrates, at least to the uprighter sort of them.'[66] He seems ill at ease about the admission of the obvious point, that Charles's jury consisted of men selected in the knowledge that they would find him guilty, 'the uprighter sort'. But Charles's tyranny is confirmed, too, by God's providential guidance of the fortunes of war; 'God and a good cause [has given] them Victory'.[67]

Major arguments pass curiously undeveloped. The case against trying the king rested in part on the special nature of kingship. To silence that argument, Milton needs to challenge the notion that kingship is divinely sanctioned and that kings stand in a unique relationship to the godhead. Merritt Hughes notes, 'David's refusal to do bodily harm to Saul... because he was "the Lord's anointed" was Grotius's crowning authority in *De Jure Belli ac Pacis*... for a famous argument for almost absolute submission to kings', and the precedent occurs in the controversy into which Milton entered.[68] Milton dismisses the argument perfunctorily: 'when any tyrant at this day can shew to be the Lords anointed, the onley mention'd reason why *David* withheld his hand, he may then but not till then presume on the same privilege.'[69]

Milton's most important contribution to the principles underpinning the controversy rests in his assertion of the transcendence of 'the Law' (as a grand abstraction), alongside defence of something approximating to individual civil rights. In recognizing when a king has become a tyrant, 'no man of cleare judgement need goe furder to be guided then by the very principles of nature in him'.[70] Predominant among those 'principles' would seem to be a straightforward sense of enlightened self-interest and indeed self-preservation. Milton assumes, in a way that seems obvious in our own age, that anyone who perceives those interests to be threatened is unlikely to be disposed to support the author of that threat. Moreover, the law stands over all: 'be he King, or Tyrant, or Emperour, the Sword of Justice is above him'; 'Justice is the onely true sovran and supreme Majesty upon earth'. But even here, his claim is not merely a secular appeal to reason, since, explicitly, 'the tryal of Justice' is 'the Sword of God, superior to all mortal things, in whose hand soever by apparent signes his testified will is to put it'.[71] The most important of those signs, presumably, were manifest at Marston Moor and Naseby, Preston and Colchester.

Those towering figures of English political philosophy in the seventeenth century, Hobbes and Locke, at pivotal points in their writings postulate foundation myths about the origins of civil society.[72] Milton, too, at his most theoretical, offers a foundation myth, though its secular thesis is leavened by its biblical resonance:

No man who knows ought, can be so stupid to deny that all men naturally were borne free, being the image and resemblance of God himself, and were by privilege above all the creatures, born to command and not to obey: and that they liv'd so. Till from the root of *Adams* transgression, falling among themselves to doe wrong and violence, and foreseeing that such courses must needs tend to the destruction of them all, they agreed by common league to bind each other from mutual injury... against any that gave disturbance or opposition to such agreement. Hence came Citties, Townes and Common-wealths. And because no faith in all was found sufficiently binding, they saw it needfull to ordaine som authoritie, that might restrain by force and punishment what was violated against peace and common right.[73]

Hence the origin of kings and magistrates. The premises for the argument resonate with the spirit of a later set of 'self-evident' truths. The myth postulates a society which moves from Edenic freedom to a contract entered into to mitigate 'the wrong and violence' which people, tainted by '*Adams* transgression', are wont to perpetrate. Civil society, as in Hobbes, is primarily a defensive structure. Milton's model allows for resistance to authority since citizens reserve the right to recall the deputed power from kings and magistrates and to hold them to account for their actions. While kings and magistrates may govern their fellows, they remain subject to the law.

It seems improbable that Milton would have maintained the historicity, the literal truth, of the story he tells, though it offers a lucid myth for the relationship of governors, subjects, and the law. Milton is a shrewder historian than political philosopher, and when the evidence is available in the sources he draws on, he cites a more probable account for the origin of at least one monarchy. Gildas, 'the most ancient of all our Historians', in his discussion of the inception of kingship among Britons before the Roman conquest, notes '*they anointed them Kings, not of God, but such as were more bloody then the rest*'.[74]

Intermittently, Milton discloses his concept of how civil society should be organized. The role of the state should diminish as it withdraws from areas of personal choice that do not concern it. Toleration remains a key principle in Milton's thinking. Society appears as a contract between individuals who are not 'the Kings slave[s], his chattell, or his possession that may be bought and sold'.[75] Instead, they employ kings and magistrates, and may dismiss them if they find good cause. Milton's most explicit enunciation of the ideal is couched in terms of the rights of autonomous property-owners, an account which Locke would have found much to agree with. A nation is not truly free while 'wanting that power, which is the root and sourse of all liberty, to dispose and *oeconomize* in the Land which God hath giv'n them, as Maisters of Family in thir own house and free inheritance'.[76] The liberty available to those who were not property-owning males remains unaddressed.

The first edition of *Tenure of Kings and Magistrates*, like the first edition of *The Doctrine and Discipline of Divorce*, proved pivotal for Milton's public career. It placed him near the forefront of a diminished band of English intellectuals still prepared to defend in print the actions of the New Model Army and its civilian allies in the Purged Parliament, much as the first divorce tract gave Milton a fairly high profile among the radical adversaries of Presbyterianism. Coincidentally, like the 1643 version of the divorce tract, *The Tenure*, too, appeared less guarded than in its subsequent, revised version. When Milton reissued it in a second edition, some time between October 1649 and February 1650,[77] he significantly augmented his quotations from authorities supportive of his views that kings may be brought to justice. In a manoeuvre perfected in *Tetrachordon*, these are drawn from Presbyterian divines of impeccable credentials. *The Tenure* is Milton's most sustained engagement with political philosophy, and it shows both his strengths and weaknesses as a thinker. As the modern reader pieces together the argument he emerges clearly as a major precursor of Locke in the definition and celebration of civil rights, not least in his articulation of universal equality before the law, in his justification for the ownership of private property, and in the freedom of citizens to hold their governors to account. Yet the argument has to be synthesized from a discourse that simultaneously is shaped to meet the exigencies of a mature debate, to defend a *coup d'état*, and to advance the interests of the faction in army and state with which he had aligned himself.

IV

1649–1660

CHAPTER II

The Purged Parliament

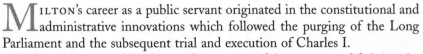

MILTON's career as a public servant originated in the constitutional and administrative innovations which followed the purging of the Long Parliament and the subsequent trial and execution of Charles I.

Before 1649 much of the day-to-day running of the country and fighting the war had been invested in successive high-level committees: the Committee of Safety, followed in 1644 by the Committee of Both Kingdoms (which also served to coordinate the combined endeavours of England and Scotland), and finally in 1648 by the Derby House Committee (or 'the Committee of Both Houses'), whose role and title changed to reflect the breach with the Scots. Each constituted 'the nearest thing that Parliament had to a supreme war council, or to a replacement for the King and the Privy Council at the head of the central executive', though a plethora of other committees and commissions operated at various times and with varying degrees of effectiveness.[1] These included the Compounding Committee, which sat at Goldsmiths' Hall and with which Milton had probably engaged as he attempted to assist his brother Christopher and his father-in-law Richard Powell senior on the collapse of the royalist cause they had supported.[2]

Besides killing the king, asserting the sovereignty and supremacy of the House of Commons, and abolishing the monarchy and the House of Lords, the Purged Parliament, in mid-February 1649, a little after the appearance of *The Tenure of Kings and Magistrates*, replaced the Derby House Committee with the first Council of State. On 15 March, it appointed Milton Secretary for Foreign Tongues, initially for a one-year period.[3] He had to move close to Whitehall, and so temporarily 'lodged at one Thomson's next door to the Bull-head Tavern at Charing-Cross, opening into the Spring Garden'.[4]

Milton was to serve the Secretariat for Foreign Tongues for four and a half years. Understanding its internal organization and its relationship to the Purged Parliament is crucial to appreciating the work that he did and the pressures and difficulties that he faced in his public capacity.

Between 13 and 17 February 1649 the Commons debated the structure of the Council of State, and an act of parliament 'carefully defined the competence of the new executive, and placed its authority on a statutory, accountable and chronologically fixed basis. It also appointed forty-one councillors'.[5]

From its inception, the Council was accountable to the full Purged Parliament. While most of its members were also MPs, the relationship nevertheless produced some vacillation in policy, as recommendations from the former could be revised or referred back by the latter. At some points, as we shall see, there was uncertainty about where the right or power to make decisions precisely rested. The Council changed on the basis of annual elections by the Purged Parliament, and half way through its life a system of compulsory rotation was introduced, in which the twenty members with least votes were replaced. While Cromwell always topped the poll and there were considerable continuities, the composition of the Council did change from year to year in ways that reflected the changing complexion of parliament, which became less militantly republican as MPs who had not supported the regicide drifted back, though the House could seem more radical as issues arose, as the external threats to the state grew or faded, and as its agenda changed. However, the engagement binding members of the Council pledged all to 'the maintenance and defence of [parliament's] resolutions concerning the settling of the government of this nation for the future in way of a Republic, without King or House of Lords'.[6]

Milton's employment by the Council was covered by two of fifteen 'instructions' which made up the Act of February 1649:

6. You shall advise, order, and direct concerning the entertaining, keeping, renewing, or settling of amity and a good correspondency with foreign kingdoms and states, and for preserving the rights of the people of this nation in foreign parts, and composing of their differences there: and you are hereby authorised to send ambassadors, agents, or messengers to any foreign kingdom or state, and to receive ambassadors, agents, or messengers from them for the ends aforesaid.

· · · · · · · · · · · · · ·

11. You have hereby power and are authorised to charge the public revenue by warrant under the seal of the Council with such sum or sums of money from time to time as you shall find necessary for defraying all charges of foreign negotiations, intelligence, and other incidencies, and for the salary of such subordinate officers and attendants as you shall judge fit to employ, and for the effectual carrying on of the service by those instructions committed to you, or by any other instructions hereafter to be given you from the Parliament.[7]

The Council had among its most pressing obligations the conduct of foreign policy, and to that end it strengthened its secretariat by the addition of Milton.

He joined a group of civil servants that would be supplemented further through the early years of the Interregnum by other men of considerable ability, as the service in general expanded, as the Council spawned further standing committees and as it developed the use of numerous temporary ad hoc committees.[8] The key appointment was Walter (or Gualter) Frost as Secretary to the Council, Milton's senior colleague. Though there were considerable continuities of employment between the civil service of the Long Parliament and that of the Purged Parliament, not all continued in post. Milton replaced the veteran Georg Rudolf Weckherlin, who had served successive administrations as secretary for foreign languages since 1625.[9] Intelligence was the portfolio of Thomas Scott, an MP and an enthusiastic regicide; he would be executed in 1660. His salary was about three times that paid to Milton.[10] Control of the entrée to parliament and Council functionally belonged to a long-time career diplomat, Sir Oliver Fleming, a cousin of Cromwell, and Master of the Ceremonies.[11]

The staffing levels supporting the Council of State rapidly outgrew the provision of the Derby House Committee. There were clerks and underclerks, a Sergeant at Arms with eight deputies, twelve messengers, a housekeeper, two porters and cleaning staff, together with the secretariat for diplomacy and foreign relations, to which Milton belonged.[12] Plainly, he was joining a well-resourced and thoughtfully planned operation at the centre of the republican project. Moreover, the Council it served was powerful, not only in its remit and authority, but also in the social and political seniority of its members. Its initial members included 'five English peers, two sons of English peers, and one Scottish peer'.[13] Thirty-four were MPs. Its President, till the office became rotational in 1652, was John Bradshaw, who had presided over the trial of Charles I. He was, in Aylmer's judgement, 'a humourless mediocrity but honest and no fool', and he seems 'to have have regarded the Lord Presidency of the Council as his due'.[14] Cromwell, and Henry Ireton, his politically astute son-in-law, regicide, and 'chief theoretician of the revolutionary army',[15] were members, as was Major-General Harrison, another regicide, who, like Thomas Scott, would be executed after the Restoration. Thomas Harrison emerged in the early 1650s as an influential figure among radical millenarians.[16]

Why did this powerful body recruit Milton? And why did he accept the appointment? Both questions are difficult to answer. Certainly, the Council needed a first-rate Latinist. For it to communicate ineptly with other states of Europe would have invited derision. In *Pro Populo Anglicano Defensio* Milton felt constrained to taunt royalist exiles, 'bishops and scholars and jurists', who 'assert that all the arts and letters fled from England in your company'.[17] The English republic had a pressing need to demonstrate the error of that view through its evident mastery in diplomatic correspondence of the highest standards of Latinity. Yet Milton had no proven record of writing excellent Latin, though his competence could probably have been confirmed by trusted authorities, such as Samuel Hartlib. In practice Milton proved his extraordinary facility in the difficult art that is now known as *retour* interpretation, translating spoken Latin into English and English into spoken Latin. Colleagues from the Council of State noted and remarked on his greater speed in communication than that of the Oldenburg delegate Hermann Mylius. His extant Latin writing is impeccable, though he evidently had some reservations about bending his Ciceronian purity to the idiom of diplomatic prose.[18] These skills, however essential, were not uniquely Milton's; decent Latinists emerged in numbers from a university system that conducted most of its pedagogy through that medium and where Latin texts dominated the curriculum to the exclusion of the English vernacular. His command of other vernaculars—fluent Italian and a working knowledge of French and Spanish—was an additional, though not essential, qualification, and he had travelled and lived in continental Europe.[19]

But Milton was certainly distinguished by his evident zeal for the regicidal process and his eloquence in its defence. Hiring him, the Council acquired someone wholly aligned with the revolutionary direction its members had taken. Moreover, *The Tenure of Kings and Magistrates*, though not, as far as we know, commissioned by the Purged Parliament, had an immediate impact, furnishing other apologists with useful material. In hiring Milton in one role, they secured the services of an accomplished and sometimes guileful pamphleteer, battle-hardened by his resistance to the Presbyterian mobilization and committed to their defence. Unlike Weckherlin, whose son had fought for the king and had followed him into exile, Milton had no question-mark over his loyalty.

Cyriack Skinner, establishing that Milton had not lobbied for the post, notes that 'hee was, without any seeking of his, by the means of a private Acquaintance, who was then a member of the new Council of State, chosen Latin Secretary'. Edward Phillips stresses the Corinthian spirit and the reluctance to enter employment that characterized the appointment: 'he was courted into the service of this new Commonwealth, and at least prevail'd with (for he never hunted after Preferment, nor affected the Tintamar and Hurry of Publick business) to take upon him the Office of *Latin* Secretary to the Counsel of State for all their Letters to Foreign Princes and States.'[20]

Biographers sometimes speculate on the role patronage played in the appointment. Three possible supporters have been identified within the Council of State. Luke Robinson, two years Milton's junior, was a student with him at Christ's College during 1627–30, and thought highly enough of his prose writings (presumably his regicide tracts) to urge the Council to facilitate their dissemination.[21] Bulstrode Whitelocke, the jurist and

MP, through the 1630s had a high profile in the region of Berkshire, Buckinghamshire, and Oxfordshire, with which the Milton family was variously associated. His principal estate of Fawley Court was about fifteen miles from Horton, which was where his mother's family lived.[22] John Bradshaw certainly knew Milton, since he had represented him in a Chancery case, and there is evidence of subsequent friendly contact.[23] They may have been distantly related. Of course, there were thirty-eight other members of the Council, who could have been the source of his nomination, or indeed a member of the secretariat.

Why did Milton accept? Then as now some parts of public service have a glamour distinctly lacking in others, and the diplomatic corps with its associated operations held an obvious attraction. It sometimes provided employment for highly cultured polymaths, towering figures of late continental humanism. Archduchess Isabella of the Spanish Netherlands used Peter Paul Rubens as an emissary, sending him to the court of Charles I to open the negotiations which ended the Anglo-Spanish war of the 1620s. Milton himself had met Hugo Grotius in Paris during his time as Swedish ambassador to France.[24] Closer to home, Weckherlin, the German émigré whom Milton in effect replaced, was a significant poet in his native tongue, 'credited with pioneering the vernacular form of German verse . . . and one of the most notable German poets of the period'.[25] Like the young Milton, he also wrote sonnets in Italian. Milton had counted among his most valued acquaintances the career diplomat Sir Henry Wotton, art collector (in the interest of the earl of Arundel and the duke of Buckingham), architectural historian, and occasional poet of some accomplishment, who had died in 1639.[26] Hermann Mylius, the Oldenburg ambassador, to whose mission we turn shortly, and Milton plainly established the easy discourse of European men of letters who were also accomplished in the ways of international diplomacy.

The emphasis by Skinner and Phillips on Milton's reluctant self-sacrifice picks up a theme from his own account in *Pro Populo Anglicano Defensio* of his motivation in accepting office:

As for me, no man has ever seen me seeking office, no man has ever seen me soliciting aught through my friends, clinging with suppliant expression to the doors of Parliament, or loitering in the hallways of the lower assemblies. I kept myself at home for the most part, and from my own revenues, though often they were in large part withheld because of the civil disturbance, I endured the tax—by no means entirely just—that was laid on me and maintained my frugal way of life.[27]

Indeed, Milton's point is a valid one: though he may have considered seriously the establishment of a private school, the project was not sustained beyond the move to his house in Barbican. Before the war, he lived well enough off private income and evidently entered with financial equanimity into marriage. During the war, he managed without evident hardship. The death of his father, which released to him his full patrimony, and the end of the war, which freed up income streams that had been interrupted, left him, at the start of 1649, considerably richer than at any other time. He had even secured the resumption of revenue from his father-in-law's estate, in lieu of the debt that was outstanding. Even after the Restoration, he lived fairly comfortably on his inherited wealth.[28]

Yet the new appointment really took his income level and, potentially, his personal wealth to a significantly higher level. Milton's annual salary at the outset was set at £288 13s. 6½ d. Quite senior officials were often paid in the range of £200–300. His salary exceeds that of a Colonel of Horse or Foot and roughly equates with a naval captain of a first-rate vessel. It is by no means a negligible sum.[29] Other income and payment in kind followed such an appointment. By November 1649 the Council of State had resolved to move Milton into lodgings in Whitehall, to be nearer to hand. Presumably he occupied these *gratis*, since in June 1650 the Council of State also allowed him a warrant 'for the furnishing of his lodgeing in Whitehall with some hangings'.[30] Members of the diplomatic secretariat could expect and in the event did receive fees for services rendered to foreign visitors, and they were obvious targets for bribery.[31] Moreover, there was the further possibility of very senior promotion within the service. Sir Philip Meadows, who had joined as Milton's assistant in 1653 (in place of Andrew Marvell, who had been Milton's choice),[32] subsequently went as an agent to Portugal and thereafter as a full ambassador to Denmark, with an allowance of £1,000 per annum. As he attempted to mediate in 1657–8 in the Dano-Swedish conflict, he was bribed by the king of Sweden with 10,000 riksdaler, then equivalent to about £1,800. As Aylmer tartly notes, 'No doubt this was more to the point than the Order of the Elephant which was bestowed upon him by the impecunious king of Denmark', though he adds that 'there is no evidence that Meadowes allowed his judgment or his reports to be influence by it'.[33]

In the event, Milton's initial appointment did not lead to that order of affluence. Nevertheless, it rendered him significantly richer than formerly. It may have prompted his decision, in April 1649, to purchase a 21-year extension to the lease he held on an investment property, the Red Rose, a large house on the west side of Bread Street, formerly held by his father on a 21-year lease, which still had four years to run. The investment was a large one. Milton eventually agreed on four half-yearly payments of £100 (to be rebated at 6 or 7 per cent for prompt settlement).[34] Though much remains elusive about Milton's finances, we do know that he had accumulated at least £2,000 in government bonds by 1660.[35] Milton and his earliest biographers represented his service of the state in terms of personal sacrifice; he was, however, very well paid.

But we should recognize the limitations of Milton's role. Socially and educationally, he had much in common with his new colleagues, who were mostly from fairly wealthy families, and among whom education at university or an inn of court (or both) was common.[36] While he was not out-of-place among the men he worked with, he was decidedly a notch below most of the men he worked for. The councillors most active in foreign affairs in the early days of the Purged Parliament were, for the most part, much wealthier than Milton. Bulstrode Whitlocke had inherited considerable estates and had pursued a successful legal career; since March 1648 he had been Keeper of the Great Seal, with an annual stipend of £1,000. Thomas Chaloner was the son of a baronet. Sir Henry Vane had been governor of Massachusetts at the age of 23 and had held high and lucrative office in the final days of the Personal Rule. Henry Mildmay held numerous lucrative offices under Charles I, and had married an heiress who brought a £3,000 dowry. The Purged Parliament awarded him £2,000 in respect of an earlier loan made to the king. Sir Henry Marten, who chaired the Committee for Foreign Affairs, as a young man had lived the life of a rake, reputedly costing his father £1,000 a year for his upkeep. He had loaned large sums to parliament and in July 1649 was richly rewarded with the grant of £1,000 per annum and vast tracts of confiscated land. The first Council of State was composed of similarly propertied and affluent men of considerable social standing, leavened by a cluster of aristocrats. The MPs had the added aura of political authority and asserted the ancient privileges of their parliamentary status. Those who held army rank were from the highest echelons of the officer cadre, and carried not only the dignity of rank and the prestige of martial heroes but also very considerable stipends. Cromwell, for example, had a salary in excess of £3,600 per annum as Lord General, plus further stipends for the colonelcies he held.[37]

Unsurprisingly, such men held Milton to be their inferior and in some respects their servant. Of course, when he interpreted in both directions between Latin and English, for the commissioners and a visiting ambassador, they sat while he stood;[38] social decorum alone would have required it, let alone the protocols of diplomatic conduct. This chapter will disclose little evidence that Milton shaped in any way the international relations for which he provided his skill as a neo-Latinist; policy was set elsewhere, and he drafted what he was instructed to draft.

Accepting office meant accepting a new kind of personal discipline. The operation of the Council of State was strictly confidential. The engagement taken by its members pledged them 'not [to] reveal or disclose anything, in whole or in part, directly or indirectly, that shall be debated or resolved upon in the Council, without the command or direction of the Parliament, or without the order or allowance of the major part of the Council or of

32. Sir Henry Vane the Younger, by William Faithorne (1662) (National Portrait Gallery, London).

the major part of them that shall be present at such debates or resolutions'.[39] That requirement was extended to its secretariat shortly after Milton's appointment.[40] But Milton seems to have accepted a far wider code of silence as a concomitant of state employment. Throughout its life, the Purged Parliament was much exercised by determining a church settlement, defining the relationship of church to state, and resolving the vexed question of how the clergy were to be funded. We know from poems written at the height of the immensely controversial tithe debate but not published till much later that Milton felt deeply about these issues and that he espoused a radical view that was a minority position within the Purged Parliament. Yet he deferred any print engagement with these concerns till 1659.[41]

Milton's new post no doubt kept him on call to translate documents into English as they arrived and to express the communications of his masters in Latin, and yet we may wonder quite how time-consuming it was. The Council of State met very frequently, but it seems evident that he was not obliged to attend all its full sessions (though he evidently worked closely with some committees and task groups); the Council was the responsibility of Gualter Frost. Milton could translate from Latin, both spoken and written, with extreme facility. There is strong evidence that a good neo-Latinist could knock out a diplomatic communication in a very few hours. Mylius evidently composed Latin communications, both formal and more casual, with extreme facility.[42] While the post was scarcely a sinecure and his role expanded to include some scrutiny of seized documents and for a while elements of press supervision, it still left Milton with ample opportunity to serve the state in other ways for which he was uniquely qualified. As Edward Phillips, who was probably still living with his uncle at the time of his appointment, recalled, 'the business of his Office came not very fast upon him, for he was scarce well warm in his Secretaryship, before other Work flow'd in upon him, which took him up for some considerable time'.[43] The Council had hired a polemicist of great energy, skill, eloquence, and guile in English, and in Latin a man who would speak for them to the nations of Europe with a distinction that would render him among continental Europeans probably second only to Cromwell in fame and notoriety among England's republicans.

Milton's appointment evidently proved a major success, and he retained office, with some adjustments to his role, through the Interregnum. Yet the service his gave was to some extent impeded by a serious illness from which he was already suffering in March 1649 and which would soon render him completely blind.[44] The fullest description of Milton's blindness is given in a letter of 28 September 1654 to Leonard Philaras, an Athenian living in Paris (where he was known as Léonard Villeré) as an agent of Ranuccio II Farnese, the duke of Parma. The letter was to be passed to the French ophthalmologist François Théverin, so Milton described his symptoms in detail:

It is ten years, I think, more or less, since I noticed my sight becoming weak and growing dim, and at the same time my spleen and all my viscera burdened and shaken with flatulence. And even in the morning, if I began as usual to read, I noticed that my eyes felt immediate pain deep within and turned from reading, though later refreshed after moderate bodily exercise; as often as I looked at a lamp, a sort of rainbow seemed to obscure it. Soon a mist appearing in the left part of the left eye (for that eye became clouded some years before the other) removed from my sight everything on that side. Objects further forward too seemed smaller, if I chanced to close my right eye. The other eye also failing slowly and gradually over a period of almost three years, some months before my sight was completely destroyed, everything which I distinguished when I myself was still seemed to swim, now to the right, now to the left. Certain permanent vapors seem to have settled upon my entire forehead and temples, which press and oppress my eyes with a sort of sleepy heaviness, especially from meal time to evening ... while considerable sight still remained, when I would first go to bed and lie on one side or the other, abundant light would dart from my closed eyes; then, as sight daily diminished, colors proportionately darker would burst with violence and a sort of crash from within; but now, pure black, marked as if with extinguished or ashy light, and as if interwoven with it, pours forth. Yet the mist which always hovers before my eyes both night and day seems always to be approaching white rather than black; and upon the eyes turning, it admits a minute quantity of light as if through a crack.[45]

The letter eloquently suggests Milton's horror at the onset and progression of the disease. But what was the cause? Some of what he says, particularly about his gastro-intestinal discomforts, may have relevance in his later illnesses, and we shall return to them, though they are probably not pertinent here.[46] We gathered the remaining details available from the early lives, most of which have something to say about the disease, and had case notes prepared that would allow the revaluation of the likely cause in light of modern medical knowledge.

It appears that Milton's sight first begins to weaken at the age of 36, first in the left eye and then the right. Symptoms gradually worsen until there is a complete loss of sight at the age of 44. Initial symptoms were of looking at a light and seeing rainbow colours obscuring it. Then a mist appeared in the bottom left part of the left eye. Milton noticed his symptoms were worst in the morning and associated with headaches. There was then a gradual, unremitting 'misting' of the vision. As symptoms progressed, he noticed occasional flashing lights as he closed his eyes; headaches became more frequent. Each eye took about three years to progress to complete blindness, left eye then right eye.

When completely blind, Milton describes the world as looking more whitish than blackish. His eyes are noted as having a normal appearance to the observer. His physician of the time (*c.*1650) tried treating him with a seton stitch; this may well have hastened his visual demise. His only other known past medical history at this point is of gout, which is not strongly associated with any putative causes of his blindness. His father had perfect vision to the age of 84. His mother had 'weak eyes' and wore glasses from the age of 30.

Thus prepared, we consulted with international glaucoma expert Mr Philip Bloom, Consultant Ophthalmologist at the Western Eye Hospital, London, who informs us that this history is very suggestive of intermittent close angle glaucoma. Although eminently treatable with modern medicine, this would have resulted in almost certain blindness in the seventeenth century.[47]

Although he was troubled by the onset of a major disability, Milton wrote two polemics for the state in the course of 1649: the 'Observations' appended to *Articles of Peace Made and Concluded with the* Irish *Rebels, and Papists* and

Eikonoklastes. The former was expressly commissioned by the Council of State, who on 28 March had ordered him 'to make some observations' on affairs in Ireland.[48] The papers of the Council do not record a similar resolution to initiate *Eikonoklastes*, though, as we shall see, it appears to have had official sanction.

The former appeared about seven weeks later; Thomason dated his copy 16 May. It appeared anonymously, though its status as an official response from the government is unequivocal: its title-page is endorsed 'Publisht by Autority'. Ireland had posed an unresolved problem to English governments since 1641 when an uprising by the Catholics against English domination not only disrupted the administration of the island but also resulted in a massacre of English and Scottish settlers, who were all Protestant and were often of a puritan inclination; the Scots were generally Presbyterian. The scale of the massacre was probably overstated, though by 1649 200,000 had wide currency as an 'official government figure'.[49] Milton writes of 'the bloud of more then 200000.... assassinated and cut in pieces by those *Irish* Barbarians'.[50] Atrocity stories, of floggings, castration, rape, sexual humiliation, genital mutilation, and even cannibalism had wide currency. The idiom and political direction of the news campaign are exemplified in Thomas Morley's *Remonstrance of the Barbarous Cruelties and Bloudy Murders Committed By the Irish Rebels Against the Protestants in Ireland... Being the examinations of many who were eye-witnesses of the same... Presented to the whole kingdome of England, that thereby they may see the Rebels inhumane dealing, prevent their pernicious practises, relieve thier poore brethrens necessities, and fight for their Religions, Laws, and Liberties* (London, 1644). Though the events and their reportage served to blacken the reputation of Charles I, who at the least had let the outrage happen, the Long Parliament had also failed to meet the challenge. Ireland descended into anarchy.

At least five warring factions operated: the 'rebels' of the Confederacy of Kilkenny, Catholics in arms against English settlement and dominion; the army led by James Butler, marquess of Ormond, loyal to Charles I and subsequently to Charles II, mobilized to suppress the rebellion; the Protestant forces of Murrough O'Brien, Baron Inchiquin, raised initially to support Ormond's efforts but, since 1645, both more militantly active than Ormond's against the Catholics and loyal to the English parliament; another Protestant army, predominately Scottish, in the north under Sir George Munro; and finally, a small parliamentary army, for the most part of Englishmen. By 1649, the last was confined to Dublin and the Pale, commanded by Colonel Michael Jones, to Londonderry, commanded by Sir Charles Coote, and to coastal enclaves in the north, commanded by Colonel George Monck. Moreover, a shift in allegiances proved critical. Ormond concluded a treaty with the Confederacy, Inchiquin switched his allegiance from parliament, and the loyalties and intentions of the newer settlers appeared decidedly uncertain as Munro's army also threw its lot in with Ormond.[51]

At the same meeting that Milton was appointed to the secretariat, the Council of State named Cromwell 'the commander-in-chief of the troops for Ireland'.[52] The Purged Parliament's move against its Irish opponents had begun in February, with the establishment of a powerful committee to organize the expedition. Ireland had proved the graveyard of many English military reputations, and Cromwell hesitated somewhat longer than Milton before accepting the invitation to command. Milton's 'Observations' were written against the background of Cromwell's sustained and purposeful efforts to assemble the men and *matériel* to ensure success. While Milton was writing, negotiations were underway to secure from the City of London huge loans towards the cause.

Milton's concern for the fate of Protestants in Ireland was deep-felt and long-standing. There is evidence that in 1642 he had made a sizeable donation, £4, for their relief.[53] He was unequivocal both in his 'Observations' and later writings in his belief in the scale and nature of the massacre Protestants had endured and in his implacable hostility to its perpetrators and those whose indifference, incompetence, or complicity had allowed it to happen. In this attitude he differed little, if at all, from Cromwell and from the overwhelming majority of the Purged Parliament and its supporters. The campaign that followed swiftly broke the back of major opposition and saw Cromwell returned to England with his reputation for invincibility further enhanced, though hostilities continued on a smaller scale till 1653 as the English met surprisingly stubborn resistance.

Cromwell's success was founded on the two notorious massacres, at Drogheda, where 2,800 soldiers were killed, 'as well as many inhabitants, including every friar who could be found'; and Wexford, where some 2,000 were slaughtered.[54] The New Model Army, in the campaigns of the English civil wars, for the most part had conducted itself well in the hours of victory. Three conditions, however, stimulated a vengeful impulse among officers and men. They reacted violently if defenders of besieged positions resisted when their defeat was inevitable, thus occasioning unnecessary loss of life among the attacking forces. A stronghold taken by storm could expect grim retribution. They habitually treated captured Catholics appallingly. They profoundly resented fighting over again men who had formerly surrendered when in arms against them. Hence, Fairfax sanctioned summary executions of Sir Charles Lucas and Sir George Lisle after the fall of Colchester. Hence, too, the massacre of 'over 100 defenceless women' when the royalist baggage train fell into the victors' hands after Naseby; they were perceived and represented 'as whores and Irishwomen'.[55] The storming of Basing House, the seat of the Catholic marquess of Winchester, whose late wife the young

Milton had lamented,[56] saw the stern treatment of a wholly Catholic garrison that had resisted, disputing 'every wall and gate. . . . Cromwell allowed his men to put a large number of the house's occupants to the sword even as they cried for mercy'.[57]

At Drogheda, all three circumstances combined. The garrison was commanded by an old enemy, Sir Arthur Aston, who had commanded Reading, where Christopher Milton had appeared in the muster roll, at the time when the town had surrendered. He had at that point been given terms of surrender that would not have precluded further service for the king, and he had fought on in England till 1646; nevertheless, it would have been galling to Cromwell's soldiers to meet again an old enemy they had already beaten. He was also, notoriously, a Catholic, and the town and garrison contained many coreligionaries. Moreover, they fought on even after the walls had been breached, leading to unnecessary English dead, including Colonel Castle, the commander of the regiment that had first broken into the town. According to legend, Castle's men clubbed Aston himself to death using his own wooden leg.[58] Wexford was in some ways a more accidental massacre, perpetrated by troops who thought a garrison which was about to surrender had resolved to resist.

Cromwell's conduct, of course, has in modern times attracted censure. Indeed, John Buchan, his staunchest hagiographer, attempted to find 'a hint of apology' in the account he rendered to Speaker Lenthall, a recognition that 'He had erred grievously and he knew it'. Even Ian Gentles, so often the clear-eyed observer of mid-century military history, finds him 'ambivalent about the slaughter he had authorized'.[59] He seems utterly remorseless, though pragmatical as well as pious, as he reports, 'I am persuaded that this is a righteous judgment of God upon these barbarous wretches, who have imbrued their hands in so much innocent blood, and that it will tend to prevent the effusion of blood for the future, which are satisfactory grounds to such actions, which otherwise cannot but work remorse and regret.'[60] So, killing many now is not regretted since it is obviously divinely sanctioned and will make other garrisons inclined to surrender quickly. Cromwell, however, is in step with English public opinion, and, indeed, with Milton's views and those of the government they both served. Newsbooks reported on Drogheda and Wexford in terms of a providential vindictiveness. At Wexford, for example, 'some preists and Friers were now killed in that Church, where they had caused many of the English to be famished to death, Thus the Lord has found out their wickednesse, and repayed it'.[61] When the Oldenburg ambassador made initial contact with officials of the Purged Parliament, the conquest of Ireland in revenge for the 200,000 dead Protestants recurs as a justification for the regicide and as an example of the new regime's religious credentials.[62] Milton returns to the theme in his defences, and he does so without a flicker of pity for the Irish dead.

Milton's 'Observations', then, serves as preparation for Cromwell's campaign. It seems, superficially, a strange publication, in that forty-four of its sixty-five pages are taken up with the reproduction of documents and declarations, for the most part from people inimical to the Purged Parliament. Its principal component is the articles agreed between Ormond and the Catholic confederacy, and it includes letters from Ormond to Michael Jones, intended to subvert his allegiance to parliament, Jones's loyal reply, and 'A Necessary Representation' issued by the Scottish Presbytery at Belfast. But the publication adapts a successful initiative of the Long Parliament in 1645, *The Kings Cabinet opened: or, Certain Packets of Secret Letters & papers Written with the Kings own Hand, and taken in his Cabinet at* Nasby-Field ... *Together, with some Annotations thereupon.* The 'Annotations' comment on forty-three pages of letters, mostly between Charles I and Henrietta Maria, which, on parliament's account, demonstrate the king's uxoriousness, his duplicity in his dealing with parliament and others, and his willingness to bring in a foreign and mercenary army. The publication, profoundly damaging to any residual reputation for honesty, appeared endorsed on its title page 'Published by speciall Order of the *Parliament*'. The king's enemies had much to gain from suggesting that they confront an attempted Catholic conspiracy, in the name of Protestantism and 'that Cause of Liberty & Religion, which the two Parliaments of *England* and *Scotland* now maintain against a combination of all the Papists in *Europe* almost, especially the bloody Tygers of *Ireland*, and some of the Prelaticall and Court Faction in *England*'.[63]

Milton's 'Observations' plays over the same game, building on a broad Protestant antipathy to Irish Catholics and feeding off the assumptions of a reading public now conditioned to look for and to find royalist and papist conspiracies, though he works more sustainedly than his predecessors to construct an English national interest. Ireland, throughout, is presented as an English property, a subordinate state belonging to the English people. The documents reproduced plainly demonstrate that Ormond and the Scottish Presbyterians in Ulster had already committed themselves to alliance with the Irish Catholics, the murderers of 200,000 fellow Protestants. Milton simply asserts his assurance in the reaction of his readers:

We may be confidently perswaded, that no true borne *English-man*, can so much as barely read them [the Articles of Peace] without indignation and disdaine, that those bloudy Rebels ... after the merciless and barbarous Massacre of so many thousand *English* ... should be now grac'd and rewarded with such freedomes and enlargements, as none of their Ancestors could ever merit.[64]

In a context in which the Purged Parliament's legitimacy would have stood little scrutiny, Milton manoeuvres his Protestant, English readers into accepting it, in its mobilization of a force to reconquer Ireland, as the protector of the faith and of national interest. In contrast, Ormond has given away Englishmen's ancient rights over Ireland, 'disallieg[ing] a whole Feudary Kingdome from the ancient Dominion of *England*'. Milton's attack on Ormond is the occasion for his first defence of Cromwell, traduced as 'some such *John* of *Leiden*', intent on becoming an elective monarch. Milton's reply contrasts the failures of the old aristocracy, exemplified by Ormond's inept attempts to suppress the Irish rebels, with Cromwell's 'more eminent and remarkable Deeds whereon to *found* Nobility in his house, though it were wanting'.[65] Laura Knoppers has remarked on the complexities of representation of Cromwell in the years of the Purged Parliament.[66] Milton's task here is relatively simple, an opposition of effective service in the national interest, based on real merit, and the incompetencies of office based merely on inherited status. The underlying assumptions, however, are profoundly republican.

Milton expends proportionately most effort in responding to the censure of the leading Scottish Presbyterians in Belfast. Milton makes something of their foreignness and their obscurity. They write 'from a barbarous nook of *Ireland*'.[67] However, his principal concerns are to address the crisis in English Presbyterianism occasioned by the coup of December 1648 and the subsequent eclipse of political Presbyterianism. Blair Worden's classic account of the Purged Parliament defines its apparent conservativism in part in terms of 'its anxiety to isolate royalists from presbyterians'. As he observes, Cromwell saw a crucial role for the conquest of Ireland in that process, along with military opposition to the new Scottish royalism, since 'These barbarous races were the enemies of the nation rather than merely of the Rump, and campaigns against them offered the government its best hope of securing the tolerance, if not the support, of presbyterian opinion in England'.[68] Milton lashes Presbyterians who are both Scots and ministers, and thus demonstrates to Presbyterians who are both English and lay that the Purged Parliament defends a national interest in which they, too, have a share. By cooperating against the Purged Parliament the Scots presbytery betrays Protestantism through 'the appearance of a co-interest and partaking with the *Irish* Rebells. Against whom, though by themselves pronounced to be the enemies of God, they goe not out to battell, as they ought, but rather by these thir doings assist and become associats.'[69] Milton labours to simplify the political choices to the simple alternatives of collaboration with or opposition to Irish Catholicism, where the issues for English lay Presbyterians were at their starkest.

Two assumptions underpin Milton's whole strategy: that Irish Catholics, manifestly, are murdering, unteachable savages, who should be both punished and controlled; and that Ireland *belongs* to England, as a dependency, acquired through conquest *by the English nation*, to be exploited by and for the

English nation. The national self-fashioning and the construction of the Irish as a race that is scarcely human are careful, racist, and imperialist, and they justify in advance a campaign that was to be marked by its extraordinary brutality and eventually by the expropriation of the ancestral homelands of the Catholic population of Ireland. Milton produced a tendentious dossier designed to launch and excuse a dubious war of aggression. He would not be the last public servant to do so; though he may, perhaps, have been the first.

Milton whole-heartedly accepted the commission to write on Ireland. His response to another instruction from the Council of State, made two days earlier on 26 March, has occasioned some speculation. He was 'appointed to make some observations on a paper lately printed, called Old and New Chains'.[70] The tracts in question are both by the Leveller leader, John Lilburne: *Englands New Chains Discovered* (Thomason dated his copy 'March 1st 1648', i.e. 1649); and *The Second Part of Englands New-Chaines Discovered* (Thomason dated his copy 'March 24 1648', i.e. 1649, just two days before the Council of State decided to act). Milton never produced the commissioned response. One sometimes adduced explanation is that he felt too sympathetic to the Leveller cause to campaign against it. After all, these two tracts celebrated the abolition of monarchy and the House of Lords, and they called for press freedom and the abolition of tithes. Lilburne's only explicit reference to Milton comes from a pamphlet of 1652, where, perhaps with some irony, he recommends to the Purged Parliament that they live up to the high-minded advice given them in the *Pro Populo Anglicano Defensio* of 'their valiant and learned Champion MR. MILTON'.[71] Milton nowhere mentions either Levellers in general or Lilburne in particular.

Milton would have been a poor choice to refute the pamphlets, not least because, in their detail, they contain much that is accurate, and the best response would have been some kind of character assassination, which he had not formerly mastered. They were published at a turning point in the relationship between Cromwell and his closest associates and the Levellers. Before the purging of parliament and the killing of the king, the army grandees had cautiously retained a dialogue with them, and had agreed a platform on the basis of their common ground, including tolerationism, an unrelenting view of the king's culpability, the rights and claims of the soldiery, and opposition to political Presbyterians in parliament. Yet their further demands for a new political settlement and constitutional reform to widen the franchise, together with a reluctance to support the planned Irish campaign and the asseveration that the MPs had simply sought power for themselves, meant that an open and irrevocable breach was much closer than Lilburne anticipated. The pamphlet and the challenge it posed 'found echo promptly from the ranks [of the New Model Army]'.[72] On 28 March, Lilburne and three other leading civilian Levellers were arrested; by the end of the day, the Council of State, probably at Cromwell's insistence, had committed them to the Tower. (Lilburne claimed to have overheard Cromwell, who, 'thumping on the Council table', had hectored his colleagues, 'if you do not break them, they will break you'.[73])

In Milton's place John Canne answered the two pamphlets, though there is no record that he did so at the direct behest of the Council of State. Canne, who seems to have been a General Baptist minister though later became a Fifth Monarchist, worked assiduously in 1649 to defend the Purged Parliament and the regicide. Whether paid to or not, he published two responses, the first of which, like the *Articles of Peace*, carried on its title page the endorsement *'Published by Authoritie'*: *The Discoverer: Wherein is set forth (to undeceive the Nation) the reall Plots and Stratagems*, and its companion piece, *The Discoverer.... The Second Part*. Again, both are, like the *Articles of Peace*, printed by Matthew Simmons. Canne's strategy is to suggest that Levellerism, in the words of the title page of the first tract, aims 'to deprive the Nation of their *Religion, Rights, Liberties, Proprieties, Lawes, Government*, &c.' His method unscrupulously involves selective quotation from a wide range of Leveller publication and a studied, disingenuous confusion of what Lilburne and his colleagues advocated with the radical agrarian communism of Gerrard Winstanley, whose tracts are cited and discussed at length.

Spring 1649 proved decisive for many radical activists. Henry Marten, a friend of Lilburne and for long sympathetic to aspects of Levellerism, silently disengaged from their cause. John Goodwin, the Independent minister in some respects closest to Milton,[74] preached in praise of their overthrow.[75] Since Cromwell was plainly identified as the Levellers' most potent adversary, and since Milton praised him fulsomely in his 'Observations', published in May, it is overwhelmingly probable that the decision not to accept the commission to write against them was practical rather than ideological. A wise judgement probably concluded that the Irish tract was more pressing, and that Milton, experienced in attacking Presbyterians, in associating his enemies with the taint of Catholicism, and well versed in the arguments for regicide, would be better at that than at attacking radicals. Yet his support for the Purged Parliament and for Cromwell against Lilburne and his associates need not be questioned. In his stead, Canne worked expeditiously enough, and Thomason received his pamphlets in June and July. By then, the dangers posed by Levellerism had passed, crushed with the crushing of the mutinies of army Levellers, which had concluded at Burford, Oxfordshire, with exemplary execution of three troopers once they had surrendered: 'For the rest of Cromwell's lifetime [the New Model Army] was his to command.'[76] Lilburne remained in the Tower.

Canne probably had some personal contact with Milton before the latter's appointment, since his own defence of the regicide, *The Golden Rule, or, Justice Advanced* was collected by Thomason only three days after he acquired *The Tenure of Kings and Magistrates*. For Milton to have influenced it, as has for long been argued, Canne must have seen the earlier tract in manuscript. Canne continued his whole-hearted support of the Purged Parliament over 1649, as he published tracts justifying the Irish campaign and defending the Purged Parliament's members from their apparent reneging on the Solemn League and Covenant, which carried on their title pages 'Published by Authority'. These, too, were published by Matthew Simmons.[77]

The Council of State plainly recognized the need to assemble as strong a team of propagandists as possible. Two months after Milton, John Hall was recruited to the service of the Council of State, 'to make Answere to such pamphletts as shall come out to the preiudice of this Commonwealth'.[78] Hall, though only 22, had a recent record as an accomplished and lively journalist, and for successive governments in the 1650s, till his death in 1656, 'he wrote works to confute William Prynne, Christopher Love, . . . and probably a number of others, including [John] Lilburne, under cover of anonymity'.[79]

Yet, unmistakeably, if only in the sheer volume of their opponents' activity, the Purged Parliament was losing the war for public opinion in press and pulpit. While the Presbyterians dominated the latter, die-hard royalists had achieved the greatest propaganda coup of the century, the publication of *Eikon Basilike: The Portraiture of His Sacred Majesty in His Solitudes and Sufferings*. Richard Royston played a pivotal role. Through the 1640s he had published anti-parliamentary propaganda, for which he suffered some close attention and occasional imprisonment. Some time before the execution of the king, he had secured a manuscript, secured the services of several printers, and had even moved a press outside London to escape detection. Thus, he ensured the book appeared on the day of the execution.[80] The book proved an immediate publishing success. In 1649 alone thirty-five editions were published in England and twenty-five elsewhere in Europe (and it was frequently reprinted for years afterwards). Though the political commitment and indeed courage of Royston and some other publishers were unquestionable, the phenomenon was further driven by its commercial success, since the market, stimulated perhaps by the frisson of oppositional transgression, supported prices out of line with the usual rates for political tracts. Indeed, Richard Holdsworth, the ejected former master of Emmanuel College, Cambridge, wrote to William Sancroft, future archbishop of Canterbury, who still held on to his Fellowship there, that copies were 'excessively dear', and that Royston's editions were going for over 6*s*.[81]

33. Charles I (attrib.), *Eikon Basilike, The pourtraicture of His Sacred Majestie in his solitudes and sufferings* (n.p., 1649), frontispiece.

Eikon Basilike posed a unique challenge even to polemicists experienced, as Milton surely was, in the business of confutation. It purported to be the late king's own account of events, or, rather, his reflections on events, and each chapter concludes with a prayer, supposedly the king's pious response to the expository section which precedes it. The insistently reflective mood allows the filtering out of hard, easily disputable details and permits the author to function at a level of grand, vague abstraction. Milton complains that the book lacks 'any moment of solidity', which makes it a very difficult target on which to land a blow, as Charles uses 'the plausibility of large and indefinite words'.[82] Only the king himself, the queen, the Prince of Wales, the first earl of Strafford, and Sir John Hotham, a turncoat commander eventually executed by the parliamentary side, are identified by name or title. Smartly, the text begins with the calling of the Long Parliament. It is decidedly elusive in

(221)

its anticipation of the eventual triumph of monarchy and the identification of the principal culprits to be dealt with, reflecting royalist uncertainties in the final months of 1648 about who could be identified as potential allies. All Charles's conduct before the autumn of 1640, about which the subsequently diverse range of puritan opinion was substantially in agreement, is omitted. William Prynne stormed against the regicide in 1649; in 1637, when his ears were cropped at the sentence of the Star Chamber, his view of the monarch and his regime was rather different. *Eikon Basilike* excluded discussion of the those days of broadly based puritan consensus, when Prynne shared the scaffold with the future Independent minister, Henry Burton, and the future hammer of Independency, John Bastwick; and when the future Leveller (and future Quaker) John Lilburne was flogged through London at the cart's tail for distributing Bastwick's books. The Scottish campaigns, so ill judged and poorly executed, are also passed over, which was an obvious advantage to a royalist project that intended to use Scotland as the base for its conquest of England. As an added problem, *Eikon Basilike*, which in the overwhelming majority of its editions appeared as a neat octavo rather than the usual quarto, scarcely looked like a work of controversy, but appeared instead like a psalter or an enchiridion of personal devotion.

Eikon Basilike, then, constituted a perceived threat to the new regime, virtually from its inception. There is no record of Milton's commission, though he clearly asserts that the work came to him as an unlooked for assignment, rather than a task that he had sought. Indeed, his comments in *Eikonoklastes* imply a puzzling lack of urgency: 'I take it on me as a work assign'd rather, then by me chos'n or affected. Which was the cause both of beginning it so late, and finishing it so leasurely, in the midst of other imployments and diversions.'[83] Posssibly Milton and his masters thought the *Eikon Basilike* phenomenon would fizzle out, or perhaps they thought another pro-Purged Parliament tract, the anonymous *Eikon Alethine*, published at the latest in mid-August (Thomason dated his copy 'August 16'), would answer it adequately.

Indeed, that alternative response presents a useful point of comparison with the polemical decisions Milton made in *Eikonoklastes*. The authorship of *Eikon Basilike* had been doubted from its earliest publication, and indeed evidence emerged after the Restoration that Dr John Gauden, a churchman on whom benefices were later showered, at the least played a major editorial role in readying the manuscript for the press.[84] *Eikon Alethine* unequivocally suggests that a high-ranking clergyman ghosted the text. As a dedicatory poem in the front matter puts it, 'By the Devotion, wit, stile, it appeares | The bishops foot was in't o're head and eares'.[85] Thereafter, the anonymous author, like Milton, simply works through *Eikon Basilike*, chapter by chapter, correcting what he represents as errors, though less assiduously than Milton; it is

Spectatum admissi risum teneatis.

The Curtain's drawne; All may perceiue the plot,
And Him who truely the blacke Babe begot :
Whose sable mantle makes me bold to say
A Phaeton Sol's charriot rulde that day.
Presumptuous Preist to skip into the throne ;
And make his King his Bastard Issue owne.
The Authour therefore hath conceiu'd it meet,
The Doctor should doe pennance in this sheet.

Ε'ΙΚΩΝ Α'ΛΗΘΙΝΗ.

THE
POVRTRAITVRE
OF

Truths moſt ſacred Majeſty truly
ſuffering, though not ſolely.

Wherein the falſe colours are waſhed off, where-
with the Painter-ſteiner had bedawbed Truth, the
late King and the Parliament, in his counterfeit
Piece entituled Εικων βασιλικη,

Publiſhed to vndeceive the World.

Εχθρὸς γὸρ μοι κεῖνος ὁμῶς Αιδαο πυλησιν Homer.
ὅς χ'ἕτερον μὲν κεύθῃ ἐνὶ φρεσὶν ἄλλο δὲ εἴπῃ 9. Iliad.

Aditum nocendi perfido præſtat fides. Sen.

Animadverto enim etiam Deos ipſos, non tam accuratis ado-
rantium precibus, quam innocentia & ſanctitate lætari :
gratieremq; exiſtimari, qui delubris eorum puram, ca-
ſtamq; mentem, quam qui meditatum carmen intulerit.
Plinii Panegyric. *Auguſt. 16*

PROV. 12. 9.
*The lip of truth ſhall be eſtabliſhed for ever ; but a lying tongue
is but for a moment.*

London printed by *Thomas Paine*, and are to be ſold by *George
Whittington* at the blew Anchor in Corn-hill. 1649.

34. Anon., *Eikon Alethine, The povrtraitvre of truths most sacred majesty truly suffering* (London, 1649), frontispiece and title page.

about half the length of *Eikonoklastes*. He often adopts a facetious tone, available to him since he is playing the old puritan game of bashing bishops, not indecorously cheeking a late and revered figure surrounded with the traditional attributes of majesty. While the strategy tries to discredit the authenticity of 'the King's book', it does so at the expense of shifting focus from the real target, Charles I himself, to old and beaten enemies.

The first edition of *Eikonoklastes*, published by Matthew Simmons no later than early October 1649 (Thomason dated his copy 'Octob 6'), unlike *Eikon Alethine* and, more significantly still, unlike Milton's 'Observations', did not appear anonymously. Its title page carries the line 'The Author I.M.'. Thomason amended his copy by adding 'ilton'. That same formula had been used on the title page of Milton's evidently influential and widely read *Tenure of Kings and Magistrates*. The authorship of *Eikonoklastes* can scarcely have been secret. However, unlike *Eikon Alethine* and *The Tenure of Kings and Magistrates*, and like 'Observations', *Eikonoklastes* carries on its title page 'Published by Authority'. Crucially, this is both an officially endorsed response to *Eikon Basilike* and the personal statement of John Milton, marking his changed status from anonymous government spokesman to principal defender of the English republic.

EIKONOKΛΑΣΤΗΣ 5:

I N

Anſwer

To a Book Intitl'd

EΙΚΩΝ ΒΑΣΙΛΙΚΗ,

T H E

PORTRATURE of his Sacred MAjesty

in his *Solitudes* and *Sufferings.*

The Author *I. Milton*

PROV. 28. 15, 16, 17.

15. *As a roaring Lyon, and a ranging Beare, fo is a wicked Ruler over the poor people.*
16. *The Prince that wanteth underſtanding, is alſo a great op-
preſſor; but he that hateth covetouſneſſe ſhall prolong his dayes.*
17. *A man that doth violence to the blood of any perſon, ſhall fly
to the pit, let no man ſtay him.*

Saluſt. Conjurat. Catilin.

Regium imperium, quod initio, conſervandæ libertatis, atque augendæ rei-
pub. causâ fuerat, in ſuperbiam, dominationemque ſe convertit.
Regibus boni, quam mali, ſuſpectiores ſunt; ſemperque his aliena virtus for-
midolola eſt.
Quidlibet impunè facere, hoc ſcilicet regium eſt.

Price 6ᵈ *Publiſhed by Authority.*

London, Printed by *Matthew Simmons,* next dore to the gilded
Lyon in Alderſgate ſtreet. 1 6 4 9.

35. John Milton,
Eikonoklastes (London,
1649), title page.

Indeed, in an extensive preface Milton establishes his own persona as reluctant but public-spirited citizen of a renewed England and explicitly its champion:

Kings most commonly, though strong in Legions, are but weak at Arguments; as they who ever have accustom'd from the Cradle to use thir will onely as thir right hand, thir reason alwayes as thir left. Whence unexpectedly constrain'd to that kind of combat, they prove but weak and puny Adversaries. Nevertheless for their sakes who through custom, simplicitie, or want of better teaching, have not more seriously considerd Kings, then in the gaudy name of Majesty, and admire them and thir doings, as if they breath'd not the same breath with other mortal men, I shall make no scruple to take up (for it seems to be the challenge both of him and all his party) to take up this Gauntlet, though a Kings, in the behalf of Libertie, and the Common-wealth.[86]

Of course, *Eikon Basilike* throws down no gauntlet; indeed, it labours to disguise its own status as a work of controversy. *Eikonoklastes* bullies it into a fight, taking its pious meditations and turning them into alleged facts, arguments, statements that can be challenged.

And challenged they are. Chapter by chapter, Milton implacably confronts what the king says with what he and his readers know to have been the case. The king asserts that he called the Long Parliament mainly of his own choice. No, he did not—'to all knowing men [this claim is] apparently not true', 'as any Child may see'. The king recalls that, as he attempted to seize the five members, he went to parliament *'attended with some Gentlemen'*. No, he did not—they were 'the ragged Infantrie of Stewes and Brothels; the spawn and shipwrack of Taverns and Dicing Houses'. At the start of the civil war, he was so bereft of resources that 'his chiefest Armes left him were those onely which the ancient Christians were wont to us against thir Persecuters, Prayers and Teares'. Milton, wondering how then the civil war proved so long, brutal and costly, interrogates him further: 'What were those thousands of blaspheming Cavaliers about him, whose mouthes let fly Oaths and Curses by the voley; were those the Praiers? and those Carouses drunk to the confusion of all things good and holy, did those minister the Teares?'[87]

Milton's use of the interrogative mood is persistent and purposeful throughout the tract.[88] He sees an obvious advantage in juxtaposing what the king says with a question: how does this square with what he says elsewhere? how may this fiction be reconciled with what you, my reader, like all good men, already know? Moreover, wherever he can, Milton attempts to recapture the spirit of broadly configured solidarity across the spectrum of puritan opinion, which had characterized the earliest years of the conflict. By invoking the stereotypical representation of the 'cavalier' as drunken, dissolute 'dammee' Milton can speak again the language of the early 1640s, a language Presbyterians and other backsliders had shared.[89] He seeks out the knowledge, beliefs and values that formerly united all the king's old enemies. Implacably, Milton works through *Eikon Basilike*, translating its pieties into substantive claims, which in turn are relentlessly discredited by reference to common knowledge and plain sense. Thus he turns the king's extraordinary book, unique within the controversies of the mid-century, into an ordinary one, another partisan account of the origins and conduct of the civil war, which can then be brought up against a different version of reality, to which those whose sympathies Milton seeks to capture would also subscribe.

Gradually, Milton accomplishes a sort of cultural mastery over Charles, whose idiom is variously represented as mawkish, indecorous, and tasteless. William Marshall's famous allegorical frontispiece, present in very many editions of *Eikon Basilike*, is associated with those literary forms most loved in court circles in the years of the Personal Rule. It is 'drawn out to the full measure of a Masking Scene'; it's a piece of 'Stagework'. When Charles writes about Henrietta Maria, he falls to 'straines that come almost to Sonnetting'.[90] Editions of *Eikon Basilike*—not the earliest ones—end with a pious coda, 'PRAYERS, Used by His Majesty in the time of his SUFFERINGS. Delivered to Doctor *Juxon* bishop of LONDON immediately before His Death'. As Milton was the first to remark in print, the first prayer was derived from the prayer of Princess Pamela in Book three, chapter six of *The Countess of Pembroke's Arcadia*.[91] Two hypotheses are possible: either Charles (or his ghost writer) was as tasteless and dim as Milton suggests; or, someone has seeded editions with material that proved easy meat to Milton's onslaught. A late seventeenth-century anecdote reports a claim that William Dugard inserted the prayer, at Milton's behest, as 'an attonement for his fault' of printing earlier editions of *Eikon Basilike*, for which he had been arrested. If it were to have happened, it would necessarily have been in early February, more than a month before Milton officially joined the service of the Council of State. The weight of opinion currently runs against acceptance of the claim. J. Milton French asserts that 'The form in which it appears sounds like unadulterated slander';[92] others would rather regard it as a subtle stroke. William Empson, by some way the subtlest Miltonist of his academic generation and himself a wartime propagandist,[93] both believed the story and thought it 'makes [Milton] a broader and more adroit kind of man than is usually thought, less pedantic and self-enclosed, more humane, more capable of entering into other people's motives and sentiments'.[94] However the prayer arrived in the text, its presence exposed Charles to a penetrating attack of accomplished contempt. His good death, as brave on the scaffold as he had been in the court, disguised his deepest corruption. Even in that extremity, he plagiarized and plagiarized, not some work of divinity, but a romance, reaching for 'the polluted orts and refuse' of a pagan prayer to inform his final orisons.[95]

In contrast to the indecorous flashiness of Charles, Milton, as in his earlier tracts of 1649, writes a disciplined, unflamboyant prose. Similes and metaphors are relatively rare. His wordplay and lexical inventiveness remain on a tight rein throughout.[96] The first person occurs infrequently, but when it does, it speaks with extraordinary *gravitas*, as in his promotion of spontaneous prayer over the contrivances of the king: 'I beleeve that God is no more mov'd with a prayer elaboratly pend, then men truely charitable are mov'd with the pen'd speech of a Begger.'[97] Milton establishes a complex image of himself as puritan, public servant, well-wisher to the commonwealth, and truth-teller; he opposes it to his alternative 'portrait' of Charles, liar, poseur, plagiarist, hypocrite, traitor, tyrant, fool.

Milton noted in his commonplace book, under the heading 'OF DUELS', 'not certain in deciding the truth'.[98] The very outcome of what Milton styled as his own duel with Charles I remains open to debate. Taking the longer view, Kevin Sharpe has argued that the failure of republicanism to survive in

English constitutional thinking reflects a failure of the images of republicanism to displace the more alluring images of monarchy in the English political consciousness.[99] But what of the shorter term? Victories of different sorts belong to both participants. *Eikon Basilike* certainly played well with those who had supported the king from the outset of his confrontation with parliament, and helped to found a cult of Charles the Martyr. Milton probably believed that readership to be as unreachable as the indocile savages of Ireland. However, for those who had supported the Long Parliament but had not endorsed Pride's Purge and the Purged Parliament, his text was powerfully persuasive, reminding them of the ceremonialism and repressiveness of the Caroline church, scaring them with the bugbear of the cavalier dammee, suggesting, too, the sorts of treatment they could expect from a restored monarchy. Most effectively, Milton reminds them of what *Eikon Basilike* was really for, namely, preparing the way for a third civil war.[100] Charles II certainly engaged in 1649–51 the active support of Presbyterians in Ireland and Scotland. In England, the Purged Parliament achieved the objective for which Milton worked: when Charles II marched south from Scotland, English Presbyterians did not flock to his standard, observing instead an acquiescent neutrality. The only significant Presbyterian conspiracy of the early republic, usually called after its most distinguished victim, Christopher Love, was discovered and suppressed in the summer before the battle of Worcester. Love's execution sent a simpler kind of message to Presbyterian royalists. Not until Booth's Rebellion of 1658 did Presbyterians take arms against the republican state, and that too was suppressed with facility.[101]

In the choice of format and dialectic, the first edition of *Eikonoklastes* did not lend itself to the development and exposition of the theoretical case against kingship. Its republicanism is inscribed in its evident value system, in its celebration of the rights of freeborn Englishmen and its denigration of the conduct of kings. Milton continued to tinker with it for some months, and a second edition appeared, some time after June 1650, endorsed on its title page, 'Publish'd now the second time, and much enlarg'd'. While Milton changed little of substance in the material he added, his political ideology emerges more clearly, not least in this remarkable passage:

Indeed if the race of Kings were eminently the best of men, as the breed of *Tutburie* is of Horses, it would in some reason then be their part onely to command, ours always to obey. But Kings by generation no way excelling others, and most commonly not being the wisest or the worthiest by far of whom they claime to have the governing, that we should yeild them subjection to our own ruin, or hold of them the right of our common safety, and our natural freedom by meer gift, as when the Conduit pisses Wine at Coronations, from the superfluity of thir royal grace and beneficence, we may be sure was never the intent of God, whose ways are just and equal; never the

(227)

intent of Nature, whose works are also regular; never of any People not wholly barbarous, whom prudence, or no more but human sense would have better guided when they first created Kings, then so to nullifie and tread to durt the rest of mankind, by exalting one person and his Linage without other merit lookt after, but the meer contingencie of a begetting, into an absolute and unaccountable dominion over them and thir posterity.[102]

Stylistically, the passage stands out from the grave austerity that characterizes much of *Eikonoklastes*. Milton premises his argument on a demeaning analogy. Tutbury had been the leading royal stud-farm, owing some of its distinction to the efforts of the first duke of Buckingham. But Charles, demonstrably, did not show the kinds of distinction over his subjects that his horses showed over ordinary nags. The old Aristotelian concept, of tyranny as the government of one person over others to whom he is not superior, becomes entangled with reductive imagery of equine bloodlines and the faintly silly notion of kings standing at stud. Coronation street parties, as the common people draw wine distributed through London's water system, appear less like festivals and more like the uncivil behaviour of the poor. The collocation of 'wine' and 'piss' suggests an unpromising vintage. Milton takes the higher ground with his account of God and Nature; each embody the force of reason, and kingship premised on heredity is incompatible with reason. 'A meer contingencie of a begetting' equates a hereditary monarch's claims to rule with the chance outcome of a random coition.

Milton's third major publication for the Council of State posed a challenge of a different kind, though the arguments shared much common ground with *Eikonoklastes*. Those around Charles II had commissioned a Latin assault on the trial of the king from Claude Saumaise, the great Claudius Salmasius. A French-born convert to Protestantism, he had established a towering reputation within the humanist tradition. He had recovered the Palatine text of the *Greek Anthology* and had edited and commented on a huge range of Greek and Latin authors. He had also achieved a reputation as historian of the early church and as a controversialist, opposing Roman Catholic claims for the primacy and supremacy of the see of Rome. He currently held the chair at Leiden made famous by Joseph Scaliger. He was a formidable neo-Latinist, and indeed his whole oeuvre was in that medium. If there had been those in the Council of State who hesitated at Milton's commission to answer *Eikon Basilike*, further anxieties may have surrounded the allocation of the later task. Milton was a proven controversialist, and he had already demonstrated his capacity to defend what had been done since December 1648. Yet he had published no Latin prose. His wider reputation, insofar as he had one, was as a libertine advocate of divorce reform and apologist for regicide. Against him, stood an academic heavyweight of the status of Grotius or Selden.

Yet the choice of Salmasius as royalist champion, though superficially attractive, was a poor one. Most significantly, he knew virtually nothing about the longer context of England's constitutional struggles. The old but still influential arguments about the ancient constitution seem to have passed him by, and his method over the first half of the huge tract (some 400 pages) that he produced is to pull the debate onto territory where he felt more comfortable. His scholarly reputation related to fields other than political philosophy and recent history. (Grotius or Selden, with their jurist backgrounds, had more pertinent expertise.) Secondly, his knowledge of recent English history was seriously incomplete. Thirdly, he was a foreigner. He may well have had the status to secure an initial interest from continental Europeans, but his alienness was off-putting to an English readership, inviting the obvious question of why the English royalist cause had found no English royalist apologist, at least in Latin. Finally, though he was a competent Latinist, he was rarely witty and smart. Milton missed none of these gaps in Salmasius's armour.

George Thomason had in his possession by 11 May 1649 Salmasius's *Defensio Regia pro Carolo I. Ad Serenissimum Magnae Britanniae Regem Carolum II. Filium natu majorem, Heredem & Successorem legitimum* (n.p., 1649) (*The Royal Defence for Charles I. To the most serene king of Great Britain Charles II. Elder-born son, heir and legitimate successor*). Though the title page of the earliest edition carries neither place of publication nor imprint, it is endorsed '*Sumptibus Regiis*' ['At royal expense'], and is as acknowledgedly official as *Eikonoklastes* had been. The title page carries, too, the royal arms, including the quartering of the Scottish lion rampant, details which Milton's response would meet with precision. Salmasius presumably emphasized the seniority of Charles II among the late king's children since Prince Henry, the duke of Gloucester, the late king's third son, was still in the hands of the Purged Parliament and the royalist interest retained a long-standing anxiety that he could be installed as their puppet.

On the whole, however, the republican response was sluggish. Salmasius worked in the United Provinces, and the text he wrote was first and most frequently printed there. The Council of State, through its representative, Walter Strickland, tried in late November 1649 to inhibit its production through representation to the States General. On 8 January 1650, the Council instructed Milton to write a response. On 18 February 1650, noting that 'several copies . . . are sent from Holland to several booksellers here', the Council ordered their 'discovery and seizure' and the prosecution of the importers, and two days later William Dugard was imprisoned for planning to print it in England.[103]

36. John Milton, *Pro Populo Anglicano Defensio* (London, 1651), title page, with inscription by the second earl of Bridgewater (see p. 402 n. 43).

JOANNIS MILTONI
Angli
PRO POPULO ANGLICANO
DEFENSIO
Contra *Claudii Anonymi*, aliàs *Salmasii*,
Defensionem REGIAM.

LONDINI,
Typis Du Gardianis. Anno Domini 1651.

It was not until 23 December 1650 that Milton presented the manuscript of his reply to the Council, who sanctioned its publication, and it was duly licensed the following week. On or about 24 February 1651 it finally appeared.[104] His continental European reputation would be founded on *Joannis Miltonii Angli pro Populo Anglicano Defensio Contra Claudii Anonymi, alias Salmasii, Defensionem Regiam*. The imprint reads 'Londini, Typis Du Gardianis', the same William Dugard who had been arrested for scheming to print Salmasius. Evidently a month in Newgate, combined with the loss of his principal employment, as a master of the Merchant Taylors' School, and the seizure of his presses, had sufficed to turn him. Milton may have played a part, too, in persuading him; Richard Dugard, the printer's uncle, is said to have been among his circle of friends, though Milton and William may have known each other at Cambridge.[105] Of course, it may have required little by way of personal influence to persuade a man that working for the republic offered better prospects than incarceration and financial and professional ruin.

Milton's title page, matching the symbolism of *Defensio Regia*, sports the arms, not of the monarch of Great Britain, but the twin crest representing

England and Ireland. That same emblem had been placed over Bradshaw's chair in the trial of Charles I, and simultaneously asserted England's claim to the country of Ireland. Scotland's arms are excluded, since, in the view of the Purged Parliament, Scotland was quite free to acclaim Charles II as its king. The old dream of James I, of the uniting of his three kingdoms, is graphically laid to rest. Milton signals in his contemptuous allusion to Salmasius's anonymity within his own text that more than a little undeferential sportiveness is to follow. Most remarkably, though, Milton's own name, John Milton, Englishman, heads the title page. Though the Council of State had commissioned the text, and indeed had required to receive the manuscript before sending it to press, Milton is allowed even more prominence than in the presentation of *Eikonoklastes*. Thus, his claimed status, as champion of the regime, is formally acknowledged. Stressing his Englishness both asserts the attempted nationalist agenda of the Purged Parliament and points up the contrast with the Frenchman the royalist émigrés have employed—Milton speaks as if for the English nation against a foreign opponent.

However, he begins defensively. The tardiness of the republic's response obviously seemed to require explanation. Moreover, he knew enough of the decorum of abuse to realize, once the counter-attack came, his imminent blindness would be known to his respondents and used pitilessly against him. Hence he offers this explanation for the twenty months of delay between the first appearance in England of *Defensio Regia* and the publication of Milton's response:

Some may wonder why we have suffered him to go in triumph so long rejoicing unassailed in our universal silence: As for others I know not, but for myself I can say with assurance that if I had been granted leisure and strength enough for writing it would have been no long laborious task to find words and arguments for the defence of a cause so just. But in the precarious health I still enjoy I must work at intervals and hardly for an hour at a time, though the task calls for continuous study and composition.[106]

The casual admission of the health problem pre-empts hysterical accusations of divine retribution (which followed in due course[107]) Milton's account also manages to suggest that the challenge posed by Salmasius was less than a pressing priority. But Milton certainly had to work hard to build his response. Nor is that task wholly one of couching in elegant Latin his now familiar defence of the judicial process against the late king. Salmasius, albeit with dubious relevance, carried the argument into some unfamiliar territory, particularly in his account of Roman precedents. Milton also honed a smart response, of drawing wherever possible on texts Salmasius had edited or written, using his previous publications against the current one. That, inevitably, entailed research and probably some wholly new reading, no doubt hampered by the rapid deterioration of his eyesight.

Milton follows the same organizing principles as he used in *Eikonoklastes*, confuting Salmasius chapter by chapter. The larger argument remains the same: indeed, some monarchs are fine, some states are best governed by monarchs. He raises, though, the issue of republican government: 'certainly the same government is fitting neither for all peoples nor for one people at all times; now one form is better, now another, as the courage and industry of the citizens waxes or wanes.'[108] There is an obvious implication that a republic is the constitutional form for a people at the height of their courage and industry. It is an argument Milton probably believed, in that he used it in a private response to Leonard Philaras in June 1652. Philaras had evidently written to Milton urging him to use his influence to secure English aid in liberating Greece from the Ottoman empire. Milton's reply, while reflecting the evident sympathies of a classically trained humanist both for a brother humanist (and diplomat) and for the sufferings of Greece, draws on the same argument, that liberation would require Philaras to 'stir and ignite the ancient courage, diligence, and endurance' which characterized the Greek people in their republican and democratic heyday.[109]

In the *Defensio* kings in general and Charles in particular are treated more abrasively than in the *Eikonoklastes* of 1649, though the idiom often echoes the additions made to the second edition, and invokes principles at least as old as Aristotle:

It is neither fitting nor proper for a man to be king unless he be far superior to all the rest; where there are many equals, and in most states there are very many, I hold that they should rule alike and in turn. Everyone agrees that it is most improper for all to be slaves of *one* who is their equal, often their inferior, and usually a fool.[110]

Rarely, then, do kings share the distinction of the breed of Tutbury. Indeed, 'Let none be so stupid, none so wicked, as to believe that kings, who are often but lazy louts, are so dear to God that the whole world must depend upon their whim and be ruled by it.'[111] Charles emerges, through cumulative reference, as a murderer, a tyrant, a fool; but Milton adds another detail, presumably based on anecdotes deriving from Caroline court masque (which was indeed characterized by the extraordinary décolletage of women masquers):[112] 'There is no need to investigate his more private habits and hidden retreats when even in the theatre he kisses women wantonly, enfolds their waists and, to mention no more openly, plays with the breasts of maids and mothers.'[113]

So much for King Charles the Martyr. A deep republican contempt runs through *Pro Populo Anglicano Defensio*, despite the theoretical concessions to foreign monarchies: 'I hate all Monarchs and the Thrones that they sitt on',[114] the second Earl of Rochester's uncompromising phrase, would summarize the tone of the tract. Yet the voice of English republicanism also at times achieves a higher register. The preface reaches its climax in a lofty assertion of uncompromising defiance, if necessary in the face of the world, embodied in a ringing period of measured symmetry:

Causam itaque pulcherrimam hac certâ fiduciâ læti aggrediamur, illinc fraudem, fallaciam, ignorantiam, atque barbariem, hinc lucem, veritatem, rationem, et seculorum omnium optimorum studia atque doctrinam nobiscum stare.[115]

Even in translation, it shares the resonance of the finest *sententiae* of *Areopagitica*:

Let us then approach this cause so righteous with hearts lifted up by a sure faith that on the other side stand deception, lies, ignorance and savagery, on our side light, truth, reason, and the hopes and teaching of all the great ages of mankind.[116]

Yet Milton well appreciated that high-flown rhetoric would not tempt continental Europeans educated in the humanist tradition to plough through nearly two hundred densely printed pages; they wanted spice—or, more precisely, they wanted salt (*sal* or wit).

As a celebrity scholar Salmasius had attracted some of the resentments that sometimes attach to academic *galácticos*. His salary was known to be, by university standards, vast, and he had entered into his Leiden appointment in a 'triumphal reception'.[117] He had already made some enemies through his controversial writing. He had alienated Catholics by his personal apostasy. Gossip abounded, including the widely believed rumour that his wife was a termagant who bossed him around while simultaneously promoting and managing his academic career with a ruthless vigour. Milton plays to a potentially receptive audience, by no means averse to seeing Salmasius humiliated.

The most personalized and pugnacious aspect of Milton's attack has for long been misunderstood. Don Wolfe, for example, complains that 'Milton is...weakened by his invective, his epithets...The tone is dominantly severe, caustic, unrelieved even by humor or lightness or originality.'[118] However, in recent times John Hale has reclaimed Milton's more vituperative Latin prose, relocating it in the tradition of academic 'saltings', aggressive, playful disputation which characterized some of his experiences of an education in early modern Cambridge and which was widely current across European higher education.

Milton engages Salmasius, twenty years his senior and much better known than himself, in rough play, a tousing that rewards the readers not only by the pleasure of the elder's discomfiture but by the wittiness of the confutation. As Hale puts it, 'when the defence is childish or threadbare or ruthless or excitable, or gamesome and captious or petty, perverse in pursuit of victory, we are hearing echoes from the Cambridge duelling-chambers."[119] Moreover, Milton 'is having *fun*' and he 'wants it to be fun for the humanist reader, because what else could sustain even that reader through hundreds of pages of demolition-job?...He was performing, in his fattest role to date, to his largest and most cosmopolitan audience...his most congenial part, to great and *pleasurable* effect."[120]

We see the game played best in passages of lexical brilliance, such as:

Atque jam tua res agitur, non nostra; *Gallus gallinaceus*, inquis, *tam maribus quàm fœminis imperitat*. Quî potest hoc fieri? Cùm tu ipse Gallus, et, ut ferunt, vel nimiùm gallinaceus, non tuæ gallinæ, sed illa tibi imperitet, et in te regnum exerceat: si gallinaceus ergo plurium fœminarum rex est, tu gallinæ mancipium tuæ, non galli-naceum te, sed stercorarium quendam esse Gallum oportet. Pro libris certè nemo te majora edit sterquilinia, et gallicinio tuo stercoreo omnes obtundis; hoc unicum galli gallinacei habes.[121]

The Columbia translator perhaps sticks a little more closely than the Yale to an impossible task:

The next point, however, is not our affair, but yours. '*Gallus gallinaceus*, the cock,' you say, 'wields imperial power over both males and females.' How can that be, since you yourself that are Gallic, and (they say) but too cocky, wield not imperial power over your hen, but she over you? So that if the gallinaceous cock be king over many females, you that are slave to your hen must needs be not Gallus gallinaceus, but some sort of Gallus stercorarius, or dunghill-cock. For the matter of books, in fact, nobody publishes huger dung-hills, and you deafen us all with your crowing over them; that is the only point in which you resemble a true cock.[122]

Salmasius had attempted a point about natural supremacy in the animal world. However, 'Gallus' means both cock and Frenchman, and this particular Frenchman is reputed to be uxorious. The chase is up and running, and lasts for a few lines more after the passage quoted. If this French cock is not a properly gallinaceous cock, perhaps he's a dunghill cock—and, dear reader, there are the dunghills, the huge piles of excrement that are his voluminous publications, over which he crows so loudly. Thus Milton dances a merry jig to the theme of Salmasius's uxoriousness. This may not, now, seem much like a game for grown-ups, let alone the appropriate discourse for high political debate; but it's a witty enough way of engaging an audience delighted by its own appreciation of Latin puns, and it allows the reiteration of a recurrent element in his representation of Salmasius.

The other, probably more pertinent, flaws in Salmasius and his text receive both bantering and more serious treatment. Milton easily proves how little he knows of contemporary English politics, for, as Cyriack Skinner loyally noted, he was 'a Forrainer, & grossly ignorant of our Laws & Constitution'.[123] He has not grasped, for example, that the Council of State is not a supreme council 'but rather appointed for a specified time by the authority of Parliament'.[124] His obsession with demonstrating the justification for monarchical absolutism ignores the fact that such a tradition is not part of English constitutional history and indeed is not characteristic of other nations.[125] But then Salmasius writes as an outsider, a foreigner; his is 'a voice abroad raving about our business'.[126] Moreover, his legendary scholarship is of the wrong sort for the immediate purpose. Even though he is a Protestant convert, he ignores the principal reformers' resistance theories in favour of what is antiquarian and obscure: 'you cannot help rushing into the utter darkness of Isidore of Seville, Gregory of Tours, and even Otto of Freising', whereas 'I have formed my battle line of Luthers, Zwinglis, Calvins, Bucers, Martyrs and Paraeuses'.[127] But then Salmasius is 'a tiresome pedant' given to 'foolish professorial talk', a man who 'till old age has spent his time thumbing anthologies and dictionaries and glossaries, instead of reading good authors with judgment and profit'.[128] Milton, however, plays another game, frequently citing Salmasius's own publications against his arguments, and crushing him with a reference to his *De Episcopis ac Presbyteris*, which demonstrates, *contra* Salmasius's current argument, that 'The Roman people preferred their republican government . . . to the unbearable yoke of the Caesars'.[129]

In the true spirit of academic *Schadenfreude* Milton's early readers were probably thoroughly engaged by his emphatic rolling over of the Salmasian fox. There is an infectious glee in his assertion that 'A man would sooner tire of thrashing him than he of presenting his back to the lash'.[130] But with that glee comes the implacable and unrelenting delivery of the republican message: yes, England's parliament had the right to try the king; yes, the king was guilty; yes, republican government is the constitutional preference for a free and courageous people; yes, kings usually are idle and stupid. In defence of the new regime, Milton takes not one backward step.

He is careful, too, to shape his polemic to the immediate exigencies of diplomatic activity. Salmasius's objective had been to render the republican regime odious across Europe; Milton writes to ease the resumption of normal diplomatic relations with other nations in general and with the United Provinces in particular. There were some obvious affinities between the countries. Both were Protestant trading nations with incipient empires. Moreover, Dutch internal politics bore some striking similarities to the conflicts within England. The government was republican, though, unlike England, federal. Each province sent representatives to a grand council, the States General, which was usually dominated by the province of Holland. Yet since the inception of the Dutch state a powerful and sometimes supreme authority had been held by the House of Orange, a quasi-royal dynasty that intermittently provided quasi-monarchical government through the hereditary office of *stadhouder* or chief magistrate. Throughout the century, Orangists and republicans engaged in the sorts of antagonisms experienced between Stuart monarchists and successive English parliaments. The Orange and Stuart families were closely connected; most recently, Mary, daughter of Charles I, had married Willem II. Willem, however, had died in 1650 of smallpox, leaving as his heir his posthumous infant son, Willem III, who would only assume office in 1672. (Eventually, in 1688, he would become, with his wife Mary, daughter of James II, monarch of the British kingdoms.) Meanwhile, the fiercely republican Johan de Witt was striving for an ascendancy over the Orangists.[131]

In 1650–1 securing friendly relations with the Dutch republic seemed an attainable and useful priority for the foreign policy of the Purged Parliament. Four months after the appearance of Milton's *Pro Populo Anglicano Defensio*, the Purged Parliament's first ambassadorial delegation set off, in great style, for The Hague. In the event, however, their grand entry into the city, with 27 coaches and almost 250 retainers, was greeted with hostile demonstrations, largely organized by Orangists and English royalist émigrés.[132]

Milton can be seen preparing the way. Thus, on occasion he addresses directly the 'most illustrious council of the Federated Netherlands [i.e. the United Provinces]' congratulating them that the attack on their ancient liberties has recently been averted by 'the most providential death of that headstrong youth', Willem II.[133] He works to demonstrate that Salmasius's arguments for royal absolutism apply as strongly in the Dutch context as the English context, and in an obvious attempt to embarrass his adversary with his employers, Milton distinguishes between the honour of the Dutch people and their ungrateful employee:

Could you [i.e. Salmasius] forget the Dutch, whose republic, after they had driven out the Spanish king in long wars successfully waged, by glorious courage won her freedom? Now at her own expense the republic supports you as a knight of the blackboard, not, we hope, that the Dutch youths may from your lying sophistry learn to be so foolish as to choose a return to Spanish slavery rather than fall heir to the glorious freedom of their fathers![134]

Again, 'no free man in any free state, much less in the renowned university of the great Dutch republic, could have written books so slavish [as *Defensio Regia*] in spirit and design that they seem rather to emanate from some slave factory or auction block.'[135]

Milton's defence achieved very quickly the desired circulation, especially in the United Provinces, where it was soon reprinted. There were at least ten further editions printed in London by the end of the year. It was translated into Dutch.[136] A pleasing notoriety soon followed. In June 1651 it was ordered to be publicly burnt in Toulouse. Shortly after, it was burnt twice in quick succession in Paris.[137]

But evidently it was also getting into the right hands. Gerard Schaep, the Dutch envoy to London, at some point early in 1651 bought copies of Milton's defence, in due course submitting to his States of Holland an expenses claim: 'Voor 25 Tractaten vande Secretaris Milton, sijnde, defensio pro Populo Anglicano contra Salmasium, om aen Verscheijden vande Heeren vande Regeringe in Hollant te senden ende bekent te sijn . . . . £4:7:6:' ['For 25 treatises by Secretary Milton, namely Defensio Pro Populo Anglicano against Salmasius, in order to send to various members of the the the government in [the province of] Holland so they may be acquainted, £4 7s. 6d.'].[138] John Toland, writing long after the event, noted that on the first appearance of the defence Milton 'was visited or invited by all the ambassadors at London, not excepting those of Crowned Heads, and particularly esteemed by Adrian Paw' [Adriaan Pauw], the Dutch anti-Orangist politician who had arrived in London on 7 June with a view to averting an Anglo-Dutch war.[139] The mission was unsuccessful, in that the First Anglo-Dutch War began with the 'Declaration against the Dutch' on 9 July 1652 and continued until 5 April 1654.[140] Correspondence between continental humanists, some of them in the service of various regimes, discloses the level of interest and the range of dispersal. In March there was a report from Leiden that both there and in Amsterdam there was an expectation that the English ambassadors would bring over copies of the defence.[141]

In the midst of this frantic activity, Milton's wife Mary gave birth to a son in their Scotland Yard apartment on the evening of 16 March; the boy was called John. Milton's sight was by this time fading quickly, but he was able to see his infant son. The birth seems not to have had any discernible effect on Milton's difficult relations with his mother-in-law, Anne Powell, with whom he was locked in a legal dispute. In 1647 Milton had secured possession of the Wheatley property as a means of keeping alive his hope of securing the money owed to him by his father-in-law. He had secured tenants for the various cottages to generate revenue, and had regularly paid Anne Powell her widow's thirds. A change in the law in 1650, however, meant that anyone who had acquired estate belonging to a royalist delinquent was liable to a fine; Milton submitted a petition to compound, but neglected to conclude the process, as a result of which his tenants were forbidden to pay rent to him. Milton paid the fine in two instalments, but was now forbidden by law to pay Anne Powell her widow's thirds. Anne petitioned repeatedly, and on 11 July 1651 asked the Commissions for Compounding to instruct Milton to pay her thirds (including arrears) 'to preserve her and her children from starving'. A few days later Anne added that 'Mr Milton is a harsh and choleric man'. The Commissioners rejected the petition and denied Anne her thirds. It is not known how Milton reacted to this verdict; it is possible that he did nothing, but equally possible that he paid Anne out of his own funds. She and her children did not starve.

However pressing family matters were, there could be no pause in Milton's professional life, which had assumed a high profile. On 19/29 March Georg Richter wrote to Christoph Arnold in Nuremburg reporting the publication of the defence.[142] Nicholas Heinsius, an old adversary of Salmasius, wrote to his friend Isaac Vossius, a former pupil of Salmasius and at that time librarian to Kristina of Sweden, attesting to the popularity of *Pro Populo Anglicano* in Leiden. By early April, Vossius replied to say that a copy had arrived in Stockholm and that Kristina had immediately borrowed it. A week later he wrote again to add that she had read it and praised both Milton's genius and his style.[143] No doubt Heinsius, and Salmasius's many other academic enemies, relished the news. By the end of the month Heinsius was reporting that there were already five different editions of Milton's tract circulating in Leiden. Soon Heinsius was sharing with Johannes Fredericus Gronovius, like Salmasius a distinguished classicist, the news that Salmasius, by then in Stockholm at the invitation of Kristina, was furious about Milton's attack.[144] Through the summer, Heinsius, Vossius, and Gronovius exchanged questions and information about Milton. By July there was some discussion of the defence in the Hartlib circle.[145] By December at least one continental humanist, the philologist Jan van Vliet (Janus Vlitius), secretary to the Dutch legation, was actively seeking to meet Milton.[146]

By this point England and the United Provinces were at war, and Milton's tasks included servicing the diplomatic arm of the conflict. In 1649 Isaac Dorislaus (whose controversial lectures Milton may have heard at Cambridge) had been sent as an ambassador to the Provinces, and had been assassinated by English royalists. The tensions provoked by this murder were exacerbated when in October 1651 parliament passed the Navigation Act, which restricted Dutch merchant vessels and foreign fishing vessels, in effect excluding the Dutch herring fleet; ships in breech of the act were subsequently seized under letters of marque and reprisal. In December the Dutch sent a three-man embassy (one of whom was the poet and emblematist Jacob Cats), accompanied by ninety officials and dignitaries. When the embassy was received by parliament, Cats delivered a conciliatory Latin oration of Miltonic eloquence, but Whitehall's spin machine ensured that it was disparaged as bombast. There is no evidence that Milton had worked on the United Provinces at an earlier stage (though someone in his office must have prepared credential letters for Dorislaus), and he was not needed when the Dutch embassy arrived, because they presented their documents in English.

The first evidence of his involvement is an entry in the diary of Herman Mylius to the effect that he had seen a Dutch visitor at Milton's house on 20/30 January 1652. When negotiations over seized ships and crews stalled, the Dutch delegation sent Jan van Vliet, secretary to the legation, and the translator Lodewijk Huygens with a document (*incipit* 'Cum nihil prius') which Milton was ordered to translate into English.[147] No copy of his translation is known to survive. A week later Milton was ordered to translate two documents into Latin in response to subsequent Dutch papers in Latin.[148] These translations launched Milton into Dutch negotiations that were to last for years.

They also manifest one of the undiplomatic aspects of his Latinity, which is a habit of distancing himself from phrases of which he disapproves in the Dutch documents. When the Dutch use the phrase *literas merc et represales* ('letters of marque and reprisal'), Milton fastidiously inserts *quae vocas* ('as you call them') or *quas vocant* ('which they call') or *vulgo dictas* ('popularly called') to avoid being tainted by neologism. He also wrestled with his English superiors on points of Latin, for example eschewing the neo-Latin *curia admiralitatis* (Admiralty Court) in favour of the classically formed *curia maritimarum causarum* ('court of maritime cases').[149] There was a war to be won, but standards of Latinity were not to be compromised. Milton was to be involved in translating the correspondence arising from the war until its conclusion in mid-1654. Leo Miller has skilfully identified and elucidated Milton's surviving contributions,[150] and it is clear from his analysis that as Milton's country waged a naval war, he used his small role to wage a small war for purity of Latin.

On 18 June 1651 the Council of State thanked Milton formally for writing *Pro Populo Anglicano Defensio* and awarded him a gratuity of £100. There is some uncertainty as to whether Milton accepted the money, and he later denied that he had been paid for his work. As he had twitted Salmasius about the fee he allegedly received, Milton may well have found it difficult to take the payment. Against that, no one surely would have believed he had gone unrewarded; Salmasius claimed he was paid £4,000.[151] Cromwell, after all, received £8,000 and the gift of Hampton Court after the battle of Worcester. MPs and their servants were not noticeably reluctant to accept whatever came their way.

Of course, Milton's first defence did not end the controversy, and a sort of pugilistic undercard rapidly developed. John Rowlands, a royalist clergyman ejected from his Kentish living and currently in exile in the Netherlands,[152] published anonymously *Pro rege et populo Anglicano apologia contra Johannis Polypragmatici (alias Miltoni Angli) defensionem destructivam regis et populi Anglicani*, which went to two editions in 1651, a third in 1652, and was translated into Dutch. Milton and his advisers evidently attributed the work to a rather more senior Laudian exile, John Bramhall, former bishop of Derry, and a man termed by Cromwell 'Ireland's Canterbury'.[153] Milton handed the case to his nephew, the 20-year-old John Phillips, still resident in his uncle's household. His brother Edward, who by then had quit Milton's home for Oxford and had perhaps already moved on to the estate he inherited in Shrewsbury about that time, recalled that his brother had submitted sections of his own tract to Milton 'for his examination and polishment'.[154] His *Joannis Philippi Angli Responsio Ad Apologiam Anonymi cujusdam tenebrionis pro Rege & Populo Anglicano infantissimam* appeared around December 1651, though it carried a 1652 imprint (a familiar publishers' trick for publications coming out near the turn of the year). Its title page is made to some extent to resemble Milton's and once more Dugard, now effectively a favoured publisher of the Purged Parliament government, was responsible, but, unlike Milton's first defence, there is no hint that this was an officially sanctioned publication. Phillips speaks for himself—or, rather, for his uncle. Not for the last time in the Latin controversies of the 1650s Milton's defective information certainly produced a misfire, for the opening pages dwell extensively on the failings of Bramhall, 'a dissolute drunkard from his youth'.[155] Rowland eventually responded to Phillips with *Polemica sive supplementum ad apologiam anonymam pro rege etc. per Jo. Rolandum pastorem Anglicanum* (Antwerp, 1653), thus acknowledging on his very title page his authorship of the earlier tract.

Milton's first defence continued to be published in sundry unauthorized editions, sometimes together with the *Defensio Regia*. Together, they offered humanist educationalists a perfect example of a disputation, a demonstration by fine neo-Latinists of the controversial arts that the early modern European pedagogic tradition had placed at the heart of its teaching practices. Republican ideology thus found an easy way into the universities of Europe. At a session of the Reichstag in Regensburg in the summer of 1653, the problem was explicitly addressed by representatives of the German states. The delegate from Braunschweig-Wolfenbüttel argued that 'aforementioned writings and particularly Milton's should be banned so that in the universities they will not be able to carry on unrestrained disputations of those principles; also those Professors who favored England must be reined in, to restrict and restrain those with this opinion.' The Reichstag agreed that:

it is very necessary to call attention to current widespread danger because of the English crime against their King, and there have been dispersed and sold openly in the Holy Roman Empire tractates and writings most injurious to the authority of governing rulers whereby dismayingly great disobedience, uprising and rebellion of subjects against their rules may be gradually aroused, all such things shall by public edicts be banned under heavy penalties, and where they are found, they shall be confiscated.[156]

There could scarcely have been a more eloquent testimony to the penetration Milton's defence had achieved. With one Latin tract he had progressed from cranky advocate of divorce reform to England's champion, shaking the foundations of tyranny from London to Vienna, the Cromwell of political controversy.

✤

Cromwell's return from Ireland had been precipitated by a threat from the north posed by Charles II. In June 1650 he had landed in Scotland, taken the Covenant, and as King of Scotland, with the help of his newly loyal subjects, had prepared to regain his southern kingdom. In September, Cromwell checked him with his remarkable victory at Dunbar, one of the few occasions he found himself constrained to fight against significant odds. Nevertheless, despite further reverses, the summer campaign saw Charles, with a considerable though predominately Scottish force, marching deep into England, shadowed as they advanced by the New Model Army. Few English sympathizers joined the incursion, which suggests that the Purged Parliament's various policies of appeasement, reconciliation, and propaganda had achieved their primary objective. The fragility of the English republic, before Cromwell's definitive victory over the royalists at Worcester in early September, sets a context for Milton's work both as a public servant and as a principal apologist for the regime. It also provided the background to the diplomatic mission of Hermann Mylius, on whose memoirs we have already drawn.

Mylius had been dispatched by Anthon Günther, count of Oldenburg, to secure for his small Baltic state a *salvaguardia* or 'safeguard', which would guarantee the neutrality of Oldenburg's shipping in case of hostilities with other adjacent countries, and would also recognize the ancient right of Oldenburg to collect tolls on river traffic on the Weser, a source of conflict with the more powerful city-state of Bremen, which occupied the opposite bank. The count had received such an undertaking from Charles I; he recognized the need to renew it under the changed political circumstances.

Most significantly for Milton studies, Mylius 'alone, of all the people who met Milton, kept a real diary'.[157] From his account, as we have noted, we learn of Milton's subordinate role as servant of the Council of State. What he has to say about Milton's attendance at the Council is less clear. Leo Miller not only vouchsafed a transcription and translation of key documents associated with the Oldenburg mission, but also offered an insightful analysis of their evidence. He concludes, since Milton made an appointment that clashed with a regular meeting of the Council, only to be called to attend, that 'he was not routinely and regularly in attendance'.[158] Indeed, since Milton's role and expertise were quite circumscribed, regular attendance would have been a waste of resource. One record superficially seems to indicate the opposite.

Milton wrote to Mylius, 'Yesterday I was present as usual in the Council, distinguished sir, with your documents', which seems to imply habitual attendance. Here, however, Miller's translation excludes an alternative interpretation available in the Latin original: 'Heri aderam pro more in Concilio, Vir clarissime, cum chartis vestris.' While 'pro more' could mean 'as usual', it could also mean 'as according to custom', that is, Milton perhaps means that he attended Council in order to present the documents, since that was the customary way in which documents were received by that body.

From Mylius comes a vivid sense of the complexities of the governmental and administrative milieu in which Milton had rapidly learnt to function. The Council of State was a committee of the Purged Parliament; it could establish further committees or commissions, as too could parliament itself. Mylius's mission sees him working with a subgroup appointed by the Council, which sends proposals and recommendations to the Council itself, which must then send them on, if it so decides, to parliament for further consideration and final ratification. Weckherlin, briefing Mylius informally, 'spoke of the confused way affairs were going on. [In the Commonwealth government] no one trusts the other, and the number of persons to be consulted is too great'. Moreover, key people supported various interests. The state of Bremen evidently had powerful figures lobbying for it.[159] There was, moreover, among those most active in foreign policy an anxiety about the intentions of Denmark towards the young republic. Frederick III was full cousin to Charles I. Intelligence suggested that royalist envoys had been well received. Oldenburg was in a very close relationship with Denmark. Anthon Günther had no legitimate heir and on his death control of Oldenburg would pass to Denmark. The Purged Parliament had reservations about making a treaty with Oldenburg which could prove ultimately to the advantage of a state whose disposition remained uncertain.[160]

Mylius's record offers a rich sense of the social context of Milton's work, not least in its depiction of the penumbra of official and semi-official government servants associated with the foreign policy of the Purged Parliament. The group includes not only the displaced and semi-retired Weckherlin, but Hartlib and members of his circle, Theodore Haak and John Dury (who in May 1651 was ordered by the Council of State to translate *Eikonoklastes* into French[161]). The secretariat, widely defined, was an enclave of continental humanism of a kind Milton had so relished in the late 1630s, cultured intellectuals engaged through their own merit. Mylius, who peppers his more informal Latin correspondence with tags from Horace, evidently found men he could talk to, among them Milton. He recorded one conversation which has attracted considerable interpretation, in which Milton discussed with him the character of the Council of State. The context may be important; Milton has just reported a setback to Mylius's request for the *salvaguardia*:

[Milton said] he sees quite clearly where the fault lies. It flowed from the inexperience and wilfullness of those who enjoyed the plurality of votes; those men were mechanics, soldiers, home-grown, strong and bold enough, in public political affairs mostly inexperienced, of whom the more powerful part of the Commonwealth consisted. The more prudent men did not even dare to reveal their true opinions. I should not blame the Commonwealth, nor the sounder men; among the forty persons who were in the Council, not more than three or four had ever been out of England, but among them there were sons of Mercury and Mars enough. Meanwhile he promised to bring it up to the Council again opportunely, and the same evening at the end of the Council session to give me word of final clarification.[162]

Milton was probably speaking guardedly, and Mylius may have used further discretion in recording the conversation, and so the tone is difficult to judge. Milton, moreover, repeats what seems to have been a commonplace— or possibly a commonly used excuse for delay; Weckherlin had previously explained that Lenthall, Speaker of the Purged Parliament, muddied the issues over foreign policy as he had never been overseas.[163] Milton, in any case, speaks too sweepingly. He surely knew that many of those sons of Mars, the senior army officers who had entered parliament through recruiter elections, had been to Ireland or Scotland. Most pertinently, the key figures in determining the foreign policy, the politicians for whom Milton worked most closely, included men like Vane, Whitelocke, and Chaloner, all of whom had travelled in continental Europe. So what Mylius's record has to tell us about Milton's view of the Purged Parliament remains elusive. It does, however, demonstrate how readily Milton fell back on a sort of brotherhood of intellectual, cosmopolitan humanism. Indeed, Mylius evidently felt privileged to meet the author of *Pro Populo Anglicano Defensio*, and on his first coming to London, put him third on his list of English intellectuals he hoped to encounter (behind Selden and the classicist and controversialist Meric Casaubon, another figure of long-standing significance in an international context).[164] Milton, of course, has been famous for months, not years, unlike the others. Both Selden and Casaubon were unavailable, living in rural retirement. Milton, too, was initially out of town, 'vier meilen von hinnen'. The phrase is ambiguous: Mylius may have meant English miles, or German miles, which would indicate a distance of eighteen English miles. We have no real sense of where he had gone—Hammersmith? Horton?—but the record demonstrates that he remained able to travel some distance despite his disability. As their relationship developed over Mylius's visit, they discussed what Mylius terms 'the drubbing of Salmasius', whereupon, perhaps with avuncular pride, Milton gave him a copy of John Phillips's *Responsio*.[165]

There was a shadier side to the easy intercourse between this brotherhood of polyglot intellectuals. Early on, Mylius was briefed by Johan Oste, secretary to the Dutch legation, about whom he must bribe. Oliver Fleming, who controlled access to parliament, figured most prominently. Schaep, the Dutch ambassador who would shortly leave for home carrying copies of Milton's defence, had given presents to his daughter. Gualter Frost, secretary to the Council of State, had three sons working as amanuenses, and Oste recommended making them presents, too. As Aylmer drily observes, Frost 'had marked nepotistic tendencies, or shall we say a strong sense of family connections'.[166] During the course of Mylius's visit, Fleming started to arouse some suspicion among his political masters that his advocacy for the Oldenburg cause had been suborned, so much so that when Mylius 'offered a recompense', he felt constrained to decline, even rejecting 'fancy trinkets for his daughter'. As Milton helped the progress of his mission, Mylius wrote, carefully choosing his words, 'I give you thanks, which will be confirmed materially before my departure.' In the event, the record of his expenses clearly shows payments equivalent to £25 to Milton and to Frost, £50 to Dury, and a gift set of Cicero's works for Weckherlin's grandson. Plainly, when public servants controlled access to the Council and its committees, when business could be advanced or retarded with facility, the objective conditions for a culture of gifts and recompense obtained. Milton evidently participated. He and his colleagues were merely doing covertly on the small scale what their political masters did more grandly and ostentatiously. Anthon Günther was among Europe's leading horse-breeders, and he had largely preserved Oldenburg's neutrality through the horrors of the Thirty Years War by judicious gifts of prize specimens. Mylius concludes his visit by arranging to send some horses to Cromwell.[167]

While the Mylius mission was in progress, Milton's personal life darkened. He lost his residual vision, and in December 1651 his increasing incapacity prompted a move from his Whitehall accommodation across St James's Park to 'a pretty garden-house in Petty France in Westminster, next door to Lord Scudamore's, and opening into the park'.[168] This was the same Lord Scudamore whom Milton had met in Paris thirteen years earlier. The new property came much closer to the kinds of house he selected when choice was unconstrained, being located on the edge of the conurbation, with access to an open space and with a garden of its own, but it was a little further from Whitehall.

Early in 1652 Milton made what seems to have been regarded as an error of professional judgement. A Latin version of the Socinian manifesto known as the Racovian Catechism (so called because the Polish original had been published in Raków, in southern Poland) had been published in London in February 1652; an English version was to follow in June. Parliament was displeased, and established an *in camera* enquiry to ascertain how this had happened. The printer (Dugard) said that Milton had licensed it, and on 21 February Milton was called before the enquiry to explain himself. There are no records of the enquiry beyond the bare fact of Milton's testimony in the *Journal of the House of Commons*, but the Dutch-born diplomat Lieuwe van Aitzema (or Leo ab Aitzema), who had arrived in London on 20 February as representative of the Hanse cities, recorded in his diary (in Dutch) that Milton had admitted licensing the Catechism and in his defence had cited the principles articulated in *Areopagitica*.[169]

Encroaching blindness, the strains of domestic relocation, and interrogation by his own government proved to be preludes to a further and greater calamity. May 1652 started wondrously with the birth of a daughter who was called Deborah. Three days later, however, Milton's wife Mary died, leaving Milton, who was by now totally blind, with four young children: Anne (aged 5), Mary (aged 3), John (aged 14 months), and the infant Deborah. The death of Milton's wife is recorded in his family Bible, but her place of death and burial is not known; it may have been Horton, as the rector seems to have stopped recording burials at this period.[170] Milton hired a nurse to look after the children, but his sorrow was not yet complete: six weeks later his son John followed his mother to the grave. Rightly or wrongly, Edward Phillips was to attribute the death of Milton's only son to 'the ill usage or bad constitution of an ill-chosen nurse'.[171]

In the midst of this sorrow Milton composed two political sonnets: 'To the Lord General Cromwell' is dated May 1652 (the month of Mary's death) in the Trinity Manuscript, and 'Vane, young in years', was composed on 3 July (a fortnight after his son John's death). Perhaps the discipline of writing panegyric afforded a measure of distraction or solace. In the Trinity Manuscript the sonnet to Cromwell (in the hand of an amanuensis) is given a title (subsequently deleted) that includes a date and an occasion: 'To the Lord Generall Cromwell May 1652 | On the proposalls of certaine ministers at the Commtee for Propagation of the Gospel'. This committee, of which Cromwell was a member, had been established by the Purged Parliament on 18 February 1652 in response to a petition, signed by fifteen Independent ministers (including John Owen, Thomas Goodwin, Philip Nye, and Sidrach Simpson) who the previous week had presented a petition against the Racovian Catechism. As the full title of the second petition explains,[172] the Independents proposed limited toleration for separatists tempered by a system of clerical licences that would stifle 'dangerous errours and blasphemies'. Milton addresses Cromwell as a member of the Committee considering these proposals, probably at this time pushing at an open door in urging him not to reduce toleration of dissenting opinion and not to yield for demands for a stipendiary clergy ('hireling wolves') funded by tithes; on the second issue, Cromwell's view was soon to shift. The octave, which spills over into the ninth line, is an apostrophe to Cromwell as a soldier; the sestet urges him to deploy the same resolution in peacetime, where

> New foes arise
> Threatening to bind our souls with secular chains.
> Help us to save free conscience from the paw
> Of hireling wolves whose gospel is their maw.

Cromwell, if he ever read the sonnet, would have seen it as wholly laudatory and hortatory, and on one level it is precisely that; it is also, however, a guarded criticism of Cromwell, who in Milton's view did not see the seriousness of the threat to religious liberty enshrined in the proposals of the Independents.

The sonnet 'To Sir Henry Vane the Younger', as it is headed in the Trinity Manuscript, is so similar in syntax (including the octave extended by a half line) and tone that it may be seen as a twin of the sonnet to Cromwell. Milton had urged Cromwell to 'save free conscience'. Vane, who shared Milton's view of the threat to liberty of worship and publication posed by the Independents, had reacted to the proposals with *Zeal Examined, or, A Discourse for Liberty of Conscience* (1652). Vane's view that the secular authorities had no right to regulate Christianity extended even to the toleration of idolaters. It may have been this tract that inspired Milton's sonnet, which he sent to Vane on 3 July 1652. And whereas the sonnet to Cromwell had pleaded, the sonnet to Vane simply praised; the difference reflects both the distinction that Milton drew between the two men, and the growing rift between Vane and Cromwell. When Milton says to Vane that 'both spiritual power and civil, what each means | What severs each, thou hast learned, which few have done', Cromwell is not counted amongst the few.

The surviving corpus of state papers during this period bulks largest with respect to the Oldenburg mission and the first Anglo-Dutch war, but it is clear that Milton was also engaged in correspondence with Hamburg, Danzig (both independent Hansa cities), Tetuán, Portugal (newly independent of Spain), Tuscany (an independent grand duchy), Venice, Denmark, the Evangelical Swiss cantons, Holstein (an imperial duchy), Spain, and the Spanish Netherlands.[173] Some of these letters, such as one to João IV of Portugal (17 April 1650), are cast in Milton's most elegant and powerful Latin. He was also involved in the translation of intercepted letters, in searches for papers and in the examination of seized papers.

The evidence of work on intercepted letters is two letters written on 13 April 1649 by Princess Sophia (princess palatine of the Rhine) in The Hague to her brothers Prince Maurice (then serving in a royalist squadron off the coast of Ireland) and Prince Rupert; the latter letter was in French, and the former in what would now be described as a mixture of Dutch and German forms (Dutch was not yet universally regarded as a separate language).[174] The margins of the Dutch/German letter are annotated with corrections and additions in Milton's hand. Roger Williams was later to recall that he taught 'Dutch' to Milton in return for instruction in other languages. The common meaning of 'Dutch' was German (*Deutsch*, or in modern Dutch, *Duits*), whereas Dutch was usually known as Low German or Low Dutch; as Williams had acquired some of the language in 'New Amsterdam', it was probably the Dutch 'dialect' of German that Milton learned. A language is a dialect with an army, so the dialect would soon be recognized as the Dutch language.

The order books show that Milton's duties included searching for subversive papers. On 24 October 1649 he was ordered (together with Edward Dendy) to seize the papers of the dissident pamphleteer Clement Walker and prepare a report for the Council;[175] a similar order (which does not name the suspect) was issued on 15 May 1650. On 25 June 1650 Milton was issued with a search warrant and ordered to search the Lincoln's Inn rooms of William Prynne, who remained actively engaged in opposing the effects of Pride's Purge.[176] He was an old adversary of Milton's, and had himself relished searching the papers of William Laud in preparation for the archbishop's trial. Milton also examined papers seized by others. On 30 May 1649 he had been ordered to examine the papers of John Ley, who was arrested on suspicion of dealing with an enemy of the state;[177] a similar order was issued on 11 June with respect to William Small, who was arrested for corresponding with an enemy of the state. On 23 June Milton was ordered to examine 'the papers of Pragmaticus' and report his findings to the Council. *Mercurius Pragmaticus* was the royalist newspaper edited by Marchamont Nedham, who was later to become a friend of Milton.[178]

Milton had become the servant of a state that was prepared to implement oppressive measures in its own defence, and in taking the republican equivalent of the king's shilling had consequently acted in ways that seem in some instances to have compromised the large ideals of liberty and tolerance he had formerly articulated. Indeed, Milton became a practitioner of the pre-publication censorship that he had deplored in *Areopagitica*. Under Bradshaw's Press Act of 20 September 1649, licensing of books published in England was no longer required (though the practice continued), but newsletters and political pamplets were subject to licensing 'by such person as shall be authorised by the state'. In December 1649 Milton licensed a book in French on the trial of Charles I.[179] He returned to licensing on 17 March 1651, when he began to license the weekly journal *Mercurius Politicus*; Milton is usually named as the licenser of *Mercurius Politicus* until no. 85 (22 January 1652), after which the licenser is usually unnamed or occasionally named as Thurloe. Since Nedham had been turned only recently from his previous allegiance to the royalist cause, close supervision was obviously advisable to be sure he did not stray off message. Five days later, on 27 January 1652, it emerged that Milton had licensed the Racovian Catechism, and defended his action by reference to *Areopagitica*. This act, which as we have noted attracted the hostile attention of his political masters,[180] seems to have led to the termination of Milton's role as a licenser.

Milton played no part in the formulation of foreign policy, but his position as a senior civil servant was inevitably noticed by former acquaintances who thought that he could be of use. Correspondence in January 1653, for example, included an exchange with Andrew Sandelands, who had overlapped with Milton at Christ's College, where he was a Fellow from 1624–30 (and the predecessor of Edward King). A letter of 15 January from Sandelands in Edinburgh to Milton 'at his house in Petite-ffrance' lobbies on the subject of a proposal to use Scottish wood for English ships, but also contains a request for the skull of the marquis of Montrose, which had for the previous three years been mounted on a spike on the Tolbooth in Edinburgh.[181] Milton seems not to have acted on the request, or was unable to oblige; the skull remained in place.

The extent to which Milton exercised patronage is difficult to assess, but there are a few telling scraps of evidence. He recommended Richard Heath, whom he had known at Cambridge, as vicar of St Alkmund's in Shrewsbury.[182] Heath became an assistant (advising on oriental languages) on Brian Walton's *Polyglot Bible*, which was a project in which Milton's patronage may be detected: Walton had been a curate at All Hallows, Bread Street from 1624 to 1628. An order of 20 July 1652 implies that it was Milton who brought the petition for assistance in the preparation and publication of the Bible to the Council of State; similarly, the records of the Council of State for 9 July 1653 allude to a letter (now lost) from Milton lending support to the request of Walton and Bruno Ryves (a former chaplain of Charles I) that they be allowed to import paper for the Polyglot free of custom and excise duties; Council duly granted permission to import 7,000 reams.[183]

The Purged Parliament was dismissed by Cromwell in April 1653, and with it the term of its Council of State expired.[184] But the administration of government continued largely undisturbed. That it did so, reflected the endurance of the cadre of public servants who had served the state since 1649, among them, Milton. However, a more recent recruit proved pivotal to the sustained business of running the state, John Thurloe. His rise had been surprising to contemporaries and continues to puzzle historians. His connections with an emerging republican establishment were not negligible. His brother-in-law, the regicide Isaac Ewer, was an army officer who had performed well in the second civil war and in Ireland, and plainly Cromwell had trusted him. He had played a part in the transfer of Charles from the Isle of Wight to await trial. On his death, from plague in Ireland, Thurloe had executed his will and become guardian of his children.[185] Thurloe had another, crucial connection: since young manhood he served Oliver St John in various secretarial roles, and had received a legal education under his patronage. St John had been a leading figure in the developing Independent grouping in the Long Parliament and held high legal office under the Purged Parliament. He was also a friend and ally of Cromwell, whose cousin he had married. Probably through this connection, Thurloe had acted as Cromwell's solicitor in 1650–1. He achieved minor office in the Chancery. In 1651 he had first entered higher-level state service, as the secretary to the embassy to the United Provinces, led by St John and Walter Strickland. In the event, he was sent home ahead of them to report on progress, and Aylmer surmises, 'this must have impressed his hearers'. He seems to have moved nimbly to transfer his primary loyalties from St John to Cromwell.

It proved timely. Gualter Frost's death in March 1652 left vacant the post of secretary to the Council of State; 'Apparently without hesitation the Council recommended, and Parliament confirmed, the appointment of John Thurloe, who had not previously been in the central secretariat at all.' Among those who had, Milton was arguably the most senior, and was already engaged in some of the activities at which Thurloe would shortly excel, particularly in foreign relations and surveillance of possible dissident elements. Just possibly, had he been well enough, he may have had an outside chance of the appointment. Milton, however, was blind, and Thurloe was better connected. In the event, he proved an inspired choice, and Milton worked with him and under him till May 1659. Fallon concludes that henceforth, just as Cromwell and Thurloe were the architects of the republic's foreign policy, so 'Milton was answerable to them alone, rather than to a Council crowded with discordant voices'.[186] As Aylmer observes, Thurloe's greatest importance came later under the Protectorate, but he provided continuity at a higher than merely clerical level from the last year of the Purged Parliament and the changes of 1653 into the Cromwellian period which followed.[187]

CHAPTER 12

The Protectorate

THE period from 20 April 1653 to 3 September 1658 witnessed significant changes in the governance of England, each redefining the republicanism of successive regimes, marking the rise or fall of groups and individuals, and challenging the integrity of its public servants. Milton remained in the employment of the state throughout, evidently accommodating himself to Cromwell's ever-more-powerful control. However, his role shifted as the extent of his incapacity became clearer. The life records no longer show him directly engaged in surveillance work or in supervising other recruits to the publicity machine of the government. He published only two major works, both Latin polemics, though he continued, somewhat intermittently, to translate state papers. At the same time, he found ways of working that allowed him to take up and pursue major research projects in systematic theology, in British history, and in classical lexicography, to translate psalms, to complete a number of short poems of considerable distinction, and to work in earnest on his long-promised vernacular epic. As he did so, he strengthened his social ties and celebrated the pleasures of friendship, he built an appropriate support network, and he remarried, though the marriage was to be short-lived.

Cromwell's motives for dismissing the Purged Parliament remain the subject of controversy and speculation. He and senior army officers had become both disappointed and alarmed by parliament's conduct over its final year, as Blair Worden and Austin Woolrych have demonstrated.[1] Within the New Model Army a wave of millenarian optimism followed the stunning victories at Dunbar and Worcester. Fifth Monarchism, with its aspiration of ushering in the rule of Christ through direct action, achieved some purchase among all ranks, and was championed at the most senior level by Major-General Thomas Harrison, nor was Cromwell himself unmoved by the apparently providential nature of the success to which he had led his troops. Yet as members who had distanced themselves from the regicide drifted back to resume their seats, a political body that was already quite conservative in its religious and social outlook became even more sceptical about extreme tolerationism, the abolition of tithes and the disestablishment of the church.

While such conduct disappointed Cromwell, the politicians' resumption of a recurrent theme of most mid-century parliaments, the reduction and control of the armed forces, created suspicion and alarm. Parliament had supplemented itself through recruiter elections but remained both under strength and without any mandate that would resist the most superficial scrutiny, and, under pressure from the same armed forces that had purged it of its less acceptable members in 1648, it began in the spring of 1653 to debate its own reform or dissolution. Woolrych has demonstrated that, contrary to the propaganda of the army leadership and contrary to the conclusions of most earlier historians, the resolution it seemed likely to carry on the day it was dismissed was not to govern in apparent perpetuity, through the addition of members through recruiter elections, but to issue writs for a new parliament, perhaps to be preceded by a period in which the current members, augmented by others, would continue to sit.

Cromwell, if that was indeed the likely outcome and if he understood it, may well have been concerned that new elections would return members even more critical of the army and its leaders and more resistant to tolerationism and a radical church settlement. The dismissal of parliament, however, proved the parting of the ways with a number of prominent republicans and parliamentarians, some of whom Milton admired and with whom he was associated. Sir Henry Vane the Younger retired to his country estates, to remain under the suspicion of the Cromwellian ascendancy at least till Oliver's death. John Bradshaw, who had presided over the trial of Charles I and who, like Vane, had served prominently on the republican Council of State, spoke out against the *coup*, perhaps too eloquently for his own good. When Cromwell dismissed the council, Bradshaw told him, 'you are mistaken to think that the parliament is dissolved: for no power under heaven can dissolve them but themselves'.[2] He lost power and influence, securing only posts as a law officer in his native Cheshire, and retaining those only with difficulty. In contrast, Milton stayed on.

Ten days after the *coup* Cromwell and his senior officers appointed a new council of state, much smaller than its predecessor. It included senior officers, Cromwell himself, Lambert, Disbrowe and William Sydenham, and civilians on whom Cromwell would depend throughout the vicissitudes that followed: Sir Gilbert Pickering, and Walter Strickland.[3]

But the officers had not despaired entirely of forming a representative body that would carry forward the settlement of the country along lines which they approved. A nominated assembly, made up of those who were believed to be sympathetic to the cause, was contrived. They would have liked to include Fairfax, Vane, to both of whom Milton had composed sonnets, and a possible past patron of Milton, Luke Robinson,[4] but none of them would serve. In a move that would anticipate much of Cromwell's political repositioning in later years, 'representatives of such houses as Howard, Montagu, Sidney, Eure, Wolseley, and Ashley Cooper were called'. There were also a good few Fifth Monarchists on the list. The representation of other sectaries was at best patchy. Perhaps significantly, from the congregation of John Goodwin, close to Milton in the early defence of the republic, not one representative was selected.[5]

The new body, 120 strong and soon to grow to 144 with co-option, met on 4 July. It decided to call itself a parliament, to which mocking contemporaries added the epithet, 'Barebone's' in allusion to its memorably named member, Praisegod Barbon, a pious leather merchant and lay-preacher.[6] At the outset it seemed collectively compliant with Cromwell, and as it formed its council of state, it incorporated all thirteen of the council he had formed, and it added among others Lieutenant-General Charles Fleetwood, who was Cromwell's son-in-law, and men who would play a significant role in the years that followed, Philip Sidney (Viscount Lisle), Edward Montagu (cousin of the earl of Manchester), and Henry Lawrence. None had been a regicide.

Cromwell regarded foreign affairs as largely his own prerogative, and over the summer months events went well. In June Dutch ambassadors were sent, unsuccessfully, to negotiate peace terms, and 31 July brought a major naval victory, and with it the death of their military genius, Admiral Maarten Harpertszoon Tromp. However, popular sentiment favoured continuing the war in order to crush the Dutch, a campaign driven on by Fifth Monarchist preachers, who saw the success as providential and as precursor to an imminent millennium. Peace would not follow till April 1654, but the tide of war ran ineluctably England's way. Attention turned to the Baltic, where England's best interest seemed served by more cordial relations with Sweden and its eccentric monarch, Queen Kristina. Cromwell's wish to widen the base of support and to rebuild old alliances probably led to the appointment of Bulstrode Whitelocke in September 1653 as ambassador to Sweden (though Whitelocke's wife, who was against his going, thought it was intended as a punishment). Whitelocke, another possible past patron of Milton's, was not a regicide, though he supported the republic and had been critical of the ejection of the Purged Parliament. He was added to the council of state in November, and warmly welcomed by Cromwell on his return from his mission.

The Barebone's Parliament busied itself about the cluster of issues relating to a new church settlement. As we have noted, Milton's own views were sketched out in his sonnet to 'Cromwell, our chief of men', from May 1652.[7] Though his proposals are vague, at that time he expressed concern about a mercenary, presumably tithed, ministry and supported a broad tolerationism and the exclusion of the civil magistrate from matters of conscience. The tracts he was to produce in 1659 broadly concur with that position.[8] In 1653, however, he observed a silence.

The parliament had been put together in such a way as to balance the zeal of the more militant enthusiasts, among whom the Fifth Monarchists were a vociferous element, with men of property, experience, and some more conservative principles. But, as Woolrych observes, even these moderates were typically 'committed men, Independents or sectaries for the most part, who would have stood out as rather radical against the prevailing political and religious background of the mid-century'.[9] While the moderates were probably the majority, the zealots were more active in the committees of parliament and shaped the proposals for law reform and for a new church settlement that advanced enough to be formulated into bills by December 1653. Only the latter was debated, and on the controversy it aroused the Barebone's Parliament was foundered and wrecked.

The more radical faction favoured a separation of church and state as radical as anything proposed by Sir Henry Vane and apparently supported, at least in 1652, by Milton, with an abolition of tithes and the withdrawal of public provision for the ministry. Such a settlement would have proved ruinous to many congregations, both Presbyterian and Independent, which were by now generally compliant with the republican regime. On 12 December the moderates withdrew from parliament to tender their resignation to Cromwell, while those remaining were cleared from the house by troopers probably under orders from Lambert, who had resisted the formation of the Barebone's Parliament and had never taken his seat, despite his co-option. Once more the New Model Army dipped very directly into English political life, though in close association with civilian allies; there is strong circumstantial evidence 'that Lambert and his colleagues were in collusion with the MPs who led the walk-out'.[10]

The *coup* of December 1653 was followed rapidly by a new constitutional initiative, based on a document that had already been prepared, as contemporaries believed, by Lambert, the Instrument of Government. It was accepted by the Council of Officers and by Cromwell. It installed the latter as Lord Protector with powers analogous to those of earlier monarchs, it established a council of state, and made provision for fresh elections. The council included men who had worked closest with Cromwell in recent months: Lawrence, who became its president, Lisle, Fleetwood, Lambert, Disbrowe, Montagu, Sydenham, Pickering, and Strickland. Whitelocke was not included, but he was confirmed in his role as ambassador to Sweden, a mission on which he had already embarked. The Council's secretariat, of which Milton remained a part, was again headed by Thurloe.

Once more, at a parting of the ways between the Cromwellians and radicals, Milton chose to remain with the Cromwellians. The Instrument dealt in detail with the vexatious issue of the new church settlement, offering a compromise of sorts:

XXXV. That the Christian religion, as contained in the Scriptures, be held forth and recommended as the public profession of these nations; and that, as soon as may be, a provision, less subject to scruple and contention, and more certain than the present, be made for the encouragement and maintenance of able and painful teachers, for the instructing the people, and for discovery and confutation of error, hereby, and whatever is contrary to sound doctrine; and until such provision be made, the present maintenance shall not be taken away or impeached.

XXXVI. That to the public profession held forth none shall be compelled by penalties or otherwise; but that endeavours be used to win them by sound doctrine and the example of good conversation.

XXXVII. That such as profess faith in God by Jesus Christ (though differing in judgment from the doctrine, worship or discipline publicly held forth) shall not be restrained from, but shall be protected in, the profession of faith and exercise of their religion; so as they abuse not this liberty to the civil injury of others and to the actual disturbance of the public peace on their parts: provided this liberty be not extended to Popery or Prelacy, nor to such as, under the profession of Christ, hold forth and practise licentiousness."

In terms of the freedoms Milton claimed for himself, this was a compromise he could live with. Tithes would be retained, though in due course they would be reformed, and so the separation of church and state was not complete. Against that, the civil magistrate had a much reduced role in matters of religion, controlling Catholicism and episcopalianism, neither of which Milton ever defended, and also 'licentiousness', presumably the sexual excesses and rowdy Adamitism attributed to ranters. There would be no obligation of church attendance, nor civil action against heterodoxy in practice or belief, thus allowing for the kinds of speculative thinking that would be part of Milton's own systematic theology. The Instrument inscribed in a written constitution all that Milton had asked for in *Areopagitica* and more: instead of the right to publish heterodox views and defend them in court, the expression of such views was taken completely outside the authority of the civil magistrate. For political reasons, Bradshaw was never reconciled to the Instrument, declining, when the First Protectoral Parliament eventually met, to take the oath that would have allowed him to sit. Harrison, as patron of Fifth Monarchism, opposed it on both political and religious grounds. Cromwell tried several times in December to talk him over, without success. He now entered the political wilderness, and by the end of December he was deprived of his military commission. Early next year he was in effect in internal exile in his Staffordshire home. Milton stayed.

In 1655 the first Protectoral parliament was replaced by direct military rule. The country was divided into eleven districts, each governed by a Major-General, with local militias and regular troops at his command. Christopher Hill observes, 'Laud and the Rump's committees had been feeble whips compared to the scorpions of the Major-Generals'.[12] Once more, despite this most repressive of developments, Milton neither commented nor resigned. He seems to have been equally unmoved by the imprisonment without trial in 1656 of Sir Henry Vane.

The second parliament of the Protectorate insisted that the rule of the Major-Generals be rescinded. However, the refinement of the Instrument of Government into the new Humble Petition and Advice reduced even further the vestigial distinctions between the role of the Lord Protector and the role of a king as it was traditionally understood by allowing Cromwell to nominate his own successor and to appoint his own council of state without reference to parliament.[13] Milton continued to draw his salary and to perform the duties which were required of him.

What were those duties? Milton's shift in employment from the Council of State to the office of the Secretary of State meant that his name disappears from the Order Books of the Council of State, except for occasional references to his salary and one to his role in Cromwell's funeral. It is therefore more difficult to track the Letters of State in which he was involved during this period. It seems safe to assume that there was some diminution in activity because of Milton's disability, but also that his duties changed with the restructuring of government, and that some of his activities cannot now be identified, because a department whose duties include intelligence-gathering is unlikely to keep records for posterity.

Under the Protectorate, Milton was involved in several diplomatic theatres, of which the most important were the United Provinces, France, Sweden, and Savoy. The most urgent was the war with the United Provinces, and Milton continued to work on that brief until the peace treaty concluding the first Anglo-Dutch War was signed in April 1654.[14] Early in 1655 René Augier left Thurloe's office, and responsibility for correspondence with France was passed to Milton.

This was a critical time for relations with France, which England needed as an ally in the Anglo-Spanish War (1654–60). What is now the French port of Dunkerque was in the mid-seventeenth century the Flemish port of Duinkerke, and part of the Spanish Netherlands; indeed, Dutch remained its principal language until World War II. Calais had been lost to France in 1558, and Cromwell was eager that England re-establish a toehold on the continent. Duinkerke had been captured by the French in 1646 but recaptured by the Spain in 1652. An Anglo-French army commanded by Henri Turenne defeated the Spanish at the Battle of the Dunes (4/14 June 1658), and in the ensuring settlement Duinkerke became the English city of Dunkirk; it was to remain English until Charles II sold it to France in 1662. In the late 1650s, Milton shared responsibility for the correspondence, probably translating incoming letters from French and certainly translating outgoing letters into Latin.[15]

Bulstrode Whitelocke had been sent on an embassy to Sweden in September 1653, but Milton did not take up the Swedish brief until August 1654. He already had an interest in Sweden, because he believed Queen Kristina had withdrawn her patronage of Salmasius in a gesture of support for Milton in response to her reading of his first *Defence*.[16] In the intervening months Queen Kristina had shocked Protestant Europe (including Milton) by converting to Catholicism and abdicating the throne (5 June 1654). In the first letter translated by Milton (29 August 1654) Cromwell congratulated her cousin Karl X on his accession to the throne.

King Karl was England's most bellicose ally, and his protracted attempts to exert Swedish control over the Baltic brought him into conflict with both Protestant and Catholic states. The letters and documents that Milton translated for Cromwell had a twofold agenda: first, Cromwell tried to support Karl's attacks on Catholic countries (e.g. Poland) while urging restraint in his attacks on Protestant countries (e.g. Denmark); second, he tried to secure the duchy of Bremen as an English foothold on the North Sea; the duchy had been created by the Peace of Westphalia (1648) from the territories of the archbishop of Bremen to the north of the city (which was not in the duchy), between the Weser and the Elbe. Under the terms of the Treaty Sweden had been given control of the city, but the city declined to submit, and in an uneasy peace (known as the Recess of Stede) instead paid tribute to King Karl. In 1657 Cromwell decided to take advantage of this instability by offering naval support to Sweden in the war against Denmark in return for English possession of the duchy of Bremen, including the city and its port. Conscious of the need to create Protestant unity in the Baltic, Cromwell prudently opened a double diplomatic initiative, sending William Jephson to Sweden and Philip Meadows to Denmark. Milton seems to have been heavily involved throughout this period and beyond into Richard Cromwell's Protectorate, translating letters (including credential papers) to Frederick III and Karl X.[17]

It is hard to judge the extent to which Milton undertook this work himself. Meadows worked as Milton's assistant until he was posted to Portugal in March 1656; he seems unlikely to have done much translating when he returned wounded from Portugal, and in any case he soon left for Hamburg. On 2 September 1657, Marvell was appointed as a clerical assistant, and six days later Meadows was formally replaced by 'Mr Sterry' (probably Nathaniel, but possibly his brother Peter),[18] so bringing the office up to strength. At about the same time 'John Driden', almost certainly the poet and future dramatist, began to assist in the office.[19] The question of the extent to which Milton was contributing to the work of the office is further complicated by documents relating to his pay. On 17 April 1655 Milton's annual salary was reduced from £288 18s. 6d. to £150 per annum but payable for life. This sounds like a pension arrangement, but it was part of a larger restructuring and reflects an improvement in Milton's terms of employment. (Gualter Frost's salary was similarly reduced but not extended for life, and the salaries of employees such as Marchamont Nedham, John Hall, and René Augier were stopped altogether.) The wage cut proved to be impermanent, in that a document of 25 October 1659 implies that Milton's salary had been partially restored, to £200 a year.[20] Moreover, as Aylmer explains, under the old system of royal administration, offices could be held on three main kinds of tenure: for life; during good behaviour; or during pleasure.[21] Parliament favoured engagements that corresponded to the last category and appointments were usually made for a specified period, though of course they were often renewed. That, previously, had been the procedure governing Milton's office-holding, and so the change to tenure for life marks a recognition, not only of past service, but also an unqualified confidence in his future role and usefulness in the administration. However, although the balance of evidence indicates that Milton continued to work, in the late 1650s he worked less, possibly because he was not needed so much after the appointment of Marvell and Sterry, and possibly because he was engaged on the composition of *De Doctrina Christiana* and *Paradise Lost*, and so a salary reduction of some sort may well have seemed appropriate and fair.

In any case Milton was certainly not poor. Indeed, he was able to invest money: he lent £500 (at 6 per cent interest) to a London goldsmith called Thomas Maundy, taking a statute staple bond for £1,000 as security. The transaction surfaces in a document of 14 January 1658, in which Maundy exchanged the bond for a leasehold mortgage on a property in Kensington; the leasehold would revert to Maundy on repayment of the debt and interest. Under the terms of the arrangement Maundy would continue to possess the property on condition that he pay £30 in interest annually (in two instalments) on the loan. In the event Milton retained the investment until 7 June 1665, when he decided to sell. The reason for the sale is not clear, though it may be related to the fact that plague was ravaging London and that Milton was preparing to leave. Milton transferred the mortgage on the Kensington property to Dr Baldwin Hamey, and received in return £500, the amount of the original loan.[22] The transaction is of interest not only because it demonstrates Milton's prosperity, and the fact that some investments survived the Restoration, but also because of the names on the document. Milton's counterpart is signed on his behalf by Jeremie Pickard, a professional scribe who worked occasionally for the Protectoral government; Pickard was soon to reappear in Milton's life as one of the two principal scribes of the treatise now known as *De Doctrina Christiana*. The document was witnessed by Pickard and by Elizabeth Woodcock, mother of Milton's second wife.[23]

Milton's contribution to diplomatic activities shaped directly a short but remarkable poem of this period. In April 1655 the forces of the duke of Savoy embarked on a massacre of the Waldenses in Piedmont, which was part of his duchy. The Waldenses (or Vaudois), whose successors are now known in Italy as the Chiesa Evangelica Valdese, trace their origins to a twelfth-century anti-sacerdotal sect founded by Pierre Vaudès.[24] The principal community of the Waldenses was in Savoy, where they had been persecuted by the ruling house since the fifteenth century. In 1487 Pope Innocent VIII had promulgated a bull ordering that the Waldenses be exterminated. At the Reformation Protestants such as Beza, Farel, and Olivétan created a pre-history of Protestantism by declaring the Waldenses to be Protestants *avant la lettre* who had kept the pure flame of the early church alive through the decadent Catholic centuries. Much effort was expended by Reformers in strengthening the power of this fiction by imposing a Protestant theology on the Waldenses; a synod held at Chanforans in 1532 (attended by Farel and Olivétan) adopted a confession of faith which affirmed the doctrine of predestination, sanctioned clerical marriage, and denied the supremacy of the pope. In 1545 the forces of Francis I had slaughtered thousands of Waldenses in Provence, and in April 1655 Carlo Emanuele II, duke of Savoy, inaugurated a similarly bloody campaign in Piedmont.

Carlo Emanuele had previously tried to convert the Waldenses by a combination of carrot (tax incentives) and stick (the Inquisition), but finally settled on extermination. On 25 January 1655 Andrea Gastaldo, the duke's deputy for heretics (*deputato per la separazione*), ordered that Waldenses refusing to convert leave the towns of the region for a list of specified upland areas; the penalty for refusing to leave was death and confiscation of property. The Waldenses petitioned the duke, but realized that the edict would not be withdrawn, and so retreated to the mountains at the height of winter. Early in April they were followed to their Alpine refuges by Savoyard troops (supplemented by French and Irish troops), and on 14/24 April the massacre began. Survivors told lurid tales of atrocities such as mothers and babies being hurled from clifftops, and news of the massacre spread to the Evangelical Swiss Cantons and thence to Protestant Europe.

37. Samuel Morland, *History of
the Evangelical Churches*
(London, 1658), 344.

Cromwell took the opportunity to seize the leadership of the Protestant world by lodging a formal protest with the duke, writing on 25 May to Louis XIV and Cardinal Mazarin urging them to intervene, and writing on the same day to the Protestant rulers of Sweden, Denmark, the United Netherlands, the Evangelical Swiss Cantons to ensure that they were acting together. Milton translated all seven letters into Latin. Samuel Morland was dispatched to Paris and Savoy, carrying the letters for Louis XIV and Cardinal Mazarin, and also carrying the text of a speech which he delivered to Carlo Emanuele in Rivale on 24 June; it is likely that the speech had been translated into Latin by Milton.[25] On 31 May Cromwell wrote to Rákoczi György II, voivode of Transylvania, responding to a letter from Rákoczi and describing the massacre, and again Milton translated the letter. Finally, Cromwell wrote to Geneva (which had seceded from Savoy in 1603) contributing £2,000 to a fund established for the relief of the Waldenses, and Milton was the translator. On 14 June a national day of humiliation and fasting was declared, and money was collected for the relief of the surviving victims.

At the height of revulsion against this attack on Protestant Europe's co-religionists, when emotions resembled those evoked by the fall of Constantinople in 1453, the St Batholomew's Day Massacre of 1572 and the attacks on the United States in 2001, Milton decided to write a sonnet on the subject. He had long had an interest in the Waldenses,[26] and he had been close to the diplomatic response to the massacre, so his indignation was informed and inflamed by his detailed knowledge of the atrocities derived from Morland's report. The resulting poem is the most passionate and highly charged that Milton ever wrote, and his *saeva indignatio* bursts out in a cry for divine vengeance:

> Avenge O Lord thy slaughtered saints, whose bones
> Lie scattered on the Alpine mountains cold,
> Even them who kept thy truth so pure of old
> When all our fathers worshipped stocks and stones,
> Forget not: in thy book record their groans
> Who were thy sheep and in their ancient fold
> Slain by the bloody Piedmontese that rolled
> Mother with infant down the rocks.[27]

The avalanche of words gathers force as the sentence thunders towards its culminating image of casual brutality.

Milton wrote no vernacular polemic under Oliver Cromwell's Protectorate. But the press war in Latin, initiated by Salmasius and continued by Milton, required two major responses from him. *Pro Populo Anglicano Defensio* had been answered by the anonymous *Regii Sanguinis Clamor* (1652). This was almost certainly the work of an ejected minister of the Church of England, Peter du Moulin, though a reformed divine, Alexander More, who held various prestigious offices in continental Europe, seems to have edited it and seen it through the press. Milton worked from the assumption that More was the principal author, a view in which he persevered despite attempts by continental well-wishers and others to correct it.[28] Milton by then had invested great efforts in ridiculing More. Since he had almost certainly played a part in the publication of the *Clamor*, the ethical issues were unproblematic. Moreover, Milton's personal onslaught really functions as the spice to reward his readers for their effort, rather than as part of the serious argument of his response. He needed a victim, and the real identity of the author was not disclosed, indeed probably was not known, to those who had tried to tip him off.

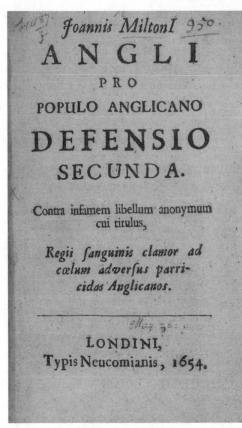

38. John Milton, *Pro populo
Anglicano Defensio Secunda*
(London, 1654), title page.

The *Defensio Secunda* (published 30 May 1654) was printed by Thomas
Newcombe and, like its predecessor, combined high politics with low scurrility.
The target was somewhat less elevated than Salmasius, and a recurrent tone
of contempt characterizes Milton's treatment of him. Much is made of
More's alleged sexual impropriety with one of Salmasius's maidservants.
More was conveniently vulnerable to *ad hominem* attack, because in 1652
Elizabeth Guerret, a servant in the Salmasius household in Leiden which
More had regularly visited, brought a breach of promise suit, naming him as
the father of her illegitimate child and alleging that he had seduced her
under promise of marriage. Reaction to the allegation was mixed: More's
powerful friends remained loyal, and the Synod of Utrecht did not revoke
his licence to preach, but he was banned from preaching in Leiden, and
Madame Saumaise sided with her former employee against More.[29]

Again, the pleasure Milton offers his continental humanist readership rests
largely in the playfulness of the attack. For paragraph after paragraph, Milton

quibbles on More's name, which means 'mulberry bush' in Latin and 'fool' or 'knave' in Greek. He would return to the sport in his third and final Latin defence.

The high politics is more complex than formerly. The English republic was in the process of fighting a very successful war against an accomplished adversary. The fragility, the sense of isolation and uncertainty, and the revolutionary excitement of *Pro Populo Anglicano Defensio* is replaced by a new assurance. Milton sticks closer to the approved message: England is not opposed to monarchs, though it reserves the right to try its own if he transgresses and to organize its government on alternative principles: 'As a good man differs from a bad, so much, I hold, does a king differ from a tyrant.'[30]

Two new elements make that argument easier to substantiate. Cromwell had assumed a quasi-monarchical role, albeit one that, as in Poland, was elective rather than hereditary. We find no hint of criticism of Cromwell in this tract. Indeed, Milton carefully aligns himself with the Lord Protector: 'Continue to curse me as being "worse than Cromwell" in your estimation— the highest praise you could bestow on me.'[31] The panegyric is concerted and sustained.[32] Cromwell was 'Commander first over himself, victor over himself'. Years on, in *Paradise Regained*, Milton would have the Son instruct Satan that such self-mastery is the basis of all sound government.[33]

Singularity is the Protector's defining characteristic: 'Cromwell, we are deserted! You alone remain. On you has fallen the whole burden of our affairs.... By your deeds you have outstripped not only the achievements of our kings, but even the legends of our heroes.' Evidently, the old plan for writing an Arthurian national epic can be subsumed in the celebration of Cromwell's achievements. Milton is saying that Cromwell *could* be king, but that would be inappropriate, for the title would set a limit on his dignity and power. He is no tyrant, because tyranny is the condition when a ruler has power over people who are at least his equals. Cromwell's qualities are transcendent.

The second helpful element is the immediate context of the Swedish embassy, which occasions a lengthy celebration of Kristina's own character and achievements: 'From now on, to be sure, the Queen of the South [i.e. the Queen of Sheba] shall not alone be celebrated. The North has now its Queen as well, and one not only worthy of setting forth to hear the sagacious king of the Jews (or any other like him) but worthy to attract others from every quarter as to the most brilliant exemplar of royal virtues and a heroine to be visited by all.'[34] From the probable pattern of Milton's diplomatic correspondence over this period, there is reason to believe that his desk had been cleared since November or December to let him get on with the *Defensio Secunda*, perhaps in recognition of its potential usefulness in seconding

Whitelocke's mission to Sweden. In the event, he evidently took a little longer than ideal, since the mission had reached its desired outcome in the Treaty of Uppsala, signed over four weeks before Milton's tract appeared. The kind words on the queen were barely timely: a week after publication, she abdicated.

Several other contemporaries are praised by name. The cluster of members of the protectoral council of state is selected to confirm the direction in which Cromwell was taking the government. It is replete with the new men of property and standing, on whom the Lord Protector would increasingly rely: 'Pickering, Strickland, Sydenham, Sidney (which glorious name I rejoice has ever been loyal to our side), Montagu, Lawrence, both of them men of supreme genius, cultivated in the liberal arts.'[35] Milton adds Whitelocke to the list. Though not a member of the council at that point, he had been honoured by his appointment as ambassador, and his new cooperativeness with the Cromwellian ascendancy was a triumph for the Lord Protector's favoured policy of incorporating former opponents into new alliances.

That policy probably explains the presence of three others in the text. Milton picks his way around Fairfax's behaviour since 1649 with some tact. The praise is gushing: 'Fairfax, in whom nature and divine favor have joined with supreme courage supreme modesty and supreme holiness.' But, as was widely known, Fairfax had withdrawn to his northern estates. Milton turns this into an endorsement of Cromwell: 'whether ill health, as I suspect, or some other reason has withdrawn you from public life, I am firmly convinced that nothing could have torn you from the needs of the State had you not seen how great a defender of liberty, how strong and faithful a pillar and support of English interests you were leaving in your successor.'[36] Indeed, in the summer of 1654 Fairfax does seem to have considered a return to the political scene, and he was elected for the West Riding of Yorkshire in the First Protectoral Parliament, which met on 3 September, although he seems not to have taken up his seat. Government courtship in Milton's tract was indeed timely. Milton has another long digression on the merits of John Bradshaw. His fortunes had certainly flickered since the heady days in 1649–51 when he had chaired the Council of State continuously, and his antipathy to the *coup* was unequivocal. Milton is probably as keen to coax him back into active collaboration as he is to recommend his merits to Cromwell and his associates. However, there does seem an element of personal pleading in Milton's comment that 'No man could hope for a patron or friend more able and fearless or more persuasive', which also seems obliquely to acknowledge Bradshaw's role in securing his initial appointment as Latin Secretary to the Council of State in 1649.[37]

The third surprise inclusion is Robert Overton. He occurs in the section which praises Cromwell's senior officers. The other names are predictable.

Charles Fleetwood—'The enemy found you brave and fearless, but also merciful in victory'—was Cromwell's son-in-law. John Disbrowe was his brother-in-law. Edward Whalley was his cousin. The inclusion of Lambert, widely acknowledged as architect of the *coup*, is a ringing endorsement of the regime. Overton stands out. He had appeared critical of Cromwell's conduct over recent times, and had seemed apprehensive about the establishment of the protectorate. Cromwell both suspected him and sought to win him over during the spring of 1654. They met and Cromwell confirmed his appointment to the military government of Scotland, where he was to assist Monck. Overton left assuring Cromwell that he would serve him loyally as long as Cromwell put the interest 'of these nations' above 'the setting up of himself'.[38] Milton's comments serve well the moment, though, as with his praise of Bradshaw, he vouchsafes a personal friendship—they have been 'linked . . . with a more than fraternal harmony' for many years.[39] Overton's rehabilitation proved short-lived. By the end of the year, he was suspected of conspiracy against the protectorate, sent to London, and committed to the Tower. He spent the next four years in prison without trial. Milton never again mentions him.

The tract also displays Milton's powerful capacity for self-presentation. His name had appeared on the title page of the first defence, and the *Clamor* had assailed him with predictable insults. Of course, the biographical sections, on Italy and on his own blindness, were carefully crafted to meet the accusations of the *Clamor*, that he had fled abroad in disgrace and that his blindness was a divine punishment. Yet the sections remain invaluable, and have been quarried by biographers from the authors of the early lives to ourselves. However, they should not be read ingenuously.

In October 1654 came a response, published in The Hague, *Alexandri Mori Ecclesiasticae et Professoris Fides Publica*, followed in the spring of 1655 by *Supplementum Fidei Publicae*, a supplementary publication, consisting chiefly of documentary evidence. More made one fair point, that he had not actually written the *Clamor*, amid a highly tendentious defence of his own conduct and further vituperation directed at Milton. Milton's answer, *Joannis Miltoni Angli Pro Se Defensio* appeared in August 1655. Attack remained the best form of defence, and Milton has much to say about More and his morals, though little about high politics. More had largely pulled the exchange into an appraisal of his reputation and personal standing with the reformed churches of continental Europe. Milton was happy to follow him onto this ground, because it allowed him to return frequently to his affair with the serving girl, and to amuse his target readership with some allusive and lexical pyrotechnics. When More came out of a summerhouse after a tryst with his Pontia, he was still sexually aroused. The gardener saw him and mistook him for Priapus, tutelary god of gardens, where his priapic statue was often placed, both in classical antiquity and in early modern times. Such objects were traditionally made of the wood of the fig tree; in this case, though, the priapic figure is made from mulberry (at last the joke: 'morus' means 'mulberry').[40] More had called Milton an upstart mushroom, but he's really the upstart; the emperor Claudius on one account was poisoned with mushrooms; mushrooms look a bit like erect penises; More copulated with someone called Claudia, the female version of the name Claudius, in a kitchen garden; so: 'Soon among the mushrooms being newly tumescent, you did not indeed destroy Claudius, but you laid Claudia on her back.'[41] Sadly, the humour has lost little in translation.

Although Milton brought no major poetry to completion during the Protectorate, he completed quite a few minor poems. In the second week of August 1653 he translated Psalms i–viii at the rate of approximately one per day. What is unclear is the occasion for the translations and for the discipline of a psalm a day. The poems invite a political reading. It is tempting to see an allusion, perhaps, to the Barebone's Parliament in 'the assembly of just men' (Psalm i) and to ponder Milton's parenthetical insertion of 'though ye rebel' in 'but I saith he | Anointed have my king (though ye rebel) | On Sion my holy hill', though the local application of those lines is bewildering. But the start of the sequence, 'Bless'd is the man who hath not walked astray | In counsel of the wicked', carries, perhaps, a personal resonance, while other passages do seem to offer assurance to an administration established, with no mandate whatsoever, on a military *coup*: 'Of many millions | The populous rout | I fear not.'[42] Such coincidences of situation perhaps drew Milton to those psalms at that time, and working over them could have provided a kind of comfort that he was right to remain in the employment of the Cromwellian regime. As technical feats, however, Milton's accomplishment is clear: he has eschewed the ballad metre that had dominated previous translations (chiefly because it was conducive to singing) in favour of a remarkable range of metres, some features of which (for example, the continuity afforded by the use of unstressed line endings) anticipate the style of *Paradise Lost*.

In the autumn of 1655 Milton again began to compose sonnets. Sonnet 17 (*incipit* 'Lawrence of virtuous father') is almost certainly addressed to Edward Lawrence, but possibly to his younger brother Henry. The 'virtuous father' of the two brothers was Henry Lawrence, a relative of Cromwell and prominent member of his government. He was also a theological radical: in the satirical *Narrative of the Late Parliament* (1657) he was to be called a Baptist, and he wrote in defence of believers' baptism, but his precise confessional sympathies are elusive, beyond the fact that in his *Plea for the Use of Gospel Ordinances* (1649) he had attacked 'spiritual Levellers' and 'holders of extravagant opinions'. He spent much of his youth in voluntary religious exile in the

Netherlands, where he became an elder in Thomas Goodwin's English church at Arnhem, and remained associated with Goodwin when both returned to London. When Cromwell seized power, Lawrence was appointed Lord President of the Council of State (16 December 1653), and also sat on the Foreign Affairs Committee, where his involvement in Anglo-Dutch negotiations (he was a Dutch speaker) and the Swedish embassy brought him into contact with Milton.[43]

Milton had included an encomium to Henry Lawrence in his *Defensio Secunda*, and in this sonnet almost certainly praised his son Edward Lawrence (1633–57), who was working as an assistant (principally as amanuensis) to his father; during this period, as Edward Phillips explains, Milton was frequently visited by 'young Laurence (the Son of him who was President of Oliver's Council)'.[44] Edward Lawrence was, like Milton, in correspondence with Henry Oldenburg, and seems to have moved in similar circles; two years after Milton wrote his poem, he was to die of smallpox. The opening line of Milton's sonnet ('Lawrence of virtuous father virtuous son') graciously adapts Horace's *O matre pulchra filia pulchrior*[45] ('o lovely mother's still lovelier daughter'), and the Horation echoes cascade through the poem in its celebration of friendship and *otium*. Milton had already celebrated leisure (*otium*) in *Tetrachordon*, noting that 'God himself conceals us not his recreations before the world was built'.[46]

Later in the year, perhaps December 1655, Milton addressed two sonnets to Cyriack Skinner, who had been Milton's pupil in the mid-1640s before entering Lincoln's Inn in 1647. From 1654 he had been living near Milton, and like Lawrence, was a regular visitor. The two sonnets both appear in the Trinity Manuscript in what seems to be Cyriack Skinner's hand, which may mean that Milton dictated them to the person to whom they are addressed.[47] As with Lawrence, Milton begins with praise of Skinner's ancestry, invoking his 'grandsire on the royal bench'; the reference is to Skinner's maternal grandfather, Sir Edward Coke, the celebrated jurist who became Chief Justice of the King's Bench in 1613. He was eventually to be regarded as England's greatest common lawyer, and his works, as Sir William Holdsworth memorably asserted, stand in relation to the common law as Shakespeare does to literature and the King James Bible to religion; in Milton's time Coke had not yet been been raised to such heights, but he was recognized by republican intellectuals (and Levellers such as John Lilburne) as the principal champion of common law against the attempt of the king to exercise royal power through the equity courts.[48] Milton's high opinion of Coke may have been reinforced by his friendship with Roger Williams, who had been Coke's secretary and amanuensis.

The first sonnet (number 18, 'Cyriack whose grandsire') is an invitation to enjoy hospitality and leisure with Milton, and so may be a companion piece to the sonnet to Lawrence; indeed, it may be an invitation to the same occasion. The second sonnet, which Edward Phillips entitled 'To Mr Cyriac Skinner upon his blindness',[49] declares Milton's blindness in the octave, and then in the sestet asks 'what supports me dost thou ask?' His answer is that he has lost his sight, 'In liberty's defence, my noble task, | Of which all Europe talks from side to side.' This fiction is a sustaining illusion of a sort that Ibsen was to dramatize in *The Wild Duck*. Milton had fashioned an image of himself in which his writings on behalf of the regicide state were represented as defences of liberty, his reputation had made him a household name in Europe and his eyes had been sacrificed in the discharging of a 'noble task'; none of these claims could withstand serious scrutiny. His Latin defences had little to say about liberty; he was famous and somewhat notorious in continental Europe but mainly among humanists interested in witty neo-Latin polemic; and the aetiology of his blindness was unconnected with working too hard. But Milton needed the comfort of such fictions to assure himself that he was 'content though blind'.

The circle of Milton, Lawrence, and Skinner also included Marvell, Oldenburg, and Lady Ranelagh. Marvell had written to Milton in 1654 saying that he was 'exceeding glad to think that Mr Skyner is got near to you'.[50] Henry Oldenburg, a friend of Milton who was later to become first president of the Royal Society (and a friend of Spinoza), had corresponded with Edward Lawrence; drafts of four letters from Oldenburg to Lawrence survive in the archives of the Royal Society: two in French, one in Italian, one in Latin. Similarly, Milton says in a letter to Oldenburg that he has passed on greetings to 'our Lawrence'.

Oldenburg was a native of Bremen, and like Milton, an excellent linguist: Milton declared that Oldenburg had 'learnt to speak our language more accurately and fluently than any other foreigner I have ever known'. They came to know each other when Oldenburg came to England to solicit the assistance of Cromwell in the dispute with Sweden over the sovereignty of Bremen, and a long correspondence began.[51] Milton introduced him to Katherine, Lady Ranelagh, an intellectual and linguist, member of the Hartlib circle and friend of Henry Lawrence.[52] In 1656 she appointed Oldenburg as tutor to her son Richard Jones, who later became Milton's pupil. Milton corresponded with Oldenburg, and also with Richard Jones. Milton had known Lady Ranelagh since the mid-1640s, and after he was twice widowed they became closer; Lady Ranelagh had long been separated from her husband, and was clearly fond of Milton. When Lady Ranelagh's daughter Frances died, Marvell wrote her epitaph ('An Epitaph upon ——'). It is a circle that includes a poet, a European intellectual, an aristocratic lady, and at least one pupil; it is in miniature a representative grouping of Milton's friends.

Sustained by his friends, Milton turned to marriage. Milton's wife Mary had died in May 1652. Four years later Milton decided to remarry. He was blind, he had three young children (daughters aged 10, 8, and 4), and as the apostle Paul had noted, it was better to marry than to burn. His choice was Katherine Woodcock, the 28-year-old daughter of Elizabeth Woodcock, a widow who since the death of her husband (an indigent gentleman) twelve years earlier had been supported in some style by relatives. Katherine is not known to have brought a dowry to the marriage, but Milton's comfortable financial circumstances obviated the need for one.[53] The wedding, on 12 November 1656, was conducted by Sir John Dethicke, whose term as Lord Mayor of London had ended three days earlier; it was a civil ceremony, as required by the Marriage Act of 1653, and probably took place in the Guildhall, where Dethicke sat as a magistrate. Katherine gave her parish as St Mary the Virgin, Aldermanbury, which may imply that she was living separately from her sister and widowed mother, who lived in Hackney.[54]

Within a few months of the wedding Katherine was pregnant, and on 19 October 1657 their daughter Katherine was born. The pleasure, if indeed the birth of a fourth daughter rather than a son afforded pleasure, was to be short-lived. On 3 February 1658 Milton's wife died, probably of consumption. Milton chose to have a heraldic funeral, a decision indicative of his current wealth and social standing. Elite funeral ceremonial was the responsibility of the College of Arms, who since the early seventeenth century had mounted funerals for nobility, knights, esquires, and gentlemen. Such funerals were expensive, and in the 1630s burial by night (as in the case of the elder Edward Phillips[55]) was used as a way of evading heraldic funerals. The regulations specified protocols that varied with the status of the deceased. The number and sex of hired mourners was specified, as was dress. If the corpse had been buried quickly (as, for example, in the case of Cromwell), then an effigy replaced the body in the procession and service. The number of heraldic funerals had declined during the civil wars and the Interregnum, so Milton was exercising a choice in commissioning a heraldic funeral. The paraphenalia of such funerals included hatchments, on which the arms of the deceased were painted. The hatchments were initially hung outside the house (in Milton's case, in Petty France) and then hung in the church (in Milton's case, St Margaret's, Westminster). A Painters' Workbook in the College of Arms records expenses of £5 3s. 4d. for Katherine Milton's funeral, and also contains sketches of the arms painted on the hatchments: a parted shield contains the Milton arms on the left and the Woodcock arms on the right; the normal practice was for a woman's husband's arms to be on the right and her father's on the left, but exceptions are not unknown, and nothing need be read into this reversal. What is clear is that Milton considered the pomp and expense of a heraldic funeral to be appropriate to his own rank and that of his late wife.[56]

More sorrow was to come, for on 17 March Milton's baby daughter Katherine died; three days later she was buried in St Margaret's Church, Westminster. Milton did not mark her passing in a public way, but he did compose a sonnet, number 19, in memory of his 'late espoused saint', his wife Katherine. Some scholars have sought to link this poem to Mary Powell, but that cannot be right: the woman commemorated in this poem was 'pure as her mind', and 'Katherine' means 'pure' in Greek. The commemorated woman had been 'washed from spot of childhood taint'; that was true of Katherine, who had lived for four months after giving birth (so beyond the period of purification specified in Leviticus), but not true of Mary, who had died three days after giving birth. Katherine's 'face was veiled', because Milton had never seen it, but also because in the ceremony of the churching of women, it was customary that the woman wear a white veil.

The poem closes with a poignant delicacy: 'But O as to embrace me she inclined | I waked, she fled, and day brought back my night.' An awareness of the erotic implications of the social context adds to that poignancy, rendering this as, recognizably, a sexual reverie, albeit decorously expressed. The ceremony of churching established 'a ritual closure' to the period of physical recovery allowed after childbirth, 'allowing the resumption of sexual relations between husband and wife'.[57] As Herrick puts it, the ceremony constitutes a sort of second wedding, to be followed with a new consummation: 'All Rites well ended, with the fair Auspice come | (As to the breaking of the Bride-cake) home: | Where ceremonious Hymen shall for thee | Provide a second Epithalamie.'[58] The rite had officially been discontinued with the promulgation of the Directory of Public Worship in 1645, but 'some people, especially royalist gentry, continued to seek out ministers to perform the office'.[59] In his dream, as in the funeral service, Milton's second marriage was marked by its ceremoniousness.

On 26 October 1656 Milton signed the autograph album of the Swiss minister Johannes Zollikofer, once again affirming (as he had with the Christoph Arnold Album) that 'I am made perfect in weakness'. Zollikoffer was proud of his trophy signature, and later added *Caecus hæc apposuit Celeberr[imus] Milton* ('the famous blind Milton wrote this here').[60]

On 24 March 1657 Milton wrote to the French humanist Emery Bigot, who owned a copy of the *Modus Tenendi Parliamentum*, a late medieval treatise on the relation between the crown and parliament.[61] In a letter now lost, Bigot, who had met Milton in the course of a visit to England and so was wholly aware of his blindness, had asked him to check certain readings and to see if the original text had survived in the Tower of London. Milton reports that he had confirmed or emended readings from manuscripts in the possession of John Bradshaw and Sir Robert Cotton, and had consulted a friend who was responsible for manuscripts in the Tower and established that there was no copy there; the friend was William Ryley, the royalist Norroy King-of-Arms.[62] It seems astonishing that Milton was willing and able to engage in textual scholarship. The extent of his engagement with scholarly matters is further revealed by the list of books that he asks Bigot to secure from a Parisian publisher. Of the six, only one was a well-known text: the *Liber Pontificalis* ('Book of Popes') then attributed to the ninth-century anti-Pope Anastasius Bibliothecarius. The others were a history of Byzantium from 1118 to 1176 (i.e. a continuation of the *Alexiad* of Anna Commena) by Joannes Kinnamos, of which the *editio princeps* had been published in 1652; the *Chronographia* of Theophanes the Confessor (covering the years 284 to 813), of which the *editio princeps* had been published in 1655; the *Brevarium Historicum* of Constantine Manasses, a 7,000-line metrical chronology from the creation to AD 1081, again published in 1655; the *Excerpta de Antiquitatibus Constantinopolitanus*, a treatise on this history, topography and monuments of Constantinople attributed to Georgios Kodinos, also published in 1655. Milton's sixth request, for the *Annales* of Michael Glycas (a chronology from the creation to AD 1118), was premature (as Milton thought it might be), in that the edition was not published until 1660. The volumes were all part of a sumptuous edition of the Byzantine historians being published by Sebastian Cramoisy under the patronage of King Louis XIV. These splendid folios, with Latin translations and notes supporting the Greek texts, were not cheap, and the request speaks eloquently of Milton's ability to pay,[63] of the support network that enabled him to read such works, of his current scholarly interest in Byzantium and of Milton's knowledge of the edition (the *Corpus Byzantinae Historiae*), which extended to knowing about work then in preparation.

But, evidently, Milton had discovered how to carry on his own work, and particularly those great projects that were underway, in the face of a daunting physical incapacity. Moreover, as his professional duties eased, especially after he had, to his own satisfaction, seen off the attacks of Alexander More, he had the time whole-heartedly to pursue them. He found time in 1657, for example, to correspond with a young French scholar called Henri de Brass about the merits of Sallust as an historian and about the writing of history.[64] Milton replied to De Brass's enquiries in two letters in Olympian Latin; both show that Milton had been thinking carefully about historical narratives, and also demonstrate that his grasp of scholarship was still formidable. Another exchange, with a German admirer called Peter Heimbach, explored the possibility of purchasing a new atlas, which seems an extraordinary aspiration for a blind man.[65] Edward Phillips, who plainly worked often alongside his uncle, gives us the richest picture of him in the mid and late 1650s:

being now quiet from State-Adversaries and publick Contests, he had leisure again for his own Studies and private Designs; which were his ... *History of England*, and a new *Thesaurus Linguae Latinae*.... But the Heighth of his Noble Fancy and Invention began now to be seriously and mainly imployed in a Subject worthy of such a Muse, *viz.* A Heroick Poem, Entituled, *Paradise Lost*; the Noblest in the general Esteem of Learned and Judicious Persons, of any yet written by any either Ancient or Modern.[66]

Phillips goes on to explain how the blind man worked on a poem of such extraordinary complexity, and to give an account of his own contribution to the project:

There is another very remarkable Passage in the Composure of this Poem, which I have a particular occasion to remember; for whereas I had the perusal of it from the very beginning; for some years, as I went from time to time, to Visit him, in a Parcel of Ten, Twenty, or Thirty Verses at a Time, which being Written by whatever hand came next, might possibly want Correction as to the Orthography and Pointing.[67]

Phillips adds the fascinating detail that Milton composed more freely between the autumn and spring equinoxes and was generally dissatisfied with whatever he produced in the summer. That quirk aside, his account shows well enough how Milton coped. Evidently, once he had mentally composed a batch of lines, he used whoever was around to write them down, and then, from time to time, had Phillips set them in good order. The manuscript from which the printers were to set Book 1 is held by the Morgan Library, New York. It clearly substantiates Phillips's claim as to his own contribution. It is a fair copy in a single unidentified hand, which Phillips has revised lightly, correcting, for the most part, accidentals of spelling and punctuation, presumably along the lines he knew his uncle to favour. The probable sequence in the production of the poem, then, is that Milton composed the verses, any one of several people captured them in manuscript, Phillips corrected them for accidentals and recopied them, Milton worked on them again, a professional scribe then copied them out (perhaps several times[68]), and Phillips then perfected one of those copies for the press.

The history of Britain would eventually see publication in 1670, though the Latin dictionary had a less happy fate.[69] Phillips seems not to have been involved in the remaining great project of his uncle's leisure, the systematic theology we now know as *De Doctrina Christiana*. Its complex manuscript has recently given up more of its secrets, to permit a reconstruction of how Milton worked on it and to answer the challenging question of how a blind man could assemble a text which contains about 8,000 biblical quotations, each carefully referenced. The manuscript is now in the National Archives at Kew.[70]

The origins of the project probably stretched back into the earliest years after Milton's return from Italy, but at some point in the 1650s Milton chose to have his working manuscript carefully and elaborately transcribed by Jeremie Pickard, the man who signed the Maundy mortgage deed on Milton's behalf. The manuscript was organized into separate fascicules, each corresponding to a chapter of the treatise. As he made the fair copy, Pickard left a wide margin on the left side, a common practice in the drafting of documents in the civil service both then and, indeed, in the present day. Milton reflected on his argument, perhaps revisiting the opinions of other systematic theologians (pre-eminently the work of William Ames and Johan Wolleb), and pondering the bible itself, read to him by one of a legion of willing helpers. He corrected some things, having them scored through in the body of the text. But most of his revisions were additions, typically of new proof texts, sometimes written interlineally, but often written, vertically, in those wide left margins, which on some pages are filled to capacity. Once material could no longer be thus accommodated, he had Pickard recopy the leaf, cutting the earlier version from the fascicule and inserting the cancellans. Pickard laboured to keep the pagination unchanged by increasing the line density and reducing the character size of the recopied pages. Once a fascicule had become too complicated for new material to be accommodated, Milton had Pickard copy the whole thing out afresh, this time without any regard to preserving the original pagination. The manuscript we have shows chapters in each of these various stages of transition, but even the fascicules which are complete fair copies remain parts of a working document to which Milton was still adding material when work was suspended.

By working in fascicules, Milton could break his task down into manageable sections, remain in control of his material, and use whatever helper happened to be available, simply directing him to specific and easily located chapters. What has come to us is a work in progress, and the contrast with the clarity of the manuscript of *Paradise Lost* which Milton submitted to his printer convincingly demonstrates that the systematic theology was still some way from being ready for the press. It remains, however, an extraordinary memorial to the adaptability, the ingenuity, the power of memory, and the sheer intellectual tenacity of its author.

De Doctrina Christiana is organized according to Ramist principles. The principal division is into books: Book I sets out what can be known about God, and Book II describes issues relating to the worship of God. The endless subdivisions of each of these categories is common to the genre of systematic theology, and Milton's wide reading in the works of his predecessors, especially Johan Wolleb and William Ames, means that verbal echoes proliferate. To say that the treatise is wholly the work of Milton is at once true and untrue; as with any genre in which the conventions are fixed (e.g. Latin grammar books), much of the material and many of the proof texts are common to all examples of the genre. If plagiarism software of the type now used by academics to identify essays that are excessively dependent on other sources were to be used on the Latin systematic theologies of the seventeenth century, the results (i.e. the percentage of material deemed to be original) would be broadly similar to those produced when a group of undergraduates write essays on a topic assigned by a tutor who has distributed a recommended reading list.

Theology was a living discipline for Milton, and his opinions on many theological issues changed in the course of his life. *De Doctrina* affords a view of his theological thinking in the 1650s. His thinking is for the most part unexceptionable, but on some issues he adopts minority opinions which he defends vigorously.

From the perspective of the modern Christian consensus, Milton's central aberration is his antitrinitarianism. Dissent from trinitarianism was, however, much more common among seventeenth-century Christians than among their twenty-first century successors. There was, for example, a widespread awareness that the doctrine of the Trinity was post-biblical, and that the central biblical proof text for the Trinity (1 John 5: 7) was a medieval forgery inserted into Bibles to support a trinitarian doctrine that had been erected on a disconcertingly thin biblical base. This verse, which is known as the Johannine Comma ('comma' is used in the prosodic sense of a phrase), was an easy target for Milton, who sought to base his theology on authentic biblical texts. With respect to God the Father, Milton took a conventional line. With respect to God the Son, however, Milton argued that he is consubstantial with the Father but not co-essential, and that he is perpetual but not eternal (i.e. that there was a time before he was generated when he did not exist, but that he will exist forever). This position does not make Milton an Arian, because he believed that the Son, in the words of the Christmas carol, was 'begotten not created'. The term 'subordinationist', as John Rumrich has helpfully observed, is a nineteenth-century coinage intended to describe a tendency within Arianism, not an ancient doctrine with which Milton can be identified.[71] Milton was defensive about his Christology, and so wrote a separate preface to the chapter (1. 5) in which he discusses it, but that was because he was distinguishing his position from that of other systematic theologians; in other circles throughout England,[72] and in continental states such as Transylvania, antitrinitarianism in various forms had assumed the standing of an orthodoxy, though there was vociferous debate about the precise nature of the Son.

Pneumatology was another battlefield. In common with other antitrinitarians Milton rejected the doctrine of the double procession of the Holy Spirit, and in *Paradise Lost* Book II memorably mocked the doctrine in his allegory of sin and death; in *De Doctrina* he dismisses the notion that the Spirit proceeded by spiration, but declares himself agnostic on the question of whether it came into being by generation or creation (*nec generari dicatur, neque creari*). Milton's Christology has no precise antecedent in patristic theology, but his pneumatology was anticipated by the Pneumatomachi ('spirit-fighters') of late antiquity.

Christians agreed that the world was created, but there was no consensus beyond that generalization. On the issue of the source material of the created world, Milton rejected the argument that the world was created out of nothing (*creatio ex nihilo*) in favour of an affirmation that the source material must derive from God (*creatio ex Deo*), a position deriving from Greek Platonic theology; this is perhaps the most striking instance of Milton's thought being aligned with that of the Cambridge Platonists. On the contentious issue of the role of the Son in creation, Milton inflects the position embodied in the Nicene Creed, in which the Son is he through whom everything was made (*per quem omnia facta sunt*), by insisting that *per quem* is indicative of a secondary role in creation. On the relation between the creation and the advent of time, Milton rejected the commonplace that the world was created in time (*in tempore*) or, in the Augustinian formulation, with time (*cum tempore*). Milton instead argues that the advent of time is signalled by the gap between the divine decree whereby God begot the Son and the act of begetting. The creation of the world, in his view, took place after the generation of the Son (and probably after the fall of the angels), and so was an event embedded in time rather than the mark of its inception. Finally, his stance on the generation of the soul, Milton favoured a traducianist position, which was the view that the soul was generated along with the body or (in Origen's variation) that the soul was pre-existent. He did, however, accommodate his thinking to the opposing creationist view, which in the seventeenth century denoted the doctrine that God created fresh a soul for each human being at the moment of birth. The distinction matters because it impinges on hamartiology: creationism is incompatible with hereditary sin. Milton's accommodation took the form of affirming both that sin was common to all humans and that sin was an act of the individual human will.

On soteriology, there was universal Protestant assent to Luther's (and Ambrosiaster's) contention that salvation was secured by faith alone (*sola fide*) rather than by works. Milton concurs, but adds that a saving faith cannot be devoid of works. On the doctrine of the atonement, Milton favours the forensic theory (also known as the penal-substitutionary theory), in which God the Father is the judge and the Son is the advocate of fallen humankind who decides to bear the penalty on behalf of his client, so fulfilling the Father's demand for satisfaction.[73] On the related doctrine of grace (the transformation of the fallen sinner on the initiative of God), Milton had long had sympathy for the Arminian position. In his youth he was a proponent of Laudian Arminianism, which was ceremonial and sacramental. He eventually shed his sympathies for ceremonialism and sacramentalism, and in the 1640s rethought the doctrine of grace. What emerges in *De Doctrina* (and, arguably, in *Paradise Lost*) is a broadly Arminian view that makes some concessions to the opposing Calvinist position. In common with other Arminians, Milton in the 1650s believed that Adam fell through the exercise of his free will, and that God predestined to salvation those whom he knew were going to have a saving faith; he was thus an advocate of general election rather than particular election. On the issue of reprobation, however, Milton parts company with traditonal Arminians by affirming that whereas election to grace may be attributed solely to the divine will, reprobation lies not so much in the divine will as in the obstinate refusal of reprobates to repent while it is in their power to do so. This is a point at which Milton's position aligns him with radical Arminians such as John Goodwin, and even Servetus. It is also a perspective that is articulated in *Paradise Lost*, and on the issue of salvation the theology of the treatise and the epic most strikingly converge.[74]

When Protestants purged purgatory from the spiritual world, they inadvertently left an awkward temporal gap between the death of the body and the last judgement. One type of response to this gap was the set of doctrines known collectively as mortalism.[75] The three variants were psychopannychism (in which the soul is deemed to sleep through the temporal gap), thnetopsychism (in which the soul dies with the body but is resurrected at the last judgement), and annihilationism (in which the soul permanently ceases to exist). In poems such as Sonnet 14 (in which Catharine Thomason is deemed to be in heaven) and *Epitaphium Damonis* (in which Diodati is said to have flown to the stars) there is no sign of mortalist sympathies, and Martin Bucer is deemed to be listening to the debate about divorce from a heavenly abode, but in the 1650s, when Milton was writing *De Doctrina*, he pugnaciously advocated thnetopsychism, so aligning himself with Arminian theologians such as Stephanus Curcellaeus.

Throughout his life Milton had taken an engaged interest in the contemporary debate about polygamy, and in *De Doctrina* included a spirited defence of the practice. Although the practice had occasional advocates among academic theologians (Luther had famously condoned the bigamy of Philip of Hesse), it was for the most part associated with radical Anabaptists, notably John of Leiden and the Anabaptists of Münster.[76] As in the case of Milton's hamartiology and thnetopsychism, his views on polygamy arise in part from his anti-Galenic embryology. His emphasis on the centrality of the male seed even affected his Christology, because he insisted that the mother of Jesus was no more than a human incubator for the divine seed; the alternative Galenic embryology would have emphasized the role of the

Virgin Mary to a point that would make Protestants like Milton feel distinctly uncomfortable.

On 4 May 1658, late in Milton registered for publication an edition of *The Cabinet Council*, a collection of 'political and polemical aphorisms' which was then attributed to Sir Walter Ralegh. Milton wrote a short preface in which he claims that the treatise was given to him many years earlier by a 'learned man' who was dying; the learned man has not been identified. There is no obvious reason to doubt his statement that he came across the manuscript 'by chance among other Books and Papers'.[77] The temptation is to read the text as an oblique comment on the late Protectorate of Cromwell. However, Milton's own comments serve to close off such interpretation, stressing that it is a document from an earlier age, recently chanced upon. Moreover, the printer, Thomas Newcombe, was currently producing the government-sponsored newsbooks and had published Milton's own, loyal, Latin defences. The little treatise appears endorsed with Milton's name, as large on the title page as the putative author's, which plainly discloses the kinds of attraction he believed himself to have for the reading public. But the text is not without contemporary relevance. The author blends the style of Francis Bacon's essays with the content of Machiavelli's *Discorsi* and *Il Principe*, as he draws on the history of early modern Italy and classical Rome, and in the process, he demonstrates that nominally monarchical governments have taken many forms, a point of general significance amid the drafting and redrafting of the constitution of England.

CHAPTER 13

From the Death of Oliver
Cromwell to the Restoration

CROMWELL died on 3 September 1658, the anniversary of his signal victories at Dunbar and Worcester. As in the establishment of the first Protectorate in succession to the dismissal of the Purged Parliament, Thurloe's role was pivotal, ensuring continuity in the administration of government. Indeed, over the following months, Richard Cromwell, Oliver's elder son and, apparently, his nominated successor, depended heavily on his close control of the apparatus of the state. He continued in his principal role as secretary to the Privy Council, a group which, under Richard, closely resembled his father's Council. Superficially at least, Milton's life was not substantially changed by the change of regime. He continued to work under the supervision of the Council and immediately under the direction of Thurloe in the undemanding tasks that had exercised him under the first Protectorate. His high standing among Cromwellian public servants is marked by a document drawn up in advance of Oliver's state funeral, which made him a grant for the purchase of mourning cloth; he appears listed alongside Andrew Marvell, John Dryden, and other colleagues from Thurloe's foreign service.[1] Presumably, since the grant seems to have been disbursed, he and the others marched in the procession which on 23 November accompanied an effigy of the first Protector to Westminster Abbey, where his body had already been interred.

Oliver had bequeathed Richard two major problems of foreign policy. The war against Spain, conducted in consort with Louis XIV of France and Cardinal Mazarin, his own first minister, continued. After the collapse of the Treaty of Roskilde, open warfare had broken out again between Sweden, under Karl X, and Denmark, under Frederick III. Oliver had interested himself in promoting the failed treaty; since the Dutch were already intervening to counterbalance the ascendancy of the Swedes, England was

39. Anon., *A Brief Chronology of the most remarkable Passages and Transactions which occurred since his late Renowned Highness, Oliver Lord Protector vas [sic] invested with the Government of the Commonwealth of England, Scotland and Ireland, and the Territories thereto belonging* (London, 1658).

perceived also to have an interest in settling the Baltic conflict. Ideologically, such an intervention served the old Cromwellian agenda of promoting amity among Protestant nations; economically, the Baltic trade was very significant, and Dutch influence needed to be countered. Thus the months of the second Protectorate saw Milton working on correspondence with the French allies and with the warring Scandinavian monarchs. In September, he translated letters of state from Richard Cromwell to Louis XIV and to Mazarin, announcing the death of his father and his own succession.[2]

Early in October Milton published the third edition of his *Pro Populo Anglicano Defensio*. This edition contains hundreds of small changes and corrections, and concludes with a freshly composed personal postscript. The voice of the postscript is constructed with a view to presenting himself as a figure of international standing who speaks not simply for England, but for all of Christendom. He claims rather vaguely that yet greater things are to come, but gives no hint of what these might be. It is possible that he was thinking of *Paradise Lost* or *De Doctrina Christiana*, both of which were in progress, but he may have had another major political work in mind, one that we now know was never to be written.

The workaday world soon intruded on such solipsistic thoughts. In late October Milton translated a letter to Karl X, commending Sir George Ayscue, a veteran commander in the first Anglo-Dutch War, who had been commissioned by the Swedish king to take command of his fleet. Ayscue evidently carried other diplomatic communications with him, and the letter requests 'quick Access, and favourable Audience'.[3] His appointment antedated the death of Oliver,[4] and the letter indicates clearly that Richard is preparing to involve England intricately in the Baltic turmoil. There were other letters to Karl X. In November (though Milton dated his published version of it as October) another guarded letter was sent.[5] In January 1659, another sought the release of English vessels detained by the Swedish navy.[6] A similar intervention petitioned the States of West Friesland in the interest of an English widow owed money by a mercenary in their service.[7] Milton translated other letters, to Louis XIV and Mazarin, and to the Afonso VI, king of Portugal.[8]

But besides these evident continuities of employment in his well-paid but scarcely time-consuming role, Milton in the autumn of 1658 reawoke to the possibility of shaping government domestic policy. Oliver's Protectorate had contented itself with a vague church settlement, which retained a nominally national church and a tithed ministry but allowed most sects to worship unhindered. Within it Presbyterian church government was permitted, though not imposed on congregations that favoured independent congregationalism, and a range of doctrine was tolerated, more or less benignly. Baptist churches were largely left alone. Ranterism had petered out in the early 1650s. However, by the end of the decade, the rapid growth of Quakerism, spread by determined and well-organized missionaries, both alarmed those in authority and raised the unwelcome issue of the limitations to be placed on toleration. Not only were Quakers studiedly undeferential but also their privileging of the spirit within over scriptural text smacked of antinomianism and rejected a central tenet of the Protestant reformation, the primacy of biblical authority. Quakers were among the most militant opponents of tithes, and at the end of Oliver's Protectorate over a hundred were in prison, most commonly for non-payment. Tithes and the larger, cognate issue of the relationship between state and church, immediately concerned the new regime, which responded by, broadly, confirming its predecessor's position. In late November 1658 Richard's Privy Council issued a proclamation ordering that the laws requiring due payment of tithes should be fully enforced.[9]

A systematic interrogation of the database of Early English Books Online discloses three distinct and non-contiguous phases of heightened controversy over the appropriate model for the maintenance of ministers of religion: 1645–7, 1651–4, and 1657–9. Milton's silence during the first may have originated in his general withdrawal from prose polemic after the hostile response to his divorce tracts, though possibly the issue, then, may have seemed of a minor order. At a practical level of personal interest, tithes were notoriously difficult to collect in the urban context. Alternatively, Milton's hostility to Presbyterianism may not yet have mutated into a wider anti-clericalism. Whatever the reason, the word 'tithe' and its cognates occur only a handful of times in his prose of the 1640s.

His reticence in the early 1650s is more illuminating. The twin panegyrical sonnets, to Cromwell and to Vane,[10] indicate sharply both his expectation from the former and his concurrence with the latter's radical and well-known views of the separation of church and state. That Milton did not participate in the press debate of the early 1650s may most likely be attributed to a public servant's respect for the protocol of his profession. Furthermore, under Oliver's Protectorate, the lord Protector was obviously intolerant of open dissent among those from whom he expected loyalty. Thus, for example, he was prepared to relieve John Lambert of his commands, once his opposition to the Humble Petition and Advice became public knowledge. The qualified criticism implicit in Milton's sonnet on Cromwell may well have been as much as he could safely do even under the Purged Parliament.

But in 1659 Milton returned to writing vernacular prose for the first time since the autumn of 1649. He developed cognate theses, on tolerationism and the exclusion of the state from the regulation of religious belief and practice, and on the organization and funding of Christian ministry. Among religious radicals in a broad spectrum from the gathered churches of the more militant wing of independency, through baptism, to the Quakers, the issues were frequently thus connected in their campaigns, to which other touchstone opinions of

English radicalism were sometimes associated. Thus, the Bedfordshire petition of June 1659 was wholly typical of the renewed agitation in linking tithes and tolerationism with settling the militia under republican command, legal reform, and elimination of an old bugbear, wardship.[11]

We have noted the part played by the rise of Quakerism in reanimating these debates. Furthermore, the death of Cromwell led those who had been discouraged about more radical reform to revive old causes. Richard Cromwell, Protector when Milton returned to vernacular prose, was relatively unknown, and his innate conservatism was scarcely apparent. In early November, his Privy Council decided to call a new parliament to meet in late January 1659. When it convened, it included several figures, missing from public life under Cromwell's Protectorate, whom Milton knew from the Council of State of the Purged Parliament, along with Milton's junior colleague, Andrew Marvell, returned as one of the members for Hull. Among the most prominent of the old faces, was Sir Arthur Hesilrige, who would prove the most influential civilian politician over the next year and a quarter. Hesilrige was no friend to radical reform and offered little hope to those who would abolish tithes and extend toleration.[12] Much more encouraging, however, was the return of Sir Henry Vane the younger, the subject of Milton's sonnet. Vane had withdrawn from political life in the immediate aftermath of Cromwell's coup of 1653. During the latter part of Oliver's Protectorate, he had emerged as a cogent and incisive critic of Cromwellian autocracy. He had published in 1656 *A Healing Question propounded and resolved upon occasion of the late publique and seasonable Call to Humiliation*, designed to reanimate the radical coalition of the late 1640s, and written 'To remove out of the minds and spirits of the Honest Partie, that still agree in the reason and justice of the good Old Cause, all things of a private Nature and selfish Concern'.[13] That tract put into play, as a rallying point for the revived republicans of the pre-Protectorate period, a ringing phrase, the Good Old Cause, that would resonate through many tracts of 1659–60, not least Milton's own. However, he was incarcerated without trial for a period thereafter.[14]

In mid-February, about three weeks after Richard's parliament convened, Milton published *A Treatise of Civil Power in Ecclesiastical causes: Shewing That it is not lawfull for any power on earth to compell in matter of Religion*. The title page was endorsed 'The author J. M.', a formula he had favoured before; the epistle, 'To THE PARLAMENT OF THE COMMONWEALTH OF ENGLAND WITH THE DOMINIONS THEROF', is signed with his full name. The book was printed by Thomas Newcombe, who was through the 1650s the printer of the pro-government newspapers, *Mercurius Politicus* and *The Publick Intelligencer*, both of which carried advertisements for the tract.[15]

Milton's epistle shows him simultaneously recalling past service and initiating a new personal direction:

Of civil libertie I have written heretofore by the appointment, and not without the approbation of civil power: of Christian liberty I write now; ... although I write this not otherwise appointed or induc'd then by an inward perswasion of the Christian dutie which I may usefully discharge herin to the common Lord and Master of us all.[16]

A certain air of retrospection, of nostalgic invocation of the early days of the republic, recurs, as in his observation, while discussing a passage from Paul's epistle to the Romans, that 'It hath twice befaln me to assert, through Gods assistance, this most wrested and vexd place of scripture; heretofore against *Salmasius* and regal tyranie over the state; now against *Erastus* and state-tyranie over the church'.[17] The force of his allusion to *Pro Populo Anglicano Defensio* is obvious, both as a reminder of his former service and an appeal to the spirit that animated the Purged Parliament at that time. The views of the sixteenth-century Swiss theologian Thomas Erastus, had been particularly influential in English politics in the early and mid-1640s, and were a factor in the inclination of a significant number of otherwise fairly conservative members of the Long Parliament to resist reformation of the Church of England on the model of Scottish Presbyterianism.[18] However, Erastians' belief that the church should not meddle in matters of state was much more agreeable to Milton than the related notion that the civil magistrate should intervene in matters of religion. The resurgence of an interest in Erastus's thought was marked in the autumn of 1659 by the publication of the first English translation of his cardinal text, *Explicatio grauissimae quaestionis vtrùm excommunicatio quatenùs religionem intelligentes & amplexantes, à sacramentorum vsu, propter admissum facinus arcet; mandato nitatur diuino, an excogitata sit ab hominibus* (London, 1589) as *The nullity of church-censures: or A dispute written by that illustrious philosopher, expert physician, and pious divine Dr Thomas Erastus, publick professor in the University of Heidelbertge, and Basil* (London, 1659). (Thomason dated his own copy 'October 1659'.)

Milton's prose style is markedly plainer than heretofore. Similes and metaphors, like word play and lexical inventiveness, are at a minimum. He cites frequently from scripture, and develops a patient exposition of the passages he cites. He writes to men whom he thinks he knows, and he offers a consciously brief and purposeful text, which he represents as stripped of 'Pomp and ostentation of reading', for, 'in matters of religion he is learnedest who is planest'.[19]

His central thesis is an advanced tolerationist argument which tidies up the contradictions inherent in *Areopagitica* while still balking at the clarity of Roger Williams's complete toleration of all religious belief.[20] The central proposition, to be substantiated from scripture, is 'That for beleef or practise in religion according to this conscientious perswasion no man ought to be punishd or molested by any outward force on earth whatsoever'. 'No man' soon receives a minor qualification: Catholicism is not to be tolerated in that it is less a religion than 'a Roman principalitie ... endevouring to keep up her old universal dominion under a new name'.[21] The distinction between civil disorder, to be punished by the magistrate, and theological error, to be tolerated, is crucial. Defining heresy in terms that primarily suggest Catholicism, he concedes the heretic is 'not alwaies punishable by the magistrate, unless he do evil against a civil Law'.[22] In practice, quietist recusancy had been winked at in an English context through the 1650s, in contrast to the more active persecutions of the previous decade.

Milton is most concerned to establish a framework for speculative theology within the Protestant confession, defined at its broadest. What unites Protestantism, across national boundaries and through ages since its foundation is the absolute primacy it gives to the scripture:

> To protestants therfore whose common rule and touchstone is the scripture, nothing can with more conscience, more equitie, nothing more protestantly can be permitted then a free and lawful debate at all times by writing, conference or disputation of what opinion soever, disputable by scripture: concluding, that no man in religion is properly a heretic at this day, but he who maintains traditions or opinions not probable by scripture.[23]

As others have noted and as we have elsewhere argued ourselves,[24] Milton is advocating a civil society that is tolerant of heterodoxy and protective of the rights of speculative theologians to develop seemingly heretical perspectives on key areas of Christian doctrine, so long as their arguments are substantiated from scripture. In so doing he is looking to build an England fit to receive his own systematic theology, known now to us as *De Doctrina Christiana*, a text pre-eminent in its massive citation and explication of the Bible. Milton could, with facility, have secured a continental publisher for his Latin text once it was ready. His controversial Latin prose had been pirated in the United Provinces, and his own Europe-wide fame and notoriety would have guaranteed a readership. But he evidently wished to prepare the ground for its domestic reception, conscious of the personal dangers posed, should a more intolerant regime come to power. Indeed, the urgency of his tract was demonstrated on 5 April 1659 when the House of Commons passed a declaration 'censuring magistrates for their laxity in punishing "heresies"'; the avowed optimism of Milton's epistle to parliament must by then have seem ill-founded. On 16 April the Commons rejected a Quaker petition for relief from persecution, replying that the petitioners should go home and behave themselves.[25]

Two letters from this period afford glimpses of other sides of Milton's life. On 26 March Moses Wall, a member of the Hartlib circle who had translated Manasseh Ben Israel's *Hope of Israel*,[26] wrote to Milton thanking him for the copy of his last book (presumably his *Treatise of Civil Power*) and urging him on with the publication of his work on 'hire'. Wall clearly felt as passionately about tithes as did Milton. The second letter, written at the end of April, was dictated by Milton for transmission to the radical pietist Jean de Labadie in Orange inviting him to succeed the late Jean Despagne as minister of the Westminster French Church, which since 1653 had worshipped in the Savoy Chapel near Somerset House.[27] Labadie was a former Jesuit who had been converted to Protestantism and was soon to found a pietist sect known as the Labadists. He and his followers believed that the Bible could only be understood with the individual assistance of the Holy Spirit; they also believed that marriage with an unregenerate person was not binding. Milton's letter modestly acknowledges his celebrity throughout Europe, and pays tribute to Labadie's sufferings for the Protestant cause. He then passes on the offer of the ministry of the French church. In the event Labadie never came, but the correspondence is nonetheless of interest, as it shows Milton's willingness to extend patronage to other heterodox thinkers.

Richard's Protectorate proved short-lived. Its principal difficulties were economic, and their cause lay in its expenditure on a considerable standing army and the absence of a funding stream to support it. Once more, this was a long-standing and intractable difficulty inherited from his father. The Commons established a committee on public revenue. On 7 April it produced its balance sheet, which showed that 'The government was now nearly £2½ million in debt, its regular revenue was falling short by nearly £333,000 per annum, and it owed the army nearly £890,000 of arrears.'[28] Two days later, it received a petition, known usually as the Humble Representation, passed on by Richard from the General Council of Officers, an organization of officers who were stationed in or near London. Arrears of pay figured largely among their complaints. At no point between the establishment of Richard's Protectorate and the eventual restoration of the king did Milton engage in print with these twin issues; his political ideology and indeed what he understood by the notion of liberty were unshaped by an appreciation of macroeconomic exigencies.

Nor did Richard and his parliament have a solution. The only options would have been to increase taxation, which would have been disastrously unpopular in the country and extremely difficult to enforce, or to reduce radically the size of the army, which the army would not have tolerated. In the event, an attempt was made to face down the challenge. Richard ordered the General Council to disperse, and the Commons began to consider restructuring the armed forces into a militia. On the night of 21 April forces loyal to General Fleetwood occupied London, and the next day Richard acceded to his demand for the dissolution of his parliament, and effective government passed temporarily to the General Council. Richard continued for a time as Protector, and Milton continued in government service, though his exact designation over the immediate period would be hard to define. On 25 April Richard signed a run-of-the-mill letter to Karl X (translated by Milton), seeking assistance with a shipment of hemp, which was needed to caulk ships of the English fleet.[29] Richard's reprieve proved transient. In late April John Lambert, the most energetic army opponent of the Humble Petition and Advice, was reinstated in the commands from which Oliver had dismissed him. Richard resigned, and, after some careful negotiation between leaders of the army and the Purged Parliament, on 6 May the General Council invited its members to return and resume the business of government.[30]

Milton probably regarded these developments with a guarded optimism. Richard's parliament had proved too resolute in resisting the calls for a wider toleration of Protestant heterodoxy. Perhaps the Purged Parliament would be more tractable to his polemic and the petitioning of others. Some early measures were encouraging. In mid-May it established a committee, including Vane and Hesilrige, to review the cases of people imprisoned for reasons of conscience and to consider them for release.

On the other hand, those restored to power included men who had nursed a determined resentment of the late Protector's ascendancy and were vengeful to some of its supporters. Parliament considered recovering the money disbursed in 'technically illegal salaries' paid to public servants since 1653, though they eventually decided against such a divisive measure.[31] The Council of State, once formed by ballot of the parliament, chose Bradshaw as its first President and soon determined to dismiss Thurloe from its secretaryship, leaving numerous uncertainties about the ordering of foreign policy. On 9 May, Thurloe wrote to Sir William Lockhart, governor of Dunkirk, 'only as a private person and as one who has no relation at all to public affairs'.[32] He was replaced by Thomas Scott, a regicide who had handled the security portfolio before Thurloe's appointment.[33] Arguably, the Purged Parliament and its Council of State, preoccupied with domestic problems, never effectively engaged with foreign affairs after its return.

Milton, however, retained his post, and produced translations of letters from the commonwealth, signed by the speaker of parliament, William Lenthall, to Karl X and Frederick III, announcing the abdication of Richard and confirming Philip Meadows, Milton's old assistant, now well launched on his diplomatic career, as English mediator in the war between Denmark and Sweden.[34] Those are the last state papers for which he was certainly responsible, although he continued to draw his salary at least until 25 October 1659, when payment was authorized by the Council of State at its own last meeting.[35]

More surprising than Thurloe's dismissal was the decision of parliament on 13 May to suspend Nedham from the editorship of the government's most effective newspaper, *Mercurius Politicus*. Milton had worked with Nedham since the latter's earliest days as apologist for the republic, and they had probably walked together in the funeral procession for Oliver. In his place, the Purged Parliament inserted John Canne, who had, with a dull mendacity, defended them against the Levellers in 1649.[36] By August Nedham was back in post.

The established view among historians is that the Purged Parliament failed, as it was doomed to do, through the short-sighted self-interest of its leading members and of the senior army officers and through its inability to face and resolve its economic difficulties, which were unchanged since Richard's Protectorate. Latterly, challenging the views of Woolrych and Hutton and the classic account of Godfrey Davies, Ruth Mayers has suggested that this analysis, shaped by the clarity of hindsight, does not recognize the skill, optimism, and the spirit of collaboration the restored members brought to their task, in which, in her view, they could have succeeded.[37] The objectives they faced, of raising revenue and reducing the army, of reconciling the religious conservatism of their majority with the fervid aspirations of their minority, were probably intractable to resolution. Moreover, their return to power depended on a military intervention from a force which most of them regarded with suspicion and which they would need to subordinate in order to achieve their other targets. Instability pervaded every aspect of their work. Nevertheless, to religious radicals, among them John Milton, in the summer of 1659 the restored Purged Parliament seemed to show the potential and perhaps the appetite to address the key issues relating to the relationship of church and state. To the members, to their Council of State, and to Milton, the restoration of monarchy surely seemed a remote danger.

The summer of 1659 saw both fervid anti-tithe agitation and ineffectual reaction to it, though the Purged Parliament proved, on balance, set against abolition. The late spring 'had been a time of great hope for the Quakers as they rehearsed and pressed home their political demands: the abolition of tithes, the state church and the universities; religious toleration; law reform'.[38] All but the last figure in Milton's next tract, which chimes closely with the contemporary idiom of extremer radicals such as Anthony Mellidge:

> We are not only free-born of England, but we have also purchased our freedome in the Nation, and the continuation thereof with many years hard service, the losse of the lives of many hundred, the spoyling of much goods, the shedding of much blood in the late war, by the which at last the Lord overturned them, who then fought to enslave our persons, and infringe our liberty in the Nation, in the which liberty now, we do expect to worship God in spirit, and in truth.[39]

The idiom is rougher than Milton's and the allusion to service in arms betrays a different contribution to the Good Old Cause, but the sentiments here, of Anthony Mellidge, a former naval officer imprisoned in the spring as a

Quaker activist,[40] differ little from those of Milton's next tract. Though the Purged Parliament in mid-June received coolly the 15,000-strong petition against tithes, moderate religious opinion, most evidently among the propertied, was alarmed by the surge in popular activism, and that anxiety may well have fuelled the royalist uprisings launched in August 1659. Certainly the leader of the only insurrection to achieve any military success, the Presbyterian Sir George Booth, a man excluded from his parliamentary seat by Pride's Purge, seems to have been motivated by concern about 'rumours of impending sectarian risings and Quaker plots'.[41]

Booth's failure indicated, even so late in the history of the republic, the weakness of the forces that could be raised against it. At a skirmish at Winnington Bridge, near Northwich in Cheshire, Lambert routed Booth's forces, which had remained close to his territorial base in the north-west midlands. The Purged Parliament rejoiced at this apparent manifestation of its army's effectiveness and obedience, awarding Lambert £1,000 (five times Milton's salary in the late 1650s) to buy a jewel; characteristically, he instead distributed the funds to his troops. Probably about the same time,[42] Milton released *Considerations touching The likeliest means to remove Hirelings out of the church. Wherein is also discourc'd Of Tithes, Church-fees, Church-revenues; And whether any maintenance of ministers can be settl'd by law* (London, 1659). The imprint reads 'Printed by *T. N.* for *L. Chapman*'. As in the case of the previous tract, the printer was Thomas Newcombe, a respectable enough figure in late republican London, and a publisher of pro-government newspapers. Livewell Chapman, however, was a more controversial figure, formerly (and perhaps currently) a Fifth Monarchist, who had suffered occasional imprisonment for publishing anti-Cromwellian texts. His involvement with Milton marks some reconfiguration of radical affiliations in that Indian summer of the Good Old Cause.[43]

Hirelings, formally, resembles *Of Civil Power*. Both carried Milton's initials on the title page, but his full name after the epistle, which once more is 'To the Parlament of the Commonwealth of England with the Dominions therof', and both, unusually within Milton's prose oeuvre, are in duodecimo. They look a matched pair, and their theses are complementary. But we find significant differences. Of course, the parliament had changed—from Richard's, elected afresh, to the members of the Purged Parliament, which about this time attracted the unlovely soubriquet 'The Rump', perhaps because it was still sitting. The opening paragraphs of the tract have bewildered commentators. Milton at once claims that the body he addresses is the same one that has guaranteed 'libertie of writing' since he first published controversial prose, eighteen years earlier; that is, the Long Parliament. He adds that it is the body which he has defended from 'an adversarie of no mean repute', obviously Salmasius; that is, the Purged Parliament. But he used the same mode of address to Richard's parliament. He appears to regard parliament as a sort of Platonic ideal variously and imperfectly embodied in several manifestations. That reading could meet the problems posed by his reference to the 'peace and safety [of these islands, which], after a short but scandalous night of interruption, is now again by a new dawning of Gods miraculous providence among us, revolvd upon your shoulders'.[44] If parliaments are all merely manifestations of 'Parliament', and if the interruption is recent (implied by 'after') and short (explicitly so), then, to us, the natural interpretation of the phrase is as an allusion to the period between the dismissal of Richard's parliament, on 22 April, and the return of the Purged Parliament on 7 May. That reading would not suggest a militantly anti-Cromwellian perspective, which would be the case were the phrase taken to allude to the whole Protectorate, though it does indicate at the least a critical perspective on the short period when England had been governed by a group of army officers.

Milton's attack on a beneficed clergy caps two decades of growing hostility. Images and phrases, used first in his anti-prelatical pamphlets and then mapped on to the divines of the Presbyterian mobilization, become generalized into a pervasive anti-clericalism that hammers the 'Simonious decimating clergie'.[45] The godly Englishman no more needs their services than he needs a king. Milton's arguments against tithes are both familiar and technical, and, as in *Of Civil Power*, the exposition is patient and assiduously tied to biblical references and analysis. The old rhetorical flourishes occasionally break through, usually at the most censorious moments:

certainly it is not necessarie to the attainment of Christian knowledge that men should sit all thir life long at the feet of a pulpited divine; while he, a lollard indeed over his elbow-cushion, in almost the seaventh part of 40. or 50. years teaches them scarce half the principles of religion; and his sheep oft-times sit the while to as little purpose of benifiting as the sheep in thir pues at *Smithfield*; and for the most part by some Simonie or other, bought and sold like them.[46]

Note the old playfulness returning in the pun on 'lollard' and the nicely turned comparison of metaphorical sheep and real sheep, real pews and metaphorical pews.

Newer and more surprising is the positive image he constructs of an ideal modern ministry. The poor are not excluded, for 'They [who first taught the gospel] were otherwise unlearned men', and the scriptures, in the Protestant tradition, are 'translated into every vulgar tonge, as being held in main matters of belief and salvation'; moreover, 'Christian religion may be easily attaind, and by meanest capacities, it cannot be much difficult to finde waies, both how the poore, yea all men may be soone taught what is to be known of Christianitie'. Saving faith is more important than a nuanced appreciation of controversial points not pertinent to salvation, and it can be imparted by 'itinerarie preaching' by people holding no benefices. The gospel may be preached anywhere: 'notwithstanding the gaudy superstition of som devoted still ignorantly to temples, we may be well assur'd that he who disdaind not to be laid in a manger, disdains not be preachd in a barn'. Some of the resource freed up by the abolition of a beneficed clergy and by the necessity of maintaining 'temples' can be redirected towards a regionally based education system, as an alternative to the two universities, 'where languages and arts may be taught free together, without the needles, unprofitable and inconvenient removing to another place'. Such a model contrasts with the self-interested arguments for the status quo in education: 'to speak freely, it were much better, there were not one divine in the universitie; no schoole-divinitie known, the idle sophistrie of monks, the canker of religion.'[47]

The steeple-house is redundant; universities are unnecessary; the gospel may be preached most effectively by unbeneficed itinerants, and that role stands open to poor men to take it on: those views are shibboleths of Quakerism in the late 1650s. Milton was not a Quaker, but their values and assumptions, their practices and their zeal have evidently struck home with him. He differs, *toto caelo*, on key areas of doctrine. His theology is bibliocentric; theirs privileges the spirit over the word in a way that invites the charge of antinomianism. But that same enthusiasm for carrying the reformation on to a kind of apostolic purity inspired Milton as surely as it inspired George Fox. Sir Henry Vane, whose ideological development so often kept step with Milton's, showed a similar rapprochement with Quakerism. In 1658 he had had his chaplain seek Fox out and invited him to his seat at Raby Castle, County Durham. The interview had gone badly, and Fox was, on his own account, later told that Vane had considered having him 'put out of his house as a madman'.[48] But he evidently worked better with less peppery Quakers. Once he had got over the apparent insult of their reluctance to doff their hats, he chaired sympathetically the committee commissioned by the Purged Parliament to review prisoners of conscience, and he had lobbied on behalf of the first great petition for the abolition of tithes.[49]

In late August 1659 Milton and Vane probably thought the government of England was both in fairly safe hands and moving towards appropriate objectives. Two principles were paramount for them—that there should be toleration for a wide spectrum of Protestant belief and that power should not be invested in a single person—and both notions, probably, commanded a majority of support within the restored parliament. Indeed, both, probably, would have been subscribed to by a majority of senior army officers, and of the junior officers and other ranks, for that matter. There ought not to have been a problem. Yet it arrived with an astonishing swiftness.

After their success against Booth, the officers of Lambert's force convened in Derby to ponder the state of the nation and the army's place in it. Old grievances, about arrears, about the settlement of the highest command, and about the security of their employment, remained unresolved. Though Lambert was not present, they resolved on a petition to the House, accusing it of dilatoriness in addressing the pressing issues it had formerly raised with them, and copies were sent out to other units to solicit their endorsement. On 22 September Hesilrige acquired a copy and broached it with the House: 'The MPs' traditional distrust of the soldiery flared up with fresh violence, and it was proposed to send Lambert to the Tower.'[50] In the event, Fleetwood and Vane and even Hesilrige himself attempted to assuage the anger, and the next day the House settled for ordering Fleetwood to admonish the army, rejecting the demands for the senior appointments the petitition sought. The General Council of Officers nevertheless responded aggressively, and on 5 October John Disbrowe delivered to the House a document demanding censure of MPs who had attacked the army and repeating the familiar requests about tenure and arrears.[51] The House hesitated, but on 11 October it took a subtly disabling decision, declaring it treason to levy a tax not imposed by parliament; plainly, they anticipated a second expulsion by the army and wanted to ensure whatever government replaced them was handicapped from raising revenue.

Their anxiety proved well founded. On 12 October, the Purged Parliament resolved to cashier nine senior army officers, including Lambert, and to revoke Fleetwood's commission as commander-in-chief; next day, Lambert's troops expelled parliament. In a period of extreme confusion, power notionally rested with the Council of State, which continued to operate till 25 October. Real power, at least over the metropolis, rested with the Council of Officers. Before the last meeting of the Council of State, a new body had been formed, the Committee of Safety, nominated by the senior officers, ten of whom sat on it, and supplemented by 'thirteen civilian collaborators', including 'the inevitable Vane', though his engagement with the new body was inconsistent.[52]

Although Milton's quarterly pay had been approved by the Council of State at its final meeting, he had not followed closely the rapidly developing crisis and would seem to have been out of touch with the business of politics. 'A Letter to a Friend, Concerning the Ruptures of the Commonwealth' is a manuscript document, dated 20 October 1659, not published in Milton's lifetime.[53] The identity of the friend to whom Milton addresses himself has been subject to speculation. We doubt that Vane dropped round in the evening, and anyway he was still in dialogue with the senior army officers. Bradshaw, once more the president of the Council of State, would be a possibility. Certainly he had responded with anger and bewilderment to the actions of the army. Yet he was terminally ill. The letter speaks of a meeting on 19 October; he died on 31 October, leaving Milton £10 in his will.[54] He lived quite close to Milton and would have been well placed to disclose to him the information about recent events on which he premises his letter. But it could, as easily, have been a member of the secretariat to the Council of State, still technically Milton's colleagues.

Milton writes as an outsider, though one confident enough to give advice to a friend still, perhaps, well enough placed to have some influence on events. He admits, frankly, that he does not understand why the army behaved as it did. Could they have overthrown parliament purely to protect the interests of nine of their number? He declines to speculate: 'I presume not to give my censure upon this action, not knowing, as I doe not, the bottome of it. I speak only what it appeares to us without doors.' Indeed, he says at the outset that, before 'the sad & serious discourse which we fell into last night', he was unaware of 'these dangerous ruptures of the common wealth'. Yet he evidently thought clearly and quickly about the peril to republican govern-ment, which threatens 'the destrucion of true religion & civill liberty'. He is faithful to the two principles that concern him in the settling of the state: wide toleration of Protestant doctrine and discipline and abjuration of rule by a single person, and he attempts to build a new coalition around those. All that is needed is that the 'senate or generall Councell of State'—evidently he remains uncertain of what will happen in the next few days—should be made up of men who also subscribe to those tenets, who then can preserve the peace, take over foreign relations, and 'lastly... raise moneys for the manage-ing of these affaires'. He has still not grasped the central significance of government finance: without settlement of arrears the army would not be placated. Moreover, in the next sentence, he is revisiting the name and nature of the supreme council, vacillating between a council of state and a Purged Parliament readmitted for a second time. He has a pragmatic solution to the mutual anxieties and suspicions of civilian politicians and army leaders: both should be confirmed in their offices for their lifetimes if they agree to the two fundamental principles. The brief text ends with an acknowledgement of Milton's own highly marginal position. It is the sum of his present thoughts 'as much as I understand these affaires', and the unnamed friend may use them as he chooses, 'put out, put in, communicate, or suppresse'.[55]

On the very day that Milton addressed his letter, another communication was being penned to the Council of State, from General George Monck. So far we have spoken of 'the army' as though it were, in 1659, monolithic; it was, in fact, deeply fissured. Besides the regiments various garrisoned around England, there were significant armies of occupation in Ireland and in Scotland. Monck commanded the latter, and he was broadly out of agreement with Fleetwood and Disbrowe and deeply hostile to the adventurous militancy of Lambert and the junior officers who looked to him for leadership. Ideologically, he stood outside the mainstream of former Cromwellians. He had been promoted by Oliver on the strength of his good service in Ireland and Scotland, and in the late 1650s he was in effect the military governor of Scotland. He was, however, a royalist turncoat, who had been imprisoned, eventually in the Tower, after his capture at Nantwich in 1644. More conservative in religion than Fleetwood and Disbrowe and in politics than Lambert, he had shared the concerns of the likes of Sir George Booth about the rise of Quakerism. He had already opened negotiation with the civilian MPs opposed to the England-based army commanders. He was monitoring the crisis in London, purging his own force of its more radical officers, and preparing it to march south. While Milton wrote to his friend, Monck wrote to the Council of State, condemning the expulsion of the Purged Parliament and, with his troops, declaring for their restoration. Hutton concludes, 'For the first time in its history, a large section of the army had turned against the rest. The Fourth Civil War seemed about to begin.'[56]

Milton certainly thought so. The curious text he wrote next carries the title 'Proposalls of certaine expedients for the preventing of a civill war now feard, & the settling of firme government'. It remained in manuscript, in the Columbia University Library, till the twentieth century. It appears to be an early draft, not ready for the press, nor does it read like a letter: it has a title, it is not addressed to anyone, it is undated. Indeed, when Milton wrote it remains a matter of surmise, though plainly it was during the period of 'the present committee of safety'.[57] It lists ten principal expedients for averting disaster, starting with recognizing that the Committee of Safety had to secure England both from internal subversion and from opportunistic attack by Spain and France, to which 'this distracted anarchy' has left the country vulnerable, not least because allies would neither honour agreements nor enter into negotiations. When Milton thinks of high politics, foreign relations top his agenda. He acknowledges the urgency of settling the concerns of the army in England, once more advocating lifetime tenure of senior posts, though again he does not recognize the importance of addressing arrears. He advocates new elections premised upon an oath of allegiance to the now familiar twin fundamental principles. The text ends with more speculative proposals: that the name 'parlament' be replaced with something more fitting; that membership of the supreme council, however it is named, should be permanent; that education and the administration of civil justice should be devolved to county towns. Most curiously, there is a proposal for economic reform, 'the just division of wast Commons, whereby the nation would become much more industrious, rich & populous', though it is not clear whether he envisages a distribution of the common treasury of the earth along the lines proposed by Gerrard Winstanley, or, perhaps more likely, another round of enclosure. 'Proposalls of certaine expedients' acknowledges the imminence of military conflict, between Monck's army and the troops loyal to Fleetwood, Disbrowe, and Lambert, which perhaps places its composition after 3 November, when Lambert was despatched north to block a possible incursion, but before 5 December, when issues of civil order within London became pressing.

The Committee of Safety never really engaged with the mechanisms that controlled all civil government in early modern England. Some law courts ceased to function. Demonstrations by apprentice boys proved difficult to control, and on 5 December troops opened fire on a near riot, killing two. Hesilrige, who had commanded a regiment in the first civil war, took up arms, raised supporters, and occupied Portsmouth in the name of the Purged Parliament. Vice-Admiral James Lawson, who commanded the strategically vital Channel fleet, gave assurances to City leaders that the navy was ready to use force to restore parliament, and on 16 December entered the Thames. The unit sent to reduce Portsmouth changed sides. The Committee of Safety attempted on 14 December a conciliatory gesture, determining to send out writs for a new parliament to meet on 24 January, but the old parliamentarian, Bulstrode Whitelock, Keeper of the Great Seal, declined to seal them. They were eventually sent on 21 December and recalled the next day as Fleetwood acknowledged the untenability of his position. On 26 December, the Purged Parliament reconvened.

That produced only the most transient hope of renewed stability. On 27 December Lambert decided to turn south to bring London to order; as he did so, his army melted away. On 30 December, Fairfax, the first commander-in-chief of the New Model Army, raised the Yorkshire gentry in anticipation of and support for Monck's next move, and on 1 January, Monck crossed the Tweed as Fairfax took York. The former pressed onward, meeting no resistance from an opposition abandoned by its former supporters and too demoralized to stand its ground. On 11 January Monck entered York; on 2 February, as the troops of the England-based commanders quit their quarters ahead of them, 'Monck's army marched into Whitehall, impressing observers with its air of discipline but watched by the crowds in cold silence, broken by the occasional shout for a free Parliament.' Their earliest action was to beat up the local Quakers, 'saying that they had come to rid England of sectaries'.[58]

The Purged Parliament proceeded as though they expected from Monck no more than loyal and obedient service. Before he arrived they had resolved to hold elections to replace members who had died or who had been secluded at Pride's Purge. They gave every impression that the clock, for them, had been turned back to April 1653 or at least October 1659, and, now they had a loyal army to instruct, they would carry on in perpetuity. More sceptical minds were less certain as to Monck's longer-term objectives. He was well known to none in the circle of Fleetwood, Disbrowe, and Lambert, who had misjudged his likely response to their October coup. From his vantage point as aide to Edward Montagu (the future first earl of Sandwich), from late February a member of the Council of State and from March commander of the navy,

Samuel Pepys watched and recorded the unfolding mystery. Even in March he noted that Monck's motivation was attracting speculation: 'Many think that he is honest yet, and some or more think him to be a fool that would raise himself, but think that he will undo himself by endeavouring it.'[59] With hindsight, it is evident that, from early January to the Restoration in May, all significant power really rested in the hands of this unknown figure and the close coterie of his own officer corps with which he had surrounded himself.

Monck was probably already in communication with the secluded members before the crisis came in his dealings with the restored Purged Parliament. On 9 February parliament, seeking to re-establish close control over the City, instructed Monck, by force if necessary, to destroy its defences and arrest supposed ringleaders of anti-parliamentary agitators. With an evident reluctance, he partially complied. By 11 February, he had decided to end the charade, instructing MPs within six days to issue the writs for new elections which would not disable any except those who had been in arms for the king. Robert Ayers notes, 'This open declaration for a free Parliament was in effect something close to a declaration for the king.'[60] The City responded, probably spontaneously, in carnival style, 'a night of "the Roasting of the Rump", possibly the greatest expression of popular rejoicing London has ever known'.[61] Yet the Purged Parliament further delayed, issuing writs on narrower qualifications which would have ensured those elected were ideologically compatible with its current members. On 21 February Monck summoned as many of the secluded members as could be rounded up, directed them to ensure that writs should be issued with fewer restrictions for a new parliament, and had them escorted back into the House, for the first time since December 1648. William Prynne, an old adversary of Milton's who had recently renewed his attacks, was in their ranks.[62] Once more the City celebrated with bonfires in the streets.

Milton had evidently been working on his own proposals for settling the state as the crisis between the Purged Parliament and Monck unfolded, turning the jottings of the 'Proposalls of certaine expedients' into an eloquent little pamphlet, some eighteen quarto pages long, *The Readie and Easie Way to Establish a Free Commonwealth, and the Excellence therof Compar'd with The inconveniences and dangers of readmitting kingship in this nation*. By the time it was ready, not only had he been overtaken by events but also he himself recognized it. Internal evidence places the *terminus a quo* for its publication at 22 February, the date on which the restored Long Parliament voted to hold new elections, and the *terminus ad quem* 3 March, when Thomason dated his copy, though as the Yale editor notes, he 'did not always receive copies promptly, or perhaps he did not always immediately date them'.[63] Once more, the imprint reads 'Printed by *T. N*[ewcombe]. and are to be sold by *Livewell Chapman*'. Milton's initials appear on the title page, and though his full name is nowhere to be found, the identity of the author can scarcely have been hard to guess.

Milton evidently wrote the first paragraph after the rest, adding it to explain how imperfectly his treatise meets the changed circumstances once the secluded members were readmitted and once the enlarged parliament had resolved to hold new elections for all seats:

> Although since the writing of this treatise, the face of things hath had some change, writs for new elections have bin recall'd, and the members at first chosen, readmitted from exclusion, to sit again in Parlament, yet not a little rejoicing to hear declar'd, the resolutions of all those who are now in power, jointly tending to the establishment of a free Commonwealth, and to remove if it be possible, this unsound humour of returning to old bondage, instilld of late by some cunning deceivers, and nourished from bad principles and fals apprehensions among too many of the people, I thought best not to suppress what I had written, hoping it may perhaps (the Parlament now sitting more full and frequent) be now much more useful then before: yet submitting what hath reference to the state of things as they then stood, to present constitutions; and so the same end be persu'd, not insisting on this or that means to obtain it.[64]

Milton puts a brave face on, but events have taken away the conditions on which he premised his argument and shifted power from those he sought primarily to address. 'The state of things as they then stood', as he wrote the body of the text, could have been perceived as one in which the Purged Parliament, restored after the collapse of the Committee of Safety, could rely on Monck's loyalty to underwrite their dominion. He wrote after that the Purged Parliament had issued writs to supplement its numbers, apparently in anticipation of thus assuring that it would sit in perpetuity. Indeed, at one point he alludes to the (now withdrawn) writs for recruiter elections as a positive move that would allay the criticism that the Purged Parliament is too small and unrepresentative.[65] Milton's arguments, against sequential parliaments and in favour of a perpetual grand council, are in broad harmony with the ambitions of men seemingly engaged in securing their own extended tenure of office. Milton certainly echoes pious statements by Monck and by the secluded members in support of settling England as 'a free Commonwealth', which probably in this context means a republic.[66] Of course, such assertions, useful for the time being, had little credibility; even the apprentice boys dancing around their bonfire at the Rump roasting knew that that action sealed the fate of the Good Old Cause, insofar as it lay with its defenders in the Purged Parliament.

Milton's rhetoric is tuned to the arrogance of his intended audience, those founders of the English republic, 'our old Patriots, the first Assertours of our religious and civil rights', brought together by divine providence a third time.[67] He celebrates the past victories of English republicanism and deplores the possibilities of 'losing by a strange aftergame of folly, all the battels we have wonne, all the treasure we have spent'.[68] Milton rehearses the merits of republican government, in terms of public service and cheapness, and the horrors of gaudy, wasteful, and irrational kingship.

Milton builds an argument for a perpetual grand council, as he prefers to term the unicameral parliament he proposes should be constituted once the new recruited members have arrived, in curiously evasive and duplicitous terms. His real reasons were probably as simple as those of the members of the Purged Parliament. Sooner or later, an election would return a membership with the potential to reinstate monarchy: no matter what oaths were administered, what restrictions put in place on the franchise or the right to stand, the risk remained of such subversion. But Milton can cite the examples of other republics: ancient Rome, Venice, the United Provinces. On the other hand, English constitutional practice always expected sequential parliaments, and if representation of the enfranchised people is of value, the arguments against, at the level of theory rather than *Realpolitik*, are hard to find. Milton resorts to a pair of improbable analogies:

The ship of the Commonwealth is alwaies undersail; they sit at the stern; and if they stear well, what need is ther to change them; it being rather dangerous? Adde to this, that the Grand Councel is both foundation and main pillar of the whole State; and to move pillars and foundations, unless they be faultie, cannot be safe for the building.[69]

The imagery seems to lack conviction. No ship is always under sail; no bit of a building can be simultaneously foundations and a pillar. His first point certainly cannot survive scrutiny in the context of early modern governance. The Council of State, the executive elected by parliament, can certainly govern alone in the interim between parliaments or during recesses. Milton is squirming away from the horror of a free election, the outcome of which can scarcely have been in doubt.

The peroration begins in studiedly laconic fashion: 'I have no more to say at present: few words will save us, well considerd; few and easie things, now seasonably don.'[70] Milton worked to convince his intended readers that all they had to do to preserve republican government, and with it a broad toleration, was nothing; just fill up the 'grand council' with men of their own political persuasion and hang on. The concluding sentences grow more flamboyant, touching on the vein of Jeremiah, whose words he echoes as he speaks 'the language of the good old cause': 'Thus much I should perhaps have said, though I were sure I should have spoken only to trees and stones, and had none to cry to, but with the Prophet, *O earth, earth, earth.*'[71]

For all the good it did, Milton could as well have directed his words to inanimate objects. However, other changes perhaps encouraged him to rethink his intended audience and to try again. On 27 February Monck secured the dismissal of Thomas Scott from the office of secretary of state, and the reinstatement of Thurloe, in tandem with one of Monck's personal staff. Of course, the subtle Thurloe had long since opened lines of communication with Monck, as early as 1658, and he, along with others, had preliminary contact with those promoting the interests of the king.[72] However, it placed Milton's former boss close to the real seat of power. There were radical changes in the Council of State. From 25 February, its president was Arthur Annesley, a young Irish aristocrat and Cromwellian protégé. Certainly in the Restoration period Annesley, created first earl of Anglesey, knew and befriended Milton. He had served in Richard's parliament and may at that time have established the friendship.[73] Annesley proved a significant figure in the transition to monarchy, though as late as 9 March he persuaded the restored Long Parliament to issue the writs for the elections 'with a republican formula', in opposition to demands from Prynne and others that they should be promulgated in the king's name.[74]

Perhaps temporarily reasssured that men of the Cromwellian Protectorates were again in positions of power and influence, Milton decided on a direct address to Monck, and around the first week of March he drafted 'The Present Means, and brief Delineation of a Free Commonwealth, Easy to be put in Practice, and without Delay. In a Letter to General *Monk*'. The text appeared first in *A Complete Collection of the Historical, Political, and Miscellaneous Works of John Milton, Both English and Latin. With som Papers never before Publish'd*, which was published in 1698 with a probably spurious Amsterdam imprint. The text is prefaced with the note, 'Publisht from the Manuscript'.[75] The transmission of the manuscript, which is not known to be extant, from 1660 to 1698 can merely be guessed at, though Edward Phillips may well have had a role. The document itself seems like a late draft, but there is no reason to dispute the traditional assumption that it was intended to be sent to Monck, probably as a private communication. Robert Ayers, with appropriate caution, notes, 'Not only is there no evidence that it was ever sent, received, or printed in Milton's lifetime; there is no evidence that it was ever in fact finished.'[76] Yet there is no reason why Milton would not have sent it, or rather a perfected version derived from it. It constituted no personal risk to himself, since his views were already widely disseminated, and he has shaped his address quite decorously to appeal to Monck, who is termed throughout 'your Excellency', and the source of whose power is called 'a faithfull Veteran Army'.[77]

Milton tries to engage Monck in thinking more innovatively about government, mapping out a plan for the devolution of most governmental authorities to regional assemblies made up of leading gentry. At one level Milton can be seen as anticipating measures not put in place in Britain till the second part of the twentieth century, a bit like his views on divorce. But there are contemporary examples which would have rendered his views as rather less zany than they are sometimes represented to be. The regional assemblies of the United Provinces are the most developed analogue. But English county structures were crucial to providing for the local administration of government and justice, through the corporations and the benches of magistrates, and the rule of the major-generals, while scarcely a blue-print for a new constitution, was essentially devolved and regional in character. Milton carries the arguments further in the second edition of *The Readie and Easie Way*. The rationale for the letter is Monck's own declarations that he sought to maintain the republic, rather than usher in a restoration of monarchy. Milton chooses to take these at face value, though his anxious awareness of the likely outcome of free elections is clear enough. So, too, is evidence of how out of touch he felt himself to be with critical developments: the original terms on which the imminent election was to be fought are 'not yet repeal'd, as I hear'.[78]

But the initiative slipped irreversibly from the republicans in the early weeks of March. On the fifth, parliament ordered the republication of the Solemn League and Covenant, including the clause about the defence of monarchy that Milton had once laboured to set aside.[79] By 10 March Monck, still to most people an enigma, was reported to have told an intimate 'that he would submit to the next Parliament if it wanted King and Lords'.[80] On 13 March parliament annulled the Engagement of 1650, which required all men over 18 to declare and promise to 'be true and faithful to the Commonwealth of England, as it is now established without a King or House of Lords'.[81] On 16 March the parliament first assembled in 1640 dissolved.

Milton's work on revising and supplementing *The Readie & Easie Way* probably occupied him from shortly after its initial publication, though it assumed a fresh urgency once more or less free elections became inevitable and then imminent. Getting it through the press proved problematic, however, in that Livewell Chapman, to whom he had turned for his earlier pamphlets of 1659–60, had attracted the attention of the Council of State as a key publisher of republican texts. Warrants for his arrest were issued on 28 March and 3 and 28 April. Though he evaded his pursuers, he was evidently no longer in a position to do much publishing. Nor could Milton find a printer willing to put his name to the new edition, which appeared, probably in the first week of April, with an imprint that simply reads 'Printed for the Author'.

Milton could have hoped to have some readership among the electorate, though some elections had already been held by the time it was published, nor is it clear how he could have hoped for much of a circulation outside London in the time available. However, it does address with some precision a new target readership, the newly royalist Presbyterians, who could confidently be expected to control the parliament that would assemble on 25 April. Milton's game is simple: he means to terrify them with the probability that Presbyterians will be persecuted and to outrage them with a more lurid depiction of the excesses of monarchical regimes, both premised on a strengthened account of the rule of Charles I. In part, he adopts a stratagem Nedham had used in August 1659 in *Interest Will Not Lie*, an ingenious tract designed to show that 'only the *Papist*' would gain by the restoration of monarchy. Milton's arguments resemble the case Nedham made in his chapter on Presbyterians.[82] Though there are considerable differences in idiom, it shares, too, the strategy of Nedham's later tract, *Newes from Brussels in a Letter from an Attendant on his Majesties Person*, which Thomason dated 'March 23'. Nedham fakes or spoofs a letter from a Cavalier exile to an England-based Cavalier conspirator, which has the supposed author explain the tactic of letting the Presbyterians settle the sectaries before the Cavaliers settle the Presbyterians:

The *Presbyter* will give up the *Phanatique*, a handsome bone to pick at first: I like it better far than all at once; excess brings surfeits: Thus half the beard they shave themselves, let us alone with t'other: Drown first the Kitlings, let the Dam that litter'd them alone a little longer.[83]

In similar vein, Milton seeks to frighten men intractable to other argumentation: 'nor let the new royaliz'd presbyterians perswade themselves that thir old doings, though now recanted, will be forgotten'.[84] Milton cleverly invokes the language and the fears of the early 1640s, when 'cavaliers' plundered the land, and he uses the evidence of the violent, sometimes obscene, publications with which promoters of the restoration were currently flooding London, 'the insolencies, the menaces, the insultings of our newly animated common enemies crept lately out of thir holes, ... the spue of every drunkard, every ribald'. 'Common' makes a play for the old days of broad puritan solidarity.

Milton does not like the Presbyterians and knows their view of him; yet they should be afraid of their new allies: 'Let our zealous backsliders forethink now with themselves, how thir necks yok'd with these tigers of Bacchus, these new fanatics of not the preaching but the sweating-tub, inspir'd with nothing holier then the Veneral pox, can draw one way ... to the establishing of church discipline.' Milton, correctly as it proves, forecasts a church settlement on the prelatical model and the relegation and suppression of Presbyterianism, along with other puritan denominations. Moreover, the Long Parliament in 1642 had been Presbyterian dominated: 'neglected and soon after discarded, if not prosecuted for old traytors; the first inciters, beginners, and more then to the third part actors of all that followd'.[85] Like Nedham, Milton knows he needs to focus Presbyterian anxiety on the dangers of unbridled cavalierism. Indeed, those Presbyterian politicians who, in spring 1660, were consciously working to bring in the king recognized their weakness. Denzil Holles, prominently among them, later disclosed that they 'pressed the royalists to be quiet, and to leave the game in their hands; for their appearing would give jealousy, and hurt that which they meant to promote'.[86]

Milton also plays on the old puritan aesthetic in government, religion, and lifestyle. He strengthens considerably his depiction of how kingship would operate, promising that 'There will be a queen also of no less charge; in most likelihood a Papist; besides a queen mother such alreadie; together with both thir courts and numerous train', and then offspring and their courts. Instead of public service, the nobility and gentry would seek instead court offices. He adds, with a shudder he expects his readers to share, that they would compete to be 'grooms, even of the close-stool', alluding to the office of 'groom of the stole' and carefully reminding us of its practical origins.[87] In place of such horrors, Milton offers a refined account of his alternative constitutional model, with further reduction in the role of national government and an increase in the power and responsibilities of regional assemblies.[88]

Milton's final publication of the republican years was *Brief Notes Upon a late Sermon, Titl'd The Fear of God and the King; Preach'd, and since Publish'd, by Matthew Griffith, D. D., And Chaplain to the late KING*. The imprint carries the name of neither printer nor bookseller. The title page has Milton's initials, and the opening paragraph alludes to *The Readie and Easie Way*; its author's identity cannot have been uncertain. It is, however, a curiously inept conclusion to Milton's spirited if doomed campaign. Griffith was a worthy and tactically appropriate adversary. A man of undaunted courage, he had preached the royalist cause in London pulpits till his arrest in November 1643. His livings were sequestrated. He had escaped to join Charles I at Oxford, thus moving into close proximity to Milton's wife and father-in-law, and had found himself among the predominately Catholic defenders of Basing House when it was taken by storm. In that carnage, he had been wounded and one of his daughters had been killed. 'Sequestered from his livings and from his temporal estate, several times violently assaulted and imprisoned, he suffered enormously during the revolutionary era.'[89] Unsurprisingly, Griffith viewed the prospect of restoration with some enthusiasm. However, he was a good example of the kind of royalist Holles and his associates wanted to marginalize. On 25 March he preached at the chapel of the Mercers' Company, taking as his text Proverbs 24: 21, 'My son, fear God and the King, and meddle not with them that be seditious, or desirous of change, &c.'[90] The sermon appeared with a second work, printed continuously with it, *The Samaritan revived*, which offers a tendentious, essentially Cavalier, account of the last twenty years, with particular attention to recent times. The sermon is relatively muted, though there is nothing mealy-mouthed about the epistle dedicatory, to Monck, telling him, 'Think not with thy self that thou shalt escape in the *Kings* House, more then the rest if thou forbearest at this time, then shall our enlargement and deliverance rise from some other place; but thou, and thy house shall be destroyed.'⁹¹ *The Samaritan revived* is much fuller in its analysis of Presbyterianism and its role in fomenting the discord that had led to the inception of the first civil war. Griffith is not minded to except the new royalists from a wider culpability, observing no distinction in those early years between them and those they would term fanatics: 'here observe by the way, that though the Presbyterians, Independents, Anabaptists, and all other Schismatiques and Sectaries, may well be called LEGION, for they are many; yet though they be never so many, and never so far differing, and disagreeing each from other, in their heads, yet like *Samsons* Foxes, they are tyed together by the tayls…they agreed like brethren in actuating this [armed rebellion], which was as capitall a crime, and as horrid an iniquity, as ever the Sun beheld. And which I may not pretermit in silence.'⁹² Silence, at the least in the short term, nevertheless did follow; on 2 April the Council of State ordered his arrest and incarceration in Newgate, where he remained till early May. His was an inconveniently plain voice in such delicate times, though one which initially found a hearing: *The Fear of God and the King* reportedly sold out all 500 copies of the impression in a few days.⁹³ Hutton observes that, 'The exiles were if anything even more furious with him, and begged their supporters not merely to be passive but to make conciliatory gestures.'⁹⁴

Milton had a perfect target but he muffed his shot. *The Samaritan revived*, most useful for his purpose, is largely ignored: 'finding it so foul a libell against all the well-affected of this land…and meeting with no more Scripture or solid reason…then hath already bin found sophisticated and adulterate, I leave your malignant narrative, as needing no other confutation, then the just censure already pass'd upon you by the Councel of State.' Instead, Milton opts to dispute the theology of Griffith's sermon, and even picks away at his 'Geographical and Historical mistakes…as…*Philip of Macedon*, who is generally understood of the great *Alexanders* father only, made contemporarie, page 31, with *T. Quintus the Roman commander*, instead of *T. Quintius* and the latter *Philip*'. It would have taken a lot more than pedantry to save the republic. Indeed, Milton at one point recognizes the game was all but lost, opening the possibility of an elective monarchy, 'chusing out of our own number one who hath best aided the people, and best merited against tyrannie'.⁹⁵ Presumably, he meant Monck.

As Milton's *Brief Notes*, the final gesture of republican polemic, appeared, Lambert as ineptly launched the last aggressive action of the New Model Army. Escaping from the Tower (and leaving his chambermaid lying in his bed to deceive his guards), he attempted to rally soldiers to resist Monck and halt the spiral into restoration. As they mustered on what had been the battlefield of Edgehill, they were dispersed and Lambert arrested by troops under Richard Ingoldsby, a regicide destined to be a gentleman of the privy chamber and knight of the Bath.

On 25 April what would soon be known as the Convention Parliament gathered, and it was dominated by members who were, in the words of Edward Hyde, the future Earl of Clarendon, 'of singular affection to the King'.[96] On 1 May the Declaration of Breda was read in parliament and the king, unanimously, was invited to return home.[97] On 29 May he entered London in triumph.

V

1660–1674

CHAPTER 14

Milton in 1660

THE mid-century decades had followed only imperfectly the aspirations and intentions evinced by Milton in the 1630s and on his return from Italy. Certainly, he had achieved fame, indeed in its more challenging sub-species, notoriety. He had published a great deal and his learning, so patiently accumulated since childhood, had been widely displayed and variously feared or praised. He had married, not one but two, not especially poor, probable virgins. Three children survived. However, from the perspective of the fairly young man who had moved from St Bride's Churchyard to a pleasant, little house, in a quiet street, with enough room for his books, the 1640s and 1650s had been disruptive and tumultuous (as, of course, they were for many who lived in England).

He had entered into the controversies surrounding church government with an initial diffidence. But the Smectymnuans' response to the notes he had provided prompted him to take on prelacy in his own person. His adoption of the familiar young man's stratagem—finding an old and illustrious target to strike at (in this case Bishop Joseph Hall)—had raised his profile. But he soon found himself staving off counter-attacks and declaring his ambition to get back to writing poetry.

His marriage once more dragged him into controversy. The first divorce tract, or rather the response it evoked, set him on a course away from his erstwhile comrades, with whose theology, particularly on the issue of salvation, he had sharp disagreements and whose newly clarified enthusiasm for a church settlement on Presbyterian lines he did not share. Tolerationism emerged as the cause to be defended. Yet by 1645, hounded by the Presbyterian mobilization, he rebuilt his social connections and resumed his scholarly and creative activities in earnest. Yet he had been radicalized into alignment with the civilian supporters of Pride's Purge and with the trial and execution of the king, and he emerged as the most eloquent defender of that process.

His appointment as public servant and leading apologist for the republican regime carried him away from fighting private battles and from promoting publicly the radical agenda on tithes, on church government, on the separation of church and state, to which he probably subscribed. Moreover, through the first five or six years after the death of the king, the task of writing on behalf of the state, in English and in Latin, posed an exhausting burden alongside the more undemanding work as Latin secretary. Meanwhile two wives had died, and his health had declined sharply. Poor vision gave way to blindness. Yet by the middle years of the 1650s, while retaining much of his salary and continuing to undertake the duties of Latin secretary, he could return in earnest to scholarship and to poetry.

He developed ways of working that allowed him to pursue the most ambitious projects. He was engaged on his history of Britain, on the poem that became *Paradise Lost*, on a Latin dictionary, and on a systematic theology. He was widely feted. Around him had formed a sort of private academy of cultured friends educated in the humanist tradition, of which he was the cynosure. He cultivated, at least till the death of Oliver Cromwell, the kinds of public reticence appropriate to a servant of the state. He was prosperous and appeared untroubled by the way England was governed. Once Cromwell died, he judged the political climate to have changed, and entered spiritedly into the renewed debate about church government, advocating a primitive style of worship that he presented as apostolic but which in the immediate context points to some sympathy, at least on such issues, with the Quakers.

Then, in 1660, he awoke to the imminence of the Restoration and the fragility of his own position. The blind Fury seemed to be making her way to Petty France, threatening not only Milton's eminence and prosperity but perhaps his freedom or even his personal survival, bringing to an end those aspirations, so long delayed and now so evidently achievable, which he had formed twenty years earlier.

CHAPTER 15

Surviving the Restoration

R ONALD Hutton has argued persuasively that two separate Restoration settlements are to be distinguished, 'of different character and produced by different groups of men working in different circumstances':[1] the first, during which a relatively irenic policy was developed under the Convention Parliament; the second, a regime of more extensive persecution under the Cavalier Parliament. The distinction helps in understanding Milton's conduct and experiences from May 1660 to the end of 1662. The sequence broadly accords with Nedham's speculation in *Newes from Brussels*, that cavaliers would deal first with the kitlings and then with their dam.[2]

Charles II's return had been premised upon assurances that reprisals would be limited and that the Presbyterian royalists who now ushered in the Restoration had nothing to fear. At the session on 1 May when the Convention Parliament unanimously invited him home, his Declaration of Breda, dated 4 April, was disclosed. This promised a process of oblivion and reconciliation with selective exceptions:

to the end that the fear of punishment may not engage any, conscious to themselves of what is past, to a perseverance in guilt for the future, by opposing the quiet and happiness of their country, in the restoration of King, Peers, and people to their just, ancient and fundamental rights, we do, by these presents, declare, that we do grant a free and general pardon, which we are ready, upon demand, to pass under our Great Seal of England, to all our subjects, of what degree or quality soever, who, within forty days after the publishing hereof, shall lay hold upon this our grace and favour, and shall, by any public act, declare their doing so, and that they return to the loyalty and obedience of good subjects; excepting only such persons as shall herafter be excepted by Parliament, those only to be excepted.[3]

The curious circularity of that final sentence alerts an anxious reader to the uncertainties it foreshadows: everyone will be pardoned except those whom parliament decides should not be pardoned. How widely would the general pardon be extended? Technically, all who had been in arms against Charles I or Charles II were traitors; but over 30,000 were currently soldiers and tens of thousands more had passed through the ranks of the New Model Army and its predecessors.

Milton was, of course, familiar with the fates of the defeated. Penalties after the first civil war had, in most cases, been financial, and he had witnessed and worked to mitigate the charges laid against his brother and the estate of his father-in-law.[4] Ring-leaders in the second and third civil wars, ended respectively at Colchester and Worcester, were sometimes executed, and among prominent conspirators of subsequent plots and insurrections, Sir George Booth was unique in escaping execution.[5] Indeed, on occasion the Protectorate had taken to itself the full panoply of quasi-regal judicial process, using the treason statute, 25 Edward III (1352), with its provision for the evisceration and dismemberment of anyone who 'compasses or imagines' the death of the 'chief magistrate'. Miles Sindercombe, a former Leveller, who in 1657 led a conspiracy to kill Cromwell, was sentenced to be hanged, drawn and quartered, though opted instead to commit suicide on the eve of the spectacle, to the evident disappointment of the officials involved. As a poor alternative, he was dragged to Tower Hill and turned naked into a pit, with a stake through his body; 'The part of the stake which remaines above ground, being all plated with Iron: which may stand as an example of terror to all Traytors for the time to come', as a newsbook, printed by Thomas Newcombe, a regular government printer at this time, observes.[6] Spectacular punishment was certainly not unprecedented in the Interregnum. Nor could those convicted of treason at the Restoration expect a cleaner death. Indeed, the regicides brought to trial were arraigned under the same statute used against Sindercombe.

How and why did Milton escape? Four variables characterized the thirty-three people finally excepted from the Bill of Indemnity and Oblivion signed by the king on 29 August 1660 and thus exposed to the possibility of capital punishment: they were directly involved in the trial and execution of Charles I; they were perceived to be still dangerous; they were of no potential utility to the new regime; they had too few powerful friends and too many powerful enemies among the new establishment. On all four counts, Milton's profile was promising. Certainly, *The Tenure of Kings and Magistrates* had justified the trial of Charles I and its arguments had been incorporated more widely into republican polemic, but it appeared after the event and had no bearing on the outcome. The ten people first to be executed included Daniel Axtell, who had commanded the guard at the trial, Francis Hacker, responsible for the custody of the king, and John Cook, the principal prosecutor, Hugh Peter, the Independent minister and Cromwell's chaplain who had unremittingly advocated the king's prosecution, and six others who had signed the death warrant. Besides Cook, only three public servants were excepted from pardon and exposed to capital prosecution, Andrew Broughton, John Phelps, and Edward Dendy, who had officiated at the trial; all absconded and died in exile.[7] Mere service of the republican state was not capitally punished. Even Thurloe, though incarcerated for six weeks over the summer of 1660, was not one of the thirty-three excepted from the Bill of Indemnity. Indeed, none of his administrative team was significantly punished.

Milton, palpably, was not dangerous. His attempts to rally support through his publications of 1660 had proved signally unsuccessful, and it is highly doubtful whether significant numbers of the second edition of *The Readie and Easie Way* actually made it into circulation. Milton, once excluded from the circles of government, was ineffectual, and could probably be hunted down were that judgement to prove unfounded. Moreover, the easiest way to control the press, as always, was not to prosecute authors but rather their printers and booksellers, which was the principal policy of the new regime. Livewell Chapman, who had published the first edition, was already on the run from warrants issued by the Council of State in the month before the Restoration.[8] Sir Henry Vane and John Lambert, however, had proved energetic and inter-mittently effective in the final months of the republic. They were indeed excepted from the Bill of Indemnity, though neither participated in the trial of the king. (Vane withdrew from parliament in protest at Pride's Purge, while Lambert was away from London, besieging Pontefract.)

However, Milton was, potentially, useful. His European reputation was very high, and, were he to have been turned in his loyalties to serve the restored monarchy, his apostasy would have resonated across the continent. There is strong evidence that, on the whole, his enemies perceived him, not as motivated by radical conviction, but as an accomplished mercenary. Others were turned. John Canne, who in 1649 had seconded Milton's efforts on behalf of the republic and who had briefly edited *Mercurius Politicus* in 1659, in the weeks before the Restoration 'launched two fresh newspapers, which supported the government [of the Convention Parliament] as firmly as the official press'.[9] Marchamont Nedham, by 1660 more notorious in England than Milton, skipped abroad but nevertheless was pardoned. The most talented popular propagandist of the age, he had twice changed sides in the 1640s—from parliament to king and from king to parliament. He evidently took some wooing, however. Not until 1676, two years before his death, did he write propaganda for Charles II, producing five pamphlets attacking the first earl of Shaftesbury; as Joseph Frank, his modern biographer, observes, 'Nedham made his last exit as a full-fledged Tory.... Nedham was back on the government payroll.'[10] Cyriack Skinner recalls that Milton, a little while after the Act of Indemnity and Oblivion, was approached: 'hee was visited ... by a Chief Officer of the State, and desir'd to imploy his Pen on thir behalfe.'[11]

Fourthly, Milton had significant connections with the new establishment. As Hutton puts it, 'The close-knit nature of the English ruling class . . . now assisted the process of granting indemnity as many republicans proved to have friends, relatives, or men who owed them gratitude, sitting in the Convention.' Such connections saved from execution far guiltier and far more prominent men than Milton. William Heveningham, a regicide, was saved from death by the Privy Council 'out of respect for his grandfather-in-law, a royalist earl', and his estate was also protected for his heirs. Colonel John Hutchinson, also a regicide, was set at liberty 'through the efforts of friends from both wartime parties'.[12] Milton's connections spread far wider than the Convention Parliament. His, after all, was a royalist family, and he had worked on behalf of both his brother, Christopher, and the Powell clan. With the king's return, Christopher's legal career picked up. By November he was called to the Bench of the Inner Temple, marking his recognition as a senior member of his inn of court.[13] Thomas Agar, whose step-sons, the Phillips brothers, Milton had in effect brought up, had lost his post of Deputy Clerk of the Crown in the Crown Office in Chancery in the 1640s. By June 1660 he was successfully petitioning the king for grant of the office of Clerk of Appeals in Chancery 'in addition to his former office'. As John Shawcross has remarked, he was strategically placed to wield some influence on Milton's behalf.[14] In late April 1660 another brother-in-law, Richard Powell, whose parents and siblings Milton had sheltered while he himself was in exile,[15] emerged among other Oxfordshire luminaries to sign a declaration, subsequently printed, that 'we do declare, that we *disdain*, and with perfect detestation *disown*, all purpose of *Revenge*, or *partial Remembrance* of things past'.[16]

The early lives point to some influence closer to the real seats of power. Edward Phillips recalls, 'the Act of Oblivion . . . prov'd as favourable to him as could be hop'd or expected, through the intercession of some that stood his Friends both in Council and Parliament; particularly in the House of Commons, Mr. *Andrew Marvel*, a member for *Hull*, acted vigorously in his behalf, and made a considerable party for him.'[17] The identity of those friends in the Council of State of the Convention Parliament is more a matter of speculation. Annesley would seem an obvious possibility since their subsequent acquaintance and indeed friendship are well evidenced. Jonathan Richardson, writing over seventy years after the event, records some oral accounts, and offers tentatively a possible account: 'I have heard that Secretary *Morrice* and Sir *Thomas Clargis* were his Friends, and manag'd Matters Artfully in his Favour; Doubtless They, or Sombody Else did, and They very Probably, as being very Powerful Friends at That time.'[18] No other early record connects Milton with Sir William Morice or Sir Thomas Clarges. However, both would have been ideal friends to have under the circumstances. Morice, a close associate of Monck, took at the Restoration the role of secretary of state formerly held by Thurloe. Clarges, who had been Monck's agent in London during his governorship of Scotland, had married his sister and had been chosen to carry the news of the 1 May vote from the Convention Parliament to the king.

Evidently, there were also debts which could be invoked. Cyriack Skinner notes, 'among others, the Grand child of the famous Spencer, a Papist suffering in his concerns in Ireland, and S[i]r William Davenant when taken Prisoner, for both of whom hee procur'd relief'.[19] The allusion to Edmund Spenser's grandson has some circumstantial plausibility. William Spenser had converted to Catholicism and in the early 1650s had been deprived of his estates; however, a successful appeal to Cromwell overturned that decision. Milton would have been in a position to support such an approach, and William Spenser, in turn, evidently had some influence at the Restoration since Cromwell's decision was finally implemented and the lands returned to him.[20] Richardson offers some support for Davenant's role, claiming to have received the anecdote from Alexander Pope, who in turn had it from Thomas Betterton, who had acted in the Duke's Company under the management of Davenant, who had related to him these events.[21] Again, there is circumstantial plausibility. Davenant, in arms for the king, had been captured in 1650 on a ship bound for Maryland or Virginia. Till 1652 he was held, at first in Jersey and later in the Tower, at some risk of prosecution for the capital offence of treason. At that point he was released and in some measure reconciled to successive Interregnum regimes.[22] Once more, Milton would have been reasonably placed to have exercised some influence on behalf of a fellow poet and masque-writer.

Of course, Milton's influence and connections may have been even more extensive than the extant records suggest. The nature of clandestine lobbying renders it extremely difficult to document even in our own age, let alone at 350 years' remove. Edward Phillips, reflecting on his uncle's failure to realize his excise bonds,[23] simply remarked on 'all the Power and Interest he had in the Great ones of those Times'.[24]

Nor should Milton's prominence in the consciousness of the Restoration authorities be overstated. In the months before and after May 1660 numerous publications issued from Cavalier writers, often in broadside, presenting lists of the guilty men whose condign punishment was anticipated. Their effect was counter-productive, given the Presbyterian royalists' concern that a spirit of reconciliation should be promoted, and Milton picked up on them effectively in his denunciation of the 'diabolical forerunning libells' that presented a rather different aspect to the impulse towards restoration from that projected by the likes of Hyde and Holles.[25] Once Milton had returned to publishing in defence of the republic, he attracted attack and refutation; unfortunately, the most assiduous adversary was Roger L'Estrange. From 1663 the surveyor of the press, charged with its close regulation, he was an awkward enemy for an author to make, though in 1660–1 his influence was slight. He had in March sneered at the ill-timing of the first edition of *The Readie and Easie Way*.[26] His most substantial assault comes in his *No Blinde Guides, in Answer To a seditious Pamphlet of J. Milton's, Intituled Brief Notes upon a late Sermon*. L'Estrange not only identifies Milton as the author of the pamphlet but also associates it with *The Readie and Easie Way, Pro Populo Anglicano Defensio*, and *Eikonoklastes*.[27] *The Readie and Easie Way* attracted a substantial, book-length response, *The Dignity of Kingship Asserted*, usually attributed to George Starkey; Thomason dated his copy 'May'. Its tone is unusually serious-minded, amid the more scabrous Cavalier publications of the time. Starkey, a Presbyterian, was formerly a member of the Hartlib circle.[28]

Milton does sometimes figure in the more general onslaughts on prominent republicans, and shares the contempt heaped upon them. Some of the allusions carry a minatory edge. Colonel Hewson, whose troops had killed several prentice-boy demonstrators in December 1659, was pilloried the following January in a tract offering a rich fantasy of the spectacular punishment appropriate for a former cobbler. He had lost an eye in the Irish campaign, which supported the gratuitous suggestion that 'The one good eye he hath left, wee'l take out of his Head, and bestow it upon blind *Milton* that it may still be worn as an Ornament in a knaves countenance, and when he leave it, it shall be given to Surgeons Hall for a rarity.'[29] An anonymous squib sometimes attributed to Samuel Butler, amid attacks on Nedham, Harrington, Bradshaw, and Hesilrige, offers a threatening though not imperceptive picture of Milton's singularity: 'he is so much an enemy to usual practices that I believe when he is condemned to travel to *Tyburn* in a cart, he will petition for the favour to be the first man that ever was driven thither in a *Wheel-barrow*.'[30]

Yet, amid the plethora of broadsides offering possible wish-lists of republican victims, Milton occurs rarely. Consider the wholly typical *Lucifers lifeguard containing a schedule, list, scrovvle or catalogue, of the first and following names of the antichristian, anabaptistical, atheistical, anarchial and infernal imps, who have been actors, contrivers, abettors, murders and destroyers, of the best religion, the best government, and the best king that ever Great Britain enjoyed* (London, 1660). In a list of sixty-two miscreants that stretches from Bradshaw to 'Dunce Owen' (presumably John Owen, an Independent divine much favoured by Cromwell[31]), Milton's name is absent from the usual litany of miscreants, though it does, perhaps surprisingly, contain that of Stephen Marshall, who had died in 1655. Nor is he among the twenty-eight named in the ballad *The Arsy Versy, or, The Second Martyrdom of the Rump* (London, 1660), or in *The History of the Second Death of the Rump* (London, 1660), where Nedham figures twice. Toland entertained the whimsy that Milton escaped prosecution because he had slipped the memory of Charles II: 'som are of opinion that he was more oblig'd to that Prince's Forgetfulness than to his Clemency.'[32] Yet in truth by May 1660 he did not stand as high in the consciousness of royalists as he had done nine or ten years before, nor as high as Nedham, frequently pilloried as a knave of diabolical accomplishment.[33]

That Milton survived, with hindsight, is unsurprising, and at the time he may have approached the crisis with guarded optimism. But he was, certainly, at risk, and his conduct from May 1660 to the end of the year shows a cautious man's careful and well-advised response to damaging and potentially deadly threats. Moreover, despite his efforts, he sustained a massive loss of personal equity. He had saved most of his salary as a public servant, accruing, according to his early biographers, £2,000 'lodg'd in the Excise'.[34] Milton, no doubt mindful of how royalists had been bled dry by financial impositions, tried to protect his investment, in anticipation that republican sympathizers would have their most obvious and accessible assets seized. On 5 May he assigned to Cyriack Skinner an excise bond dating back to 13 May 1651, to the value of £400. The endorsement, written and witnessed by Jeremie Pickard, one of the last dateable documents linking him to Milton, assigned to Skinner the interest payable since 13 November 1659, together with the principal on its maturity.[35] It is reasonable to assume that Milton at the least tried to place bonds for the remaining £1,600 lent to former governments in equally safe hands. Skinner had done nothing to attract hostile attention from the Restoration regime.

In the event, the attempt proved fruitless: 'those men who had advanced money to the Interregnum governments now forfeited both principal and interest.'[36] Milton, who had recently lost his public salary, lost now capital capable of generating about £160 per annum. He was not, however, impoverished. Presumably he had at this time the £1,500 he left at his death, worth at the usual rate about £120 per annum. He had, too, the leasehold of the Bread Street property, which he had inherited from his father, though that would be lost in 1666.[37] Edward Phillips writes of another sizeable investment, 'another great Sum, [lost] by mismanagement and for want of good advice'.[38] We can only speculate; the ways of losing money in early modern England were legion.

Milton also left his home in Petty France. That house had been fairly convenient for his continuing work for successive Councils of State, since it was quite a short walk from Whitehall and the Palace of Westminster. Its other charm was 'a door into [St James's] Park'. However, its proximity to the complex of royal palaces at Whitehall and its immediate adjacency to St James's Palace made it a dangerously conspicuous place for Milton to remain. Cyriack Skinner noted that he 'prudently left his house' once the court returned; prudently perhaps, Skinner later deleted the adverb and inserted 'in good manners'.[39] In Petty France Milton was altogether too exposed to rough treatment by cavalier courtiers, who were perhaps indulging a nocturnal ramble in the Park in the spirit celebrated a little later by the second earl of Rochester.[40]

Milton moved into hiding, as Phillips notes, in 'a Friend's House in *Bartholomew-Close*'.⁴¹ It is in the clandestine nature of this concealment that the friend remains unidentified. About this time, John Rowe, an Independent minister who had preached Bradshaw's funeral service, moved there to minister to a new congregation.⁴² However, there would have been dubious wisdom in a notorious fugitive seeking refuge with another dissident already well known to their mutual enemies. Milton stayed in his hiding place there till the Bill of Indemnity and Oblivion received royal assent.⁴³

Biographers of Milton face a temptation to fictionalize about his probable emotional state, what he must have felt, over those summer months. There is no evidence. A pious man in an age of faith, he may, for all we know, simply have trusted in divine providence. A well-connected and experienced political activist, he may have confidently looked to the measures put in place to ensure his inclusion in the general pardon.

But the campaign to save him ran into problems early in June. The Convention Parliament's debate on who should be excepted proceeded with curious vacillations and relative moderation 'due to the tendency of the two Houses to reject each other's victims'.⁴⁴ However, in due course the Commons turned to consider the case, not of regicides and those who promoted the execution of Charles I, but of the apologists for the action. Together with John Goodwin, the Independent Arminian minister whose intellectual affinities with Milton we have already considered,⁴⁵ he was the subject of orders and resolutions of the Commons made on 16 June.⁴⁶ The House resolved to petition the king to issue a proclamation calling in *Eikonoklastes* and *Pro Populo Anglicano Defensio*, together with Goodwin's *Hybristodikai. The obstructours of justice. Or a defence of the honourable sentence passed upon the late King, by the High Court of Justice* (London, 1649), itself indebted to Milton's *Tenure of Kings and Magistrates*. The House was acting in accordance with its principal concerns, of focusing on the events surrounding the execution and on the maltreatment of the late king, a policy with obvious attraction for those members who had been active opponents of Charles I in the early 1640s. Curiously, Milton's later Latin defences and his more theoretical but in some ways much more radical *Tenure* escape mention. Charles II moved only slowly in response to this petition. Not until 13 August was a proclamation issued, requiring all copies of the named texts to be surrendered within ten days and instructing magistrates and university vice-chancellors to seek out any copies still retained, reporting the offenders to the Privy Council.⁴⁷ The books were to be burnt by the common hangman. 'Several copies' were reportedly burnt at the Old Bailey on 27 August, and perhaps again in early September. The Bodleian Library seems to have retained its copies, at least of Milton's works.⁴⁸ Judicially sanctioned book-burning in the early modern period functioned much more as a symbolic judgement than as a practical measure to curtail circulation; these are not today exceptionally rare books for their period.

The second action of the House of Commons was more alarming and had longer-term implications. It instructed the Attorney General to proceed against Milton and Goodwin 'by way of Indictment, or Information' against them with respect to the offending books, and it resolved 'That Mr. *Milton*, and Mr. *John Goodwin*, be forthwith sent for, in Custody, by the Serjeant at Arms attending this House'. But the birds had flown. Goodwin, like Milton, was in hiding, in his case in Bethnal Green and then in the Essex town of Leigh.[49] But the parliamentary resolution was to occasion Milton's temporary incarceration later in the year.

Nevertheless, when the Act was finally promulgated, Milton was in no measure excluded from the general pardon, while Goodwin was merely excluded from holding any position of public trust. Since he had been ejected from his living and presumably entertained no aspirations for preferment under the Restoration regime, the measure was perhaps no great impairment. As for Milton, in Edward Phillips's words, the Act, 'it pleased God, prov'd as favourable to him as could be hop'd or expected'.[50]

While Milton lay concealed, a handful of glancing print attacks appeared, some of them perhaps inadvertently helpful to his cause. His blindness was again deemed providential—the old canard recurs as a slight, though it probably supported an argument from his defenders that he had been punished already. He is sometimes called 'mercenary', which again suggests he was a mere hireling, not a dangerous fanatic acting out of conviction. But much more prominent miscreants dominated events in the autumn. In October, during a parliamentary recess, all the regicides in custody were tried and condemned, and 'all except one of the eleven immediately vulnerable were hanged, drawn and quartered . . . amidst the atmosphere of a bearbaiting'.[51] Milton certainly knew personally at least some of the victims, though there is no evidence that any was a close friend. On its return, parliament passed a bill of attainder, convicting fugitive regicides and confiscating their property, along with that of colleagues who were already dead. It then resolved to mark the twelfth anniversary of the king's execution by exhuming the bodies of Cromwell, Ireton, and Bradshaw, gibbeting them briefly from the Tyburn scaffold, and burying them in an adjacent pit. Their skulls were exhibited on spikes on Westminster Hall, and for the rest of Milton's life remained there; they were blown down by a storm in the 1680s. Milton, of course, had known Bradshaw before the trial of the king, and had been a minor beneficiary of his will.[52] Pepys, not sentimental for the Good Old Cause, found the desecration of Cromwell's corpse gratuitous and upsetting: it 'doth trouble me, that a man of so great courage as he was should have that dishonour', though George Fox rejoiced in the infamous

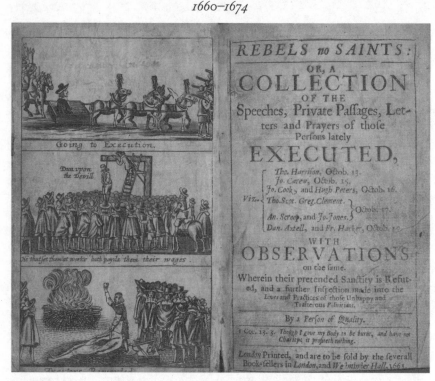

40. W.S., *Rebels no Saints* (London, 1661), title page and frontispiece.

exposure of one who had failed to protect Quakers.[53] Milton's contemporary response to these events is unrecorded.

From late August Milton once more moved freely. He took a house in Holborn near Red Lion Fields,[54] by chance close to the inn where the three exhumed bodies were kept on the eve of the gibbeting. Phillips notes that he stayed there 'not long before his Pardon having pass'd the Seal'.[55] The phrase is more problematic than at first it seems. The Act of Oblivion was a general pardon. However, Milton seems to have received a specific pardon, apparently not extant, no later than mid-December 1660, which related to a brief period of incarceration, perhaps since November, possibly a little longer.[56] The warrant presumably originated in the House of Commons resolution of 16 June, which called for him to be sent for and to come, in custody, to the House. There is no record to suggest he appeared before the House. Instead, he was lodged in the Tower of London, though, as required in the resolution, 'in Custody of the Serjeant at Arms attending this House'.[57] Again, the dangers of fictionalizing his response to these events are considerable. Of course, for a blind man such an experience could well be especially traumatic. The Tower of London, however, offered a range of accommodation, some of it fit for its occasional aristocratic prisoners. Milton, on his release, was obliged to pay fees of £150, demanded by the serjeant, probably including fees for incarceration as well as arrest. The sum was exorbitant, and the subject of a complaint in parliament, though it may be indicative that Milton, and quite probably a friend or servant carer, were lodged well. The outcome of the protest, launched by Marvell in the Commons, is unknown. Two phrases in early accounts merit attention. A Dutch periodical noted that Milton 'was freed through good promises'.[58] This implies that Milton gave some explicit undertaking as to his future conduct as part of his release from the Tower; it could at least in part explain his long abstention from writing controversial prose. Cyriack Skinner says, 'hee early sued out his Pardon; and by means of that, when the Serjeant of the house of Commons had officiously seisd him, was quickly set at liberty'.[59] This is even more enigmatic. Skinner may mean that he invoked his inclusion in the general pardon of August to escape detention in December, though if the pardon alluded to is the specific pardon, now lost, the account broadly confirms the Dutch report.

It was probably the only time he was imprisoned and the last time he faced prosecution. On his release, he shortly moved house once more, to Jewin Street, off Aldersgate Street where he had lived in the early 1640s.[60] New and reissued responses to his controversial prose trickled unanswered from the press. Ephraim Pagitt's *Heresiography* appeared in a sixth edition in 1661.[61] There was a new edition of *Regii Sanguinis Clamor*, from a press in The Hague.[62] Starkey reissued *The Dignity of Kingship Asserted* as *Monarchy Triumphing Over Traiterous Republicans* (London, 1661).[63] A London edition of Salmasius's posthumous and incomplete response to *Pro Populo Anglicano Defensio* appeared, probably while Milton was in prison.[64] To none of these Milton replied.

Thus Milton began the business of living prudently under the restored monarchy. London and the regime, however, were shaken by a minor incident with spectacular results. On 17 January 1661, Thomas Venner and about fifty other Fifth Monarchists attempted to usher in the millennium by resort to armed insurrection. He had tried this before, organizing a conspiracy against Cromwell in 1657, for which he had been imprisoned in the Tower. Thomas Harrison, a hero to Fifth Monarchists, had been among the regicides to perish in the previous October, and Venner's group, who worshipped in his chapel in Coleman Street, seems to have been encouraged by his display of equanimity during his execution. (Pepys had noted, drily, that Harrison was 'looking as cheerfully as any man could do in that condition'.[65]) The fifty or so rebels briefly fought off Charles's lifeguard, before a final skirmish in which about half died and most of the rest were captured. Fourteen were hanged, drawn, and quartered. Venner at his trial and even on the gallows with a rope around his neck echoed Harrison's speech to his own judges, asserting, 'All the Doctrines that ever I have preached are truth,... according to the word and the best light which I had within me, and the same I now seale with my Blood.'[66] Milton had manifested no affinities or enthusiasm for Fifth Monarchists. Their actions in 1661 succeeded only in bringing on the sorts of suffering that a wide range of sectaries had dreaded. Charles and Hyde had held off such persecution, and the king had even interviewed leading Quakers and liberated 700 from gaols; 'He seems to have found them entertaining.' But after the Venner rebellion, royal proclamations forbad sectaries from meeting and authorized the search of their houses. Within six weeks 'at least 4,688 Quakers were in prison, and the sufferings of the gathered churches were probably as great in proportion to their numbers'.[67] Simply surviving had become more difficult.

Yet thus far Milton's vision, projected in his tracts of 1660, had not materialized. The fanatics of the sweating tub had not yet brought low the Presbyterian royalists; indeed, through the months of the Convention Parliament, the agenda set by Hyde accorded well with the ambitions and expectations of men like Holles. But vindication of Milton's warnings followed soon.

In March and April 1661 elections were held for a new parliament, a body which would in time acquire and live up to the soubriquet 'the Cavalier Parliament'; 'nearly half of its number *were* "cavaliers", in the sense of men who had been fined for royalism, or their sons, or conspirators of the 1650s'. Peace and reconciliation were not objectives for men who had learned little and forgotten nothing. Contemporary estimates place the number still committed to the policies of the Convention Parliament at about a third of the members. Only about fifty were Presbyterians.[68] The coronation of Charles took place, amid great splendour, in late April. Royal honours were distributed to old friends and to the men who had brought the king home. Monck became the duke of Albemarle, Hyde the earl of Clarendon, Holles and Milton's probable protector, Annesley, became respectively Baron Holles and the earl of Anglesey. In what Hutton has termed the second Restoration settlement the Cavalier Parliament then turned its attention to suppressing not only separatists, a work already begun, but also the Presbyterians.

In an act of resonant symbolism, parliament ordered the public burning of the Solemn League and Covenant, with other documents from the mid-century decades. Milton had struggled to eliminate it from the debates surrounding the trial of the king.[69] Around it, the political philosophy of Presbyterianism had cohered, in that it made provision for the puritan measure of aligning the Church of England with Scottish Presbyterianism and at the same time asserted the responsibility of protecting the English monarchy. Plainly, in the eyes of a majority of the new parliament, the latter scarcely compensated for the former. In another measure, bishops were returned to the House of Lords.

What of the puritans in the Church of England? Under the Convention Parliament, the Act for Confirming Ministers, passed in September 1660, recognized the legitimacy of non-episcopal ordination, and no liturgical or ceremonial test was imposed on ministers, the vast majority of whom were confirmed in the livings they had held in the Interregnum church. But in June 1661 the Cavalier Parliament returned, in a very different spirit, to settling the church. In May 1662 assent was given to the Act for the Uniformity of Publique Prayers and Administrations. Its provisions included a requirement that every minister should use the Book of Common Prayer, and only the Book of Common Prayer, and should never pray or preach without it. All other forms of worship were outlawed. Every minister was required on 24 August, the last Sunday before St Barthomew's Day, to declare his consent to all aspects of the Book of Common Prayer, and any minister not episcopally ordained by St Bartholomew's Day was to be deprived of his living.

Most, of course, assented, though a substantial number felt unable to comply.[70] Among Milton's old Smectymnuan allies, Stephen Marshall and Thomas Young had died before the Restoration; Edmund Calamy was ejected in 1662 and went into retirement; Matthew Newcomen, also ejected, took up a living at Leiden; and William Spurstowe, also ejected, attempted to continue his ministry, for which he was incarcerated in Newgate for a fortnight in January 1663.[71] Milton at least had the dubious satisfaction of being right. Under every settlement of the 1650s Presbyterians were wholly free to hold livings in the Church of England, to worship using their chosen forms, and to organize into Presbyterian classes; their sole constraint was that they could not require others against conscience to conform to their doctrine and discipline. As Milton had predicted, those freedoms now were lost.

Henceforth, legislation caught all nonconformists alike. The subtle gradations of puritan radicalism, which stretched from Presbyterianism, through Independent congregationalism, to the gathered churches of the baptists and to the Quakers, were elided: each believer was either a communicant of the English church or a miscreant subject to a rapidly developing legal restraint. The Act to Prevent and Suppresse Seditious Conventicles became law in 1664. It prohibited 'all but the most private prayers' unless the Book of Common Prayer was used; a third offence could be punished by transportation for seven years. The Act for Restraining Non-Conformists from inhabiting in Corporations (1665) required ejected ministers to keep at least five miles away from the community where they had held their living.[72]

Such measures, while devastating to old adversaries and erstwhile friends, probably left Milton largely unscathed. In the 1640s we have conjectured that his own theological development may have been stimulated by some contact with radical congregations such as John Goodwin's or those of the general baptists.[73] But evidence is largely circumstantial. No church claimed to hold his allegiance in the 1650s, and it is difficult to see what attraction communal worship would have held for him once his generalized anti-clericalism matured in the late 1650s. Though in the tracts of 1659 he showed some sympathy with aspects of contemporary Quaker practice, his bibliocentric theology, committed to close exegesis of sacred text, precluded his convincement. The legislation was much tougher on those who wished to worship communally outside the Church of England than on those who simply did not wish to worship communally at all. Moreover, there is some evidence of at the least occasional conformity on Milton's part, for example at the time of his third marriage. His interment surely accorded with the rites of the Book of Common Prayer, though the choice may not have been his own.[74]

Besides occasional glancing blows from anti-puritan or anti-republican publications, Milton remained as inconspicuous as possible through 1662 as the Cavalier Parliament continued its work. One act of vindictiveness produced a probably unlooked for and perhaps unwelcome Miltonic publication in the late summer. Proceedings had begun in early summer against Vane and Lambert, and though the latter, through apparent contrition, escaped with a life sentence, Vane was condemned to be beheaded. The measure, carried out on 14 June, occasioned popular revulsion, and there appeared shortly afterwards *The Life and Death of Sir Henry Vane, Kt.* The work is anonymous, though subsequently attributed to George Sikes, and the colophon carries the name of neither printer nor bookseller. Its hagiographical account spends considerable effort on summarizing Vane's views, some of which, particularly on the relationship of church and state, of course accord closely with Milton's own. There are several testimonies to Vane's achievements, carefully anonymized. Milton's sonnet on Vane, printed for the first time, is attributed to 'a learned Gentleman, and sent to him [Vane], *July* 3. 1652'.[75] Other objectives, too important to Milton for them to be placed in jeopardy for such a transient gesture, urgently awaited him.

CHAPTER 16

Plague, Fire, and *Paradise Lost*

T wo people of considerable significance to Milton's life and well-being were drawn to his attention sometime around late 1661 or very early 1662 by Nathan Paget. He was a singularly well-connected man of radical and speculative inclination. His uncle, Thomas Paget, had been prominent in shaping the Amsterdam Presbyterian church, serving as minister from 1607 to 1639, and his father was also a puritan divine of moderate inclination. Nathan himself was a physician, who had studied at Leiden. His circle and Milton's overlapped at several points. Both corresponded with Hartlib. Like many of the Cromwellian establishment, Paget was related to Cromwell; he had married his cousin's daughter; perhaps through this connection, he had been granted by the Council of State of the Purged Parliament the office of physician to the Tower of London.[1] He lived in Coleman Street and worshipped at St Stephen, where John Goodwin, whose life and work inter- mittently intersect with Milton's, was minister. Isaac Penington, regicide MP and sometime mayor of London, worshipped there too. His son, Isaac Pening- ton the younger, 'had an intimate Acquaintance' with Paget, and Paget, on Edward Phillips's account, was 'an old Friend' of Milton's.[2] Through that chain of familiarity, Thomas Ellwood, sought out the company of Milton.

Ellwood became a considerable figure in the early history of the Quakers. He was a major controversialist, an office holder in several capacities, once Quaker central organization matured, and the editor of the posthumous edition of George Fox's *Journal*. In the early 1660s his principal significance was that, like the younger Penington and like William Penn the Younger, the son of an admiral under Cromwell and Charles II, he broke the stereotype of the Quaker as propertyless fanatic, for he, too, came from a relatively affluent background. His father was a JP and magistrate, and in his early brushes with the law, as he describes them in his autobiography, those sent to arrest him seemed embarrassed to do so, conscious of his father's local standing, and they were inclined to treat him rather better than his poorer colleagues.[3]

Ellwood claims to have been prompted towards seeking Milton's acquaintance by an awareness that, though he (like Milton) unreservedly subscribed to the view that a learned ministry was unnecessary, it opened up Quakers to the reproach that they despised humane learning. However, (unlike Milton) he had lost the scholarship he had demonstrated as a boy, and his friend the younger Penington suggested he would make better progress in his attempts to remedy the deficiency by seeking out Milton.[4] Ellwood's account offers a valuable supplement to Edward Phillips's explanation of how the blind Milton created around him a support network that allowed him to study and to write. He confirms the watchful retirement in which he lived 'a private and retired Life in *London*'. Milton 'kept always a Man to read to him, which usually was the Son of some Gentleman of his Acquaintance, whom, in Kindness, he took to improve his Learning'. A little later, Ellwood turned up in London, and Paget introduced him to Milton, who evidently knew of Penington the Younger and 'bore a good Respect' towards him. Ellwood undertook to read to him every afternoon, except Mondays, 'such Books in the *Latin Tongue*, as he pleased to hear me read'. Milton rapidly licked his aide into shape, amending his English pronunciation of Latin to the Italian manner, which was obviously more euphonious for Milton, while assuring him it would allow him to converse better with continental Europeans. Milton remained a natural teacher, noting when Ellwood struggled to understand what he was reading and 'open[ing] the most difficult passages to me'.[5] Ellwood will shortly recur in our narrative.

Paget also 'recommended' Milton's third wife to him. She was Elizabeth Minshull, the granddaughter of Paget's aunt. She came from a minor gentry background, and her family connections were for the most part around south Cheshire, with relatives associated with property in Crewe, Wistaston, and Nantwich; the last was her own place of origin, to which she would retire in widowhood.[6] Why she had come to London remains uncertain, though for a daughter, perhaps without a role in the family home, to be placed in the household of a more prosperous kinsman, or at least under his general supervision, is unremarkable. When she married Milton, her parish of residence was given as St Andrew, Holborn, some way from Paget's home, which invites the speculation that she was in some sort of upper domestic capacity, perhaps as a governess or housekeeper.[7]

Milton evidently needed a wife. His three daughters by Mary Powell were still living with him, though there is no evidence to indicate whether they had accompanied him into hiding or, if not, who looked after them. Much later, in 1674, Elizabeth Fisher, then employed by Milton as a maid, recalled that his daughter Mary, then about 14, said all the children urged 'his Maidservant' (presumably, a different one from Fisher) to chisel money when she went to market, and they were stealing and selling some of his books. She also remembered Mary remark that the news of his marriage was 'noe Newes' but 'if shee could heare of his death that was something'.[8] The account belongs in the context of a somewhat acrimonious probate process, though, given the disruptions the children had endured—the death of their mother and first step-mother, the arrival and death of two siblings, the disruptions caused by their father's flight and concealment—some anti-social conduct would not be surprising.

We have no way of assessing the possible motives for Milton's third marriage—affection, desire, practical necessity, perhaps any combination. The age gap between husband and wife was greater than the sixteen years that separated him from Mary Powell. He was 54; Elizabeth Minshull was 24. Yet his marriage has attracted far less comment, either in the early lives or from recent biographers. The former felt obliged to meet contemporary slurs and to account for Milton's views on divorce by rehearsing the circumstances of his relationship with Mary Powell; the latter have followed their lead, not least because there is plausible and relatively detailed information.

Milton's third marriage proved stable, though childless. Milton and Elizabeth declared their intention to marry on 11 February 1663, requesting a licence to marry in either St George in Southwark or St Mary Aldermary in London. Neither venue was the home parish of either participant; though canon law had tried to restrict the practice of marrying elsewhere, enforcement and regulation of this, as of other components of the process, were highly problematic, and would remain so till Lord Hardwicke's Marriage Act of 1753.[9] The ceremony, necessarily conducted according to the Book of Common Prayer, took place on 24 February at St Mary Aldermary.

The venue was perhaps doubly propitious. The church, destroyed in 1665, was singularly impressive. For centuries patronized by the London mercantile elite,[10] it had been rebuilt in the early sixteenth century, with a new tower completed in 1629. It was a city church on the stately scale, reflected in Wren's replacement, which stands on the same site. Secondly, its rector, Dr Robert Gell, was an old acquaintance and perhaps old friend of Milton's. He had been a Fellow of Christ's College during Milton's student days, when Milton may have collaborated with him.[11] After a long academic career, he had been appointed rector in 1641, shortly before his own marriage, and he had retained the living through the mid-century decades and was confirmed in it at the Restoration. He seems to have entertained some sympathy with aspects of Quakerism. He had shown an inclination towards scientific and theological speculation. He preached to 'the learned Society of Astrologers' on the Magi of the Nativity.[12] To the same group, he preached, too, a patient exposition of the biblical evidence for the nature and role of angels, a topic of considerable interest to Milton.[13] In 1660 he published a substantial pamphlet, *Eirenikon, or, A Treatise of peace between the two visible divided parties* (London, 1660), in which he sought to reconcile Presbyterians and episcopalians by assuaging the traditional concerns of the former, and invoking the spirit of the first Restoration settlement: 'my brethren, *Episcopal*, glory not in your *service*... Nor despise you... my brethren of Presbyterian perswasion, in regard of their *service of God*, as *superstitious*.'[14] He was also an immensely learned theologian, thoroughly accomplished in the languages of the Bible. In 1659 he published a huge treatise, *An Essay toward the Amendment of the Last English-Translation of the Bible* (London, 1659), in which he worked scrupulously over the text of the Pentateuch as rendered in the Authorized Version, in comparison with the Hebrew original. Gell was as ideologically acceptable to Milton as any conformist minister currently in holy orders, and his scholarly interests overlapped very considerably with his own. The choice of St Mary Aldermary for his wedding is unmysterious.

Shortly after the wedding Milton moved from Jewin Street to 'a House in *Artillery*-walk leading to *Bunhill Fields*... his last stage in this World, but... of many years continuance', as Edward Phillips remarks.[15] It was on the northern edge of the conurbation, outside the London Wall, a part of the city he had previously been drawn to, and the location would prove fortunate. Residence continued without interruption till the plague year of 1665. By the time he moved there, he was very probably close to completing one of the three great projects on which he had laboured through the 1650s.

Paradise Lost may well have been almost ready for the press no later than February 1665. The evidence comes from the whereabouts and the role of Edward Phillips himself. We considered earlier the mode of working Milton had developed. The manuscript for Book I, now in the Morgan Library and Museum, New York, shows the final stages of his involvement, but also evidences other work in bringing the poem to press. It is written throughout by a single, unidentified scribe of high competence. This must be a fair copy, quite probably made from the version Phillips produced from the text taken piecemeal by several hands directly from Milton's dictation.[16] From 1662 to 1664 Phillips worked as a research assistant to Elias Ashmole, translating and transcribing documents for his treatise on the Order of the Garter, which finally appeared in 1672 as *The Institution, Laws and Ceremonies of the Most Noble Order of the Garter*. Such work would not have precluded rendering assistance on the preparation of *Paradise Lost*. In late October 1663, Phillips found employment as a tutor to the son of the diarist John Evelyn at his considerable estate at Deptford. Evelyn, who would remain a patron of Phillips, noted in his diary for 24 October that he was 'not at all infected' with the republican principles of his notorious uncle.[17] However, in February 1665 he moved to Wilton House to act as tutor to Philip Herbert (the future seventh earl of Pembroke), a post he held till 1669. Deptford to Bunhill Fields was a tedious but fairly short journey; Wilton was much less accessible. The Morgan manuscript shows Phillips carefully checking

41. Anon., *Londons Loud Cryes to the Lord by Prayer* (London, 1665).

through what we know to have been the copytext for the first edition, introducing corrections, mostly to punctuation and orthography, in final preparation for the press. It is altogether likelier that this work would have been done before he set off for the depths of Wiltshire. The obvious question is why Milton hesitated to send the manuscript to the press, though, as we shall see, the better question is why Milton chose to do so at the time he did.

While Milton wrote on in his watchful and creative retirement, the restored regime experienced a series of probably gratifying reverses. Charles II and his courtiers proved to be as dissolute as Milton had predicted, fitting heirs to the stereotypical cavaliers of the early 1640s. In the autumn of 1662 the king's first-born bastard was created duke of Monmouth. By then, Charles had married an outlandish and papist bride, again as predicted, though he continued to busy himself among increasingly high-profile mistresses, of whom Barbara Palmer, countess of Castlemaine was the most prominent and by whom, since the Restoration, he had already acknowledged his first child, rumoured to have been christened at a Catholic ceremony.[18]

Domestic policy saw hues and cries after several real or imaginary uprisings, and an associated intensification of the persecution of dissenters, including, under the Conventicle Act of 1664, transportation to the tropical colonies for seven years. By the end of that year 'every surviving leader of the [Quaker] movement had been gaoled'.[19] Foreign policy took a belligerent turn as friction over colonial ambitions and trade triggered the second Anglo-Dutch war, which would soon prove catastrophic for England. Then in 1665 a tragedy of a different kind swept the country and devastated London: a major outbreak of bubonic plague.

Milton had experienced serious plague years before. This was the eighth visitation of the century, and 1625 saw a major epidemic on the scale of 1603 or 1665, and Milton may well have stayed at university through the long vacation, possibly shifting to join his parents in country retreat as eventually it spread to Cambridge.[20] In 1636, another conspicuously bad year, he was probably in Horton. This time, with his wife and his children, he sought refuge in Chalfont St Giles. The initiative was Milton's own, and he knew the locale he had selected was an enclave of dissent and held a substantial Quaker community. Indeed, Ellwood was his agent. He recalled:

Some little time before I went to *Alesbury* Prison, I was desired by my quondam Master *Milton* to take an House for him, in the Neighbourhood where I dwelt, that he might go out of the City, for the Safety of himself and his Family, the *Pestilence* then growing hot in *London*. I took a pretty box for him in *Giles-Chalfont*, a Mile from me; of which I gave him notice: and intended to have waited on him and seen him well settled in it; but was prevented by that Imprisonment.[21]

'That Imprisonment' was the month he spent in gaol after his arrest on 1 July with Isaac Penington and others, at a Quaker funeral in Amersham.[22] Milton evidently had sufficient help to move himself in Ellwood's absence. The property itself was pleasant enough, more of a small house than the diminutive tweeness implied by 'cottage' or 'pretty Box', and large enough for a married couple, three children, and a servant or two, without unbearable overcrowding.[23] Penington's family lived nearby at Bottrels in Chalfont, though for much of 1665 Penington himself was in Aylesbury gaol.[24]

The house Milton rented belonged to the estate centred on The Vache, Chalfont St Giles, the ancestral home of the regicide, George Fleetwood, who had signed Charles I's death warrant. He had remained politically active through the 1650s. His death sentence had been commuted, but he was kept in captivity, where, at some indeterminate date, he died. His Buckingham estates were given to James, duke of York. Technically, we believe, Milton was the tenant of the future James II.[25] However, Fleetwood's mother, Anne, still lived at The Vache, and the family successfully petitioned to retain the estates during her lifetime. (She expired in 1673, at which point the regicide's widow, now homeless, moved to join a Quaker family at Jordans, Chalfont St Giles.[26]) Milton's withdrawal from London no doubt accorded with the practice of most of his friends and relations. As Richard Baxter observed, 'The richer sort removing out of the City, the greatest Blow fell on the Poor.'[27] During that summer and autumn, across the metropolis (and including the suburbs) nearly 100,000 people died, nearly six times the normal death rate; within the city walls of London, over 15,000 died, almost two-thirds of them attributed to plague.[28] We know of no friend or relative of Milton's who died in the pestilence. Yet there remained an element of risk even for the cautious. Anne Fleetwood also gave shelter in Chalfont St Giles to some Presbyterian clergymen, and Baxter noted a single plague death within their house.[29]

By the time Ellwood could visit Milton, presumably in August, *Paradise Lost* was already in a fit state for limited manuscript circulation, and probably existed in several copies. Ellwood recalled, 'After some common discourses had passed between us, he called for a Manuscript of his, which being brought he delivered to me, bidding me take it home with me, and read it at my Leisure, and when I had so done, return it to him, with my Judgment thereupon.'[30] It would have been absurd for Milton to commit a unique copy of a poem that had been so long in the making to a radical activist who could have been arrested at any time, and we thus conclude other copies were extant and perhaps also in limited circulation. Indeed, Andrew Marvell read the poem in manuscript, at some undeterminable date between his return from an embassy to Russia in early March 1665 and the composition of his brilliant satire, *The Last Instructions to a Painter*, in the late summer of 1667, for he echoes Milton's epic in his own verse.[31]

42. Milton's Cottage, Chalfont St Giles.

Ellwood was already a spirited controversialist and plainly he strove to acquire a richer understanding of the broad literary tradition and the writing of classical world; that was what moved him to study with Milton in the first place. In later life, he would develop a secondary interest in writing poetry. His most ambitious project, *Davideis. The Life of David King of Israel: A Sacred Poem in Five Books*, first published in 1712, went into five editions. It appears to owe little to Milton, presenting a plain narrative in competent, if not especially artful, couplets, though the invocation to book one has a certain Miltonic resonance.[32] Milton could well have been interested in the responses of one so eminently a member of his intended readership, since he was godly, responsive to creative writing, and fairly well educated.

Nor need we assume he dismissed Ellwood's comments: 'He asked me how I liked it, and what I thought of it; which I modestly but freely told him: and after some further Discourse about it, I pleasantly said to him, Thou hast said much here of *Paradise Lost*; but what hast thou to say of *Paradise Found?* He made me no Answer, but sate some time in a Muse: then brake off that Discourse, and fell upon another Subject.' On some later occasion, once Milton had returned to London, Ellwood called on him as he usually did when in the city, and Milton showed him the manuscript of *Paradise Regained*: 'in a pleasant Tone [he] said to me, *This is owing to you: for you put it into my Head, by the Question you put to me at* Chalfont; *which before I had not thought of.*'[33]

Milton 'sate some time in a Muse'. Of course, facetious interpretations are available. He could have been nonplussed by Ellwood's stupidity, or uncertain how to respond without hurting his feelings. The later conversation about *Paradise Regained* could have been a private joke at the expense of a young ingénu. Ellwood, however, was no intellectual lightweight and certainly no fool. He had spent hours in Milton's company on numerous occasions and continued to do so into the 1670s and probably for the rest of Milton's life. The anecdotes come, gratuitously, in a long digression amid what is a detailed history of early Quaker experiences.

Taken at face value, as we believe they should be, the events he describes mark a turning point in Milton's ideological development and psychological healing, a point of transition from the steely but passive endurance commemorated in *Paradise Lost* to the abrasive confidence of the Son in *Paradise Regained*. Milton spent the summer of 1665 in a rural idyll with his new, young wife. He was among religious radicals, who knew and respected his contribution to English puritanism and to tolerationism, and was visited by brave, buoyant young Quakers, at least one of whom hero-worshipped him. Instead of the desperate and discredited men with whom he worked in the 1650s, now hanging on to life and liberty as best they could, these embodied a new generation of dissent. He had, moreover, completed one of the three great projects that had preoccupied him for many years; he had written an epic to court comparison with those of Homer and Virgil. Possibly, his children, removed from the world of petty crime into which they had drifted, had been brought to heel by the new Mrs Milton.

Yet the next years proved financially damaging, though relieved by the satisfaction of governmental incompetence, the eclipse of enemies, and the satirical observations of Marvell and others. It is reasonable to assume that he extended his stay in Buckinghamshire well past the downturn in plague deaths. To do otherwise would have been foolhardy.

The hot, dry summer of 1666 passed without a return of the epidemic. On 2 September, however, a fire broke out in a bakery in Pudding Lane, in the south-east corner of the City. Since Milton lived north of the City wall he and his family were in no personal danger. Yet as the fire spread, driven by a strong easterly wind, it destroyed many of the London sites associated with him. By the fourth day, it had burnt the Guildhall and St Mary Aldermary, where he had married his second and third wives; St Paul's and the associated school, where he had been educated, perished; so did Jewin Street, his previous home. Most significantly, all the property in Bread Street was destroyed. Milton, fortunately, had surrendered in July 1656 the leasehold on the Red Rose, a house in Bread Street, which he had inherited from his father and which he had expensively extended in 1649.[34] However, he retained the leasehold on the Spread Eagle, his probable birthplace, in the same street. Skinner and Wood note that this 'was all the Real Estate hee had'.[35] Leaseholds, it seems, perished with the property, though the owners of the freehold, in Milton's case Eton College, retained their rights to the land. Milton's disaster was repeated thousands of times across a city in which leasehold properties were habitually acquired to be rented out as a relatively safe way of securing a regular return from capital. The loss of rental income devastated numerous households.[36] Of course, Milton did not qualify for the limited charitable relief which was disbursed to the indigent.

He was, however, lucky in another respect. About 13,000 houses were destroyed, leaving between 65,000 and 80,000 people homeless.[37] Many sought accommodation with relatives in the metropolis. After the fall of Reading and Oxford, Milton's household had received a considerable influx of people and responsibilities. This time, probably, he evaded the problem. John Phillips was probably 'the John Phillips, schoolmaster, who was living in Aldersgate Street [most of which was beyond the fire[38]] in 1666', while Edward retained his post at Wilton House.[39] Brother Christopher had chambers in the Inner Temple, which was severely damaged, but retained a practice and a family home in Ipswich.[40] Most of Coleman Street perished, though if Nathan Paget lived at the north end, his house would have escaped. That he was still living in Coleman Street when he died in 1679 lends some support.[41] So, for Milton, the impact of the fire came in financial losses rather than household disruption.

The catastrophe did bring one significant benefit for dissenters: since England at the time was at war with the Dutch and the French, it stimulated waves of xenophobia, against all foreigners, and anti-Catholic sentiment. The latter fed off the ancient Protestant argument that Catholics constituted a threat to security because they subordinated loyalty towards the monarch to loyalty towards the pope. Even as the fire burnt, Londoners were searching out and attacking supposed incendiaries. There were several incidents of very rough justice; 'a woman carrying chicks in her apron was taken for a bearer of fire-balls by a hysterical mob which clubbed her and cut off her breasts'.[42] After the event, a French watchmaker, Robert Hubert, was arrested at Romford apparently trying to flee the country. He confessed to arson,

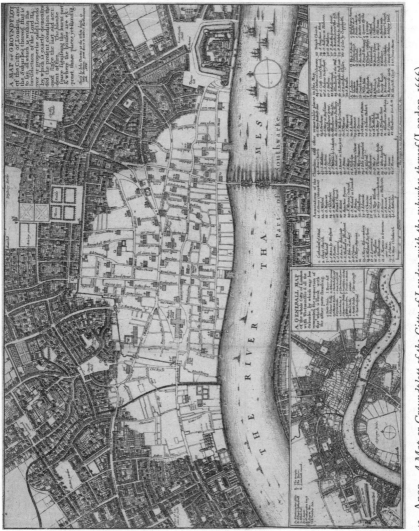

43. Anon., *A Map or Groundplott of the Citty of London with the suburbes thereof* (London, 1666).

claiming to have been agent of France, and was hanged late in October.[43] Though the Privy Council remained convinced that the fire originated by accident and was spread through an unfortunate coincidence of meteorological conditions, the conspiracy theories, usually focused on Catholics or foreigners, had wide and long-lived currency. Indeed, in 1681 a sentence was added to the one of the three Latin inscriptions on the Monument, which stands near the site of the source of the fire, asserting that it was 'begun and carried on by the treachery and malice of the Popish faction'.[44] Across the community there emerged a consensus that Protestants shared sufficient common ground to collaborate in the face of a perceived Catholic threat.

Thus the fire gave added vigour to a more tolerant approach to dissent that was discernible over 1665–7. Prosecutions under the Conventicle Act fell sharply, and from early 1666 even Quakers were meeting in relative safety in London and elsewhere. The reasons are complex and uncertain. An understandable wish to avenge the indignities of the mid-century decades no doubt animated much of the cavalier backlash in the early 1660s. Moreover, the fears of uprisings and new rebellion which had stoked that anger substantially had faded. Other imperatives preoccupied magistrates, among them managing the plague, raising war-taxation, and ensuring the orderly and effective operation of impressment. The king himself seems to have relaxed his earlier antipathy to dissent, while among senior churchmen a wider comprehension once more found support.[45] In the broader context, England was evolving into a society more tolerant of Protestant heterodoxy, and more likely to receive tolerantly an epic by Milton.

In the spring of 1667 Milton set about publishing *Paradise Lost*. He did so at a time of singular confusion within the book trade, which had been clustered around St Paul's Cathedral. Booksellers and printers had attempted to save their stock of paper and printed material by caching it in St Faith's, a church under the cathedral, in Stationers' Hall, and in Christ Church, Greyfriars, but all were destroyed. Estimates for the total value ranged from £150,000 to £200,000. Perhaps a few of Milton's publications were among the back-lists that were lost, though Humphrey Moseley had died in 1661 and his wife had ceased to trade in 1664. The immediate impact of the disaster was complex. It made the press harder to control, since booksellers and printers could set up in improvised premises. It made the demand for new titles the keener and increased the prices of the second-hand trade.[46]

On 27 April Milton entered into a contract with a printer unaffected by the fire, Samuel Simmons of Aldersgate Street. Proximity—Milton lived a little to the north of Simmons, whose parish church was St Botolph's Without the

Wall—and the happy chance of the printer's survival may have been influential factors in bringing them together, though Milton had probably known him since his childhood. His father, Matthew Simmons, was associated with numerous Independent and republican publications, and, much favoured by the Purged Parliament, he had printed all Milton's tracts of 1649 (and some of the divorce tracts). He perhaps was the printer of *Areopagitica, Of Education, Tetrachordon,* and *Colasterion.* When Matthew died in 1654, his widow, Mary, continued the business, and was joined by their son, Samuel, whose name appears on imprints from 1662 onwards.[47] He was, however, young in the trade, and *Paradise Lost* was the first title he entered under his own name in the Stationers' Register. Simmons had not lost paper stock in the fire and he still had his presses, and while the booksellers he did business with were badly hit, the knock-on effect on his cash-flow was probably slighter than in the case of printers who had been working inside the zone of devastation.

The contract he entered into with Milton on 27 April 1667 reflects the changes occurring in the relationship between the book trade and authors in the 1660s, of which John Dryden's complex, honourable and fairly lucrative dealings with Henry Herringman provide the best example. Like Dryden's work, Milton's great poem had scarcely circulated in manuscript; it was written to be printed, from authorized copy, and supplied in return for some remuneration. The contract does not differ very significantly in its stipulations from the agreements still current between authors and publishers. In return for £5, 'now paid', Milton assigned to Simmons, his executors and assignees, the copy of his poem, 'now lately Licensed to be printed', with all benefit accruing from it, with the right to all future editions. When Simmons had sold thirteen hundred copies, he was to pay Milton a further £5, with another £5 for each of a second and third impression, neither of which was to exceed fifteen hundred copies. Simmons gave an undertaking to provide an account of the copies sold on Milton's request or pay a forfeit of £5. Milton stood at most to make £20 from the deal, which has occasioned over the centuries intermittent moralizing complaint.

Was he really hard up for £10 or £20? Certainly not, but if that was what the market offered, in what we may perceive as the age of Dryden, even a gentleman scholar could stoop with equanimity to collect it. In a couple of decades, the most prestigious writers, pre-eminently Dryden, would make very considerable sums from new patterns of publication, not least by subscription. But in the 1660s, the transition was at an early stage. Alastair Fowler may well be right in his judgement that the contract offered 'then a reasonable remuneration'.[48]

Simmons proceeded energetically in marketing the printed books, though his efforts reflect the current disruptions to the book trade. Several issues were produced, each with its own title page, showing a gradual accretion in front matter. He placed the copies with six booksellers, whose location is signficant.

44. John Milton, *Paradise Lost. A Poem Written in Ten Books* (London, 1667).

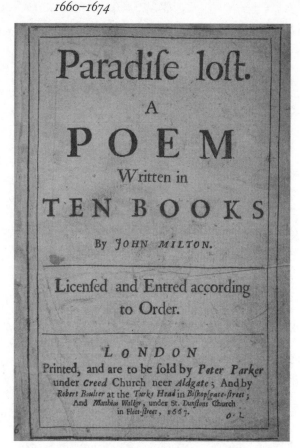

Paradiſe loſt.
A
POEM
Written in
TEN BOOKS
By *JOHN MILTON.*

Licenſed and Entred according
to Order.

L O N D O N
Printed, and are to be ſold by *Peter Parker*
under *Creed* Church neer *Aldgate* ; And by
Robert Boulter at the *Turks Head* in *Biſhopſgate-ſtreet* ;
And *Matthias Walker*, under St. *Dunſtons* Church
in *Fleet-ſtreet*, 1667. *o·l*

Like himself, all operated outside the zone devastated by the fire: Peter Parker, near Aldgate; Robert Boulter, in Bishopsgate Street; Matthias Walker in Fleet Street; Thomas Helder in Little Britain; Samuel Thomson, in Duck Lane; and Henry Mortlack, in Westminster Hall. Among these, Parker, Boulter, Walker, Thomson, and perhaps Mortlack had lost in the Great Fire their shops around St Paul's and the streets to the east of there.[49] Simmons was operating with energy and ingenuity in changed and disrupted trading circumstances to get Milton's poem to retailers, some of whom were also improvising. Possibly the complexities of the distribution reflect cash-flow difficulties among those involved, each taking only a small parcel of the total imprint.

The copy Milton supplied to Simmons came in all probability bound into fascicules, one for each of the ten books. The evidence for this comes, circumstantially, from the way we know Milton worked on the manuscript of *De Doctrina Christiana.*[50] More materially, the Morgan manuscript of Book 1 is itself bound within an original outer cover of plain, stout paper.

That manuscript also contains the imprimatur, permitting Simmons to register his copyright and print the book. It reads:

> Imprimatur
> Tho. Tomkyns RRmo. in
> Christo patri ac Domino
> D[omi]no Gilberto divina Providentia
> Archiepiscop Cantuarensi a
> Sacris domesticis.
>   Richard Royston
>   Int[ratu]r p[er] Geo: Tokefeilde Cl[ericum]

(Let it be printed. Thomas Tomkyns, one of the religious servants of the most reverent father and lord in Christ, Lord Gilbert, by divine providence archbishop of Canterbury. Richard Royston. Entered by George Tokefield, clerk.[51])

Richard Royston was a veteran bookseller, by this time patronized by the king as his 'stationer' and currently a warden of the Stationers' Company. His involvement perhaps suggests a high-level interest in ensuring the unquestionable legality of the transaction. Thomas Tomkins was Robert Gell's successor as rector of St Mary Aldermary, where Milton had married, and a chaplain to Gilbert Sheldon, archbishop of Canterbury. The imprimatur allowed Simmons to register his copyright on 20 August 1667. The manuscript was preserved in the possession of the Tonson family, and had been acquired when Jacob Tonson the elder bought the rights to *Paradise Lost*, not from Simmons, but from Brabazon Aylmer, to whom they had been sold on. Its retention, through changes of ownership, probably reflects a concern to keep the unequivocal evidence that the manuscript of the notorious John Milton had indeed been cleared for publication.

Censorship in the mid-1660s was quite complex. The Licensing Act of 1662 substantially reintroduced the mechanisms in place before the Long Parliament. For books other than those on law, politics, and affairs of state, the appointees of the archbishop of Canterbury or of the bishop of London were charged with responsibility to read them and to license them if they deemed that appropriate. Since 1663, as an added measure of control, the energetic Roger L'Estrange had been 'Surveyor of the Press', charged with hunting out clandestine and treasonous printing; his malign presence pervaded the print culture of that decade and the next, and we have noted already his particular antipathy to the writings of Milton.[52] Tomkins, who was himself a polemicist against nonconformists, had something of a reputation for dealing in partisan fashion with the manuscripts of his opponents.[53]

Yet he treated Milton's poem tolerantly. Toland is the sole source for the information that 'we had like to be eternally depriv'd of this Treasure by the Ignorance or Malice of the Licenser; who, among other frivolous Exceptions, would need suppress the whole Poem for imaginary Treason in the following line'.[54] He then quotes:

> as when the sun new ris'n
> Looks through the horizontal misty air
> Shorn of his beams, or from behind the moon
> In dim eclipse disastrous twilight sheds
> On half the nations, and with fear of change
> Perplexes monarchs.[55]

Given the disasters that had overwhelmed the kingdom in the two previous years, a certain jitteriness on Tomkins's part seems wholly reasonable. But he did indeed allow that passage through, nor does the manuscript carry any evidence whatsoever of censorship, at least as far as Book 1 is concerned.

Why was Milton treated so lightly? Current interpretative orthodoxy asserts that the epic is thoroughly replete with oppositional, anti-clerical and, indeed, republican values and sentiment, a cairn of critical endeavour to which we shortly add our own pebble. It is sometimes suggested that Tomkins gave the manuscript a light-touch scrutiny because he was overwhelmed with the scale of his task. Yet he was scrupulous enough with the manuscripts of Richard Baxter, among others; Milton was notorious; and L'Estrange, an extremely dangerous man one would not wish to cross, had a known interest in him.

There are, we think, two principal factors, besides a general softening of attitudes, already noted, towards nonconfirmity. The industrial scale of censorship and repression in some totalitarian states in the last century has distorted understanding of seventeenth-century English practice. Indeed, men found printing seditious literature in the 1660s were severely punished, even executed. Indeed, political activists mistrusted by the state were imprisoned or killed. But there were no gulags for creative writers, and poetry of a non-satirical kind was treated gently, even when its authors were anti-government. Richard Lovelace, an active and fairly effective cavalier, had problems getting out his first collection, *Lucasta* (London, 1648), but it was eventually published. Creative writing, to be read by a small cultural elite, was a low priority for government authorities much more concerned with managing news and suppressing open sedition. Secondly, Thomas Tomkins, though almost thirty years his junior, may well have been an old acquaintance of Milton. He was born in and as a child had lived in Aldersgate Street, where Milton had his home in the early 1640s. Perhaps more significantly, Thomas's father, John, and his uncles, Giles and Thomas, were musicians and composers who certainly moved in the same circles as Milton's own father, and in the musical ensembles of the Caroline court, where Milton's own friend and collaborator, Henry Lawes, was a major luminary.[56] Thomas

Tomkins no doubt loathed Milton's politics, but he may well have respected his art, and may even have liked him personally.

⚜

Twenty-five years separates the publication of *Paradise Lost* from Milton's statement in the digression to *The Reason of Church-Government* that his 'mind in the spacious circuits of her musing' was considering the composition of either a neoclassical epic on a patriotic theme or perhaps a play modelled on the practice of Sophocles and Euripides.[57] His poem became, through the advocacy and critical interpretation of Joseph Addison, the iconic English Protestant poem, 'a Work which does an Honour to the *English* Nation'.[58] One would struggle to find anything patriotic in Milton's epic, except insofar as it is written in English and thus demonstrates that the most demanding genre fell within the scope of vernacular expression. It is, however, unmistakably Protestant. Here, at least, the child proved father to the man. The wordplay and bantering humour of his poems on the Gunpowder Plot recur in the gratuitous quips which pepper his depiction of the entry of Sin and Death into the fallen world:

> The aggregated soil
> Death with his mace petrific, cold and dry,
> As with a trident smote....
>
> Now had they brought the work by wondrous art
> Pontifical, a ridge of pendent rock
> Over the vexed abyss.[59]

In a surprising and strange satirical digression, which divides Milton's first depiction of heaven from Satan's entry into Paradise, Milton depicts the opaceous outer shell of the universe as a limbo prepared for monsters and for fools who have pursued 'all things transitory and vain', among whom devout Catholics figure largely:

> Embryos and idiots, eremites and friars
> White, black and gray, with all their trumpery.
> Here pilgrims roam, that strayed so far to seek
> In Golgotha him dead, who lives in heaven;
> And they who to be sure of Paradise
> Dying put on the weeds of Dominic,
> Or in Franciscan think to pass disguised ...

In a brief but vivid fantasy, he imagines their confusion, swept 'by a violent cross wind' just as they thought they approached heaven:

> then might ye see
> Cowls, hoods and habits with their wearers tossed

(337)

And fluttered into rags, then relics, beads,
Indulgences, dispenses, pardons, bulls,
The sport of winds: all these upwhirled aloft
Fly o'er the backside of the world far off
Into a limbo large and broad, since called
The Paradise of Fools.[60]

The deeper game, and one which was substantially won by the time of publication, is to reconfigure the polarities of contemporary Christian belief, replacing the Cavalier Parliament's opposition of dissent and conformity with the opposition of Catholicism and a widely defined Protestantism.

Soteriologically, the poem is again inclusively Protestant. The most elaborate and explicit exposition of doctrine comes in Book 3 as the Father and the Son discuss how humankind will be saved, at least in part. He carefully incorporates predestination, for a few, in language that resonates with English Calvinist discourse: 'Some I have chosen of peculiar grace | Elect above the rest.'[61] But the larger perspective is explicitly Arminian, as the Father explains his intention to renew at least partially the power of faith and reason on fallen people, so they may choose to accept and work synergistically with his grace, which is extended to all. Those are saved who 'to the end persisting, safe arrive'.[62] Arminian soteriology remained a minority position among dissenters, although in the Restoration Church of England, following its status among leading Caroline divines, it was broadly endorsed. Milton could feel confident that the expression of this doctrine, one in which he had believed for decades, could be utterly explicit without provoking the charge of heresy.

Of course, Milton was a heterodox thinker in a number of doctrinal areas. However, unless one has *De Doctrina Christiana* open at one's elbow, his points of disagreement with the mainstream would often pass unremarked. Nor should we necessarily attribute to *Paradise Lost* views Milton had held when work on his systematic theology was, we surmise, necessarily interrupted. His representation of the Son in conversation with the Father, in the opening half of Book 3, carefully establishes that both share the characteristic of omniscience, though the Father manifests divine justice, while the Son expresses divine love towards humankind. Less orthodox, however, is the status of the Son as not eternal; he is, in Milton's studied distinction, perpetual rather than eternal, in that he has a beginning but no end.

Milton's view of prelapsarian sexuality shows, more emphatically, subscription to another minority position. Several views had currency in the cauldron of Protestant opinion.[63] Prelapsarian sexuality was sometimes represented as technically different from its fallen manifestation, more a function of reason, rather than passion, with male arousal as a voluntary, dispassionate choice, rather than an involuntary and passionate response. Or else, sexuality was attributed wholly to the fallen condition, sometimes seen as a sort of consolation for having to work for a living. Milton asserts both that penetrative sex occurred before the fall and that it was in kind and in moral status continuous with postlapsarian sex among the godly. As he and his readers avert their gaze from the bower of Adam and Eve, where we leave them probably engaged in 'the rites | Mysterious of connubial love', he launches a lofty apostrophe ('Hail wedded love'), which unequivocally identifies human sexuality as the basis of personal, familial, and societal stability and happiness, and equates its later manifestation with its paradisal form.[64] The young Milton may have looked with bewildered disdain on the fornications of his student contemporaries, and celebrated, in his masque, the victory of unconquerable chastity, but the thrice-married older man, newly wed to his much younger bride, displays an evident enthusiasm.

Other aspects of how he represents the relationship of Adam and Eve carry a wider, rather than simply personal, implication. The view that the late seventeenth century saw a shift in interpersonal relations towards companionate marriage has been subject to challenge; David Cressy observes that 'The ideal of a companionate marriage based on "mutual society, help and comfort" was enshrined in the prayer book from its inception'. But the ideal had for long been promoted with particular vigour by puritans, and it was especially strong among dissenters, where a stout and reciprocal affection between partners seemed to support them in an age of persecution.[65] Adam and Eve initiate their own spiritual regeneration process in dialogue, albeit of a fraught and initially recriminatory nature. They leave Paradise hand in hand, as they were when first we encounter them.[66] As N. H. Keeble observes, this offers 'an image of equal companionship, of a relationship restored and enduring . . . The greatest poem of the age shares with the least nonconformist tract a belief in the sanctity of human affection.'[67] Adam speaks transhistorically when, capping an argument with Raphael with a point the angel does not challenge, he praises 'Harmony to behold in wedded pair | More grateful than harmonious sound to the ear'.[68]

Though the affection of Adam and Eve chimes with the coping strategies of Restoration dissenters, the evident asymmetry between the couple seems a plain rehearsal of the familiar patriarchalism of the period. Even their physical appearance allows Satan to draw, presumably correctly from Milton's perspective, a conclusion about their disparity:

> For contemplation he and valour formed,
> For softness she and sweet attractive grace,
> He for God only, she for God in him:
> His fair large front and eye sublime declared
> Absolute rule.[69]

Milton observes a Pauline orthodoxy.[70] Yet Adam, after as before the fall, engages both affectionately and intellectually with Eve. Moreover, Milton, closely echoing Genesis 3: 16 ('he shall rule over thee'), notes that a sterner patriarchy results from the fall, and, like pain in childbirth, constitutes the punishment of Eve and her daughters, distinct from the ideal Edenic relationship he has depicted.[71]

On top of a Miltonic variation on Protestant doctrine, Milton lays a seam of insistent, if low-key and rather defeatist, radical ideology. Tomkins had been concerned, not with its theology, but with the politics of the poem, and with reason. Milton had warned in *The Readie and Easie Way* that cavaliers in a position of domination would outrage the godly. By mid-decade, his predictions had not only come to pass, such debauchery and outrage were widely recognized as wholly characteristic of the ruling elite. As cavaliers gave way to rakehells, 'Neither women nor inferiors were safe when they took to the streets'. 'Bestial, predatory and violent' is Keeble's verdict on a court that centred on a king who had already acquired a well-founded reputation for debauchery.[72] When Milton from time to time in *Paradise Lost* depicts degenerate societies, they bear an unmistakable likeness to the widely current view of the society the Restoration had ushered in. Thus, the children of Cain manifest the kinds of obsession with bold, shameless women that Charles and his intimates shared, women bred 'to sing, to dance, | To dress, and troll the tongue, and roll the eye'.[73] By Noah's time,

> All was now turned to jollity and game,
> To luxury and riot, feast and dance,
> Marrying or prostituting, as befell,
> Rape or adultery, where passing fair
> Allured them; thence from cups to civil broils.[74]

Milton's allusion to his own condition, threatened by 'the barbarous dissonance | Of Bacchus and his revellers',[75] ties the depravities of antediluvian times to the present age.

Monarchs abound throughout the poem. Regal qualities are displayed by morally sound figures from the Son through good angels to Adam and Eve. Even the moon, 'Rising in clouded majesty', throws 'o'er the dark her silver mantle'.[76] Good kings are genuinely distinguished by their superiority over the ordinary, and, for the most part, their conduct is not marked by state rituals and pomp. When unfallen Adam meets Raphael, he

> walks forth, without more train
> Accompanied than with his own complete
> Perfections, in himself was all his state,
> More solemn than the tedious pomp that waits
> On princes, when their rich retinue long
> Of horses led, and grooms besmeared with gold
> Dazzles the crowd, and sets them all agape.[77]

The minds of contemporary readers would inevitably have turned to recollect the sumptuous pre-coronation entry and procession of Charles II. Pepys noted, 'So glorious was the show with gold and silver that we were not able to look at it—our eyes at last being so much overcome with it.' The horse of Lord Warton 'exceeded all for diamonds'; some estimated the cost of those trappings at £8,000.[78] Satan's supporters show him the wrong sorts of reverence as 'Towards him they | Bend with awful reverence prone; and as a god | Extol him equal to the highest in heaven'.[79] A few early readers, those who had managed to secure a copy of *The Readie and Easie Way*, could have recalled the prediction there that the restored monarch would require to be worshipped 'like a Demigod'.[80] Satan shows all the worst traits of the worst kings, 'High on a throne of royal state ... by merit raised | To that bad eminence'.[81]

Milton's review of antediluvian history permits an oblique restatement of the central principle of his case against the English monarchy: namely, that domination over his equals (or superiors) by a ruler who is not himself inherently superior constitutes tyranny. The case of Nimrod, one of the most developed sections of what Michael has to tell Adam and much elaborated from the account in Genesis 10, carries the argument:

> [Nimrod] Above his brethren, to himself assuming
> Authority usurped, from God not given:
> He gave us only over beast, fish, fowl
> Dominion absolute; that right we hold
> By his donation; but man over men
> He made not lord; such title to himself
> Reserving, human left from human free.[82]

Michael confirms and extends these observations from Adam:

> Justly thou abhorr'st
> That son, who on the quiet state of men
> Such trouble brought, affecting to subdue
> Rational liberty; yet know withal,
> Since thy original lapse, true liberty
> Is lost, which always with right reason dwells
> Twinned, and from her hath no dividual being:
> Reason in man obscured, or not obeyed,
> Immediately inordinate desires
> And upstart passions catch the government
> From reason, and to servitude reduce
> Man till then free.[83]

Nimrod's reign originates in an act of usurping the sovereignty held collectively by his brethren, and it marks a falling off from rational liberty to irrational servitude. Nimrod's only claim to eminence is his status as a hunter—and his will to power, a 'proud ambitious heart' and a resolve to overthrow 'fair equality, fraternal state'.[84] Just as Charles I and his son were no Tutbury stallions, so Nimrod has no natural superiority to justify his claims to monarchy.[85]

Anticlericalism as well as republicanism resurfaces subtly within the epic. Among the attributes of Belial is his capacity to seduce the clergy: 'who more oft than he | In temples and at altars, when the priest | Turns atheist'.[86] The present tense implies a transhistorical and continuing influence. Once more, the fullest attack comes in the last part of the poem. Michael describes the sharp and continuing decline as the primitive religion of the apostolic age gives way to the ministry of professional clergy. Then,

> Wolves shall succeed for teachers, grievous wolves,
> Who all the sacred mysteries of heaven
> To their own vile advantage shall turn
> Of lucre and ambition, and the truth
> With superstitions and traditions taint,
> Left only in those written records pure,
> Though not but by the Spirit understood.
> Then shall they seek to avail themselves of names,
> Places and titles, and with these to join
> Secular power, though feigning still to act
> By spiritual, to themselves appropriating
> The Spirit of God, promised alike and giv'n
> To all believers; and from that pretence,
> Spiritual laws by carnal power shall force
> On every conscience.[87]

The passage resonates with the language of the 1640s and 1650s. Princely bishops can be recognized among those seeking titles, but the clergy in general, even most Independents, had sought to invoke the civil magistrate to control religious observance and belief of radical sectaries. The post-apostolic wolves still prowl the chancels of the late-Stuart church.

The larger political resonances, however, invoke the experience of defeat much more than the resilient commitment to the values of the Good Old Cause. Milton represents himself as isolated and threatened, 'fallen on evil days, | On evil days though fallen, and evil tongues; | In darkness, and with dangers compassed round, | And solitude'.[88] An early life recalls that he had in the Restoration a recurrent anxiety that he would be assassinated.[89] It was scarcely fanciful. In the republican years, two ambassadors, Isaac Dorislaus and Anthony Ascham, were killed while serving abroad. More recently, the regicide and prominent office-holder in the 1650s, John Lisle, who had fled abroad at the Restoration, had been shot dead by a royalist assassin in 1664.[90] Milton probably knew them all personally.

The history Michael foreshadows for Adam discloses a recurrent pattern of social degeneration resisted by a tiny godly remnant. Enoch 'old and young | Exploded, and had seized with violent hands, | Had not a cloud descending snatched him thence'.[91] Noah and his family are 'The only righteous in a world perverse'.[92] Thus, 'shall the world go on, | To good malignant, to bad men benign'.[93] Remarkably, Milton has Adam raise the suggestion that the followers of the Son in this fallen world would be treated worse than he was; Michael confirms his surmise: 'Be sure they will'.[94]

The role of the godly is one of small gestures that keep alive their faith and principles, 'by small | Accomplishing great things, by things deemed weak | Subverting worldly strong, and worldy wise | By simply meek'. Not to them will it fall to overthrow the mighty, for theirs is a life of 'suffering for truth's sake', in which 'fortitude' is the the 'highest victory'.[95] Michael does offer a millenarian vision of sorts, when the day will come 'of respiration to the just, | And vengeance to the wicked'.[96] Yet it is a millennium almost infinitely postponed, wholly lacking the urgency and imminence of the violent fantasy with which, in 1641, Milton concluded *Of Reformation.*[97]

We have argued that Milton probably began work on *Paradise Lost* in the 1640s, and wrote much of it in the 1650s, basing our case on the evidence of the early lives and the life records. How then could he have produced a poem so replete with the watchful and anxious pessimism of the early 1660s? We may merely speculate. However, the more melancholy sections are quite narrowly confined, to the preamble to Book 7[98] and to Michael's mission in the concluding section. Without those, the epic would much more straight-forwardly celebrate the generosity and sacrifice of the Son and the regenerate strength of Adam and Eve, leaving them to walk from Paradise with a less gloomy fate for the progeny hanging over them.

Milton's experience as polemicist and public servant contributes a different kind of depth to the poem, for heaven and hell, and to a lesser extent earth, are profoundly political environments. In the 1640s he had mastered the craft of meeting and destroying the polemic of others. Disputations and debates abound throughout the poem, in heaven, earth and hell, and with facility he finds the arguments for the occasion. Satan's harangue of his troops owes something to republican rhetoric, while Abdiel's reply draws on the concept of the godly remnant much in the manner of Milton's defence of the Good Old Cause.[99] It is a critical commonplace that Eve's case for leaving Adam despite the warning of Raphael shares common ground with elements of *Areopagitica.*[100]

In the 1650s Milton moved among politicians, heard them at work, and he came to understand how the control of information lies at the centre of power. He had taken an oath of secrecy, and in the twilight of the republic, as he attempted to improvise a resilient form of government, the preservation of secrecy in the state remained an important imperative. His superior, Thurloe, was head of intelligence. He ran the Post Office and under his administration the collection of intercepts from foreign and royalist correspondence was perfected.[101] Milton was evidently privy to at least some of these activities. Indeed, somewhat gratuitously, Edward Phillips concludes his own life of Milton with two anecdotes demonstrating the accomplishment of the state's intelligence service in the 1650s, explicitly noting that 'they hapned during [Milton's] publick employ, and consequently fell most especially under his cognisance'.[102] Milton was probably Phillips's only source.

Thurloe would have envied the godhead's powers of surveillance, not least because they were substantially hidden from those who are being watched. The rebel angels had no idea, before the revolt, just how powerful were the forces ranged against them.[103] As Beelzebub and Satan plot their uprising, they withdraw their legions to the north because, near the throne of God, 'more in this place | To utter is not safe'.[104] Little do they realize that nowhere is 'safe' from the all-seeing eye of God, and the Father is 'smiling' as he discusses with the Son the response they shall make.[105] Similarly, Adam and Eve, fearing judgement, think they can hide 'among | The thickest trees'.[106]

Typically the Father operates on a strictly defined need-to-know basis. When the rebel angels conceal their weapons of mass destruction within their battle formation, a hollow cube, the Father, all-seeing, certainly knows about them, but chooses not to inform the unfallen angels, who thus may demonstrate their loyalty and fortitude by taking their full blast: 'down they fell | By thousands, angel on archangel rolled'.[107] The knowledge angels, both good and bad, have about earth and its inhabitants is decidedly fragmentary. Satan taps into the conversation of Adam and Eve to learn about the rules that govern them: 'Yet let me not forget what I have gained | From their own mouths; all is not theirs it seems'.[108] Raphael missed out on witnessing the creation and asks Adam to tell him what he evidently does not know. Nor is the angel loose-lipped in answering astronomical queries: 'Solicit not thy thoughts with matters hid, | Leave them to God above'.[109] Indeed, the Father dispatched Raphael with a narrow and purposeful brief, to tell Adam and Eve only what they needed to know to make their choice informed and thus indefensible, thus 'render[ing] man inexcusable'.[110] Half a century ago, William Empson, no stranger to the workings of government, found Milton 'like Kafka' because 'both seem to have had a kind of foreknowledge of the Totalitarian State'.[111] Yet, more probably, Milton, sharing Machiavelli's ambition to identify principles that determine the operation of all states, has by drawing on his own experience stumbled across a pervasive enthusiasm of many organizations in controlling what is known.

Fallen creatures in *Paradise Lost* manifest the sorts of predictable machinations no doubt wearyingly familiar to Milton from his own years in government office. Thus, Eve, having sinned, quickly runs a risk assessment on whether it is safer or not to share her forbidden knowledge with Adam; not to would give her an edge, but if punishment follows it would perhaps be more bearable for her if he too were indicted.[112] Satan shows a guileful use of a clandestinely briefed colleague, Beelzebub, in floating the scheme he intends his council of state to follow.[113] Once his colleagues have accepted his mission, he rapidly closes the meeting,

> Prudent, lest from his resolution raised
> Others among the chief might offer now
> (Certain to be refused) what erst they feared;
> And so refused might in opinion stand
> His rivals, winning cheap the high repute
> Which he through hazard huge must earn.[114]

Milton's poem offers a series of temptations, to the angels, to Adam and Eve, perhaps in a sense to the Son as he accepts the challenge of atoning for fallen humankind. The challenge to Adam and Eve he found, albeit somewhat sketchily developed, in Genesis. He seems to have drawn on his own immediate experience in constructing the challenge to the angels' loyalty. He had seen close-to a dreadful example of how not to transfer power in the succession of Richard Cromwell to the Protectorate. In a process improvised by Thurloe, supposedly on the dying word of the old Protector, power passed to Oliver's son, a figure hitherto virtually unknown, wholly innocent of military or political prowess or profile. In so doing, leading figures among both civilian republicans and senior officers in the New Model Army faced a challenge to their obedience that, after an initial show of assent, proved overwhelming and disastrous. The Father's disclosure to his assembled angels of this Son and the declaration of his future rule over them form a temptation which a third of them find irresistible. Milton well knew, in the bitter legacy of the Restoration, how best to irk and irritate the ambitious and the vain.

Of course, we are not arguing that Milton is saying Richard Cromwell is a Christ figure, any more than Oliver was Satanic or Thurloe godlike in his powers. Rather, among the many elements assembled to make the epic, there is an awareness of how the political animal, in its hopes, fears, and longings, behaves. Milton forfeited at the Restoration much of what he had earned in the 1650s, but the years as public servant most certainly were not without profit of a less tangible kind.

The poem has the stamp of Milton's political experience, but it also contains a version of himself in the invocations that begin Books 1, 3, 7, and 9 and in the occasional interjections of the narrator into the narrative. This figure of the poet is a character that spills out of the poem into the accounts of Milton's practice of composition, all of which seem to originate with Milton. The mould into which he casts his character is distinctly Virgilian. Just as the youthful Virgil announced in Catalepton 14 that he would one day write an epic, so Milton often reminded his readers of his similar aspiration. The accounts of his composition practices have similar origins. Richardson, for example, explained that while writing *Paradise Lost* Milton 'frequently Compos'd lying in Bed in a Morning... He would Dictate many, perhaps 40 lines as it were in a Breath, and then reduce them to half the Number'.[115] Similarly, Donatus said of Virgil that

It is said that when he was writing the *Georgics* that early each morning he would dictate a large number of lines which he had composed, and then devote the day to working on them and reducing them to a few lines. He used to say that he wrote poetry as a bear treats her cubs, licking them gradually into shape.[116]

It would seem that the same muse that visited Milton's slumbers when the morn purples the east had many centuries earlier visited Virgil's bedside. It is a Christian version of this Virgilian character that Milton creates for himself within the poem; Milton's character, however, is competitive: Virgil's muses will accompany him from the Aonian summit (*Aonio... vertice*) but Milton's will soar *above* the Aonian mount. Virgil planned to write a *templum* for Caesar, and Milton's character announces that the Spirit 'dost prefer | Before all Temples the upright heart and pure'. Milton creates for himself a character who has been inspired by God to write his poem.

Claims to divine inspiration are sometimes embarrassing for a modern secular reader and possibly blasphemous for a modern Christian reader. There was a similar spread of views in the late seventeenth century. Thomas Hobbes, writing in 1650, rails against the 'foolish custome, by which a man, enabled to speak wisely from the principles of nature and his own inspiration, loves rather to be thought to speak by inspiration, like a Bagpipe'. In the same volume, Davenant reproaches poets who 'assume such saucy familiarity with a true God'.[117] Milton defied contrary opinion, as he had in his polemical writings, and created a version of himself inspired by God. In Book 1 he invokes the aid of the spirit in his 'adventurous song'; in Book 3, he reminds the reader that he is blind, like all the best classical poets and prophets, and that he is visited by his muse by night (as had Virgil been); in Book 7 he presents himself as a heroic figure who has overcome the hardship of having fallen on 'evil days', with 'dangers compassed round', seeking inspiration from the muse who 'visit'st my slumbers nightly'. In Book 9 he speaks once more of 'nightly visitation' of his celestial patroness, who 'dictates to me slumbering, or inspires | Easy my unpremeditated verse'.[118] Milton had presumed to speak for England in many of his tracts, and now he was speaking for the God whose conduit he had become.

CHAPTER 17

The Sunlit Uplands

Two intertwined issues dominated English politics from late 1667 to the end of Milton's life: toleration (and repression) and Anglo-Dutch relations; a third, the increasing odium in which Charles's audaciously outrageous court was held by most of the political nation, provided an ever-present background. Milton's engagement with events on the national scale was for the most part tenuous, but he still had friends close to power (and from 1673 his engagement became closer). Arthur Annesley, since 1661 earl of Anglesey, remained a privy counsellor, intermittently holding high office, as treasurer of the navy and Lord Privy Seal, though for some of the time a senior role in the administration of Ireland kept him abroad. Andrew Marvell retained his seat in the Commons, where he had represented Hull since the inception of the Cavalier Parliament (and, indeed, during the Convention Parliament and Richard Cromwell's). Marvell became active on behalf of the emerging anti-court group, the incipient 'country party' or, as they are sometimes known to modern historians, the 'proto-whigs'. He looked to Annesley for protection and patronage, though from the turn of the decade he was associated with the increasingly oppositional figure of George Villiers, second duke of Buckingham. Marvell's Restoration writings, both verse and prose, sit illuminatingly alongside Milton's own, and we shall return to them. From Marvell and Annesley—and there were probably others—Milton would have known rather more about national affairs than was disclosed in the newsbooks permitted by Sir Roger L'Estrange.

In the months before the first publication of *Paradise Lost* the Second Anglo-Dutch War was concluded on generally poor terms. The Dutch had ended the war with a daring and lethal blow, overwhelming the fort that protected the entrance to the Medway, burning or seizing three of the largest vessels of the Royal Navy, and settling down to blockade the Thames; 'Charles's first war as effective king had ended in humiliation and defeat.' The Treaty of Breda was ratified in late August 1667, and produced at least one outcome gratifying to an old republican. Charles's chief minister, the earl of Clarendon, a major architect of the Restoration, was dismissed and shortly afterwards exiled, to be replaced in effect by Henry Bennet, first earl of Arlington (and future employer of Edward Phillips). Another probable object of Milton's hatred, George Monck, first duke of Albemarle, to whom he had abortively appealed in the twilight of the republic, entered a sharp and visible decline, dying of dropsy in January 1670. His state funeral, perhaps again gratifyingly, was delayed for nearly five months while Charles scraped together enough funds. Edward Montague, first earl of Sandwich, another who profited hugely from betraying the republic, died in 1672 at the battle of Southwold Bay.[2]

Not only old enemies were dying. In March 1668 Milton's nephew Christopher, the eldest son of his brother, died. Child mortality was a grim but normal part of life in seventeenth-century England, but the death of an adult son was not. The younger Christopher had followed his father to the Inner Temple in 1661, and had been called to the Bar on 9 February 1668; a month later he was dead. In December 1669 another adult son, 17-year-old John, who was a student at Pembroke College Cambridge, followed his brother to the grave.[3]

Charles's relations with the Cavalier Parliament fluctuated considerably after the fall of Clarendon. Besides the permanently disaffected, like Marvell, others were at various times critical of foreign policy and the conduct of the wars, suspicious of his apparent inclination to tolerate Catholics or dissenters, or simply shocked by the debauchery of his court. Charles entertained no particular affection for the Church of England. Veiling toleration for popery under a general toleration that embraced dissent recurred as government policy, though fitfully, through the rest of Milton's life. As we noted in the previous chapter, by 1667 dissenters could reasonably have concluded that their faith communities would not be persecuted to extinction. Indeed, by the autumn of 1667 Charles was urging on parliament the principle of religious comprehension which would have eased considerably the residual concerns of the nonconformists. The first Conventicle Act was allowed to expire.

But Charles both vacillated in his own perspective on dissent and sought to reassure those Anglican zealots in parliament who had promoted the formulation of the Clarendon Code.[4] Policy was reversed frequently over the final years of Milton's life, in ways which certainly touched the well-being of at least the Quakers in his immediate circle. Throughout 1668 and early 1669, 'reports reached the government that [dissenters] were taking their impunity for granted rather than as a privilege that might be withdrawn'. Charles's attitude hardened and in mid-1670 a second Conventicle Act went into force 'wherever there were magistrates prepared to execute it, and there turned out to be a great many of them'. This, in turn, improved relations with the majority of the Cavalier Parliament. However, on 13 March 1672, Charles issued a Declaration of Indulgence, in effect decriminalizing the activities of both dissenters and Catholics, satisfying his new ally and patron Louis XIV, protecting Catholics close to the throne, and ensuring some support from dissenters and their defenders. In the process he once more alienated the majority of his parliament. Two days later, he declared war on the Dutch, so inaugurating the Third Anglo-Dutch War. For the next year, nonconformists could reasonably regard the legality of their actitivities as secured, as their chapels were licensed. John Bunyan, amid the release of many Quakers from prison, also found himself at liberty. But by spring 1673 Charles felt con-strained to withdraw the Declaration, returning the legal status of dissent to confusion.[5] Milton's own responses to these vagaries reflect the complexities of events on the national stage, as we shall see.

About the court's morals the political nation was altogether clearer: its conduct was outrageous. Charles had tolerated around him aristocrats and courtiers, whose behaviour in the years immediately following the Restoration we have considered already. Nothing restrained them over the rest of the reign. Moreover, the king's own sexual impropriety was widely known and discussed. John Evelyn, quondam employer of Edward Phillips and best known now as a diarist, had been fiercely loyal to the royalist cause, and during the second and third Anglo-Dutch wars served conscientiously as a commissioner for the sick and wounded.[6] He looked on appalled at the court's excesses, noting in October 1671 that during its sojourn at Newmarket (for the horse racing) it more resembled 'a luxurious and abandoned rout than a Christian court'.[7] The most vivid depiction of court morals came from within its charmed circle, in the writings of John Wilmot, second earl of Rochester, a young man often indulged by the king. His satirical writing and writing attributed to him, widely circulated in manuscript, established indelibly the image of a Charles as 'A merry Monarch, scandalous and poore', parading publicly his illegitimate children and rolling 'about from Whore to Whore'.[8]

The reputation of the court was further diminished by the apparent indulgence of Catholicism: 'The King's wife, his mistresses Cleveland and Querouaille, and (or so many suspected) his brother were Catholics.'[9] In 1670, Charles struck a secret treaty, the Treaty of Dover, with Louis XIV, by which he received a substantial annual subsidy in return for undertaking, eventually, to declare his own conversion and to engage with France against the Dutch. To Protestant Englishmen, the Dutch as coreligionaries seemed in some respects natural allies, and the French natural enemies, as papists ruled by a dangerously ambitious and expansionist king: 'for the rest of his life Charles II would be a French client and prey to constant anxiety that Louis would leak the details of their agreement.'[10] Indeed, when England returned to war with the Dutch in 1672, it was in alliance with the French. The war did not go well. Moreover, parliament made anti-Catholic legislation a condition of voting supply. The Test Act of 1673 flushed out the Duke of York's conversion, and required him to resign all government offices. By February 1674, the war concluded, Charles's relations with parliament had deteriorated so far that he prorogued it for several months; in the month of Milton's death, he prorogued it for an unprecedented fifteen months.

Enemies of the court could certainly feel the tide was running with them. In 1667 Marvell had concluded *The Last Instructions to a Painter* with the representation of Charles II alone in his chamber. To him appear the spectral forms of his grandfather, the assassinated Henri IV of France, who 'in his open side | The grisly wound' reveals, and his own father, 'the ghastly Charles', who turn his collar down to show 'The purple thread about his neck'.[11] They serve to remind Charles that monarchies are fragile and the violent death of monarchs has close and pertinent precedent. By 1674, that minatory edge had not diminished.

The first edition of *Paradise Lost* sold solidly in the years immediately following its publication. London in 1667, at least within the city walls, was as devastated as Hamburg and Dresden were by 1945, though there had been no firestorm and the slow advance of the fire had claimed property but few lives. As we noted, Samuel Simmons had made ingenious provision for distributing the print run through several booksellers and over six issues, each with its own title page, thus improvising in the context of a devastated booktrade and a metropolis close to ruin. From an analysis of surviving copies H. F. Fletcher has convincingly conjectured that sales accelerated over 1668 and 1669.[12]

One anecdote, recorded by Jonathan Richardson, tells of a spectacular response to the poem by a poet of some former accomplishment:

Sir *George Hungerford*, an Ancient Member of Parliament, told me, many Years ago, that Sir *John Denham* came into the House one Morning with a Sheet, Wet from the Press, in his Hand. What have you there, *Sir John?* Part of the Noblest Poem that was ever Wrote in Any Language, or in Any Age. This was *Paradise Lost*.[13]

Since Westminster is a fair walk from Aldersgate Street, where the poem was printed, it seems altogether unlikely that Denham did indeed have a sheet wet from the press. Yet he could well have bought the poem unbound, and his enthusiasm is by no means beyond credibility. Not only had he been among the finest poets of the late Caroline period but also he had revived an interest in his own creative writing, and was gathering his own poetry together for new publication. Moreover, not least because he resented his current notoriety as a man cuckolded by James, duke of York, he was fiercely anti-Catholic and would have found enough to relish in Milton's epic on that point.

There is also evidence from the correspondence of the period that the poem was finding appreciative readers. John Beale discussed it in a series of letters to John Evelyn,[14] and Sir John Hobart spoke approvingly of it in letters to his son John Hobart.[15] Similarly, as we noted,[16] Marvell paid it the compliment of imitation in his 'Last Instructions to a Painter'.[17] A second issue of *Paradise Lost* was published late in 1667, and in 1668 two more issues were published; in the third issue Milton's name was withheld (the poem is said to have been written by 'The Author J.M.'[18]) but in the fourth it was restored. Since Milton was often represented by his initials on title pages this need not mark an attempt to suppress his authorship. It would be a curious way to sell a book to suggest it was written by an unknown rather than an author legendary for his learning and notorious for his politics.

This fourth issue has significant changes in the prefatory material. In a note from 'The Printer to the Reader', Samuel Simmons[19] explains that in response to requests from readers he has procured a summary ('argument') for each book from the author, and 'withall a reason of that which stumbled many others, why the Poem Rimes not'. Milton's note on the verse offers an explanation of why the poem is unrhymed; in tones that range from the spirited to the defiant he explains that rhyme 'is the invention of a barbarous age to set off wretched matter and lame metre'. Warming to his theme, he explains that while the lack of rhyme may be deemed a defect by 'vulgar readers', his practice should be 'esteemed an example set, the first in English, of ancient liberty recovered to heroic poem from the troublesome and modern bondage of rhyming'. Milton was clearly not in a mood to cater to the ephemeral tastes of vulgar readers, but he nonetheless supplied the 'arguments' that are now printed at the beginning of each book of *Paradise Lost*.

In 1669 two more issues of *Paradise Lost* were published, and on 26 April Milton received an additional £5 for the poem. The receipt, which may be the most famous in English literary history, was signed on Milton's behalf by a helper, probably Thomas Ellwood. It is now in Christ's College, Cambridge.

At the end of June (probably 28 June 1669) Samuel Simmons published Milton's *Accedence Commenc't Grammar*, so inaugurating the process whereby in his last years Milton sought to publish some of his early works. 'Accidence', as it is now spelt, denotes the variable forms of words (especially inflections), and Milton's title indicates that the teaching of accidence should precede grammar. The full title indicates the aim of the work: *Accedence Commenc't Grammar, supply'd with sufficient rules for the use of such as, Younger or Elder, are desirous without more trouble then needs, to attain the Latin Tongue; the elder sort especially, with little teaching, and their own industry.* It is not clear when Milton wrote this primer. It may be a product of his years as a teacher in the 1640s, but may reflect his experience of teaching older pupils in later years. What is striking about the pedagogy of the volume is Milton's insistence that fluency is more important than competence: the deep understanding that comes with a knowledge of Latin grammar takes second place to a command of the language sufficient to access its literature and write coherent Latin. Much of the material in the *Accedence* reaches back to Lily's *Introduction to Grammar* (1540), but Milton's approach has been coloured by his engagement with Comenius and the Hartlib circle, and its most distinctive feature is the urgency with which he proposes to guide his pupils through the basics of the language in order to move away from constructed examples to real Latin.

Apart from his months in Chalfont St Giles, Milton had been living in Artillery Walk (now Bunhill Row) since spring 1663, but at some point in 1670 he moved temporarily into the house of the bookseller Edward Milli-ngton, whose shop and home were then at the Pelican in Duck Lane, off Little Britain, which was a street dominated by booksellers from the late sixteenth to the early eighteenth century. Millington later became a publisher and then an auctioneer, but at this stage he was a seller of second-hand books. The circumstances of this temporary residence are not known, nor is it clear that Milton was accompanied by his wife Elizabeth. The move may have been connected with Milton's decision to sell a large part of his library on the grounds that the collection would be of no use to his heirs, and that, as Toland explained, 'he thought he might sell it more to their advantage than they could be able to do so themselves'.[20]

On or shortly before 1 November 1670 Milton's *History of Britain* was published.[21] The first four books had been drafted in February and March 1649, and the last two books seem to have been written in the mid-1650s, possibly in 1655. The most problematical element in the *History* is the digression, a passage in Book 3 which was omitted from all editions until 1738, but published separately in 1681 as *Character of the Long Parliament*; this comparison of the ancient Britons at the time of the Roman withdrawal with the English in Milton's own time was probably written in 1648, but a case for composition in 1660 has been advanced.[22]

At the front of the *History of Britain* is an engraved portrait of Milton by William Faithorne the elder.[23] The image bears a problematical relationship to a pastel portrait in the Princeton University library;[24] it is possible that it is a preliminary *ad vivum* drawing for the engraving, but its quality, by com-parison with the usual high quality of Faithorne's chalk portraits, is distinctly mediocre. In the case of the engraving, however, there can be no reasonable doubt about the sitter or the artist. The engraving, which claims in its inscription to be an image of Milton at the age of 62 (which he did not reach until December 1670), presents a harsher image than the pastel: the collar and the mouth, which are softly drawn in the pastel, are hardened (and in the case of the collar, squared) in the engraving. In both cases Milton's sightless eyes are presented as if focused on the viewer.

Two recurrent rhetorical strategies adopted by Milton in his *History* prove stumbling blocks to the modern reader. The modesty topos which Milton uses in the *Defensio Secunda*, suggests that the project is a liberal pastime sacrificed on the altar of English republicanism, given up in defence of the cause of the Commonwealth.[25] The account suggests both the range of Milton's liberal humanism and his commitment to the cause, but it prompts the modern reader to view the history as somehow an abandoned work, albeit one resumed after a fashion. David Loewenstein's telling epithet is 'aborted'.[26] But it is surely not quite that. Rather, it is a reconfigured work, its *terminus ad quem* adjusted to something more achievable in changed personal circumstances. What we have is a work of some accomplishment, in all probability carefully revised close to its first publication date of 1670, between the first appearances of his two epics, although we have observed his engagement with the project over the mid-century decades.[27] Milton closes his account of English history with a contemporary reference which, as others have noted, makes rather more sense as a comment on the immediate age than the 1640s or early 1650. His closing depiction is of an age of gluttony, drunkenness, debauching of servants and 'then turning them off to the Stews',[28] which does not suggest the decades shaped by the movement that culminated in the Adultery Act of 1650, with its provision for the death penalty for married women convicted of adultery and three months in gaol for fornication.[29] It is, moreover, an age 'in the midst of her security' and characterized by the perseverance of a godly remnant—'Not but that some few of all sort were much better among them; but such was the generality'.[30] This echoes a familiar way for Restoration dissent to represent itself in the late 1660s. If Milton was tinkering with the end, we may certainly entertain the notion of his preparing the rest of the volume with some precision for the press. Its publication comes amid a flurry of such activity as Milton brought other long-term projects, his late poems and the second edition of his anthology of minor poetry, into readiness for the press. Moreover, we should note that he secured for the first edition an index of over 50 pages (to a text of 308 pages), sure evidence that it has been worked up into a proper state of revision and completion.

Within the text itself, its modern reception is further inhibited by a second rhetorical manoeuvre: Milton seeks readers' benevolence by seeming useful, though to our own age he sounds tired, resentful, and a little peevish. Thus, as he negotiates the *Anglo-Saxon Chronicle*, available to him in Abraham Wheelocke's 1643 edition, which printed the Old English in parallel with a Latin translation, he represents himself as cutting through 'extravagant fansies and metaphors, as bar [his author] quite beside the scope of being understood', to summarize his source 'in usual language'. Working through Geoffrey of Monmouth, a text replete in legends 'Whereto I neither oblige the belief of another person, nor over-hastily subscribe mine own', he is like 'one who had set out on his way by night, and travail'd through a Regioun of

45. John Milton, *The History of Britain* (London, 1670), title page and portrait frontispiece by William Faithorne.

smooth or idle Dreams'. Bede offers 'a scatter'd story pickt out heer and there, with some trouble and tedious work', while his successors offer 'obscure and blockish Chronicles'.[31]

In part, this is a manoeuvre adopted, more transparently, in the posthumously published *Brief History of Moscovia* (1682), where he observes, '*What was scatter'd in many Volumes, and observ'd at several times by Eye-witnesses, with no cursory pains I laid together, to save the Reader a far longer travaile of wandering so many desert Authours*'.[32] Indeed, Milton actually suffixes the *Brief History* with a nineteen-item bibliography. George B. Parks, its modern editor, seems shocked, constrained to observe not once but twice that 'Actually... he did all his searching in two volumes [of Hakluyt and Purchas]' and 'it was they who had "laid together" chronologically "what was scatter'd in many volumes," though often in manuscript reports'.[33] The 'Names of the Authours from whence these Relations have been taken'[34] carries us away from those comfortable arguments about the rather different concept of authorship in the early modern period and close to commonsense unease about fakery.

In *The History of Britain* Milton's policy is more complicated. Certainly Milton constructs himself as a helpful guide through a body of material so ghastly to read that his task appears heroic. But he has another purpose, to

46. Portrait of John Milton, attributed to William Faithorne (Princeton University Library).

fashion himself as a liberal humanist, a cool neoclassicist, who despises his medieval sources both for their style and for their monkish assumptions. His purpose is perhaps pre-emptive, for his history compares poorly in terms of its scholarly methodology and its thoroughness with the achievements of contemporary antiquaries. Here Graham Parry's masterful study, *The Tro-phies of Time: English Antiquarians of The Seventeenth Century*,[35] offers an important corrective. Milton emerges as utterly marginal to one of the greatest academic endeavours of the early modern period, the labours—genuine, not merely asserted—of Camden, Cotton, Selden, Ussher, Spelman and—perhaps most significantly in this context—Sir William Dugdale.

Milton suggests that no liberal scholar would waste his time on the kind of dross the antiquaries worked on. Certainly, he did not, basing his history wholly on published sources. Dugdale, the most prominent among a cluster of antiquaries to recognize the richness of the records still preserved from monastic foundations, was toiling on his mighty *Monasticon Anglicanum* as Milton fashioned his own, slighter, narrative of pre-Conquest history. The first volume appeared in 1655. Dugdale worked in uncongenial times, since 'the prevailing mood of the Commonwealth years was hostile to antiquarian research...[and thus] the booksellers were not eager to publish Dugdale'.[36] It is a knowing Milton, a Milton aware of this rival tradition and of his own relatively shallow scholarship, that plays the liberal-humanist card when he observes, 'This travail rather then not know at once what may be known about antient story, sifted from Fables and impertinences, I voluntarily undergo; and to save others, if they please the like unpleasing labour; except those who take pleasure to be all thir life time, rakeing in the Foundations of old Abbies and Cathedrals.'[37]

Milton, we believe, had been researching and writing the history, inter-mittently, for about twenty-five years, and the tone of such comments can strike at least modern readers as perplexing. If he does not enjoy such primary material, then why not leave the whole subject alone? *The History of Britain*, in effect on his own account, appears a work of drudgery. This in turn leads us away from recognizing it for what it really is—a work of verve, wit, and playfulness; a spirited rehearsal of Miltonic themes and values; and a cardinal text in his ideas about history and about government.

There are silences of great significance. Milton does not present a national history that celebrates either Britain or England. Rather, early history depicts primitivism, ignorance, corruption, and depravity. He represents his Britons as no better than savages. Milton usually displays the Englishman's easy contempt for the other peoples of the British isles, for the Scots (less evident here than elsewhere), for the Welsh in their 'Mountanous and Barren Cor-ner', for the '*wild Irish*' in their 'Bogs'. But his forefathers, it seems, were no better, unless they were beaten, like children, into a temporary civility by the Romans.[38] Here is no prehistory of a chosen people; whatever the subsequent history of England, it owes nothing to that past. Milton's indifference to precedent and to the contemporary consequence of what may have happened formerly leads him to ignore the arguments of radical constitutionalists that pre-Conquest England manifested a legal system or an ancient and mixed constitution that could usefully be invoked in his own age.

Helpfully, no doubt, for the republican position, the past he establishes does not show the customary and time-hallowed status of monarchism because numerous forms of government are to be found in the pre-Conquest period. Vortigern was 'chief rather than sole King'. The early Saxon settlers had '7 absolute Kingdoms'. Edward 'had the whole Iland in subjection, yet so as petty Kings reign'd under him'. There is even a republic, somewhat longer lived than the English republic of his own day, in Northumbria after the death of Ethelred, and an obvious glee informs his comments: 'thir Kings one after another so oft'n slain by the people, no man dareing, though never so ambitious, to take up the Scepter which many had found so hot, (the only effectual cure of ambition that I have read) for the space of 33 years'; the parenthesis seems purposeful. Milton seems to savour attempts to assert the ancient status of royal lineages. Hengist and Horsa are allegedly 'descended in the fourth degree from *Woden*; of whom, deify'd for the fame of his acts, most Kings of those Nations derive thir pedigree'. Ethelwolf's chroniclers 'write... his Pedigree, from Son to Father, up to *Adam*', an amusing anticipation of Sir Robert Filmer's perspective, perhaps.[39]

Miltonic preoccupations recur, not all of them congenial to the modern reader. This is probably his most misogynistic work, sometimes embarrassingly so. Boadicea has been flogged and her daughters raped by the civilizing Romans Milton so much admires; in the sources she invokes this experience to motivate her army, an action, Milton says, worse than her injury, for these were 'things worthier silence, retirement, and a Vail, then for a Woeman to repeat, as done to her own person, or to hear repeated before an host of men'. It is the gratuitousness that makes the judgement particularly disturbing. But Boadicea represents in extreme form female presumption in the sphere of government, a recurrent concern.[40] In the *History* Milton produces a cumulative image of the malign impact of female influence on government that gives a backdrop to his charge against Charles I of 'effeminacy', that is of subordinating his judgement to his wife's, which finds expression and development in *Eikonoklastes*.[41] But Milton knows such 'effeminacy' to be wrong both from first principles and from a consideration of his own age. It is not a lesson learnt from remote history but a mistake repeated in remote history.

Polyandry fascinates and repels him: 'certain it is that whereas other Nations us'd a liberty not unnatural for one man to have many Wives, the *Britans* altogether more licentious, but more absurd and preposterous in thir licence, had one or many Wives in common among ten or twelve Husbands'. Polygamy, he slyly insinuates, is natural, and it receives intermittent though tangential praise: 'King *Edward* thus nobly doing,... a builder and restorer eev'n in War, not a destroyer of his Land. He had by several Wives many Childern.'[42]

A playful anti-clericalism and an abrasive puritanical Protestantism pervade the text, and support its best jokes. When Augustine meets with Ethelbert as a prelude to the conversion of England, the king 'chose a place to meet them under the open Sky, possest with an old perswasion, that all Spells, if they should use any to deceive him, so it were not within doors, would be unavailable'. Milton describes from his source, Bede, how Augustine's party advance, with their standard, their silver cross, their 'painted image' of Christ, 'singing thir solemn Litanies', and adds, tartly, his own observation that thus, probably, they increased his suspicion that a spell was being wrought; so much for gay antiphons still favoured by papists and prelates in his own age. The monk Elmer not only claimed the power of prophecy but also sustained serious injury in an experiment in manned flight; how strange he 'could not foresee, when time was, the breaking of his own Legs for soaring too high'.[43]

Milton uses the lamentations of his sources as a route into a broader and transhistorical attack on the clergy. Those 'suttle Prowlers, Pastors in Name, but indeed Wolves ... seising on the Ministry as a Trade, not a Spiritual Charge', occupy the same ethical status as the Presbyterian divines in *The Tenure of Kings and Magistrates*, 'rambling from Benefice to Benefice, like rav'nous Wolves seeking where they may devour the biggest', and the post-apostolic ministers of whom Michael warns Adam.[44]

To justify monastic retirement, Gildas needed to excoriate both civil and religious establishments;[45] this suits Milton well as a platform to attack both the Long Parliament and the Presbyterian-dominated Westminster Assembly of Divines. His 'digression', which survives in a non-holograph manuscript, was pulled from *The History* at some point before its 1670 publication; it appeared in print posthumously in 1681, evidently from a Tory bookseller under the patronage of Sir Roger L'Estrange, and published as part of the controversial literature surrounding the Exclusion Crisis, as has been well established. Quite how the Tories found copy remains uncertain. Edward Phillips recalled that Milton had 'presented' the earl of Anglesey 'with a Copy of the unlicensed Papers of his History'.[46]

If the passage were withdrawn at the insistence of the licenser, the effect was useful to the larger coherence of *The History*. If it were written in the late 1640s but before Pride's Purge, the digression had only a transient relevance. Gildas's text reflected a society that was both doomed to foreign incursion and poised for a monastic revival; by 1649, Milton's targets had been sidelined, the religious tolerationism that he promoted had substantially triumphed, England had a republican administration and Milton was its leading apologist; by the 1670s Presbyterians were merely one kind of dissenter, legally excluded from toleration like all the other nonconformists. To retain the digression would have been risking ridicule.

But we should not be surprised that Milton's work was appropriated in 1681, for in a sense *The History of Britain* as a whole is a proto-Tory history. Within canonical literature its closest analogue is the Glubbdubdrib passage of *Gulliver's Travels* where, vouchsafed an encounter with ghosts of figures from modern history, Gulliver reels back from 'How many Villains had been exalted to the highest Places of Trust, Power, Dignity, and Profit'.[47] Milton's own historiographical adventure is mirrored in Gulliver's. It is a journey away from grand narratives. Milton abandons the myth of England as a chosen and privileged nation. He abandons the legacy of sixteenth-century Protestant historiography, the legacy of John Foxe and John Bale, with its patient chronicling of the sufferings and triumph of the godly in the providential progress towards an English reformation. He virtually abandons a providential view of history altogether. Good men frequently suffer; bad men may triumph, few are punished for their actions but each successive civilisation ends in disaster. He steps away, too, from the principles of Guicciardini and Machiavelli, that the study of history can give lessons by which subsequent ages can conduct themselves politically, for political action emerges as unworthy or ineffectual.

Milton's is a narrative without heroes and without consequence. It begins doubting the enterprise of historiography:

Certainly oft-times we see that wise men, and of best abilitie have forborn to write the Acts of thir own daies, while they beheld with a just loathing and disdain, not only how unworthy, how pervers, how corrupt, but often how ignoble, how petty, how below all History the persons and thir actions were; who either by fortune, or som rude election had attain'd as a sore judgment, and ignominie upon the Land, to have cheif sway in managing the Commonwealth.[48]

It ends, echoing William of Malmesbury, with a general reflection that evidently merited italics '*as the long suffering of God permits bad men to enjoy prosperous daies with their good, so his severity oft times exempts not good men from thir share in evil times with the bad*'.[49]

On 2 July 1670 *Paradise Regained* was licensed by Thomas Tomkins, and on 10 September it was registered for publication, together with *Samson Agonistes*. The composition of *Paradise Regained* certainly postdates the completion of *Paradise Lost*, and may well owe something to Thomas Ellwood's observations on the earlier poem.[50] The dating of its companion piece has proved less certain. Edward Phillips noted, 'It cannot certainly be concluded when he wrote his excellent Tragedy entitled *Samson Agonistes*, but sure enough it is that it came forth after his publication of *Paradice lost*, together with his other Poem call'd *Paradice regain'd*, which doubtless was begun and finisht and

Printed after the other was publisht, and that in a wonderful short space considering the sublimeness of it.'[51] The passage offers several points of interest. We note that, for Phillips, who had worked closely with Milton as he composed *Paradise Lost*, four years for the production of the two thousand lines of the brief epic seemed like quick work, which lends support to our argument about the protracted period over which Milton was working on his first epic, which is five times as long.

Phillips was away from London and its environs for much of the period 1648–55 and again from 1665 to some time between 1669 and 1672. Either could correspond with the composition of *Samson Agonistes*, and each has its proponents.[52] Given the precedent of *Paradise Lost*, we need not regard the alternatives as mutually exclusive. Indeed, the closet drama has a potent resonance in the England of the third Anglo-Dutch war, but its intimate and empathetic engagement with the problems of personal adjustment to blindness suggest, too, that Milton may have worked on it in the earliest years of his disability.

It is not, of course, a work of encrypted autobiography. Milton, whether in 1654 or 1669, cut a very different figure from his representation of Samson. Samson acknowledged a culpability in his blindness: 'Whom have I to complain of but myself?'; 'of what I now suffer | She [Dalila] was not the prime cause, but myself'; 'Nothing of all these evils hath befall'n me | but justly; I myself have brought them on'.[53] In sharp contrast, Milton laboured to represent his own blindness as concommitant on his heroic endeavours, despite his doctors' warnings, in defence of the English republican against the disparagements of Salmasius.[54] Again, Samson declines to escape prison, where he toils in the interest of his Philistian captors, accepting it as a fit punishment for his sin of garrulity. There he lives 'captive, poor, and blind | Into a dungeon thrust, to work with slaves'.[55] He resists the attempts of his father, Manoa, to secure his release. At the Restoration, Milton through the intercession of friends sought to secure his inclusion in the Act of Oblivion and to be delivered promptly from jail, using methods quite similar to Manoa's.[56] Indeed, Manoa's advice, 'if the punishment | Thou canst avoid, self-preservation bids',[57] accords closely with Milton's own policy. When Dalila in vain reminds Samson that for the blind, 'Life yet hath many solaces, enjoyed | Where other senses want not their delights | At home in leisure and domestic ease',[58] Milton perhaps recalls his own pleasure in a young wife and a warm bed.

Yet, as in *Paradise Lost*, both the experiences and the principles of the 1640s and 1650s are clearly to be seen, together with some shrewd hits at Restoration mores. The court of Charles II was bedevilled with a cult of duelling, which was 'positively fashionable among soldiers and courtiers'.[59] In the most notorious encounter of the period, the duke of Buckingham 'destroyed his reputation in the nation at large by killing the Earl of Shrewsbury, husband of

47. John Milton, *Paradise Regain'd. A Poem in IV Books. To which is added Samson Agonistes* (London, 1671), title page and imprimatur.

his mistress ... and gossip reported that the Countess had witnessed the fight disguised as a page, or that she and Buckingham had made love afterwards while his clothes were still stained with blood'.[60] With nothing to support the incident in Judges, Milton fashions a depiction of a would-be duellist in the swaggering Harapha, though the Philistine evades putting his own courage, skill, and strength to the test of combat. With an astuteness probably honed in the circles of power in which he once moved, Milton has Samson analyse his probable conduct. The Chorus worry that Harapha will report his own aggression to his Philistian masters; Samson offers the observation that he could not do that without incurring the risk that they would press him to take up the challenge.[61]

The poem concludes with a report of the slaughter Samson effects on the celebrating Philistines. There is a passing anti-court and anti-clerical blow: Samson observes that 'Lords are lordliest in their wine; | And the well-feasted priest then soonest fired | With zeal'.[62] Samson strikes them when they are in their cups, much like Charles's court at Newmarket, 'While their hearts were jocund and sublime, | Drunk with idolatry, drunk with wine'.[63] He strikes, too, with guile, pretending to rest against the pillars of the temple before pulling them down, using a kindly gesture by his guide to bring down devastation.[64] Milton's addition to the biblical account, that the 'choice nobility and flower' were killed while 'The vulgar only scaped who stood without',[65] probably has nothing to do with sympathy for the propertiless and merely celebrates the death of what another age of conflict would term 'high-value targets'.[66] We see no reason to doubt that the poem endorses the exultation over the carnage shown by Manoa and the Chorus, the latter of whom has choric status!

In its original context the poem invites interpretation as a gleeful fantasy, in which the downcast champion of an oppressed people slaughters their oppressors as they gloat. The wish fulfilled, we surmise, is that the gleeful court of Charles II could somehow share their fate. It is not, however, a terrorists' handbook, and to associate Milton's representation of Samson with the terrorists of our own age is to misunderstand both the poem and the nature of modern terrorism. Terrorism seeks to influence political action by small-scale but bloody outrages. Those who perpetrate them may entertain notions that they exercise some kind of religious or revolutionary justice, but the larger rationale aims instead at shifting the policy of the regimes that are attacked. Samson does not show much concern for Philistian public opinion, nor can Milton have intended what he depicts to scare the regime into better behaviour. Rather, perhaps sickened by Charles's endless caprice in his treatment of dissent, he entertains a reverie about the death on a substantial scale of members of his ungodly court, with Catholics well-represented among them.

The tone is disturbing. Manoa had complained about the vindictiveness of some of the Philistian lords while welcoming the 'magnanimity' of others. Within 250 lines he is joyously anticipating the Philistines' 'years of mourning, | And lamentation'.[67] Milton's was often a merciless age, and he sometimes shares its most distressing values and assumptions. The obvious analogues are to the wholesale slaughter of Catholics, for example at Drogheda or Wexford or in the so-called Black Vespers of 1623. In the last case, a large group of Catholics, who had met clandestinely for a mass, perished when a floor collapsed. The incident was contemporaneously celebrated as providential punishment for the reprobate. In contemporary illustrations, the scene, with its crushed bodies and fallen classical columns, resembles the carnage Samson causes. Indeed, as Leo Miller noted, Alexander Gil, at that time a friend of Milton's, wrote a poem comparing the collapse of the chapel with Samson's destruction of the temple.[68]

One obsession from Milton's days as a public servant still retains a value for him: keeping secrets from one's enemies. Samson as riddler had played tricks on the Philistines that depended on his knowing more than they did: such is the nature of riddling. But Samson attributes his eventual undoing wholly to 'my crime, |Shameful garrulity':

> To have revealed
> Secrets of men, the secrets of a friend,
> How heinous had the fact been, how deserving
> Contempt, and scorn of all, to be excluded
> All friendship, and avoided as a blab,
> The mark of fool set on his front!
> But I God's counsel have not kept, his holy secret
> Presumptuously have published, impiously,
> Weakly at least, and shamefully.... [69]

Thurloe would emphatically have agreed.

The relationship between the component parts of the 1671 volume poses interpretative conundrums. Formally, connections are easily made. Each consists of a series of exchanges between an isolated protagonist and those who variously tempt or challenge him, though in *Samson Agonistes* some temptations are benign—to the alternative versions of *otium* on offer from Dalila and Manoa—and in *Paradise Regained* the Son faces one tempter in several guises. The pieces are similarly proportioned and at their conclusions some lines approximate closely to each other:

> To fetch him [Samson] hence and solemnly attend
> With silent obsequy his funeral train
> Home to his father's house.... [70]
> Thus they the son of God our Saviour meek
> Sung victor, and from heavenly feast refreshed
> Brought on his way with joy; he unobserved
> Home to his mother's house private returned. [71]

One is a funeral procession, the other a kind of clandestine and muted triumph. Milton invites his readers to consider which is preferable, or, perhaps more accurately, which is more pertinent, and he gives a strong cultural guidance as to how the questions posed are to be answered.

It comes in the puzzlingly and seemingly gratuitous debate on the relative merits of Greek and Hebrew literary traditions, which, without any biblical authority, he generates between the Son and Satan. The Son moves from the subordination of classical scholarship to internal wisdom and then to the transcendence of Hebrew writings over Greek, 'Where God is praised aright': 'Such are from God inspired, not such from thee [Satan]'. [72] Of course, the model for *Samson Agonistes* is Greek drama; the model for *Paradise Regained*, as Barbara Lewalski long ago established, is the paradigmatic brief epic, the Book of Job. [73]

Moreover, while 'Samson hath quit himself | Like Samson, and heroicly hath finished | A life heroic', [74] the remit of *Paradise Regained* is to celebrate 'deeds | Above heroic, though in secret done'. [75] *Samson Agonistes* leaves its readers with a problem resolved, how Samson can endure his sufferings, and a sense of relief: the 'calm of mind all passion spent'[76] sums up both the feelings of the Chorus and of readers who have, like them, witnessed the struggle. But in the brief epic, the greatest problem is posed to Satan, while the Son, though struggling to understand his divine status and his mission, simply trusts to providence: 'Who brought me hither | Will bring me hence, no other guide I seek.'[77]

Paradise Lost showed a radical revision of Milton's millenarian thinking, as the second coming appears both certain and at the same time almost infinitely postponed. In *Paradise Regained*, only Satan and his associates are concerned about its timing. The Son exhibits an extraordinary passivity and a complete refusal to consider any of the practical measures Satan suggests to bring his kingdom on. Indeed, his perspective diametrically opposes the belief of Fifth Monarchists that direct action could hurry in the millennium. As others have noted, a Quakerish pacifism characterizes his responses to Satan's temptations. Indeed, a fundamental principle of the modern-day Society of Friends originates in 'the famous Peace Testimony of the movement', issued in the aftermath of the Venner Uprising in an attempt to forestall a wave of persecution by a regime in panic.[78]

Once more, however, the Miltonic values of the 1640s and 1650s colour the work, to which is added explicit reflection of Milton's own political experiences. When Satan shows the Son a vision of Roman political life, the latter comments in particular detail on the work of diplomacy:

> then embassies thou show'st
> From nations far and nigh; what honour that,
> But tedious waste of time to seat and hear
> So many hollow compliments and lies,
> Outlandish flatteries?[79]

So much for the delicately turned compliments of Hermann Mylius.[80]

Milton, a little slyly, lets Satan make the anti-clerical points on this occasion, as he tells the Son:

> Thy father, who is holy, wise and pure,
> Suffers the hypocrite or atheous priest
> To tread his sacred courts, and minister
> About his altar, handling holy things,
> Praying or vowing.[81]

The Son does not dispute his assertion. Another point of contemporary significance receives more substantial discussion. Arguments about the cost of standing armies and the threat they pose to civil liberties recur persistently from the 1640s deep into the Hanoverian period. The level of forces to be maintained in peacetime was controversial in the 1660s. Moreover, Milton wrote *Paradise Regained* against the background of a more general national mobilization to meet the needs of the third Anglo-Dutch war. The poem ridicules at length the display of military might. Satan shows the Son a massive display of army manoeuvres, while the narration is characterized by a witty wordplay unusual within the poem: 'numbers numberless | The city gates outpoured, light-armed troops | In coats of mail and military pride', and so on. The Son picks up the idiom, dismissing such 'ostentation vain of fleshly arm, | And fragile arms'. He adds, conclusively, 'that cumbersome | Luggage of war' is indicative of 'human weakness rather than of strength'.[82]

The Son uses Satan's temptations as the basis for the construction of his version of true kingship. Thus, in debate he deprecates what Satan calls 'The monarchies of the earth, their pomp and state', dismissing 'this grandeur and majestic show | Of luxury, though called magnificence'.[83] To monarchy, and the rule of emperors, the Son opposes two alternative concepts. The first is a metaphor, in which each individual is like a little kingdom. Reason and virtue should rule within the human mind:

> Yet he who reigns within himself, and rules
> Passions, desires, and fears, is more a king;
> Which every wise and virtuous man attains;
> And who attains not, ill aspires to rule
> Cities of men, or headstrong multitudes,
> Subject himself to anarchy within.[84]

The larger argument, here, points towards the integrity of the individual and the kind of interiority that offers a hope of comfort in a troubled and hostile world, a Paradise within ruled by king reason and queen virtue. But the Son is not everyman; Milton shows that he accepts that his is a historic mission. The Son explains to Satan, as best as he can given his remaining uncertainties about that mission, what will distinguish his kingdom:

> Know therefore when my season comes to sit
> On David's throne, it shall be like a tree
> Spreading and overshadowing all the earth,
> Or as a stone that shall to pieces dash
> All monarchies besides throughout the world,
> And of my kingdom there shall be no end:
> Means there shall be to this, but what the means,
> Is not for thee to know, nor me to tell.[85]

Milton's text closely echoes Daniel and the gospels, as editors note, and there is no option of denying the kingship of the Son. The more radical regiments of the New Model Army sometimes took as their mottos, inscribed on their battle standards, 'Christ the only king'. Milton knows that to be merely aspirational; his world was full of kings. Instead, he has the Son, darkly, suggest a transcendent kind of monarchy that sets worldly kingship at nothing, although the date of its coming remains undisclosed. As in *Samson Agonistes*, secrecy is a virtue, and the Son is no blab.

Milton's enthusiasm for the Quaker style of Christian mission, first noted in his tracts of 1659, received a final endorsement. In *The Likeliest Means to Remove Hirelings*, he observed that 'he who disdaind not to be laid in a manger, disdains not to be preachd in a barn' and 'such meetings as these' are 'most apostolical and primitive'. The earliest who could be identified as Protestant reformers were 'for the meanenes of thir condition calld, *the poore men of Lions*'.[86] With particular emphasis, Milton in *Paradise Regained* stresses the poverty of the Son ('A carpenter thy father known, thyself | Bred up in poverty and straits at home') and the humble status of the earliest apostles: 'Plain fishermen, no greater men them call, | Close in a cottage low together got.'[87] There is another, anti-prelatical, point. Who would have an interest in talking up the social status of the apostles? Who but those princes of the church who would justify episcopalian church government by claiming its apostolic status?

In May 1672 Milton published his *Artis logicae plenior institutio ad Petri Rami methodum concinnata, adjuncta est praxis analytica & Petri Rami vita* ('A fuller course in the art of logic, arranged according to the method of Pierre de la Ramée; an analytical exercise and a life of La Ramée are appended'). The *Artis logicae* is in one sense a reworking of the 1572 edition of Ramus's *Dialectica*, but its debt to the Latin commentary on Petrus Ramus by George Downham is so substantial that Milton's work is in another sense an edition of Downham; similarly, the biography is a condensed version of the life of Ramus by Johann Freige.[88] Enthusiasm for the logic of Ramus and his method now seems misplaced, as he made no lasting contribution to the history of logic, but the sheer scale of Ramus's influence cannot be ignored. There were more than 1,000 editions of Ramus's logic and rhetoric published before Milton published his edition, which was the last English recension of Ramus. The extent to which a knowledge of Ramus was deemed essential by Protestant writers may be gauged by an edition of Ramus published in America in the same year as Milton's: it was an interlinear translation of the *Dialectica* into English and Massachusett Algonquian by John Eliot, the 'Apostle to the Indians'. The logic of Ramus was deemed to be important for ministers, physicians, orators, mathematicians, and lawyers, and Antony Wotton argued that it was invaluable 'even in the managing of your horse'.[89] In Milton's case his treatise on Ramus articulates the organizational principles that inform both *Accedence*

Commenc't Grammar and *De Doctrina Christiana*, but it is less clear whether it informed the management of his horse.

Of True Religion, Heresy, Schism, Toleration, And what best means may be us'd against the growth of Popery, appeared in May 1673, thirteen years after his last prose polemic. It sits curiously alongside Milton's earlier prose. Stylistically, there is a distinct shift towards a simpler sort of exposition. The syntax of Milton's vernacular polemic had remained substantially unchanged across his career. As he returned to the genre after so long an interruption, he did so writing, in some sense, less demandingly, in sentences that are markedly shorter than those that formerly characterized his style.[90] In this, he may reflect changing norms for the genre, which in turn would indicate a shift in expectations about readership. The public domain of politics, perhaps like the public sphere itself, was contemporaneously widening.

Indeed, reflected too in the deliberations and actions of the Cavalier Parliament, public opinion in 1672–3 was increasingly animated about the conduct of the third Anglo-Dutch war, and increasingly alarmed about the role of Catholics in the highest offices of the state. In March 1673 parliament both forced Charles II to withdraw the Declaration of Indulgence and to pass the Test Act, making the grant of supply, on which continuation of the war depended, conditional on the latter measure. By June James, Duke of York, was excluded from office. Before parliament was adjourned, attempts were made to moderate legislation against nonconformists, though without agreement between the houses; 'the status of nonconformity was left confused, as both King and Commons had signalled their desire to end the Conventicle Act, yet this was still technically in force.'[91] As John Spurr remarks, 'who knew where the court was veering?'[92]

Nonconformists, nevertheless, would have felt singularly confident in the spring of 1673. A great feat had been accomplished: a broad Protestant front had emerged against popery, which recast the polarity, imposed since 1662, between conformity and dissent into the opposition of Protestantism and Catholicism. It remains unresolved on current evidence whether Milton's tract was published before or after the adjournment, though on balance it seems likelier at least to have been written before. The issue is not critical to interpretation, because it is a contribution to a campaign that was to continue unabated over the decade and beyond, tying together his old enthusiasm, tolerationism (for Protestants) into an emerging and soon to be dominant project, the exclusion of James from succession. *Of True Religion* was licensed, though its title page bears the name of neither bookseller nor printer; Milton appears as 'J.M.', a familiar *nom de guerre*.[93] The effect is to give the tract an air of *samizdat* danger, which it scarcely merits.

Besides its syntactic innovation, another new feature characterizes the tract: Milton offers something of an olive branch to supporters of the mainstream Church of England. In so doing, he follows astutely the strategy of the current campaign. He finds something to praise in the Thirty-Nine Articles, noting the 'good and Religious Reason' embodied in 'Artic. 6*th*, 19*th*, 20*th*, 21*st*, and elsewhere'.[94] His tolerationist thesis is twofold: that salvation depends on a small number of tenets that are unambiguously defined in the Bible and common to a broad spectrum of Protestant denominations; and that the remaining disputed doctrines, debated by professional and amateur theologians, are inevitable, are pursued in good faith, may contain errors, and are not crucial to salvation. He builds his argument carefully, to incorporate Lutherans and Calvinists alongside more heterodox thinkers:

The Lutheran holds Consubstantiation; an error indeed, but not mortal. The Calvinist is taxt with Predestination, and to make God the Author of sin; not with any dishonourable thought of God, but it may be over zealously asserting his absolute power, not without plea of Scripture. The Anabaptist is accus'd of Denying Infants their right to Baptism; again they say, they deny nothing but what the Scripture denies them. The Arian and Socinian are charg'd to dispute against the Trinity.... The *Arminian* lastly is condemn'd for setting up free will against free grace; but that Imputation he disclaims in all his writings, and grounds himself largely upon Scripture only.

Milton declines to identify himself with any of these views. They include tenets held by most men in holy orders in the Church of England at that time, who subscribed in terms of their soteriological beliefs either to predestination, a notion in decline outside dissenting groups, or to the Arminian notion of the synergy of free will aligned with freely vouchsafed grace. It remains uncertain quite how such men would have relished inclusion in Milton's audaciously broad category, 'all these sects or Opinions'.[95]

Milton uses the moment, surfing a wave of anti-Catholic sentiment, conscious that 'it is unknown to no man, who knows ought of concernment among us, that the increase of Popery is at this day no small trouble and offence to the greatest part of the Nation'.[96] Perhaps the sense of a new freedom for Protestant nonconformists led Milton to a further initiative in 1673, the decision to republish his minor poetry.

Around November there appeared *Poems, &c. upon Several Occasions. By Mr. John Milton: Both English and Latin, &c Composed at several times. With a small Tractate of Education To Mr. Hartlib.* Thomas Dring was the bookseller, an interesting choice. Around this time, his list contained a lot of creative writing, though mainly plays: he published work by William Wycherley, Aphra Behn, and *The Rehearsal* by the second duke of Buckingham and collaborators, though his list was broader, including a new edition of the work that recorded the debate which made William Laud's name as a theologian, *A Relation of the Conference between William Laud...and Mr. Fisher the Jesuite* (London, 1673), first published in 1624.

We know from the catalogues issued from time to time by Humphrey Moseley, who had published in 1645 the first edition of the poems, that they had remained in print into the 1650s. Moseley had died in 1661 and his wife, who inherited his business and the copyrights he held, retired a little while afterwards, though she did not die till 1673.[97] Presumably most of whatever unsold copies of the collection remained in the hands of other booksellers perished in the Great Fire. Milton picked his moment well, while judging with care how far he could push the bounds of what was permitted to a man of his notoriety. Of the poems he had written since 1645 he includes all his extant psalm translations, the sonnets to Henry Lawes, Cyriack Skinner, his own late wife, the late Mrs Thomason, and on his blindness. No one in 1673 risked anything by attacking Presbyterians, and so the inclusion of 'A book was writ of late' and 'I did but prompt the age' was unproblematic, except insofar as it recalled past discord among Protestants. Perhaps more challengingly, he includes 'Lawrence of virtuous father virtuous son', with its explicit praise of the Lord President of Oliver Cromwell's council of state, and the sonnet on the massacres of the Waldensians, which commemorated, in effect, a triumph for Cromwellian foreign policy. 'Lycidas' retains the headnote first included in 1645, 'And by occasion foretells, the ruine of our corrupted Clergie then in their height'. But the poems to Vane, Cromwell, and Fairfax are absent.

The collection differs presentationally from its precursor, in ways that reflect shifts in the publishing industry. Moseley had been a pathfinder in the publication of creative writing by living authors. The 1645 edition of the minor poems came with his introduction. Moreover, lest Milton be confused with a hack writer publishing for immediate gain, it includes a letter to the author from Sir Henry Wotton, and the aristocratic entertainments came with notes on their precise provenance, including, in the case of 'A Masque', the aristocratic cast list. Dring publishes in an age in which Dryden's usual publisher at the time, Henry Herringman, held the eminence Moseley himself had achieved; to him, publication of the poems and plays of living writers, and pre-eminently Dryden himself, suggested no hint of the stigma that such activities once perhaps carried. Milton's 1673 collection does retain as a prefix to the Latin poems the commendatory Latin and Italian verse of his academician friends, but the other metatextual material is omitted.

The addition of *Of Education* seems initially curious, since without it this was already a substantial publication and it needed no makeweight. However, the first edition of the little tract, privately published and circulated, had probably acquired only a very limited readership, principally among Hartlib's acquaintance. In the context of the early 1670s, its reissue was a timely contribution to renewed interest in godly pedagogy as dissenter communities, sensing the changes in the political climate towards greater toleration, considered how best to educate children excluded from the universities.[98] Indeed,

Charles Morton's academy at Newington Green, where Daniel Defoe would be educated, was established no later than 1675, and he may have been running an educational establishment as early as 1672.[99]

Milton's final prose work is *A Declaration, or, Letters Patent*, an English translation of the Latin version of the formal announcement of the election to the Polish throne of Jan III Sobieski. It shows, rather like *Of True Religion*, that Milton was prepared to engage tactically with the developing political crisis of the regime, and further marks his return to the role of political activist. Indeed, the document presents an account of a monarchical constitution in operation. But it serves to show that kingship can be organized on more than one model, and that the principle of heredity, the basis of James's heir-apparency, is not the only option. Crucially, the Polish monarchy was elective from among a ruling caste. It could be argued that a similar mechanism was finally operated in 1688 at the point at which the grandees of English politics decided James II should be ousted, and William of Orange, with his wife Anne, should be installed. The publisher was Brabazon Aylmer, a young bookseller fairly new to the trade, who also published Milton's *Epistolae Familiares* and the *Brief History of Muscovia*.[100]

In the event, 1674 was to be the last of Milton's life. John Dryden, who had worked with Milton in the late 1650s, secured permission from Milton to produce a rimed version of *Paradise Lost* that could be used for a dramatic performance, and on 17 April it was registered as *State of Innocence*. The new Theatre Royal opened in Drury Lane in 1674, and Dryden may well have intended his adaptation to take advantage of the improved facilities the venue offered for the staging of operatic spectaculars.[101] In the event what Dryden wrote proved too expensive to stage: 'The first Scene represents a Chaos, or a confus'd Mass of Matter, the Stage is almost wholly dark: A symphony of Warlike Music is heard for some time, then from the Heavens (which are opened) fall the rebellious Angels wheeling in the Air, and seeming transfix'd with Thunderbolts: The bottom of the Stage being opened, receives the Angels.'[102] Plainly, the epic poet enjoys some advantages over the playwright in the depiction of such events. Nevertheless, the work enjoyed considerable success once it was printed in 1677, going through nine editions, no doubt far outselling *Paradise Lost*, though in the process perhaps doing something to raise the profile of Milton's work.

Dryden's reworking rewards study. It demonstrates his extraordinary prosodic facility; turning Milton's blank verse into couplets seems to come easily: 'That's worth our fall; thus low tho' we are driven, | Better to Rule in Hell, than serve in Heaven.'[103] His omissions are informative. The actions which in Milton are performed by the godhead are attributed to angels; God remained excluded from dramatic representation. Dryden strips out the scholarly allusiveness of the original. Vallombrosa disappears, leaving the fallen angels merely 'like scatter'd Leaves in Autumn'.[104] In part, such changes reflect the shift of genre: opera should be immediately understandable. But it points, too, to Dryden's sense of shifting cultural preferences and the emergence of a cooler and perhaps more elegant literary discourse. Unsurprisingly, he also strips out all the subversive and encoded republican and anticlerical sentiment. In a curious irony, he dedicates his opera to Mary of Modena, since 1673 Duchess of York, and he accompanies it with an epistle dedicatory that is fulsome even by his own standards. Milton's name, tactfully, is missing from the title page and the epistle. But Nathaniel Lee's prefatory poem alludes to the origins of Dryden's project. Inevitably, Milton is disadvantageously compared: Milton 'roughly drew, on an old fashion'd ground, | A Chaos, for no perfect World was found, | Till through the heap, your [Dryden's] mighty Genius shin'd'. Dryden himself prefixes the opera with a scholarly and astute defence of 'Heroique Poetry and Poetique Licence', and, though he mainly draws his examples from Homer and Virgil, Milton, too, is defended, particularly from the charge of overreaching himself in his choice of theme.[105] For all its guardedness, *The State of Innocence* marks a stage in Milton's rehabilitation with a wider reading public unsympathetic to his political beliefs. Tories, too, could admire his epic, at least after his death.

In May 1674 Milton published a volume containing a collection of thirty-one private letters (*Epistolae Familiares*) and the Latin Prolusions that he had delivered while a student in Cambridge. On 1 June his daughter Deborah married a weaver called Abraham Clarke in Dublin;[106] Deborah's sisters had not heard about the wedding before their father died, so it seems unlikely that Milton had been told of it. Some estrangement had presumably occurred.

Around 6 July a second edition of *Paradise Lost* was published by Samuel Simmons, under the terms of the original contract he had agreed with Milton. Evidently, the first edition was sold out and he correctly judged there to be a strong enough market for a second. The title page carries the statement, 'The Second Edition | Revised and Augmented by the same Author', with the first three words in a heavy Gothic font. Presumably Simmons entertained the aspiration of attracting some trade from customers who had already bought the first edition. Little is really different between the two versions of the poem. The second edition introduces thirty-seven substantive variants, comprising, in the judgement of Alastair Fowler, 'eight where it [1667] is superior and thirteen where *1667* is inferior with sixteen indifferent'. There are about 800 places where the editions disagree in spelling or punctuation. Currently, there is no convincing evidence that someone—the obvious candidate would be Edward Phillips, who saw the first edition through the press and attended to such details and who was probably living in London at the time—oversaw the systematic emendation of these accidentals.[107] However, the second edition does some tidying up, distributing the headnotes to the start of the appropriate books, and absorbing (while sometimes forgetting) errata.

The second edition is prefaced by two poems, 'In Paradisum Amissam [sic] Summi Poetae Johannis Miltoni' and 'On Paradise Lost'. The former, signed '*S. B. M. D.*', is usually ascribed to Samuel Barrow. His otherwise unknown connection with Milton raises fascinating questions. He had a double career, as a distinguished physician and as judge-advocate, first of Monck's army in Scotland, and he later held the same post 'to the first permanent establishment of guards'. More significantly, he was a close confidant of Monck in the crucial period before the Restoration, and thereafter he became a physician to the king. His recent biographer speculates that he may have been among those who helped Milton to escape retribution.[108] He published no other Latin verse that is known, and while his poem is a gentlemanly exercise it throws little light on the reception of the epic. It does, however, make clear that for Barrow the core of the epic was the war in heaven in Book 6; this is not a judgement that many modern readers would be likely to make.

The vernacular poem, signed only with initials, is by Marvell. It apparently indicates that even he had reservations about the scope of the subject and the choice of unrhymed verse, on the basis of which he turns a measured compliment; Milton's triumph satisfied his anxieties on both points. The comments indicate that the prosodic innovation, which had prompted Simmons to include an explanation of the verse in some issues of the first edition, still struck some contemporaries as challenging. Moreover, he corroborates Dryden's admission, in the essay which accompanied *The State of Innocence* when it was eventually printed, that Milton's ambitious depiction of divine events attracted some contemporary criticism.

Marvell's poem approaches sibling rivalry in its gratuitous and mean-spirited attack on Dryden. Milton, as he acceded to Dryden's request for permission to adapt *Paradise Lost* for the stage, alluded to its transposition into heroic couplets as the prosodic equivalent of 'tagging' his verse.[109] Presumably, Milton, sportively but a little demeaningly, meant that, by forming couplets which tied together the ends of the lines, Dryden behaved as a serving man behaved when he tied together the pieces of ribbon used to hold together his master's hose and doublet. Marvell combines the disdainful term with an allusion to Dryden as 'Bayes', the character recently created to ridicule him on the stage in *The Rehearsal*, by the second duke of Buckingham, to whom Marvell contemporaneously looked for patronage:

> Well mightest thou [Milton] scorn thy readers to allure
> With tinkling rhyme, of thy own sense secure;
> While the town-Bayes writes all the while and spells,
> And like a pack-horse tires without his bells;

Their fancies like our bushy-points appear,
The poets tag them, we for fashion wear.[110]

The most noticeable difference is the restructuring into twelve books through the division of books seven and ten of the first edition, and the addition of brief transitional passages at the start of books eight and twelve of the second edition. Milton's motives remain a matter of speculation. At the most mundane, books six and ten were the longest of the first edition and, at 1,290 and 1,423 lines respectively, they exceed the length of books in the epics of Homer and Virgil. Both books are episodic and their later division poses no challenges to their narrative coherence. The twelve-book structure mirrors that of Virgil's *Aeneid*, and may indicate a wish to insist on comparison with the transcendent achievement of classical Rome. As such, it could also mark a direct challenge to Dryden, who had laboured to make the Virgilian idiom so much his own mode of celebrating the reign of Charles II.[111]

The last books published in Milton's lifetime, the second edition of *Paradise Lost* and his collected Latin letters, the *Epistolae Familiares* appeared in July 1674, concluding the remarkable period of his life which had been ushered in by the first edition of his great epic. Projects on which he had toiled for decades were finally accomplished—his brilliant, playful (though, even now, critically undervalued) *History of Britain* and perhaps *Samson Agonistes*, while *Paradise Lost* itself was set into its definitive form. His revised and extended second edition of his shorter poems both reminded new generations of his achievements as a poet in the Jacobean and Caroline eras and demonstrated how he had continued to innovate within those minor genres, while *Paradise Regained* showed that his boldness in developing literary forms remained undimmed. The republication of *Of Education* confirmed his commitments to educational reform in a period as replete with opportunity as had seemed the case when Hartlib and friends had strutted the English intellectual stage. He confirmed his status as a pedagogic innovator by making public his textbooks on logic and on teaching and learning Latin, while the collection of letters displayed to a more sceptical and in some ways more introverted England a little of the social conduct and inner life of an old-style humanist and scholar, while his Prolusions revealed that wit and verve were not opposed to learning.

But these were years, not only of retrospection, but also of a renewed engagement with political activism. As his late works of controversial prose demonstrate, whatever inhibitions or undertakings had kept him silent on the political crises since 1660 no longer restrained him as he eased his way, cautiously and guilefully, into the ranks of the opponents of the current regime. By November 1674 Milton had at least six publications in print and advertised for sale.[112] The *History of Britain* was priced at 6*s.*, *Of True Religion* at 3*d.*, *Poems* and *Paradise Regained with Samson Agonistes* each at 2*s.* 6*d.*, *Accedence* at 8*d.*, *Artis Logicae* at 2*s.*, *Epistolarum Familiarum* at 1*s.*, and *Of True Religion* at 3*d.* As a poet and scholar, he strode the sunlit uplands, fulfilled in his ambitions; as an old republican, perhaps he reminded himself that the race is not always to the swift, nor the battle to the strong, that the Good Old Cause was not dead but sleeping.

The creative, scholarly, and polemical achievements were premised on a domestic stability, unbroken by death among his closest family. His third marriage underpinned the coping strategies he had developed in order to live with his blindness. His youngest daughter, Deborah, had left the family home to marry a weaver; her absence was perhaps unlamented.[113] The move to Artillery Walk had proved congenial, and he continued to be lionized by a succession of admiring visitors, and served by friends and informal pupils, who read to him and wrote for him at his behest. Two great projects remained incomplete. He had interrupted his work of systematic theology many years before, nor had the Latin dictionary, for which he had collected material over decades of reading, reached anything like a fit state to send to the press.[114]

His final illness came quite suddenly. In late July 1674, he had made a nuncupative will. This was an oral declaration, duly witnessed, to his brother, whom he appointed his executor, in which he made provision for the distribution of his estate.[115] It is unclear why he adopted this procedure. Seventeenth-century wills are often elaborate professions to the faith and beliefs of their makers. Perhaps Milton, unconvinced of the imminence of his own end, was reluctant to set time aside for such an avowal. Perhaps, since his brother was evidently acting as his legal adviser, a sensitivity to their ideological and theological differences inhibited him. The simplest explanation, however, is that suddenly Milton was indeed seriously ill, and he knew it. Urgency would then have prompted the declaration he made. In early modern England about half of wills proved in court were drawn up shortly before death, and nuncupative wills were a frequent accompaniment to the deathbed scene.[116]

Yet, whatever that alarm, Milton evidently recovered. Early biographers describe his death with tantalizing inadequacy of detail from a diagnostic perspective. Cyriack Skinner notes, 'Hee dy'd in a fitt of the Gout, but with so little pain or Emotion, that the time of his expiring was not perceiv'd by those in the room'. Aubrey has it that 'He died of the gowt struck in the 9th or 10th of Novemb. as appears by his Apothecaryes Booke.'[117] We are unclear whether he cites the evidence of the apothecary to confirm the date of death or the putative cause. Milton, as his early biographers note, had long suffered from gout, and had endured it patiently. It occurs often as a concomitant of kidney disease. However, it is unlikely that he succumbed to chronic renal failure, as this would have been preceded by prolonged and clinically overt illness. In fact, since all causes of death associated with gout would almost certainly be the end stage of a chronic and progressive illness, his cause of death is probably not related to the history of gout.

The passage from Skinner suggests some circumstances that would go against the final illness being a chronic one. Descriptions of death in early modern England are profoundly shaped by a strict decorum and associated tropes. If Milton had died in bed, the deathbed scene would almost certainly have figured in the account.[118] Milton was evidently in a room, presumably his sitting room, in the company of others who were not particularly attentive to him. This is not a death watch, a last pious vigil, at a bedside.

Sudden death due to a heart attack or dissecting aortic aneurysm is usually accompanied by excruciating pain of a kind that could not go unnoticed by the people with him. Sudden death due to painless causes could include massive pulmonary embolus, stroke or cardiac arrhythmia; however, he had no known risk factors for these conditions. We are drawn to a new hypothesis, that death came as a consequence of a massive and undetected gastrointestinal haemorrhage, such as could be caused by a peptic ulcer eroding into an artery. Besides gout, Milton's other chronic complaints certainly included abdominal discomfort and bloating, consonant with underlying peptic ulcer disease.[119]

The last years had been ones of frantic, brilliant achievement, and he had lived them as if to exemplify another text of Ecclesiastes, 'Whatsoever thy hand findeth to do, do it with thy might; for there is no work, nor device, nor knowledge, nor wisdom, in the grave, whither thou goest.'

VI

1674 and after

CHAPTER 18

Posthumous Life and *Nachlass*

❧

MILTON died on the night of 9–10 November 1674. He was buried beside his father near the altar in St Giles Cripplegate on 12 November. The significance of burial in a conformist church is difficult to ascertain, especially as it is not clear whether the choice was Milton's or that of one of his surviving relatives. Bunhill Fields, the cemetery of puritan England, might have been a more fitting and convenient choice; Milton's home was almost opposite it. But the timing made interment there less likely than would have been the case a few years later. Cartloads of bones from the charnel house in St Paul's churchyard had been buried there in 1549, and in 1665 it was decided to use the site for a plague pit. A brick wall and gates were constructed to define the area, but in the event plague victims seem not to have been buried there. There is no evidence that the ground has ever been consecrated, and nonconformists eventually realized that they could inter their dead there without the rites of the Book of Common Prayer. Dissenters began to take advantage of this loophole in the 1680s, when prominent figures such as John Owen and John Bunyan were buried there. Milton died too soon for Bunhill Fields to be appropriate. In any case, there is no evidence to link Milton with any dissenting group. As Toland recorded, Milton 'was not a profest Member of any Sect among Christians, he frequented none of their Assemblies, nor made use of their particular Rites in his Family'.[1]

Two early biographers comment on Milton's funeral. Edward Phillips records that he

had a very decent interment according to his Quality, in the Church of St *Giles Cripplegate*, being attended from his House to the Church by several Gentlemen then in Town, his principal wellwishers and admirers.[2]

The phrase 'according to his Quality' indicates Milton's standing as a gentleman, which determined the protocols to be observed at his funeral. Toland notes (as does the parish register) that Milton was buried in the chancel (another indicator of social standing) and emphasizes the size of the funeral procession:

48. St Giles Cripplegate, London.

All his learned and great Friends in London, not without a friendly concourse of the Vulgar, accompany'd his Body to the Church of S. Giles near Cripplegate, where he lies buried in the Chancel.[3]

Milton's interment beside his father moved Cyriack Skinner to invoke the language of the Bible to say that he 'had this Elogy in common with the Patriarchs and Kings of Israel that he was gathered to his people'.[4]

These funereal sentiments were soon swept aside by a family dispute about Milton's will. A few months before his death Milton had dictated a nuncupative will with the help of his brother Christopher. Such wills (which were abolished in 1837 except for the military on active service) were declared orally and proved by the evidence of witnesses. On 23 November 1674, a fortnight after Milton's death, his brother Christopher wrote the will as he recalled it, and then read it to Elizabeth Fisher (John Milton's maidservant) to ensure that their recollections concurred before lodging it with the Prerogative Court of Canterbury at Doctors' Commons.[5] Christopher later testified that he had met Milton's widow in the chamber of Sir Thomas Exton, an advocate at Doctors' Commons, and that he had lent her two half-crowns. Clearly she was short of money, so she moved quickly to have Milton's will proved in order that probate might be granted. The Court required assurance that the will was valid, and therefore called for statements of affirmation and objection; the terms of the will, which left his estate to the disposal of

Milton's 'loving wife' and nothing to his 'unkind children', clearly invited both. The two daughters in England (Anne, who was described as 'lame, and almost helpless', and Mary) hired a solicitor through whom they posed on behalf of all three sisters nine questions ('interrogatories') to the three witnesses to the will (Christopher Milton, Elizabeth Fisher and her sister Mary Fisher). The daughters had caught wind of their stepmother's intention to divide any residue of the estate in excess of £1,000 to Christopher's children, but seemed not to know that their sister Deborah (in Dublin) was now married. The questions that they posed were hardly neutral: at exactly what date and time was the nuncupative will declared? Was the deceased in perfect health? Was he in an angry humour against some or one of his children by his former wife? Did Christopher Milton's family not stand to profit by the will as it had been reported? Christopher replied on 5 December, followed by Elizabeth and Mary Fisher on 15 December.[6]

At this point the documentary trail peters out. It is possible that Sir Leoline Jenkins, the judge of the Prerogative Court, declared the will to be invalid, but there is no record of such a decision. It is equally possible that the four lawyers involved (Christopher Milton, Richard Powell, the Mr Thompson who acted for the widow, and the Mr Clements who acted for the daughters) had a private meeting and hammered out a deal. Whatever the means, the result is clear: probate was not granted, and Elizabeth Milton instead emerged from the court with letters of administration, according to which she was obliged to pay any outstanding debts and then distribute the estate.[7] Had she been granted probate, she would have received the entire estate; under administration, she received two-thirds (one-third as widow and one-third as administrator), and divided the remaining third among the three daughters. They each received £100, which implies that the estate was worth £900 (not £1,500, as Edward Phillips estimated).[8] The discrepancy, which is not negligible, could reflect poor recollection or imperfect information on the nephew's part, or perhaps some of the estate had been disposed of before Milton's death; lawyers have always found ways of presenting the value of estates to the advantage of their clients.

As it was worth less than £1,000 there was nothing for Christopher's children, but as he had never heard his brother make such an undertaking, he was content not to object. In a similarly magnanimous (or practical) spirit, Elizabeth granted to the daughters the dowry debt that her late husband had so scornfully assigned to them. This was a legitimate debt, and she felt that should it ever be repaid, the beneficiaries should be her stepdaughters rather than herself. In another transaction which cannot now be fully understood, Christopher Milton gave a bond of £200 to Richard Powell; its precise purpose is not known, but it seems likely to be related to the unpaid dowry. Powell was a surviving blood relative of Milton's daughters, and so had a duty of care that the family was willing to honour, in the same way that Milton had taken in his nephews when their mother died.[9] On 22 February 1675 Mary signed an agreement ('release') that gave her £100 from Elizabeth Milton, and on the same day her sister Anne made her mark on a virtually identical document; Deborah signed a similar document on 27 March.[10]

Milton's daughter Anne died in childbirth within four years of her father; Mary died, apparently unmarried, at an unknown date between 1681 and 1694; his daughter Deborah died in 1727. The family line ended in the mid-eighteenth century, when Deborah's daughter Elizabeth (Clarke) Foster died in Islington in 1754; another branch of the family, descended through Deborah's son Caleb, ended in Madras at about the same time.[11] By the time of her death in 1727 the widow Elizabeth had returned to her native south Cheshire. She is buried in Nantwich. The inventory of her estate suggests straitened but not impoverished circumstances, nor had she disposed of all her Miltonic memorabilia; it lists among her possessions '2 Books of Paradice'.[12]

Milton's brother Christopher may have converted to Roman Catholicism; if so, that might explain why his daughter Anne described him as 'deceased' on her marriage to a Protestant minister. Such a conversion might also explain why in April 1686 James II appointed him serjeant-at-law (21 April) and baron of the exchequer (24 April) and knighted him (25 April); the following year, on 14 April 1687, Milton was appointed justice of the common pleas with an annual salary of £1,000. This eminence was to be short-lived because Christopher retired, perhaps involuntarily, on 6 July 1688. He had acquired a country home at Rushmere St Andrew, about two miles from Ipswich, and he lived there until his death in 1693. There are now no direct descendants of Milton, but there are collateral descendants, certainly through his sister Anne and possibly through his brother Christopher. Of the orphaned nephews, in whose lives he played so significant a part, Edward died abut 1696 and John no earlier than 1706. Both were prolific minor writers over a wide range of genres, though, except for Edward's life of his uncle, they produced nothing of abiding significance.[13] As for Milton's own mortal remains, they were dug up and parts were sold as mementos by an enterprising sexton in 1790; what was left was reburied within the church.

Milton left a variety of unpublished papers on his death, many of which were scooped up by Daniel Skinner, whose acquisitions included Milton's state papers, his Commonplace Book, the Trinity manuscript, the page now in Texas that contains some juvenilia and *De Doctrina Christiana*. The first of these furtive items to be published was a collection of state papers, though it was not printed from Skinner's collection, which he evidently failed to bring to press and which remained in manuscript. The first edition, *Literae pseudo-senatûs Anglicani Cromwellii reliquorumque perduellium nomine ac jussu conscriptae a Joanne Miltono* ('Letters written by John Milton in the name and by the order of the so-called English parliament of Cromwell and other traitors'), was printed by two different printers (in Amsterdam and Brussels) in October 1676; a preface carefully distances the edition from the politics of the reviled interregnum government by insisting disingenuously that the sole interest of the letters lies in their exemplary Latin style. The *Brief History of Moscovia*, which, as the bookseller Brabazon Aylmer explains in a prefatory note, had been prepared for the press before Milton's death, finally saw publication in 1682.

Many items in the Milton *Nachlass* have been rediscovered in succeeding centuries, but most are only of scholarly interest (such as the Commonplace Book and Skinner's collection of the state papers); a few, such as the manuscripts of projects in classical philology on which Milton was working, have not been recovered. The one work that created a popular sensation when it was discovered was *De Doctrina Christiana*, which was found in November 1823 in the State Paper Office. That discovery, and the story of the travels of the manuscript before it was lodged in the State Paper Office, deserved a book in its own right.[14]

Abbreviations Used in Notes and Bibliography

BL	British Library
BLR	*Bodleian Library Record*
BNYPL	*Bulletin of the New York Public Library*
Burmann	Pieter Burmann (ed.), *Sylloges Epistolarum* (5 vols., Leiden, 1727)
CPW	*Complete Prose Works of John Milton*, gen. ed. Don M. Wolfe (8 vols. in 10, New Haven: Yale University Press, 1953–82)
CSP	John Milton, *Complete Shorter Poems*, ed. John Carey (2nd edn., London and New York: Longman, 1997)
Darbishire	Helen Darbishire (ed.), *The Early Lives of Milton* (London: Constable, 1932)
DBI	*Dizionario Biografico degli Italiani* (62 vols. to date, A–Labriola)
ELR	*English Literary Renaissance*
Grove Art	*The Grove Dictionary of Art*, ed. Jane Turner (34 vols., Oxford: Oxford University Press, 1996)
Grove Music	*The New Grove Dictionary of Music and Musicians*, ed. Stanley Sadie and John Tyrrell (2nd edn., 29 volumes, Oxford: Oxford University Press, 2001)
HistJ	*The Historical Journal*
HLQ	*Huntington Library Quarterly*
HMC	Royal Commission on Historical Manuscripts (subsumed into the National Archive in 2003)
JEGP	*Journal of English and Germanic Philology*
JWCI	*Journal of the Warburg and Courtauld Institutes*
LR	J. M. French (ed.), *The Life Records of John Milton* (New Brunswick, NJ: Rutgers University Press, 1949–58)
Masson	David Masson, *The Life of John Milton: Narrated in Connexion with the Political Ecclesiastical and Literary History of his Time* (7 vols., London: Macmillan, 1859–94)
MLN	*Modern Language Notes*
MP	*Modern Philology*
MQ	*Milton Quarterly*
MRTS	*Medieval and Renaissance Texts and Studies*
MS	*Milton Studies*
N&Q	*Notes and Queries*

NDB	*Neue Deutsche Biographie* (22 vols. to date, A–Schinkel)
ODNB	*Oxford Dictionary of National Biography*
Parker	W. R. Parker, *Milton: A Biography*, ed. Gordon Campbell (2nd edn., Oxford: Clarendon Press, 1996)
Peile	John Peile, *Biographical Register of Christ's College, 1505–1905, and of the earlier foundation, God's House, 1448–1505*, ed. J. A. Venn (2 vols., Cambridge: Cambridge University Press, 1910, 1913)
PBSA	*Publications of the Bibliographical Society of America*
PCC	Prerogative Court of Canterbury
PHSR	*Publications of the Harleian Society, Registers*
PL	John Milton, *Paradise Lost*, ed. Alastair Fowler (2nd edn., London and New York: Longman, 1998)
PMLA	*Publications of the Modern Language Association of America*
PQ	*Philological Quarterly*
PRO	National Archives, Kew (in which the Public Record Office was subsumed in 2003)
RES	*Review of English Studies*
SB	*Studies in Bibliography*
SEL	*Studies in English Literature, 1500–1900*
SR	*A Transcript of the Registers of the Company of Stationers, 1554–1640*, ed. E. Arber (5 vols., London and Birmingham: privately printed, 1875–7, 1894, 1950); *A Transcript of the Registers of the Company of Stationers, 1641–1708*, ed. G. E. B. Eyre and H. R. Plomer (3 vols., London: privately printed, 1913–14)
TCBS	*Transactions of the Cambridge Bibliographical Society*
TMS	Trinity College Cambridge, MS R3.4 (Milton's workbooks, known collectively as the Trinity Manuscript)
WJM	*The Works of John Milton*, gen. ed. F. A. Patterson (18 vols. in 21, New York: Columbia University Press, 1931–8).
YES	*Yearbook of English Studies*

Notes

INTRODUCTION

1. *Letters of State, Written by John Milton...to which is added, An Account of his Life* (London, 1694).
2. Bodleian Library, MS Aubrey 8, fols. 63–8.
3. Bodleian Library, MS Wood D4, fols. 140–4.
4. Anthony Wood, *Athenae Oxoniensis* (2 vols., Oxford, 1691–2); the life of Milton is in the *Fasti Oxoniensis*, 1. cols. 880–4.
5. All most helpfully have been available in a scholarly edition: Helen Darbishire (ed.), *The Early Lives of Milton* (London: Constable, 1932). Darbishire's transcription of the anonymous life (which she attributes to John Phillips rather than Cyriack Skinner) is not always accurate; a better transcription is distributed through the five volumes of French's *Life Records* (see next note).
6. W. R. Parker, *Milton: A Biography*, ed. Gordon Campbell, 2 vols. (1969; 2nd edn., 2 vols., Oxford: Clarendon Press, 1996); J. M. French (ed.), *The Life Records of John Milton* (New Brunswick, NJ: Rutgers University Press, 1949–58), abbreviated hereafter as *LR*.
7. For example, consider the anonymous pamphet called *Théorie de la royauté, d'après la doctrine de Milton* (Paris, 1789), sometimes attributed to Mirabeau.
8. See Tony Davies, 'Borrowed Language: Milton, Jefferson, Mirabeau', in David Armitage, Armand Himy, and Quentin Skinner (eds.), *Milton and Republicanism* (Cambridge: Cambridge University Press, 1995), 254–71, and Christophe Tournu, *Milton et Mirabeau: Rencontre révolutionnaire* (Paris: Edimaf, 2002).
9. Kennedy addressed the issue of his Catholicism in a speech to the Greater Houston Ministerial Association, ringingly delivered on 12 September 1960. The exclusion of Catholics from the British throne was enshrined in the Act of Settlement of 1701, and was confirmed in 1927, when other discriminatory legislation was repealed.'
10. *CPW* 4. 583.

I CHILDHOOD

1. The date and time are recorded in Milton's hand in his family Bible (British Library Add MS 32,310) and confirmed in Milton's horoscope, which was cast some time after the publication of *Eikonoklastes* in October 1649; the horoscope is in the Bodleian Library (Ashmole MS 436, Part I, fol. 119); on the horoscope see Harry Rusche, 'A Reading of John Milton's Horoscope', *MQ* 13 (1979), 6–11.
2. Parish Register, All Hallows Church, Guildhall Library MS 5031; the Register is printed in *PHSR* 43 (1913).
3. In Henry Milton's will he left an estate of £6. 19s. to his wife Agnes, his children Isabel and Richard, and two other relations named Roland and Alice Milton (Oxfordshire

Archives, Wills 182/236); Agnes's will was signed on 9 March 1561 and proved on 14 June 1561 (Oxfordshire Archives, Wills 184/2).

4. Stanton St John is six miles east of Oxford city centre, and less than a mile from Forest Hill, the home of Mary Powell, the first wife of the poet.

5. Shotover Forest was a Royal Forest from the Norman Conquest until 1660, when it was disafforested; it now survives only in vestigial form (e.g. Brasenose Wood and Shotover Hill); rangers enforced forest laws relating to hunting, trespass, and passage through the forest. The information about Richard Milton's occupation comes from Wood (Darbishire, 35); Elizabeth Foster, who was Richard's great-great-granddaughter (granddaughter of the poet through her mother Deborah) told Thomas Birch that Richard Milton was born in France. Parker cleverly triangulates Richard's date of birth and concludes that he was born in the last quarter of 1562. A French birth is possible, but it seems an unlikely time for an English Catholic family to be living in France: the first of the eight civil wars that constitute the Wars of Religion continued from March 1552 to March 1553, and in September 1552 Louis de Bourbon, prince of Condé, had concluded the Treaty of Richmond with England, which agreed to supply (Protestant) troops and finance in return for the temporary possession of Le Havre (then called 'Newhaven' by the English), which would be exchanged for Calais at the cessation of hostilities.

6. On the excommunication see Bodleian MS O.A.P. Oxon.e.11, fol. 182v; on the conviction for recusancy see PRO E377/29d/10.

7. The conversion and disinheritance are attested by Cyriack Skinner, Wood, Edward Phillips and Aubrey (Darbishire, 1, 18, 35, and 50–1).

8. Christopher Brooks, 'Apprenticeship, Social Mobility and the Middling Sort, 1500–1800', in Jonathan Barry and Christopher Brooks (eds.), *The Middling Sort of People: Culture, Society and Politics in England, 1550–1800* (Houndsmill: Macmillan, 1994), 70.

9. Below, 40.

10. Guildhall MS 5370, p. 162.

11. Paul Jeffrey(s) (*c*.1528–83) was a native of East Hanningfield (Essex) who was made free of the Company of Merchant Taylors in 1559. Ellen's maiden name is not known, but there are three possibilities. Francis Peck reported that a letter from Roger Comberbach to William Cowper (15 December 1736) recorded that Sara Milton was a Haughton; she was a Jeffrey, but her mother could have been Ellen Haughton. Second, Edward Phillips reported that Sara Milton was 'of the family of the *Castons*' (Darbishire, 52), so her mother could have been Ellen Caston. Third, Aubrey gave Sara Milton's maiden name as Sara Bradshaw, and recorded at the outset of his account that the poet's 'mother was a Bradshaw' (Darbishire, 1, 8).

12. The possibility that Milton and Bradshaw were relatives might help to explain why Milton chose Bradshaw as his attorney when he was sued by Sir Robert Pye (11 February 1647), and why Bradshaw left Milton £10 in his will (10 December 1655; PRO PROB 11/296/549). In the 19th century Thomas Bradshaw-Isherwood of Marple Hall (Cheshire), the ancestral home of the Bradshaws, reported that his library had once contained a copy of a book by Milton inscribed 'to my cousin Bradshaw'; if the book was *Defensio Secunda*, which Andrew Marvell had presented on behalf of the poet, the inscription may have been in Marvell's hand, as Milton was blind. The evidence is contained in a letter from Marvell to Milton (2 June 1654), of which an 18th-century copy survives in BL Add MSS 4292, fol. 264–264ᵛ.

13. Sir Baptist Hicks (1551?–1629), later Viscount Campden, was a mercer and moneylender; see *ODNB*. A tenement is a portion of a building, tenanted as a separate dwelling.

14. Eton College, MS Records 13; see Noel Blakiston, 'Milton's Birthplace', *London Topographical Record* 19, no. 80 (1947), 6–12 and plates.

15. It is not clear why Milton the elder rented a large cellar, as none of his known business activities required storage facilities on such a scale. Similarly, he had a second property on Bread Street called the Rose, but it is not clear to what use he put it. It is remotely possible that this rather than the Spread Eagle was the family home: Milton's widow told Aubrey that he had been born at the Rose, but Christopher Milton told him that he had actually been born at the Spread Eagle, and Aubrey corrected his note (Darbishire, 1).

16. Little is known of Anne Milton; neither her date of birth nor her date of death is known (though she was certainly dead by 1651). She was twice married, first in 1623 to Edward Phillips (father of Milton's nephews Edward and John Phillips) and then in 1632 to Thomas Agar.

17. The term 'servant' is ambiguous, in that it may refer to apprentices. One such servant, Oliver Lowe, was buried on 9 January 1610 (Parish Register, All Hallows); another, William Bold, witnessed a bond on 2 December 1617 (BL MS Cart. Harl, 112.D.19).

18. Sara Milton was baptized on 15 July 1612 and buried three weeks later, on 6 August. Tabitha Milton was baptized on 30 January 1614 and buried 18 months later on 3 August 1615. Christopher Milton studied law and then became a lawyer and judge; see *ODNB*.

19. John Stow, *A Survey of London*, ed. Charles Lethbridge Kingsford (3 vols., Oxford: Clarendon Press, 1908–27).

20. Bread Street now ends at Cannon Street, but then extended to Thames Street, below which lanes led to the river.

21. For a checklist of the elder Milton's business transactions, see Parker, 689–93 (to 1625) and 735–7 (1625–32).

22. Peter Earle, 'The Middling Sort in London', in Barry and Brooks (eds.), *The Middling Sort*, 152.

23. Anne Milton, the scrivener's daughter and the poet's elder sister, was married on 22 November 1623 at a service conducted by the rector of St Stephen Walbrook, Thomas Myriell, apparently her father's musical friend of that name.

24. Darbishire, 12.

25. PRO E112/221/1215 and E125/27 fols. 199–200; the originals are in the National Archives, and were found because Herbert Berry noticed transcriptions in the Huntington Library. See his 'The Miltons and the Blackfriars Playhouse', *MP* 89 (1992), 510–14.

26. *ODNB*.

27. Glynne Wickham, Herbert Berry, and William Ingram (eds.), *English Professional Theatre, 1530–1660* (Cambridge: Cambridge University Press, 2000), 522–3.

28. Lines 131–4, *CSP* 143.

29. See Gordon Campbell, 'Shakespeare and the Youth of Milton', *MQ* 33 (1999), 95–105.

30. Murray Tolmie, *The Triumph of the Saints: The Separate Churches of London 1616–1649* (Cambridge: Cambridge University Press, 1977), 7–12.

31. Kenneth Fincham, 'Introduction', in Kenneth Fincham (ed.), *The Early Stuart Church, 1603–1642* (Houndmills: Macmillan, 1993), 12; he is quoting Nicholas Tyacke.

32. The church was destroyed in the Great Fire, and rebuilt to Wren's design (1680–4); Wren's church was demolished in 1877.

33. On Stock (*c.*1569–1626) see *ODNB*. The curates whose names appear in the Parish Register were [Henry?] Shaw (*c.*1617–18), [William?] Skepper (1619), Phineas Cockraine (1620–3), Nathaniel Stock (1623) and Brian Walton (1624–8); Walton (see *ODNB*), who rose to become bishop of Chester, was the compiler of the *Biblia Sacra Polyglotta* (6 vols., 1654–7), a project which Milton seems to have supported by bringing Walton's proposal for the project to the Council of State (20 July 1652; PRO SP 25/30, 54) and assisting with the importing of paper for the project (9 July 1653; PRO SP 25/70, 32).

34. On Whitaker see *ODNB*; the quotation comes from the *ODNB* article on Stock.

35. On Montagu, Cope and Knollys see *ODNB*; the entry on Stock claims that he was chaplain to 'Sir Anthony Cope of Canons Ashby' but that was the residence of Sir Anthony's cousin Sir Edward Cope.

36. The translation of Whitaker is *An answere to the ten reasons of Edmund Campian* (1606); the sermons are collected as *The Doctrine and Use of Repentance* (1606); the Paul's Cross sermon is *A Sermon preached at Paules Cross the second of November 1606* (1609); the funeral sermon in which Stock thanked the Countess of Bedford was for her brother John Harington of Exton, and was published as *The Churches Lamentation for the Losse of the Godly* (1614). Gataker's funeral sermon is *Abrahams decease* (1627).

37. The Feoffees for Impropriation was a City organization established in 1625 with a view to buying lay impropriations (the rights of laymen to appoint clergy to posts) and using them to appoint puritans to lectureships. The organization was abolished by Laud in 1633.

38. On Jane Paulet, marchioness of Winchester, see below, 57; on Katherine Jones, Viscountess Ranelagh, see below, 267.

39. See R. C. Bald, *John Donne: A Life* (Oxford, 1970), 284. Sir Henry Wotton was a friend of Donne and part of the same circle (he had, for example, stayed with Casaubon in Geneva), and it is possible that Donne effected Milton's introduction to Wotton; below, 104.

40. On Young (*c.*1587–1655) see *ODNB* and Edward Jones 'The Wills of Edward Goodall and Thomas Young and the Life of John Milton', forthcoming in *John Milton: 'Reasoning Words'*, ed. Charles Durham and Kristin Pruitt (Selingrove, Pa.).

41. Darbishire, 2.

42. On Patrick Young see *ODNB*. The evidence that this dauntingly learned man taught Milton is a letter of 29 May/ 8 June 1651 from Isaac Vossius to Nicholas Heinsius in which Vossius says that he has learned from his uncle Junius that Milton is a multilingual Latin secretary, not a nobleman but at least a gentleman, and a disciple of Patrick Young (the Latin original is in Burmann, 3. 318). 'Patrick' may be a slip for 'Thomas', Milton's known tutor, but Francis Junius is unlikely to have confused his fellow scholar-librarian Patrick Young with the Smectymnuan Thomas Young, who did not move in such circles. Another piece of evidence (if such it be) is that on 4 March 1645 Milton sent Patrick Young (by then the King's Librarian) a volume containing ten of his tracts; the volume is now in Trinity College Dublin (R.dd.39). If Patrick Young did teach Milton, he may well have provided the letter of introduction to his friend Lukas Holste, the Barberini librarian in Rome (see below, 123).

43. On the portrait see Leo Miller, 'Milton's Portraits: An Impartial Inquiry into Their Authentication' (*MQ* special issue, 1976); on Janssen see *ODNB* (under Johnson) and *Grove Art* (under Jonson van Ceulen, Cornelis, I).

2 ST PAUL'S SCHOOL

1. On the history of St Paul's in the Early Modern period see M. McDonnell, *The Annals of St Paul's School* (privately printed, Cambridge, 1959), 202–20 and M. McDonnell (ed.), *The Registers of St Paul's School, 1509–1748* (privately printed, London, 1977), 117–22.

2. Darbishire, 53 and 10. Christopher does not say that the school was St Paul's, so it is possible that he was referring to a school in Essex to which his brother may have been sent at an earlier stage.

3. *CPW*, 4. 612.

4. Darbishire, 10.

5. The number was chosen because Jesus pulled 153 fish from the sea; it had the additional attraction of being the lowest of four (the others are 370, 371 and 407) narcissistic numbers known to be the sum of the cubes of each of its digits ($1^3 + 5^3 + 3^3 = 1 + 125 + 27 = 153$) and a triangular number (it is the sum of the first seventeen integers). In the description that Erasmus gave in 1521, there were to be nine forms of seventeen pupils each, but by the late 16th century the catechumens had been merged with the first form of the grammar school, and upper forms had more pupils than the lower. See T. W. Baldwin, 'Number of Forms in Paul's Grammar School', Appendix III of *William Shakespere's Small Latine & Lesse Greeke* (2 vols., Urbana: University of Illinois Press, 1944), 2. 702–5.

6. The poor used tallow instead of beeswax, which was expensive. Tallow candles are smoky and smelly, but beeswax candles burn clean. The rule remained in effect till 1820.

7. In 1602 the merger of the class of catechumens with the first form of the grammar school was recognized when the chaplain officially became known as the under-usher, and taught both catechism and accidence to the first-year boys ('petties').

8. On Gil the elder and Mulcaster see *ODNB*; Wood, *Athenae Oxoniensis* 2. 597–600.

9. If he began earlier, Milton would have studied Ovid's *Tristia* in the third form (1619), and in the fourth form (1620) would have read more Ovid (*Epistles* and *Metamorphoses*), with Caesar for history (especially warfare).

10. On the syllabus and teaching methods see Donald Clark, *John Milton at St Paul's School* (New York: Columbia University Press, 1948); Foster Watson, *The English Grammar Schools to 1660* (Cambridge: Cambridge University Press, 1908); Baldwin, op. cit.

11. It is possible that the event, or Gil's comparison of the collapse of the chapel to Samson's destruction of the arena, coloured the conclusion of Milton's *Samson Agonistes*; see Leo Miller, 'On Some Verses by Alexander Gil which John Milton Read', *MQ* 24 (1990), 22–5.

12. Anthony Milton, *Catholic and Reformed: The Roman and Protestant Churches in English Protestant Thought 1600–1640* (Cambridge: Cambridge University Press, 1995), 42–3.

13. Thomas Cogswell, *The Blessed Revolution: English Politics and the Coming of War, 1621–1624* (Cambridge: Cambridge University Press, 1989), 6–9.

14. Below, 35.

15. On Charles and Theodore Diodati see *ODNB*. The standard work on the English branch of the family is Donald Dorian's *The English Diodatis* (New Brunswick, NJ: Rutgers University Press, 1950).

16. See below, 49.
17. See *ODNB* under Evelyn, John (1655–1699).
18. On the ages of Oxford undergraduates during this period, see Stephen Porter, 'University and Society', in *Seventeenth-Century Oxford* (vol. 4 of *The History of the University of Oxford*), ed. Nicholas Tyacke (Oxford: Clarendon Press, 1997), 54–7.
19. *Camdeni insignia* (Oxford, 1624), Sig E4^r.
20. For a detailed comparison of the two psalm paraphrases with Sylvester's Du Bartas (in the 1621 folio edition) see Charles Dunster, *Considerations on Milton's Early Reading* (London, 1800), 16–32.
21. Cit. Susan Snyder in her *ODNB* entry on Sylvester.
22. Snyder notes that Dryden in his dedication of *The Spanish Fryar* to Lord Haughton (1681) records the reversal in his own sensibility: 'I remember, when I was a boy, I thought inimitable Spencer a mean Poet, in comparison of Sylvester's Dubartas: and was rapt into an ecstasie when I read these lines: "Now, when the Winter's keener breath began | To Chrystallize the Baltick Ocean; | To glaze the Lakes, to bridle up the Floods, | And periwig with Snow the bald-pate Woods". I am much deceiv'd if this be not abominable fustian.'
23. See George C. Taylor, *Milton's Use of Du Bartas* (Cambridge, Mass.: Harvard University Press, 1934).
24. Lines 1–4, *CSP* 7.
25. Wilkes' setting was first printed in *Hymns Ancient and Modern* (1861), in which the Monkland tune is also used for Sir Henry William Baker's 'Harvest'. Milton's hymn (with the Monkland tune) now appears in the hymnals of the Anglican communion (e.g. *The Hymnal (1982)* of the American Episcopal Church) and in those of other Protestant denominations (e.g. the *Baptist Hymnal*, the *Lutheran Book of Worship* and the *Presbyterian Hymnal*).
26. The Latin name of Battista Spagnoli (1447–1516); his name in Latin and Italian (Il Mantovano) refers to his birthplace, Mantua. He was a Carmelite friar with a prodigious literary output that includes eclogues, narrative poems, and religious verse; Erasmus proclaimed him as the 'Christian Virgil'.
27. See Harris Fletcher, 'Milton's *Apologus* and its Mantuan Model', *JEGP* 55 (1956), 230–3 and Estelle Haan, 'Milton, Manso and the Fruit of that Forbidden Tree', *Medievalia et Humanistica* 25 (1998) 75–92.
28. In English Renaissance verse, the best-known example of the metre is Sidney's 'O sweet woods, the delight of solitariness' (in the *Arcadia*); the standard modern example is Auden's 'In due season'.
29. On Ravenscroft and Lane see *ODNB*. On Milton's sonnet to Lane and Lane's response see Campbell, 'Shakespeare and the Youth of Milton'.
30. Parish Register, St Stephen, Walbrook, Guildhall Library MS 8319; the register is printed in *PHSR* 69 (1919).
31. The marriage settlement, dated 17 November, was witnessed by (among others) John Milton the younger and his mother Sara (Morgan Library, New York, MS MA 953); this is the earliest recorded signature of Milton and the only recorded signature of his mother.
32. Their parish church was St Martin in the Fields, where their first child, a boy called John, was baptized on 16 January 1625. This John Phillips died on 15 March 1629; his better-known namesake was probably born in October 1631.

33. Peter Earle, 'The Middling Sort in London', in Barry and Brooks (eds.), *The Middling Sort*, 143–5.

3 CAMBRIDGE: THE UNDERGRADUATE YEARS

1. As Aubrey (probably on the authority of Christopher Milton) and Edward Phillips stated independently that Milton went up to Cambridge at the age of 15, it is possible that he had already been in residence for several months before he was formally admitted to the College on 12 February.
2. On Chappell see *ODNB*; the reference to the university disputation in which Chappell is said to have 'got the better of King James' in 1624 is an error that may originate in Thomas Fuller's account; the disputation took place during the visit of the king in 1615.
3. On Preston and Ussher see *ODNB*.
4. Masson, 1. 129; on Richard Thomson, who had been born in the Netherlands and had met Arminius, see *ODNB*.
5. See Christopher Brooke, 'Chambers', in Victor Morgan, with Christopher Brooke, *A History of the University of Cambridge*, vol. 2, *1546–1750*, (Cambridge: Cambridge University Press, 2004), 32–7.
6. The Great Bed of Ware, now in the Victoria and Albert Museum, could accommodate up to fifteen sleepers at the White Hart Inn.
7. In descending order of size, Trinity, St John's, Christ's, Emmanuel, Queens', Gonville and Caius, Clare Hall, Peterhouse, Pembroke, King's, Sidney Sussex, Corpus Christi, Jesus, Magdalene, Catharine Hall, and Trinity Hall.
8. N. Goose, 'Household Size and Structure in Early-Stuart Cambridge', *Social History* 5 (1980), 347–85.
9. The semi-circular channel known as the King's Ditch left the River Cam near what is now Mill Lane and re-entered it near Magdalene College; its course took it by Christ's College down what is now Hobson Street.
10. The master was Thomas Bainbridge (*ODNB*). The Fellows, in order of seniority, were William Power, William Siddall, William Chappell (*ODNB*), Joseph Mede (*ODNB*), John Knowsley, Michael Honywood (*ODNB*), Francis Cooke, Nathaniel Tovey (*ODNB*), Arthur Scott, Robert Gell (*ODNB*), John Alsop, John Simpson, and Andrew Sandelands. On those not in *ODNB*, see Parker (727), and John Peile, *Biographical Register of Christ's College, 1505–1905, and of the Earlier Foundation, God's House, 1448–1505*, ed. J. A. Venn (2 vols., Cambridge: Cambridge University Press, 1910, 1913). Andrew Sandelands and Milton were to re-establish contact in 1653; see below, 248.
11. Anthony Milton, *Catholic and Reformed: The Roman and Protestant Churches in English Protestant Thought, 1600–1640* (Cambridge: Cambridge University Press, 1995), 119.
12. See Brooke, in Morgan, *History of University of Cambridge*, 32–58.
13. 'Johannes Milton. Londiniensis filius Johannis institutus fuit in literatū elementis sub Mᵗᵒ Gill Gymnasij Paulini præfecto. Admissus est pensionarius minor. ffeb. 12. 1624. sub Mᵗᵒ Chappell. Soluitqz pro ingressu ... 10ˢ.' The year is stated as 1624 because of the convention that the year started in 25 March.
14. Robert Pory (*ODNB*) was to stay on at Cambridge for his BD (1634), serving as Burrell Lecturer in Rhetoric (1634–9). He married the niece of Bishop William Juxon (*ODNB*), who promptly presented him for the rectorship of St Margaret, New Fish Street Hill

(London). He was 'sequestered on the basis of allegations that he had taught Arminian doctrines, and had refused to read parliamentary declarations before deserting his cure' (*ODNB*). After the Restoration he became archdeacon of Middlesex; he is not known to have maintained contact with Milton, though Henry Oxinden (*ODNB*), who was later to comment on Milton's blindness, was known to both.

15. Thomas Baldwin, Thomas Chote, William Jackson, Robert Pory, Roger Rutley, Philip Smith; see Peile, *Biographical Register*.

16. The other was Edmund Barwell (d. 1667), descendant and namesake of a former Master of Christ's; see Peile, *Biographical Register*.

17. W. T. Costello, *The Scholastic Curriculum of Early Seventeenth Century Cambridge* (Cambridge, Mass.: Harvard University Press, 1958).

18. Nicholas Tyacke (ed.), *The History of the University of Oxford*, vol. 4, *Seventeenth-Century Oxford* (Oxford, Clarendon Press, 1997).

19. Victor Morgan with Christopher Brooke, *A History of the University of Cambridge*, vol. 2, *1546–1750* (Cambridge, Cambridge University Press, 2004).

20. The plague of 1625 was, except in terms of the total number of deaths, even more serious than the 'Great Plague' of 1665; see Paul Slack, *The Impact of Plague in Tudor and Stuart England* (2nd edn., Oxford: Oxford University Press, 1990), 150.

21. Masson, I, 162; French, *LR* I. 99. *CPW* evades the problem by mistranslating *anemesetos* as 'with humility' rather than 'without offence'.

22. J. Karl Franson, 'The Diodatis in Chester', *N&Q* 234 (1989), 435. It is possible that the letter is a reply to one in Greek by Diodati (British Library Add MS 5016*; printed in *LR* I. 104–5).

23. *CSP* 19.

24. The best recent study of the four poems is John Hale's 'Praising Dead Worthies, 1626', in Hale's *Milton's Cambridge Latin: Performing in the Genres 1625–1632* (Tempe, Ariz.: 2005), 127–45. See also Thomas N. Corns, 'Milton before "Lycidas" ', in Graham Parry and Joad Raymond (eds.), *Milton and the Terms of Liberty* (Cambridge: D. S. Brewer, 2002), 23–36.

25. On Andrewes, Felton and Gostlin see *ODNB*.

26. Lines 54–5, *CSP* 55.

27. 'Bedell' and 'bedel' are archaic spellings of 'beadle' retained at both Cambridge (where there are two) and Oxford (where there are four). Cambridge distinguished esquire bedells from yeoman bedels; Ridding was the former, and at the time of his death was senior bedell. For an example of the intervention of a Cambridge bedell in a college mastership election in 1635, see Morgan, 381–3. See also H. P. Stokes, 'The Esquire Bedells of the University of Cambridge', *Cambridge Antiquarian Society Publications* 45 (1911), 39, 93–5.

28. The Duke of Buckingham (who was officially informed of his election by Ridding) presented three silver maces for the use of Esquire Bedels during his chancellorship (1626–8); two are pictured in Morgan, *History of University of Cambridge*, 157. See A. P. Humphry, 'On the maces of the Esquire Bedells', *Cambridge Antiquarian Communications* 21 (1881), 207–18.

29. Line 6, *CSP* 27.

30. The term was a priestly title in classical Rome; line 13, *CSP* 27.

31. Milton, *Of Reformation*, *CPW* I. 549. On Mountain (or Montaigne), later Archbishop of York, see *ODNB*.

32. See Hale, *Milton's Cambridge Latin*, 151–8.

33. In the 1645 *Poemata* the poem is said to have been written *anno aetatis 17* ('at the age of 17'). Scholars who believe that Milton's poem is indebted to Phineas Fletcher's *Locustae*, which was printed in Cambridge in 1627, either assume that Milton saw Fletcher's poem in manuscript or that Milton's recollection of his age was wrong, and that his poem should be dated 1627.

34. See Estelle Haan, 'Milton's *In Quintum Novembris* and the Anglo-Latin Gunpowder Epic', *Humanistica Lovaniensia* 41 (1992), 221–95 and 42 (1993), 368–93; on the occasion see Hale, *Milton's Cambridge Latin*, 147–84.

35. Lines 5, 31–2, 223–6, *CSP* 47, 50.

36. Morgan, *History of University of Cambridge*, 129–30.

37. Hale, *Milton's Cambridge Latin*; on disputations see 15–31, and on declamations 67–90.

38. Morgan, *History of University of Cambridge*, 128. The *Spectator* article is in no. 485, Tuesday 16 September 1712.

39. See Donald L. Clark, 'Ancient Rhetoric and English Renaissance Literature', *Shakespeare Quarterly* 2 (1951), 202.

40. J. T. Shawcross, 'The Dating of Certain Poems, Letters and Prolusions written by Milton', *ELN* 2 (1965), 261–6; Leo Miller, 'Milton's Clash with Chappell: A Suggested Reconstruction', *MQ* 14 (1980), 77–87; Gordon Campbell, *A Milton Chronology* (Basingstoke, 1997), 31–41.

41. *PL* 7.31; *PR* 3.50.

42. In *Epistolares Familiares* the letter (no. 1) is mistakenly dated 26 March 1625. In the letter Milton describes a companion poem which must be *Elegia IV*. He dates the poem *anno aetatis 18*, which confirms that the year must be 1627, when Milton was 18; lines 33–8 place the composition of the poem between the vernal equinox (11 March in the Julian calendar) and the beginning of the ancient festival of Chloris on 28 April. The Hebrew Bible is lost.

43. *Patria parens* is unlikely to include Scotland, so Milton must be thinking of Young as an English resident; lines 87–94, *CSP* 60.

44. Lines 71–4; *CSP* 59.

45. On 29 May Milton signed (together with his father) an indenture recording the purchase of property in St Martin the Fields (PRO C54/2715/20); on 11 June he signed an agreement by which his father lent £300 to Richard Powell (see n. 56 below).

46. The accusation in *A Modest Confutation* (London, 1642), sig. A3ᵛ, that Milton had been 'vomited out' of Cambridge may be an allusion to the rustication, but is equally likely to be a hostile way of saying 'graduated'.

47. The letter survives only in printed form (see *LR* 3. 375), so the error whereby Christ's College is called 'Christ Church', which a Cambridge graduate would be unlikely to make, may be transcriptional. Bramhall's papers are in the Hastings papers (his daughter married into the family), and the letter is not listed in the HMC account of Bramhall's correspondence (vol. 78, Report on the Hastings Manuscripts, vol. 4, 55–136), so it must have been removed long before the Hastings manuscripts were acquired by the Huntington Library. On Bramhall see *ODNB*.

48. Below, 240.

49. On Atherton see *ODNB*; on Mede's view of Power, see his denunciation of Power as a 'son of Belial' in his letter of 19 May 1627 to Sir Martin Stuteville (BL Harleian MS 389).

50. Darbishire, 10.

51. Below, 152.

52. In *Bartholomew Fair* I. 2 Jonson's Littlewit refers to the clothes worn in 'Moorfields, Pimlico Path or the Exchange, in a summer evening'. Moorfields (a park since 1606), the Pimlico path in Hoxton and the New Exchange (the shopping arcade opened in the Strand in 1609) were all fashionable places for promenading, as were Lincoln's Inn Fields, Gray's Inn Fields, and the Temple Gardens.

53. Milton was later to date this poem *anno aetatis undevigesimo*, and this unique use of a Latin ordinal number makes it likely that it means 'in his nineteenth year', i.e. 1627, rather than 'at the age of 19', which is what *anno aetatis 19*, his usual formulation, would have meant.

54. Nathaniel Tovey had lived in the Harington household until 1612. Theodore Diodati had been the tutor (*c*.1599–1607) to John Harington (1592–1614, later the second baron), who had travelled to Italy with John Tovey; in 1614 Richard Stock had preached the funeral sermon of Harington (*The Churches Lamentation for the Losse of the Godly*, 1614).

55. On the Powell family see Parker, 866–70 and French, *Milton in Chancery*, 71–99, 167–80. The loan document is PRO C152/61, and the statute staple (which mentions the younger Milton), recorded the same day, is PRO LC4/56.

56. A staple was a designation given to a number of towns and cities (including London) that regulated specified areas of trade and commerce. Courts of the Staple had jurisdiction in pleas concerning debt and covenant; the law applied was the Law Merchant rather than the common law. A statute staple was a bond of record acknowledged in the presence of the Clerk of the Staple, in this case Sir Thomas Hampson; he was still Clerk in 1646 when he endorsed the bond on 15 or 16 December, shortly before Powell's death.

57. Maximum interest rates were fixed by statute; in 1624 the rate was fixed at 8 per cent, and that became the common rate for loans; below, 150.

58. Below, 150.

59. Parish Register, St Martin in the Fields, City of Westminster Archive Centre; printed in PHSR 66 (1936).

60. Milton's nephew Edward Phillips said that the subject of the poem was 'one of his [Milton's] Sister's Children (a Daughter) who died in her Infancy' (Darbishire, 62). The principal objection to the 1628 date is that in the 1673 *Poems*, Milton added the caption '*anno aetatis 17*', which would place the poem between 9 December 1625 and 8 December 1626; such a date would be consistent with the reference to the 'slaughter-ing pestilence' of 1625. If the poem was written in 1626, its subject would not have been Anne, but rather an unidentified child who, as lines 3–5 seem to imply, did not survive a single winter.

61. Lines 71–7, *CSP* 18.

62. The baby, Elizabeth Phillips, was baptized at St Martin in the Fields on 9 April 1628; like her sister, Elizabeth died in infancy, and was buried at St Martin in the Fields on 19 February 1631.

63. An act, in the language of Cambridge, is an academic exercise, which in the seven-teenth century usually took the form of a disputation.

64. On Gell see *ODNB*, where Louise Curth records that 'on 24 August 1658, Matthew Poole, the presbyterian rector of St Michael-le-Querne, told Richard Baxter that he had heard Gell "once or twice & I find him run much upon Arminian and some Popish errours"'. See below 323.

65. John Hale, 'Milton's Philosophic Verses and the Cambridge Act Verses', in Hale's *Milton's Cambridge Latin*, 33–65. On *Naturam* see also Estelle Haan, 'Milton's *Naturam non pati senium* and Hakewill', *Medievalia et Humanistica* 24 (997), 147–67.

66. The letter (*CPW* 1. 313–15) is dated 2 July 1628 in *Epistolae Familiares* (where it is no. 3), but it is possible that it was written on 2 July 1631; see J. T. Shawcross, 'The Dating of Certain Poems, Letters and Prolusions Written by Milton', *ELN* 2 (1965), 261–6.

67. Cambridge University Archives, Supplicats 1627, 1628, 1629, fol. 331. The granting of the BA is recorded in Grace Book Z, 158.

68. In the 1646 *Poemata* Milton dated the poem 'anno aetatis 20', which fixes the date of composition; Parker's remark is on p. 56.

69. *CSP* 92 (Sonnet 1) and 84 (*Elegia Quinta*).

70. Diodati had proceeded MA at Oxford a year earlier, on 8 July 1628. Incorporation is a method of conferring degrees by adoption; see pp. 86–7.

71. The Iceni were the Celtic tribe of Norfolk and north Suffolk; Milton fancifully extends their territory to include Stowmarket. The Poikile ('Painted') Stoa associated with Zeno was in Athens; the villa of Cicero was at Tusculum, near Rome; Caius Atilius Regulus Serranus and Manius Curius Dentatus were Roman farmers who were also consuls.

72. PRO, SP 16/117; on Chillingworth's betrayal of Gil see *ODNB* (s.n. Chillingworth).

73. The Court of Assistants argued that it enjoyed the prerogative to deal with Gil as it judged appropriate. Laud, in defending Gil, appealed to canon law in formulating his view that Gil's bishop would have to be party to any decision to dismiss him. Laud's appeal to canon law not only failed to save Gil from dismissal but also contributed to his own fate, in that it formed the last of the ten supplementary charges brought against him at his trial in 1644.

74. *Records of Early English Drama: Cambridge*, ed. Alan H. Nelson. (2 vols., Toronto, Buffalo, and London: University of Toronto Press, 1989).

75. *An Apology*, *CPW* 1. 887. The meaning of 'atticisme' is not clear; it may simply refer to the rhetorical balancing of the sentence, but more likely alludes to Milton's debt in the passage to the oration of Demosthenes 'On the Crown' (*De Corona*), in which Demosthenes defends himself against vituperative allegations about his private and public life; Andrew Downes had lectured on *De Corona* in 1619, and possibly later.

76. *The Plot Discovered and Counterplotted* (1641). The parallel was first noted by Thomas Kranidas, 'Milton's Trinculo', *N&Q* 26 (1979), 416.

77. On 24 September 1629, for example, the chancellor Henry Rich, earl of Holland, and the French ambassador M. de Chasteauneuf visited Cambridge, and Edmund Stubbe's *Fraus Honesta* was performed. The argument that Milton was present is advanced by Alan Nelson, 'Women in the Audience of Cambridge Plays', *Shakespeare Quarterly* 41 (1990), 335.

78. Below, 322.

79. See Leo Miller, 'Milton's Portraits: An Impartial Inquiry into Their Authentication', special issue of *MQ* (1976), 9–15, 19–25.

4 CAMBRIDGE: THE POSTGRADUATE YEARS

1. Richard Cust, *The Forced Loan and English Politics 1626–1628* (Oxford: Clarendon Press,1987), 185.
2. *ODNB.*
3. Peter Lake, 'The Laudian Style: Order, Uniformity and the Pursuit of the Beauty of Holiness in the 1630s', in Fincham (ed.), *Early Stuart Church*, 161–85 (162).
4. M. H. Curtis, *Oxford and Cambridge in Transition, 1558–1642* (Oxford: Clarendon Press, 1959), 91, 97.
5. See Mordechai Feingold's discussion of modern languages at Oxford in Nicholas Tyacke (ed.), *Seventeenth-Century Oxford* (vol. 4 of *The History of the University of Oxford*, Oxford: Clarendon Press, 1997), 270–5.
6. Stefano Villani, 'The Italian Protestant Church of London in the Seventeenth Century', forthcoming in Barbara Schaff (ed.), *Exiles, Emigres and Go-Betweens: Anglo-Italian Cultural Mediations,* (Amsterdam and New York: Rodopi).
7. The volume is now in the New York Public Library (Rare Book Room *KB 1529). On the marginalia see Maurice Kelley, 'Milton's Dante—Della Casa—Varchi volume', *BNYPL* 66 (1962), 499–504.
8. The phrase *patriis cicutis* is ambiguous. We have assumed, with John Carey ('The Date of Milton's Italian Poems', *RES* 14 (1963), 383–6), that the phrase refers to Italian, Diodati's ancestral language; alternatively, the phrase could refer to Milton's native language, in which case the line may continue the reference to the 'Nativity Ode' or refer to another English poem.
9. Lines 1–2, *CSP* 94.
10. The identification was first made by J. S. Smart in his edition of *The Sonnets of Milton* (Glasgow: Maclehose, Jackson, 1921), 137–44.
11. A *canzone* is an Italian lyric which normally consists of several long stanzas with lines of irregular length and a short concluding stanza called the *commiato* (dismissal). Milton's *canzone* would more accurately be called a *stanza di canzone*, since it consists of only one stanza and a *commiato*.
12. Sonnet 4 lines 11–12, *CSP* 97; *PL* 2. 665.
13. On Shelford, see *ODNB.*
14. Lake, 'Laudian Style', 175.
15. *CSP* 111.
16. Diane McColley, *Poetry and Music in Seventeenth-Century England* (Cambridge: Cambridge University Press, 1997), 196.
17. Thomas N. Corns, ' "On the Morning of Christ's Nativity", "Upon the Circumcision" and "The Passion" ', in Thomas N. Corns (ed.), *A Companion to Milton* (Oxford: Blackwell, 2001), 221.
18. Christopher Hill, *Puritanism and Revolution* (1958; London: Panther, 1969), 313.
19. Above, 28.
20. H. Neville Davies, 'Milton's Nativity Ode and Drummond's "An Hymne of the Ascension" ', *Scottish Literary Journal* 12 (1985), 5–23; Corns, ' "On the Morning" ', *passim*. On Drummond, see *ODNB.*
21. Lines 24–6, *CSP* 105.
22. Lines 227–8, *CSP* 115.

23. Lines 55–6, *CSP* 125.
24. *PL* 12. 411–14.
25. Richard Crashaw, 'Upon the body of Our Bl. Lord, Naked and Bloody', lines 1–4, in *The Poems, English, Latin, and Greek, of Richard Crashaw*, ed. L. C. Martin (2nd edn., Oxford: Clarendon, 1957), 290.
26. Corns, '"On the Morning"', 219.
27. See Gordon Campbell, 'Shakespeare and the Youth of Milton', *MQ* 33 (1999), 95–105.
28. Matricula Studiosorum, in Bibliothèque Publique et Universitaire de Genève, MS fr. 141C (Inv. 345), fol. 9ᵛ.
29. See below 125.
30. The letter (*CPW* I. 316–17) is dated 20 May 1628 in *Epistolae Familiares* (where it is number 2), but it seems to allude to Gil's poem on the fall of 's-Hertogenbosch in September 1629. See Eugenia Chifas, 'Milton's Letter to Gill, May 20, 1628', *MLN* 62 (1947), 37–9, and J. T. Shawcross, 'The Dating of Certain Poems, Letters and Prolusions Written by Milton', *ELN* 2 (1965), 261–6. Sylva-Ducis is the Latin term for 's-Hertogenbosch (French Bois le Duc).
31. On King see *ODNB* and Norman Postlethwaite and Gordon Campbell (eds.), 'Edward King, Milton's Lycidas: Poems and Documents', special issue of *MQ* 28 (December 1994), 77–111.
32. On Hobson (1545–1631) see *ODNB*, on which our account relies; the portrait is owned by the National Portrait Gallery in London and hangs in Montacute House in Somerset.
33. See W. D. Bushell, *Hobson's Conduit: The New River at Cambridge Commonly Called Hobson's River* (1938). The monument to Hobson, originally a fountain in the market, was moved in 1856 to the point at which the conduit crosses Lensfield Road.
34. Milton's second Hobson poem (*incipit* 'Here lieth one') was printed in *A Banquet of Jests* (1640), where it is followed by an unattributed epitaph on Hobson (incipit 'Here Hobson lies'); it was also printed in *Wit Restor'd* (1658), in which Milton's first Hobson poem (incipit 'Here lies old Hobson') also appears.
35. Lines 14–19; *CSP* 128.
36. BL C.60.1.7. On the annotations see Maurice Kelley and Samuel Atkins, 'Milton's Annotations of Aratus', *PMLA* 70 (1955), 1090–106. In the same year Milton is said to have acquired a silver gilt watch (now in the British Museum, Registration no. 1862, 8–1.1) inscribed 'Ioanni Miltoni 1631'. The inscription could be retrospective, but is probably spurious; the maker, William Bunting, was not made free of the Company of Clockmakers until 1647, and the style of the watch is that of the 1650s.
37. Below, 177.
38. BL Sloane MS 1446, fols. 37–8. John Walrond, brother of the colonial administrator Humphrey Walrond (on whom see *ODNB*), was secretary to Francis Willoughby (fifth Baron Willoughby of Parham; see *ODNB*), who had no known connection with Milton, though after the Restoration his daughter Elizabeth married Milton's pupil Richard Jones.
39. Two pieces of evidence are adduced for the traditional date. First, Milton describes himself as the emergency leader of the sophisters, a term that could denote junior sophisters (second-year undergraduates) or a senior sophisters (third-year undergraduates); there is, however, no reason why the sophisters could not be led by a

'bachelor' (i.e. postgraduate); see John Shawcross, *Rethinking Milton Studies: Time Present and Time Past* (Newark, NJ: University of Delaware, 2005), 182 n. 1. Second, Milton dated the English poem 'anno aetatis 19' in 1674, and Milton was 19 in July 1628; this seems likely to be a *lapsus memoriae*.

40. John King may have left after taking his BA in early 1624, but Edward King (later Milton's Lycidas) and his brother Roger were admitted on 9 June 1626, and Henry and Adam King were admitted on 9 June 1631.

41. Milton refers to 'several' geese (*complures*), so two is, strictly speaking, an insufficient number, but the phrase is likely to represent a rhetorical inflation of the numbers.

42. The College 'Accounts, 1622–39' is in the archive of Christ's College, as is the Admissions Book. Data on the students has been gathered by John Peile, *A Biographical Record of Christ's College, 1505–1905, and of the Earlier Foundation, God's House, 1448–1505*, ed. J. A. Venn (2 vols., Cambridge: Cambridge University Press, 1910, 1913).

43. Parker, 740 n. 55; see Gordon Campbell, 'Milton and the Water Supply of Cambridge', in B. Sokolova and E. Pancheva (eds.) *Essays for Alexander Shurbanov* (Sofia, 2001), 38–43, reprinted in revised form in *South African Journal of Medieval and Renaissance Studies* 15 (2006 for 2005), 121–6.

44. The manuscript in the Cambridge University Archives is in the *Acta Curia* (Proceedings of the Vice-Chancellor's Court, VCCt.1.52, fols. 132–3). The two postgraduates were Ewers Gower (BA 1627, later BD) and Richard Buckenham (BA 1629, MA 1632, and so Milton's exact contemporary); the three undergraduates were William Troutback (BA 1632, MA 1635), Henry Bate (matriculated 1628, did not graduate) and Alexander Kirby (BA 1632, MA 1635).

45. The genre was established by Roslyn Richek, 'Thomas Randolph's Salting (1627), its Text, and John Milton's Sixth Prolusion as Another Salting', in *ELR* 12 (1982), 102–31, and has been the subject of detailed study (including an edition) by John Hale in *Milton's Cambridge Latin*, 195–293.

46. Lines 37–42, *CSP* 146.

47. A. Milton, *Catholic and Reformed*, 317.

48. Lines 156–60, *CSP* 151.

49. Lines 161–6, *CSP* 151.

50. *CPW* 3. 552, 558.

51. Parish register, St Martin in the Fields, City of Westminster Archive Centre; printed in *PHSR* 66 (1936). The subversion of government-sponsored heraldic funerals organized by the College of Arms (as in the case of the funeral of Milton's second wife) began with King James, who buried his mother at night. The practice became popular in the 1630s (despite the attempt of the king to stamp it out), partly because private nocturnal funerals were cheaper (the extra fees charged by clergy were amply offset by the savings in sets of mourning clothes), but also because the protocols of heraldic funerals included a requirement that the principal mourner be the same sex as the deceased, which meant that a surviving spouse could not be the principal mourner unless the funeral was held privately at night.

52. The Deputy Clerkship was destined to stay in the family: when Agar died in 1673 he was succeeded by his nephew Thomas Milton (bap. 1647, d. 1694), who was the son of Christopher Milton.

53. The king and queen arrived in Cambridge on 19 March 1632. The plays, both in English, were *The Rival Friends* (by Peter Hausted of Queens') and *The Jealous Lovers* (by Thomas Randolph of Trinity); the Vice-Chancellor was Henry Butts.

54. Cambridge University Archives, Subscr. 1, 377. The granting of the MA is recorded in Grace Book Z, 224.

55. On receiving the MA Milton became a 'regent' or 'regent master', and so had a (wholly fictional) responsibility to lecture as well as study. Regent House, the assembly of regent masters, was the senior executive body of the university, but its decisions could be overturned by the Non-Regent House, which consisted of senior academics who no longer had any obligation to lecture.

5 HAMMERSMITH

1. The Hammersmith depositions in which the elder Milton identifies himself as a resident of Hammersmith are PRO C24/587/46 (14 September 1632), PRO C24/591/2 (17 April 1634), PRO C24/596/33 (5 August 1734), and PRO C24/600/37 (8 January 1635). On the records discovered in 1996 see notes 3 and 4.

2. See *ODNB* s.n. 'Sheffield'; the *ODNB* article does not mention Butterwick House, later Bradmore House, which stood on Broadway, Hammersmith, and was demolished in 1836. In October 1646 Lord Sheffield was buried in the chapel-of-ease that he had founded.

3. Hammersmith and Fulham Record Office, DD/818/56.

4. On the history of Hammersmith and its church see Thomas Faulkner, *The history and antiquities of the parish of Hammersmith: interspersed with biographical notices of illustrious and eminent persons, who have been born, or who have resided in the parish, during the three preceding centuries* (London: Nichols & Son, 1839). See, also, William Laud, *The Works of the Most Reverend Father in God, William Laud* (7 vols. in 9; Oxford: J. H. Parker, 1847–60), 6.

5. Hammersmith and Fulham Record Office, PAF/1/21, fol. 68; the final payment was made on 25 March 1632. The assessments for Hammersmith side for 1633, 1634, and 1635 seem to be lost, but Milton the elder was presumably assessed during those years.

6. Inner Temple Archive, Admissions Book 1571–1640, 593.

7. Cedric Brown, *John Milton's Aristocratic Entertainments* (Cambridge: Cambridge University Press, 1985), 47. Our reading of *Arcades* is indebted to Brown's account.

8. *ODNB* s.n. Spencer, Alice.

9. J. H. Baker, in the *ODNB* entry on Sir Thomas Egerton.

10. Line 108, *CSP* 167.

11. F. R. Fogle, ' "Such a rural queen": The Countess Dowager of Derby as Patron', in F. R. Fogle and L. A. Knafla (eds.), *Patronage in Late Renaissance England* (Los Angeles: William Andrews Clark Memorial Library, University of California, 1983), 3–29.

12. There are *ODNB* articles on Mervin Touchet, James Touchet, George Touchet, and Grey Brydges. There are accounts of the trial in MS in the House of Lords Record Office, The Huntington Library (the Ellesmere MSS and the Hastings MSS), the Leicestershire Record Office (the Braye MSS), the National Library of Scotland, the Northamptonshire Record Office (Finch–Hatton MSS and Isham–Lamport MSS) and the National Archives. Printed accounts of the trial include *The tryal and condemnation of Mervin, Lord Audley Earl of Castle-Haven, at Westminster, April the 5th 1631, for abetting a rape upon his Countess, committing sodomy with his servants, and commanding and countenancing the debauching his daughter* (1699); *The trial of Lord Audley, earl of Castlehaven for inhumanely causing his own wife to be ravished and for buggery* (1679); *The arraignment and conviction of Mervin, Lord Audley, earl of Castle-haven, (who was by 26 peers of the realm found guilty of committing rapine and sodomy) at*

Westminster, on Monday, April 25, 1631 (1642); *The case of sodomy, in the trial of Mervin, Lord Audley, earl of Castlehaven, for committing a rape and sodomy with two of his servants* (1708). The most recent account of the trial is Cynthia Herrup's *A House in Gross Disorder: Sex, Law and the 2nd Earl of Castlehaven* (Oxford: Oxford University Press, 1999).

13. PRO, SP 16/175/2.

14. On Lady Eleanor Davies see *ODNB*.

15. The argument was developed by Barbara Breasted in 'Comus and the Castlehaven Scandal', *MS* 3 (1971), 202–24; for a contrary view see John Creaser, 'Milton's *Comus*: The Irrelevance of the Castlehaven Scandal', *N&Q* 229 (1984), 307–17, reprinted in *MQ* 21 (1987), 24–34. See also Cedric Brown's account (*Entertainments*, 174–8) of the possibility that the scandal may have coloured the editing of the Bridgewater MS of *A Maske*.

16. Quoted by Brown, *Entertainments*, 21.

17. Elizabeth on 14 November, Anne on 30 November.

18. The tradition embodied in several accounts (e.g. the Victoria County History entry on Harefield) that Burbage's company performed *Othello* on the occasion of the queen's visit is based on a Collier forgery in the Egerton papers now at the Huntington Library.

19. Early in 1633 Milton wrote the 'Letter to an unknown friend', in which he describes this sonnet as a 'Petrarchian stanza' which he had composed 'some while since'; December 1632 therefore seems a possible date.

20. *CSP* 153.

21. *CSP* 171. In what may be the earliest manuscript of the poem (Bodleian Ashmole MS 36, 37, fol 22ʳ) Milton entitled the poem 'Upon a clock case, or dyall'; in the Trinity MS he initially called it 'To be set on a clock case' and later changed the title to 'On Time'. On the date of the Ashmole MS see Frederic B. Tromly, 'Milton Responds to Donne: "On Time" and "Death Be Not Proud" ', *MP* 80, no. 4 (May 1983), 390–3.

22. Herrick, 'Another New-yeeres Gift, or Song for the Circumcision', lines 7–9, *Poetical Works*, 367.

23. Milton, 'Upon the Circumcision', lines 26–8, *CSP* 173.

24. Francis Quarles, 'Of our Saviours Circumcision, or New-years day', lines 11–12, in *Hosanna or Divine Poems on the Passion of Christ and Threnodes*, ed. John Horden (Liverpool: Liverpool University Press, 1969), 9. See Thomas Corns, 'On the Morning of Christ's Nativity', in Corns (ed.), *Companion*, 215–31 (at 219–21), for other examples of analogues to Milton's poem.

25. Below, 290.

26. The friend seems to be older than Milton, and may be in holy orders; Milton had visited him the previous day, so he is likely to be based in London rather than Cambridge. Thomas Young might be a candidate, but Milton normally wrote to him in Latin. Another possibility, as Parker observes (783 n. 13) is John Lawson, rector of All Hallows from 1628 to 1642.

27. The letter is printed in *CPW* 1. 318–21; the quoted passage is on 319.

28. *CPW* 3. 319–20.

29. Below, 101.

30. *PL* 3. 365–71.

31. The Lycophron is an edition of *Alexandria* (Geneva, 1601), which Milton bought for 13 shillings, recording the purchase on the flyleaf; it is now in the University of Illinois

(MS /x q821 M64/ BF63+). The Euripides is a collected edition, *Tragoediae quae extant* (2 vols., Geneva, 1602); it is now in the Bodleian Library (Don.d.27, 28). The annotations in the Euripides have been studied by Maurice Kelley and Samuel Atkins, 'Milton's Annotations of Euripides', *JEGP* 60 (1961), 680–7.

32. On the earl of Bridgewater see *ODNB*, s.n. Egerton; on the Council Wales see Caroline Skeel, *The Council in the Marches of Wales* (Cambridge: Girton College, Girton College Studies, 1904).

33. For an argument to the effect that this case is related to Milton's *Masque*, see Leah Marcus in 'The Milieu of Milton's *Comus*: Judicial Reform at Ludlow and the Problem of Sexual Assault', *Criticism* 25 (1983), 193–327; for a contrary view, see Brown, *Entertainments*, 26, where the Evans case is described as 'an instance of [Egerton's] general conscientiousness'.

34. Many details of the progress are drawn from Brown, *Entertainments*, 28–35.

35. On Henry Lawes see *ODNB* and Ian Spink, *Henry Lawes: Cavalier Songwriter* (Oxford: Oxford University Press, 2000); Milton's Sonnet 13 (1646) is dedicated to 'Mr H. Lawes, on his Airs'; see below, 184.

36. On Richard Newport see *ODNB*; Eyton Hall was demolished in 1867, but one of its two banqueting towers survives, and is now rented to tourists; it was in one of these towers that the Egerton family was entertained.

37. On the Myddeltons see *ODNB*; Chirk Castle is now owned by the National Trust.

38. 'Keeper of the rolls', i.e. custodian of the legal records under the commission of the peace; the *custos* was the principal justice of the peace and the principal crown servant of the county. Myddelton much later took part in Booth's uprising; see below, 287.

39. On Salusbury see *ODNB*; for the text of the entertainment see Cedric Brown, 'The Chirk Castle Entertainment of 1634', *MQ* 11 (1977), 76–86.

40. On Sir Roger Mostyn and Robert Cholmondeley, see *ODNB*. Bretton Hall was the home of the Ravenscroft family. Thomas Egerton (later the first Viscount Brackley; see *ODNB*) was the illegitimate son of a landowner and a servant; he spent his childhood with the Ravenscroft family, and married his step-sister Elizabeth, who grew up in the same house. Bachymbyd Fawr, Mostyn Hall, and Cholmondeley Castle are all private houses; Dunham Massey Hall is owned by the National Trust; Lyme Park, which was rebuilt as an Italianate palazzo in the eighteenth century, was owned by the Legh family for 600 years, and is now owned by the National Trust.

41. The suggestion that the production of *A Masque* was 'essentially a children's party' was made by Parker, 142; the necessary corrective was offered by John Creaser, '"The present aid of this occasion": The Setting of *Comus*', in David Lindley (ed.), *The Court Masque* (Manchester: Manchester University Press, 1984), 111–34.

42. The suggestion that the masque was substantially influenced by the Castlehaven scandal was first advanced by Betty Irwin in 'Milton's Ludlow Masque: An Historical approach' (unpublished MA thesis, University of Northern Illinois, 1960). See above n. 15.

43. Lady Alice, b. 13 June 1619, married Richard Vaughan, second earl of Carbery, in 1652; she died in 1689. On Viscount Brackley (later second earl of Bridgewater, b. 29 May 1623) see *ODNB* s.n. Egerton, John. He was later to own a copy of Milton's *Defensio* (1651; now in the Huntington Library) which he inscribed with the words *Liber igne, author furcâ dignissimi* ('this book is most deserving of burning, its author

of the gallows' (see plate 36, p. 230). Thomas Egerton (b. 11 June 1625) died unmarried *c*.1648.

44. Lines 84–88, *CSP* 184–5.

45. Line 478, *CSP* 204.

46. Lines 30–36, *CSP* 181–2. As in 'Arcades', the 'state' is the chair on which the earl is seated.

47. The music survives in two manuscripts in the British Library, Add MS 11518 (in a scribal hand) and Add MS 52723, in the hand of Henry Lawes.

48. Lines 413–20, *CSP* 201.

49. Compare *PL* 4. 748–9, 'Our maker bids increase, who bids abstain | But our destroyer, foe to God and man?'

50. For a summary, see Thomas Corns, *A History of Seventeenth-Century Literature* (Oxford: Basil Blackwell, 2007), 38–40, 176–82.

51. Corns, 'Milton before "Lycidas" ', 34–5.

52. Line 77, *CSP* 185.

53. Lines 1021–2, *CSP* 234. Milton was to quote these lines in Camillo Cardoini's *album amicorum*, which he signed in Geneva; see below, 126.

54. Lines 12–4, *CSP* 180.

55. *PL* 3. 173–5.

56. Lines 910–17, *CSP* 227.

57. Lake, 'Laudian Style', 164, quoting Thomas Laurence, a protégé of Laud, on whom see *ODNB*.

58. John Milton, *A Maske Presented at Ludlow Castle, 1634*, sig. A2^{r-v}.

59. The issues are reviewed in Corns, *History*, 18–21, 94–7.

60. For an account of the changes see Brown, *Entertainments*, 132–52.

61. The poem is in the East Sussex Record Office (FRE 690); see Leo Miller. 'On Some Verses by Alexander Gil which John Milton Read', *MQ* 24 (1990), 22–5. On Noel see *ODNB*.

62. On Simeon Foxe see *ODNB*; Foxe was an Italian speaker, and so may have had links with the Diodati family and other members of the London Italian community.

63. The Library of the College of Physicians ('Royal College of Physicians' since 1674) had core holdings of medical books but also collected in other fields: in the policy formulated by William Harvey in 1656 he declared an intention to collect books of geometry, geography, cosmography, astronomy, music, optics, natural history, physics, and mechanics, and 'those that treat of journeys to remote regions of the Earth'.

64. Sion College, which was a society of clergymen rather than an educational establishment, had been founded in 1624, secured a royal charter in 1630 and in 1631 erected buildings (the college and almshouses) between Philip Lane and St Alfege London Wall. There was a library from the outset, but it was not a significant size till it received books from St Paul's Cathedral library in 1647.

65. Wood, in Darbishire, 35; the friend may be John Aubrey. Those who doubt the incorporation include Nicholas von Maltzahn in 'Wood, Allam and the Oxford Milton', *MS* 31 (1994), 155–77.

66. Laudian Statutes of 1636 (Tit IX sectio 8, *De incorporatione*).

67. On Pinck see *ODNB*.

6 HORTON

1. Hyde Clarke, *Athenaeum* 2746 (12 June 1888), 760–1. The document that Clarke cites can no longer be identified.
2. The escape from plague proved to be temporary, for throughout 1637 there was a succession of deaths by plague in Colnbrook.
3. Below, 206.
4. In 1636 Milton bought for 18 shillings Chrysostom's *Orationes LXXX* (Paris, 1604), at some point entering textual corrections on four pages; the book is now in the Cambridge University Library (Ely.a.272). In 1637 he bought for 5 shillings the *Allegoriae in Homeri fabulas de diis* (Basel, 1544) then attributed to the philosopher Heraclides Pontius but now believed to be the work of an otherwise unknown 1st-century rhetorician called Heraclides; the book is now in the library of the University of Illinois.
5. On the Kedermister (sometimes spelt 'Kederminster') Library see Jane Francis, 'The Kedermister Library: An Account of its Origins and a Reconstruction of its Contents and Arrangement', *Records of Buckinghamshire* 36 (1994), 62–85.
6. BL Add MS 36,354. It is not clear whether Milton took the Commonplace Book with him on his continental journey.
7. See Gordon Campbell, 'Milton's *Index Theologicus* and Bellarmine's *Disputationes De Controversiis Christianae Fidei Adversus Huius Temporis Haereticos*', *MQ* 11 (1977), 12–16.
8. Italic is the term used to denote the style of handwriting that emerged in 15th-century Italy and by the early 17th century was evolving into early copperplate. See B. L. Ullman, *The Origin and Development of Humanistic Script* (Rome: Edizioni di Storia e letteratura, 1960).
9. On Goodall and the presentation see Edward Jones 'The Wills of Thomas Young and Edward Goodall and the Life of John Milton', forthcoming in *John Milton: 'Reasoning Words'*, ed. Charles Durham and Kristin Pruitt (Selingrove, Pa.).
10. Below, 137.
11. 'In term time I have letters of intelligence from my friends: but out of term when they are gone, I live in darkness and ignorance and know not which end of the world stands upwards', letter from Nathaniel Tovey to his brother-in-law George Warner (PRO SP 46/83/46).
12. Herrick, *Poetical Works*, 19.
13. *CPW* 4. 613–14.
14. The point is made by Edward Jones on his account of Milton in Horton: ' "Filling in a blank in the canvas": Milton, Horton, and the Kedermister Library', *RES* 53 (2002), 31–60. Many details in this chapter derive from this article.
15. Below, 194.
16. Kenneth Fincham, 'Episcopal Government, 1603–1640', in Fincham (ed.), *The Early Stuart Church*, 71–91 (78–9).
17. Kevin Sharpe, *The Personal Rule of Charles I* (New Haven and London: Yale University Press, 1992), 842–3.
18. The Court of Requests was a minor Court of Equity (as opposed to a Court of Common Law), widely used in the Stuart period as an alternative to the Court of Star Chamber and the Court of Chancery. Courts of Common Law denied the legality of the Court of Requests, which was abolished in 1641 (indirectly, by the abolishment of its jurisdiction in England); its records are now in the National Archives: PRO Req 1

consists of 210 volumes of the Miscellaneous Books of the Court, and PRO Req 2 consists of 829 bundles of Proceedings.

19. John Bowers declared on 8 April 1637 that Milton had handled Cotton's investments 'for thirty years or thereabouts' (BL, Cottonian Charters 1/5/2). Milton the elder declared on 13 April that he had been handling Cotton's investments 'for the space of neere forty years' and that the investment amounted to 'a good value about Three thousand pounds' (PRO Req 2/630; there is another copy (not identical) in BL, Cottonian Charters 1/5/1).

20. Thomas Bower served an apprenticeship with Milton the elder from 1617 to 29 June 1624, when he was admitted to the Company of Scriveners (Guildhall MS 5370, 215); he was a witness to the marriage settlement of Anne Milton (the scrivener's daughter and poet's sister) to Edward Phillips on 27 November 1623 (Morgan Library MA 953). He seems to have entered into partnership with the elder Milton in 1625.

21. The allegation is contained in the action initiated by Sir Thomas Cotton on 28 May 1636 (PRO Req 2/630; there is another copy (not identical) in BL, Cottonian Charters 1/5/5).

22. Milton's view is embedded in his answer to Cotton's action on 6 May 1636 (PRO Req 2/630; there is another copy (not identical) in BL, Cottonian Charters 1/5/1).

23. BL, Cottonian Charters 1/5/4.

24. PRO PROB 11/170, Pile 2.

25. On Sir Thomas Cotton (1594–1662) see *ODNB* under Cotton, Sir Robert Bruce (the nephew of John Cotton).

26. The document recording these penalties was seen by Masson among the records of the Court of Requests (Masson, 1. 630), but subsequent scholars have not been able to identify it.

27. The Latin (which means 'we have given the power') is the opening phrase of a writ that empowers someone who is not a judge to act in place of a judge.

28. PRO Req 2/360.

29. Thomas Agar was the second husband of Anne Milton. John Agar was his brother, and may have been the person at that time who was studying at the Inner Temple, to which he had been admitted on 27 May 1636.

30. PRO Req 1/141 fol. 218.

31. BL, Cottonian Charters 1/5/5.

32. Sara Milton's death (3 April) and burial (6 April) are recorded in the Horton parish register (Buckinghamshire County Record Office, Aylesbury, PR 107/1/1). French (*LR* 1. 321) was puzzled by the presence of the astronomical sign for Jupiter, but it is merely shorthand for 'Thursday', the day on which she was buried; the figure of Mars that he wrongly discerned in the entry means 'Tuesday'.

33. BL, Cottonian Charters 1/5/5; the copy in the records of the Court of Requests cannot now be found.

34. The Court of Star Chamber was a court of criminal equity that was housed in the Star Chamber, a room in the Palace of Westminster in which *starra* (deeds and bonds of Jews) had once been deposited. Under the Stuarts the criminal jurisdiction of the Court dealt with misdemeanours of a public character such as riot, forgery, libel and conspiracy; as a equity court free from the constraints of common law, it used fines, imprisonment, whipping, branding and mutilation as instruments for the repression of puritans. The Court's tyrannical and illegal exercise of its powers led to its abolition in 1641.

35. Sharpe, *Personal Rule*, 759.
36. Ibid. 763.
37. His account of the mutilation is in *Discovery of the Prelates Tyranny* (1641) no pagination.
38. Sharpe, *Personal Rule*, 764.
39. Below, 222.
40. On Williams's career see *ODNB*.
41. The report was discovered by Edward Jones. See his ' "Church-outed by the Prelats": Milton and the 1637 Inspection of the Horton Parish Church', *JEGP* 102 (2003), 42–58.
42. On Edward King see *ODNB* and N. Postlethwaite and G. Campbell, 'Edward King, Milton's 'Lycidas': Poems and Documents', *MQ* 28 (December 1994).
43. *TMS* 31; *CSP* 243.
44. *ODNB*.
45. Lines 114–15, *CSP* 251.
46. Sharpe, *Personal Rule*, 234, 290.
47. Lines 128–9 and n., *CSP* 252.
48. Lines 75, 77, *CSP* 248; see John Leonard, ' "Trembling Ear": The Historical Moment of "Lycidas" ', *JMRS* 21 (1991), 59–81.
49. In *Epistolae Familiares* (1674) the first letter (no. 6) is dated 2 September and its sequel (no. 7) 23 September. These dates conflict with the internal evidence of both the first letter (which refers to the onset of autumn as an event in the past) and the second letter (which tells Diodati to hurry because winter is imminent). It seems likely that Milton dated the letters '2.ix.1637' and '23.ix.1637', and that the printer of the 1674 edition understood the Roman numerals to refer to the ninth month of the year beginning in January (i.e. September) rather than the ninth month of the year beginning in March (i.e. November).
50. The letter is *Epistolae Familiares* no. 7 in the 1674 edition.
51. See Wilfred Prest, 'Legal Education of the Gentry at the Inns of Court, 1500–1640', *Past and Present* 38 (1967), 20–39, and Prest's *The Inns of Court under Elizabeth I and the Early Stuarts, 1590–1640* (London, 1972).
52. It is possible that Milton had some sort of link with Gray's Inn. Many years later Edward Phillips recalled that after he returned from Italy, Milton would socialize with a couple of friends from Gray's Inn; see below, 134.
53. F. A. Inderwick, *A Calendar of the Inner Temple Records* (5 vols. 1896–1936), 2. 239.
54. Milton's father wrote a six-line prefatory epigram for John Lane's unpublished continuation of Chaucer's 'Squire's Tale' (Bodleian Douce 170) and a prefatory sonnet for Lane's unpublished continuation of Lydgate's Guy Earl of Warwick (BL MS Harleian 5243). He may also have been the author of a poem signed 'I.M.' in the First Folio of Shakespeare, as discussed in the previous chapter.

7 ITALY

1. On the journey to Italy in the 17th century, see Edward Chaney, *The Grand Tour and the Great Rebellion* (Geneva: Slatkin, 1985) and *The Evolution of the Grand Tour: Anglo-Italian Cultural Relations since the Renaissance* (rev. edn., London: Frank Cass, 2000).
2. The author of *Regii sanguinis clamor* (1652) (below, 260–4) asserted that Milton had been expelled from Cambridge and fled to Italy in shame. John Bramhall, in a letter to

his son (9/19 May 1654) also hinted at a scandal that should have resulted in Milton being forced 'out of the University and out of the society of men'.

3. The Cinque Ports are the five south-coast ports of Dover, Hastings, Romney, Hythe, and Sandwich. Appointments to the wardenship were customarily made for life; those appointed also served as Constable of Dover, so the incumbent had responsibilities that were naval and military (as Warden) and judicial (as Constable).

4. See *ODNB* under Howard, Theophilus. The earl's patron was the duke of Buckingham, who in July 1628 had resigned his wardenship of the Cinque Ports in Suffolk's favour; Suffolk was Warden (and Constable of Dover) until his death in 1640.

5. BL Add MS 36,354. On the back of the letter Milton wrote the couplet 'Fix here'. The smudged word in square brackets has traditionally been transcribed as 'wryte', but 'ryde' makes more sense; the reading is the suggestion of Victor Stater, author of the *ODNB* article on the second earl of Suffolk.

6. Suffolk House, later Northumberland House, was a grand house on the Strand, on what is now the south side of Trafalgar Square; it was demolished in 1874.

7. The MS version in the BL (Add MS 28,637) seems to be an 18th-century copy based on the lost original rather than on the printed text. 'Dorique' here means 'pastoral'.

8. On Wotton and Hales see *ODNB*; the quotation about the Synod of Dort is from Hales's *Golden Remains* (1659), sig. A4^v. Marvell was later to describe Hales as 'a most learned Divine. . . . [and] one of the clearest heads and best prepared brests in Christendom' (*Rehearsal Transpos'd*, ed. Martin Dzelzainis, in *The Prose Works of Andrew Marvell*, ed. id. and Annabelle Patterson (2 vols., New Haven: Yale University Press, 2003), I. 130.

9. On Randolph see *ODNB*. Wotton says that he had already received from 'our common friend Mr R' a volume in which Milton's *Masque* and Randolph's *Poems* were bound together, but no such copy is known, nor has the friend been identified. The friend had not revealed Milton's authorship of the Masque (possibly because he did not know who had written it).

10. Below, 134.

11. See *ODNB* under 'Scudamore, John, first viscount', 'Scudamore family', 'Sidney, Robert, second earl of Leicester', 'Sidney, Algernon', and 'Sidney, Philip, third earl of Leicester'. See also Ian Atherton, *Ambition and Failure in Stuart England: The Career of John, First Viscount Scudamore* (Manchester and New York: Manchester University Press, 1999); ch. 6 (171–219) is devoted to 'Scudamore as ambassador [in Paris], 1635–39'.

12. *Life and Letters of Sir Henry Wotton*, ed. L. Pearsall Smith (Oxford: Clarendon Press, 1907), 2. 382; for Wotton's other uses of the aphorism see 1. 21–2.

13. The report of Salmasius's allegations is contained in a letter from Vossius to Heinsius written on 21/31 January 1653, printed in *LR* 3. 316: '*Miltonum* passim Catamitum vocat, aitque eum in Italia vilissimum fuisse scortum, & paucis nummis nates prostituisse' ('he sometimes calls Milton a catamite, denouncing him as the vilest prostitute in Italy and saying that he sold his buttocks for a few pence'). The allegation did not survive into the posthumously published version of the *Responsio* (1660).

14. The original bond is lost, but its conditions can be inferred from Milton's suit against the Copes of 16 June 1654 (PRO C8/120/72 and C7/452/60). The interest of £12 a year (i.e. 8 per cent) was paid quarterly, apparently on 3 February, 3 May, 3 August, and 3 November. Milton's bill of 1654 implies that payments were made until November 1641.

15. The Miltons had bought the property on 25 May 1627 (PRO C54/2715/20).
16. Sir Matthew Lister was a court physician who specialized in chemical and Paracelsian remedies (see *ODNB*). He had been the tenant, but may not have been the occupier; the property may have been used as a second home by the Milton family or occupied by the Phillipses. See Rose Clavering and John Shawcross, 'Anne Milton and the Milton Residences', *JEGP* 59 (1960), 680–90.
17. PRO CP 25/2/458, 14 Charles I E.
18. Phillips, in Darbishire, 56.
19. BL Add MS 11044, 91 ff.
20. Tetrachordon, *CPW* 2. 715; *Doctrine and Discipline of Divorce*, *CPW* 2. 238; *Judgement of Martin Bucer*, *CPW* 2. 434.
21. Bodleian Wood MS D4, fol. 140^v; Darbishire, 19; cf. Wood, who says that 'he touched at Paris . . . but the manners and genius of that place being not agreeable to his mind, he soon left it' (36–7).
22. Below, 258.
23. In *Defensio Secunda* he writes *mox Liburnum* ('I arrived soon after at Livorno'); the phrase may imply a quick voyage, but may mean that he only stayed in Genoa for a short time.
24. The *Description* is included in the Columbia MS of Milton's State Papers (Columbia University Library MS X823 M64/S52) and was printed in the Columbia Milton (18. 122). The other essay in the MS, 'Of statues & antiquities', is the work of 'someone who had travelled in Turkey and Greece: probably the earl of Arundel's brilliant (Anglican) agent, William Petty' (Edward Chaney, untitled review in *English Historical Review*, 108 (1993), 720).
25. The passage, he had been assured by Wotton, was as diurnal as a Gravesend barge.
26. *CPW* 4. 615–16.
27. On the Svogliati see Estelle Haan, *From Academia to Amicitia: Milton's Latin Writings and the Italian Academies* (Philadelphia: Transactions of the American Philosophical Society, vol. 88. pt. 6, 1998), 10–28.
28. Biblioteca Nazionale Centrale di Firenze, MS Palatino E.B. 15,2, Striscia 1406. See Neil Harris, 'Galileo as Symbol: the "Tuscan Artist" in *Paradise Lost*', *Annali dell'Istituto e Museo di Storia della Scienza di Firenze* 10 (1985), 3–29.
29. On Gaddi see Haan, *Academia to Amicitia*, 10–15. By the time of Milton's visit Gaddi had published *Poematum Libri Duo* (Padua, 1628), *Adlocutiones et Elogia* (Florence, 1636), *Corollarium Poeticum* (Florence, 1636), and *Elogia Historica* (Florence, 1637).
30. Biblioteca Nazionale Centrale di Firenze, MS Magliabechiano, Cl. IX, cod. 60, fol. 46^v); subsequent references in the text are to fols. 47 and 48.
31. Of Milton's other poems in hexameters, neither 'Epitaphium Damonis' nor 'Mansus' had yet been written, and 'In Quintum Novembris' would have been a discourteous choice.
32. Charles Diodati was buried on 27 August (Guildhall Library, MS 4508, Parish Register of St Anne Blackfriars).
33. Register of St Andrew, Holborn, Guildhall Library, MS 6668. The record was discovered by Edward Jones in 2006.
34. The collection seems not to have been published, but a manuscript was found on a London bookstall in 1750 and printed in an undated volume (variously estimated to be anywhere between 1757 and 1860); the manuscript has subsequently been lost.

35. The letter to Dati (20 April 1647) is now in the New York Public Library, but is not available for inspection; the NYPL also has what appears to be an 18th-century copy of the letter.

36. On Buonmattei see *DBI* and A. A. Cinquemani, *Glad to Go for a Feast: Milton, Buonmattei and the Florentine Accademici* (New York: P. Lang, 1998).

37. The letter, which survives only in printed form (*Epistolae Familiares* no. 8) was written on 31 August/10 September 1638.

38. In France the most important claim for the vernacular was Joachim du Bellay's *La deffence, et illustration de la langue françoyse* (Paris, 1549). In Spanish Naples Juan de Valdés wrote *Diálogo de la lengua* (1535, published Madrid, 1737); on the Spanish debate see Avelina Carrera de la Red, *El 'problema de la lengua' en el humanismo renacentista español* (Valladolid: Universidad de Valladolid, Secretariado de Publicaciones; [Salamanca]: Caja de Ahorros y Monte de Piedad de Salamanca, 1988).

39. On the debate in Italy see Cecil Grayson, *A Renaissance Controversy: Latin or Italian* (Oxford: Clarendon Press, 1960); Giancarlo Mazzacurati, *La questione della lingua dal Bembo all' Accademia fiorentina* (Naples: Liguori, 1965); M. Tavoni, *Latino, grammatica, volgare: storia di una questione umanistica* (Padua: Antenore, 1984); Maurizio Vitale, *La questione della lingua* (2nd edn., Palermo: Palumbo, 1984); Maria Antonietta Passarelli, *La lingua della patria: Leon Battista Alberti e la questione del volgare* (Rome: Bagatto Libri, 1999).

40. *CPW* 2. 538. The Secretary of the Congregation of the Index (the body that produced the *Index Librorum Prohibitorum*) was always a Dominican; occasionally books were referred to the Jesuits for a specialist opinion, but there were no Franciscan 'licensers', as theirs was not a learned order. The congregation's activities were independent of the Roman Inquisition (see below) from 1571 until 1917, when responsibility for the Index was passed to the Holy Office.

41. Galileo had completed the book several years earlier, but had withheld it from publication until the accession of Pope Urban VIII, a Florentine (Maffeo Barberini) with whom Galileo had long enjoyed a personal friendship. It was nonetheless under Urban's pontificate that Galileo was condemned for the second time and forced under threat of torture to abjure Copernican cosmology on 22 June 1633.

42. The Inquisizione Romano was governed by the Holy Office in Rome, and so was wholly distinct from the Spanish and Portuguese Inquisitions, which were administered by secular powers. The Roman Inquisition had successfully expunged Protestantism from Italy; its most famous victim was Giordano Bruno, who had been burnt in 1600. See P. F. Grendler, *The Roman Inquisition and the Venetian Press* (Princeton: Princeton University Press, 1977) and R. Canosa, *Storia dell' Inquisizione in Italia della metà del Cinquecento alla fine del Settocento* (5 vols., Rome: Sapere, 1986–90).

43. The documents are cited by Harris, 'Galileo as Symbol'.

44. On Coltellini (1613–93) see *DBI*.

45. Alessandro Lazzeri, *Intellettuali e consenso nella Toscana del Seicento: L'Accademia degli Apatisti* (Milan: A. Giuffrè, 1983); see Haan, *Academia to Amicitia*, 29–37.

46. On Dati (1619–76) see *DBI* and *Grove Art*; on Dati and Milton see Haan, op. cit. 43–80. Dati's most enduring book, *Vite dei pittori antichi* ('Lives of the ancient painters') was published (like *Paradise Lost*) in 1667, and was last reprinted in 1953. Dati is mentioned (along with Francini) in Milton's *Epitaphium Damonis* 137; one of Milton's letters to Dati survives (see n. 30), as do two of Dati's letters to Milton.

47. On Frescobaldi (d. 12 December 1654) see R. M. Frye, 'Milton's Florentine Friend, Bishop Frescobaldi: A Biographical Note and Portrait', *MQ* 7 (1973), 74–5.

48. On Chimentelli see *DBI* and Edward Rosen, 'A Friend of John Milton: Valerio Chimentelli and his Copy of Viviani's *De Maximis et minimus*', *BNYPL* 57 (1953), 159–74.

49. Quoted by Haan, *Academia to Amicitia*, 23.

50. See Gordon Campbell, 'Milton's Spanish', in *MQ* 30 (1996), 127–32.

51. On Rovai see Haan, *Academia to Amicitia*, 61–71.

52. *CPW* 1. 809–10.

53. *PL* 1. 302–4.

54. See Edward Chaney, 'Milton's Visit to Vallombrosa: A Literary Tradition', in Mario Di Cesare (ed.), *Milton in Italy: Contexts, Images, Contradictions* (Binghamton, NY: MRTS, 1991), 113–46, reprinted with illustrations in Chaney, *Evolution*, 278–313. The best case for the view that Milton may have visited Vallombrosa (though not in the autumn, if our understanding of the chronology of the tour is correct) is made by Neil Harris, 'The Vallombrosa Simile and the Image of the Poet in *Paradise Lost*', in Di Cesare, *Milton in Italy*, 71–94.

55. The suggestion, first advanced in 1931 (R. W. Smith, 'The Source of Milton's Pandemonium', *MP* 39 (1931), 187–98), that Milton's Pandemonium (*PL* 1. 710–30) might be modelled on St Peter's is supported by details such as the bronze doors, the pilasters, the carved roof, the gilding and even the bee simile (there were bees in the arms of Urban VIII, who was pope at the time of Milton's visit), but there are no Doric pillars in the Basilica, and the late date of Bernini's Doric colonnade would seem to obviate any possibility that Milton's model was St Peter's.

56. See Michael Williams, *The Venerable English College, Rome: A History, 1579–1979* (London: Associated Catholic Publications, 1979).

57. The identification of Milton's fellow guests was the subject of two independent investigations: Leo Miller, 'Milton Dines at the Jesuit College: Reconstructing the Evening of October 30, 1638', *MQ* 13 (1979), 142–6, and Chaney, *The Grand Tour*, 245, 282–4.

58. On Cary see *ODNB*. His poems were edited by Sir Walter Scott; the standard modern edition is *The Poems of Patrick Cary*, ed. V. Delany (Oxford: Clarendon Press, 1978).

59. On Holden see *ODNB*.

60. See *ODNB*, which names Sir Nicholas as Milton's fellow diner.

61. On Salzilli see J. A. Freeman, 'Milton's Roman Connection: Giovanni Salzilli', in *MS* 19 (1984), 87–104, and Haan, *Academia to Amicitia*, 82–98.

62. The identification of Selvaggi as Codner was made by Chaney, *Grand Tour*, 244–51. See also David Lunn, *The English Benedictines, 1540–1688* (London, 1980), 123–4, 152–3, 157–8. The couplet imitates Propertius 2. 34. 65–6 (in praise of Virgil), as do Salzilli's epigram and lines 30–40 of Samuel Barrow's poem on *Paradise Lost*.

63. On Gawen (1612–84) see *ODNB*, Chaney, *Grand Tour*, 389–92 and Allan Pritchard, 'Milton in Rome: According to Wood', *MQ* 14 (1980), 92–7.

64. On Manso see Angelo Borzelli, *Giovan Battista Manso* (Naples, 1916). On Manso and Milton see Anthony Low, '*Mansus* in its Context', *MS* 19 (1984), 105–26 and Haan, *Academia to Amicitia*, 118–64.

65. The family had owned a second villa at Bisaccio, but by the time of Milton's visit it was no longer in Manso's possession. The precise location of the Puteoli villa is not

known. See Haan, *Academia to Amicitia*, 122 and Joseph Walker, 'An attempt to ascertain the site of the villa near Naples in which the Marquis Manso received Tasso and Milton', Appendix V of Walker's *Historical Memoir on Italian Tragedy* (London, 1799). Manso's written account of the eruption of Vesuvius in December 1631, which he witnessed from his villa, is regularly cited in accounts of the eruption, which killed more than 3,000 people. Manso's villa was close to the Solfatara, a dormant crater with bubbling pools of sulphurous hot water that may have influenced Milton's description of Hell; see Marjorie Nicolson, 'Milton's Hell and the Phlegraean Fields', *University of Toronto Quarterly* 7 (1938), 500–13.

66. Part of the Palazzo still stands; the interior has been rebuilt, but (except for some later statuary), Domenico Fontana's façade now looks the same as it did in 1638.

67. On Manso's and Milton's use of Gregory's pun (as recorded by Bede) see Haan, *Academia to Amicitia*, 130–6.

68. In *Epitaphium Damonis*, 181 Milton again mentioned Manso, who had given him 'two cups' (*bina...pocula*), which were probably his own books rather than cups. See Michelle De Filippis, 'Milton and Manso: Cups or Books?' *PMLA* 51 (1936), 745–56.

69. *Quin et in has quondam pervenit Tityrus oras* (*Mansus* 34) has traditionally been seen as an allusion to Chaucer's visits to Italy, and so in John Hale's sparkling translation is rendered 'Our Chaucer came before me to this land' (John Milton, *Latin Writings: A Selection*, ed. and trans. John Hale (Assen and Tempe: *MRTS*, 1998), 107); Hale's note, however, notes the suggestion of David Money that Tityrus is not Chaucer (though that is the pastoral name given to him by Spenser) but rather Virgil's Tityrus. The context, which speaks of the Thames, makes Money's the more likely interpretation.

70. *CPW* 4. 619.

71. On travellers to Sicily see Chaney, *Evolution*, 1–40.

72. Quoted in *ODNB* under Lithgow, William.

73. See Diana Treviño Benet, 'The Escape from Rome: Milton's *Second Defense* and a Renaissance Genre', in Di Cesare, *Milton in Italy*, 29–49.

74. See Gordon Campbell, 'Nathaniel Tovey: Milton's Second Tutor', *MQ* 21 (1987), 81–90.

75. Francesco Barberini the elder (1597–1679), on whom see *DBI*, was the eponymous founder of the library that remained in Palazzo Barberini until 1902, when it was acquired by Pope Leo XIII and transferred with the original shelving into the Vatican.

76. The wing that contained the theatre was demolished in 1926 to make way for the Via Barberini. On Barberini patronage see Frederick Hammond, *Music and Spectacle in Baroque Rome: Barberini Patronage under Urban VIII* (New Haven: Yale University Press, 1994).

77. On both composers see *Grove Music*; Massocchi was a member of the household of Antonio Barberini.

78. The brothers were nephews of Pope Urban VIII; on Antonio Barberini the younger (1607–71) see *DBI*.

79. See Margaret Byard, '"Adventrous Song": Milton and the Music of Rome', in Di Cesare *Milton in Italy*, 305–28.

80. On Leonora Baroni (1611–70) see *DBI*, *Grove Music*, Byard (in previous note), and Haan, *Academia to Amicitia*, 99–117.

81. *Aurea maternae fila movere lyrae.* Leonora and Adriana were sometimes joined by Leonora's sister Caterina, but she seems not to have been present on this occasion.

82. Vincenzo Costazuti (ed.), *Applausi poetici alle glorie della signora Leonora Baroni* (Rome, 1639).
83. On Holste (1596–1661) see *NDB*.
84. Barberini's copy, still in the Vatican Library, is catalogued as Stamp. Barb. JJJ.VI.67.
85. Above, 18.
86. *Demophili Democratis et secundi veterum philosophorum sententiæ morales* (Rome, 1638); the book, which was published in December 1638 (shortly before Milton's return to Rome), was identified by Leo Miller, 'Milton and Holstenius Reconsidered', in Di Cesare, *Milton in Italy*, 573–87. The presentation copy has disappeared.
87. The letter to Holste is catalogued as Barb. Lat. 2181, fols. 57–8ᵛ; the version printed in *Epistolae Familiares* (no. 9) is dated 30 March 1639. The other surviving holograph letter is Milton's letter to Carlo Dati (20 April 1647), which is now in the NYPL.
88. Eco Haitsma Mulier, *The Myth of Venice and Dutch Republican Thought in the Seventeenth Century* (Assen, Netherlands: Van Gorcum, 1980); C. Kallendorf, *Virgil and the Myth of Venice: Books and Readers in the Italian Renaissance* (Oxford: Clarendon Press, 1999); D. C. McPherson, *Shakespeare, Jonson and the Myth of Venice* (Newark: University of Delaware Press, 1990).
89. Below, 262.
90. *Grove Music* has entries on all four composers. Claudio Monteverdi (1567–1643) was still living in Venice at the time of Milton's visit; Luca Marenzio (1553/4–1599) was a composer of madrigals who worked in a succession of North Italian courts and in Poland; Orazio Vecchi (1550–1605) was a Modenese composer who mainly wrote sacred music, but also composed canzonettas and madrigals; Antonio Cifra (1584–1629) was a composer of madrigals and sacred music who had worked in Loreto and Rome; Carlo Gesualdo (*c.*1561–1613) was a prince of Venosa who composed in Naples until, after murdering his wife and her lover, he retreated to Gesualdo; he subsequently married Eleonora d'Este and thereafter composed for the Ferrarese court.
91. Donald Dorian, *The English Diodatis* (New Brunswick, NJ: Rutgers University Press, 1950), 133.
92. The album is now in the Houghton Library in Harvard (Sumner 84). Cardoini's precise identity is not known. The Camillo Cardoini who was physician to the earl of Leicester and settled in Geneva was an established physician by the 1580s, and would not have been alive at the time of Milton's visit. His son Andrea, who was born in Geneva in 1595, was still living there at the time of Milton's visit. Cardoini is sometimes described as a 'count', but the Latin is *eques*, which in Italian is *cavaliere; conte* would have been rendered in Latin as *comes*. The manuscript of Leo Miller's unpublished 'Milton in Geneva and the Significance of the Cardoini Album' is held by the Colorado University Library in Boulder (Collection Box XXII, File 17).
93. Below, 134.

8 THE CRISIS OF GOVERNMENT

1. *Defensio Secunda*, *CPW* 4. 620.
2. Roy Strong, *Britannia Triumphans: Inigo Jones, Rubens and the Whitehall Palace* (London: Thames and Hudson, 1980); the third kingdom, Ireland, stood outside these ambitions.
3. Kevin Sharpe, *The Personal Rule of Charles I* (New Haven: Yale University Press, 1992), 782.

4. Ibid. 786.
5. Conrad Russell, *The Fall of the British Monarchies, 1637–1642* (Oxford: Clarendon Press, 1995; 1st pub. 1991), 82.
6. Sharpe, *Personal Rule*, 821.
7. Russell, *Fall*, 146.
8. This was Robert Russell; see John T. Shawcross, *The Arms of the Family: The Significance of John Milton's Relatives and Associates* (Lexington: University Press of Kentucky, 2004), 238 n. 42.
9. The house was in Lamb Alley (later called Maidenhead Court), which until the Barbican was built in the 1980s ran from Aldersgate Street to Nicholls Square; from 1644 the land beside the house was occupied by Inigo Jones's Thanet House (later Shaftsbury House), and the house that Milton rented was in its garden.
10. Darbishire, 60, 62.
11. Lawrence Stone, *The Family, Sex and Marriage In England 1500–1800*, abridged edition (Harmondsworth: Penguin, 1979), 83–4.
12. See below, 180.
13. PRO E179/252/1(A).
14. Darbishire, 62; 'make bold with his body' remains a puzzling phrase.
15. Parker, 846.
16. Wilfred R. Prest, *The Inns of Court under Elizabeth I and the Early Stuarts 1590–1640* (London: Longman, 1972), *passim*.
17. *OED*, s.v. 'spark', sb.2, sig. 2; 'beau', sb.; sig. 1, 'gaudy', sb., sig.4; William Shakespeare, *Antony and Cleopatra*, III. xiii. 18.
18. *CSP* 270.
19. Above, III, 126.
20. *CSP* 272, 282.
21. Line 108, *CSP* 276, 284.
22. Parker, 840.
23. Lines 161–8, *CSP* 279.
24. line 169, *CSP* 279.
25. Sharpe, *Personal Rule*, 877. On Robert Rich (second earl of Warwick), William Fiennes (first Viscount Saye and Sele), Robert Greville (second Baron Brooke), Pym, Hampden, and Erle see *ODNB*.
26. Shawcross, *Arms*, 48.
27. See above, 45.
28. *ODNB*.
29. See above, 17.
30. Russell, *Fall*, offers the most detailed account.
31. On Russell, Calamy, Spurstowe, Newcomen, and Marshall see *ODNB*.
32. Joseph Hall, *Episcopacy by Divine Right* (London, 1640), 259.
33. Ibid. 177.
34. Joseph Hall, *An Humble Remonstrance to the High Court of Parliament* (London, 1640 [?1641]), 23.
35. Masson, 2. 244.
36. David L. Hoover and Thomas N. Corns, 'The Authorship of the Postscript to *An Answer to a Booke Entituled, An Humble Remonstrance*', *MQ* 38 (2004), 59–75.
37. On the bibliographical complexities of the Postscript pages, see *CPW* 1. 965.

38. Smectymnuus, *An Answer to a Booke Entituled, An Humble Remonstrance* (London, 1641), '85' [i.e. 95].
39. Smectymnuus, *A Vindication of the Answer to the Humble Remonstrance* (London, 1641), 78.
40. Joseph Hall, *A Defence of the Humble Remonstrance* (London: April 1641), *A Short Answer to the Tedious Vindication of Smectymnuus* (London: July 1641); Smectymnuus, *A Defence of the Humble Remonstrance* (London: June, 1641).
41. Joseph Hall, *Divers Treatises Written upon severall Occasions by Joseph Hall* (London, 1662).
42. Hall, *Short Answer*, 1.
43. Hall, *Defence*, 159; Hall alludes to Alexander Leighton's *An Appeal to the Parliament: or, Sions Plea against the Prelacie* (n.p., 1629) and William Prynne's *A Breviate of the Prelates Intolerable Usurpations* (London, 1637). The term 'Pasquin' derives from Pasquino, the name given in the 16th century to an ancient marble statue of Menelaus with the body of Patroclus in the Piazza Pasquino. Satirical messages (then in Latin verse, now in Italian prose) have been posted on the statue since it was placed there in 1501; the term is now used generically to refer to lampoons, but in Milton's time retained the sense of allusion to the most famous of Rome's 'talking statues'.
44. Hoover and Corns, 'Authorship', 71–3.
45. Hall, *Defence*, 159.
46. *CPW*, 1. 556–7.
47. Thomas N. Corns, *The Development of Milton's Prose Style* (Oxford: Clarendon Press, 1982), 40.
48. Corns, *Development*, 43–63.
49. *CPW* 1. 549.
50. *CPW* 1. 616.
51. *PL* 12. 551.
52. H. R. Trevor Roper, *Archbishop Laud, 1573–1645* (2nd edn., London: Macmillan, 1962), 427.
53. *CPW* 1. 617.
54. *ODNB*.
55. *CPW* 1. 639.
56. Above, 60.
57. *CPW* 1. 678, 683, 726.
58. Robert Greville, Lord Brooke, *A Discourse Opening the Nature of that Episcopacie, which is Exercised in England* (London: November, 1641), esp. 67–8. For a discussion of the apparent debt, see Parker, 850.
59. *CPW* 2. 560.
60. Masson, 2. 272.
61. PRO E179/252/1(F); Campbell, *Chronology*, 72.
62. Samuel Rawson Gardiner (ed.) *The Constitutional Documents of the Puritan Revolution 1625–1660* (3rd edn., Oxford: Clarendon Press, 1979; first printed 1906), 203.
63. For an account of the uprising and Milton's response to it, see below, 212.
64. Russell, *Fall*, 455.
65. 'Lycidas', line 71, *CSP* 248.
66. *CPW* 1. 897; for a useful discussion by Frederick Lovett Taft, the *CPW* editor, see 1. 863.

67. *CPW* I. 863.
68. *CPW* I. 860; discussed 738.
69. Anon., *A Modest Confutation of A Slandrous and Scurrilous Libelll, Entituled, Animadversions upon the Remonstrants Defense against Smectymnuus* (London, 1642), sig. A3^r.
70. *Modest Confutation*, sig. A3^v, 22.
71. *CPW* I. 804, 808.
72. *Modest Confutation*, sig. A3^v.
73. *CPW* I. 818.
74. *CPW*, I. 823 and n. 161; above, 43, 63.
75. *CPW*, I. 884–92; above, 146.
76. *CPW* I. 929.
77. Stone, *Family*, 46.
78. *CPW* I. 894.
79. Thomas N. Corns, 'Studies in the Development of Milton's Prose Style', D. Phil. dissertation, Oxford, 1977, 3–10.
80. *Modest Confutation*, 6.
81. R. S. Paul, *Assembly of the Lord: Politics and Religion in the Westminster Assembly and the 'Grand Debate'* (Edinburgh: T. & T. Clark, 1985), 119–21; Tom Webster, *Godly Clergy in Early Stuart England: The Caroline Puritan Movement c.1620–1643* (Cambridge: Cambridge University Press, 1997), 327.
82. Thomas Edwards, *Gangraena, or, A Catalogue and Discovery of the Many of the Errours, Heresies, Blasphemies and Pernicious Practices of the Sectaries of this Time*, three parts (London, 1646); on Milton and Edwards, see below, 167.
83. Masson, 2. 377–8.
84. Masson, 2. 382.
85. Masson, 2. 596.
86. *CPW* I. 837; on Milton and congregational independency, see below, 194.
87. Darbishire, 22.
88. Ibid. 63.
89. PRO C152/61, PRO LC 4/46; Eric Kerridge, *Trade and Banking in Early Modern England* (Manchester: Manchester University Press, 1988), 36; above, 40.
90. Kerridge, *Trade*, ch. 4, esp. 66–7.
91. Darbishire, 63.
92. Parker, 866–70.
93. Stone, *Family*, 72.
94. PRO PROB 18/6; see below, 381.

9 THE FIRST CIVIL WAR

1. Darbishire, 64, 22, 14.
2. Stone, *Family*, 117.
3. Above, 137.
4. Darbishire, 64.
5. Ibid. 65.
6. There were few matriculations from 1643–9 (except for Magdalen Hall); see Tyacke, *History of the University of Oxford*, 727 and, more generally, 687–731 ('Oxford and the Civil Wars') and 773–802 ('College Finances 1640–60').

7. *VCH*, Oxfordshire, 5. 124; David Eddershaw,with a contribution by Eleanor Roberts, *The Civil War in Oxfordshire* (Stroud: Sutton, 1995), 76.

8. Ronald Hutton, *The Royalist War Effort 1642–1646* (London and New York: Longman, 1982), 96.

9. Ibid. 99.

10. Masson, 2. 389; Campbell, *Chronology*, 70–1.

11. TMS 9.

12. *CSP* 289.

13. Darbishire, 67.

14. Thomas N. Corns, *Uncloistered Virtue: English Political Literature 1640–1660* (Oxford: Clarendon Press, 1992), 7.

15. Philip Tennant, *The People's War in the South Midlands, 1642–45* (Stroud: Alan Sutton, 1992), 27–8 *et passim*; Keith Lindley, *Popular Politics and Religion in Civil War London* (Aldershot: Scolar, 1997), 222.

16. Darbishire, 64–5.

17. *CPW* 1. 406.

18. *ODNB*.

19. Masson, 2. 490.

20. Parker, 234.

21. *ODNB*.

22. Paul, *Assembly of the Lord*, 69.

23. Ibid., 70.

24. The sonnets appear after Sonnet 8 (November 1642) in the Trinity MS, and were published in the 1645 Poems.

25. Darbishire, 65.

26. See *ODNB* on Ley, Whitelock, and Sherfield.

27. On Henderson, Gillespie, Baillie, and Rutherford, see *ODNB*; see also the *ODNB* survey article on 'Members of the Westminster assembly and Scottish commissioners (1643–1652)'.

28. Ann Hughes, Gangraena *and the Struggle for the English Revolution* (Oxford: Oxford University Press, 2004), *passim*.

29. Paul, *Assembly of the Lord*, 131.

30. *ODNB*, s.n. Nye, Philip, and Nye, John.

31. *CPW* 2. 278–9; Milton lists old bugbears from the writings of anti-sectaries. 'Anabaptism' was term widely used of those who opposed the rite of infant baptism, as opposed to believer baptism; 'Familism' alludes to the mysterious old sect, the 'Family of Love'; 'Antinomianism' is the label applied to radicals who allegedly believed their inner sense of personal redemption freed them from the constraints of moral law.

32. *CPW* 2. 248.

33. Canons and Constitutionals Ecclesiastical, ratified Canterbury 1604 and York 1606.

34. Lawrence Stone, *Road to Divorce England 1530–1987* (Oxford and New York: Oxford University Press, 1992; 1st pub. 1990), 4; on the legal framework, see 24–7, on ecclesiastical jurisdiction, see 308. See also M. Ingram, *Church Courts, Sex and Marriage in England, 1570–1640* (Cambridge: Cambridge University Press, 1987).

35. *CPW* 2. 240.

36. *CPW* 2. 259–60.

37. *CPW* 2. 247.
38. Matthew 19: 3.
39. *CPW* 2. 330–1.
40. Genesis 1: 28.
41. Genesis 2: 18.
42. *CPW* 2. 356 and n. 19; the texts he echoes are I Corinthians 15: 7 and I Timothy 1: 5.
43. *CPW* 2. 436.
44. *CPW* 2. 434.
45. *ODNB*.
46. Herbert Palmer, *The Glasse of Gods Providence towards His Faithfull Ones* (London, 1644), title page.
47. Ibid. 57.
48. *CPW* 2. 233; the title page is signed 'J.M.'; Milton discussed the decision on his *Judgement of Martin Bucer, CPW* 2. 434.
49. *LR* 2. 107.
50. William Prynne, *Twelve Considerable Serious Questions touching Church Government* (London, 1644), 7; for Williams, see below, 173.
51. Anon., *Answer to a Book, Intituled, The Doctrine and Discipline of Divorce, or, A Plea for Ladies and Gentlewomen, and all other Maried Women against Divorce* (London, 1644), 41.
52. Below, 170.
53. *Answer to a Book*, 28, 14.
54. Ibid. 39, 8–9.
55. Stone, *Road to Divorce*, 5.
56. *LR* 2. 116–17.
57. On Hartlib and Milton, see below, 180.
58. *ODNB*.
59. Darbishire, 24.
60. Anon., *A Brief Collection Out of Master Pagits Book Called Heresiography* (London, 1646).
61. Ephraim Pagitt, *Heresiography: or, A description of the Heretickes and Sectaries of these latter times* (London, 1645), sig. A3ᵛ; the account is more substantial in subsequent editions.
62. Robert Baillie, *A Dissuasive from the Errours of the Time* (London, 1645), 76.
63. Hughes, Gangraena, 2, 18, 23, 43.
64. Ibid. 24.
65. Thomas Edwards, *The Second Part of Gangraena* (London, 1646), 10–11; discussed by Hughes, Gangraena, 244–5. On Mrs Attaway see *ODNB*.
66. Lines 1–3, *CSP* 297, our emphasis; the issues recur in Sonnet 11, sometimes dated a little later; see *CSP* 307.
67. The four courts were the consistory, classis, synod and national assembly. This was the last occasion on which Milton was to use the word 'Christ' in an English poem.
68. *CPW* 2. 222.
69. Thomas N. Corns, *John Milton: The Prose Works* (New York and London: Twayne and Prentice Hall, 1998), 46–7; *Development*, especially ch. 10.
70. *CPW* 2. 430.
71. *CPW* 2. 440.

72. *Colasterion, CPW* 2. 724.
73. *CPW* 2. 726–7.
74. *CPW* 2. 743, 746.
75. *CPW* 2. 734.
76. *CPW* 2. 692–718.
77. PRO E179/252/14. The manuscript is in poor condition, and the evidence for the donation is strongly circumstantial rather than conclusive.
78. John Coffey, *Persecution and Toleration in Protestant England, 1558–1689* (Harlow: Longman, 2000), 134–42.
79. *CPW* 2. 565.
80. See Thomas N. Corns, 'John Milton, Roger Williams, and the Limitations of Toleration', in Sharon Achinstein and Elizabeth Sauer (eds.), *Milton and Toleration* (Oxford: Oxford University Press, 2007), 72–81.
81. John Goodwin, *Theomachia, or, The grand imprudence of men running the hazard of fighting against God in suppressing any way, doctrine, or practice concerning which they know not certainly whether it be from God or no* (London, 1644), 52.
82. *CPW* 2. 492.
83. Darbishire, 22, 67.
84. Ibid. 66–7. William Blackborough was a leatherseller in St Martin's Le Grand, a precinct (now a street) populated by tailors; on his relation to Milton see Parker, 925 n. 23. Isabel Webber lived near St Clement Danes, in the Strand.
85. Corns, 'Early Lives', forthcoming.
86. Stone, *Road to Divorce*, 64–6.
87. Ian Roy, 'The City of Oxford, 1640–1660', in R. C. Richardson (ed.), *Town and Countryside in the English Revolution* (Manchester: Manchester University Press, 1992), 151, 153; *VCH*, Oxfordshire 5. 127, Campbell, *Chronology*, 88.
88. Paul Hardacre, *The Royalists During the Puritan Revolution* (The Hague: Martinus Nijhoff, 1956), 24.
89. Eddershaw, with Roberts, *Civil War in Oxfordshire*, 159.
90. Above, 58; below, 214.
91. Hutton, *Royalist War Effort*, 199–200.
92. Christopher subscribed to the National Covenant (i.e. the Solemn League and Covenant), which included a pledge to extirpate popery and prelacy, on 20 April 1646; the subscription was administered by William Barton, minister of the church of St John Zachary (which is no longer extant). The oath confirming his subscription was sworn before one Thomas Vincent, who endorsed the certificate, which is PRO SP 23/187, 199.
93. PRO SP 23/187, 196–7.
94. PRO SP 23/54, 681–2; cf SP 23/187, which confirms the larger fine. A tenth was supposed to approximate two years' rent, but was in practice calculated at two-fifteenths of the capital value of the land, in this case £600; thirds were also calculated on the basis of two years' rent, and as Christopher's tenancy of the Cross Keys in Ludgate Hill (which he had recently inherited from his father) was valued at £40 a year, he was fined £80.
95. Christopher paid on 24 September (PRO SP 23/42, 60) and 24 December (PRO SP 23/82, 653; payment is an inference from a tick against his name).
96. Darbishire, 52.
97. Powell's petition is PRO SP 23/194, 400; the inventory of 21 November is PRO SP 23/194, 403 and SP 23/110 60; the record of Covenant and Oath on 4 December is PRO

SP 23/194, 401, and the oath affirming his debts on 406; the fine is recorded in SP 23/194, 387.

98. On Powell's finances see J. Milton French, *Milton in Chancery: New Chapters in The Lives of the Poet and his Father* (New York: Modern Languages Association of America, 1939), 71–99 and 167–80, and Parker, 866–70.

99. *ODNB.*

100. For an account of the proceedings see Parker, 308–11.

101. Darbishire, 66.

102. *LR* 2. 128.

103. PRO PROB 11/199/52.

104. PRO SP Dom 2/110; *LR* 2. 173.

105. Below, 330.

106. *ODNB.*

107. *LR* 2. 100, 104, 115; *ODNB.*

108. *CPW* 2. 369.

109. *CPW* 2. 379–80.

110. *CPW* 2. 378–9.

111. *CPW* 2. 411.

112. Corns, *John Milton: The Prose Works*, 63.

113. *ODNB.*

114. *LR* 2. 132.

115. Corns, 'Early Lives', forthcoming.

116. *CPW* 2. 379; Darbishire, 67.

117. Thomason dated his copy 2 January 1645 (i.e. 1646).

118. John Milton, *A Maske Presented At Ludlow Castle, 1634* (London, 1637), sig. A2^{r-v}.

119. Daniel Featley, *The Dippers Dipt* (London, 1645), sig. B2^v.

120. '[On the Engraver of his Portrait]', *CSP* 293.

121. Compare Hall, *Humble Remonstrance*, 1–2.

122. John Milton, *Poems of Mr. John Milton, Both English and Latin, Compos'd at several times* (London, 1645), sigs. a3^r, a4^v.

123. Ibid., sig. a4^r.

124. Thomas N. Corns, 'Milton's Quest for Respectability', *MLR* 77 (1982), 769–79.

125. Nicholas McDowell, 'Dante and the Distraction of Lyric in "To my Friend Mr Henry Lawes"', *RES* (in press).

126. TMS 43; 'Sonnet XIII. To Mr H. Lawes, on his Airs', lines 2–3, *CSP* 294.

127. Guildhall Library MSS 10,343–10,348, Parish Register, St Dunstan in the West, ed. T. C. Ferguson (1898–1901); on George Thomason see *ODNB*. The version of Milton's poem in the Trinity Manuscript is headed 'On the religious memorie of Mrs Catharine Thomason my christian freind deceas'd 16 Decem. 1646'. As 16 December was the date of her interment, it seems likely that Milton's date is either a mistake or the day on which he wrote the poem.

128. *CPW* 7, rev. edn., 255; compare *De Doctrina Christiana*, which is divided into faith or the knowledge of God, and worship, or the love of God.

129. The volume is now in the library of Trinity College Dublin (R.dd.39); on Young see *ODNB.*

130. Above, 18.

131. 'Ad Joannem Rousium Oxoniensis Academiae Bibliothecarium', line 16, *CSP* 303.

10 THE ROAD TO REGICIDE

1. Above, 178.
2. Darbishire, 68. When the thirty-two houses built in Lincoln's Inn Fields by William Newton were completed in the early 1640s, the square became very fashionable, and a house that backed onto the Fields would have been particularly prestigious.
3. BL Add MS 32,310, BL Add MS 4344 fol. 52^v, Parish Register, St Giles in the Fields; Campbell, *Chronology*, 96.
4. The holograph is dated (in Latin) 'the third day of Easter 1647'; Easter Sunday fell on 18 April, so the third day was 20 April. The date of 21 April in the printed *Epistolae* of 1674 (where it is no. 10) must be wrong, though it is consistent with the date of Easter in 1674. The letter has been held in the New York Public Library's Conservation Division since 1988, and we were not allowed to see it in 2007, but it has since been displayed in NYPL's *John Milton at 400 exhibition* (2008). Thomason is not known to have returned to Italy after his visit of 1646, so the letter was probably carried by James Allestree.
5. The manuscript is in the New York Public Library and is available for scholarly scrutiny; it is probably the holograph sent to Milton, but could be Dati's file copy.
6. *Poesie de Francesco Rovai*, ed. N. Rovai (Florence, 1652). On Rovai see Haan, *From Academia to Amicitia*, 61–71.
7. Shawcross, *Bibliography*, distinguishes four editions: the first and second in 1645, the third and fourth in 1647, with a reissue of the fourth edition in 1648.
8. *ODNB.*
9. Below, 188.
10. *LR*, 2. 185.
11. *ODNB.*
12. Robert Baron, *Erotopaignion, or The Cyprian Academy* (London, 1647), 55.
13. Bodleian Tanner MS 466, 34–5 (Psalm 136) and 60–6 (Nativity Ode); *ODNB*.
14. Darbishire, 68.
15. Ian Gentles, *The New Model Army in England, Ireland and Scotland, 1645–1653* (Oxford: Blackwell, 1992), 95–101.
16. Mark Kishlansky, *The Rise of the New Model Army* (Cambridge: Cambridge University Press, 1979).
17. Hughes, Gangraena, 388–9, Gentles, *New Model Army*, 101.
18. Gentles, *New Model Army*, 153.
19. Ibid. 169.
20. Ibid. 235.
21. Ibid. 256.
22. Ibid. 259.
23. Ibid. 276.
24. J. M. French, *Milton in Chancery: New Chapters in the Lives of the Poet and his Father* (New York: MLA, 1939), 113; see above, 178.
25. Below, 207.
26. Campbell, *Chronology*, 97.
27. TMS 47.
28. *CSP* 324–5.
29. *CSP* 323.
30. Gentles, *New Model Army*, 265.

31. Andrew Marvell, 'An Horatian Ode upon Cromwell's Return from Ireland', lines 101–2; *The Poems of Andrew Marvell*, ed. Nigel Smith (London and New York: Pearson Longman, 2003), 278.

32. For example, *CPW* 3. 241; see below, 196.

33. John Milton, *Poems, &c. upon Several Occasions*, 143.

34. *CSP* 309.

35. Psalm lxxx, lines 25–32, *CSP* 311. Carey's text loses something by not printing the marginal note (*Jilgnagu*, the verb meaning 'scorn') and the markers for the three synonyms, the effect of which is to link the languages of England and Israel.

36. Campbell, *Chronology*, 95.

37. Darbishire, 69.

38. Parker, 903–17. See below, 359.

39. G. N. Shuster, *The English Ode from Milton to Keats* (New York: Columbia University Press, 1940), 76.

40. Above, 149.

41. Darbishire, 72–3.

42. See below, 271.

43. *WJM* 14. 4, 6.

44. Gordon Campbell, Thomas N. Corns, John K. Hale, and Fiona J. Tweedie, *Milton and the Manuscript of* De Doctrina Christiana (Oxford: Oxford University Press, 2007), 64–5.

45. See below, 273.

46. Murray Tolmie, *The Triumph of the Saints: The Separate Churches of London 1616–1649* (Cambridge: Cambridge University Press, 1977) 72; *ODNB*.

47. Tolmie, *Triumph*, 72–3, 78, 81, 82.

48. Ibid. 76.

49. For example, consider the conduct of Arise Evans, *ODNB*.

50. Campbell et al., *Milton and the Manuscript*, 89–120; see below, 273–6.

51. Tolmie, *Triumph*, 73.

52. Ibid. 81; above, 168.

53. Quoted by John Coffey, *John Goodwin and the Puritan Revolution* (Woodbridge: Boydell, 2006), 60.

54. *ODNB*; Coffey, *Goodwin, passim* but esp. 44–5, 54.

55. Coffey, *Goodwin*, 180.

56. *CPW* 3. 191.

57. *CPW* 3. 195 and n. 23, 'A glance at Prynne's *A Briefe Memento* (January 4, 1649)'.

58. *CPW* 3. 101–25.

59. *CPW* 3. 194.

60. *CPW* 3. 258.

61. *CPW* 3. 233.

62. Gardiner, *Constitutional Documents*, 269.

63. *CPW* 3. 194.

64. *CPW* 3. 232. Covenant was one of two types of contract (the other was debt), and denoted a promise under seal.

65. *CPW* 3. 212.

66. *CPW* 3. 197.

67. *CPW* 3. 192.

68. *CPW* 3. 216 n. 93.
69. *CPW* 3. 216.
70. *CPW* 3. 212.
71. *CPW* 3. 197, 237, 193.
72. See Thomas Hobbes, *Leviathan* (London, 1651), for example, ch. 14; John Locke, *Two Treatises of Government* (London, 1698), for example, Book II, ch. 5.
73. *CPW* 3. 198–9.
74. *CPW* 3. 221.
75. *CPW* 3. 203; slaves were chattel, which was owned property that could be bought and sold; they could also be leased, in which case they were possessed but not owned by their masters.
76. *CPW* 3. 237.
77. Campbell, *Chronology*, 106.

11 THE PURGED PARLIAMENT

1. G. E. Aylmer, *The State's Servants: The Civil Service of the English Republic 1649–1660* (London and Boston, Routledge and Kegan Paul, 1973), 9–11.
2. Above, 177–8.
3. PRO SP 25/62, 89.
4. Edward Phillips, in Darbishire, 71. Thomson has not been identified. The Bull-head Tavern was on the site of what is now the Royal Bank of Scotland at 49 Charing Cross. Spring Garden was a fashionable park laid out early in the seventeenth century, but was soon to be closed until the Restoration; the street that was subsequently built on the garden is called Spring Gardens. The location is on foot less than ten minutes away from the centre of the Whitehall Palace, which functioned as a government compound.
5. Sean Kelsey, 'The Foundation of the Council of State', in Chris R. Kyle and Jason Peacey (eds.), *Parliament at Work: Parliamentary Committees, Political Power and Public Access in Early Modern England* (Woodbridge: Boydell, 2002), 129–48 [131].
6. Gardiner, *Constitutional Documents*, 384.
7. Ibid. 382–3.
8. Aylmer, *State's Servants*, 17–19.
9. *ODNB*.
10. *ODNB*.
11. *ODNB*. The master of the ceremonies was the official responsible for welcoming ambassadors with appropriate ceremony and escorting them to audiences with the head of state. The office had been established by James I and was replaced in 1820 by that of Marshal of the Diplomatic Corps. On Fleming's agreement on pay and support staff, see *ODNB*.
12. Aylmer, *State's Servants*, 21.
13. Kelsey, 'Foundation', 131–2.
14. Aylmer, *State's Servants*, 22.
15. *ODNB*.
16. On Ireton, Scott, and Harrison see *ODNB*.
17. *CPW* 4. 527.
18. Below, 239.
19. Milton took French lessons as a child (*Ad Patrem*), was complimented on his French by Carlo Dati (who had probably not heard him speak it) and read French historians in

French (recorded in the Commonplace Book). He worked on documents in French for the secretariat. His preference for reading Du Bartas in Sylvester's translation probably reflects an enthusiastic appreciation of the translator's poetic craftsmanship. On his competence in Spanish see Gordon Campbell, 'Milton's Spanish', *MQ* 30 (1996), 127–32.

20. Darbishire, 26, 69; 'tintamarre', as it is now spelt, means 'hubbub'.
21. *ODNB*.
22. *ODNB*.
23. See above, 190.
24. Above, 106.
25. *ODNB*.
26. See above, 104; *ODNB*.
27. *CPW* 4. 627.
28. Above, 179; below, 313.
29. Aylmer, *State's Servants*, 106–10.
30. PRO SP 25/63, 249, PRO SP 25/64, 447. The apartment into which Milton moved had been occupied by the MP Sir John Hippisley; it was in the Scotland Yard section of the Palace of Whitehall, which was so named because it was the section of the palace reserved for the kings of Scotland. The biographical entry for Sir John Hippisley (completed 2003) will be included in the volume due to be published by the History of Parliament Trust in 2016. The warrant, which was issued on 18 June (PRO SP 25/64, 460), was redeemable at the sale of the king's collection of art and furniture at nearby Somerset House.
31. See the discussion of the Oldenburg embassy, below, 244.
32. On Meadows see *ODNB*. Milton's letter recommending Marvell is PRO SP 18/33, 75; below, 257.
33. Aylmer, *State's Servants*, 165; on Meadows, see *ODNB*.
34. Goldsmiths' Company, Court Book, fols. 46 and 96; in the event, the property perished in the Great Fire of 1666, though Milton had by then relinquished his interest in it.
35. Below, 313.
36. Aylmer, *State's Servants*, ch. 4.
37. Ibid. 110.
38. Leo Miller, *John Milton and the Oldenburg Safeguard* (New York: Loewenthal Press, 1985), 70.
39. Gardiner, *Constitutional Documents*, 384.
40. PRO SP 25/62, 94.
41. Below, 280.
42. Miller, *Safeguard, passim*.
43. Darbishire, 69.
44. The earliest record of total blindness is contained in an inscription in the hand of Henry Oxinden in a copy of the 1650 *Eikonoklastes* now in Canterbury Cathedral (Elham 732): 'the man that wrot this booke is now growne blind and is led up and down'; the entry is dated 9 July 1652.
45. *CPW* 4. 871.
46. Below, 375.
47. We are indebted to medical practioners Sarah Carroll and Robert Corns for assistance with this investigation.

48. PRO SP 25/62, 125.

49. Mylius was briefed on the massacre and its significance for the parliamentary government very shortly after his arrival in England; again, 200,000 was the death toll cited (Miller, *Safeguard*, 33–4).

50. 'Observations', *CPW* 3. 308; he adopted a figure of 200,000 in Ulster alone in the first edition of *Pro Populo Anglicano Defensio* (*CPW* 4. 431).

51. Ian Gentles, *The New Model Army in England, Ireland and Scotland, 1645–1653* (Oxford: Blackwell, 1992), 355.

52. PRO SP 25/62, 88.

53. PRO E179/252/14.

54. Gentles, *New Model Army*, 361, 367.

55. Ibid. 60.

56. Above, 57.

57. Gentles, *New Model Army*, 77.

58. Ibid. 359–61.

59. John Buchan, *Oliver Cromwell* (1934; London: Hodder and Stoughton, 1935), 346, 353; Gentles, *New Model Army*, 361.

60. Quoted by Gentles, ibid. 362–3.

61. Anon., *A perfect and particuler Relation Of the severall Marches and proceedings of the Armie in Ireland* (London, 1649), 8.

62. Miller, *Safeguard*, 33.

63. Anon., *The Kings Cabinet opened: or, Certain Packets of Secret Letters & papers Written with the Kings own Hand, and taken in his Cabinet at* Nasby-Field... *Together, with some Annotations thereupon* (London, 1645), sig. A3ᵛ.

64. *CPW* 3. 301.

65. *CPW* 3. 307, 291, 312.

66. Laura Lunger Knoppers, *Constructing Cromwell: Ceremony, Portrait, and Print 1645–1661* (Cambridge, Cambridge University Press, 2000), 66.

67. *CPW* 3. 327.

68. Blair Worden, *The Rump Parliament 1648–1653* (1974; Cambridge: Cambridge University Press, 1977), 80, 191.

69. *CPW* 3. 334.

70. PRO SP 25/62, 117.

71. John Lilburne, *As You Were: or The Lord General Cromwel and the Grand Officers of the Armie their Remembrancer* ([Amsterdam?], 1652), 16.

72. H. N. Brailsford, *The Levellers and the English Revolution*, ed. Christopher Hill (1961; Nottingham: Spokesman, 1983), 474.

73. Quoted Brailsford, *Levellers*, 484.

74. Above, 194.

75. Brailsford, *Levellers*, 520.

76. Ibid. 523.

77. John Canne, *The Improvement of Mercy: or a short Treatise, shewing how, and in what manner, Our Rulers and all well-affected to the present government should make a right and profitable use of the late great victory in Ireland* (London, 1649); *The Snare is broken, Wherein is proved by Scripture, Law and Reason, that the National Covenant and Oath was unlawfully given and taken* (London, 1649).

78. PRO SP 25/62/303.

79. *ODNB.*

80. *ODNB*; Charles I, *Eikon Basilike: The Portraiture of His Sacred Majesty in His Solitudes and Sufferings, with selections from Eikonoklastes*, edited by Jim Daems and Holly Faith Nelson (Peterborough, Ont.: Broadview Press, 2006), 'Introduction', 13–14; all references are to this edition.

81. Andrew Lacey, *The Cult of King Charles the Martyr* (Woodbridge: Boydell, 2003), 85; Sandcroft had intended to buy half a dozen copies, but Royston thought that price would be prohibitive.

82. *CPW* 3. 339, 456.

83. *CPW* 3. 339.

84. For a recent review of the evidence, see *Eikon Basilike*, ed. cit., 16–21.

85. Anon., *Eikon Alethine. The Pourtraiture of Truths most sacred Majesty truly suffering, though not solely* (London, 1649), sig. a2^v.

86. *CPW* 3. 337–8.

87. *CPW* 3. 352, 354, 380–1, 452.

88. Thomas Corns, *Uncloistered Virtue: English Political Literature, 1640–1660* (Oxford: Clarendon Press, 1992), 212.

89. Ibid., ch. 1.

90. *CPW* 3. 342, 530, 420–1.

91. *Eikon Basilike*, ed. cit., 205 and n.

92. *LR* 2. 226.

93. *ODNB.*

94. William Empson, *Milton's God* (rev. edn., London: Chatto and Windus, 1965), 317–18.

95. *CPW* 3. 364.

96. Corns, *Development*, chs. 8 and 10.

97. *CPW* 3. 553.

98. *CPW* 1. 374.

99. Kevin Sharpe, *Remapping Early Modern England: The Culture of Seventeenth-Century Politics* (Cambridge: Cambridge University Press, 2000), esp. ch. 7.

100. *CPW* 3. 339.

101. Below, 287.

102. *CPW* 3. 487.

103. PRO SP 25/63, 486; PRO SP 25/95, 3; Guildhall Library MS 34275, 179–80 (Scholars' Register, Merchant Taylors' Company, letter of 7 March 1649/50), 179–80.

104. The date is an inference from *Nouvelles Ordinaires de Londres*, no. 34, 20 February/2 March–27 February/9 March 1651.

105. *ODNB.*

106. *CPW* 4. 307.

107. Below, 264, 315–16.

108. *CPW* 4. 392.

109. *CPW* 4. 852–3. Milton's letter (*Epistolae* no. 12) was written from London rather than Westminster, which may be indicative of the domestic disruption consequent upon the death of his wife and son.

110. *CPW* 4. 366–7.

111. *CPW* 4. 359.

112. Consider, for example, Inigo Jones's designs for the costumes of Henrietta Maria and her ladies in *Chloridia* or *Tempe Restored*, her Shrovetide masques of 1631 and 1632. See

Stephen Orgel and Roy Strong, *Inigo Jones: The Theatre of the Stuart Court* (London and Berkeley and Los Angeles: Sotheby Parke Bernet and University of California Press, 1973), 2. 441–8, 498–503.

113. *CPW* 4. 408.
114. John Wilmot, Earl of Rochester, 'Satyr', lines 33–4, *The Works of John Wilmot, Earl of Rochester*, ed. Harold Love (Oxford: Oxford University Press, 1999), 86.
115. *WJM* 7. 12.
116. *CPW* 4. 307.
117. *CPW* 4. 963.
118. *CPW* 4. 112; for a similar misreading, see Corns, *Prose Works*, 93.
119. John K. Hale, *Milton's Cambridge Latin: Performing in the Genres 1625–1632* (Tempe: Arizona Center for Medieval and Renaissance Studies, 2005), 121.
120. John K. Hale, *Milton's Languages* (Cambridge: Cambridge University Press, 1997), 96–8.
121. *WJM* 7. 280.
122. *WJM* 7. 281.
123. Darbishire, 26.
124. *CPW* 4. 317.
125. *CPW* 4. 340–1.
126. *CPW* 4. 474.
127. *CPW* 4. 395–6.
128. *CPW* 4. 307, 338.
129. *CPW* 4. 390–1.
130. *CPW* 4. 399.
131. On Mary (1631–60), princess royal and princess of Orange, see *ODNB*; she was 9 when she married 14-year-old Willem of Orange (from 1647 Willem II), who died at the age of 24, a week before his son Willem III (on whom see *ODNB* s.n. 'William III and II') was born. The mathematician Johan de Witt (1625–72) was Grand Pensionary (Raadspensionaris) of Holland from 1652 until his death at the hands of a mob.
132. For an account of the mission, see Robert Fallon, *Milton in Government* (University Park, Pa.: Pennsylvania University Press, 1993), 73–88.
133. *CPW* 4. 312.
134. *CPW* 4. 430.
135. *CPW* 4. 341.
136. John Milton, *Ioannis Miltons Engelsmans Verdedigingh des gemeene Volcks van Engelandt, tegens Claudius sonder Naem, alias Salmasius Konincklijcke Verdedigingh. Wt het Latijn overgeset na de Copy gedruckt tot Londen, by Du Gardianis* (Gouda, 1651).
137. Bibliothèque Nationale MS F.L. 602, fols. 21–2, MS F.L. 602, fols. 23, 23a.
138. Leo Miller, 'Milton's Defensio Ordered Wholesale for the States of Holland', *N&Q* 231 (1986), 33.
139. Darbishire, 160.
140. On Pauw's mission see Leo Miller, *John Milton's Writings in the Anglo-Dutch Negotiations, 1651–1654* (Pittsburgh, Pa.: Duquesne University Press, 1992), 49–55); on the war, below, 255.
141. *Mercurius Politicus*, no. 39.
142. The letter is printed in *LR* 3. 9; French's translation reverses sender and recipient and in the headnote translates Lugdunum as Lyons rather than Leiden.

143. Amsterdam Universiteits-Bibliotheek, MS III.E.40; Burmann, 3. 595–6.

144. Burmann, 3. 600, 257–9.

145. Hartlib 62/30/1a–4b.

146. Burmann, 3. 742.

147. Order Book 23 January 1652, PRO SP 25/66/252; the Latin text is printed in Miller, *Writings*, where it is mistakenly described as Milton's translation. Lodewijk was the brother of the mathematician Christiaan Huygens and the son of Constantijn Huygens, the poet, composer, and diplomat.

148. See Miller, *Writings*, 14–15 and 304. The orders to Milton are PRO SP 25/66/257 and 267.

149. Miller, *Writings*, 16–20 provides other examples.

150. Edited versions of the documents are printed in Miller, *Writings*, 94–293.

151. PRO SP/20, 44, 46. The issue has been frequently discussed. See, for example, Campbell, *Chronology*, 119.

152. *ODNB*.

153. *ODNB*.

154. Darbishire, 71; *ODNB*.

155. *CPW* 4. 892.

156. Quoted and translated in Miller, *Safeguard*, 278–9.

157. Ibid. 1.

158. Ibid. 75.

159. Ibid. 141, 146.

160. Ibid. 41, 180, 196. On Anthon Günther's death, control of Oldenburg did revert to Denmark, though the issue remained contentious among Baltic states for some time.

161. PRO SP 25/19, 146.

162. Miller, *Safeguard*, 171–2.

163. Ibid. 141.

164. Ibid. 26.

165. Ibid. 128.

166. Aylmer, *State's Servants*, 19.

167. Miller, *Safeguard*, 200, 219, 176, 215, 219.

168. Edward Phillips, in Darbishire, 71. Petty France was so called because it was formerly inhabited by French wool merchants. The house that Milton rented was later owned by Jeremy Bentham, whose tenant from 1811 was William Hazlitt; John Stuart Mill was a later resident. The house survived until 1877, when it was demolished by the Metropolitan Railway Company.

169. Leo Miller, 'New Milton Texts and Data from the Aitzema Mission, 1652', *N&Q* 235 (1990), 279–88.

170. Mary's death and Deborah's birth are recorded in Milton's family Bible (BL Add MS 32,310); Deborah's birth is also recorded in Birch's transcription of Mary's (lost) Bible (BL Add MS 4244, fol. 52ᵛ). We owe the suggestion of burial in Horton to Edward Jones. If correct, it would point towards a continuing interest, perhaps financial, perhaps social, in the place of his father's retirement.

171. Darbishire, 71.

172. 'The humble proposals of Mr Owen, Mr Tho. Goodwin, Mr Nye, Mr Sympson, and other ministers: who presented the petition to the Parliament, and other persons, Febr. 11. under debate by a committee this 31 of March, 1652. for the furtherance and

propagation of the Gospel in this nation. Wherein they having had equall respects to all persons fearing God, though of differing judgements, doe hope also that they will tend to union and peace. With additionall propositions humbly tendred to the Committee for propagating the Gospel, as easie and speedy means for supply of all parishes in England with able, godly, and orthodox ministers. For, setling of right constituted churches, and for preventing persons of corrupt judgements, from publishing dangerous errours, and blasphemies in assemblies and meetings, by other godly persons, ministers, and others.' On the four named ministers see *ODNB*.

173. Fallon, *Milton in Government*, has elucidated the correspondence with Hamburg (34–43), Portugal (43–53), Oldenburg (53–65), the United Provinces (73–88), Spain (88–100), Denmark (100–11), and Tuscany (111–22).

174. On Sophia, Maurice, and Rupert see *ODNB*; Sophia had lived in Leiden, The Hague, and Heidelberg.

175. On Walker, who subsequently died in prison while awaiting trial for treason, see *ODNB*.

176. The search warrant is now in the library of the University of Illinois; the entry in the Order Book (in which Milton's name is missing) is PRO SP 25/64/283.

177. PRO SP 25/62/373; on Ley see *ODNB*.

178. PRO SP 25/62/422; PRO SP 25/62/464b. On Nedham see *ODNB* and Joseph Frank, *Cromwell's Press Agent: A Critical Biography of Marchamont Nedham* (Lanham, Md.: University Press of America, 1980).

179. Stationers' Register, i. 333; the book was *Histoire . . . du Procès de Charles Stuart*, which was published in London by John Grismond in March 1650.

180. Above, 245.

181. PRO SP 18/23/6.

182. Register of Presentations, 1649–54, BL Add MS 36792; see Austin Woolrych, 'Milton and Richard Heath', PQ 53 (1974), 132–5.

183. The Order of 20 July 1652 is PRO SP 25/30/54; the record of 9 July 1653 is PRO SP 25/70/32; on Bruno Ryves (or Reeves) see *ODNB*.

184. Below, 250–1.

185. *ODNB*.

186. Fallon, *Milton in Government*, 22.

187. Aylmer, *State's Servants*, 68, 23; *ODNB*.

12 THE PROTECTORATE

1. Worden, *Rump*; Woolrych, *Commonwealth*.

2. Woolrych, *Commonwealth*, 104.

3. On Sydenham, Pickering, and Strickland, see *ODNB*.

4. Above, 206.

5. Woolrych, *Commonwealth*, 123–5.

6. On Barbon (or Barebone), see *ODNB*.

7. Above, 245.

8. Below, 280.

9. Woolrych, *Commonwealth*, 394.

10. Ibid. 352.

11. Gardiner, *Constitutional Documents*, 416.

12. Hill, *Milton*, 175.

13. Gardiner, *Constitutional Documents*, 448–9.
14. See above, 237 and Leo Miller, *John Milton in the Anglo-Dutch Negotiations, 1651–1654* (Pittsburgh: Duquesne University Press, 1992).
15. On Milton's correspondence with France, see Fallon, *Milton in Government*, 151–60.
16. *CPW* 4. 557; above, 238.
17. On Milton's correspondence with Sweden and its antagonists, see Fallon, *Milton in Government*, 160–76.
18. PRO SP 25/78/132; there is a blank where the forename should be.
19. Dryden signed a receipt for £50 on 19 October 1657 (PRO SP 18/180/95; see Paul Hammond, 'Dryden's Employment by Cromwell's Government', *Transactions of the Cambridge Bibliographical Society* 8 (1981), Part I, 130–6, plates 3 and 4.
20. PRO SP 25/55/28 (17 April 1655); PRO SP 25/107/143 (25 October 1659).
21. Aylmer, *State's Servants*, 82.
22. Milton's counterpart of the mortgage deed is in the Rosenbach Museum in Philadelphia (810/25); the acquittance (i.e. receipt) is in the Folger Library in Washington (MS 960.1). In 1665 Milton sold the mortgage bond to Jeremy Hamey, who bought the bond in trust for his brother Dr Baldwin Hamey; on Baldwin Hamey, who may at one time have been Milton's physician, see *ODNB*.
23. On Milton's second wife, Katherine Woodcock, see below, 268–9. The fact that her mother was at this time living with the family suggests that she was perhaps attending to her daughter, who died a few weeks later of consumption.
24. Also known as Pierre de Vaux, Peter Valdo, and Peter Waldo; on the early history of the sect, see Gabriel Audisio, *The Waldensian Dissent: Persecution and Survival, c.1170–c.1570*, Cambridge Medieval Textbooks (Cambridge: Cambridge University Press, 1990).
25. On Milton's correspondence with Savoy, see Fallon, *Milton in Government*, 139–51.
26. Milton had read Pierre Gilles' *Histoire ecclesiastique des églises reformées, recueillies en quelques valées de Piedmont ... autrefois appelées Eglises Vaudoises* (Geneva, 1644), and made a note on it in his Commonplace Book (*CPW* 1. 379)].
27. Lines 1–8, *CSP* 342–3.
28. John Dury to Samuel Hartlib in letters from Amsterdam (Hartlib 4/3/1A-1B, Hartlib 4/3/2A-2B); Willem Nieuport to Alexander More in a letter from Westminster (*LR*, 3. 399–402); unsigned letter, apparently to More (Bodleian MS Rawlinson A.16, fol. 455).
29. *ODNB*, s.n. More, Alexander.
30. *CPW* 4. 561.
31. *CPW* 4. 595.
32. *CPW* 4. 664–72.
33. Below, 365.
34. *CPW* 4. 605–6.
35. *CPW* 4. 676–7. Almost certainly, Philip Sidney, Viscount Lisle is intended, and not, as the *CPW* editor suggests (n. 524) his younger brother, Algernon.
36. *CPW* 4. 669–70.
37. *CPW* 4. 639; above, 207.
38. *ODNB*.
39. *CPW* 4. 676.
40. *CPW* 4. 756.

41. *CPW* 4. 819 and n. 308.
42. Line 14, Psalm i; lines 12–4, Psalm ii; lines 1–2, Psalm i; lines 15–7, Psalm iii; *CSP*, 334–5.
43. On Henry Lawrence, *see ODNB*.
44. Darbishire, 74.
45. Horace, *Odes* 1.16.1.
46. *CPW* 2.596. On otium see Brian Vickers, 'Leisure and Idleness in the Renaissance: The Ambivalence of Otium', *Renaissance Studies* 4 (1994), 1–37, 107–54.
47. The first quatrain of 'Cyriack whose grandsire' is missing, as it was on a page (now lost) of a separate booklet with small pages which Milton used for sonnets; the outside pages were those now numbered 45 and 49.
48. On Coke (pronounced 'Cook') and his reputation *see ODNB*.
49. Unnumbered in *CSP*.
50. The letter, dated 2 June 1654, also describes Marvell's presentation of the *Defensio Secunda* to John Bradshaw; the letter survives in an eighteenth-century transcription by Josiah Owen (BL Add MS 4292, fol. 264.
51. On 6 July 1653 Milton wrote to Oldenburg about the authorship of the *Clamor*; on 27 October 1653 Milton wrote to acknowledge receipt of a letter delivered by Oldenburg; on 25 June 1656 Milton wrote to Oldenburg in Oxford, passing on the greetings of Cyriack Skinner; on 1 August 1657 Milton wrote to Oldenburg (and Richard Jones) in Saumur, deploring the appointment of Morus as minister in Charenton; Milton's final letter to Oldenburg was written on 20 December 1659. These letters, all in Latin, are printed in *Epistolae Familiares*. On 28 December 1656 Oldenburg wrote to Milton from Oxford about the date of Christmas (Royal Society MS I, fol. 11), and on 4/14 October he wrote from Saumur (Royal Society MS I, fol. 30).
52. On Lady Ranelagh, *see ODNB*, s.n. Katherine Jones, Viscountess Ranelagh. She was led to the Hartlib circle by her aunt, Dorothy Moore (née King, later Durie; see *ODNB*, s.n. Durie], who was the sister of Edward King, Milton's Lycidas.
53. For details of Katherine and her family, see J. S. Smart (ed.), *The Sonnets of Milton* (Glasgow: Maclehose, Jackson, 1921), 121–4, 175–88, and Parker, 480–1, 1053–5.
54. The banns and the record of the marriage are recorded in the Parish Register of St Mary the Virgin, Aldermanbury (Guildhall Library MS 3572, printed *PHSR* 61, 62, 65 (1931–5).
55. Above, 62.
56. College of Arms, Painters' Workbook I.B.7, fol. 46b; on heraldic funerals, see C. Gittings, *Death, Burial and the Individual in Early Modern England* (London: Croom Helm, 1984).
57. David Cressy, *Birth, Marriage, and Death: Ritual, Religion, and the Life-Cycle in Tudor and Stuart England* (Oxford, Oxford University Press, 1997), 204.
58. 'Julia's Churching, or Purification', quoted and discussed by Cressy, *Birth*, 204.
59. Cressy, *Birth*, 225.
60. The album is in the Stadbibliothek Vadiana, St Gallen, Switzerland; see Leo Miller, 'Milton in the Zollikoffer and Arnold Albums', *MQ* 24 (1990), 99–104.
61. Milton's Latin letter is printed in *Epistolae Familiares*, no. 21. On Bigot, see *DBF* and Leonard Doucette, *Emery Bigot: Seventeenth-Century French Humanist* (Toronto, 1970); on the treatise, see V. H. Galbraith, 'The *Modus Tenendi Parliamentum*', *JWCI* 16 (1953), 81–99.

62. On Cotton and Ryley, see *ODNB*.

63. Milton has arranged for payment and shipping to be handled by Jean-Baptiste Stouppe, a Swiss minister, who had written on the Piedmont massacre and was working as an agent for Thurloe.

64. The letters are *Epistolae Familiares* no. 23 (15 July 1657) and 26 (16 December 1657); Henri de Brass has not been properly identified.

65. The letters to Heimbach are *Epistolae Familiares* no. 20 (8 November 1656) and 27 (18 December 1657). The unidentified atlas about which Milton has enquired is said to cost 130 florins, which Milton decides is too much for a blind man to pay for maps. Heimbach has not been properly identified.

66. Darbishire, 72.

67. Ibid. 73.

68. On conjectured manuscript circulation, see below, 327.

69. Below, 352, 382.

70. For the fullest account of the making of the manuscript, see Gordon Campbell, Thomas N. Corns, John K. Hale, and Fiona J. Tweedie, *Milton and the Manuscript of* De Doctrina Christiana (Oxford: Oxford University Press, 2007), especially ch. 3. The manuscript is catalogued as PRO SP 9/61.

71. Steven R. Dobranski and John P. Rumrich (eds.), *Milton and Heresy* (Cambridge: Cambridge University Press, 1988), 80–1.

72. See Hill, *Milton*, 285–96.

73. On the four dominant theories of the atonement (recapitulation, ransom, satisfaction and forensic), see C. A. Patrides, *Milton and the Christian Tradition* (Oxford: Oxford University Press, 1966), 132–42.

74. *PL* 3. 183–8; discussed below, 338.

75. On the doctrine of mortalism, see Norman T. Burns, *Christian Mortalism from Tyndale to Milton* (Cambridge, Mass.: Harvard University Press, 1972).

76. On polygamy, see Leo Miller, *John Milton among the Polygamophiles* (New York: Loewenthal Press, 1974).

77. Sir Walter Ralegh [attrib. incorrectly], *The Cabinet-Council: Containing the Chief Arts of Empire and Mysteries of State* (London, 1658), sigs. A2^{r-v}.

13 FROM THE DEATH OF OLIVER CROMWELL TO THE RESTORATION

1. PRO SP/182/90 fol. 2.

2. *WJM* 13. 400–5.

3. *WJM*, 13. 411.

4. In August; *ODNB*.

5. *WJM* 13. 406–9.

6. *WJM* 13. 412–15.

7. *WJM* 13. 414–17.

8. *WJM* 13. 416–27. In the printed and MS collections of the State Papers the letter to the king of Portugal is addressed to Afonso's late father, João IV, who had died in November 1656; only the Lünig collection of the State Papers (J. C. Lünig (ed.) *Literae Procurem Europae* (Leipzig, 1712)) correctly addresses the letter to Afonso.

9. Ronald Hutton, *The Restoration: A Political and Religious History of England and Wales 1658–1667* (1985; Oxford: Oxford University Press, 1987), 25; the final years of the

republic is a tale often told, and our narrative, where events are related without citation, draws on a synthesis of Hutton's study and Austin Woolrych's fine introduction to *CPW*, 7, rev. edn. 1–228, augmented by Ruth E. Mayers, *1659: The Crisis of the Commonwealth* (Woodbridge: Boydell, 2004) and N. H. Keeble, *The Restoration: England in the 1660s* (Oxford: Blackwell, 2002).

10. Above, 245.

11. Anon., *To Parliament. The humble Representation and desires of divers Freeholders and others inhabiting within the County of Bedford* (London, 1659), broadside.

12. On Hesilrige see *ODNB*.

13. Sir Henry Vane the younger, *A Healing Question propounded and resolved upon occasion of the late publique and seasonable Call to Humiliation* (London, 1656), sig, D1ʳ.

14. *ODNB*.

15. *Mercurius Politicus* No. 554, 10–17 February 1659 and *The Publick Intelligencer* no. 163, 7–14 February 1659. On Newcombe see *ODNB*.

16. *CPW* 7, rev. edn., 240.

17. *CPW* 7, rev. edn., 252.

18. Above, 160.

19. *CPW* 7, rev. edn., 272.

20. Above, 169, 173.

21. *CPW* 7, rev. edn., 242, 255.

22. *CPW* 7, rev. edn., 252. Civil law is here set in opposition to church law (the *corpus iuris civilis* as opposed to the *corpus iuris canonici*).

23. *CPW* 7, rev. edn., 249.

24. Parker, 518–20; Campbell et al., *Manuscript of* De Doctrina Christiana, 64–5.

25. Hutton, *Restoration*, 35–7.

26. On Wall see R. H. Popkin, 'A Note on Moses Wall', in Menasseh ben Israel, *The Hope of Israel*, ed. H. Méchoulan and G. Nahon (Oxford, 1987), 165–70. On the date of the letter, which is 26 May in the surviving transcription, see Campbell's note in Parker, 1251.

27. The letter is dated 21 April in Milton's *Epistolae*, but Jean Despagne did not die till 25 April, so '21 April' must be a misprint for a later date. On Jean Despagne see *ODNB* and *DBF*; on Labadie see T. J. Saxby, *The Quest for the New Jerusalem: Jean de Labadie and the Labadists, 1610–1744* (Dordrecht and Boston: Martinus Nijhoff, 1987). The French church in London was on Threadneedle Street, but Westminster had a separate congregation. It did not meet in the chapel in Somerset House (a Catholic chapel built in anticipation of the Spanish match and subsequently desecrated) but in the nearby Savoy Chapel.

28. Hutton, *Restoration*, 35.

29. *WJM* 13. 462–5.

30. On George Fleetwood and John Lambert see *ODNB*.

31. Mayers, *1659*, 41.

32. Quoted by Philip Aubrey, *Mr Secretary Thurloe: Cromwell's Secretary of State 1652–1660* (London: Athlone, 1990), 150.

33. On Lockhart and Scott see *ODNB*.

34. *WJM* 13. 428–33.

35. PRO SP 25/107, 143.

36. Above, 219; on Canne see *ODNB*.

37. Godfrey Davies, *The Restoration of Charles II, 1658–1660* (San Marino, Calif.: Huntington Library, 1955); Mayers, *1659, passim*.

38. Barry Reay, *The Quakers and the English Revolution* (New York: St Martin's Press, 1985).

39. Anthony Mellidge, quoted by Reay, *Quakers*, 82–3.

40. For an account of his suffering see, Anthony Mellidge, *Winchester Prison the 21th day of the 1 month, 59 If the measure of my sufferings under the creuel hands of unreasonale men, be finished in this noysome prison by the laying down of my life* (London: 1659).

41. Reay, *Quakers*, 93–5. On Booth see *ODNB*.

42. Thomason dates his copy 'Aug'; it was not advertised till a notice in *Mercurius Politicus*, no. 585, 1–8 September 1659.

43. On Chapman see *ODNB*; he was to publish Milton's *Readie and Easie Way*. See below, 294.

44. *CPW* 7, rev. edn., 274; discussed extensively, 85–7.

45. *CPW* 7, rev. edn., 275; Corns, *Uncloistered Virtue*, 272–3.

46. *CPW* 7, rev. edn., 302. Smithfield, a 10-acre area just outside the city walls, has been a meat market since the twelfth century.

47. *CPW* 7, rev. edn., 302–5, 317.

48. George Fox, *The Journal*, ed. Nigel Smith (Harmondsworth: Penguin, 1998), 257–9.

49. Hutton, *Restoration*, 49.

50. Ibid. 64.

51. On Disbrowe (or Desborough) see *ODNB*.

52. Hutton, *Restoration*, 67; *ODNB*.

53. The *CPW* edition is based on a manuscript copy in the Columbia University Library.

54. Bradshaw added the codicil bequeathing £10 to Milton on 10 September 1655 (PRO PROB 11/296/549); the will was proved on 16 December 1659.

55. *CPW* 7, rev. edn., 326–7, 324, 328–32.

56. Hutton, *Restoration*, 67.

57. *CPW* 7, rev. edn., 336.

58. Hutton, *Restoration*, 91.

59. Samuel Pepys, *The Diary of Samuel Pepys*, ed. Robert Latham and William Mathews (11 vols., London: Bell, 1970–83), 1. 79.

60. *CPW* 7, rev. edn., 342.

61. Hutton, *Restoration*, 93.

62. Prynne had twice attacked the *Pro Populo Anglicano Defensio* in May 1659, in *The Re-Publicans* and *A True and Perfect Narrative*.

63. *CPW* 7, rev. edn., 345 n. 26.

64. *CPW* 7, rev. edn., 353–5.

65. *CPW* 7, rev. edn., 367.

66. *CPW* 7, rev. edn., 354 n. 2.

67. *CPW* 7, rev. edn., 356; the three times were at the inception of the Long Parliament, at the restoration of the Purged Parliament in May 1659 and again in December; the words were omitted when Milton revised the pamphlet for its second edition.

68. *CPW* 7, rev. edn., 358.

69. *CPW* 7, rev. edn., 369.

70. *CPW* 7, rev. edn., 385.

71. *CPW* 7, rev. edn., 388.
72. Aubrey, *Thurloe*, 156–8.
73. Darbishire, 76.
74. Hutton, *Restoration*, 103. On Annesley see *ODNB*.
75. John Milton, *A Complete Collection of the Historical, Political, and Miscellaneous Works of John Milton, Both English and Latin. With som Papers never before Publish'd* ('Amsterdam' [actually London]: 1698), 799; *CPW* 7, rev. edn., 393.
76. *CPW* 7, rev. edn., 389.
77. *CPW* 7, rev. edn., 395.
78. *CPW* 7, rev. edn., 392.
79. See above, 196.
80. Hutton, *Restoration*, 106.
81. Gardiner, *Constitutional Documents*, 391.
82. Marchamont Nedham, *Interest Will Not Lie, or, A View of England's True Interest* (London, 1659), title page, 11–16.
83. Marchamont Nedham, *Newes from Brussels in a Letter from an Attendant on his Majesties Person* ([London], 1660), 6. Kitlings are kittens.
84. *CPW* 7, rev. edn., 389.
85. *CPW* 7, rev. edn., 389, 452–4.
86. Quoted Keeble, *Restoration*, 25; on Denzil Holles see *ODNB*.
87. *CPW* 7, rev. edn., 425; *OED*, s.v. 'groom of the stole', 1.
88. *CPW* 7, rev. edn., 437–44.
89. *ODNB*.
90. Matthew Griffith, *The Fear of God and the King* (London, 1660), 1.
91. Ibid., sig. A4^v–A5^r.
92. Ibid., '91' [i.e. 81]–82.
93. *ODNB*.
94. Hutton, *Restoration*, 111.
95. *CPW* 7, rev. edn., 485–6, 477, 482.
96. Quoted Keeble, *Restoration*, 29.
97. On the Declaration of Breda, see below, 307.

15 SURVIVING THE RESTORATION

1. Hutton, *Restoration*, 125.
2. Above, 299.
3. Gardiner, *Constitutional Documents*, 465–6.
4. Above, 177–8.
5. Hutton, *Restoration*, 59.
6. Anon., *The VVhole business of Sindercome, from first to last, it being a perfect narrative of his carriage, during the time of his imprisonment in the Tower of London* (London, 1657), 8–9, 16. On Sindercombe see *ODNB*.
7. On Axtell, Hacker, Cook, Peter, Broughton, Phelps, and Dendy see *ODNB*; see also the *ODNB* survey entry on 'regicides'.
8. *ODNB*.
9. Hutton, *Restoration*, 115.
10. Joseph Frank, *Cromwell's Press Agent: A Critical Biography of Marchamont Nedham* (Lanham, Md.: University Press of America, 1980), 153.

11. Darbishire, 32.
12. Hutton, *Restoration*, 133; *ODNB*.
13. F. A. Inderwick, *A Calendar of the Inner Temple Records* (5 vols., London: Sotheran & Co., 1896–1936), 3. 1.
14. Shawcross, *Arms*, 69–71.
15. Above, 179.
16. Montague Bertie, earl of Lindsey, et al., *A declaration of the nobility, knights & gentry of the County of Oxon which have adhered to the late King* (London, 1660), single sheet.
17. Darbishire, 74.
18. Ibid. 271; on Morice and Clarges see *ODNB*.
19. Darbishire, 30.
20. *ODNB*.
21. Darbishire, 272.
22. *ODNB*.
23. Below, 313.
24. Darbishire, 78.
25. *CPW* 7. rev. edn., 452.
26. Roger L'Estrange, *Be Merry and Wise; or, A Seasonable Word to the Nation* (London, 1660), 86.
27. Roger L'Estrange, *No Blinde Guides, in Answer To a seditious Pamphlet of J. Milton's, Intituled Brief Notes upon a late Sermon* (London, 1660), 11, 1–2; the imprint dates it 20 April.
28. On Starkey, who was also a medical polemicist, see *ODNB*; *The Dignity of Kingship*, in which the author is identified by the initials G.S., has occasionally been attributed to George Searle or Gilbert Sheldon, but W. R. Parker's identification of the author as Starkey in his facsimile edition of 1942 is now generally accepted.
29. Anon., *The Out-Cry of the London Prentices for Justice to be Executed upon John Lord Hewson* (London, 1659), 6; Thomason dated his copy 'Jan: 16' [1659], that is, 1660. On John Hewson see *ODNB*. The Barber-Surgeons' Hall in Monkwell Street maintained a collection of medical oddities.
30. Anon., *The Character of the Rump* (London, 1660), 2–3; Thomason dates his copy 'March 17 1659', i.e. 1660. On the attribution to Butler see Nicholas von Maltzahn, 'Samuel Butler's Milton', *SP* 92 (1995), 482–9.
31. See *ODNB*, which has a section on 'reputation' that would seem to clinch the identification.
32. Darbishire, 177.
33. Frank, *Nedham*, 125–7, 143–5.
34. Darbishire, 32.
35. *LR* 4. 317–18; the document was offered for sale on 29 June 1995, and is reproduced in the Christie's catalogue of that date, but was subsequently withdrawn. See Campbell et al., *Milton and the Manuscript*, 31–2. On Picard, see above, 000.
36. Hutton, *Restoration*, 135.
37. Below, 330.
38. Darbishire, 78.
39. Ibid. 32 and n.
40. See Wilmot, 'A Ramble in St. James's Park', *Works*, 76–80.

41. Darbishire, 74. Bartholomew Close, by the church of St Bartholomew the Great, was principally occupied by printers. It was (and remains) a narrow street amid a maze of such streets.

42. *ODNB.*

43. Darbishire, 74.

44. Hutton, *Restoration*, 133.

45. Above, 194.

46. *Journal of the House of Commons* 8. 65–6; *Parliamentary Intelligencer* no. '26' (i.e. 25); *The Diary of Bulstrode Whitelock, 1605–1675*, ed. Ruth Spalding (Oxford: Published for the British Academy by Oxford University Press, 1991), 606.

47. *A proclamation for calling in, and suppressing of two books written by John Milton the one intituled, Johannis Miltoni Angli pro populo Anglicano defensio, contra Claudii Anonymi aliàs Salmasii, defensionem regiam; and the other in answer to a book intituled, The pourtraicture of His Sacred Majesty in his solitude and sufferings. And also a third book intituled, The obstructors of justice, written by John Goodwin* (London, 1660), broadside.

48. *LR* 4. 334, 338, 323.

49. *ODNB.* The Attorney-General was Sir Geoffrey Palmer, who had preceded Milton at Christ's; Palmer was memorably described by the fugitive regicide, Edmund Ludlow, as 'one of the tyrant's bloodhounds at the bar', thirsting for the blood of innocent lambs (*A Voyce from the Watch Tower*, ed. A. B. Worden, *CS*, 4th ser., 21 (1978), 315), cit. *ODNB.*

50. Darbishire, 74.

51. Hutton, *Restoration*, 134.

52. Above, 290.

53. Pepys, *Diary*, 1. 309; Fox, *Journal*, 293.

54. The house was in the parish of St Giles in the Fields, where Milton's daughter Mary had been baptized in 1648; Red Lion Fields was laid out as what is now Red Lion Square in 1684.

55. Darbishire, 75.

56. The pardon is listed in the PRO's Index to Warrant Books, 1660–1722, A-P, (IND/1/ 8911, 201) and the Index to the Signet Office Docket Bookss, 1660–1737 (PRO SO 4/5 fol. 164), both under December 1660.

57. *Journals of the House of Commons*, 8. 208.

58. 'Nu uytging door goe beloften'; *Hollandsche Mercurius*, no. 249 (1661), 163.

59. Darbishire, 32.

60. The house was in the parish of St Giles Cripplegate, so must have been at the Redcrosse end of Jewin Street (which was destroyed during World War II, and is now under the site of the Barbican complex) rather than the Aldersgate Street end.

61. Ephraim Pagitt, *Heresiography Or A Description of the Hereticks and Sectaries of these Latter times* (London, 1645; 6th edn., 1661); see above, 167.

62. *Regii Sanguinis Clamor* (The Hague, 1661); see above, 260.

63. G.S. [i.e., George Starkey], *Monarchy Triumphing Over Traiterous Republicans* (London, 1661); see above, 312.

64. Claudius Salmasius, *Claudii Salmasii ad Johannem Miltonum Responsio, Opus Posthumum* (London, 1660).

65. Pepys, *Diary*, 1. 265. On Venner and Harrison see *ODNB.*

66. Anon., *The last speech and prayer with other passages of Thomas Venner, the chief incourager and promoter of the late horrid rebellion immediately before his execution in*

Coleman-street on Saturday last being the 19th of Ianuary, 1660 [i. e. 1661]: together with the names of the rest that were condemned for the same fact (London, 1660 [i. e. 1661]), 6; compare Harrison's words, quoted in C. V. Wedgwood, *The Trial of Charles I* (1964; London: Reprint Society, 1966), 233.

67. Hutton, *Restoration*, 147, 151.
68. Ibid. 152–3; Keeble, *Restoration*, 115. The cluster of measures introduced by this parliament are often known, collectively, as 'the Clarendon Code'.
69. Above, 196.
70. Keeble, *Restoration*, 118–19.
71. *ODNB.*
72. Keeble, *Restoration*, 120–1.
73. Above, 194.
74. Below, 379.
75. George Sikes (?), *The Life and Death of Sir Henry Vane, Kt.* (London, 1652), 93–4; Hutton, *Restoration*, 162–3.

16 PLAGUE, FIRE, AND *PARADISE LOST*

1. *ODNB.*
2. Thomas Ellwood, *The History of the Life of Thomas Ellwood* (2nd edn., London: 1714), 154; Darbishire, 75.
3. Ellwood, *History, passim.*
4. Ibid. 153.
5. Ibid. 154–8.
6. *LR* 4. 381–3; below 382.
7. Declaration of Intention to Marry, Lambeth Palace MS FMI/3B fol. 149.
8. PRO PROB 24/13/312–313ᵛ.
9. Stone, *The Family*, 31–4.
10. John Stow, *A Survey of London*, ed. Charles Lethbridge Kingsford (3 vols., 1908–27; Oxford: Clarendon Press, 1971), I. 252–3.
11. Above, 41.
12. Robert Gell, *Stella nova, a new starre, leading wisemen unto Christ* (London, 1649); *ODNB.*
13. Robert Gell, *Aggelokratia theon, or, A sermon touching Gods government of the world by angels* (London, 1650).
14. 'Irenaus Philadelphus Philanthropus', *Eirenikon, or, A Treatise of peace between the two visible divided parties* (London, 1660), 102.
15. Darbishire, 75.
16. Above, 271.
17. *ODNB*, s.n. Phillips, Edward.
18. *ODNB.*
19. Hutton, *Restoration*, 211.
20. Above, 31.
21. Ellwood, *History*, 246.
22. *ODNB.*
23. Alone of the properties Milton lived in, it still survives, and, with the support of the Milton Cottage Trust, houses a collection of Milton memorabilia.
24. *ODNB.*

25. *ODNB*.
26. *ODNB*, s.n. Fleetwood, Hester.
27. Richard Baxter, *Reliquiae Baxterianae*, ed. Matthew Sylvester (London, 1696), 3. 1.
28. Stephen Porter, *The Great Fire of London* (Stroud: Sutton, 1996), 2–3, 17.
29. Baxter, *Reliquiae*, 3. 2.
30. Ellwood, *History*, 264.
31. Marvell, 'The Last Instructions to the Painter', lines 131–2, 146, 964; *Poems*, 364 (comment), 369, 371, 393 (text and notes).
32. Thomas Ellwood, *Davideis. the Life of David King of Israel: A Sacred Poem in Five Books* (London, 1712).
33. Ellwood, *History*, 246–7.
34. Above, 208.
35. Darbishire, 33, 48.
36. Walter George Bell, *The Great Fire of London in 1666* (1920; London: Bodley Head, 1951), 222–5.
37. Porter, *Fire*, 71.
38. Bell, *Fire*, 112.
39. *ODNB*.
40. Bell, *Fire*, 153–4; *ODNB*.
41. Porter, *Fire*, 52–3.
42. Hutton, *Restoration*, 249.
43. Porter, *Fire*, 86–7.
44. Ibid. 173; this part of the inscription was removed in 1830.
45. Hutton, *Restoration*, 263–6, reviews the issues.
46. Porter, *Fire*, 77–9.
47. On the Simmons family see *ODNB* and D. F. McKenzie, 'Milton's Printers: Matthew, Mary and Samuel Simmons', *MQ* 14 (1980), 87–91.
48. *PL* 5; Peter Lindenbaum, 'Milton's Contract', *Cardozo Arts and Entertainment Law Journal* 10 (1992), 439–54, reprinted in Martha Woodmansee and Peter Jaszi (eds.), *The Construction of Authorship: Textual Appropriation in Law and Literature* (Durham, NC: Duke University Press, 1994), 175–90.
49. Based on a scrutiny of imprints, 1660–9, facilitated by the search facility of *Early English Books Online*.
50. Campbell et al., *Milton and Manuscript*, ch. 3.
51. French's translation, *LR* 4. 434.
52. Above, 311.
53. Keeble, *Restoration*, 148–50.
54. Darbishire, 180.
55. *PL* 1. 594–9.
56. On Lawes see *ODNB* and Ian Spink, *Henry Lawes: Cavalier Songwriter* (Oxford, 2000); on Tomkins see *ODNB* and Denis Stevens, *Thomas Tomkins, 1572–1656* (London: Macmillan, 1957).
57. *CPW* 1. 812–14.
58. Joseph Addison and Richard Steele, *The Spectator*, ed. D. F. Bond (Oxford: Clarendon Press, 1965), 3. 391.

59. *PL* 10. 293–5, 312–14; *PL 1667*, 9. 293–5, 312–14. Books 1–6 in the 1667 edition are unchanged in 1674, on which *PL* is based. For the remaining four books, we include also a reference to the first edition.

60. *PL* 3. 446, 474–80, 487, 489–96.

61. *PL* 3. 184–5 and n.; Thomas N. Corns, *Regaining* Paradise Lost (Harlow: Longman, 1994), 83.

62. *PL* 3. 197.

63. James Grantham Turner, *One Flesh: Paradisal Marriage and Sexual Relations in the Age of Milton* (Oxford: Clarendon Press, 1987), *passim*.

64. *PL* 4. 742–73.

65. Stone, *Family*, esp. ch. 8; David Cressy, *Birth, Marriage, and Death: Ritual, Religion, and the Life-Cycle in Tudor and Stuart England* (1997; Oxford: Oxford University Press, 1999), 297.

66. *PL* 4. 321; 12. 648.

67. N. H. Keeble, *The Literary Culture of Nonconformity in Later Seventeenth-Century England* (Leicester: Leicester University Press, 1987), 91–2.

68. *PL* 8. 605–6; *PL 1667*, 7. 1242–3.

69. *PL* 4. 297–301.

70. See 1 Corinthians, esp. chs. 11 and 14; Corns, *Regaining*, 71–3.

71. *PL* 10. 196; *PL 1667*, 9. 196.

72. Keeble, *Restoration*, 176–82.

73. *PL* 11. 619–20; *PL 1667*, 10. 616–17.

74. *PL* 11. 714–18; *PL 1667*, 10. 710–14.

75. *PL* 7. 32–3; *PL 1667*, 7. 32–3.

76. *PL* 4. 406–9.

77. *PL* 5. 351–7.

78. Keeble, *Restoration*, 43–6.

79. *PL* 2. 477–9.

80. *CPW* 7, rev. edn., 425.

81. *PL* 2. 2–6.

82. *PL* 12. 65–71; *PL 1667*, 10. '956–62' [i.e. 957–63].

83. *PL* 12. 79–90; *PL 1667*, 10. '971–81' [i.e. 972–82].

84. *PL* 12. 25–6; *PL 1667*, 10. '916–17' [i.e. 917–18].

85. *Tenure*, *CPW* 3. 486; see above, 227–8.

86. *PL* 1. 493–5.

87. *PL* 12. 508–22; *PL 1667*, 10. '1399–413' [i.e. 1400–14].

88. *PL* 8. 25–8; *PL 1667*, 7. 25–8.

89. Darbishire, 276.

90. *ODNB*.

91. *PL* 11. 668–70; *PL 1667*, 10. 664–6.

92. *PL* 11. 701; *PL 1667*, 10. 697.

93. *PL* 12. 537–8; *PL 1667*, 10. '1429–30' [i.e. 1430–1].

94. *PL* 12. 479–85; *PL 1667*, 10. '1376' [i.e. 1377].

95. *PL* 12. 566–70; *PL 1667*, 10. '1457–61' [i.e. 1458–62].

96. *PL* 12. 540–1; *PL 1667*, 10. '1431–2' [i.e. 1432–3].

97. Above, 142.

98. In both *PL* and *PL 1667*.

99. *PL* 5. 771–895.
100. *PL* 9. 273–341; *PL 1667*, 10. 273–341.
101. Aubrey, *Thurloe*, 127.
102. Darbishire, 78–9.
103. *PL* 1. 93–4, 143–4, 640–2.
104. *PL* 5. 682–3.
105. *PL* 5. 718.
106. *PL* 10. 100–1; *PL 1667*, 9. 100–1.
107. *PL* 6. 593–4.
108. *PL* 4. 513–14.
109. *PL* 8. 224–48, 168–9; *PL 1667*, 7. 861–85, 804–5.
110. *PL* 5. 229–45, 'The Argument'.
111. Empson, *Milton's God*, 146.
112. *PL* 9. 817–33; *PL 1667*, 8. 817–35.
113. *PL* 2. 378–82.
114. *PL* 2. 468–73.
115. Darbishire, 291.
116. *Vitae Virgilianae Antiquae*, ed. Colin Hardie (rev. edn., Oxford: Clarendon Press, 1966), 11: *cum Georgica scriberet, traditur cotidie meditatos mane plurimos versus dictare solitus ac per totum diem retractando ad paucissimos redigere, non absurde carmen se ursae more parer dicens et lambendo deum effingere.*
117. Sir William Davenant, *A Discourse upon Gondibert . . . with an answer to it by Mr Hobbs* (Paris, 1650).
118. *PL* 9. 22–4.

17 THE SUNLIT UPLANDS

1. Ronald Hutton, *Charles II, King of England, Scotland, and Ireland* (1989; Oxford: Oxford University Press, 1991), 249.
2. *ODNB.*
3. On the admission of the younger Christopher to the Inner Temple 'at his father's request' on 30 June 1661 see F. A. Inderwick, *A Calendar of the Inner Temple Records* (5 vols., London: H. Sotheran & Co., 1896–1936) 2. 3; on his calling to the Bar see Inderwick, *Calendar*, 3. 49; his burial is recorded in the Register of St Nicholas Ipswich (Suffolk Record Office; printed edition ed. E. Cookson, Parish Register Society, 1897). It is assumed by Parker that John was 26 when he died, but Cambridge did not accept what would now be called 'mature students', and John's age when he entered Pembroke College, Cambridge in January 1668 was given as 15. It is likely that John was the name given to two sons, one baptized in 1643 who died as a child, and another who entered Pembroke College, Cambridge, in 1668, aged 15.
4. On the Clarendon Code, see above, 318 and n. 68.
5. Hutton, *Charles II*, 266–93.
6. *ODNB.*
7. Quoted Hutton, *Charles II*, 278.
8. 'Satyr', in John Wilmot, second earl of Rochester, *The Works of John Wilmot, Earl of Rochester*, edited by Harold Love (Oxford: Oxford University Press, 1999), 86.
9. John Spurr, *England in the 1670s: 'This Masquerading Age'* (Oxford: Blackwell, 2000), 40.

10. Ibid. 13.

11. Lines 919–20, 922, in Andrew Marvell, *The Poems of Andrew Marvell*, ed. Nigel Smith (London: Pearson Longman, 2003), 376.

12. John Milton, *John Milton's Complete Poetical Works Reproduced in Photographic Facsimile*, ed. Harris Francis Fletcher (Urbana: University of Illinois Press, 1943–8), 2. 208.

13. Darbishire, 295; see also *ODNB*.

14. On John Beale, pomiculturalist, Fellow of the Royal Society, chaplain-extraordinary to Charles II and member of the Hartlib circle, see *ODNB*. John Evelyn is the diarist, whose son was taught by Milton's nephew Edward Phillips; he knew Beale through Hartlib's 'Office of address for communications'. The letters which mention Milton are now in the Evelyn manuscripts in the British Library, and are dated 31 August 1667 (Evelyn MSS Letters 63), 11 September 1667 (Letters 64), 16 October 1667 (Letters 67), 11 November 1667 (Letters 69; seems to allude to *Paradise Lost*), 18 November 1667 (Letters 68, bound out of sequence; discusses *Paradise Lost*), 2 April 1668 (Letters, 71; mentions *Paradise Lost*). On these letters see Nicholas von Maltzahn, 'Laureate, Republican, Calvinist: An Early Response to *Paradise Lost* (1667)', in *MS* 29 (1992), 181–98.

15. On Sir John Hobart, a supporter of Cromwell's government who changed sides at the Restoration, see *ODNB*. The letters to his son are in the Bodleian; one is dated 27 January 1668 (Bodleian MS Tanner 45, fol. 264) and the other 30 January 1668 (fol. 271). See James Rosenheim, 'An early appreciation of *Paradise Lost*', *MP* 75 (1978), 280–2.

16. Above, 327.

17. In Bodleian MS Eng. Poet. d.49 the poem is dated 4 September 1667; if this date is correct, Marvell must have read the poem before publication.

18. This issue exists in two states known as Issue 3A and Issue 3B; the latter (not in Wing) has a full stop after the word 'BOOKS'.

19. Samuel Simmons was the son of Matthew and Mary Simmons (not their nephew, as Parker thought). See D. F. McKenzie, 'Milton's Printers: Matthew, Mary and Samuel Simmons', *MQ* 14 (1980), 87–91; McKenzie also identifies the workmen who printed *Paradise Lost*.

20. On Edward Millington see *ODNB*. Richardson is the only early biographer to mention the move (which he mentions twice); see Darbishire, 203, 275. For Toland's remark see Darbishire, 192–3. Pepys noted the views of a bookseller acquaintance in the aftermath of the fire that the price of particularly foreign and Latin books, would be sharply inflated; see Pepys, 8. 309. Such books were certainly a significant part of Milton's personal collection.

21. On 1 November the publication of the *History* was noted in a letter from Thomas Blount to Anthony Wood (Bodleian MS Wood 40, fol. 80); the price was 6s. The first issue was printed 'for James Allestry', who died on 3 November; a second title page (dated 1671 and naming Spencer Hickman as publisher) was quickly printed.

22. On the historiographical context of the *History* see Nicholas von Maltzahn, *Milton's History of Britain: Republican Historiography in the English Revolution* (Oxford: Oxford University Press, 1991). On the date of the Digression, von Maltzahn defends 1648 in 'Dating the *Digression* in Milton's *History of Britain*', *HistJ* 36 (1993), 945–56; the alternative date of 1660 was proposed by Austin Woolrych, 'The Date of the *Digression* in Milton's *History of Britain*', in R. Ollard and P. Tudor Craig (eds.), *For Veronica Wedgwood: These Studies in Seventeenth-Century History* (Oxford, 1986),

217–46 and the same author's 'Dating Milton's History of Britain', *HistJ* 36 (1993), 929–43.

23. On Faithorne see *ODNB* and *Grove Art*.

24. On the pastel portrait see J. R. Martin, *The Portrait of John Milton at Princeton and its Place in Milton Iconography* (Princeton: Princeton University Library, 1961), David Piper, 'The Portraits of John Milton', in *Christ's College Magazine* 60 no. 195 (May 1970), 155–61, and Leo Miller, 'Milton's Portraits: An Impartial Inquiry into Their Authentication', special issue of *Milton Quarterly* (1976). Martin thinks the pastel a preliminary drawing, and Piper thinks it a derivative. In the Milton literature this portrait is known as the 'Crayon Drawing', but the term is unhelpful, as 'crayon' may denote chalk (of which pastel is a type), *crayons de couleur* (wood-encased crayons), oil, charcoal, conté, lithograph, and wax crayons as well as pastel.

25. *CPW* 4. 627–8.

26. David Loewenstein, *Milton and the Drama of History: Historical Vision, Iconoclasm, and the Literary Imagination* (Cambridge: Cambridge University Press, 1990), 81.

27. Above, 271.

28. *CPW* 4. 402.

29. *An Act for suppressing the detestable sins of incest, adultery and fornication* (London, 1650); in the event the death penalty was never exacted.

30. *CPW* 5. 402.

31. *CPW* 5. 308, 37, 229–30.

32. *CPW* 8. 475; below, 383.

33. *CPW* 8. 475; see also 478.

34. *CPW* 8. 537–8.

35. Graham Parry, *The Trophies of Time: English Antiquarians of The Seventeenth Century* (Oxford: Oxford University Press, 1995).

36. Parry, *Trophies*, 188.

37. *CPW* 5. 230.

38. *CPW* 5. 183, 59, 58, 101, 61.

39. *CPW* 5. 141, 185, 304, 255, 145, 268.

40. *CPW* 5. 79, 32, 72, 320.

41. *CPW* 3. 421.

42. *CPW* 5. 103, 303. See Leo Miller, *John Milton Among the Polygamophiles* (New York: Loewenthal Press, 1974).

43. *CPW* 5. 188 and n. 12, 394. Elmer (or Eilmer) of Malmesbury was a Benedictine monk who leapt from the roof of Malmesbury Abbey with artificial wings.

44. *CPW* 5. 175; 3. 241.

45. John Morris, 'Historical Introduction', in Gildas, *The Ruin of Britain and other Documents*, ed. and trans. Michael Winterbottom (London and Chichester, 1978), 2–3. On Gildas see *ODNB*.

46. Darbishire, 76. For a fine overview of the publication, see von Maltzahn, *Milton's History, passim.*

47. Jonathan Swift, *Gulliver's Travels 1726*, ed. Harold Williams (Oxford: Blackwell, 1941), 183.

48. *CPW* 5. 1–2.

49. *CPW* 5. 403; the italics are found, too, in his source: 403 n. 24.

50. Above, 329.

51. Darbishire, 75.
52. Reviewed usefully in *CSP* 349–50.
53. *SA* 46, 233–4, 374–5.
54. Above, 264, 267.
55. *SA* 366–7.
56. Above, 310.
57. *SA* 504–5.
58. *SA* 915–17.
59. Spurr, *1670s*, 70.
60. Hutton, *Charles II*, 256.
61. *SA* 1253–6.
62. *SA* 1418–20.
63. *SA* 1669–70.
64. *SA* 1630–5.
65. *SA* 1654, 1659.
66. The issues are reviewed in Thomas N. Corns, 'Milton and Class', in David Brooks and Brian Kiernan (eds.), *Running Wild: Essays, Fictions and Memoirs Presented to Michael Wilding* (New Delhi: Manohar for the Sydney Association for Studies in Society and Culture, 2004), 55–6; see, for an opposite view, Christopher Hill, *The Experience of Defeat: Milton and Some Contemporaries* (London: Faber, 1984), 314–15.
67. *SA*, 1457–70, 1712–13.
68. Alexander Walsham, '"Fatal Vespers": Providentialism and Anti-Popery in Late Jacobean London', *Past and Present*, 144 (1994), 36–87; Miller, 'Verses by Gil', 22–5.
69. *SA* 490–9.
70. *SA* 1731–3.
71. *PR* 4. 636–9.
72. *PR* 4. 348, 350.
73. Barbara K. Lewalski, *Milton's Brief Epic: The Genre, Meaning, and Art of* Paradise Regained (Providence, RI, and London: Brown University Press and Methuen, 1966), esp. ch. 2.
74. *SA* 1709–11.
75. *PR* 1. 14–5.
76. *SA* 1758.
77. *PR* 1. 335–6.
78. Above, 317; Hutton, *Restoration*, 151.
79. *PR* 4. 121–5.
80. Above, 243; Fallon, *Milton in Government*, 177.
81. *PR* 1. 486–90.
82. *PR* 3. 310–12, 387–8, 400–3.
83. *PR* 3. 246; 4. 110–11.
84. *PR* 2. 466–71.
85. *PR* 4. 146–53.
86. *CPW* 7, rev. edn. 304, 302; above, 288. The early Waldenses were known as the *pauvres de Lyon*.
87. *PR* 2. 414–15, 27–8.
88. On George Downham see *ODNB*; on the debt to Downham, see Francine Lusignan, 'L'Artis Logicae Plenior Institutio de John Milton: État de la question et position', Ph.D. thesis, Université de Montréal, 1974; on Milton's editing of Friege, see Leo

Miller, 'Milton edits Freigius' "Life of Ramus"', *Renaissance and Reformation* 8 (1972), 112–14.

89. Eliot's primer is *The Logical Primer. Some logical notions to initiate the Indians into the knowledge of the rule of reason* (Cambridge, Mass., 1672); claims for occupational usefulness are those of Roland MacIlmaine, *The Logic of P. Ramus Martyr* (London, 1574), 13–14; the usefulness for lawyers was also claimed by Abraham Fraunce, *The Lawiers Logike* (London, 1588); the usefulness for equine management (and archery and good posture) was claimed by Wotton in *The Art of Logike, gathered out of Aristotle . . . by P. Ramus* (London, 1626), sigs A2^v–A3^r.

90. Corns, *Development*, 31–42.

91. Hutton, *Charles II*, 306.

92. Spurr, *1670s*, 21.

93. *Term Catalogues*, 1. 135, which makes clear that the tract is to be sold by Thomas Sawbridge, a younger relative of the illustrious printer and bookseller, George Sawbridge, and himself in the 1670s a competent entrepreneur with a varied list. His shop was in Little Britain, and thus handy for Artillery Walk.

94. *CPW* 8. 419–20.

95. *CPW* 8. 424–6.

96. *CPW* 8. 417.

97. John Curtis Read, 'Humphrey Moseley, Publisher', *Oxford Bibliographical Society Proceedings and Papers* 2 (1927–30), 61–72, 139–42.

98. We owe this suggestion to Sharon Achinstein (private communication).

99. *ODNB*.

100. *ODNB*; 371, below, 383.

101. *ODNB*.

102. John Dryden, *The State of Innocence, and Fall of Man: An Opera Written in Heroique Verse* (London, 1677), 1.

103. Ibid. 3.

104. Ibid. 2.

105. Ibid., sigs. A4^r, b1^r, c2^v.

106. Parish Register, St Peter and St Kevin, in the Representative Church Body Library MS P.45.1.1; printed in *Parish Register Society of Dublin* 9 (1911).

107. *PL* 5–6; for a careful assessment of the textual relationship between the editions, see R. G. Moyles, *The Text of* Paradise Lost: *A Study in Editorial Procedure* (Toronto: University of Toronto Press, 1985), *passim*, with whose conclusions Fowler concurs.

108. *ODNB*. See also Nicholas von Maltzahn, '"I admird thee": Samuel Barrow, Doctor and Poet', *MQ* 29 (1995), 25–8.

109. The anecdote is recorded by Aubrey, in Darbishire, 7, and substantiated by Marvell's subsequent allusion.

110. *PL* 54.

111. Corns, *History*, 360–8.

112. Advertised in Robert Clavell, *The General Catalogues of Books Printed in England* (London, 1675), 34, 47, 76, 82, 83 (2), 104 (2), 113 (2), 118, 199; on Clavell see *ODNB*.

113. According to Elizabeth Foster, Milton's granddaughter, her mother Deborah had married 'a weaver in Spitalfields'. The marriage took place in Dublin, where Deborah and her husband Abraham Clarke settled; they were still there in 1688 when Elizabeth was born.

114. Below, 382.
115. Below, 380.
116. Cressy, *Birth*, 393.
117. Darbishire, 33, 5.
118. On the decorum of mortality, see Cressy, *Birth*, ch. 17.
119. Above, 212. We are indebted to Robert Corns, MRCS, for his advice on the probable diagnosis of Milton's fatal illness.

18 POSTHUMOUS LIFE AND *NACHLASS*

1. Darbishire, 195.
2. Ibid. 76.
3. Ibid. 193.
4. Ibid. 34.
5. PRO PROB 20/1817/fol. 238ᵛ. Wills were proved and administered by ecclesiastical courts, in this case the Prerogative Court of Canterbury, which exercised the testamentary jurisdiction of the archbishop of Canterbury. The court sat in Doctors' Commons, on Paternoster Row. On Sir Thomas Exton see *ODNB*.
6. The allegation initiated by Milton's widow should be among the Allegations for 1674 in PRO PROB 18/6, but is not there, nor is it listed in the indices; it seems not to have been seen since the mid-19th century. Warton's transcription of this document and of the list of nine questions is printed in *LR* 5. 207–12. Christopher Milton's reply is PRO PROB 24/13/238ᵛ; the replies of the Fisher sisters are PRO PROB 24/13/311–13.
7. PRO PROB 6/50/14.
8. Darbishire, 78.
9. See above, 212.
10. The three releases are now in the NYPL. Deborah's release, which seems to have been prepared and signed in Dublin (the handwriting and witnesses are different) contains the reference to the (lost) bond given by Christopher Milton to Richard Powell.
11. See Gordon Campbell, 'Milton in Madras' *MQ* 31 (1997), 61–3.
12. Cheshire Record Office, Chester, WS 1727 (contains will and inventory).
13. On the later lives of Sir Christopher Milton, Edward Phillips, and John Phillips, see *ODNB*.
14. Campbell et al., *Milton and the Manuscript*.

Bibliography

I. MANUSCRIPTS

(including books with manuscript annotations)

Amsterdam, Universiteits-Bibliotheek
MS III.E.9 (letters from Nicolas Heinsius to Isaac Vossius).

Austin, Texas, Harry Ranson Humanities Research Center
Pre-1700 Manuscript 127 (a page of Milton's juvenilia).
PFORZ 714 (*A Masque Presented at Ludlow*. Copy of 1637 edition with nine corrections apparently in Milton's hand; as the volume comes from the Bridgwater House Library, of which J. P. Collier was librarian, it is possible that the corrections are a Collier forgery).

Aylesbury, Centre for Buckinghamshire Studies
D/A/T 107 (Horton, Bishop's Transcript, 1637).
D/A/V 15 (Archidiaconal Visitation Books).
PR 107/1/1 (Parish Register, St Michael, Horton).

Bedford, Bedfordshire Record Office
MS P 11/28/2, fols. 309, 313–15 (document dated 24 June 1695 signed by Elizabeth Milton at Mainwarings Coffee House in Fleet Street assigning copyright of Milton's prose works—which are listed in full—to Joseph Watts for a payment of 10 guineas).

Bloomington, Lilly Library, Indiana University
DA407.V2 S5 George Sikes, *The Life and Death of Sir Henry Vane* (copy presented by Lady Vane to Sarah Calvert; the dated inscription means that the book—and Milton's sonnet—must have been published on or before 5 September 1662).

Boston, Massachusetts Historical Society
Winthrop Papers.

Boulder, Colorado University Library
Leo Miller Collection Box XXII, File 17 (Leo Miller, 'Milton in Geneva and the significance of the Cardoini Album').

Brussels, Bibliothèque Royale
MS II 4109 MUS. Fétis 3095 (a collection of 100 songs in the hand of Thomas Myriell).

Cambridge, Christ's College
Admissions Book.
MS 8 ('Milton Autographs').

Cambridge, Trinity College
MS R3.4 (Milton's workbooks).
MS R5.5 (Anne Sadleir's letterbook).

Bibliography

MS O.ii.68 (MS copy of John Lane's *Triton's Trumpet*).

C.9.179 (copy of Milton's *Eikonoklastes* that belonged to Richard Vaughan, earl of Carbery and from July 1652 husband of Lady Alice Egerton, the Lady of Milton's 'Masque').

Cambridge, University Library

MS 154 (copy of *Justa Edouardo King* annotated by Milton).

Ely. A.272 (copy of Chrysostom, *Oratiobes LXXX* (Paris, 1604) bought by Milton in 1636; he subsequently added textual corrections on four pages).

Ely.c.281 (copy of Polycarp and Ignatius, *Epistolae* (Oxford, 1644); Milton is said to have owned and annotated this volume, but the handwriting may not be his).

Cambridge University Archives (in University Library)

Grace Book Z.

Matriculation Book.

Subscription Book.

Supplicats 1627, 1628, 1629.

Supplicats 1630, 1631, 1632.

VCCt.1.52 (*Acta Curia*; Proceedings of the Vice-Chancellor's Court).

Cambridge, Mass., Harvard University, Houghton Library

MS Sumner 84, Lobby XL3.43 (Cardoini Album, signed by Milton).

14496.13.4.10F (copy of Milton's *Defensio* presented by Hartlib to Peter Pells, a Swedish diplomat, on 17 February 1652).

14497.100* Lobby XI.3.40 (annotated copy of Thomas Farnaby's *Systema Grammaticum* (1641); the notes are no longer believed to be in Milton's hand).

F Br 98.319* Lobby XI.4.24 (Gildas, *De excidio & conquestu Britanniæ epistola*, in *Rerum britannicarum, id est Angliæ, Scotiæ, vicinarumqve insularum ac regionum* (Heidelberg, 1587). The notes are said to be in Milton's hand, but he did not ordinarily write in minuscules, and in any case the annotations are transcriptions of the printed marginalia in Josseline's edition of 1558; see W. H. Davies in Printed Books and Articles, below).

*FC6 R115 Zz620p (copy of Olympia, *Pythia, Nemea*, Isthmia (Saumur, 1620) said to have been bought by Milton on 15 November 1629 and subsequently annotated by him, but the handwriting is not his; see Kelley and Atkins, 'Milton and the Harvard Pindar', in Printed Books and Articles, below).

MS Eng 901 Lobby XI.2.69 (manuscript of Digression in Milton's *History of Britain*).

*OLC.T272.635 (copy of Terence, *Comoediae sex* (Leiden, 1635) said to be signed by Milton, but the signature is not in his hand).

Canterbury, Cathedral Library

Elham 732 (copy of Milton's *Eikonoklastes* with a note of his blindness by Henry Oxinden).

Chennai, Fort St George Museum

Parish Register, St Mary's Church (transcription made in 1739 by Alexander Wynch).

Chester, Cheshire Record Office

Parish Register, Wistaston.

WS 1727 (Elizabeth Milton's will and inventory).

Copenhagen, Kongelige Bibliotek

GKS 3579, 8vo (MS copy of Milton's *Defensio*).

GKS 2259, 4to (MS of unpublished pseudonymous answer (written by Henrik Ernst) to the preface to Milton's *Defensio*).

NKS 373c, 4to (Oluf Borck 'Itinerarium').

Rostgaard 39, 4to (contains Wilhelmus Worm's attribution to Milton of the republican inscription in the niche in the Old Exchange from which the statue of Charles I had been taken).

Dublin, Archbishop Marsh's Library
Z2.2.16(9) (contains letters from the Marquis Turon de Beyrie to Elie Bouhéreau).

Dublin, The Representative Church Body Library (Church of Ireland)
MS P.45.1.1 (Parish Register, St Peter's Church, Dublin); printed in *Parish Register Society of Dublin* 9 (1911).

Dublin, Trinity College
R.dd.39 (volume of ten of Milton's tracts with his autograph inscription to Patrick Young, the King's Librarian).

Ely Cathedral Library
[see Cambridge University Library, in which the Ely library and archives have been deposited].

Eton College Library
MS Records 16 (survey of the Spread Eagle in Bread Street).

Exeter Cathedral Library
T2/18 Milton, John, *Tenure of Kings and Magistrates* (presentation copy apparently for John or Henry Bradshaw).

Florence, Biblioteca Marucelliana
MS A.36 (Anton Francesco Gori's notes on the Accademia degli Apatisti).

Florence, Biblioteca Nazionale
MS Magliabecchiana Cl. IX cod. 60 (Svogliati Academy, Minute Book).
MS Palatina E.E. 152 (Descrizione del numero delle case e delle persone delle città di Firenze fatta l'anno MDCXXXII).
MS Panciatichi 194 (letters from Emery Bigot to Antonio Magliabecchi and Lorenzo Panciatichi).

Geneva, Bibliothèque Publique et Universitaire
MS fr. 14lC/Inv. 345 (Matricula Studiosorum).

The Hague, Algemeen Rijksarchief
MS Leg. Arch. 8582 (Gerald Schaep's accounts).

Herefordshire County Record Office
MS K11/3232/3/23 (indenture signed by Milton's father).

Ipswich, Suffolk Record Office
Parish Register, St Nicholas (ed. E. Cookson, Parish Register Society, 1897).

Leeds, Brotherton Library
Marten/Loder-Symonds MSS, 3rd series.

Leiden, Rijksuniversiteitsbibliotheek
BPL 1923/3I (Letters from Emery Bigot to Nicolas Heinsius).

Lewes, East Sussex Record Office
FRE 690 (contains epithalamium by Alexander Gil).

London, British Library
Add Chart 10,260 (deeds related to the hundreds of Carlford and Colneis, Suffolk).

Add MS 4,180 (Thomas Birch's transcriptions of papers of Sir Edward Nicolas).

Add MS 4,244 (miscellaneous biographical and literary memoranda by Thomas Birch).

Add MS 4,292 (transcriptions by Thomas Birch).

Add MSS 4,300–23 (letters addressed to Thomas Birch).

Add MS 4,364 (State Papers relating to the Swiss Evangelical Cantons and Piedmont).

Add MS 4,472 (Literary diary of Thomas Birch, 1754–64).

Add MS 4478 (Catalogue of Birch's MSS).

Add MS 5,016* (Letters including several related to Milton).

Add MS 11,044 (Letters and Papers of John Scudamore).

Add MS 11,518 (Henry Lawes's five songs for Milton's *Masque*).

Add MS 18,861 (contract for *Paradise Lost*).

Add MS 19,142 (vol. 28 *of* Pedigrees of Suffolk, 43 vols.).

Add MSS 24,487–92 (Joseph Hunter's 'Chorus Vatum Anglicanorum').

Add MS 24,501 (collections of Joseph Hunter relating to Milton and his family).

Add MS 28,637 (Francis Peck's transcriptions of Milton's poems).

Add MS 28,954 (Notebook of John Ellis).

Add MSS 29,372–7 (part-books of Thomas Myriell's 'Tristitiae Remedium').

Add MS 29,427 (anonymous collection of anthems and madrigals).

Add MS 32,310 (Milton's family Bible).

Add MS 33,509 (Notebook of Thomas Stringer).

Add MS 34,326 (Petitions to Parliament and Council of State, 1648–54).

Add MSS 35,396–400 (Hardwicke Papers, correspondence of Philip Yorke and Thomas Birch).

Add MS 36,354 (Milton's Commonplace Book).

Add MS 36,792 (Register of Presentations to Benefices, 1649–54).

Add MS 38,100 (Dispatches from agents and ambassadors to King Karl X of Sweden).

Add MS 52,723 (songs from Milton's *Masque* in the hand of Henry Lawes).

C.21.c.42 (*Justa Edouardo King*, 1638; annotated by Milton).

C.38.h.21 [Thomason, George?], Catalogue of the Thomason Collection of Civil War Tracts, 12 vols. (1665?); another transcription, 12 vols. (1669?) is catalogued as C.37.h.13.

C.60.1.7 (Aratus, *Phenomena*, 1635; annotated by Milton).

C.114.6.37 (Milton, *Defensio Pro Populo Anglicano*, 1651; presentation copy to John Morris. See T. A. Birrell in Printed Books and Articles, below).

MS Cart Harl 112.

MS Cottonian Charters 1/5/4.

MS Egerton 1324 (Christoph Arnold's *album amicorum*).

MSS Egerton 2533–62 (papers of Sir Edward Nicholas, 30 vols.).

MSS Evelyn (605 volumes and unnumbered papers).

MS Harleian 389 and 390 (Letters of Joseph Mede).

MS Harleian 1557 (Visitation of Oxfordshire, 1634).

MS Harleian 5243 (John Lane, 'Historie of Sir Gwy, Earl of Warwick').

MS Harleian 6802.

MS Harleian 7003.

MS Lansdowne 95 (Milton in Cromwell's funeral procession).

MS Ref. 17 B xv (Lane).

MS Roy. App. 63 (MS version of Leighton's *Teares*, with music by Milton's father).

MS Sloane 649.

MS Sloane 1325.
MS Some 1446 (copy of Milton's 'Epitaph on the Marchioness of Winchester').
MS Stowe 76 (Roger Ley, 'Gesta Britannica').
MS Stowe 142/41 (the 'Ashburnham Document').
MSS Stowe 305/6 (transcription of Milton's *Eikonoklastes*).
MS Tanner 466 (William Sandcroft's MS anthology).
MS Trumbull Misc 22.
Thomason Tract Collection (2,235 pieces in 2,008 volumes; for printed catalogue *see* Fortescue).

London, City of Westminster Archives Centre
Parish Register, St Martin in the Fields, printed in *PHSR* 66 (1936).
Parish Register, St Clement Danes (unpublished).

London, College of Arms
Painters Workbook I.B.7.

London, Corporation of London Records Office
Historical Papers 1/11 (bond witnessed by Milton's father).

London, Dr Williams's Library
Baxter Correspondence, 6 vols. (see *Calendar of the Correspondence of Richard Baxter*, ed. N. H. Keeble and Geoffrey Nuttall, 2 vols., Oxford: Clarendon Press, 1991).

London, Dulwich College
Muniment 503 (document witnessed by Milton's father).

London, Goldsmiths' Hall
Committee of Contractors and Leases, 1641, 1651–62 (No. 1915.B393).
Committee of Survey, 1651.
Court Book, 1648–51.
Extracts of Leases, 1650–75.

London, Guildhall Library
MS 1503 (Miscellaneous Rate and Subsidy Assessments, St Botolph's Parish, Aldersgate).
MS 34275 (Nomina descipulorum qui admissi sunt in scholam mercatorum. scissorum Gulielmo Dugard Archididascalo, 1644–62; Scholar's Register, Merchant Taylor's Company).
MS 3572 (Parish Register, St Mary the Virgin, Aldermanbury; printed in *PHSR* 61, 62, 65, 1931–5).
MS 4508 (Parish Register, St Anne Blackfriars; unpublished).
MS 5031 (Parish Register, All Hallows, Bread Street; printed in *PHSR* 43, 1913).
MS 5370 (Common Paper of the Company of Scriveners; printed in Steer, q.v.).
MS 6419 (Parish Register, St Giles without Cripplegate; *Records* ed. W. Denton, 1883).
MS 6668 (Parish Register, St Andrew Holborn, unpublished).
MS 7857 (Parish Register, St Dunstan in the East; printed in *PHSR* 69–70, 84–87 (1939–58)).
MS 8319 (Parish Register, St Stephen Walbrook; printed in *PHSR* 69, 1919).
MS 8716 (Charters, Company of Scriveners).
MS 8820 (Parish Register, St Peter's upon Cornhill, printed in *PHSR* 1 and 4, 1877–9).
MS 8990 (Parish Register, St Mary, Aldermary; printed in *PHSR* 5, 1880).
MSS 10343–10348 (Parish Register, St Dunstan in the West; ed. T. C. Ferguson, 1890–1901).

London, Hammersmith and Fulham Archives and Local History Centre
DD/818/56 (Copies of Papers Relating to Hammersmith Chapel).
PAF/1/21 (Rate Books of the Vestry of Fulham).

London, Inner Temple Archive
Admissions Book, 1571–1640.

London, Lambeth Palace Library
MS FM1/3B (Allegations for Marriage Licences).

London, National Archive (formerly Public Record Office)
C2 (Chancery Proceedings, Series I, 2,240 bundles).
C5 (Chancery Proceedings, Bridges, 640 bundles).
C7 (Chancery Proceedings, Hamilton, 671 bundles).
C8 (Chancery Proceedings, Mitford, 658 bundles).
C10 (Chancery Proceedings, Whittington, 546 bundles).
C21 (Chancery County Depositions, 767 bundles).
C22 (Chancery County Depositions, 1,052 bundles).
C24 (Chancery Town Depositions, 2,509 bundles).
C33 (Chancery Entry Books of Decrees and Orders, 1,262 vols.).
C38 (Chancery Reports and Certificates, 3,330 vols.).
C54 (Chancery Close Rolls, 20,899 rolls).
C66 (Chancery Patent Rolls, 5,573 rolls and vols.).
C152 (Chancery Certificates and Recognizances of Statute Staple, Rolls Chapel Office, 12 bundles, numbered 55–66.
C228 (Chancery Proceedings on the Statute Staple, Petty Bag Office, 35 bundles).
CP24/3 (Court of Common Pleas, Concords of Fines, Charles I, 33 files).
CP25/2 (Court of Common Pleas, Feet of Fines Files, 1,574 files).
CP40 (Court of Common Pleas, Plea Rolls, 4,135 rolls).
E112 (Exchequer Bills, Answers etc., 2,387 bundles).
E125 (Exchequer Entry Books of Decrees and Orders, Series III, 39 vols.).
E179 (Exchequer Subsidy Rolls, 401 boxes).
E372 (Exchequer Pipe Rolls, Pipe Office, 676 rolls).
E377 (Exchequer Recusant Rolls, Pipe Office Series, 82 rolls).
IND/1/1926 (Index to Chancery Reports and Certificates, 1657).
IND/1/8911 (Index to Warrant Books, 1660–1722, A–P).
LC4 (Lord Chamberlain's Department, Recognizance Rolls, 219 rolls and vols.).
PC2 (Privy Council Office, Registers, 872 vols.).
PROB 6 (PCC Administration Act Books, 206 vols.).
PROB 10 (Registered Copy Wills, PCC and other probate jurisdictions, 7,457 vols.).
PROB 11 (PCC Registered Copy Wills, 2,263 vols.).
PROB 18 (PCC Allegations, 149 vols.).
PROB 20 (PCC Supplementary Wills Series I).
PROB 24 (PCC Deposition Books, 114 vols.).
Req 1 (Court of Requests, Miscellaneous Books, 210 vols.).
Req 2 (Court of Requests, Proceedings, 829 bundles).
SO4 (Indexes to Signet Office Docket Books, 15 vols.).
SP9 (State Papers Domestic, Miscellaneous, 273 vols., built around the collection of Joseph Williamson, Keeper of the State Papers 1661–1702).
SP14 (State Papers Domestic, James I, 218 vols.).
SP18 (State Papers Domestic, Interregnum, 228 vols.).
SP23 (State Papers Domestic, Interregnum, Committee for Compounding Delinquents: Books and Papers, 269 vols.).

SP25 (State Papers Domestic, Interregnum: Council of State, 138 vols.).
SP29 (State Papers Domestic, Charles II, 450 vols.).
SP45 (State Papers Domestic, Various, 89 vols.).
SP46 (State Papers Supplementary).
SP82 (State Papers Foreign, Hamburg and Hanse Towns, 103 vols.).
T52 (Treasury, King's Warrants, 122 vols.).
T53 (Treasury, Warrants Relating to Money, 68 vols.).

London, Royal College of Music
MS 1940 (contains songs by Milton's father).

London, Royal Society
MS 1 (Notebook of Henry Oldenburg).
MS 5 (Correspondence of Henry Oldenbug).

London, St Giles in the Fields
Parish Register (unpublished, kept in the church).

London, Society of Antiquaries
MS 138 (volume of state papers collected by Milton).

London, Westminster Abbey
Muniment 28,515 (bond witnessed by Milton's father).
Muniment 33,770 (erection of John Rysbrack's monument to Milton in Westminster Abbey).
Parish Register, St Margaret, Westminster; printed in *PHSR*, 64 (1935) and 88 (1968).

Longleat, The Marquess of Bath's Collection
MS 124a Sir Bulstrode Whitelocke, 'Journal of the Swedish Embassy'.
Sir Bulstrode Whitelocke, Collected Papers, 30 vols. and 9 parcels.

Munich, Bayerisches Hauptstaatsachiv
Bestand Kurbayern, Lit. 2636.

New Brunswick, NJ, Rutgers University Library
DA396.A3S32 1652 Milton, John, *Defensio Pro Populo Anglicano*, (1652) (copy in which Milton's release from prison is noted).

New Haven, Yale University Library
James Osborn Collection b63 (MS copy of Comus dated 1658) I.

New York, Columbia University Library
MS X823 M64/S52 (Milton's Letters of State).

New York, The Morgan Library and Museum
MA 954 (Indenture signed by Christopher and Richard Milton).
MA 953 (marriage settlement of Anne Milton and Edward Phillips, witnessed by Milton).
MA 307 (manuscript of Book I of *Paradise Lost*).
PML 17280 (Milton, John, *Defensio Pro Populo Anglicano* (1651); presentation copy inscribed in the hand of the unknown recipient).
'MA Unassigned', Rulers of England Box 09, Charles II, Part 2, no. 016 (Letter from John Durel to William Edgeman recording his intention (never realized) to answer Milton's *Eikonklastes*).

Bibliography

New York Public Library

John Milton papers, 1647–1882 (includes Milton family manuscripts, a letter from Milton to Carlo Dati (held in Conservation Department since 1988) and a letter from Carlo Dati to Milton).

*KB 1529 (volume signed and dated by Milton, containing Della Casa's *Rime e Prose*, Dante's *Convivio*, and Varchi's *Sonetti*).

Northampton, Northamptonshire Record Office

MS 1(0)18 (letter from Brian Duppa to Sir Justinian Isham, alluding to Milton's divorce tracts).

Oldenburg, Niedersächsische Staatsarchiv

Best. 20, Tit. 38, No. 73, fasc 13 (Hermann Mylius's diary and correspondence with Milton, including seven letters by Milton in the hand of an amanuensis).

Oxford, Bodleian Library

Pamph.84 (39) (Paul Best, *Mysteries Discovered*, 1647; copy sometimes said in error to have been annotated by Milton).

Don.d.2728 (Euripides, *Tragoedia*, 2 vols., Geneva, 1602; bought by Milton for 12/6, and subsequently annotated by Milton).

b.36 (Library Records, Bills to 1763).

Matriculation Register (University Archives).

E.H.2.20.Art (presentation copy of Milton's *Defensio Pro Populo Anglicano*, apparently inscribed by John Rous, Bodley's Librarian).

MS 4O.Rawl 408 (presentation copy of second edition of Milton's *Eikonoklastes*; the inscription is not in his hand).

4°.F.56.Th, kept at Arch.G.e.44 (copy of Milton's 1645 *Poems* with corrections apparently in his hand).

MS Add B.5 (Notebook of Christopher Wase, apparently in the hand of Henry Some).

MS Ashmole 36,37 (English poetry, including verses by Alexander Gil).

MS Ashmole 436, part I (Nativities, including Milton's horoscope).

MS Aubrey 6–9 (John Aubrey's 'Brief Lives'; Aubrey 8, fols. 63–8, contains his notes on the life of Milton).

MS Aubrey 13 (Letters to Aubrey).

MSS Clarendon (Papers of Edward Hyde, earl of Clarendon, 152 vols.).

MS Douce 170 (John Lane's continuation of Chaucer's 'Squire's Tale').

MS Lat. misc. d.77, kept at Arch.G.f.17 (MS of Milton's *Ad Joannern Rousiarn*).

MS Locke d.10 (John Locke's 'Lemmata Ethica Argumenta et Authores 1659').

MSS Nalson (State and Parliamentary Papers, 20 vols.).

MS OAP Oxon.e.11 (Oxford Archdeaconry Papers: Visitation Books).

MSS Rawlinson A (English history, including papers of Thurloe and Pepys, 499 vols.).

MS Rawlinson D.51 (fols. 23–41 are the Annual Catalogue of the Company of Scriveners printed in Steer, 76–127) I.

MS Rawlinson D.230 (MS copy of Milton's *Defensio*).

MS Rawlinson E.69 (Sermon by Robert South).

MSS Tanner (papers of Thomas Tanner, 473 vols., including papers of Archbishop Sandcroft, 144 vols.).

MS Top. Oxon.c.289 (copy of Richard Powell's will, witnessed by Milton).

Bibliography

MS Wood D4 (fols. 140–4 contain the anonymous life of Milton by Cyriack Skinner; printed in Darbishire, who attributes it to John Phillips).
MS Wood F39–F45 (letters to Anthony Wood).
MS Wood F51.
Wood 515 (Wood's printed book collection).

Oxford, Christ Church College Library
MS 44 (collection of music in the hand of Thomas Myriell, including a setting by Milton's father).

Oxford, Oxfordshire Record Office
Wills 183/236 (Henry Milton's will).
Wills 184/2 (Agnes Milton's will).

Paris, Bibliothèque Nationale
MS F.L. 602 (burning of Milton's *Defensio* in Toulouse and Paris).
MS FR 10712 (letters from Gaston de Comminges).
Nouvelles acquisitions françaises 1343 (letters from Emery Bigot to Gilles Ménage).

Philadelphia, Historical Society of Pennsylvania
Ferdinand Dreer Collection 115.2 (receipt signed by Milton).

Philadelphia, Rosenbach Museum
MS 810/25 (Maundy's statute staple, signed on Milton's behalf; at the same time Milton authorized an acquittance (i.e. a receipt) for £500; the acquittance, also signed on Milton's behalf, is in the Folger Library).

Philadelphia, University of Pennsylvania Library
Thomas Flatman MS ENG 28 (formerly 821/F61I).

Reading, Berkshire Record Office.
Parish Register, St Laurence, Reading.
MS R/HMC XXXIX (Corporation of Reading, Muster Roll, 1642).

Rome, English College
Pilgrim Book.

Rome, Vatican Library
MS Barb. Lat. 2181 fols. 57–8 (autograph letter from Milton to Lukas Holste).

St Gallen, Stadtbibliothek Vadiana
MS 92a (*album amicorum* of Johanna Zollikofer with Milton's signature).

San Marino, California, Henry E. Huntington Library
105644 (copy of Milton's *Defensio* (1651) with a hostile inscription by the Earl of Bridgewater, who as a child had acted in Milton's Masque). See above 230, plate 36.
87103 (copy of Johannes Crecellius's *Collectanea* (Frankfurt, 1614) apparently signed and dated by Milton (21 October 1633), but the inscription is not in Milton's hand).

Sheffield University Library
Hartlib Collection, published on CD-ROM by UMI (1995).

Urbana, Illinois University Library
IUA01704 (copy of Boiardo's *Orlando Innamorato* (Venice, 1608) sent to Milton by Daniel Oxenbridge).
X 881 H2151544 (copy of Heraclitus of Pontus's *Allegoriae in Homerii fibula de diis* (Basel, 1544) bought by Milton for five shillings).

Bibliography

881 L71601 (copy of Lycophron, *Alexandra* (Geneva, 1601) bought by Milton for thirteen shillings; see H. F. Fletcher, ed. John Shawcross, in Printed Books and Articles, below).

Pre-1650 MS 168 (warrant issued to Milton to search William Prynne's rooms at Lincoln's Inn, 25 June 1650).

Vienna, Österreichische Nationalbibliothek

MS 19287 (translation into German of Milton's father's 'Thou God of might').

Washington DC, Folger Shakespeare Library

MS X.d.161 (acquittance signed on Milton's behalf; see Philadelphia, Rosenbach Museum).

Wolfenbüttel Herzog-August-Bibliothek

MS Fol 609.84.12. Extrav. ('Commercium literarium Joh. Christiani de Boineburg et Hermanni Conringii a. 1660–1664').

Zürich, Staatsarchiv

MS Acta Anglicana EII 457c (letter in French from John Dury denying any intention of translating Milton's *Defensio*).

MS Acta Anglicana EII 457d (letter in French from Jean-Baptiste Stouppe about Morus and the *Clamor*).

2. PRINTED BOOKS AND ARTICLES

An Act for suppressing the detestable sins of incest, adultery and fornication (London, 1650).

Answer to a Book, Intituled, The Doctrine and Discipline of Divorce, or, A Plea for Ladies and Gentlewomen, and all other Maried Women against Divorce (London, 1644).

The arraignment and conviction of Mervin, Lord Audley, earl of Castlehaven, (who was by 26 peers of the realm found guilty of committing rapine and sodomy) at Westminster, on Monday, April 25, 1631 (London, 1642).

The Arsy Versy, or, The Second Martyrdom of the Rump (London, 1660).

A Brief Collection Out of Master Pagits Book Called Heresiography (London, 1646).

Camdeni Insignia (Oxford, 1624).

The case of sodomy, in the trial of Mervin, Lord Audley, earl of Castlehaven, for committing a rape and sodomy with two of his servants (London, 1707).

A Catalogue of the Several Sects and Opinions in England and other Nations (London, 1647).

Certaine Briefe Treatises, Written by Diverse Learned Men (Oxford, 1641).

The Character of the Rump (London, 1660).

Eikon Alethine. The Pourtraiture of Truths most sacred Majesty truly suffering, though not solely (London, 1649).

Histoire entiere & veritable du procez de Charles Stuart, Roy d'Angleterre: contenant, en forme de journal, tout ce qui s'est faict & passé sur ce sujet dans le Parlement, & en la haute cour de justice; et la facon en laquelle il a esté mis à mort. Au mois de janvier, 1649/8. A quoy sont adjoustées quelques declarations du Parlement cy-devant publiées, pour faire voir plus amplement, quels ont esté les motifs & raisons d'une procedure si extraordinaire. Le tout fidelement receüilly des pieces authentiques & traduit de l'anglois (London, 1650).

The History of the Second Death of the Rump (London, 1660).

Justa Edouardo King naufrago, ab Amicis mœrentibus, amoris & μνείας χάριν (Cambridge, 1638).

The Kings Cabinet opened: or, Certain Packets of Secret Letters & papers Written with the Kings own Hand, and taken in his Cabinet at Nasby-Field... *Together, with some Annotations thereupon* (London, 1645).

Bibliography

The last speech and prayer with other passages of Thomas Venner, the chief incourager and promoter of the late horrid rebellion immediately before his execution in Coleman-street on Saturday last being the 19th of Ianuary, 1660: together with the names of the rest that were condemned for the same fact (London, 1660).

Lucifers Life-guard (London, 1660).

A Modest Confutation of A Slandrous and Scurrilous Libelll, Entituled, Animadversions upon the Remonstrants Defense against Smectymnuus (London[?], 1642).

The Out-Cry of the London Prentices for Justice to be Executed upon John Lord Hewson (London, 1659).

To Parliament. The humble Representation and desires of divers Freeholders and others inhabiting within the County of Bedford (London, 1659).

A perfect and particuler Relation Of the severall Marches and proceedings of the Armie in Ireland (London, 1649).

The Plot Discovered and Counterplotted (London, 1641).

A proclamation for calling in, and suppressing of two books written by John Milton the one intituled, Johannis Miltoni Angli pro populo Anglicano defensio, contra Claudii Anonymi aliàs Salmasii, defensionem regiam; and the other in answer to a book intituled, The pourtraicture of His Sacred Majesty in his solitude and sufferings. And also a third book intituled, The obstructors of justice, written by John Goodwin (London, 1660).

Regii sanguinis clamor (The Hague, 1661).

Théorie de la royauté d'après la doctrine de Milton (Paris, 1789).

These Trades-men are Preachers in and about the City of LONDON (London, 1647).

The trial of Lord Audley, earl of Castlehaven for inhumanely causing his own wife to be ravished and for buggery (London, 1679).

The tryal and condemnation of Mervin, Lord Audley Earl of Castle-Haven, at Westminster, April the 5th 1631, for abetting a rape upon his Countess, committing sodomy with his servants, and commanding and countenancing the debauching his daughter (London, 1699).

The VVhole business of Sindercome, from first to last, it being a perfect narrative of his carriage, during the time of his imprisonment in the Tower of London (London, 1657).

Alblas, Jacques, 'Milton's *The Doctrine and Discipline of Divorce*: The Unknown Dutch Translation Discovered', *MQ* 28 (1994), 35–9.

Addison, Joseph, and Richard Steele, *The Spectator*, ed. D. F. Bond (5 vols., Oxford: Clarendon Press, 1965).

Armitage, David, Armand Himy, and Quentin Skinner (eds.), *Milton and Republicanism* (Cambridge: Cambridge University Press, 1995).

Atherton, Ian, *Ambition and Failure in Stuart England: The Career of John, First Viscount Scudamore* (Manchester and New York: Manchester University Press, 1999).

Aubrey, Philip, *Mr Secretary Thurloe: Cromwell's Secretary of State 1652–1660* (London: Athlone, 1990).

Audisio, Gabriel, *The Waldensian Dissent: Persecution and Survival, c.1170–c.1570*, Cambridge Medieval Textbooks (Cambridge: Cambridge University Press, 1990).

Aylmer, G. E., *The State's Servants: The Civil Service of the English Republic 1649–1660* (London and Boston: Routledge and Kegan Paul, 1973).

Baillie, Robert, *A Dissuasive from the Errours of the Time* (London, 1645).

Bald, R. C., *John Donne: A Life* (Oxford: Clarendon Press, 1970).

Baldwin, T. W., *William Shakespere's Small Latine & Lesse Greeke* (2 vols., Urbana: University of Illinois Press, 1944).

Bibliography

Baron, Robert, *Erotopaignion, or The Cyprian Academy* (London, 1647).

Barry, Jonathan, and Christopher Brooks (eds.), *The Middling Sort of People: Culture, Society and Politics in England, 1550–1800* (Basingstoke: Macmillan, 1994).

Baxter, Richard, *Reliquiae Baxterianae*, ed. Matthew Sylvester (London, 1696).

Beal, Peter, 'Milton', in *Index of English Literary Manuscripts*, vol. 2, part 2, *1625–1700* (London: Mansell, 1993), 69–104.

Bell, Walter George, *The Great Fire of London in 1666* (1920; London: Bodley Head, 1951).

Berghaus, Günter, 'A Case of Censorship of Milton in Germany: On an Unknown Edition of the *Pro Populo Anglicano*', *MQ* 17 (1983), 61–70.

Berry, Herbert, 'The Miltons and the Blackfriars Playhouse', *MP* 89 (1992), 510–14.

Bertie, Montague, earl of Lindsey, et al., *A declaration of the nobility, knights & gentry of the County of Oxon which have adhered to the late King* (London, 1660).

Birrell, T. A., *The Library of John Morris: The Reconstruction of a Seventeenth Century Collection* (London: British Museum Publications Ltd for the British Library, 1976). See MSS, British Library, C.114.6.37.

Blakiston, Noel, 'Milton's Birthplace', *London Topographical Record* 19, no. 80 (1947), 6–12 and plates.

Borzelli, Angelo, *Giovan Battista Manso* (Naples: Federico & Ardia, 1916).

Bradley, S. A. J., 'Ambiorix Ariovistus, Detractor of Milton's *Defensio*, Identified', *MP* 73 (1976), 382–8.

Brailsford, H. N., *The Levellers and the English Revolution*, ed. Christopher Hill (1961; Nottingham: Spokesman, 1983).

Breasted, Barbara, '*Comus* and the Castlehaven Scandal', *MS* 3 (1971), 202–24.

Brooks, Christopher, 'Apprenticeship, Social Mobility and the Middling Sort, 1500–1800', in Barry and Brooks (eds.), *Middling Sort*, 51–83.

Brown, Cedric, 'The Chirk Castle Entertainment of 1634', *MQ* 11 (1977), 76–86.

—— *John Milton's Aristocratic Entertainments* (Cambridge: Cambridge University Press, 1985).

—— 'Milton's "Arcades" in the Trinity Manuscript' *RES* n.s. 37 (1986), 542–9.

—— *John Milton: A Literary Life* (London and New York: Macmillan, 1995).

Buchan, John, *Oliver Cromwell* (1934; London: Hodder and Stoughton, 1935).

Burmann, Pieter, *Sylloges Epistolarum* (5 vols., Leiden, 1727).

Burns, Norman T., *Christian Mortalism from Tyndale to Milton* (Cambridge, Mass.: Harvard University Press, 1972).

Bushell, W. D., *Hobson's Conduit: The New River at Cambridge Commonly Called Hobson's River* (Cambridge: Cambridge University Press, 1938).

Campbell, Gordon, 'Milton's *Index Theologicus* and Bellarmine's *Disputationes De Controversiis Christianae Fidei Adversus Huius Temporis Haereticos*', *MQ* 11 (1977), 12–16.

—— 'Milton and the Lives of the Ancients', *JWCI* 47 (1984), 234–8.

—— 'Nathaniel Tovey: Milton's Second Tutor', *MQ* 21 (1987), 81–90.

—— 'Milton's Spanish', *MQ* 30 (1996), 127–32.

—— 'Milton in Madras', *MQ* 31 (1997), 61–3.

—— *A Milton Chronology* (Basingstoke: Macmillan, 1997).

—— 'Shakespeare and the Youth of Milton', *MQ* 33 (1999), 95–105.

—— 'Milton and the Water Supply of Cambridge', in B. Sokolova and E. Pancheva (eds.), *Essays for Alexander Shurbanov* (Sofia, 2001), 38–43, reprinted in revised form in *South African Journal of Medieval and Renaissance Studies* 15 (2006 for 2005), 121–6.

Bibliography

Campbell, Gordon, Thomas N. Corns, John K. Hale, and Fiona J. Tweedie, *Milton and the Manuscript of* De Doctrina Christiana (Oxford: Oxford University Press, 2007).

Canne, John, *The Improvement of Mercy: or a short Treatise, shewing how, and in what manner, Our Rulers and all well-affected to the persent government should make a right and profitable use of the late great victory in Ireland* (London, 1649).

—— *The Snare is broken, Wherein is proved by Scripture, Law and Reason, that the National Covenant and Oath was unlawfully given and taken* (London, 1649).

Canosa, Romano, *Storia dell'Inquisizione in Italia della metà del Cinquecento alla fine del Settocento* (5 vols., Rome: Sapere, 1986–90).

Carey, John (1963), 'The Date of Milton's Italian Poems', *RES* 14 (1963), 383–6.

Carrera de la Red, Avelina, *El 'problema de la lengua' en el humanismo renacentista* (Valladolid: Universidad de Valladolid, Secretariado de Publicaciones; [Salamanca]: Caja de Ahorros y Monte de Piedad de Salamanca, 1988).

Cary, Patrick, *The Poems of Patrick Cary*, ed. V. Delany (Oxford: Clarendon Press, 1978).

Chaney, Edward (1985), *The Grand Tour and the Great Rebellion: Richard Lassels and 'The voyage of Italy' in the seventeenth century* (Geneva: Slatkin, 1985).

—— [untitled review], *English Historical Review* 108 (1993), 720.

—— *The Evolution of the Grand Tour: Anglo-Italian Cultural Relations since the Renaissance* (rev. edn., London: Frank Cass, 2000).

Charles I, *Eikon Basilike: The Portraiture of His Sacred Majesty in His Solitudes and Sufferings, with selections from Eikonoklastes*, ed. Jim Daems and Holly Faith Nelson (Peterborough, Ont.: Broadview Press, 2006).

Chifas, Eugenia, 'Milton's Letter to Gill, May 20, 1628', *MLN* 62 (1947), 37–9.

Cinquemani, A. A., *Glad to Go for a Feast: Milton, Buonmattei and the Florentine Accademici* (New York: Peter Lang, 1998).

Clark, Donald L., *John Milton at St Paul's School* (New York: Columbia University Press, 1948).

—— 'Ancient Rhetoric and English Renaissance Literature', *Shakespeare Quarterly* 2 (1951), 195–204.

Clarke, Hyde, *Athenæum* 2746 (12 June 1888), 760–1.

Clavell, Robert, *The General Catalogues of Books Printed in England* (London, 1675).

Clavering, Rose, and John Shawcross, 'Anne Milton and the Milton Residences', *JEGP* 59 (1960), 680–90.

Coffey, John, *Persecution and Toleration in Protestant England, 1558–1689* (Harlow: Longman, 2000).

—— *John Goodwin and the Puritan Revolution* (Woodbridge: Boydell, 2006).

Cogswell, Thomas, *The Blessed Revolution: English Politics and the Coming of War, 1621–1624* (Cambridge: Cambridge University Press, 1989).

Corns, Thomas 'Studies in the Development of Milton's Prose Style', D. Phil. dissertation, Oxford, 1977.

—— *Milton's Language* (Oxford: Blackwell, 1990).

—— *The Development of Milton's Prose Style* (Oxford: Clarendon Press, 1982).

—— 'Milton's Quest for Respectability', *MLR* 77 (1982), 769–79.

—— *Uncloistered Virtue: English Political Literature, 1640–1660* (Oxford: Clarendon Press, 1992).

—— *Regaining* Paradise Lost (Harlow: Longman, 1994).

—— *John Milton: The Prose Works* (New York: Twayne; London: Prentice Hall International, 1998).

—— 'Milton before "Lycidas"', in Parry and Raymond (eds.), *Milton and the Terms of Liberty*, 23–36.

—— 'Milton and Class', in David Brooks and Brian Kiernan (eds.), *Running Wild: Essays, Fictions and Memoirs Presented to Michael Wilding* (New Delhi: Manohar for the Sydney Association for Studies in Society and Culture, 2004), 55–68.

—— *A History of Seventeenth-Century English Literature* (Oxford: Blackwell, 2007).

—— 'John Milton, Roger Williams, and the Limits of Toleration', in Sharon Achinstein and Elizabeth Sauer (eds.), *Milton and Toleration* (Oxford: Oxford University Press, 2007), 72–81.

—— 'Milton's Early Lives', in Kevin Sharpe and Steven N. Zwicker (eds.), *Writing Lives* (Oxford: Oxford University Press, 2008), 75–90.

—— (ed.), *A Companion to Milton* (Oxford: Blackwell, 2001).

Costazuti, Vincenzo (ed.), *Applausi poetici alle glorie della signora Leonora Baroni* (Rome, 1639).

Costello, W. T., *The Scholastic Curriculum of Seventeenth-Century Cambridge* (Cambridge, Mass.: Harvard University Press, 1958).

Coyet, P. J., *Swedish Diplomats at Cromwell's Court, 1655–1656*, trans. Michael Roberts (London: Royal Historical Society, 1988).

Crashaw, Richard, *The Poems, English, Latin and Greek*, ed. L. C. Martin (2nd edn., Oxford: Clarendon Press, 1957).

Creaser, John, 'Milton's *Comus*: The Irrelevance of the Castlehaven Scandal', *N&Q* 229 (1984), 307–17, reprinted in *MQ* 21 (1987), 24–34.

—— '"The present aid of this occasion": The Setting of *Comus*', in David Lindley (ed.), *The Court Masque* (Manchester: Manchester University Press, 1984), 111–34.

Cressy, David, *Birth, Marriage, and Death: Ritual, Religion, and the Life-Cycle in Tudor and Stuart England* (1997; Oxford, Oxford University Press, 1999).

Curtis, M. H., *Oxford and Cambridge in Transition, 1558–1642* (Oxford: Clarendon, 1959).

Cust, Richard, *The Forced Loan and English Politics, 1626–1628* (Oxford: Clarendon Press, 1987).

Darbishire, Helen, *The Early Lives of Milton* (London: Constable, 1932).

Dati, Carlo, *Vite dei pittori antichi* (Florence, 1667).

Davenant, Sir William, *A Discourse upon Gondibert . . . with an answer to it by Mr Hobbs* (Paris, 1650).

Davies, Godfrey, *The Restoration of Charles II, 1658–1660* (San Marino, Calif.: Huntington Library, 1955).

Davies, H. Neville, 'Milton's Nativity Ode and Drummond's "An Hymne of the Ascension"', *Scottish Literary Journal* 12 (1985), 5–23.

Davies, Tony, 'Borrowed Language: Milton, Jefferson, Mirabeau', in Armitage, et al. (eds.), *Milton and Republicanism*, 254–71.

Davies, W. H., 'A Note on Milton's Annotated Copy of Gildas in the Harvard University (Widener) Library', *Papers of the British School at Rome* 15 (1939), 49–51.

De Filippis, Michelle, 'Milton and Manso: Cups or Books?', *PMLA* 51 (1936), 745–56.

Di Cesare, Mario (ed.), *Milton in Italy: Contexts, Images, Contradictions* (Binghamton: MRTS, 1991).

Diekhoff, John S. (ed.), *Milton on Himself: Milton's Utterances upon Himself and his Works* (London: Oxford University Press, 1939).

Dobranski, Steven R., and John P. Rumrich (eds.), *Milton and Heresy* (Cambridge: Cambridge University Press, 1988).

Bibliography

Dorian, Donald, *The English Diodatis* (New Brunswick, NJ: Rutgers University Press, 1950).

Doucette, Leonard, *Emery Bigot: Seventeenth-Century French Humanist* (Toronto: University of Toronto Press, 1970).

Dryden, John, *The State of Innocence, and Fall of Man: An Opera Written in Heroique Verse* (London: 1677).

Du Bellay, Joachim, *La deffence, et illustration de la langue françoyse* (Paris, 1549).

[Du Moulin, Peter], *Regii sanguinis clamor ad cœlum adversus parricidas Anglicanos* (The Hague, 1652); dedication by Alexander Morus.

Dunster, Charles, *Considerations on Milton's Early Reading* (London, 1800).

Dzelzainis, Martin, 'Milton's *Of True Religion* and the Earl of Castlemaine', *The Seventeenth Century* 7 (1992), 53–9.

Earle, Peter, 'The Middling Sort in London', in Barry and Brooks (eds.), *Middling Sort*, 141–58.

Eddershaw, David, with a contribution by Eleanor Roberts, *The Civil War in Oxfordshire* (Stroud: Sutton, 1995).

Edwards, Thomas, *Gangraena, or, A Catalogue and Discovery of the Many of the Errours, Heresies, Blasphemies and Pernicious Practices of the Sectaries of this Time*, three parts (London, 1646).

—— *The Second Part of Gangraena* (London, 1646).

—— *The Third Part of Gangraena* (London, 1646).

Eliot, John, *The Logical Primer. Some logical notions to initiate the Indians into the knowledge of the rule of reason* (Cambridge, Mass., 1672).

Ellwood, Thomas, *Davideis. the Life of David King of Israel: A Sacred Poem in Five Books* (London, 1712).

—— *The History of the Life of Thomas Ellwood*, (2nd edn., London: 1714).

Empson, William, *Milton's God* (rev. edn., London: Chatto and Windus, 1965).

Erastus, Thomas, *Explication grauissimae quaestionis* (London, 1589).

—— *The nullity of church-censures* (London, 1659).

Fallon, Robert, *Milton in Government* (University Park, Pa.: Pennsylvania State University Press, 1993).

Fatio, Guillaume, 'Milton et Byron à la Villa Diodati', in Jules Crosnier, *Nos Anciens et leurs Oeuvres*, (ed.), (Geneva, 1912), 21–66.

Faulkner, Thomas, *The history and antiquities of the parish of Hammersmith: interspersed with biographical notices of illustrious and eminent persons, who have been born, or who have resided in the parish, during the three preceding centuries* (London: Nichols & Son, 1839).

Featley, Daniel, *The Dippers Dipt* (London, 1645).

Fincham, Kenneth, 'Episcopal Government, 1603–1640', in Fincham (ed.), *Early Stuart Church*, 71–91.

—— and Peter Lake, 'The Ecclesiastical Policies of James I and Charles I', in Fincham (ed.), *Early Stuart Church*, 23–50.

—— (ed.), *The Early Stuart Church 1603–1642* (Basingstoke: Macmillan, 1993).

Fletcher, H. F., 'Milton's *Apologus* and its Mantuan Model', *JEGP* 55 (1956), 230–3.

—— 'John Milton's Copy of Lycophon's *Alexandra* in the Library of the University of Illinois', ed. John Shawcross, *MQ* 23 (1989), 129–58.

Fogle, F. R., '"Such a rural queen": The Countess Dowager of Derby as Patron', in F. R. Fogle and L. A. Knafla (eds.), *Patronage in Late Renaissance England* (Los Angeles: William Andrews Clark Memorial Library, University of California, 1983), 3–29.

Bibliography

Fortescue, G. K., *Catalogue* of *the Pamphlets... Collected by George Thomason, 1640–1661* (2 vols., London: British Museum, 1908).

Fox, George, *The Journal*, ed. Nigel Smith (Harmondsworth: Penguin, 1998).

Francis, Jane, 'The Kedermister Library: An Account of its Origins and a Reconstruction of its Contents and Arrangement', Records of Buckinghamshire 36 (1994), 62–85.

Frank, Joseph, *Cromwell's Press Agent: A Critical Biography of Marchamont Nedham* (Lanham, Md.: University Press of America, 1980).

Franson, J. Karl, 'The Diodatis in Chester', *N&Q* 234 (1989), 435.

Fraunce, Abraham, *The Lawiers Logike* (London, 1588).

Freeman, James, 'Milton's Roman Connection: Giovanni Salsilli', *MS* 19 (1984), 87–104.

French, J. M., *Milton in Chancery: New Chapters in the Lives of the Poet and his Father* (New York: Modern Language Association of America, 1939).

—— 'Milton's Supplicats', *HLQ* 5 (1942), 349–51.

—— (ed.), *The Life Records of John Milton* (New Brunswick, NJ: Rutgers University Press, 1949–58).

Frye, R. M., 'Milton's Florentine Friend, Bishop Frescobaldi: A Biographical Note and Portrait', *MQ* 7 (1973), 74–5.

Gaddi, Jacopo, *Poematum Libri Duo* (Padua, 1628).

—— *Adlocutiones et Elogia* (Florence, 1636).

—— *Corollarium Poeticum* (Florence, 1636).

—— *Elogia Historica* (Florence, 1637).

Galbraith, V. H., 'The *Modus Tenendi Parliamentum*', *JWCI* 16 (1953), 81–99.

Gardiner, Samuel Rawson (ed.), *The Constitutional Documents of the Puritan Revolution 1625–1660* (3rd edn., Oxford: Clarendon Press, 1979).

Gataker, Thomas, *Abrahams decease* (London, 1627).

Gell, Robert, *Stella nova, a new starre, leading wisemen unto Christ* (London, 1649).

—— *Aggelokratia theon, or, A sermon touching Gods government of the world by angels* (London, 1650).

—— [pseudonym 'Irenaus Philadelphus Philanthropus'], *Eirenikon, or, A Treatise of peace between the two visible divided parties* (London, 1660).

—— *An Essay towards the Amendment of the Last-English Translation of the Bible* (London, 1659).

Gentles, Ian, *The New Model Army in England, Ireland and Scotland, 1645–1653* (Oxford: Blackwell, 1992).

Gil, Alexander, *Parerga, sive Poetici Conatus Alexandri Gil* (London, 1632).

Gildas, *The Ruin of Britain and other Documents*, ed. and trans. Michael Winterbottom (London and Chichester, 1978).

Gilles, Pierre, *Histoire ecclesiastique des églises reformées, recueillies en quelques valées de Piedmont... autrefois appelées Eglises Vaudoises* (Geneva, 1644).

Gittings, C., *Death, Burial and the Individual in Early Modern England* (London: Croom Helm, 1984).

Goodwin, John, *Theomachia, or, The grand imprudence of men running the hazard of fighting against God in suppressing any way, doctrine, or practice concerning which they know not certainly whether it be from God or no* (London, 1644).

—— *Hybristodikai. The obstructours of justice* (London, 1649).

Goose, N., 'Household Size and Structure in Early-Stuart Cambridge', *Social History* 5 (1980), 347–85.

Bibliography

Grayson, Cecil, *A Renaissance Controversy: Latin or Italian* (Oxford: Clarendon Press, 1960).

Grendler, P. F., *The Roman Inquisition and the Venetian Press* (Princeton: Princeton University Press, 1977).

Greville, Robert (Lord Brooke), *A Discourse Opening the Nature of that Episcopacie, which is Exercised in England* (London: November, 1641).

Griffith, Matthew, *The Fear of God and the King* (London, 1660).

Haan, Estelle, Milton's *In Quintum Novembris* and the Anglo-Latin Gunpowder Epic', *Humanistica Lovaniensia* 41 (1992), 221–95 and 42 (1993), 368–93.

—— 'Milton's *Naturam non pati senium* and Hakewell', *Medievalia et Humanistica* 24 (1997), 147–67.

—— 'Milton, Manso, and the Fruit of that Forbidden Tree', *Medievalia et Humanistica* 25 (1998), 75–92.

—— *From Academia to Amicitia: Milton's Latin Writings and the Italian Academies* (Transactions of the American Philosophical Society, vol. 88, pt. 6, Philadelphia, 1998).

Haitsma Mulier, Eco, *The Myth of Venice and Dutch Republican Thought in the Seventeenth Century* (Assen, Netherlands: Van Gorcum, 1980).

Hale, John K., *Milton's Languages* (Cambridge: Cambridge University Press, 1997).

—— *Milton's Cambridge Latin: Performing in the Genres, 1625–1632* (Tempe, Ariz.: Arizona Center for Medieval and Renaissance Studies, 2005).

Hall, Joseph, *Episcopacy by Divine Right* (London, 1640).

—— *An Humble Remonstrance to the High Court of Parliament* (London, 1640 [?1641]).

—— *A Short Answer to the Tedious Vindication of Smectymnuus* (London, 1641).

—— *A Defence of the Humble Remonstrance* (London: 1641).

—— *Divers Treatises Written upon severall Occasions by Joseph Hall* (London, 1662).

Hammond, Fredrick, *Music and Spectacle in Baroque Rome: Barberini Patronage under Urban VIII* (New Haven: Yale University Press, 1994).

Hammond, Paul, 'Dryden's Employment by Cromwell's Government', *Transactions of the Cambridge Bibliographical Society* 8 (1981), pt. I, 130–6, plates III and IV.

Hampshire, G., 'An Unusual Bodleian Purchase in 1645', *BLR* 10 (1982), 339–48.

Hanford, J. H., 'The Chronology of Milton's Private Studies', *PMLA* 36 (1921), 251–314.

Hardacre, Paul, *The Royalists During the Puritan Revolution* (The Hague: Martinus Nijhoff, 1956).

Hardie, Colin (ed.), *Vitae Virgilianae Antiquae* (rev. edn., Oxford: Clarendon Press, 1966).

Harris, Neil, 'Galileo as Symbol: The "Tuscan Artist" in *Paradise Lost*', *Annali dell'Istituto e Museo di Storia della Scienza di Firenze* 10 (1985), 3–29.

Herrick, Robert, *The Poetical Works of Robert Herrick*, ed. L. C. Martin (Oxford: Clarendon Press, 1956).

Herrup, Cynthia, *A House in Gross Disorder: Sex, Law and the 2nd Earl of Castlehaven* (Oxford: Oxford University Press, 1999).

Hill, Christopher, *Puritanism and Revolution* (1958; London: Panther, 1969).

—— *Milton and the English Revolution* (London: Faber and Faber, 1977).

—— *The Experience of Defeat: Milton and Some Contemporaries* (London: Faber, 1984).

Hindmarsh, Bruce, *The Evangelical Conversion Narrative: Spiritual Biography in Early Modern England* (Oxford: Oxford University Press, 2005).

Hobbes, Thomas, *Leviathan* (London, 1651).

Hoover, David. L., and Thomas N. Corns, 'The Authorship of the Postscript to *An Answer to a Booke Entituled, An Humble Remonstrance*', *MQ, 38* (2004), 59–75.

Hughes, Ann, *The Causes of the English Civil War* (2nd edn., Basingstoke: Macmillan, 1998).

—— *Gangraena and the Struggle for the English Revolution* (Oxford: Oxford University Press, 2004).

Humphry, A. P., 'On the Maces of the Esquire Bedells', *Cambridge Antiquarian Communications* 21 (1881), 207–18.

Hutton, Ronald, *The Royalist War Effort, 1642–1646* (London: Longman, 1982).

—— *The Restoration: A Political and Religious History of England and Wales, 1658–1667* (Oxford: Clarendon, 1985).

—— *Charles II, King of England, Scotland, and Ireland* (1989; Oxford: Clarendon Press, 1991).

—— *The British Republic, 1649–1660* (2nd edn., Basingstoke: Macmillan, 2000).

Inderwick, F. A., *A Calendar of the Inner Temple Records* (5 vols., London: H. Sotheran & Co., 1896–1936).

Ingram, M., *Church Courts, Sex and Marriage in England, 1570–1640* (Cambridge: Cambridge University Press, 1987).

Irwin, Betty, 'Milton's Ludlow Masque: An Historical Approach' (unpublished MA thesis, University of Northern Illinois, 1960).

Jones, Edward, '"Filling a Blank in the Canvas": Milton, Horton, and the Kedermister Library', *RES* 53 (2002), 31–60.

—— '"Church-Outed by the Prelates": Milton and the 1637 Inspection of the Horton Parish Church', *JEGP* 102 (2003), 42–58.

—— 'The Loyalty and Subsidy Returns of 1641 and 1642: What They Can Tell Us About the Milton Family', in Kristin A. Pruitt and Charles W. Durham (eds.), *Milton's Legacy* (Selinsgrove: Susquehanna University Press, 2005), 234–47.

—— 'The Wills of Thomas Young and Edward Goodall and the Life of John Milton', forthcoming in Charles Durham and Kristin Pruitt (eds.), *John Milton: 'Reasoning Words'* (Selinsgrove, Pa: Susquehanna University Press).

Kallendorf, C. *Virgil and the Myth of Venice: Books and Readers in the Italian Renaissance* (Oxford: Clarendon Press, 1999).

Keeble, N. H., *The Literary Culture of Nonconformity in Later Seventeenth-Century England* (Leicester: Leicester University Press, 1987).

—— *The Restoration: England in the 1660s* (Oxford: Blackwell, 2002).

Kelley, Maurice, 'Milton's Dante—Della Casa—Varchi Volume', *BNYPL* 66 (1962), 499–504.

—— 'Additional Texts of Milton's State Papers', *MLN* 67 (1952), 18–19.

Kelley, Maurice, and Samuel Atkins, 'Milton's Annotations of Aratus', *PMLA* 70 (1955), 1090–106.

—— —— 'Milton's Annotations of Euripides', *JEGP* 60 (1961), 680–7.

—— —— 'Milton and the Harvard Pindar', *SB* 17 (1964), 77–82.

Kelsey, Sean, 'The Foundation of the Council of State', in Chris R. Kyle and Jason Peacey (eds.) *Parliament at Work: Parliamentary Committees, Political Power and Public Access in Early Modern England* (Woodbridge: Boydell, 2002), 129–48.

Kerridge, Eric, *Trade and Banking in Early Modern England* (Manchester: Manchester University Press, 1988).

Bibliography

Kishlansky, Mark, *The Rise of the New Model Army* (Cambridge: Cambridge University Press, 1979).

Knoppers, Laura Lunger, *Constructing Cromwell: Ceremony, Portrait, and Print 1645–1661* (Cambridge, Cambridge University Press, 2000).

Kranidas, Thomas, 'Milton's Trinculo', *N&Q* 26 (1979), 416.

Kyle, Chris R., and Jason Peacey (eds), *Parliament at Work: Parliamentary Committees, Political Power and Public Access in Early Modern England* (Woodbridge: Boydell, 2002).

Lacey, Andrew, *The Cult of King Charles the Martyr* (Woodbridge: Boydell, 2003).

Lake, Peter, 'The Laudian Style: Order, Uniformity and the Pursuit of the Beauty of Holiness in the 1630s', in Fincham (ed.), *Early Stuart Church*, 161–85.

Laud, William, *The Works of the Most Reverend Father in God*, William Laud (7 vols. in 9; Oxford: J. H. Parker, 1847–60).

Lazzeri, Alessandro, *Intellettuali e consenso nella Toscana del Seicento: L'Accademia degli Apatisti* (Milan: A. Giuffrè, 1983).

Leighton, Alexander, *An Appeal to the Parliament: or, Sions Plea against the Prelacie* (n. p., 1629).

Leighton, William, *The Tears or Lamentations of a Sorrowful Soul* (London, 1614).

Leonard, John, '"Trembling Ear": The Historical Moment of "Lycidas"' *Journal of Medieval and Renaissance Studies* 21 (1991), 59–81.

L'Estrange, Sir Roger, *Be Merry and Wise; or, A Seasonable Word to the Nation* (London, 1660).

—— *No Blinde Guides, in Answer To a seditious Pamphlet of J. Milton's, Intituled Brief Notes upon a late Sermon* (London, 1660).

Lewalski, Barbara, *Milton's Brief Epic: The Genre, Meaning, and Art of Paradise Regained* (Providence, RI, and London: Brown University Press and Methuen, 1966).

—— *The Life of John Milton: A Critical Biography* (rev. edn., Oxford: Blackwell, 2003).

Lilburne, John, *Englands New Chains Discovered* (London, 1649).

—— *The Second Part of Englands New-Chains Discovered* (London, 1649).

—— *As You Were: or The Lord General Cromwel and the Grand Officers of the Armie their Remembrancer* ([Amsterdam?], 1652).

Lindenbaum, Peter, 'John Milton and the Republican Mode of Literary Production', *YES* 21 (1991), 121–36.

—— 'Milton's Contract', *Cardozo Arts and Entertainment Law Journal* 10 (1992), 439–54, repr. in Martha Woodmansee and Peter Jaszi (eds.), *The Construction of Authorship: Textual Appropriation in Law and Literature* (Durham, NC: Duke University Press, 1994), 175–90.

—— 'Authors and Publishers in the Late Seventeenth Century: New Evidence on Their Relations, *Library* 17 (1995), 250–69.

Lindley, Keith, *Popular Politics and Religion in Civil War* (Aldershot: Scolar, 1997).

Locke, John, *Two Treatises of Government* (London, 1698).

Loewenstein, David, *Milton and the Drama of History: Historical Vision, Iconoclasm, and the Literary Imagination* (Cambridge: Cambridge University Press, 1990).

Low, Anthony, '*Mansus* in its Context', *MS* 19 (1984), 105–26.

Lünig, J. C. (ed.), *Literae Procurem Europae* (Leipzig, 1712).

Lunn, David, *The English Benedictines, 1540–1688* (London: Barnes & Noble, 1980).

Lusignan, Francine, 'L'Artis Logicae Plenior Institutio de John Milton: État de la question et position', Ph.D. thesis, Université de Montréal, 1974.

Bibliography

McColley, Diane, *Poetry and Music in Seventeenth-Century England* (Cambridge: Cambridge University Press, 1997).

McDonnell, Sir Michael, *The Annals of St Paul's School* (Cambridge: privately printed, 1959).

—— *The Registers of St Paul's School, 1509–1748* (London: privately printed, 1977).

McDowell, Nicholas, 'Dante and the Distraction of Lyric in "To my Friend Mr Henry Lawes" ', *RES* (in press).

MacIlmaine, Roland, *The Logic of P. Ramus Martyr* (London, 1574).

McKenzie, D. F., 'Milton's Printers: Matthew, Mary and Samuel Simmons', *MQ* 14 (1980), 87–91.

McPherson, D. C., *Shakespeare, Jonson and the Myth of Venice* (Newark, NJ: University of Delaware Press, 1990).

Maltzahn, Nicholas von, *Milton's* History of Britain: *Republican Historiography in the English Revolution* (Oxford: Oxford University Press, 1991).

—— 'Laureate, Republican, Calvinist: An Early Response to *Paradise Lost* (1667)', *MS* 29 (1992), 181–98.

—— 'Dating the *Digression* in Milton's History of Britain', *HistJ* 36 (1993), 945–56.

—— 'Naming the Author: Some Seventeenth-Century Milton Allusions', *MQ* 27 (1993), 1-19.

—— Wood, Allam, and the Oxford Milton', *MS* 31 (1994), 155–77.

—— 'Samuel Butler's Milton', *SP* 92 (1995), 482–95.

—— '"I admird Thee": Samuel Barrow, Doctor and Poet', *MQ* 29 (1995), 25–8.

—— 'The First Reception of *Paradise Lost* (1667)', *RES* 47 (1996), 479–99.

Marcus, Leah, 'The Milieu of Milton's *Comus*: Judicial Reform at Ludlow and the Problem of Sexual Assault', *Criticism* 25 (1983), 293–327.

Martin, J. R., *The Portrait of John Milton at Princeton and its Place in Milton Iconography* (Princeton: Princeton University Library, 1961).

Marvell, Andrew, *The Poems of Andrew Marvell*, ed. Nigel Smith (London: Pearson Longman, 2003).

—— *The Prose Works of Andrew Marvell*, ed. Martin Dzelzainis and Annabel Patterson (2 vols., New Haven: Yale University Press, 2003).

Masson, David, *The Life of John Milton: Narrated in Connexion with the Political, Ecclesiastical and Literary History of his Time* (7 vols., London: Macmillan, 1859–94).

Mayers, Ruth E. *1659: The Crisis of the Commonwealth* (Woodbridge: Boydell, 2004).

Mazzacurati, Giancarlo, *La questione della lingua dal Bembo all' Accademia fiorentina* (Naples: Liguori, 1965).

Mede, Joseph, *Clavis apocalyptica* (Cambridge, 1627).

Mellidge, Anthony, *Winchester Prison the 21th day of the 1 month, 59 If the measure of my sufferings under the creuel hands of unreasonable men, be finished in this noysome prison by the laying down of my life* (London: 1659).

Menasseh ben Israel, *The Hope of Israel*, ed. H. Méchoulan and G. Nahon (Oxford: Oxford University Press, 1987).

Miller, Leo, 'Peloni Almoni, Cosmopolites', *N&Q* 205 (1960), 424.

—— 'Milton's State Letters: The Lünig Version', *N&Q* 215 (1970), 412–14.

—— 'The Italian Imprimaturs in Milton's *Areopagitica*, *PBSA* 65 (1971), 345–55.

—— 'Milton edits Freigius' "Life of Ramus"', in *Renaissance and Reformation* 8 (1972), 112–14.

Miller, Leo, 'Milton and Lassenius', *MQ* 6 (1972), 92–5.

—— *John Milton among the Polygamophiles* (New York: Loewenthal Press, 1974).

—— 'Salmasius's *Responsio*: Addenda to the Milton Life Records', *N&Q* 219 (1974), 95.

—— 'Milton, Fichlau, Bensen and Conring: Addenda to the Life Records of John Milton', *PBSA* 68 (1974), 107–18.

—— 'Milton's "Areopagitica": Price 4d', *N&Q* 220 (1975), 309.

—— '"Milton's" (sic) *Eikon Alethine* Located', *MQ* 9 (1975), 65.

—— 'Milton, Salmasius and *vapulandum*: Who Should be Flogged?', *MQ* 9 (1975), 70–5.

—— 'Milton's Portraits: An Impartial Inquiry into Their Authentication' *MQ* (Special Issue, 1976).

—— 'Miltoniana: Some Hitherto Unrecognised Items', *PBSA* (1976), 107–10.

—— 'Milton Cited in Germany, 1652: A Further Note', *MQ* 12 (1978), 28–31.

Miller, Leo, 'Milton Dines at the Jesuit College: Reconstructing the Evening of October 30, 1638', *MQ* 13 (1979), 142–6.

—— 'Milton's Clash with Chappell: A Suggested Reconstruction', *MQ*, 14 (1980), 77–87.

—— 'Milton's 1626 Obituaries Dated', *N&Q* 225 (1980), 323–4.

—— 'Milton's *Patriis* Cicutis', *N&Q* 226 (1981), 41–2.

—— 'Milton and Weckherlin', *MQ* 16 (1982), 1–3.

—— 'Milton's Contemporary Reputation: A Footnote to Parker and French', *MQ* 17 (1983), 56–7.

—— 'The Date of Christoph Arnold's Letter', *N&Q* 229 (1984), 323–4.

—— *John Milton and the Oldenburg Safeguard* (New York: Loewenthal Press, 1985).

—— 'Two Milton State Letters: New Dates and New Insights', *N&Q* 231 (1986), 461–4.

—— 'Milton's *Defensio* Ordered Wholesale for the States of Holland', *N&Q* 231 (1986), 33.

—— 'Milton's Conversations with Schlezer and his Letters to Brandenburg', *N&Q* 232 (1987), 321.

—— 'Before Milton was Famous: January 8, 1649–50', *MQ* 21 (1987), 1–6.

—— 'Another Milton State Paper Recovered and a Mystery Demystified', *ELN* 25 (1987), 30–1.

—— 'The Burning of Milton's Books in 1660: Two Mysteries', *ELR* 18 (1988), 424–35.

—— 'Milton's "Oxenbridge" Boiardo Validated', *MQ* 23 (1989), 26–8.

—— 'A 1647 German Critique of *Areopagitica*', *N&Q* 234 (1989), 29–30.

—— 'Milton and Vlacq: Addenda 1644–1688', *PBSA* 83 (1989), 533–8.

—— 'On Some Verses by Alexander Gil which John Milton Read', *MQ* 24 (1990), 22–5.

—— 'Milton in the Zollikoffer and Arnold Albums', *MQ* 24 (1990), 99–104.

—— 'The Milton/Cromwell Letter to Transylvania', *N&Q* 234 (1990), 435–42.

—— 'New Milton Texts and Data from the Aitzema Mission, 1652', *N&Q* 235 (1990), 279–8.

—— *John Milton in the Anglo-Dutch Negotiations 1651–1654* (Pittsburgh Pa.: Duquesne University Press, 1992).

—— 'Milton in Geneva and the Significance of the Cardoini Album': see Manuscripts, s.n. 'Boulder'.

Milton, Anthony, *Catholic and Reformed: The Roman and Protestant Churches in English Protestant Thought, 1600–1640* (Cambridge: Cambridge University Press, 1995).

Milton, John, *A Maske Presented at Ludlow Castle, 1634* (London, 1637).

—— *Epitaphium Damonis* ([London], [1640]).

—— *Poems of Mr. John Milton, Both English and Latin, Compos'd at several times* (London, 1645).

—— *Ioannis Miltons Engelsmans Verdedigingh des gemeene Volcks van Engelandt, tegens Claudius sonder Naem, alias Salmasius Konincklijcke Verdedigingh. Wt het Latijn overgeset na de Copy gedruckt tot Londen, by Du Gardianis* (Gouda, 1651).

—— *Poems, &c. upon Several Occasions* (London, 1673).

—— *Letters of State, Written by John Milton . . . to which is added, An Account of his Life* (London, 1694).

—— *A Complete Collection of the Historical, Political, and Miscellaneous Works of John Milton, Both English and Latin. With som Papers never before Publish'd* ('Amsterdam' [actually London]: 1698).

—— *The Sonnets of Milton*, ed. J. S. Smart (Glasgow: Maclehose, Jackson, 1921).

—— *The Works of John Milton*, gen. ed. F. A. Patterson (18 vols. in 21, New York: Columbia University Press, 1931–8).

—— *John Milton's Complete Poetical Works Reproduced in Photographic Facsimile*, ed. Harris Francis Fletcher (Urbana: University of Illinois Press, 1943–8).

—— *Complete Prose Works of John Milton*, gen. ed. Don M. Wolfe (8 vols. in 10, New Haven: Yale University Press, 1953–82).

—— *Complete Shorter Poems*, ed. John Carey (2nd edn., London and New York: Longman, 1997).

—— *Paradise Lost*, ed. Alastair Fowler (2nd edn., London and New York: Longman, 1998).

—— *Latin Writings: A Selection*, ed. and trans. John Hale (Assen and Tempe: *MRTS* 1998).

Morgan, Victor, with Christopher Brooke, *A History of the University of Cambridge*, vol. 2, *1546–1750* (Cambridge: Cambridge University Press, 2004).

Morley, Thomas, *The Triumphs of Oriana* (London, 1601).

Morley, Thomas, *Remonstrance of the Barbarous Cruelties and Bloudy Murders Committed by the Irish Rebels Against the Protestants in Ireland* (London, 1644).

Moyles, R. G., *The Text of* Paradise Lost*: A Study in Editorial Procedure* (Toronto: Univerity of Toronto Press, 1985).

Nedham, Marchamont, *Interest Will Not Lie, or, A View of England's True Interest* (London, 1659).

—— *Newes from Brussels in a Letter from an Attendant on his Majesties Person* ([London], 1660).

Nelson, Alan H., *Records of Early English Drama: Cambridge* (2 vols., Toronto, Buffalo and London: University of Toronto Press, 1989).

—— 'Women in the Audience of Cambridge Plays', *Shakespeare Quarterly* 41 (1990), 333–6.

Nicolson, Marjorie, 'Milton's Hell and the Phlegraean Fields', *University of Toronto Quarterly* 7 (1938), 500–13.

Norbrook, David, *Writing the English Republic: Poetry, Rhetoric, and Politics, 1627–1660* (Cambridge: Cambridge University Press, 1998).

Orgel, Stephen, and Roy Strong, *Inigo Jones: The Theatre of the Stuart Court* (London and Berkeley and Los Angeles: Sotheby Parke Bernet and University of California Press, 1973).

O[verton?], R[ichard?], *Mans Mortallitie* (Amsterdam [?], 1643).

Owen, John, et al., *The humble proposals of Mr Owen, Mr Tho. Goodwin, Mr Nye, Mr Sympson, and other ministers: who presented the petition to the Parliament, and other persons, Febr. 11. under debate by a committee this 31 of March, 1652. for the furtherance and propagation of the Gospel in this nation* (London, 1652).

Pagitt, Ephraim, *Heresiography: or, A description of the Hereticks and Sectaries of these latter times* (London, 1645).

Palmer, Herbert, *The Glasse of Gods Providence towards His Faithfull Ones* (London, 1644).

Parker, W. R., 'Milton and Thomas Young, 1620–1628', *MLN* 53 (1938), 399–407.

—— 'Milton and the News of Charles Diodati's Death', *MLN* 72 (1957), 486–8.

—— *Milton: A Biography*, ed. Gordon Campbell (2nd edn., 2 vols., Oxford: Clarendon Press, 1996).

Parry, Graham, *The Trophies of Time: English Antiquarians of The Seventeenth Century* (Oxford: Oxford University Press, 1995).

Parry, Graham, and Joad Raymond (eds.), *Milton and the Terms of Liberty* (Cambridge: D. S. Brewer, 2002).

Passarelli, Maria Antonietta, *La lingua della patria: Leon Battista Alberti e la questione del volgare* (Rome: Bagatto Libri, 1999).

Patin, Gui, *Lettres*, ed. J.-H. Reveille-Parise (3 vols., Paris, 1846).

Patrick, J. Max, 'The Date of Milton's *Of Prelatical Episcopacy*', *HLQ* 13 (1950), 303–11.

Patrides, C. A., *Milton and the Christian Tradition* (Oxford: Clarendon Press, 1966).

Paul, R. S., *Assembly of the Lord: Politics and Religion in the Westminster Assembly and the 'Grand Debate'* (Edinburgh: T. & T. Clark, 1985).

Peile, John, *Biographical Register of Christ's College, 1505–1905, and of the Earlier Foundation, God's House, 1448–1505*, ed. J. A. Venn (2 vols., Cambridge: Cambridge University Press, 1910, 1913).

Pepys, Samuel, *The Diary of Samuel Pepys*, ed. Robert Latham and William Mathews (11 vols., London: Bell, 1970–83).

Phelps, W. H., 'The Date of Ben Jonson's Death', *N&Q* 225 (1980), 146–9.

Phillips, John, *Joannis Philippi Angli Responsio Ad Apologiam Anonymi cujusdam tenebrionis pro Rege & Populo Anglicano infantissimam* (London, 1652 [actually 1651]).

Piper, David, 'The Portraits of John Milton', in *Christ's College Magazine* 60, no. 195 (May 1970), 155–61.

Porter, Stephen, *The Great Fire of London* (Stroud: Sutton, 1996).

Postlethwaite, Norman, and Gordon Campbell (eds.), 'Edward King, Milton's Lycidas: Poems and Documents', special issue of *MQ* 28 (December 1994), 77–111.

Prest, Wilfred, 'Legal Education of the Gentry at the Inns of Court, 1500–1640', *Past and Present* 38 (1967), 20–39.

—— *The Inns of Court under Elizabeth I and the Early Stuarts, 1590–1640* (London: Longman, 1972).

Prideaux, Sir W. S. (1896), *Memorials of the Goldsmiths' Company* (2 vols., London: Printed for private circulation by Eyre and Spottiswoode, 1896–7).

Pritchard, Allan, 'Milton in Rome: According to Wood', *MQ* 14 (1980), 92–7.

Prynne, William, *Histrio-mastix: The Players Scourge, or, actors tragaedie* (London: 1633).

—— *A Breviate of the Prelates Intolerable Usurpations* (London, 1637).

—— *Discovery of the Prelates Tyranny* (London, 1641).

—— *Twelve Considerable Serious Questions touching Church Government* (London, 1644).

Quarles, Francis, *Hosanna or Divine Poems on the Passion of Christ and Threnodes*, ed. John Hordern (Liverpool: Liverpool University Press, 1969).

Bibliography

Ralegh, Sir Walter [attributed incorrectly], *The Cabinet-Council: Containing the Chief Arts of Empire and Mysteries of State* (London, 1658).

Ravenscroft, Thomas, *The Whole Book of Psalmes* (London, 1621).

Raylor, Timothy, 'New Light on Milton and Hartlib', *MQ* 27 (1993), 19–31.

Raymond, Joad, *Pamphlets and Pamphleteering in Early Modern Britain* (Cambridge: Cambridge University Press, 2003).

—— *The Invention of the Newspaper: English Newsbooks, 1641–1649* (2nd edn., Oxford: Clarendon Press, 2005).

Read, John Curtis, 'Humphrey Moseley, Publisher', *Oxford Bibliographical Society Proceedings and Papers*, 2 (1927–30), 61–72, 139–42.

Reay, Barry, *The Quakers and the English Revolution* (New York: St Martin's Press, 1985).

Richardson, R. C (ed.), *Town and Countryside in the English Revolution* (Manchester: Manchester University Press, 1992).

Richek, Roslyn, 'Thomas Randolph's Salting (1627), its Text, and John Milton's Sixth Prolusion as Another Salting', *ELR* 12 (1982), 102–31.

Rosen, Edward, 'A Friend of John Milton: Valerio Chimentelli and his Copy of Viviani's *De Maximis et minimus*', *BNYPL* 57 (1953), 159–74.

Rosenblatt, Jason, *Renaissance England's Chief Rabbi: John Selden* (Oxford: Oxford University Press, 2006).

Rosenheim, James (1978), 'An Early Appreciation of *Paradise Lost*', *MP* 75 (1978), 280–2.

Rovai, Francesco, *Poesie de Francesco Rovai*, ed. N. Rovai (Florence, 1652).

Rusche, Harry, 'A Reading of John Milton's Horoscope', *MQ* 13 (1979), 6–11.

Russell, Conrad, *The Fall of the British Monarchies, 1637–1642* (Oxford: Clarendon Press, 1995).

Salmasius, Claudius, *Defensio regia pro Carolo I ad Serenissimum Magnae Britanniae Regem Carolum II filium natu majorem, heredem & successorem legitimum* (n.p., 1649).

—— *Claudii Salmasii ad Johannem Miltonum Responsio, Opus Posthumum* (Dijon, 1660).

Saxby, T. J., *The Quest for the New Jerusalem: Jean de Labadie and the Labadists, 1610–1744* (Dordrecht and Boston: M. Nijhoff, 1987).

Sellin, Paul, 'Alexander Morus before the Hof van Holland: Some Insight into Seventeenth-Century Polemics with John Milton', *Studies in Netherlandic Culture and Literature* (Publications of the American Association for Netherlandic Studies, 7, 1994), 1–11.

—— 'Alexander Morus and John Milton II: Milton, Morus and Infanticide', *Contemporary Exploration in the Culture of the Low Countries* (Publications of the American Association for Netherlandic Studies, 9, 1995), 277–86.

—— 'Alexander Morus before the Synod of Utrecht', *HLQ* 58 (1996), 239–48.

Sharpe, Kevin, *Criticism and Compliment: The Politics of Literature in the England of Charles I* (Cambridge: Cambridge University Press, 1987).

—— *The Personal Rule of Charles I* (New Haven and London: Yale University Press, 1992).

—— *Remapping Early Modern England: The Culture of Seventeenth-Century Politics* (Cambridge: Cambridge University Press, 2000).

Shawcross, John T., 'Milton's Sonnet 23', *N&Q* 201 (1956), 202–4.

—— 'Notes on Milton's Amanuenses' *JEGP*, 58 (1959), 29–38.

—— 'Speculations on the Dating of the Trinity MS of Milton's Poems', *MLN* 75 (1960), 11–17.

—— 'The Chronology of Milton's Major Poems', *PMLA* 76 (1961), 345–58.

Shawcross, John T., 'Of Chronology and the Dates of Milton's Translation from Horace and the "New Forcers of Conscience"', *SEL* 3 (1963), 77–84.

—— 'What We Can Learn from Milton's Spelling', *HLQ* 26 (1963), 351–61.

—— 'The Date of the Separate Edition of Milton's *Epitaphium Damonis*', *SB* 18 (1965), 262–5.

—— 'The Dating of Certain Poems, Letters, and Prolusions Written by Milton', *ELN* 2 (1965), 261–6.

—— 'Milton's *Tenure of Kings and Magistrates*: Date of Composition, Editions and Issues', *PBSA* 60 (1966), 1–8.

—— *Milton: A Bibliography for the Years 1624–1700* (Binghamton: MRTS, 1984).

—— *Milton: A Bibliography for the Years 1624–1700: Addenda and Corrigenda* (Binghamton: MRTS, 1984).

—— 'A Note on a Copy of Milton's Poems', *MQ* 25 (1991), 107–8.

—— *John Milton: The Self and the World* (Lexington: University Press of Kentucky, 1993).

—— *'Arms of the Family': The significance of John Milton's Relatives and Associates* (Lexington: University Press of Kentucky, 2004).

—— *Rethinking Milton Studies: Time Present and Time Past* (Newark, NJ: University of Delaware Press, 2005).

Shuster, G. N., *The English Ode from Milton to Keats* (New York, 1940).

Sikes, George (?) *The Life and Death of Sir Henry Vane, Kt.* (London, 1662).

Sirluck, Ernest, 'Milton's Idle Right Hand', *JEGP* 60 (1961), 749–85.

Skeel, Caroline, *The Council in the Marches of Wales* (Cambridge, Girton College: Girton College Studies, 1904).

Slack, Paul, *The Impact of Plague on Tudor and Stuart England* (2nd edn., Oxford: Clarendon Press, 1990).

Smectymnuus, *An Answer to a Booke Entituled, An Humble Remonstrance* (London, 1641).

—— *A Vindication of the Answer to the Humble Remonstrance* (London: 1641).

Smith, R. W., 'The Source of Milton's Pandemonium', *MP* 39 (1931), 187–98.

Sotheby, S. L., *Ramblings in Elucidation of Milton* (n.p., 1861).

Spink, Ian, *Henry Lawes: Cavalier Songwriter* (Oxford: Oxford University Press, 2000).

Spurr, John, *England in the 1670s: 'This Masquerading Age'* (Oxford: Blackwell, 2000).

S[tarkey?], G[eorge?], *The Dignity of Kingship* (London, 1660).

—— *Monarchy Triumphing Over Traiterous Republicans* (London, 1661).

Steer, Francis, 'Scriveners' *Company Common Paper* 1357–1628, with a continuation to 1678', (London Record Society, 4, 1969).

Stevens, Denis, *Thomas Tomkins, 1572–1656* (London: Macmillan, 1957).

Stock, Richard, *The Doctrine and Use of Repentance* (London, 1604).

—— trans., William Whitaker, *An ansvvere to the Ten reasons of Edmund Campian the Jesuit* (London, 1606) (translation of *Ad Rationes decem Edmundi Campiani Jesuit responsio* (London, 1581)).

—— *A Sermon preached at Paules Cross the second of November 1606* (London, 1609).

—— *The Churches Lamentation for the Losse of the Godly* (London, 1614).

Stokes, H. P., 'The Esquire Bedells of the University of Cambridge', *Cambridge Antiquarian Society Publications* 45 (1911), 39, 93–5.

Stone, Lawrence, *The Family, Sex and Marriage in England 1500–1800* (abridged edn., Harmondsworth: Penguin, 1979).

—— *Road to Divorce England 1530–1987* (Oxford and New York: Oxford University Press, 1992; first pub. 1990).

Stow, John, *A Survey of London*, ed. Charles Lethbridge Kingsford (3 vols., 1908–27; Oxford: Clarendon Press, 1971).

Strong, Roy, *Britannia Triumphans: Inigo Jones, Rubens and the Whitehall Palace* (London: Thames and Hudson, 1980).

Swift, Jonathan, *Gulliver's Travels 1726*, ed. Harold Williams (Oxford, Blackwell, 1941).

Tavoni, M., *Latino, grammatica, volgare: storia di una questione umanistica* (Padua: Antenore, 1984).

Taylor, George C., *Milton's use of Du Bartas* (Cambridge, Mass.: Harvard University Press, 1934).

Tennant, Philip, *The People's War in the South Midlands, 1642–45* (Stroud: Alan Sutton, 1992).

Tolmie, Murray, *The Triumph of the Saints: The Separate Churches of London 1616–1649* (Cambridge: Cambridge University Press, 1977).

Tournu, Christophe, *Milton and Mirabeau: Rencontre révolutionnaire* (Paris: Edimaf, 2002).

Trevor Roper, H. R., *Archbishop Laud, 1573–1645* (2nd edn., London: Macmillan, 1962).

Tromly, Frederick B., 'Milton Responds to Donne: "On Time" and "Death be not proud"', in *MP* 80 (1983), 390–3.

Turner, James Grantham, *One Flesh: Paradisal Marriage and Sexual Relations in the Age of Milton* (Oxford: Clarendon Press, 1987).

Tyacke, Nicholas, *Anti-Calvinists: The Rise of English Arminianism c.1590–1640* (Oxford: Clarendon Press, 1987).

—— 'Archbishop Laud', in Fincham (ed.), *Early Stuart Church*, 51–70.

—— (ed.), *Seventeenth-Century Oxford* (vol. 4 of *The History of the University of Oxford*, Oxford: Clarendon Press, 1997).

Ullman, B. L., *The Origin and Development of Humanistic Script* (Rome: Edizioni di Storia e letteratura, 1960).

Ussher, James, *The Judgement of Doctor Rainoldes* (London, 1641).

Valdés, Juan de, *Diálogo de la lengua* (1535, pub. Madrid, 1737).

Vane, Sir Henry, the younger, *A Healing Question propounded and resolved upon occasion of the late publique and seasonable Call to Humiliation* (London, 1656).

Vickers, Brian, 'Leisure and Idleness in the Renaissance: The Ambivalence of Otium', *Renaissance Studies* 4 (1994), 1–37, 107–54.

Villani, Stefano, 'The Italian Protestant Church of London in the Seventeenth Century', forthcoming in Barbara Schaff (ed.), *Exiles, Emigres and Go-Betweens: Anglo-Italian Cultural Mediations* (Amsterdam and New York: Rodopi).

Vitale, Maurizio, *La questione della lingua* (2nd edn., Palermo: Palumbo, 1984).

Walker, Joseph, 'An attempt to ascertain the site of the villa near Naples in which the Marquis Manso received Tasso and Milton', Appendix V of Walker's *Historical Memoir on Italian Tragedy* (London, 1799).

Walsham, Alexander, ' "Fatal Vespers": Providentialism and Anti-Popery in Late Jacobean London', *Past and Present* 144 (1994), 36–87.

Walton, Brian (ed.), *Biblia Sacra Polyglotta* (6 vols., London, 1654–7).

Watson, Foster, *The English Grammar Schools to 1660* (Cambridge: Cambridge University Press, 1908).

Bibliography

Webster, Tom, *Godly Clergy in Early Stuart England: The Caroline Puritan Movement c.1620–1643* (Cambridge: Cambridge University Press, 1997).

Wedgwood, C. V., *The Trial of Charles I* (1964; London: Reprint Society, 1966).

Whitelocke, Bulstrode, *The Diary of Bulstrode Whitelocke, 1605–1675*, ed. Ruth Spalding (Oxford: Published for the British Academy by Oxford University Press, 1991).

Wickham, Glynne, Herbert Berry, and William Ingram (eds.), *English Professional Theatre, 1530–1660* (Cambridge: Cambridge University Press, 2000).

Williams, Michael, *The Venerable English College, Rome: A History, 1579–1979* (London: Associated Catholic Publications, 1979).

Williams, Roger, *The Bloudy Tenent of Persecution* (London, 1644).

Wilmot, John, *The Works of John Wilmot, Earl of Rochester*, ed. Harold Love (Oxford: Oxford University Press, 1999).

Wood, Anthony, *Athenae Oxoniensis* (2 vols., Oxford, 1691–2); Wood's life of Milton is in the *Fasti Oxoniensis*, 1, cols. 880–4.

Woodward, Hezekiah, *Inquiries into the Causes of our Miseries* (London, 1644).

Woolrych, Austin, 'Milton and Richard Heath', *PQ* 53 (1974), 132–5.

—— *Commonwealth to Protectorate* (Oxford: Clarendon Press, 1982).

—— 'The Date of the *Digression* in Milton's *History of* Britain', in R. Ollard and P. Tudor Craig (eds.), *For Veronica Wedgwood: These Studies in Seventeenth-Century History* (London: Collins, 1986), 217–46.

—— 'Dating Milton's *History of Britain*', *HistJ* 36 (1993), 929–43.

—— *Britain in Revolution, 1625–1660* (Oxford: Oxford University Press, 2002).

Worden, Blair, *The Rump Parliament 1648–1653* (1974; Cambridge: Cambridge University Press, 1977).

Wotton, Antony, *The Art of Logike, gathered out of Aristotle . . . by P. Ramus* (London, 1626).

Wotton, Sir Henry, *Life and Letters of Sir Henry Wotton*, ed. L. Pearsall Smith (2 vols., Oxford: Clarendon Press, 1907).

Acknowledgements

W$_E$ have both devoted a substantial portion of our professional lives to Milton, and so have incurred debts to a large number of individuals, not all of whom can be named here. Of the biographers we owe a substantial debt to heroic figures such as David Masson, Alfred Stern, J. M. French, and W. R. Parker, and to later toilers in the archival vineyard such as John Shawcross, Leo Miller, Peter Beal, Edward Jones, and Nicholas von Maltzahn. Other scholars have written illuminatingly on particular areas: Robert Fallon on the state papers, Edward Chaney and Neil Harris on the Italian journey, Paul Sellin on the Dutch dimension, Peter Lindenbaum and Donald McKenzie on the printing houses, Mordechai Feingold and Victor Morgan on the universities, Cedric Brown and John Creaser on the aristo-cratic entertainments, Martin Dzelzainis on Milton's legal knowledge, John K. Hale and Estelle Haan on Milton's Latin. Christopher Hill plotted the topography of seventeenth-century religious heterodoxy. Barbara Lewalski's life of Milton set a standard for biographical interpretation of complex literary texts and a stimulus and challenge to our own thinking on numerous issues crucial to our project. The history of the period has been recast by a new generation of revisionist historians, among whom we have very consid-erable debts; citations of their works fill our footnotes.

In the course of our research we have had occasion to consult the holdings of many archives and libraries. We should particularly like to thank the Archivio General (Simancas), the Algemeen Rijksarchief (The Hague), Archbishop Marsh's Library (Dublin), the Bayerisches Hauptstaatsarchiv (Munich), the Bedfordshire County Record Office (Bedford), the Berkshire Record Office (Reading), the Bethlem Royal Hospital Archives and Mu-seum (Beckenham), the Biblioteca Marucelliana (Florence), the Biblioteca Nazionale (Florence), the Bibliothèque Nationale (Paris), the Bibliothèque Publique et Universitaire (Geneva), the Bibliothèque Royale (Brussels), the Bodleian Library (Oxford), the British Library, the Brotherton Library (Leeds), the Buckinghamshire County Record Office (Aylesbury), the Cambridge University Library, the Canterbury Cathedral Library, the Carl H. Pforzheimer Library (New York), the Cheshire Record Office (Chester), Christ Church College (Oxford), Christ's College (Cambridge), the City of Westminster Archive Centre (London), the College of Arms (London), the

Colorado University Library (Boulder), the Columbia University Library (New York), the Corporation of London Records Office, Dulwich College (London), the East Sussex Record Office (Lewes), Eton College (Windsor), Exeter Cathedral Library, the Folger Shakespeare Library (Washington), the Fort St George Museum (Chennai), the Goldsmiths' Company (London), the Guildhall Library (London), the Hammersmith and Fulham Record Office (London), the Harry Ranson Humanities Research Center (Austin), the Henry E. Huntington Library (San Marino), the Hereford and Worcester County Record Office (Hereford), the Herzog-August-Bibliothek (Wolfenbüttel), the Historical Society of Pennsylvania (Philadelphia), the Houghton Library at Harvard University, the House of Lords Record Office, the Illinois University Library (Urbana), the Inner Temple (London), the Kongelige Bibliotek (Copenhagen), the Lambeth Palace Library (London), the Leicestershire, Leicester, and Rutland Record Office (Wigston Magna), the Lilly Library of Indiana University (Bloomington), the Massachusetts Historical Society (Boston), the Marquess of Bath's Collection (Longleat House), the Merchant Taylors' Company (London), the Morgan Library (New York), the National Archives (Kew), the National Maritime Museum (Greenwich), the Niedersächsisches Staatsarchiv (Oldenburg), the New York Public Library, the Northamptonshire Record Office (Northampton), the Österreichische Nationalbibliothek (Vienna), Oxfordshire Archives (Oxford), the Representative Church Body Library (Dublin), the Rijksuniversiteitsbibliotheek (Leiden), the Rosenbach Museum (Philadephia), the Royal College of Music (London), the Royal Society (London), the Rutgers University Library (New Brunswick, NJ), St Giles-in-the-Fields (London), St Paul's School, the Sheffield University Library, the Society of Antiquaries (London), the Staatsarchiv (Zürich), the Stadtarchiv (Leipzig), the Stationers' and Newspaper Makers' Company, the Stadtbibliothek Vadiana (St Gallen), Stonyhurst College (Clitheroe), the Suffolk Country Record Office (Ipswich), Trinity College (Cambridge), Trinity College (Dublin), the Universiteits-Bibliothek (Amsterdam), the University of Pennsylvania Library (Philadelphia), the Vatican Library and Secret Archives, the Venerable English College (Rome), Westminster Abbey, and the Yale University Library (New Haven). Our working libraries, the Bangor University Library and the University of Leicester Library, have both been heavily used in the cause of this biography, and we are grateful. We owe much to two resources on which scholars in our field increasingly and appropriately depend, *The Oxford Dictionary of National Biography*, the online version of which allowed new approaches to investigating our subject's milieu, and *Early English Books Online*, which placed on our desks in suburban Leicester and the foothills of Snowdonia the finest collection of seventeenth-century books ever to be assembled. We also thank medical practitioners Philip Bloom, Sarah Carroll, and Robert Corns for advice and guidance on Milton's illnesses. Our personal debts also include Ceri Sullivan, Neil Harris, Edward Jones, and Sarah Knight, each of whom commented constructively on portions of our manuscript. In the final stages of writing our universities both granted us periods of study leave that enabled us to finish the book on time.

One of the advantages of writing for Oxford University Press is the informed understanding of those who work there. This biography was commissioned by the poet Andrew McNeillie, who has been characteristically enthusiastic and helpful; we are also grateful for the support of the biographer Hermione Lee, who is the OUP Delegate with responsibility for Literature. Our debt to the Press extends to Jacqueline Baker (who piloted the book through the Press), the marketing teams in Oxford (Phil Henderson, Emily Wroe, and Coleen Hatrick) and New York (Cassie Ammerman and Samara Stob), the production team (Claire Thompson, Tom Chandler, and Mary Payne), and our picture researcher (Zoe Spilberg).

Despite this substantial assistance from so many quarters, there may be errors in the book, for which we blame each other.

GC; TNC

Leicester and Bangor
2008

We should like to acknowledge the following sources of illustrations:

Alamy: **12**; Author's photographs: **15**, **16**; Bodleian Library, University of Oxford: **6** (Bodleian Gough maps 75), **14**, **19** (Bodleian copy 8 P 117 Art, between pp 434–5), **20** (Bodleian copy 8 P 117 Art, between pp 100–1), **22** (Bodleian copy 8 P 117 Art, between pp 196–7), **23** (Bodleian copy 8 P 117 Art, between pp 334–5), **25** (Bodleian copy 8 P 117 Art, between pp 6–7), **29** (Bodleian Library Wing/ 1769:04), **37** (Bodleian Fol.BS.136 (image on p. 344)); British Library: **Map 1** (Maps Roll 17.a.3), **Map 2** (BL 863.k.5), **2** (BL C.30.d.17), **3 (BL C.30.d.19)**, **11** (BL shelfmark E84 (2)), **13** (BL C.34.d.46), **17** (BL 239.k.36), **26** (BL E.208 (10)), **30** (BL E. 1126 (1)), **34** (BL E. 569 (16)), **35** (BLE.578 (5)), **38** (BL E.1487 (3)), **39** (BL 816.m.1 (92)), **41** (BL 816.m.9 (26)), **44** (BL C.69.ff.5 or Ashley 11.82), **45** (BL 598.e.1 or G.4879), **47** (BL 684.d.33 or Ashley 1184)); Cambridge University Library: **18** (Adv.d.38.5); Corbis/Michael Nicholson: **42**; Corpus Christi College, Cambridge: **7** (Parker Library MS 121, p 431); Guildhall Library, City of London/The Bridgeman Art Library: **1**; Henry E. Huntington Library and Art Gallery: **33**, **36**; National Portrait Gallery, London: **8**, **9**, **10**, **27**, **28**, **31**, **32**; Morgan Library and Museum, New York: **5**; Princeton University Library, Rare Books and Special Collections: **46**; Rex Features/Dan Sparham: **48**; Robert Corns: **21**, **24**; Trinity College, Cambridge: **43** (K.15.121 (188)); Union Theological Seminary, New York Library: **4**, **40**.

Index